Principles and Practice of Constraint Programming

Principles and Practice of Constraint Programming
The Newport Papers

edited by
Vijay Saraswat and Pascal Van Hentenryck

advising editors:
Paris Kanellakis, Jean-Louis Lassez, Ralph Wachter

The MIT Press
Cambridge, Massachusetts
London, England

This book was printed and bound in the United States of America.

Library of Congress Cataloging-in-Publication Data

Principles and practice of constraint programming: the Newport papers /
    edited by Vijay Saraswat and Pascal Van Hentenryck; advising editors, Paris
Kanellakis, Jean-Louis Lassez, Ralph Wachter.
        p.   cm.
    Includes bibliographical references.
    ISBN 0-262-19361-2
    1. Constraint programming (Computer Science)—Congresses. I. Saraswat,
    Vijay. II. Van Hentenryck, Pascal.
QA76.612.P75   1995
005.13′1—dc20   94-44871
                                                                      CIP

Contents

Preface

The integration of constraint technology in programming languages is a promising direction in the development of software solutions for problems with complex modeling or problem-solving requirements. Programming with constraints as primitives, or Constraint Programming (CP), is appealing because constraints are the normal language of discourse for a wide range of applications. Currently, CP is contributing exciting new research directions in a number of distinct areas such as: artificial intelligence, concurrent computing, database systems, graphical interfaces, hardware verification, operations research and combinatorial optimization, programming language design and implementation, reactive systems, symbolic computing algorithms and systems.

This book is an edited collection of papers on the state of the art of constraint programming. The articles address both unifying principles for constraint programming as well as the wide spectrum of its practical applications. The collection was selected from a set of high-quality papers submitted by participants of the First Workshop on the Principles and Practice of Constraint Programming (PPCP), held in Newport, Rhode Island, USA, April 1993. The majority of the articles included in this book are the expanded and revised versions of material communicated in preliminary form at that meeting. All submitted papers were reviewed for originality, completeness and clarity of presentation.

Constraint Programming: Some Background

Early studies, in the 60s and 70s, introduced and made use of CP in graphics and in artificial intelligence. Indeed, computing with constraints has been an important research activity in these areas for the last two decades. Given the declarative nature of CP, it has been a natural tool for graphical user interface design as well as for knowledge representation and model-based reasoning in artificial intelligence. However, already in the late 70s, the initial appeal of CP was tempered by the cost of storing and solving constraints efficiently and by the lack of efficient, robust, general-purpose implementations.

Perhaps the most important CP advance in the 80s has been the discovery of general-purpose computational frameworks based on constraints. Research in extensions of logic programming (LP) led to the development of the notion of constraint logic programming (CLP): the realization that all the interesting theoretical properties of logic programming continue to hold if unification is replaced by constraint-solving in more general structures. Even more, existing implementation technology can readily be transferred to this more general setting. This has led to the development of a number of concrete CLP systems, with dramatic improvements in efficiency over LP systems. These systems have been applied to a number of real-life operations research problems, e.g., involving scheduling or decision-support, with considerable success.

The generality of constraint programming has meant that it can be applied to very general computational tasks (such as the specification of communication and control in concurrent systems) not traditionally thought of as constraint programming. The basic ideas of CLP have been generalized to the setting of concurrent constraint programming. The key principle is to replace the notion of "process store = assignment of values to variables" by the notion of "process store = set of assignments of values to variables (i.e., constraints)". Computation progresses by accumulating constraints; processes synchronize by suspending until the information content of the store crosses a given threshold. The resulting framework greatly extends conventional concurrent programming languages.

In the last five years, CP has been applied with some success to a number of computer science areas. Constraint query languages have been used for the natural description and efficient manipulation of spatial or temporal data, areas where traditional database systems have been weak. The emergence of real-time computing as an active area of research has led to the focus on integrating timing constraints into high-level programming notations and hardware verification systems. There is growing interest in software engineering for the use of constraints for maintaining and monitoring programs, for analyzing programs statically, for developing incremental syntax-based programming environments, and for reasoning about programs. Reactive systems design, e.g., robotics and hybrid systems, offer challenging opportunities for constraint programming. The many applications of constraint programming have revived interest in symbolic computation algorithms and systems and have generated advances in this fundamental technology.

Finally, improvements in graphical and high-performance working environments have meant that more of the computational overhead of constraint systems (general-purpose or application-specific) can be tolerated by the user. Constraint-based computation seems to be a realistic task for the 1990s.

The Newport Workshop

In the fall of 1992, we felt that the interdisciplinary area of constraint programming had developed a discernible identity, promising in terms both of simple and general foundations and of significative practical applications. We also realized that the new area needed a forum where results could be compared and new lines of development charted. So we decided to organize the First Workshop on the Principles and Practice of Constraint Programming. The workshop was partly sponsored by the Office of Naval Research and held April 28-30, 1993 in Newport, Rhode Island, USA. (It has been followed in 1994 with a second workshop on Orcas Island, Washington, USA and plans are under way for an international conference in Marseilles, France in 1995.)

The workshop program committee reflected the diversity and extent of constraint programming. It consisted of: Alan Borning (Univ. of Washington, Seattle), Jacques Cohen (Brandeis Univ.), Johan de Kleer (Xerox PARC), David Dill (Stanford Univ.), Eugene Freuder (Univ. of New Hampshire), John Hooker (CMU), Joxan Jaffar (IBM Watson), Paris Kanellakis (Brown Univ.), Deepak Kapur (SUNY Albany), Dexter Kozen (Cornell Univ.), Jean-Louis Lassez (IBM Watson), Jean-Claude Latombe (Stanford Univ.), Nancy Lynch (MIT), David McAllester (MIT), Albert Meyer (MIT), Anil Nerode (Cornell Univ.), Fernando Pereira (AT&T Bell Labs), Raghu Ramakrishnan (Univ. of Wisconsin), Vijay Saraswat (Xerox PARC), Pascal Van Hentenryck (Brown Univ.). The committee donated its time and expertise generously, and put together a program of 37 position papers from 94 submissions to the workshop. The extended abstracts of the papers presented at the meeting are available by anonymous ftp from `wilma.cs.brown.edu` in `pub/ppcp`.

The meeting was small and informal. General approaches to constraint programming were presented by three invited speakers: Alain Colmerauer (Marseilles), Hervé Gallaire (Xerox) and Anil Nerode (Cornell Univ.). There were short presentations of position papers, panels, many discussions, and New England seafood.

The Newport Papers

Starting from the material and synergy generated by the Newport workshop, MIT Press agreed to publish a volume on the Principles and Practice of Constraint Programming. The editors solicited submissions, managed the review process, and contributed their time to the composition of this volume. The selection was made by the editors (with some feedback from the advisory editors) on the basis of: either strong technical results on established themes or development of innovative themes. Of the 23 articles presented here, 20 are journal versions of position papers from the Newport workshop, and 3 are additional contributions.

The collection of papers is organized around a number of themes: concurrency, reactive systems, languages and environments, constraint-solving algorithms and consistency techniques, and computer graphics. These are all in the scope of constraint programming, as mentioned above, and described in more detail as follows.

Concurrency: The use of constraints for synchronization and communication of concurrent agents is mainly due to the foundational work of Maher and Saraswat, building upon constraint logic programming and concurrent logic programming. Concurrent constraint languages, as those discussed in the two papers of the first part, are organized around a constraint store. Agents synchronize by asking if a constraint is entailed by the constraint store while they communicate by adding constraints to the store. The first paper in this part, *A Concurrent Semantics for Concurrent Constraint Programs via Contextual Nets* by U. Montanari and F. Rossi, proposes a semantics for concurrent constraint languages in terms of contextual nets, a generalization of Petri nets. The key aspect of the semantics is to represent explicitly the concurrency and nondeterminism of the program. Applications of this semantics to run-time and compile-time optimizations are also discussed. The second paper, *Object-Oriented Concurrent Constraint Programming in Oz* by M. Henz, G. Smolka and J. Würtz, presents the design of a new concurrent constraint programming language. The salient features of *Oz* are its higher-order aspects and the new notion of a cell, which enable a wide variety of object-oriented programming techniques to be supported in a natural and concise way.

Reactive Systems: Reactive systems is a new research and application area for constraint programming. These systems have several features that distinguish them from many previous applications of constraint programming: they interact with an environment; they evolve in time; and they often have real-time requirements. The first paper in this part, *Constraint Programming in Constraint Nets* by Y. Zhang and A. Mackworth, presents a framework, called constraint nets, in which constraint satisfaction is a dynamic process with the solution set as an attractor of the process. The paper argues that this view of constraint programming is particularly appropriate for reactive systems and explores various implementation schemes. The second paper, *Robot Programming and Constraints* by D. Pai, explores the use of constraints for robot motion planning. The original feature of this new approach, called the least constraint framework, is the declarative specification of robot motions through constraints, enabling the system to be more flexible and extensible. The approach is illustrated by the dynamic walking of a simulated human-like biped. The third paper, *Constraint Logic Programming: Hybrid Control, Logic as Linear Programming* by W. Kohn, A. Nerode and V.S. Subrahmanian, explores the use of integer linear programming to implement predicate logic and shows how these techniques can be used to implement the Kohn-Nerode theory for controlling hybrid systems such as nuclear plants and traffic control systems.

Languages and Environments: The design of programming languages and environments based on constraints has been a very active research area in the last decade. Constraints bring a declarative component in this area by specifying "what" needs to be achieved instead of "how" to achieve it. Languages and environments then rest upon specific constraint solvers to meet the specifications. This area has witnessed a major development in recent years: the development of the Constraint Logic Programming (CLP) scheme by Jaffar and Lassez, a class of programming languages whose basic operations are defined on constraints, and the design and implementation of CLP systems such as Prolog III by Colmerauer, CLP($\Re$) by Jaffar and Michaylov, and CHIP by Dincbas, Simonis, and Van Hentenryck. This recent activity has nurtured new developments in programming languages inside and, more recently, outside logic programming. The first paper of this part, *2LP: Linear Programming and Logic Programming* by K. McAloon and C. Tretkoff, presents an imperative constraint language integrating two fundamental features of constraint logic programming: constraint solving and nondeterminism. Some applications of the language are presented in detail. The second paper in this part, *A Constraint-Based Scientific Programming Language* by R. Zippel, is devoted to a constraint-based scientific programming language. The language is based on a new approach which applies not only traditional compiler optimizations but also domain-specific (i.e., scientific) transformations. The work is primarily motivated by the inherent complexity of designing scientific programs. The third paper, *Designing Constraint Logic Programming Languages using Computational Systems* by C. Kirchner, H. Kirchner and M. Vittek, presents a framework, called computational systems, to express constraint solvers and operational semantics. The key feature of computational systems consists in extending the rewrite logic of P. Meseguer with the notion of strategy. The fourth paper, *Aggregation in Constraint Databases* by G. Kuper, considers constraint query languages proposed by P. Kanellakis, G. Kuper and P. Revesz. Constraint query languages are a generalization of relational databases where the notion of tuples is replaced by a conjunction of constraints. Kuper studies how to add aggregation to such a language. This extension is difficult in general since the constraint language may not be closed under aggregation, and Kuper explores possible solutions. The fifth paper, *Synthesis of Constraint Algorithms* by D. Smith and S. Westfold, proposes to use knowledge-based tools to synthesize constraint programs based on the global search paradigm. The key motivation is to exploit not only the constraint domain but also the specific feature of the application at hand. The development of constraint-based systems raises new issues in environments and debugging, since it is often difficult, if not impossible, to follow the exact flow of control. The sixth paper, *Exploiting Constraint Dependency Information For Debugging and Explanation* by W. Keirouz, G. Kramer and J. Pabon, shows how to exploit dependency information for debugging and explaining constraint algorithms. In particular, their algorithms are instrumental in identifying constraints that cause a model to be over-constrained for some classes of applications. The last paper in this part, *Constraining the Structure and Style of Object-Oriented Programs* by S. Meyers, C. Duby, and S. Reiss, proposes a tool, called *CCEL*, to express and check constraints on the structure and the style of object-oriented programs. *CCEL* shares some spirit with *lint* but its key novelty is to let software designers express their own constraints. *CCEL* then checks the actual program for possible violations.

Constraint-solving Algorithms: At the core of any constraint language lies a constraint solver for one or several given constraint domains. It is therefore not surprising that constraint programming has generated further interest in constraint-solving algorithms. The papers in this part consider various aspects of constraint solving. The first paper, *Fourier's Elimination: Which to Choose?* by J.L. Imbert, considers variable elimination in linear real constraints using Fourier's elimination. Variable elimination is important for many reasons. For instance, in constraint logic programming, it is used to express the result in terms of the query variables only, removing all intermediary values. The paper contrasts, clarifies, and shows how to combine several methods proposed in the past. New improvements are also proposed and their benefits illustrated. The paper, *An Approach for Solving Systems of Parametric Polynomial Equations* by D. Kapur, considers nonlinear polynomial equations and shows how several existing methods can be extended to cope with parameters. The key idea is to obtain a parametric solved form, from which specific solutions can be extracted by substituting values for the parameters. The paper discusses both Groebner basis computations and characteristic set computations. The paper, *Verifying Logic Circuits by Benders Decomposition* by J. Hooker and H. Yan, considers an important problem in hardware design: verifying that a circuit meets its specification. A traditional tool which applies to a variety of combinational circuits is binary decision diagrams proposed by R. Bryant. The present paper proposes a method based on Benders decomposition and compares it with binary decision diagrams. The method is particularly effective on circuits without exclusive-ors. Constraint hierarchies were introduced by Borning and his colleagues to distinguish between hard constraints (i.e., constraints that must be enforced) and soft constraints (i.e., constraints which express preferences). The paper, *An Incremental Hierarchical Constraint Solver* by F. Menezes and P. Barahona, presents an incremental algorithm for solving hierarchies of constraints where variables range over a finite set of integers. The algorithm is based on techniques from intelligent backtracking and its application to time-table scheduling, and set-covering is also discussed.

Artificial Intelligence: Constraint satisfaction has always an important part of artificial intelligence since the seminal work of Freuder, Fikes, Mackworth, Montanari, and Waltz, to name a few. Much research in this area has focused on finite constraint satisfaction problems (CSPs). Typically, a CSP consists of a set of variables, their associated domains of values, and a set of constraints. A solution consists in finding an assignment of values to the variables such that all constraints are satisfied. The first paper in this part, *A Disjunctive Decomposition Control Schema for Constraint Satisfaction* by E. Freuder and P. Hubbe, proposes a disjunctive decomposition schema encompassing several established search algorithms as well as some recent proposals. The schema sheds new light on these algorithms and may be instrumental in discovering new ones. A fundamental idea behind much work on CSPs is the use of constraints to prune the set of possible values for each variable. This has led to various notions of local consistency. The second paper in this part, *Local Consistency in Parallel Constraint-Satisfaction Networks* by S. Kasif and A. Delcher, studies fast parallel algorithms to enforce one such notion: arc-consistency. Since the general problem is P-complete, the paper identifies several classes of CSPs where parallel computation can achieve significant speed-ups. As a side-note, the paper also proposes a very simple formulation of an optimal algorithm for achieving k-consistency. The last paper in this part, *Terminological Reasoning with Constraint Handling Rules* by T. Frühwirth and P. Hanschke, considers constraint handling rules, a formalism to express constraint solvers, and shows how they can be used to implement terminological reasoning. Of particular interest is the simplicity of the approach to obtain a working implementation.

Computer Graphics: Constraint programming and computer graphics have a long common history since the seminal work of Sutherland on *Sketchpad* and of Borning on *ThingLab*. Once again, constraints bring a declarative component to an otherwise rather imperative area. A typical graphical constraint would require two objects to be aligned and the constraint would be maintained whenever one of the objects or both are moved. Computer graphics imposes strong requirements on the constraint solver which must be incremental and very fast. The first paper in this part, *The SkyBlue Constraint Solver and Its Applications* by M. Sannella, proposes a new algorithm, called *SkyBlue*, which maintains a constraint hierarchy by using multi-way local propagation. *SkyBlue* is a successor to *DeltaBlue* and addresses two of its limitations: cycles of constraints (which cannot be solved using local propagation only) and the restriction to a single output variable. The paper, *Practical Issues in Graphical Constraints* by M. Gleicher, takes the view that solving nonlinear constraints is unavoidable in interactive graphics. It reviews techniques to solve them and shows how they could be used in a graphical system to achieve a reasonable efficiency. The paper, *Constraint Management in a Declarative Design Method for 3D Scene Sketch Modeling* by S. Donikian and G. Hégron, describes an intelligent CAD system to model architectural scene sketch. The system elegantly combines symbolic and numerical constraints to describe and visualize a scene. The paper, *Expressing Constraints for Data Display Specification: A Visual Approach* by I. Cruz, introduces a constraint-based visual language to specify, in a declarative way, the display of data. The language allows the specification of a variety of displays such as graphs and pie charts. Of special interest are the declarative aspects of the language and the ease of integration in an object-oriented framework.

Acknowledgments

We wish to thank all the authors for their contributions and the referees for their invaluable service. A special acknowledgment is due to the Office of Naval Research for its support of constraint programming in general and for making the Newport workshop a reality. Finally, we thank Bob Prior of MIT Press for his patience with us and his ability to relax constraints.

Vijay Saraswat (Xerox PARC)
Editor
Pascal Van Hentenryck (Brown Univ.)
Editor
Paris Kanellakis (Brown Univ.)
Advising Editor
Jean-Louis Lassez (IBM Watson)
Advising Editor
Ralph Wachter (ONR)
Advising Editor

Principles and Practice of Constraint Programming

I CONCURRENCY

1 A Concurrent Semantics for Concurrent Constraint Programs via Contextual Nets

Ugo Montanari and Francesca Rossi

Abstract

We propose a concurrent semantics for concurrent constraint (CC) programs. Such semantics is based on structures called contextual nets, that is, Petri nets extended with context conditions, besides the usual pre- and post-conditions. Context conditions are items which have to be present in order for an event to take place, but which are not affected by the event, and are very useful for describing situations where different events share a common resource and want to read it simultaneously. The reasons we use contextual nets to give a semantics to CC programs are mainly two: naturality (CC programs are naturally context-dependent, since the ask operation is a generalized read) and expressiveness (contextual nets allow for an explicit representation of all the concurrency and the nondeterminism available in a CC program). The information contained in our semantics, possibly abstracted to have a finite structure even for recursive programs, can be of great help to a scheduler in order to obtain an efficient execution of the program, or also to a compile-time optimizer.

1.1 Introduction

A concurrent semantics is a semantics where concurrency can be realistically represented and naturally described. We believe that every concurrent language should be provided with a formal concurrent semantics. In fact, this would allow a deeper understanding of the way concurrent agents interact, and such understanding could then be fruitfully used by a scheduler or a compile-time optimizer in order to make program execution more efficient. Instead, usually, concurrent languages are provided with a formal sequential semantics and an informal concurrent semantics. This allows one to reason about simple properties of the programs, but usually not about complex ones. For example, semantics based on input-output relations or sequences of agent operations (like the ones already proposed for CC programs [16, 17, 2]) are usually not able to provide enough knowledge about the amount of parallelism available in the program and the causality between agent interactions, and therefore identify too many programs.

For this reason, we propose here a concurrent semantics for concurrent constraint (CC) programs [18]. Such programs are based on a very simple model, consisting of a collection of concurrent agents sharing a set of variables which are subject to some constraints. Each agent may perform two basic operations over the common constraint: either add a new constraint, or test whether a new constraint is entailed. The constraints are defined and handled by an underlying constraint system, which can be described very generally as a set of primitive constraints and an entailment relation among subsets of them.

We start by defining in a novel way the operational behaviour of CC programs. We do that by adopting context-dependent rewrite rules, whose applications represent the computation steps. Each rule has a left hand side, a right hand side, and a context. A rule is applicable if both its left hand side and its context are present in the current state of the computation, and its application removes the left hand side (but not the context) and adds the right hand side. The context-dependent nature of such rules is important, since context objects allow one to model faithfully the concept of asked constraints. The evolution of each of the agents in a CC program, as well as the declarations of the program and its underlying constraint system, are all expressible by sets of such rules. In this way each computation step, i.e., the application of one of such rules, represents either the evolution of an agent, or the expansion of a declaration, or the entailment of some new token.

Note that such an operational semantics is fundamentally different from those presented elsewhere. First, there are no structural axioms that a computation state has to satisfy (apart from the usual axioms for multisets), since a state for us is a flat structure which can be thought of as the standard representative of a class of states up to such axioms. Second, no inference rules are used in defining the possible state-to-state transitions, since the rewrite rules describe local changes that can be applied to any state (if some conditions are met). Third, agent evolutions and constraint generations are described uniformly and at the same level. This is crucial if one is interested in exploiting the maximal possible parallelism available at both the program level and the constraint system level. In fact, had we considered the constraint system as a black box, as is usually done in the other approaches, we would have lost parallelism both within the constraint system (because a monolithic description allows only one evolution at a time) and among the agents (since two agents which need different parts of the constraint store would have been, possibly unnecessarily, sequentialized).

From such an operational semantics of CC programs, consisting of all the sequences of rule applications, we then obtain a concurrent semantics by constructing a suitable contextual net. A contextual net [13] is just a Petri net [14] where each event may have context conditions, besides the usual pre- and post-conditions. The idea is that preconditions represent objects which are cancelled by the event, postconditions represent objects which are generated by the event, while context conditions represent objects which are needed for the event to take place but are not affected by the event (i.e., they are neither cancelled nor generated). In this way a context object is an object which is checked for presence (or, in some sense, read), but which is not consumed.

Given a(n acyclic) contextual net (formally: a contextual occurrence net), it is possible to derive three relations among its objects (either conditions or events), describing respectively the *causal dependency*, the *mutual exclusion*, and the *concurrency* among such objects. By using contextual occurrence nets to give a semantics to CC program, these relations are then interpreted as describing, respectively, the necessary sequentialization, the possible simultaneity, and the nondeterministic choices among steps of CC computations.

The main reason we used (a variant of) the Petri net formalism to express the concurrent semantics of a CC program is that such structures are able to express all the concurrency actually present in the program executions. Thus, by looking at such nets, or at an abstraction of them, one can find the maximal amount of possible parallelism that it is possible to exploit by executing the given program.

Our concurrent semantics cannot be fairly compared to the concurrent semantic approaches for process algebras. Instead, it has to be considered as a semantic domain upon which any observation mechanism can later be applied. In fact, in our approach, the equivalence classes of computations contain just those computations which differ for the order of concurrent steps. Thus any other added mechanism could enlarge such equivalence classes, possibly providing the semantics with additional properties.

We have started applying our concurrent semantics to various optimization tasks. In particular, we have used it to improve the analysis needed in order to parallelize (C)LP goals in a way which is both correct and efficient [3]. The advantage of using our approach for such a task consists of 1) a formal description of the parallel execution model, and 2) the possibility of recognizing much more parallelism. In fact, our semantics describes the parallelism at the smallest level of granularity. Therefore goals which appeared to be not parallelizable at all in the usual approach [7, 6] because of conflicts in small subparts of their execution trees, can be now partially parallelized.

The paper is organized as follows. Section 1.2 describes the CC framework. Then, Section 1.3 gives the operational semantics for CC programs, Section 1.4 defines contextual nets, and Section 1.5 proposes the concurrent semantics based on contextual nets, and relates the operational and the concurrent semantics. Finally, Section 1.6 concludes the paper by informally describing some possible abstractions and applications of the semantics structure. A shorter version of this article can be found in [12], while a comparison of (a version of) the concurrent semantics based on contextual nets with that based on graph rewriting and another one based on event structures can be found in [15]. Moreover, the semantics presented here is a conservative extension of the one in [10, 11], since by restricting the obtained contextual net to subnets without mutual exclusion, we get essentially the partial orders defined in that semantics.

1.2   Concurrent Constraint Programming

A CC program [18, 16, 17] consists of a set of agents interacting through a shared store, which is a set of constraints on some variables. The framework is parametric w.r.t. the kind of constraints that can be handled. The concurrent agents do not communicate with each other, but only with the shared store, by either checking if it entails a given constraint (ask operation) or adding a new constraint to it (tell operation). Therefore computations proceed by monotonically accumulating information (that is, constraints) to the shared store. The following grammar describes the CC language we consider:

$P ::= F.A$
$F ::= p(\vec{x}) :: A \mid F.F$
$A ::= success \mid failure \mid tell(c) \rightarrow A \mid \sum_{i=1,\dots,n} ask(c_i) \rightarrow A_i \mid A \parallel A \mid \exists \vec{x}.A \mid p(\vec{x})$

where P is the class of programs, F is the class of sequences of procedure declarations, A is the class of agents, c ranges over constraints, and $\vec{x}$ is a tuple of variables. Each procedure is defined once, thus nondeterminism is expressed via the + combinator only (which is here denoted by $\sum$). We also assume that, in $p(\vec{x}) :: A$, $vars(A) \subseteq \vec{x}$, where $vars(A)$ is the set of all variables occurring free in agent A. In a program $P = F.A$, A is called initial agent, to be executed in the context of the set of declarations F.

Given a program P, in the following we will refer to $Ag(P)$ as the set of all agents (and subagents) occurring in P, i.e., all the elements of type A occurring in a derivation of P according to the above grammar.

In the CC paradigm, the underlying constraint system can be described ([17]) as a *system of partial information* (derived from the *information system* introduced in [19]) of the form $\langle D, \vdash \rangle$ where D is a set of *tokens* (or primitive constraints) and $\vdash \subseteq \wp(D) \times D$ is the entailment relation which states which tokens are entailed by which sets of other tokens. The relation $\vdash$ has to satisfy the following axioms:

$u \vdash x$ if $x \in u$ (reflexivity), and
$u \vdash x$ if $v \vdash x$ and, for all $y \in v$, $u \vdash y$ (transitivity).

Given D, $\mid D \mid$ is the set of all subsets of D closed under entailment. Then, a constraint in a constraint system $\langle D, \vdash \rangle$ is simply an element of $\mid D \mid$ (that is, a set of tokens). In the following, we will assume that the constraint system is closed under negation. That is, if $c \in \wp(D)$, then also $\neg c \in \wp(D)$.

1.3   The Operational Semantics

Each state of a CC computation consists of the active agents and of the already generated tokens. However, a state consists of a *multiset* of agents and tokens, rather than a set, since the same agent (and also the same token) may occur in a state with multiplicity higher than one (just consider the computations of $A \parallel A$). Both agents and tokens will have associated the variables they involve. Then, each computation step will model either the evolution of a single agent, or the entailment of a new token through the $\vdash$ relation. Such a change in the state of the computation will be performed via the application of a rewrite rule.

DEFINITION 1.1 (COMPUTATION STATE) Given a program $P = F.A$ with a constraint system $\langle D, \vdash \rangle$, a state is a multiset of elements of $Ag(P) \cup D.\square$

Each item in a state involves some variables, and usually we will explicitly write these variables. For example, if t involves variables $x_1, \ldots, x_n$, then we will write $t(x_1, \ldots, x_n)$. Since each state of the computation is a multiset, when in the following we will use the operations of union and difference, as well as the inclusion predicate, we will always consider their multiset interpretation. In a multiset, the multiplicity of each item is the natural number associated to it. For example, if an item A appears n times in the multiset, then its multiplicity is n and we will write nA.

DEFINITION 1.2 (REWRITE RULES) A rewrite rule has the form

$$r : L(r)(\vec{x}) \stackrel{c(r)(\vec{x})}{\rightsquigarrow} R(r)(\vec{x}\vec{y})$$

where $L(r)$ is an agent, $c(r)$ is a constraint, and $R(r)$ is a state. Moreover, $\vec{x}$ is the tuple of variables appearing free both in $L(r) \cup c(r)$ and in $R(r)$, while $\vec{y}$ is the tuple of variables appearing free only in $R(r).\square$

The intuitive meaning of a rule is that $L(r)$, which is called the left hand side of the rule, is rewritten into (or replaced by) $R(r)$, i.e., the right hand side, if $c(r)$ is present in the current state. $R(r)$ could contain some variables not appearing in $L(r)$ nor in $c(r)$ (i.e., the tuple $\vec{y}$). The application of r would then rename such variables to constants which are different from all the others already in use.

The items in $c(r)$ have to be interpreted as a context, since it is necessary for the application of the rule but it is not affected by such application. The possibility of having a context-dependent formalism is very significant if we are interested in the causal dependencies among the objects involved in a computation. In fact, consider for example two rule applications with overlapping contexts but with disjoint left hand sides. Then, in a context-dependent formalism they can be applied independently. On the other hand, a context-independent formalism would simulate a context object by first cancelling it and then generating it again, and thus would not be able to express the simultaneous execution of the same rules, but only their sequential execution in any order. The CC framework is obviously context-dependent, since a constraint to be asked to the store is naturally interpreted as an object which is needed for the computation to evolve but which is not affected by such evolution. Therefore, the modelling of CC computations via a context-dependent formalism provides a more faithful description of this framework.

Note that the variables appearing in a rule are "really" variables, since they can be instantiated and aliased whenever the rule is applied. However, the variables appearing in a computation state can never be aliased via substitutions (although a constraint could state that they are equal). Thus they can be treated as constants without loss of generality. This is what we will do in the rest of the paper. More precisely, a rule r will be assumed to involve a tuple of variables $\vec{x}$, while a state of the computation S will involve a tuple of constants $\vec{a}$.

DEFINITION 1.3 (COMPUTATION STEPS) Consider a computation state $S_1(\vec{a})$ and a rule $r : L(r)(\vec{x}) \overset{c(r)(\vec{x})}{\rightsquigarrow} R(r)(\vec{x}\vec{y})$. Suppose also that $(L(r) \cup c(r))[\vec{a}/\vec{x}] \subseteq S_1(\vec{a})$. Then the application of r to S_1 is a computation step which yields a new computation state $S_2 = (S_1 - L(r)[\vec{a}/\vec{x}]) \cup R(r)[\vec{a}/\vec{x}][\vec{b}/\vec{y}]$, where the constants in $\vec{b}$ are fresh, i.e. they do not appear in S_1. We will write[1] $S_1 \overset{r[\vec{a}/\vec{x}][\vec{b}/\vec{y}]}{\Longrightarrow} S_2$. $\square$

In words, a rule r can be applied to a state S_1 if both the left hand side of the rule and its context can be found (via a suitable substitution) in S_1. Then, the

---

[1] The application of a substitution θ to a rule r, written $r\theta$, is a new rule whose left hand side, right hand side, and context are obtained by applying θ to the corresponding constituents of r.

application of r removes from S_1 the left hand side of r and adds its right hand side.

DEFINITION 1.4 (FROM PROGRAMS TO RULES) The rules corresponding to agents, declarations, and entailment pairs are given as follows:

$(tell(c) \rightarrow A) \rightsquigarrow c, A$

$A_1 \parallel A_2 \rightsquigarrow A_1, A_2$

$\exists \vec{x}.A \rightsquigarrow A$

$(\sum_{i=1,\ldots,n} ask(c_i) \rightarrow A_i) \overset{c_j}{\rightsquigarrow} A_j$ for all $j = 1, \ldots, n$

$(\sum_{i=1,\ldots,n} ask(c_i) \rightarrow A_i) \overset{\neg c_j}{\rightsquigarrow} success$ for all $j = 1, \ldots, n$

$p(\vec{x}) \rightsquigarrow A$ for all $p(\vec{x}) :: A$

$\overset{S}{\rightsquigarrow} t$ for all $S \vdash t$

Given a CC program $P = F.A$ and its underlying constraint system $\langle D, \vdash \rangle$, we will call $RR(P)$ the set of rewrite rules associated to P, which consists of the rules corresponding to all agents in $Ag(P)$, plus the rules representing the declarations in F, plus those rules representing the pairs of the entailment relation $\vdash$.□

That is, if the agent $(tell(c) \rightarrow A)$ is found in the current state, then such agent can be replaced by the agent A together with the constraint c. In other words, $(tell(c) \rightarrow A)$ is cancelled by the current state, while both c and A are added.

Agent $A_1 \parallel A_2$ is instead replaced by the multiset containing the two agents A_1 and A_2. Note that if $A_1 = A_2 = A$ we would still have two distinct elements, since a state is a multiset of elements. Therefore, in that case we would denote by $2A$ the new computation state.

Agent $\exists \vec{x}.A$ is replaced by agent A. This is the only rule where the right hand side has more variables than the left hand side.

Agent $\sum_{i=1,\ldots,n} ask(c_i) \rightarrow A_i$ gives rise to as many rewrite rules as the number of possible nondeterministic choices. In each of such branches, say branch j, the whole agent is replaced by agent A_j only if c_j is present already in the store. Note that only this rule, which corresponds to an ask agent, needs a context. In fact, as noted before, asked constraints in CC programming are directly related to context objects in our context-dependent formalism. If instead c_j is inconsistent with the current store (thus is modelled by the fact that $\neg c_j$ is in the store), then the whole alternative j disappears.

The other rules are needed for describing the environment in which agents evolve. Such environment is made up of the declarations in the given program and of the underlying constraint system. For declarations, the head of the clause (if declarations are seen as clauses in the logic programming sense) is replaced by its body.

This is an unfolding rule which allows to pass from the agent $p(\vec{x})$ to the agent A, which will then evolve via the rules given above. For entailment pairs, the rules have an empty left hand side. In fact, the presence of the context S is enough to add the token t to the current store.

EXAMPLE 1.1 (COMPUTATION STEP) Consider a computation state containing agent

$$A(a_1, a_2) = ask(t_1(a_1, a_2)) \to A'(a_2)$$

and tokens $t_1(a_1, a_2)$ and $t_2(a_2, a_3)$. Consider also the rewrite rule

$$(ask(t_1(x_1, x_2)) \to A'(x_2)) \overset{t_1(x_1, x_2)}{\leadsto} A'(x_2).$$

Then, since there exists a matching between the left hand side of the rule and (a subset of) the state (via the substitution $\{a_1/x_1, a_2/x_2\}$), the rule can be applied, yielding the new state containing agent $A'(a_2)$ and tokens $t_1(a_1, a_2)$ and $t_2(a_2, a_3)$. Note that token $t_1(a_1, a_2)$ has not been cancelled by the rewrite rule, since it was in its context part.□

DEFINITION 1.5 (COMPUTATIONS) Given a CC program $P = F.A$, a computation segment for P is any sequence of computation steps

$$S_1 \overset{r_1[\vec{a_1}/\vec{x_1}]}{\Longrightarrow} S_2 \overset{r_2[\vec{a_2}/\vec{x_2}]}{\Longrightarrow} S_3 \ldots$$

such that $S_1 = \{A\}$ and $r_i \in RR(P)$, i = 1, 2, ... Two computation segments which are the same except that different fresh constants are employed in the various steps, are called α-equivalent. A computation is a computation segment, say CS, such that for any other computation segment, say CS', of which CS is a prefix, CS' adds to CS only steps applying rules for the entailment relation.□

DEFINITION 1.6 (SUCCESSFUL, SUSPENDED, AND FAILING COMPUTATIONS)
A successful computation is a finite computation where the last state contains only a set of constraints, say S, and $S \not\vdash \bot$. A suspended computation is a finite computation where the last state does not contain tell agents but contains ask agents, and its set of constraints S is such that $S \not\vdash \bot$. A failing computation is a computation which is neither successful nor suspended. □

In the following we will only consider either finite computations or infinite computations which are fair. Here fairness means, informally, that if a rule can continuously be applied from some point onwards, then it will eventually be applied. This implies that both the goal selection (among several goals in the current state) and the rule selection (among several rules applicable to a goal) are fair.

DEFINITION 1.7 (OPERATIONAL SEMANTICS) Given a CC program $P = F.A$, its operational semantics, say $O(P)$, is the set of all its computations. □

1.4 Contextual Nets

In classical nets, as defined for example in [14], each element of the set of conditions can be a precondition (if it belongs to the pre-set of an event) or a postcondition (if it belongs to the post-set of an event). We now add the possibility, for a condition, to be considered as a *context* for an event. Informally, a context is something which is necessary for the event to be enabled, but which is not affected by the firing of that event. In other words, a context condition can be interpreted as an item which is *read without being consumed* by the event, in the same sense as preconditions can be considered being *read and consumed* and postconditions being instead simply *written*.

The formal technique which we use to introduce contexts consists of adding a new relation, beside the usual flow relation, which we call the *context relation*. Such relations state which conditions are to be considered as a context for which event. Nets with such contexts will be called *context-dependent nets*.

In the following, we assume the reader to be familiar with the classical notions of nets, C/E systems, occurrence nets, and relatives. For the formal definitions missing here we refer to [14]. Moreover, a longer and more detailed treatment of contextual nets and their process-based semantics can be found in [13].

DEFINITION 1.8 (CONTEXT-DEPENDENT NETS) A context-dependent net CN is a quadruple $(B, E; F_1, F_2)$ where

- $B \cap E = \emptyset$, where elements of B are called conditions and elements of E are called events;
- $F_1 \subseteq (B \times E) \cup (E \times B)$ and it is called the flow relation;
- $F_2 \subseteq (B \times E)$ and it is called the context relation;
- $(F_1 \cup F_1^{-1}) \cap F_2 = \emptyset$.□

It is immediate to see that context-dependent nets are more general than classical nets. In fact, a net is simply a context-dependent net where $F_2 = \emptyset$.

EXAMPLE 1.2 (CONTEXT-DEPENDENT NETS) Context-dependent nets will be graphically represented in the same way as nets. I.e., conditions are circles, events are boxes, and the flow relation is represented by directed arcs from circles to boxes or vice-versa. We choose to represent the context relation by undirected arcs (since the direction of such relation is unambiguous, i.e., from elements of B to elements of E). An example of a context-dependent net can be found in Figure 1.1, where there are five events $e_1, \ldots, e_5$ and nine conditions $b_1, \ldots, b_9$. In particular, event e_2 has b_2 and b_3 as preconditions, b_5 as postcondition, and b_7 as a context. Note, however, that b_7 is not a context for all events. In fact, it is a precondition for e_4 and a context for e_3, for which b_6 is a context as well, while b_4 is a precondition and b_8 is a postcondition.□

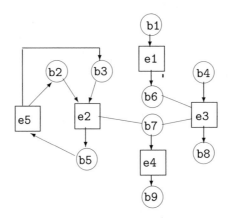

Figure 1.1
A context-dependent net.

DEFINITION 1.9 (PRE-SET, POST-SET, AND CONTEXT)
Given a context-dependent net $CN = (B, E; F_1, F_2)$ and an element $x \in B \cup E$,

- the pre-set of x is the set $^\bullet x = \{y \mid F_1(y, x)\}$,
- the post-set of x is the set $x^\bullet = \{y \mid F_1(x, y)\}$, and
- the context of x is defined if $x \in E$ and it is the set $\widehat{x} = \{y \mid F_2(y, x)\}$.□

The concept which we will use to give a truly concurrent semantics to CC programs is the notion of a contextual process, which is a contextual occurrence net together with a suitable mapping of the events onto the rewrite rules. Informally, a contextual occurrence net is just an acyclic context dependent net. More precisely, the main feature of a contextual occurrence net is the following: given a context dependent net, it is possible to derive an associated dependency relation among its items (events and conditions); then, in a contextual occurrence net such associated relation is a partial order.

The idea is that such relation (seen as a set of pairs) contains all pairs in F_1, plus other pairs, derived by the combination of F_1 and F_2. In fact, if an element b is a postcondition of $e1$ and a context condition of $e2$, then $e2$ depends on $e1$ and this has to be reflected in the partial order. The same holds when b is a context condition of $e1$ and a precondition of $e2$. In fact, in this last case, in any computation where both e_1 and e_2 are present, e_1 must happen before e_2 (that is, b cannot be cancelled before being read).

DEFINITION 1.10 (DEPENDENCY)
Consider a context-dependent net $N = (B, E; F_1, F_2)$. Then we define a corresponding structure $(B \cup E, \leq_N)$, where the dependency relation $\leq_N$ is the minimal relation which is reflexive, transitive, and which satisfies the following conditions:

- xF_1y implies $x \leq_N y$;
- $e1F_1b$ and bF_2e2 implies $e1 \leq_N e2$;
- bF_2e1 and bF_1e2 implies $e1 \leq_N e2.\square$

Therefore in the following we will say that x depends on y whenever $y \leq_N x$. However, a context-dependent net not only gives information about dependency of events and conditions, but also about their mutual exclusion (or conflict). In fact, given one such net, it is possible to derive two relations, besides the dependency relation just defined, all of which are sets of pairs of elements of $(B \cup E)$, which express 1) concurrency and 2) mutual exclusion.

DEFINITION 1.11 (MUTUAL EXCLUSION AND CONCURRENCY)
Consider a context-dependent net $N = (B, E; F_1, F_2)$ and the associated dependency relation $\leq_N$. Assume also that $\leq$ is antisymmetric. Then

- The mutual exclusion relation $\#_N \subseteq ((B \cup E) \times (B \cup E))$ is defined as follows. First we define $x\#'y$ iff $x, y \in E$ and $\exists z \in B$ such that zF_1x and zF_1y. Then, $\#_N$ is the minimal relation which includes $\#'$ and which is symmetric and hereditary (i.e., if $x\#_Ny$ and $x \leq z$, then $z\#_Ny$).
- The concurrency relation co_N is just $((B \cup E) \times (B \cup E)) - (\leq_N \cup \leq_N^{-1} \cup \#_N).\square$

In words, the mutual exclusion is originated by the existence of conditions which cause more than one event, and then it is propagated downwards via the partial order. Finally, two items are concurrent if they are not dependent on each other nor mutually exclusive.

We now come to the notion of a contextual occurrence net, which is just a context-dependent net where the dependency relation is a partial order, there are no "forwards conflicts" (i.e., different events with a common postcondition), and $\#_N$ is irreflexive.

DEFINITION 1.12 (CONTEXTUAL OCCURRENCE NET) A contextual occurrence net is a a context-dependent net $N = (B, E; F_1, F_2)$ where

- $\leq_N$ is antisymmetric;
- $b \in B$ implies $\mid {}^\bullet b \mid \leq_N 1$;
- $\#_N$ is irreflexive.$\square$

A useful special case of a contextual occurrence net occurs when the mutual exclusion relation is empty. This means that, taken any two items in the net, they are either concurrent or dependent. Since no conflict is expressed in such nets, they represent a completely deterministic behaviour. For this reason they are called deterministic occurrence nets.

DEFINITION 1.13 (DETERMINISTIC CONTEXTUAL OCCURRENCE NET) A deterministic contextual occurrence net is a quadruple $N = (B, E; F_1, F_2)$ such that N is a contextual occurrence net with $\#_N = \emptyset$.$\square$

EXAMPLE 1.3 (CONTEXTUAL OCCURRENCE NETS) Consider for example the deterministic contextual occurrence net in Figure 1.2 a). Then its dependency partial order can be seen in Figure 1.2 b).$\square$

Given a (nondeterministic) contextual occurrence net, it is easy to derive the set of all its subnets which are deterministic.

DEFINITION 1.14 Consider a contextual occurrence net $N = (B, E; F_1, F_2)$ and the associated relations $\leq$, $\#$, and co. Then a deterministic contextual occurrence net of N is a deterministic contextual occurrence net $N' = (B', E'; F_1', F_2')$ where

- $B' \subseteq B$ and $E' \subseteq E'$;
- F_1' and F_2' are the restrictions to B' and E' of F_1 and F_2 respectively ;
- $x \in (B' \cup E')$ and $y \in (B \cup E)$ such that $y \leq x$ implies that $y \in (B' \cup E')$.$\square$

The last condition states that the set $B' \cup E'$ is left-closed w.r.t. relation $\leq_N$. That is, the causes of the elements in $B' \cup E'$ are in $B' \cup E'$ as well. The intuition behind this condition is that deterministic nets which are not left-closed represent meaningless computations, since there are objects which are causally inconsistent.

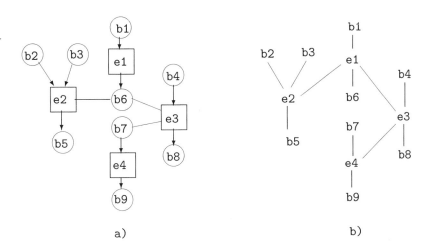

Figure 1.2
A deterministic contextual occurrence net and the associated partial order.

Let us now try to relate (nondeterministic) contextual occurrence nets to CC programs. We will do that by defining a contextual process, which is just a contextual occurrence net plus a suitable mapping from the items of the net (i.e., conditions and events) to the agents of the CC program and the rules representing it.

DEFINITION 1.15 (CONTEXTUAL PROCESS) Given a CC program P with initial agent A, and the associated sets of rewrite rules $RR(P)$, of agents $Ag(P)$, and of constraints D, consider the sets $RB = \{b\theta\}$ and $RE = \{r\theta\}$, with $b \in (Ag(P) \cup D)$, $r \in RR(P)$ and θ any substitution. Then a contextual process is a pair $\langle N, \pi \rangle$, where

- $N = (B, E; F_1, F_2)$ is a nondeterministic contextual occurrence net;
- $\pi : (B \cup E) \to (RB \cup RE)$ is a mapping with
    - $b \in B$ implies $\pi(b) \in RB$;
    - $e \in E$ implies $\pi(e) \in RE$;
    - consider $^\circ N = \{x \in B \mid \nexists y \in (B \cup E) \mid y \leq_N x\}$. Then $\pi(^\circ N) = A$;
    - let $\pi(e) = r\theta$, with $r = L \overset{c}{\rightsquigarrow} R$. Then we have $\pi(^\bullet e) = L\theta$, $\pi(\hat{e}) = c\theta$, and $\pi(e^\bullet) = R\theta$. Notice that here and in the previous definition we homomorphically extended π to a function from sets to multisets: the multiplicity of an item in the result is simply the cardinality of its inverse image;

- for each $e \in E$, consider $\pi(e) = r\theta'_e\theta''_e$, where θ''_e replaces the variables which are in R but not in L nor in c. Then for all events e and e' and variables x and x' we have:
    * let constant a occur in the initial agent A. Then $x\theta''_e \neq a$
    * $x\theta''_e = x'\theta''_{e'}$ implies $x = x'$ and $e = e'$

    i.e. the constants introduced by the rewrite rule instantiations associated to events must be fresh, namely they must be all different and different from the constants in the initial state.☐

1.5   The Concurrent Semantics

The idea is to take the set of rewrite rules $RR(P)$ associated to a given CC program P and to incrementally construct a corresponding contextual process. Such process is then shown to be able to represent all possible computations of the CC program P in a single partial-order-based structure (and not as a set of structures, as in [10, 11]).

DEFINITION 1.16 (FROM REWRITE RULES TO A CONTEXTUAL PROCESS)
Given a CC program P, the pair $CP(P) = \langle (B, E; F_1, F_2), \pi \rangle$ is constructed by means of the following two inference rules:

- $A(\vec{a})$ initial agent of P
  implies
  $\langle A(\vec{a}), \emptyset, 1 \rangle \in B$;
- $\{s_1, \ldots, s_n\} \subseteq B$, where s_i co s_j for all i, j, $i \neq j$, $i, j = 1, \ldots, n$, and $s_i = \langle e_i, B_i(\vec{a_i}), k_i \rangle$ for all $i = 1, \ldots, n$, $r \in RR(P)$ such that $L(r) = \{B_1(\vec{x_1}), \ldots, B_j(\vec{x_j})\}$, and $c(r) = \{B_{j+1}(\vec{x_{j+1}}), \ldots, B_n(\vec{x_n})\}$, and $\exists$ a substitution $[\vec{a}/\vec{x}]$ such that $B_i(\vec{x_i})[\vec{a}/\vec{x}] = B_i(\vec{a_i})$
  implies
    - $e = \langle r[\vec{a}/\vec{x}], \{s_1, \ldots, s_n\}, 1 \rangle \in E$,
    - $s_i F_1 e$ for all $i = 1, \ldots, j$,
    - $s_i F_2 e$ for all $i = j+1, \ldots, n$,
    - let h be the multiplicity of $B(\vec{x}, y_1, \ldots, y_m)$ in $R(r)$. Then for all $l = 1, \ldots, h$,
      $b_l = \langle B[\vec{a}/\vec{x}][\langle e, y_1 \rangle/y_1] \ldots [\langle e, y_m \rangle/y_m], e, l \rangle \in B$, and eF_1b_l.

Moreover, for any item $x = \langle x_1, x_2, x_3 \rangle \in (B \cup E)$, $\pi(x) = x_1$.☐

Informally, we apply the rewrite rules, starting from the initial agent, in any possible way, so that different occurrences of the same rule are represented by different events of the net and generate different conditions. The technique used to achieve that consists of generating a new event representing the rule application and new conditions representing the right hand side of the rule, and by structuring each event or condition as a triple, where the first element contains the object being represented (either an agent, or a token, or a rule application), while the second element contains the whole history of the event or condition, and the third element is a number which allows us to distinguish different occurrences with the same history (we recall that a state is a multiset, while here we are generating a set of conditions). If there is only one of such occurrences, then the number will be 1, otherwise, the k-th occurrence will have number k. Note that, for the language we consider, k is always either 1 or 2, since there cannot be more than two occurrences with the same history. In fact, the only rule which may generate a multiset containing different occurrences of the same element is the one associated to the agent $A \parallel A$. However, our approach can also handle languages where an agent may fork into more than two agents. Note that we don't have to handle the problem of different rules generating different occurrences of the same agent, since the identity of such occurrences is automatically made distinct by the fact that they will have different histories. Moreover, the mapping π tells us either the rule or the object represented (with the applied substitution). In the following we will often omit the mapping π, since we know that π always maps a triple to its first element.

The first inference rule creates one condition which represents the initial agent A of the given program P. Such term, $\langle A(\vec{a}), \emptyset, 1 \rangle$, has the agent A as the first element of the triple, the empty set as the second element, and the number 1 as the third element. This means that agent A has no element it depends on, which is reasonable since it is the first agent of each computation. A. The second inference rule creates the event representing the application of a rewrite rule r, as well as the objects in the right hand side of r. To apply r, we have to find a set of conditions, already in B, which match the left hand side and the context of r. These are the conditions s_i, each of which is the triple $\langle e_i, B_i(\vec{a}), k_i \rangle$. This means that each s_i represents the object B_i, which can be either an agent or a token, involves constants $\vec{a}$, depends on term e_i, and it is the k_i-th occurrence of B_i. Note that if agents B_i contain different sets of constants, we assume that tuple $\vec{a}$ contains their union. The matching condition is expressed by the substitution $[\vec{a}/\vec{x}]$, which is able to make the left hand side and the context of a rule to coincide with a subset of terms already generated. Furthermore, such conditions must be concurrent (i.e., $s_i \, co \, s_j$).

This means that they have the possibility of being all together simultaneously in a computation. With these preconditions satisfied, the inference rule creates a new event and new conditions. The event is $e = \langle r[\vec{a}/\vec{x}], \{s_1, \ldots, s_n\}, 1\rangle$: it represents the application of r, which depends on its left hand side and its context (this is why the second element of the triple contains the set $\{s_1, \ldots, s_n\}$). This event is then related to the conditions s_i by means of the two relation F_1 and F_2. More precisely, F_1 is used to relate it to the conditions representing the left hand side of the rule (which are $s_1, \ldots, s_j$), while F_2 is used to relate it to the conditions representing the context of the rule (which are $s_{j+1}, \ldots, s_n$). The conditions which are generated represent all the objects (either tokens or agents) in the right hand side of r. Thus, for each of such objects, say B, which involves the variables in the left hand side of r (i.e., $\vec{x}$) and possibly some other variables (i.e., $y_1, \ldots, y_m$), we create the condition $\langle B[\vec{a}/\vec{x}][\langle e, y_1\rangle/y_1] \ldots [\langle e, y_m\rangle/y_m], e, l\rangle$, and we make it dependent on event e via relation F_1. This condition represents the l-th occurrence of object B with variables $\vec{x}$ suitably substituted by the constants $\vec{a}$ (which is the matching needed for the application of the rule), plus the other variables, which have been renamed to contain term e, which is the term representing the rule application. In this way, such variables are different from any other variable ever used in the computation. It is worthwhile to notice that the technique of embedding the history of an object in the term representing the object, applied to the variables y_i, allows a formal handling of the so-called "standardization apart" step in logic programming ([9]), which informally says that all existential variables found in a clause should be renamed to be "fresh variables". The second element of the triple representing B is the event e, because B obviously depends only on the rule application (and thus on the term representing such application).

EXAMPLE 1.4 (CC PROGRAMS AND CONTEXTUAL PROCESSES)
Consider the CC program P consisting of the initial agent $IA = tell(c_1, c_2, c) \rightarrow A$, where
$A = (ask(c_1) \rightarrow A_1 + ask(c_2) \rightarrow success)$,
$A_1 = A_2 \parallel A_2$,
$A_2 = ask(c) \rightarrow success$,
and no declarations. The rules for such an agent and all its subagents are:
$r_1 : IA \rightsquigarrow c_1, c_2, c, A$
$r_2 : A \overset{c_1}{\rightsquigarrow} A_1$
$r_3 : A \overset{c_2}{\rightsquigarrow} success$
$r_4 : A_1 \rightsquigarrow 2A_2$
$r_5 : A_2 \overset{c}{\rightsquigarrow} success$.

For simplicity, we assume the entailment relation to be empty (or not relevant to the constraints involved in such program). Furthermore, the variables are not taken into consideration. This program has two alternative finite computations, depending on how agent A evolves. In one case, we have the parallel evolution of two occurrences of A_2 (even though they both ask for the same constraint c), and in the other case we have one computation step generating the success agent.

The process that is generated for this program is as follows (again, we will not explicitly write the mapping π, since each triple is mapped by π to its first element). First, condition $s_1 = \langle IA, \emptyset, 1 \rangle$ is generated for the initial agent IA. At this point, rule r_1 can be applied, and thus we generate event $e_1 = \langle r_1, \{s_1\}, 1 \rangle$ to represent the rule application, and conditions $s_2 = \langle A, e_1, 1 \rangle$, $s_3 = \langle c_1, e_1, 1 \rangle$, $s_4 = \langle c_2, e_1, 1 \rangle$, and $s_5 = \langle c, e_1, 1 \rangle$ to represent its right hand side. Moreover, we set $s_1 F_1 e_1$, and $e_1 F_1 s_i$ for $i = 2, \ldots, 5$.

Since there are conditions representing A, c_1, and c_2 (i.e., s_2, s_3, and s_4), rules r_2 and r_3 can now be applied, and thus we have events $e_2 = \langle r_2, \{s_2, s_3\}, 1 \rangle$ and $e_3 = \langle r_3, \{s_2, s_4\}, 1 \rangle$, as well as conditions $s_6 = \langle A_1, e_2, 1 \rangle$ and $s_7 = \langle success, e_3, 2 \rangle$. Moreover, we also have $s_2 F_1 e_2$, $s_3 F_2 e_2$, $e_2 F_1 s_6$, $s_2 F_1 e_3$, $s_4 F_2 e_3$, $e_3 F_1 s_7$.

Now there is a condition representing A_1, thus rule r_4 can be applied, and we have the event $e_4 = \langle r_4, \{s_6\}, 1 \rangle$, and the conditions $s_8 = \langle A_2, e_4, 1 \rangle$ and $s_9 = \langle A_2, e_4, 2 \rangle$. Moreover, $s_6 F_1 e_4$, $e_4 F_1 s_8$, and $e_4 F_1 s_9$.

Now both s_8 and s_9 match the left hand side of rule r_5, and there is a condition representing c (i.e., s_5), therefore we can apply twice rule r_5, obtaining $e_5 = \langle r_5, \{s_5, s_8\}, 1 \rangle$, $s_{10} = \langle success, e_5, 1 \rangle$, $s_8 F_1 e_5$, $s_5 F_2 e_5$, and $e_5 F_1 s_{10}$ for the first application, and $e_6 = \langle r_5, \{s_5, s_9\}, 1 \rangle$, $s_{11} = \langle success, e_6, 1 \rangle$, $s_9 F_1 e_6$, $s_5 F_2 e_6$, and $e_6 F_1 s_{11}$ for the second application.

Thus we obtained the contextual process $\langle N, \pi \rangle$, where $N = (B, E; F_1, F_2)$, and $B = \{s_1, \ldots, s_{11}\}$, $E = \{e_1 \ldots, e_6\}$, and F_1 and F_2 are as defined above. Figure 1.3 shows such a net N. In N, it is easy to see that e_2 causally depends on e_1, since they are related by a chain of F_1 pairs. Similarly, e_3 depends on e_1. However, e_3 and e_2 do not depend on each other, and they are not even concurrent. In fact, they are mutually exclusive, since they have a common precondition. This means the the rules represented by e_2 and e_3, i.e., r_2 and r_3, cannot be applied in the same computation, but only in two alternative computations. Then, we have that e_4 depends on e_2 because of a chain of F_1 pairs. Also, e_5 depends on e_4. Finally, e_6 depends on e_4 as well. However, e_5 and e_6 are concurrent, since they do not depend on each other and they are not mutually exclusive. Note that e_5 and e_6 have a common context condition. However, this does not generate any dependency, as desired.$\square$

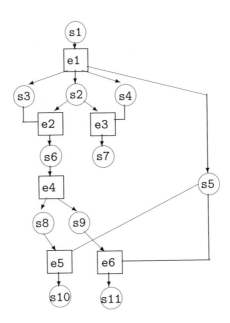

Figure 1.3
The contextual occurrence net corresponding to a CC program.

THEOREM 1.1 ($CP(P)$ IS A CONTEXTUAL PROCESS) Given a CC program P, consider the structure $CP(P)$ as defined above. Then, $CP(P)$ is a contextual process.□

The construction of the contextual process $CP(P)$, as described in Definition 1.16, is completely deterministic, in the sense that it is independent of the order in which the rules in $RR(P)$ are selected to create new events and conditions of the net. This construction of the process $CP(P)$ has been originally inspired by the one proposed in [20] to obtain a (possibly nondeterministic) occurrence net from a Petri net. Furthermore, the aim coincides, since in both cases the idea is to find a structure which represents all possible computations (of the Petri net in the case of [20], and of the given CC program in our case). However, there are four main differences. First, we do not start from a given net, but from a set of rules. Second, our definition of the mutual exclusion and dependency relations, as noted above, has to take into account the two types of resources in a CC program (i.e., agents and tokens), which are faithfully represented in a contextual net via the use of relations F_1 and F_2, while Petri net computations only involve consumable resources. In fact, as we noted above, Petri nets in their classical formulation are a context-independent formalism, and therefore they cannot express non-consumable resources. Third, variables are not present in the Petri net formalism, while we have to consider them for a faithful description of the CC framework. In this respect, it is therefore original the extension to the existential variables of the technique which puts together each element and its history. Finally, we have to deal with the possibility of having different instances of the same object in a computation state, and thus we have to use a numbering technique to distinguish among such different occurrences. A by-product of the strong relationship between the construction in [20] and ours is that, in both cases, the set of events of the process $CP(P)$, together with the dependency and mutual exclusion relations, can be seen as what is called an "event structure" in [20].

The process $CP(P)$ is able to represent all deterministic computations possible for the given CC program P. The following theorem formalizes this claim.

THEOREM 1.2 (SOUNDNESS AND COMPLETENESS OF $CP(P)$) Let P be a CC program and let $CP(P) = \langle N, \pi \rangle$ be the corresponding contextual process. Given a computation of P, there is:

- an α-equivalent computation

$$S_1 \overset{r_1[\vec{a_1}/\vec{x_1}]}{\Longrightarrow} S_2 \overset{r_2[\vec{a_2}/\vec{x_2}]}{\Longrightarrow} S_3 \dots$$

- a deterministic contextual occurrence net of N, say N', with associated partial order $\leq'$, and one of its linearizations (restricted to events), say $e_1 e_2, \dots$,

such that $\pi(e_i) = r_i[\vec{a_i}/\vec{x_i}]$ for all $i = 1, 2, \dots$.
Also, for any linearization $e_1 e_2 \dots$ of the partial order associated to a deterministic contextual occurrence net of N, there is a computation of P

$$S_1 \overset{r_1[\vec{a_1}/\vec{x_1}]}{\Longrightarrow} S_2 \overset{r_2[\vec{a_2}/\vec{x_2}]}{\Longrightarrow} S_3 \dots$$

such that, if $e_i = \langle e_{i1}, e_{i2}, e_{i3} \rangle$ and $\pi(e_i) = r$, then $r_i[\vec{a_i}/\vec{x_i}] = r$ for all $i = 1, \dots$. $\square$

Note that there is no bijective correspondence between (α-equivalence classes of) computations of P and deterministic contextual occurrence nets of N, since, as it is always the case in true concurrency, there may be different computations which are represented by the same deterministic partial order. However, there is not even a bijection between classes of computations and linearizations of partial orders associated to deterministic contextual occurrence nets. This depends on the fact that the definition of computation given by Definition 1.5, and usually employed in the literature, is not able to distinguish computations which use the same sequence of rules but where the items with multiplicity larger than one represent occurrences which are exchanged. This problem could be solved by adopting a different notion of computation which is based on states which are labelled sets (instead of multisets) and on the notion of "abstract derivations". This approach has been introduced in [4, 5] for a correct handling of graph derivations, and we believe that it can also be successfully used for CC computations.

1.6   Abstractions

The concurrent semantics we propose in this paper has to be considered only as a formal basis upon which to reason about CC programs. In fact, the explicit presence of all the information about concurrency, dependency, and mutual exclusion, can be useful in order to understand better the behaviour of CC programs with respect to such concepts. However, it is only a basis in the sense that, once a particular application had been chosen, it could be necessary to tailor the semantics for that application, possibly simplifying the net structure by some sort of abstraction, which allows either to forget some elements of the contextual net, or to identify several nets, or both. The two abstraction dimensions, being orthogonal, can be straightforwardly combined. The idea is to first decide which elements to forget, thus obtaining a smaller set of smaller nets, and then to choose a particular observation equivalence on the remaining nets.

For example, if we want to know the maximal level of concurrency of a given program, then such information can be obtained by just looking at the events of the net, and by computing the maximum number of concurrent events: e.g., the net derived for the program in the previous section has maximal concurrency two, since there are no three events which are concurrent. If instead we want to know which agent depends on which constraint, then events can be forgotten. The restriction to only some kind of elements can possibly be done after the net has been generated, by first obtaining the three relations of the net (concurrency, dependency, and mutual exclusion), and then deleting from them all the pairs which involve some element of the non-desired sort.

As for identifications of different nets, this can be useful whenever we feel that the programs which correspond to different nets should be identified. For example, if we wish to recover the input-output semantics for CC programs, then we would identify all those nets which "produce" the same set of constraints. A formal way of saying that a net produces a set of constraints $S = \{c_1, \ldots, c_n\}$ is that such a net has n maximal deterministic subnets, say $N_1, \ldots, N_n$, such that the set of tokens appearing in N_i is logically equivalent to c_i. Our semantics, as it is now, makes no identifications at all, since the syntax of the program itself is contained in the semantics, via the mapping π of the process.

It is possible that there are abstractions of the net which are common to most applications. If this is the case, then such abstractions should (and will) be developed and defined from the semantics once and for all. A possible example of such commonly desirable abstractions is the fact that events representing forkings of parallel agents, or also those representing declaration expansions, are usually not important, and can thus be forgotten. Another typical example, more crucial perhaps, is the fact that, while our semantics can in general be an infinite structure, any realistic use of our semantics will have to start from a finite description of it, for any given CC program and constraint system. Giving a finite, possibly canonical description of an infinite net, we may obviously loose some information. Thus the aim would be to loose as little dependency and concurrency information as possible, since this is the kind of information that cannot be extracted from other available semantics, which are not concurrent.

1.7 Applications

As noted above, the convenient applications for our semantics are all those tasks where some knowledge of dependency and of causality is useful. In fact, such knowledge cannot be derived by semantics, like those that have been proposed for CC programs so far, which do not have an explicit way of representing concurrency.

1.7.1 CLP Parallelization

A typical task where the concepts of dependency and concurrency are essential is the automatic parallelization of logic programs [9] or constraint logic programs (CLP) [8]. The aim is to run in parallel, independently, as many goals as possible while of course not loosing any solution (soundness) nor taking a longer time (efficiency) w.r.t. the sequential execution of the same program [7, 6]. The restriction to only sound and efficient parallelizations means that only goals which do not affect each other, that is, which are independent, can be run in parallel. Therefore any tool that can help understand whether two goals are independent or not would be of great help to such parallelization task. Our semantics can be used with profit to this extent. In fact, suppose we consider a CLP program as a CC program (it would just be a CC program without any ask agent, and with nondeterminism intended as don't know nondeterminism). Then the contextual net associated to such program would contain all the dependency and concurrency information needed to decide which goals to run in parallel safely. In fact, if two agents turn out to be concurrent in the net, then it means that they do not need each other during the computations of the program, and thus are independent. Note however that some adjustment has to be made to our semantics, since we must be able to model the conflicting situation in which different agents attempt to accomplish inconsistent tells. This can be done by adding one more relation to the three already there, called the inconsistency relation, which contains those sets of elements (agents, events, or tokens) which are inconsistent with each other, or generate inconsistency if run together. The existence of this relation can then be used to add some more dependency links (besides those generated during the construction phase) in order to force, only for the inconsistent pairs, the left-to-right execution order given by the CLP programmer in the clauses. In this way, the events that can be safely executed in parallel are all those which are still concurrent after the addition of such new links. By adopting our semantics, not only goals, i.e., entire computation trees, can be run in parallel, but also parts of computation trees. In fact, our semantics gives the independence information at the smallest level of granularity. A more detailed description of how to use our concurrent semantics to help the automatic parallelization of CLP programs can be found in [3].

1.7.2   CC Scheduling

A task which is in some sense dual to the previous one consists of running a CC program on a sequential machine in the most efficient way. In fact, if an agent A_1 depends on an agent A_2, then A_1 should be scheduled after A_2. Otherwise, the suspension of A_1 until A_2 is executed has to be taken care of (thus wasting time). For this task, our semantics can help derive the best scheduling. In fact, a sequential scheduling (but there may be many if the program is nondeterministic) where no agent ever has to wait, if it exists, is given by a linearization of one of the deterministic subnets of the contextual net which respects the dependency relation.

1.7.3   Non-Monotonic CC Programming

The CC programming paradigm, as it is considered in this paper, is completely monotonic. In fact, constraints can only be added to the store, but never deleted. However, one could imagine a more complex (and, for some applications, much more natural) situation where constraints can also be retracted. A first attempt to define such novel non-monotonic CC paradigm can be found in [1]. Consider therefore a basic non-monotonic operator, retract(c), which deletes constraint c

from the current store. Note that this operator can then be used to implement other derived non-monotonic operators, like update(c), which adds a new constraint c to the store, while deleting all the constraints already in the store which are inconsistent with c. If we want to retain the declarative reading of CC languages, and to be independent from the relative speeds of the concurrent agents, as we are in the monotonic case, then the intended meaning of retract(c) is that not only c is deleted from the store, but also everything that had been derived because of c (either via the entailment relation, or via the agents, or a combination of both). Therefore it is important to know which agents depend on c (because of an ask over c or any constraint entailed by c in the current store). This information is obviously contained in our semantics. In fact, any computation step which depends on c must have either c or a constraint dependent on c as a context. Therefore following the dependency relation we will know which part of the computation has to be retracted (together with all the constraints generated by it) because of the retraction of c. Moreover, the distinction, which is natural in our semantics, between constraints and constraint instances, allows to recognize when a constraint is generated by more than one agent. This is important, since the retraction of c has to remove only the constraint instances derived from c, but not those derived from somewhere else. For example, if constraint d has been derived by c and also by another constraint c' (which is not retracted), then d, as a constraint, should be present in the store following the retraction, since only one of its two instances is retracted.

Acknowledgments

This research has been partially supported by the GRAGRA Basic Research Esprit Working Group n.7183, by the ACCLAIM Basic Research Esprit Working Group n.7195 and by Alenia S.p.A.

References

[1] F.S. De Boer, J.N. Kok, C. Palamidessi, and J.J.M.M. Rutten. Non-monotonic concurrent constraint programming. In *Proc. ILPS93*. MIT Press, 1993.

[2] F.S. De Boer and C. Palamidessi. A fully abstract model for concurrent constraint programming. In *Proc. CAAP*. Springer-Verlag, 1991.

[3] U. Montanari and F. Rossi. From Eventual to Atomic and Locally Atomic CC Programs: A Concurrent Semantics. Proc. Int. Conference on Algebraic and

Logic Programming (ALP94), 1994.

[4] A. Corradini, H. Ehrig, M. Lowe, U. Montanari, and F. Rossi. Standard representation of graphs and graph derivations. Technical report, TU Berlin, 1992.

[5] A. Corradini, H. Ehrig, M. Lowe, U. Montanari, and F. Rossi. Abstract graph derivations in the double pushout approach. Submitted for publication, 1993.

[6] M. Garcia de la Banda, M. Hermenegildo, and K. Marriott. Independence in constraint logic programs. In *Proc. International Logic Programming Symposium*. MIT Press, 1993.

[7] M. Hermenegildo and F. Rossi. Non strict independent and-parallelism. In *Proc. ICLP90*. MIT Press, 1990.

[8] J. Jaffar and J.L. Lassez. Constraint logic programming. In *Proc. POPL*. ACM, 1987.

[9] J. W. Lloyd. *Foundations of Logic Programming*. Springer Verlag, 1987.

[10] U. Montanari and F. Rossi. True concurrency in concurrent constraint programming. In *Proc. ILPS91*. MIT Press, 1991.

[11] U. Montanari and F. Rossi. Graph rewriting for a partial ordering semantics of concurrent constraint programming. *Theoretical Computer Science*, 1992. special issue on graph grammars, Courcelle B. and Rozenberg eds.

[12] U. Montanari and F. Rossi. Contextual occurrence nets and concurrent constraint programming. In *Proc. Dagstuhl Seminar on Graph Transformations in Computer Science*. Springer-Verlag, LNCS, 1993.

[13] U. Montanari and F. Rossi. Contextual nets. *Acta Informatica*, 1994. To appear.

[14] W. Reisig. *Petri Nets: An Introduction*. EATCS Monographs on Theoretical Computer Science. Springer Verlag, 1985.

[15] F. Rossi and U. Montanari. Concurrent semantics for concurrent constraint programming. In Constraint Programming. B. Mayoh, E. Tyugu, J. Penjam eds., NATO ASI Series, 1994.

[16] V. A. Saraswat and M. Rinard. Concurrent constraint programming. In *Proc. POPL*. ACM, 1990.

[17] V. A. Saraswat, M. Rinard, and P. Panangaden. Semantic foundations of concurrent constraint programming. In *Proc. POPL*. ACM, 1991.

[18] V.A. Saraswat. *Concurrent Constraint Programming*. MIT Press, 1993.

[19] D. S. Scott. Domains for denotational semantics. In *Proc. ICALP*. Springer-Verlag, 1982.

[20] G. Winskel. Event structures. In *Petri nets: applications and relationships to other models of concurrency*. Springer-Verlag, LNCS 255, 1986.

2 Object-Oriented Concurrent Constraint Programming in Oz

Martin Henz, Gert Smolka, and Jörg Würtz

Abstract

Oz is a higher-order concurrent constraint programming system under development at DFKI. It combines ideas from logic and concurrent programming in a simple yet expressive language. From logic programming Oz inherits logic variables and logic data structures, which provide for a programming style where partial information about the values of variables is imposed concurrently and incrementally. A novel feature of Oz is the support of higher-order programming without sacrificing that denotation and equality of variables are captured by first-order logic. Another new feature of Oz are cells, a concurrent construct providing a minimal form of state fully compatible with logic data structures. These two features allow to express objects as procedures with state, avoiding the problems of stream communication, the conventional communication mechanism employed in concurrent logic programming.

Based on cells and higher-order programming, Oz readily supports concurrent object-oriented programming including object identity, late method binding, multiple inheritance, "self", "super", batches, synchronous and asynchronous communication.

2.1 Introduction

Oz [6, 21, 20, 17, 16, 7] is an attempt to create a high-level concurrent programming language bringing together the merits of logic and object-oriented programming.

Our starting point was concurrent constraint programming [14], which brings together ideas from constraint and concurrent logic programming. Constraint logic programming [8, 1], on the one hand, originated with Prolog II [4] and was prompted by the need to integrate numbers and data structures in an operationally efficient, yet logically sound manner. Concurrent logic programming [18], on the other hand, originated with the Relational Language [3] and was promoted by the Japanese Fifth Generation Project, where logic programming was conceived as the basic system programming language and thus had to account for concurrency, synchronization and indeterminism. For this purpose, the conventional SLD-resolution scheme had to be replaced with a new computation model based on the notion of committed choice. At first, the new model was an ad hoc construction, but finally Maher [11] realized that commitment of agents can be captured logically as constraint entailment. A major landmark in the new field of concurrent constraint programming is AKL [9], the first implemented concurrent constraint language combining encapsulated search with committed choice.

The concurrent constraint model [14] can accommodate object-oriented programming along the lines of Shapiro and Takeuchi's stream-based model for Concurrent Prolog [19, 10]. Unfortunately, this model is intolerably low-level, which becomes fully apparent when one considers inheritance [5]. Vulcan, Polka, and A'UM are attempts to create high-level object-oriented languages on top of concurrent logic languages (see [10] for references). Due to the wide gap these languages have to bridge, they however lose the simplicity and flexibility of the underlying base languages.

Oz avoids these difficulties by extending the concurrent constraint model with the features needed for a high-level object model: a higher-order programming facility and a primitive to express concurrent state. With these extensions the need for a separate object-oriented language disappears, since the base language itself can express objects and inheritance in a concise and elegant way.

The way Oz provides for higher-order programming is unique in that denotation and equality of variables are nevertheless captured by first-order logic only. In fact, denotation of variables and the facility for higher-order programming are completely orthogonal concepts in Oz. This is in contrast to existing approaches to higher-order logic programming [13, 2].

Cells are a concurrent construct providing a minimal form of state fully compatible with constraints. They simply model a mutable binding of a name to a value, which can be changed by an atomic operation combining reading and writing.

Oz is based on a formal computation model accommodating concurrent computation as rewriting of a class of expressions modulo a structural congruence. This setup is known from a recent version of Milner's π-calculus [12]. It proves particularly useful for concurrent constraint computation since the structural congruence can elegantly model propagation and simplification of constraints.

Oz is fully implemented including garbage collection, incremental compilation and a window system based on Tcl/Tk. In terms of efficiency, it is competitive with emulated Sicstus Prolog. The Oz System and its documentation can be obtained via ftp from `ps-ftp.dfki.uni-sb.de` or through WWW from `http://ps-www.dfki.uni-sb.de/`.

A novel feature of Oz not treated in this paper is a higher-order combinator providing for encapsulated search [16, 17]. The search combinator allows to program different search strategies, including depth first and best solution (branch and bound) search.

The paper is organized as follows. Section 2.2 shows how the constraint system of Oz accommodates records. Section 2.3 gives an informal account of the computation model underlying Oz. Section 2.4 introduces the concrete language. Section 2.5 shows how objects can be modeled in Oz.

2.2   The Oz Universe

This section describes a fragment of the Oz Universe that suffices for the purpose of this paper.

The **Oz Universe** is a mathematical model of the data structures Oz computes with. It is defined as a structure of first-order predicate logic with equality. All variables in Oz range over the elements of the Oz Universe, called **values**. First-order formulas over its signature are called **constraints**. The value we consider are records and integers.

We describe the semantics of records informally; the mathematical details of the underlying construction are given in [22].

Records are composed using literals, denoted by l. A literal is either an atom or a name. An atom is a string (e.g., val, set). Names do not have a concrete syntax in Oz. It suffices to know that there are infinitely many names.

A **record** is either a literal or a proper record. A **proper record** is an unordered tree

where l is a literal, $l_1, \ldots, l_n$ are pairwise distinct literals, $v_1, \ldots, v_n$ are values, and $n > 0$.

Records are written as $l(l_1\!:\!v_1 \ldots l_n\!:\!v_n)$, $n \geq 0$, where $l()$ stands for l. Two proper records are equal if and only if they have the same linear notation up to permutation of named fields $l_i\!:\!v_i$.

Given a record t of the form $l(l_1\!:\!v_1 \ldots l_n\!:\!v_n)$, we call the literal l the **label**, the values $v_1, \ldots, v_n$ the **fields**, the integer n the **width**, and the literals $l_1, \ldots, l_n$ the **features** of t. Moreover, we call v_i the **field or subtree of t at l_i**.

An important operation on records is adjunction. The **adjunction** of two records s and t is the record $s * t$ defined as follows: the label of $s * t$ is the label of t; the features of $s * t$ are the features of s together with the features of t; and v is the subtree of $s * t$ at l if and only if either v is the subtree of t at l, or if l is not a feature of t and v is the subtree of s at l. Thus record adjunction amounts to record concatenation, where for shared features the right argument takes priority. For instance, the adjunction $l(a\colon 1\ b\colon 2\ c\colon 3) * k(b\colon 77\ d\colon 4)$ results in $k(a\colon 1\ b\colon 77\ c\colon 3\ d\colon 4)$.

The **signature of the Oz Universe** consists of literals and integers (constants denoting themselves) and some predicates called **constraint predicates**. The constraint predicates for records are defined as follows:

- $label(x, y)$ holds if and only if x is a record whose label is y.

- $width(x, y)$ holds if and only if x is a record whose width is y.

- $subtree(x, y, z)$ holds if and only if x is a tuple or record, y is a feature of x, and z is the subtree of x at y.

- $adjoin(x, y, z)$ is the predicate corresponding to record adjunction.

- $adjoinAt(x, y, z, u)$ holds if and only if x and u are records such that $x * l(y\colon z) = u$, where l is the label of x.

Constraint predicates for integers are $intPlus(x, y, z)$, $intMinus(x, y, z)$ and $intMult(x, y, z)$ corresponding to the addition, subtraction and multiplication functions on integers.

2.3   An Informal Computation Model

This section gives an informal presentation of the basic computation model underlying a sublanguage of Oz that suffices for the purpose of this paper[1] (see [20] for a formal presentation). A full description of Kernel Oz, a semantically complete sublanguage of Oz is given in [6].

2.3.1   The Computation Space

Oz generalizes the model of concurrent constraint programming [15] by providing for higher-order programming and cells. Central to the computation model of Oz is the notion of a **computation space**. A computation space consists of a number of **elaborators** connected to a **blackboard**.

Blackboard

Elaborator $\cdots$ Elaborator

---

[1] We omit deep guard computation, disjunction, encapsulated search, and finite domains.

The elaborators read the blackboard and reduce once the blackboard contains sufficient information. The elaborators may reduce in parallel, however the effect must always be achievable by a sequence of single elaborator reductions (interleaving semantics).

The blackboard stores a constraint (constraints are closed under conjunction, hence one constraint suffices) and name bindings. Name bindings map names to abstractions or variables as explained later in this section.

The constraint on the blackboard is always satisfiable in the universe and becomes monotonically stronger over time. We say that a blackboard entails a constraint ψ if the implication $\phi \to \psi$ is valid in the universe, where ϕ is the constraint stored on the blackboard. We say that the blackboard is consistent with a constraint ψ if the conjunction $\phi \wedge \psi$ is satisfiable in the universe, where ϕ is the constraint stored on the blackboard.

2.3.2   Elaboration of Expressions

Elaborators reduce expressions. When an elaborator reduces, it may put new information on the blackboard and create new elaborators. The elaborators of the computation space are short-lived: once they reduce they disappear.

The abstract syntax of expressions is defined as follows:

E	$::=$	ϕ	constraint
	$\mid$	$x \colon \overline{y}/E$	abstraction
	$\mid$	$x \colon y$	cell
	$\mid$	$E\ F$	composition
	$\mid$	**local** $\overline{x}$ **in** E **end**	declaration
	$\mid$	$x\ y_1 \ldots y_n$	application
	$\mid$	**exch**$[x, y, z]$	exchange
	$\mid$	**if** $\overline{x}$ **in** ϕ **then** E **else** F **fi**	conditional

$x, y, z \quad ::= \quad \langle variable \rangle$

$\overline{x}, \overline{y} \quad ::= \quad \langle possibly\ empty\ sequence\ of\ variables \rangle$

By **elaboration** of an expression E we mean the reduction of an elaborator for E. Elaboration of

- **a constraint** ϕ checks whether ϕ is consistent with the blackboard. If this is the case, ϕ is conjoined to the constraint on the blackboard; otherwise, an error is reported. Elaboration of a constraint corresponds to the eventual tell operation in concurrent constraint programming [15].

- **an abstraction** $x\colon \overline{y}/E$ chooses a fresh name a, binds a to the abstraction $\overline{y}/E$ (name binding) and creates an elaborator for the constraint $x \doteq a$. Since fresh names are chosen whenever a name binding is written on the blackboard, a name cannot be bound to more than one abstraction. Thus elaboration of an abstraction provides it with a unique identity. Since the variable x refers to a name rather than to the abstraction, we can test for equality between x and other variables.

- **a cell** $x\colon y$ chooses a fresh name a, binds a to y (name binding), and creates an elaborator for the constraint $x \doteq a$.

- **a composition** $E\,F$ creates two separate elaborators for E and F.

- **a variable declaration** local x in E end chooses a fresh variable y and an elaborator for the expression $E[y/x]$. The notation $E[y/x]$ stands for the expression that is obtained from E by replacing all free occurrences of x with y. A multiple variable declaration local $x\ \overline{x}$ in E end is treated as a nested declaration local x in local $\overline{x}$ in E end end.

- **an application** $x\ y_1\ \ldots\ y_n$ waits until there is a name a such that the blackboard entails $x \doteq a$. If a is bound to an abstraction $y_1 \ldots y_n/E$, an elaborator for $E[\overline{y}/\overline{z}]$ (a copy of the body of the abstraction, where the actual arguments replace the formal arguments) is created. Otherwise, the application cannot reduce.

- **an exchange** exch$[x, y_1, y_2]$ waits until there is a name a such that the blackboard entails $x \doteq a$. If a is bound to a variable z, an elaborator for the constraint $y_1 = z$ is created and the name binding for a is changed such that a is now bound to the variable y_2. Otherwise, the exchange cannot reduce.

- **a conditional** if $\overline{x}$ in ϕ then E else F fi waits until the blackboard either entails $\exists \overline{x}\ \phi$, in which case an elaborator for the expression local $\overline{x}$ in $\phi\ E$ end is created, or disentails $\exists \overline{x}\ \phi$, in which case an elaborator for F is created.

The treatment of abstractions and applications provides for all higher-order programming techniques [21]. By making variables denote names rather than higher-order values, we obtain a smooth combination of first-order constraints with higher-order programming.

While the constraint on the blackboard becomes monotonically stronger over time and bindings of names to abstractions do not change, an exchange may change the binding of a name to a variable. Thus, cells provide a primitive to express state.

2.4   The Programming Language

Having introduced an informal computation model for Oz using the abstract syntax
of expressions, we can now present the concrete programming language. In the
concrete syntax of Oz, abstractions, applications, cells, exchanges and constraints
may not be used directly. Instead the concrete syntax given in Section 2.4.1 must
be used for abstraction and application, the concrete syntax given in Section 2.4.2
for cells and exchanges and the concrete syntax given in 2.4.3 for constraints. The
execution of a program E amounts to the creation of an elaborator for the expansion
of E according to the following sections.

2.4.1   Procedures

In the concrete syntax, variables start with a capital letter to distinguish them from
atoms. A procedure P taking n arguments can be defined with the concrete syntax

  proc {P $X_1 \dots X_n$} E **end**

standing for the expression

  local A **in**
     A:$X_1 \dots X_n/E$
     P=procedure(`NAME`:A `ARITY`:n)
  end

Thus, a procedure is represented by a record (the concrete syntax for record
construction will be explained in Section 2.4.3). This record has the name to which
the abstraction is bound as subtree at feature `NAME`. The variables `NAME`
and `ARITY` are constrained to names and may not be used in programs.

An application of a procedure P to the arguments $X_1, \dots, X_n$ can be written with
the concrete syntax

  {P $X_1 \dots X_n$}

standing for the expression

  if A **in**
     $label$(P,procedure)
     $subtree$(P,`NAME`,A)
     $subtree$(P,`ARITY`,n)
  then A $X_1 \dots X_n$
  else false fi

Introducing abstractions and applications indirectly in this way enhances programming security in that no application $x\ y_1 \dots y_n$ may become elaborated unless
there exists a name a such that the blackboard entails $x = a$ and a is bound to

an *n*-ary abstraction. If x is constrained to something else but a name, or if the name is not bound to an abstraction or if the arity does not match the arity of the application, the constraint **false** is elaborated, resulting in a run-time error. The effect is a form of dynamic type checking. The representation of procedures by records has additional benefits for objects (see Section 2.5).

2.4.2   Cells

The same form of dynamic type checking as for procedures applies to cells in the concrete syntax of Oz. A cell is created by applying the procedure NewCell, defined by

```
proc {NewCell Init C}
    local A in
        A:Init
        C = cell(`NAME`:A)
    end
end
```

and an exchange is performed using the procedure Exchange defined as

```
proc {Exchange C X Y}
    if A in
        label(C,cell)
        subtree(C,`NAME`,A)
    then exch[A, X, Y]
    fi
end
```

Note that the default for the missing **else** part of the conditional is **else false**.

2.4.3   Constraints

Because the Oz Universe provides for integers with constraint predicates for addition and multiplication, satisfiability of constraints is undecidable even for conjunctions of atomic integer constraints (Hilbert's Tenth Problem). Therefore, the concrete syntax restricts the use of constraints such that satisfiability and entailment of the occurring constraints is efficiently decidable.

The procedure Det plays a key role in the rest of this section. Informally {Det X} is entailed whenever X becomes determined, i.e. constrained to a record or an integer. The procedure Det is defined by

```
proc {Det X}
    if X=1 then true else true fi
end
```

The concrete syntax allows to enter arithmetic constraints like $intPlus(X, Y, Z)$ only by expressions of the form $Z = X + Y$ which expands to the expression

if $\{\text{Det } X\} \{\text{Det } Y\}$ **then** $intPlus(X, Y, Z)$ **fi**

This treatment of arithmetic constraints avoids the undecidability problem because the elaboration of a constraint $intPlus(X, Y, Z)$ either fails or is equivalent to $Z = n$ where n is the sum of the integers X and Y.

We ask the reader to accept a technical inaccuracy here: According to Section 2.3, the guard must consist of a constraint and not contain applications like $\{\text{Det } X\}$ (flat guards). Due to space limitations, we will not describe the more complex deep-guard computation here (see [20] for a complete description).

A similar technique as for arithmetic constraints is used to weaken the semantics of record constraints. Instead of using the constraint predicates *label*, *adjoin* and *adjoinAt*, we use the procedures Label, Adjoin and AdjoinAt:

proc $\{\text{Label X Y}\}$
    if $\{\text{Det } X\}$ **then** $label(X, Y)$ **fi**
end
proc $\{\text{Adjoin X Y Z}\}$
    if $\{\text{Det } X\} \{\text{Det } Y\}$ **then** $adjoin(X, Y, Z)$ **fi**
end
proc $\{\text{AdjoinAt X Y Z U}\}$
    if $\{\text{Det } X\} \{\text{Det } Y\}$ **then** $adjoinAt(X, Y, Z, U)$ **fi**
end

The expression $X.Y = Z$ stands for

if $\{\text{Det } X\} \{\text{Det } Y\}$ **then** $subtree(X, Y, Z)$ **fi**

For record construction, we use the syntax

$X = Y(Y_1 : Z_1 \ldots Y_n : Z_n)$

which stands for

if $\{\text{Det } Y\} \{\text{Det } Y_1\} \cdots \{\text{Det } Y_n\}$
then $label(X, Y)\ width(X, n)\ subtree(X, Y_1, Z_1) \ldots subtree(X, Y_n, Z_n)$ **fi**

We write $Y(Z_1 \ldots Z_n)$ as a short hand for $Y('1' : Z_1 \ldots 'n' : Z_n)$. Thus we obtain Prolog's finite trees as a special case of records. The outlined constraint system is in fact a conservative extension of Prolog II's rational tree system.

2.4.4 Examples

Cells are used to express objects as procedures with state. A simple procedure with state is shown in Program 2.4.1.

Program 2.4.1 A Procedure With State

```
local Cell
in
    {NewCell 0 Cell}
    proc {Num X}
        local Y in {Exchange Cell X Y}  Y = X + 1 end
    end
end
```

Elaboration of this expression creates a local variable Cell and an elaborator for the composition. Elaboration of the composition constrains the variables Cell and Num to records and writes two name bindings on the blackboard.

Suppose the computation space contains the applications

{Num X} {Num Y} {Num Z}

The abstraction realizing the procedure Num will be applied concurrently to the variables X, Y, and Z. They will be equated to different numbers and the internal counter of Num will be incremented three times. One possible outcome is X=0 Y=2 Z=1. The procedure Num builds a state sequence

$$X_1, X_2, X_3, \ldots, X_k$$

whose members are linked by constraints $X_{k+1} = X_k + 1$, and whose respective last member is held in Cell. Concurrent applications of Num create concurrent exchange requests for Cell, which are performed in indeterminate order. Reduction of an application {Exchange Cell X Y} will equate X to the current end of the sequence and make Y the new end of the sequence.

Object-oriented programming in Oz makes use of records to represent states, messages, and method tables. An example for the state of an object is

CounterState=state(val:0)

The procedure Inc

```
proc {Inc State Message Self NewState}
    if Message=inc then {AdjoinAt State val State.val + 1 NewState} fi
end
```

increments the value in field val of the argument State, resulting in NewState. We use functional notation in the **then** part which stands for

```
local X Y Z in
    X = val
    Y = State.X
    Z = Y + 1
    {AdjoinAt State X Z NewState}
end
```

The application {Inc CounterState inc _ NewCounterState}, where the symbol _ denotes an anonymous variable occurring only once, constrains NewCounterState to state(val:1). The third formal parameter Self of the procedure Inc is not used in its body, but will serve to capture the notion of "self" in Section 2.5.2 in similar procedures.

Similarly, the procedure Get

```
proc {Get State Message Self NewState}
    if X in Message=get(X) then NewState=State  X=State.val fi
end
```

serves to access the value in field val and leaves the State unchanged. The application
{Get NewCounterState get(X) _ NewCounterState2} equates NewCounterState2 to NewCounterState and the variable X to 1.

The variable CounterMethodTable in

CounterMethodTable=methods(inc: Inc get: Get)

is constrained to a record that contains the procedures Inc and Get. The application of Inc above can now be written as

{CounterMethodTable.inc CounterState inc _ NewCounterState}

2.5 Objects

Our goal are objects with the following properties:

- **Identity and state.** While enjoying persistent indentity, an object changes its behavior over time depending on its state. The manipulation of this state happens in a controlled manner.

- **Structured programming.** The behavior of objects is described in a way that allows code reuse (multiple inheritance, "self").

- **Concurrency.** Objects may be dynamically created and interact with each other in a concurrent setting.

The first goal, we achieve by representing an object by a procedure with state similar to the procedure Num in Program 2.4.1. In Section 2.5.1, we refine this scheme by incorporating late method binding and a generic mechanism to create objects.

The second goal is achieved by encoding the behavior of an object by a method table, a record containing methods. Methods are procedures

$$method: state \times message \times object \rightarrow state$$

When the object is applied to a message (represented as a record), the appropriate method is retrieved from the object's method table and applied to the current state, the message, and the object itself, resulting in a new state. We represent method tables by records. In Section 2.5.3, we will show how we can express multiple inheritance by adjunction of method tables, and how the notion of "self" can be captured.

Objects are concurrent due to the inherent concurrency of Oz. In Section 2.5.3, we show how we can nonetheless preserve the order of messages and how objects are synchronized.

2.5.1 Objects Are Procedures With State

Objects are procedures with state whose behavior is determined by a method table. Procedures with state were already discussed in Section 2.4.4.

Program 2.5.1 defines an object Counter, employing late method binding. The variable CounterMethodTable refers to the record given in Section 2.4.4 on page 39. In the following, we discuss Program 2.5.1 top-down.

Program 2.5.1 A Counter Object

```
local Cell in
   {NewCell state(val:0) Cell}
   proc {Counter Message}
      local State NewState in
         {Exchange Cell State NewState}
         if {Det State}
         then {CounterMethodTable.{Label Message}
               State Message Counter NewState}
         fi
      end
   end
end
```

The state of the object is represented by a record and stored in Cell. The initial content of the cell is the record state(val:0).

When the object Counter is applied to a message like {Counter inc}, the current State is obtained from Cell and exchanged with the fresh variable NewState. If State is determined, the appropriate method Inc is retrieved from CounterMethodTable using the label inc of the message. The method is then applied to State, the message inc, Counter and NewState. Thus, if {Counter inc} is the first application of Counter, Cell will hold the new state state(val:1).

Since objects are represented as procedures, they enjoy persistent identity (recall the translation of **proc** ⋯ **end** given in Section 2.4.1). Thus one can test for identity of two objects Counter, Counter2 using a conditional **if** Counter = Counter2 **then** ⋯ **fi**.

Note that many agents may know the object Counter and thus may concurrently attempt to apply Counter. Representing the state by a cell ensures mutual exclusion: the respective method applications are implicitly and indeterministically sequentialized.

Generic Object Creation

Since procedures are first-class citizens, we can write a generic procedure shown in Program 2.5.2 that creates a new object O from an initial state IState and a MethodTable.

Program 2.5.2 Generic Object Creation

```
proc {Create IState MethodTable O}
    local Cell in
        {NewCell IState Cell}
        proc {O Message}
            . . .
        end
    end
end
```

When Create is applied as in

{Create state(val:7) CounterMethodTable Counter2}

a new counter Counter2 is created with initial value 7.

2.5.2   Inheritance

The behavior of an object is determined by its method table. Inheritance thus
means that the method table of a new object is obtained by combining and extending method tables of existing objects. Since method tables are represented
by records, combining and extending them is straightforward (e.g., by record adjunction). To make the methods of an object accessible, we will now enrich the
representation of objects with information used for inheritance. Since objects are
procedures and procedures are represented by records on the blackboard, we can
construct an enriched object OInh by adjoining inheritance information to an object
O. Program 2.5.3 modifies Program 2.5.2 to incorporate inheritance.

Program 2.5.3 Incorporating Inheritance

```
proc {Create FromObjects IState NewMethodTable OInh}
   local Cell MethodTable in
      {NewCell IState Cell}
      {Inherit FromObjects NewMethodTable MethodTable}
      proc {O Message}  ···  end
      {AdjoinAt O methods MethodTable OInh}
   end
end
```

The procedure Create now has an additional argument FromObjects, a list of
objects from which the new object OInh inherits. The argument NewMethodTable
refers to the new methods of the new object. The MethodTable is constructed
by the procedure Inherit by adjoining all method tables of inherited objects and
the NewMethodTable (we assume the procedure FoldL to be known from functional
programming).

```
proc {Inherit From NMT MT}
   {Adjoin {FoldL
               From proc {I E O} {Adjoin I E.methods O} end methods}
      NMT MT}
end
```

Record adjunction (see Section 2.2) takes care of the usual method overriding in
object-oriented languages.

MethodTable is adjoined to the created procedure O to provide the object OInh
with information that can be used when another object inherits from OInh. For
example, in Program 2.5.4 a DecCounter is created that inherits from Counter and
additionally understands a message dec.

Program 2.5.4 Example for Inheritance

```
{Create nil state(val:7) CounterMethodTable Counter3}
local DecMethodTable in
   DecMethodTable
         =methods(dec: proc {State Message Self NewState}
                           if Message=dec
                           then {AdjoinAt
                                      State val State.val − 1 NewState}
                           fi
                     end
               )
   DecCounter={Create Counter3|nil state(val:10) DecMethodTable}
end
```

Syntactic Extension

Oz supports a syntactic extension for object creation and method definition, which allows writing the expression in Program 2.5.4 including CounterMethodTable in Section 2.4.4 as shown in Program 2.5.5.

Program 2.5.5 Objects in Sugared Syntax

```
create Counter3
   from UrObject
   attr val:7
   meth inc    val ← @val + 1 end
   meth set(X) val ← X        end
   meth get(X) X = @val       end
end
create DecCounter
   from Counter
   attr val:10
   meth dec val ← @val − 1 end
end
```

The first and the last argument of methods are the incoming State and the outgoing NewState of the object (see Program 2.5.1). In the body of methods, NewState is computed from State. During this computation, it may be necessary to introduce several auxiliary state variables. Thus one can say, that the state of the object is threaded through the body of methods. In the syntactic extension, this threading is done by the compiler. The two expressions that implicitly refer to the state are attribute access (@) and assignment (←). Syntactic limitations guarantee that there is always only one reference to the state of an object at runtime. Therefore, we can implement assignment such that the construction of a new record as in AdjoinAt is avoided (compile-time garbage collection).

Observe that our model alleviates the distinction between classes and their instances by combining object creation and inheritance into one single operation.

Self

The third formal parameter of the methods is the variable Self. Since methods are called with the receiving object as third actual parameter, the variable Self used in the body of methods has the semantics familiar from object-oriented languages. In the syntactic extension, the keyword **self** represents that variable. For example, the object Counter4 in Program 2.5.6 sends the message inc twice to itself when it receives the message inc2.

Program 2.5.6 Example for **self**

```
create Counter4
    from Counter
    attr val:0
    meth inc2 {self inc} {self inc} end
end
```

Method Application

In Section 2.5.2, we saw that attribute access and assignment implicitly refer to the state. In this section, we describe a third such expression, called **method application**.

Assume that the object Counter4 in Program 2.5.6 has received the message inc2. Due to concurrent execution, a message, say get(X), may be received by **self** after the first and before the second inc message. To avoid such situations, Oz provides for method application, a way to apply a method locally to the available state. For example, consider

```
create Counter5
    from Counter
    attr val:0
    meth inc2 ⟨⟨self inc⟩⟩ ⟨⟨self inc⟩⟩ end
end
```

The state is threaded through the two consecutive method applications introducing an intermediate state

   local TmpState in $^{\text{State}}\langle\!\langle$self inc$\rangle\!\rangle^{\text{TmpState}}$ $^{\text{TmpState}}\langle\!\langle$self inc$\rangle\!\rangle^{\text{NewState}}$ end

and a threaded method application

   $^{\text{InState}}\langle\!\langle$O Message$\rangle\!\rangle^{\text{OutState}}$

expands to

   {O.methods.{Label Message} InState Message Self OutState}

The notation for method application exploits the fact that in our model every method m of every object O can be referred to by O.methods.m. Incidentally, our notation for method application also serves the purpose of Smalltalk's "super" notation. For example, the method inc in

```
create Counter6
    from Counter
    attr val:0
    meth inc(X) ⟨⟨Counter inc⟩⟩ ⟨⟨self get(X)⟩⟩ end
end
```

is defined in terms of Counter's method inc and Counter6's own method get.

2.5.3 Concurrency Issues

We saw in the previous section that the execution order of applications may not coincide with the textual order of the applications. Using method application, we can define batch methods as a way to enforce an order on messages like in

```
create BatchObject
    meth M|Mr ⟨⟨self M⟩⟩ ⟨⟨self Mr⟩⟩ end
    meth nil  true end
end
```

The object Counter4 in Program 2.5.6 can be reformulated using the batch methods.

```
create Counter7
    from Counter BatchObject
    attr val:0
    meth inc2 ⟨⟨self inc|inc|nil⟩⟩ end
end
```

Observe the use of multiple inheritance. Sending the message

   {Counter7 inc|get(X)|inc|nil}

guarantees that no other application {Counter7 get(Y)} can be sent such that X=Y.

So far, the application of an object to messages was done in an asynchronous fashion. We can synchronize objects by using messages that are constrained by the object. For example, in

```
{Counter7 inc|get(X)|nil}
if {Det X} then E fi
```

the expression E is only elaborated after Counter7 is incremented.

2.6 Summary

Oz is an attempt to create a high-level concurrent programming language bringing together the merits of logic and object-oriented programming. For this purpose, we extend the concurrent constraint model with a facility for higher-order programming and the notion of cells. We presented aspects of the underlying constraint system and an informal model of computation of a sublanguage of Oz, based on elaboration of expressions.

We have shown how concurrent objects can be expressed concisely and naturally in Oz. Being represented by named procedures, objects enjoy persistent identity. An object can refer to an encapsulated state, stored in a cell that can only be accessed by calling the object.

Structured programming is supported by late method binding, which is achieved by method lookup in a method table represented by a record. We gave a straightforward implementation of "self" and presented how methods can be applied directly within methods, generalizing the concept of "super". We showed how method tables of several objects may be combined providing for multiple inheritance.

Objects in Oz are concurrent due to the inherent concurrency of Oz. We showed programming techniques that nonetheless enforce an order on messages and allow for synchronization of objects.

Acknowledgments

We thank all members of the Programming Systems Lab at DFKI for inspiring discussions on all kinds of subjects and objects. The research reported in this paper has been supported by the Bundesminister für Forschung und Technologie, contract ITW 9105 (Hydra), and by the ESPRIT basic research project 7195 (ACCLAIM).

References

[1] F. Benhamou and A. Comerauer, editors. *Constraint Logic Programming*. ISBN0-262-02353-9 III. Series. MIT Press, 1993. Selected Research.

[2] W. Chen, M. Kifer, and D. S. Warren. HiLog: A foundation for higher-order logic programming. *Journal of Logic Programming*, 15:187–230, 1993.

[3] K. Clark and S. Gregory. A relational language for parallel programming. In *Proc. of the ACM Conference on Functional Programming Languages and Computer Architecture*, pages 171–178, 1981.

[4] A. Colmerauer, H. Kanoui, and M. V. Caneghem. Prolog, theoretical principles and current trends. *Technology and Science of Informatics*, 2(4):255–292, 1983.

[5] Y. Goldberg, W. Silverman, and E. Shapiro. Logic programs with inheritance. In *Proceedings of the International Conference on Fifth Generation Computer Systems*, pages 951–960, Tokyo, Japan, 1992. ICOT.

[6] M. Henz, M. Mehl, M. Müller, T. Müller, J. Niehren, R. Scheidhauer, C. Schulte, G. Smolka, R. Treinen, and J. Würtz. The Oz Handbook. Research Report RR-94-09, dfki, dfkiaddr, 1994. Available through anonymous ftp from `ps-ftp.dfki.uni-sb.de` or through www from `http://ps-www.dfki.uni-sb.de`.

[7] M. Henz, G. Smolka, and J. Würtz. Oz—a programming language for multi-agent systems. In *13th International Joint Conference on Artificial Intelligence*, volume 1, pages 404–409, Chambéry, France, 1993. Morgan Kaufmann Publishers.

[8] J. Jaffar and M. Maher. Constraint logic programming - a survey. *The Journal of Logic Programming*, 1994. Special issue on 10 years of logic programming.

[9] S. Janson and S. Haridi. Programming paradigms of the Andorra kernel language. In V. Saraswat and K. Ueda, editors, *Logic Programming, Proceedings of the 1991 International Symposium*, pages 167–186, San Diego, USA, 1991. The MIT Press.

[10] K. Kahn. Objects: A fresh look. In *Proceedings of the Third European Conference on Object Oriented Programming*, pages 207–223. Cambridge University Press, Cambridge, MA, 1989.

[11] M. J. Maher. Logic semantics for a class of committed-choice programs. In J.-L. Lassez, editor, *Logic Programming, Proceedings of the Fourth International Conference*, pages 858–876, Cambridge, MA, 1987. The MIT Press.

[12] R. Milner. Functions as Processes. *Mathematical Structures in Computer Science*, 2(2):119–141, 1992.

[13] G. Nadathur and D. Miller. An overview of λProlog. In R. A. Kowalski and K. A. Bowen, editors, *Proceedings of the Fifth International Conference and*

Symposium on Logic Programming, pages 810–827, Seattle, Wash., 1988. The MIT Press.

[14] V. Saraswat and M. Rinard. Concurrent constraint programming. In *Proceedings of the 7th Annual ACM Symposium on Principles of Programming Languages*, pages 232–245, San Francisco, CA, January 1990.

[15] V. A. Saraswat. *Concurrent Constraint Programming*. The MIT Press, Cambridge, Mass., 1993.

[16] C. Schulte and G. Smolka. Encapsulated search in higher-order concurrent constraint programming. In M. Bruynooghe, editor, *Logic Programming: Proceedings of the 1994 International Symposium*, Ithaca, New York, USA, Nov. 1994. The MIT Press.

[17] C. Schulte, G. Smolka, and J. Würtz. Encapsulated search and constraint programming in Oz. In *Second Workshop on Principles and Practice of Constraint Programming*, Orcas Island, Washington, USA, May 1994. Springer-Verlag, LNCS. to appear.

[18] E. Shapiro. The family of concurrent logic programming languages. *ACM Computing Surveys*, 21(3):413–511, September 1989.

[19] E. Shapiro and A. Takeuchi. Object oriented programming in Concurrent Prolog. *New Generation Computing*, 1:24–48, 1983.

[20] G. Smolka. A calculus for higher-order concurrent constraint programming with deep guards. Research Report RR-94-03, DFKI, Feb. 1994. Available through anonymous ftp from `ps-ftp.dfki.uni-sb.de`.

[21] G. Smolka. A foundation for higher-order concurrent constraint programming. In J.-P. Jouannaud, editor, *1st International Conference on Constraints in Computational Logics*, Lecture Notes in Computer Science, München, Germany, 7–9 Sept. 1994. Springer-Verlag. Invited Lecture. To appear.

[22] G. Smolka and R. Treinen. Records for logic programming. *The Journal of Logic Programming*, 18(3):229–258, Apr. 1994.

II REACTIVE SYSTEMS

3 Constraint Programming in Constraint Nets

Ying Zhang and Alan K. Mackworth

Abstract

We view constraints as relations and constraint satisfaction as a dynamic process of approaching the solution set of the constraints. We have developed a semantic model for dynamic systems, called Constraint Nets, to provide a real-time programming semantics and to model and analyze dynamic systems. In this paper, we explore the relationship between constraint satisfaction and constraint nets by showing how to implement various constraint methods on constraint nets. In particular, we examine discrete and continuous methods for discrete and continuous domain constraint satisfaction problems. Hard and soft constraints within the framework of unconstrained and constrained optimization are considered. Finally, we present an application of the framework to robot control systems.

3.1   Motivation

Constraints are relations among entities. Constraint satisfaction can be viewed in two different ways. In a logical deductive view, a constraint system is a structure $\langle D, \vdash \rangle$ where D is a set of constraints and $\vdash$ is an entailment relation between constraints [20]. In this view, constraint satisfaction is seen as a process involving multiple agents concurrently interacting on a store-as-constraint system by checking entailment and consistency relations and refining the system monotonically. This approach is useful in database or knowledge-based systems, and can be embedded in logic programming languages [2, 5, 9]. Characteristically, the global constraint is not explicitly represented, though for any given relation tuple the system is able to check whether or not the relation tuple is entailed.

In an alternative view, which in our opinion is more appropriate for real-time embedded systems, the constraint satisfaction problem is formulated as finding a relation tuple that is entailed by a given set of constraints [12]. In this paper, we present a new approach in which constraint satisfaction is a dynamic process with the solution set as an attractor of the process. "Monotonicity" is characterized by a Liapunov function, measuring the "distance" to the set of solutions over time. Moreover, both soft and hard constraints can be represented and solved. This approach has been taken in neural nets [18], optimization, graphical simulation [16] and robot control [15]. However, it has not yet been investigated seriously in the area of constraint programming.

We have developed a semantic model for dynamic systems, called Constraint Nets, to provide a real-time programming semantics [24] and to model and analyze robotic systems [25]. Here we investigate the relationship between constraint satisfaction and constraint nets. The rest of this paper is organized as follows. Section 3.2 describes some basic concepts of dynamic processes. Section 3.3 introduces Constraint Nets and constraint solvers. Section 3.4 presents various constraint methods for solving global consistency and optimization problems. Section 3.5 summarizes the framework. Section 3.6 discusses an application to control synthesis for robotic systems.

3.2   Properties of Dynamic Processes

In this section, we define dynamic processes and discuss the relationship between dynamic processes and Liapunov functions.

3.2.1   Metric Spaces

Let $\mathcal{R}$ be the set of real numbers and $\mathcal{R}^+$ be the set of nonnegative real numbers. A *metric* on a set X is a function $d : X \times X \to \mathcal{R}^+$ satisfying the following axioms for all $x, y, z \in X$:

1. $d(x, y) = d(y, x)$.
2. $d(x, y) + d(y, z) \geq d(x, z)$.
3. $d(x, y) = 0$ iff $x = y$.

A *metric space* is a pair $\langle X, d \rangle$ where X is a set and d is a metric on X. In a metric space $\langle X, d \rangle$, $d(x, y)$ is called "the distance between x and y." We will use X to denote the metric space $\langle X, d \rangle$ if no ambiguity arises.

Given a metric space $\langle X, d \rangle$, we can define the distance between a point and a set of points as $d(x, X^*) = \inf_{x^* \in X^*}\{d(x, x^*)\}$. For $x^* \in X$ and $\epsilon > 0$, the set $N^\epsilon(x^*) = \{x | d(x, x^*) < \epsilon\}$ is an ϵ-*neighborhood* of x^*; it is *strict* if it has at least one point other than x^*. For $X^* \subset X$, $N^\epsilon(X^*) = \bigcup_{x^* \in X^*} N^\epsilon(x^*)$ is an ϵ-*neighborhood* of X^*; it is *strict* if it is a strict superset of X^*.

Let $\mathcal{T}$ be a set of linearly ordered *time* points with a least element $\mathbf{0}$. $\mathcal{T}$ can be either discrete or continuous. Let X be a metric space representing a discrete or continuous *domain*. A *trace* $v : \mathcal{T} \to X$ is a function from time to a domain. We use $X^\mathcal{T}$ to denote the set of all traces from $\mathcal{T}$ to X, a *trace space*. Given a metric space $\langle X, d \rangle$ and a trace $v : \mathcal{T} \to X$, we say v *approaches a point* $x^* \in X$ iff $\lim_{t \to \infty} d(v(t), x^*) = 0$; v *approaches a set* $X^* \subset X$ iff $\lim_{t \to \infty} d(v(t), X^*) = 0$.

3.2.2 Dynamic Processes

Let $p : X \rightarrow X^{\mathcal{T}}$ be a mapping from a domain X to a trace space $X^{\mathcal{T}}$ and $\phi_p(x) = \{p(x)(t)|t \in \mathcal{T}\}$ be the set of values in trace $p(x)$, p is a *dynamic process* iff p satisfies the following three conditions:

1. $\forall x, p(x)(\mathbf{0}) = x$.
2. $\forall x, y, t$, if $p(x)(t) = p(y)(t)$ then $\forall t' \geq t, p(x)(t') = p(y)(t')$.
3. $\forall x, y$, if $y \in \phi_p(x)$ then $\phi_p(y) \subseteq \phi_p(x)$.

Intuitively, p characterizes a state-based and time-invariant dynamic system. Furthermore, let $\phi_p(X^*) = \bigcup_{x \in X^*} \phi_p(x)$ for any $X^* \subset X$.

A point $x^* \in X$ is an *equilibrium* (or *fixpoint*) of a dynamic process p iff $\forall t, p(x^*)(t) = x^*$, or $\phi_p(x^*) = \{x^*\}$. A set $X^* \subset X$ is an *equilibrium* of a dynamic process p iff $\phi_p(X^*) = X^*$. An equilibrium X^* is *stable* [13] iff $\forall \epsilon \exists \delta, \phi_p(N^\delta(X^*)) \subseteq N^\epsilon(X^*)$.

A set $X^* \subset X$ is an *attractor* [19] of a dynamic process p iff there exists a strict ϵ-neighborhood $N^\epsilon(X^*)$ such that $\forall x \in N^\epsilon(X^*)$, $p(x)$ approaches X^*. The largest neighborhood of X^* satisfying this property is called the *attraction basin* of X^*. X^* is an *attractor in the large* iff $\forall x \in X$, $p(x)$ approaches X^*, that is the attraction basin of X^* is X. If X^* is an attractor (in the large) and X^* is a stable equilibrium, X^* is called an *asymptotically* stable equilibrium (in the large).

LEMMA 3.1 If $\{X_i\}_{i \in I}$ are ((asymptotically) stable) equilibria, then $\bigcup_I X_i$ is an ((asymptotically) stable) equilibrium.

3.2.3 Liapunov Functions

Let $\langle X, d \rangle$ be a metric space, $p : X \rightarrow X^{\mathcal{T}}$ be a dynamic process and $X^* \subset X$. A *Liapunov function* for p and X^* is a function $V : \Omega \rightarrow \mathcal{R}$, where Ω is a strict neighborhood of X^*, satisfying:

1. V is continuous, i.e., $d(x, x') \rightarrow 0$ implies $|V(x) - V(x')| \rightarrow 0$.
2. V has its unique minimum within Ω at X^*.
3. $\forall x \in \Omega, \forall t, V(p(x)(t)) \leq V(x)$.

The following two theorems are similar to those in [10].

THEOREM 3.1 $X^* \subset X$ is a stable equilibrium of a dynamic process p iff there exists a Liapunov function V for p and X^*.

PROOF: The if part: Let V be a Liapunov function for p and X^*. First of all, X^* is an equilibrium since V takes the unique minimum at X^*. Suppose Ω is the domain of V. Given any ϵ, let $\epsilon' \leq \epsilon$ such that $N^{\epsilon'}(X^*) \subseteq \Omega$, and γ be the minimum over the boundary of $N^{\epsilon'}(X^*)$. $\gamma > V(X^*)$ since X^* is the unique minimum. Because V is continuous, there exists a δ-neighborhood $N^\delta(X^*)$ such that $\forall x \in N^\delta(X^*), V(x) < \gamma$. Therefore, $\phi_p(N^\delta(X^*)) \subseteq N^{\epsilon'}(X^*) \subseteq N^\epsilon(X^*)$.

The only if part: If X^* is a stable equilibrium of p, let $V(x) = \sup_{x' \in \phi_p(x)} \{d(x', X^*)\}$. We have (1) $V(X^*) = 0$ since X^* is an equilibrium, (2) $V(p(x)(t)) \leq V(x)$ since $\phi_p(p(x)(t)) \subseteq \phi_p(x)$, and (3) V is continuous since X^* is stable. Therefore, V is a Liapunov function for p and X^*. $\square$

THEOREM 3.2 $X^* \subset X$ is an asymptotically stable equilibrium of a dynamic process p iff there exists a Liapunov function $V : \Omega \to \mathcal{R}$ for X^* and p, such that $\forall x \in \Omega, \lim_{t\to\infty} V(p(x)(t)) = V(X^*)$. Furthermore, if $\Omega = X$, X^* is an asymptotically stable equilibrium in the large.

PROOF: Since X^* is the unique minimum in Ω, $p(x)$ approaches $X^*, \forall x \in \Omega$. Given V defined as the same as that in the previous proof, if X^* is an asymptotically stable equilibrium, $V(p(x)(t))$ approaches $V(X^*)$. $\square$

3.3   Constraint Nets and Constraint Solvers

In this section, we first introduce Constraint Nets, a model for dynamic systems, then examine the relationship between constraint nets and constraint satisfaction via constraint solvers.

3.3.1   Constraint Nets

A dynamic system can be modeled by a constraint net. Intuitively, a constraint net consists of a finite set of locations, a finite set of transductions, each with a finite set of input ports and an output port, and a finite set of connections between locations and ports of transductions.

A *location* can be regarded as a wire, a channel, a variable, or a memory cell, whose value may change over time.

A *transduction* is a mapping from input traces to output traces which is causal, viz., the output value at any time is determined by the input values up to that time. Transductions are mathematical models of transformational processes. For example, a *transliteration* $f_\mathcal{T}$ is a transduction whose output value at any time $t \in \mathcal{T}$ is the function f of the input value at that time only. Intuitively, a transliteration is a transformational process without memory or internal state, for example, a combinational circuit. We use f to denote the transliteration f_T if no ambiguity arises. On the other hand, unit delays and temporal integrations are transductions modeling sequential processes. A *unit delay* $\delta(v_0)$ is a transduction defined mainly for discrete time structures, such that the output value at initial time $\mathbf{0}$ is v_0 and the rest of the output values are the input values at the previous time. A unit delay acts as a unit memory in discrete time dynamic systems. Corresponding to a unit delay, a *temporal integration* is a typical transduction in continuous time. We use $\int(v_0)$ to denote the temporal integration with initial output value v_0.

A *connection* links a location with a port of a transduction. The set of connections has the following restrictions: (1) there is at most one output port connected to each location, (2) each port of a transduction connects to a unique location and (3) no location is isolated.

A location l is an *input location* of a transduction F iff l connects to an input port of F; l is the *output location* of F iff l connects to the output port of F. A location is an *input* if it is not connected to the output location of any transduction; it is otherwise an *output*. A constraint net is *open* if there is an input; it is otherwise *closed*.

The graphical representation of a constraint net is a bipartite directed graph where locations are depicted by circles, transductions by boxes and connections by arcs, each from a port of a transduction to a location or vice versa.

Semantically, a transduction F denotes an equation $l_0 = F(l_1, \cdots, l_n)$ where l_0 is the output location of F and $\langle l_1, \cdots, l_n \rangle$ is the tuple of input locations of F. A constraint net CN denotes a set of equations, $\vec{o} = \vec{F}(\vec{i}, \vec{o})$, each corresponds to a transduction in CN. The semantics of CN is a "solution" of the set of equations [24].

In general, constraint nets can model hybrid dynamic systems, with components operating on different time structures possibly triggered by events. In this paper, we focus only on two types of constraint net: discrete transition systems and continuous integration systems, corresponding respectively to two different types of constraint solver.

3.3.2   Constraint Solvers

We view a *constraint* as a possibly implicit relation on a set of variables. The *constraint satisfaction problem* is defined as follows. Given a set of variables V with the associated domains $\{D_v\}_{v \in V}$ and a set of constraints $\{C_j\}_{j \in J}$ each on a subset of the variables, i.e., $C_j \subseteq \times_{V_j} D_v$ where $V_j \subseteq V$, find an explicit relation tuple $x \in \times_V D_v$ that satisfies all the given constraints, i.e., for all $j \in J$, $x_{|V_j} \in C_j$ where $x_{|S}$ denotes the restriction of x onto $S \subseteq V$. If $C = \{C_j\}_{j \in J}$ is a set of constraints, we use $sol(C)$ to denote the set of solutions, called *the solution set*.

A constraint solver for a constraint satisfaction problem is a closed constraint net whose semantics is a dynamic process approaching the solution set of the constraints. Formally, a closed constraint net CS^V is a *constraint solver* for a constraint satisfaction problem C on domain $X = \times_V D_v$ iff (1) the semantics of CS^V is a dynamic process $[\![CS^V]\!] : X \to X^T$ and (2) $sol(C)$ is an asymptotically stable equilibrium of $[\![CS^V]\!]$. CS^V solves C *globally* iff $sol(C)$ an asymptotically stable equilibrium of $[\![CS^V]\!]$ in the large.

LEMMA 3.2 If a constraint solver CS^V solves a set of constraints C on variables V globally, every equilibrium of $[\![CS^V]\!]$ is a solution of C.

We discuss here two basic types of constraint solver: state transition systems for discrete methods and state integration systems for continuous methods.

A *state transition system* is a pair $\langle S, f \rangle$ where S is a set of states and $f : S \to S$ is a *state transition function*. A state transition system can be represented by a constraint net with a transliteration f and a unit delay $\delta(s_0)$ where $s_0 \in S$ is an initial state (Figure 3.1). The semantics of this net is a dynamic process $p : S \to S^N$ with $p(s_0)$ as an infinite sequence $\langle s_0, f(s_0), \cdots, f^n(s_0), \cdots \rangle$. A state $s^* \in S$ is an

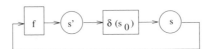

Figure 3.1
A constraint net representing $\langle S, f \rangle$

equilibrium of $\langle S, f \rangle$ iff $s^* = f(s^*)$.

LEMMA 3.3 If $V : \Omega \to \mathcal{R}$ is a Liapunov function for $\langle S, f \rangle$ and $S^* = \{s^*|s^* = f(s^*)\} \subset \Omega$, then $V(f(x)) \leq V(x), \forall x \in \Omega$. In addition, if f is continuous and $V(f(x)) < V(x), \forall x \notin S^*$, S^* is an asymptotically stable equilibrium.

PROOF: If $\lim_{n \to \infty} V(f^n(s)) = \epsilon > V(S^*)$, let $X = \{s|V(s) \leq \epsilon\} \supset S^*$, $f^n(s)$ approaches X. If f is continuous, however, $f^n(s)$ approaches $f(X) \subset X$ and $\lim_{n \to \infty} V(f^n(s)) < \epsilon$, contradiction. $\square$

For continuous time structures and domains, integration is used to replace the unit delay. A *state integration system* is a differential equation $\dot{s} = f(s)$ that can be represented by a closed constraint net with a transliteration f and an integration $\int(s_0)$ where s_0 is an initial state (Figure 3.2). The semantics of this net is a dynamic process $p : S \to S^{\mathcal{R}^+}$ with $p(s_0)$ as the solution of $\dot{s} = f(s)$ and $s(0) = s_0$. A state

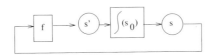

Figure 3.2
A constraint net representing $\dot{s} = f(s)$

$s^* \in S$ is an equilibrium of $\dot{s} = f(s)$ iff $f(s^*) = 0$.

LEMMA 3.4 A set $S^* = \{s^*|f(s^*) = 0\} \subset \Omega$ is an asymptotically stable equilibrium of the state integration system $\dot{s} = f(s)$ if f is continuous at S^* and S^* is the unique minimum of $- \int f(s)ds$ in Ω. If $\Omega = S$, S^* is an asymptotically stable equilibrium in the large.

PROOF: Let $V(s) = - \int f(s)ds$ be defined on a neighborhood of S^*. V is a Liapunov function for $\dot{s} = f(s)$ and S^* since $\dot{V}(s) = -f^2(s) \leq 0$. Furthermore, $\dot{V}(s) < 0, \forall s \notin S^*$ since $f(s) \neq 0$. $\square$

3.4 Dynamic Properties of Constraint Methods

In this section, we examine some typical constraint methods and their dynamic properties. In particular, we discuss two types of constraint satisfaction problem, namely, global consistency and optimization, for four classes of relation: relations on finite domains, and linear, convex and nonlinear relations in n-dimensional Euclidean space $\langle \mathcal{R}^n, d_n \rangle$, where $d_n(x, y) = |x - y| = \sqrt{\Sigma_{i=1}^n (x_i - y_i)^2}$.

  Global consistency corresponds to solving hard constraints and *unconstrained optimization* corresponds to solving soft constraints. A problem of the first kind can be translated into one of the second by introducing an energy function representing the degree of global consistency. On the other hand, *constrained optimization* can be considered as a combination of the two, which corresponds to solving the soft constraints within the solution set of the hard constraints.

  There are two types of constraint method, discrete relaxation, which can be implemented as state transition systems, and differential optimization, which can be implemented as state integration systems. In the rest of this section, we demonstrate the use of both types of constraint method.

3.4.1   Global Consistency

The problem of *global consistency* is to find a solution tuple which satisfies all the given constraints. Here we first discuss a projection method (PM) for solving convex constraints, and then study a method for solving global consistency of finite domain constraints (FM).

Projection Method   The projection method [8] can be used for solving convex constraints. A function $f : \mathcal{R}^n \to \mathcal{R}$ is *convex* iff for any $\lambda \in (0, 1)$, $f(\lambda x + (1 - \lambda)y) \leq \lambda f(x) + (1 - \lambda)f(y)$; it is *strictly* convex iff the inequality is strict. A strictly convex function has a unique minimal point. Linear functions are convex, but not strictly convex. A quadratic function $x^T M x + c^T x$ is convex if M is semi-positive definite; it is strictly convex if M is positive definite. A set $R \subseteq \mathcal{R}^n$ is *convex* iff for any $\lambda \in (0, 1), x, y \in R$ implies $\lambda x + (1 - \lambda)y \in R$. If g is a convex function, $\{x | g(x) \leq 0\}$ is a convex set.

A *projection* of a point x to a set R in a metric space $\langle X, d \rangle$ is a point $P_R(x) \in R$, such that $d(x, P_R(x)) = d(x, R)$. Projections in the n-dimensional Euclidean space $\langle \mathcal{R}^n, d_n \rangle$ share the following properties.

LEMMA 3.5 (From [8]) Let $R \subset \mathcal{R}^n$ be closed and convex. The projection $P_R(x)$ of x to R exists and is unique for every x, and $(x - P_R(x))^T (y - P_R(x)) \leq 0$ for any $y \in R$.

Suppose we are given a system of convex and closed sets, $\{X_i\}_{i \in I}$, each representing a constraint. The problem is to solve $\{X_i\}_{i \in I}$, or to find $\cap_I X_i$. Let $P(x) = P_{X_l}(x)$ be a projection of x to a least satisfied set X_l, i.e., $d(x, X_l) = \max_I d(x, X_i)$. The *projection method* [8] for this problem defines a state transition system $\langle \mathcal{R}^n, f \rangle$ where $f(x) = x + \lambda(P(x) - x)$ for $0 < \lambda < 2$.

Let PM be a constraint net representing the projection method. The following theorem is derived from [8].

THEOREM 3.3 PM solves $\{X_i\}_{i \in I}$ globally if all the X_i's are convex.

PROOF: Let $X^* = \cap_I X_i$ be the solution set of the problem. First of all, it is easy to see that if $x^* \in X^*$ is a solution, then $x^* = f(x^*)$, i.e., x^* is an equilibrium. Moreover, we can prove that $|f(x) - x^*| \leq |x - x^*|$ for any x and $x^* \in X^*$ as follows.

$$|f(x) - x^*|^2 = |x + \lambda(P(x) - x) - x^*|^2$$

$$= |x - x^*|^2 + \lambda^2 |P(x) - x|^2 + 2\lambda(x - x^*)^T (P(x) - x)$$

$$= |x - x^*|^2 + (\lambda^2 - 2\lambda)|P(x) - x|^2 + 2\lambda(P(x) - x)^T (P(x) - x^*)$$

$$\leq |x - x^*|^2 - \lambda(2 - \lambda)|P(x) - x|^2 \quad \text{according to Lemma 3.5}$$

$$\leq |x - x^*|^2 \quad \text{since } 0 < \lambda < 2.$$

Therefore, $d(f(x), X^*) \leq d(x, X^*)$. Thus, X^* is stable.

Furthermore, $|f^k(x) - x^*|$ is nonincreasing and bounded below. Therefore, $|f^k(x) - x^*|$ has a limit and $\max_I d(f^k(x), X_i)$ approaches 0. According to [8], $\lim_{k \to \infty} d(f^k(x), X^*) = 0$, since $\mathcal{R}^n$ is finite dimensional. Thus, X^* is an asymptotically stable equilibrium of PM in the large, i.e., PM solves the problem globally. $\square$

The projection method can be used to solve a set of inequality constraints, i.e., $X_i = \{x | g_i(x) \leq 0\}$, where each g_i is a convex function. Linear functions are convex. Therefore, the projection method can be applied to a set of linear inequalities $Ax \leq b$, where $x = \langle x_1, \cdots, x_n \rangle \in \mathcal{R}^n$. Let A_i be the ith row of A. The projection of a point x to a half space $A_i x - b_i \leq 0$ is defined as

$$P_i(x) = \begin{cases} x & \text{if } A_i x - b_i \leq 0 \\ x - cA_i^T & \text{otherwise} \end{cases}$$

where $c = (A_i x - b_i)/|A_i^T|^2$. This reduces to the method described in [1]. Without any modification, this method can be also applied to a set of linear equalities, by simply replacing each linear equality $g_i(x) = 0$ with two linear inequalities: $g_i(x) \leq 0$ and $-g_i(x) \leq 0$.

There are various ways to modify this method for faster convergence. For instance, a simultaneous projection method is given in [3], in which $f(x) = x + \lambda \Sigma_{j \in J} w_j (P_j(x) - x)$ where $J \subseteq I$ is an index set of violated constraints, $w_j > 0$ and $\Sigma_{j \in J} w_j = 1$. A similar method is given in [21] in which $f(x) = x + \lambda(P_S(x) - x)$ where $S = \{x | \Sigma_{j \in J} w_j g_j(x) \leq 0\}$, with the same assumption about J and w_j. Furthermore, for a large set of inequalities, the problem can be decomposed into a set of K subproblems with f_k corresponding to the transition function of the kth subproblem. The whole problem can be solved by combining the results of $\{f_1, \cdots, f_K\}$.

Finite Constraint Satisfaction   Many problems can be formalized as finite constraint satisfaction problems (FCSPs), which can be represented by constraint networks [23]. Formally, a *constraint network* C is a quadruple $\langle V, dom, A, con \rangle$ where

* V is a set of variables, $\{v_1, v_2, \cdots, v_N\}$,
* associated with each variable v_i is a finite domain $d_i = dom(v_i)$,
* A is a set of arcs, $\{a_1, a_2, \cdots, a_n\}$,
* associated with each arc a_i is a constraint $con(a_i) = r_i(R_i)$ where $R_i \subseteq V$ is a

relation scheme and r_i is a set of relation tuples on R_i.

The FCSP problem is to find one or all relation tuples in $sol(C) = r_1 \bowtie \cdots \bowtie r_n$.

An FCSP can be solved using various methods [4, 6, 11, 12, 14], one of which is to find the minimal network [14]. Let $Scheme(C) = \{R_1, \cdots, R_n\}$ be the scheme of a constraint network C. The *minimal network of a constraint network* C is a network C^*, with $sol(C) = sol(C^*)$, $Scheme(C) = Scheme(C^*)$, and $r_i^* = \Pi_{R_i}(sol(C^*))$ where Π_{R_i} is a projection operator. Here we present a relaxation method (FM) which finds the minimal network of a constraint network with an acyclic scheme. Such methods have been studied by many researchers, for instance, [7, 17, 23]. We examine the properties of the method within the framework of dynamic processes.

Let $\mathcal{C}$ be the set of constraint networks with the same scheme and solutions. We define a state transition system $\langle \mathcal{C}, f \rangle$ where $f = \{f_i\}_{a_i \in A}$ with $f_i(r) = \bigcap_{\{j \mid R_i \cap R_j \neq \emptyset\}} \Pi_{R_i}(r_i \bowtie r_j)$.

Let FM be a constraint net representing a state transition system $\langle \mathcal{C}, f \rangle$.

THEOREM 3.4 FM solves the minimal network problem globally for $\mathcal{C}$ if the scheme of $\mathcal{C}$ is acyclic.

PROOF: It is clear that a minimal network C^* is an equilibrium of the state transition system. Now let us define a metric on the set $\mathcal{C}$. Given a relation scheme R, the distance between two sets of relation tuples r_1, r_2 on the same relation scheme R can be defined as $d_R(r_1, r_2) = |(r_1 - r_2) \cup (r_2 - r_1)|$ where $|r|$ denotes the number of relation tuples. The distance between two constraint networks in $\mathcal{C}$ can be defined as $d(C_1, C_2) = \sqrt{\Sigma_{Scheme(C)} d_R^2(r_1, r_2)}$. Let us define a function L on $\mathcal{C}$ as $L(C) = \sqrt{\Sigma_{Scheme(C)} |r|^2}$. It is easy to check that L is a Liapunov function for $\langle \mathcal{C}, f \rangle$ and C^*.

If the scheme of $\mathcal{C}$ is acyclic, an equilibrium implies a minimal network [23], i.e., if $C \neq C^*$, $L(f(C)) < L(C)$. Furthermore, f is continuous since the metric space on $\mathcal{C}$ is discrete. According to Lemma 3.3, C^* is an asymptotically stable equilibrium.
□

3.4.2 Unconstrained Optimization

The problem of *unconstrained optimization* is to minimize a function $\mathcal{E} : \mathcal{R}^n \to \mathcal{R}$. Global consistency can be solved via unconstrained optimization. For instance, given a set of equations $g_i(x) = 0, i = 1 \cdots n$, let $\mathcal{E}_g(x) = \Sigma_{i=1}^k w_i g_i^2(x)$ where $w_i > 0$ and $\Sigma_{i=1}^k w_i = 1$. If a constraint solver CS solves $\min \mathcal{E}_g(x)$, CS solves $g(x) = 0$. Inequality constraints can be transformed into equality constraints. There are two approaches. Let $g_i(x) \le 0$ be an inequality constraint: the equivalent equality constraint is (i) $\max(0, g_i(x)) = 0$ or (ii) $g_i(x) + z^2 = 0$ where z is introduced as an extra variable. Here we first discuss two methods for this problem: the gradient method (GM) and Newton's method (NM), and then study the schema model (SM) for solving finite constraint satisfaction problems by minimizing an energy function $\mathcal{E} : [0, 1]^n \to \mathcal{R}$.

Gradient Method The gradient method [16] is based on the *gradient descent* algorithm, where state variables slide downhill in the direction opposed to the gradient. Formally, if the function to be minimized is $\mathcal{E}(x)$ where $x = \langle x_1, \cdots, x_n \rangle$, then at any point, the vector that points in the direction of maximum increase of $\mathcal{E}$ is the gradient of $\mathcal{E}$. Therefore, the following gradient descent equations model the *gradient method*:

$$\dot{x}_i = -k_i \frac{\partial \mathcal{E}}{\partial x_i}, \quad k_i > 0. \tag{3.4.1}$$

Let $\mathcal{E} : \mathcal{R}^n \to \mathcal{R}$ be a function. Let GM be a constraint net representing the gradient descent equations (3.4.1). The following theorem specifies conditions under which GM solves the problem of local minimization of $\mathcal{E}$.

THEOREM 3.5 Let X^* be the set of local minima of $\mathcal{E}$. GM solves the problem if $\frac{\partial \mathcal{E}}{\partial x}$ is continuous at X^*. GM solves the problem globally if, in addition, $\mathcal{E}$ is convex.

PROOF: According to Lemma 3.4, a local minimum is an asymptotically stable equilibrium. A set of local minima is also an asymptotically stable equilibrium. If $\mathcal{E}$ is convex, X^* is the unique minimal set, which is an attractor in the large. $\square$

Newton's Method Newton's method [19] minimizes a second-order approximation of the given function, at each iterative step. Let $\Delta \mathcal{E} = \frac{\partial \mathcal{E}}{\partial x}$ and J be the Jacobian of $\Delta \mathcal{E}$. At each step with current point $x^{(k)}$, Newton's method minimizes the function:

$$\mathcal{E}_a(x) = \mathcal{E}(x^{(k)}) + \Delta \mathcal{E}^T(x^{(k)})(x - x^{(k)}) + \frac{1}{2}(x - x^{(k)})^T J(x^{(k)})(x - x^{(k)}).$$

Let $\frac{\partial \mathcal{E}_a}{\partial x} = 0$, we have:

$$\Delta \mathcal{E}(x^{(k)}) + J(x^{(k)})(x - x^{(k)}) = 0.$$

The solution of the above equation becomes the next point, i.e.,

$$x^{(k+1)} = x^{(k)} - J^{-1}(x^{(k)})\Delta\mathcal{E}.$$

Newton's method defines a state transition system $\langle \mathcal{R}^n, f \rangle$ where $f(x) = x - J^{-1}(x)\Delta\mathcal{E}(x)$.

Let NM be a constraint net representing Newton's method. The following theorem specifies conditions under which NM solves the problem of local minimization of a function $\mathcal{E}$.

THEOREM 3.6 Let $X^* \in \mathcal{R}^n$ be the set of local minima of $\mathcal{E}$. NM solves the problem if $|J(x^*)| \neq 0$, $\forall x^* \in X^*$, i.e., $\mathcal{E}$ is strictly convex at each local minimal point. NM solves the problem globally if, in addition, $\mathcal{E}$ is convex.

PROOF: First, we prove that $\forall x^* \in X^*$, $x^* = f(x^*)$ and $|J(x^*)| \neq 0$ imply that x^* is asymptotically stable. Let R be the Jacobian of f. It is easy to check that $|R(x^*)| = 0$. There exists a neighborhood of x^*, $N^\epsilon(x^*)$, for any $x \in N^\epsilon(x^*)$, $|f(x) - f(x^*)| \leq \lambda |x - x^*|$ for $0 < \lambda < 1$. Therefore, $\lim_{k \to \infty} |f^k(x) - x^*| = 0$ and x^* is asymptotically stable. Therefore, X^* is an asymptotically stable equilibrium. If $\mathcal{E}$ is convex, x^* is the unique minimal point, which is an attractor in the large. $\square$

Here we assume that the Jacobian and its inverse are obtained off-line. Newton's method can also be used to solve a nonlinear equation $g(x) = 0$ by replacing $\Delta\mathcal{E}$ with g.

Schema Model The schema model has been used for finite constraint satisfaction in the PDP framework [18]. Basically, there is a set of units $\{x_i\}$, each can be on or off; constraints between units are represented by weights $\{w_{ij}\}$ on connections. An energy function is defined typically as a quadratic function in the following form:

$$\mathcal{E}(x) = -(\Sigma_{ij} w_{ij} x_i x_j + \Sigma_i b_i x_i) = -(x^T W x + b^T x)$$

where $x_i \in [0, 1]$ indicates the activation value and b_i specifies the bias for unit i. Value w_{ij} represents the constraint between two units i and j: w_{ij} is positive if units i and j support each other, it is negative if the units are against each other and it is zero if the units have no effect on each other. The problem is to minimize $\mathcal{E}$ within the closed set $[0, 1]^n$.

There are various methods for solving this problem. The schema model [18] provides the simplest discrete relaxation method. Let $n_i(x) = \frac{\partial \mathcal{E}}{\partial x_i} = -\Sigma_j w_{ij} x_j - b_i$. The *schema model* defines a state transition system $\langle [0,1]^n, f \rangle$ where $f = \langle f_1, \cdots, f_n \rangle$ and f_i is defined as follows: $f_i(x) = x_i - n_i(x) x_i$ if $n_i(x) > 0$ and $f_i(x) = x_i - n_i(x)(1 - x_i)$ otherwise. In other words, $f_i(x) = (1 - |n_i(x)|) x_i - \min(0, n_i(x))$.

Let SM be a constraint net representing the schema model.

THEOREM 3.7 SM solves the problem of minimizing $\mathcal{E}$ if $|n_i(x)| \leq 1$ for any i and x.

PROOF: Let X^* be the set of minima of $\mathcal{E}$. Let $x^{(k+1)}$ denote $f(x^{(k)})$. First, because $|n_i(x)| \leq 1$, $x^{(k)} \in [0,1]^n$ implies $x^{(k+1)} \in [0,1]^n$. Therefore, f is well-defined. Second, for each minimum x^* of $\mathcal{E}$, and for any i, either (1) $n_i(x^*) = 0$ or (2) $n_i(x^*) > 0$ and $x_i^* = 0$ or (3) $n_i(x^*) < 0$ and $x_i^* = 1$. Therefore, x^* is an equilibrium. Now we prove that x^* is stable. Let Ω be an ϵ-neighborhood of x^* such that $\forall x \in \Omega$ and for any i: if $n_i(x^*) \neq 0$, then $n_i(x)$ and $n_i(x^*)$ have the same sign, otherwise if $n_i(x) \geq 0$, then $x_i \geq x_i^*$ and if $n_i(x) \leq 0$, then $x_i \leq x_i^*$. Such a neighborhood exists because n_i is continuous. Considering $|f_i(x) - x_i^*|$, there are four cases.

1. $n_i(x^*) > 0$: In this case, $x_i^* = 0$ and $|f_i(x) - x_i^*| = |f_i(x)| = |1 - n_i(x)| \times |x_i| \leq |x_i - x_i^*|$.

2. $n_i(x^*) < 0$: In this case, $x_i^* = 1$ and $|f_i(x) - x_i^*| = |f_i(x) - 1| = |1 + n_i(x)| \times |x_i - 1| \leq |x_i - x_i^*|$.

3. $n_i(x^*) = 0$ and $n_i(x) \geq 0$: $|f_i(x) - x_i^*| = |(1 - n_i(x)) x_i - x_i^*| = |x_i - x_i^* - n_i(x) x_i| \leq |x_i - x_i^*|$.

4. $n_i(x^*) = 0$ and $n_i(x) \leq 0$: $|f_i(x) - x_i^*| = |(1 + n_i(x)) x_i - n_i(x) - x_i^*| = |x_i - x_i^* - n_i(x)(1 - x_i)| \leq |x_i - x_i^*|$.

Therefore, $\forall x \in \Omega, |f_i(x) - x_i^*| \leq |x_i - x_i^*|$ and $|f(x) - x^*| \leq |x - x^*|$. Therefore, x^* is stable. Thus, X^* is a stable equilibrium.

Furthermore, let $X_0^* \subseteq X^*$ be a set which takes a unique minimum in its neighborhood. X_0^* is convex and closed since it is an intersection of a set of linear equations on or within the boundary. Let Ω be a strict neighborhood of X_0^*. If $x \in \Omega - X_0^*$, let x^* be the projection of x on X_0^*. There exists x_i, $|f_i(x) - x_i^*| < |x_i - x_i^*|$, so $|f(x) - x^*| < |x - x^*|$ and $d(f(x), X_0^*) < d(x, X_0^*)$. Since f is continuous, according to Lemma 3.3 (with $V(x) = d(x, X^*)$), X_0^* is asymptotically stable, so is X^*. $\square$

3.4.3   Constrained Optimization

Unconstrained optimization can be used to solve soft constraints as well as hard constraints. *Constrained optimization* is a problem of solving (soft) constraints subject to the satisfaction of a set of hard constraints, or solving a constraint satisfaction problem within a subspace characterized by the set of hard constraints.

The prototypical constrained optimization problem can be stated as [16]: locally minimize $f(x)$, subject to $g(x) = 0$, where $g(x) = 0$ is a set of equations describing a manifold of the state space. There are various methods for solving the constrained optimization problem. Here we focus on methods derived from the gradient method. During constrained optimization, the state x should be attracted to the manifold $g(x) = 0$ and slide along the manifold until it reaches the locally smallest value of $f(x)$ on $g(x) = 0$.

Different methods arise from the design of the energy function $\mathcal{E}$ for minimizing $f(x)$ under constraints $g_k(x) = 0$ for $k = 0 \cdots m$. Let $\mathcal{E}_c$ be the energy function generated from the constraints, we have $\mathcal{E}(x) = f(x) + \mathcal{E}_c(x)$.

∗ *Penalty Methods*: The penalty method constructs an energy term that penalizes violations of the constraints, i.e., $\mathcal{E}_c(x) = \Sigma_{k=0}^{m} c_k g_k^2(x)$.

∗ *Lagrange Multipliers*: The Lagrange multiplier method introduces a Lagrange multiplier λ for each constraint and λ varies as long as its constraint is not satisfied, i.e., $\mathcal{E}_c(x) = \Sigma_{k=0}^{m} \lambda_k g_k(x)$. In addition, there is a set of differential equations for λ, i.e., $\dot{\lambda}_k = g_k(x)$.

The advantage of the penalty method is its simplicity; however, the constrained optimization problem may not be solved with finite c_i. The advantage of the Lagrange multiplier method is its ability to satisfy the hard constraints.

Let LM be the constraint net representing the Lagrange multiplier method. The following theorem specifies a condition under which LM solves the constrained optimization problem globally.

THEOREM 3.8   Let A be a matrix where $A_{ij} = \frac{\partial^2 f}{\partial x_i \partial x_j} + \Sigma_{k=0}^{m} \lambda_k \frac{\partial^2 g_k}{\partial x_i \partial x_j}$. If A is positive definite, LM solves the constrained optimization problem $\min f(x)$ subject to $g_k(x) = 0$ globally.

PROOF: Let

$$V(x) = \frac{1}{2} \Sigma_i \dot{x}_i^2 + \frac{1}{2} \Sigma_k g_k^2(x).$$

It has been shown in [16] that

$$\dot{V} = -\Sigma_{i,j} \dot{x}_i A_{ij} \dot{x}_j.$$

V is a Liapunov function for LM and the solution set. □

3.5   Summary

We have presented here a framework for constraint satisfaction. Figure 3.3 illustrates the overall approach. First, we view constraints as relations and constraint

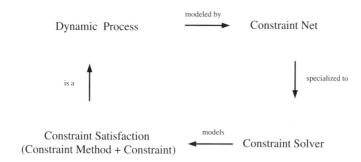

Figure 3.3
A framework for constraint satisfaction

satisfaction as a dynamic process of approaching the solution set of the constraints. Then, we explore the relationship between constraint satisfaction and constraint nets through constraint solvers.

Within this framework, *constraint programming* is seen as the creation of a constraint solver that solves the set of constraints. A constraint solver "solves" a set of constraints in the following sense (Figure 3.4). Given a constraint satisfaction problem C, and a discrete or continuous (time) constraint method, a constraint solver CS is generated. Starting from any initial state in the attraction basin of $sol(C)$, CS will approach $sol(C)$ asymptotically. In this framework, constraint programming is off-line and constraint satisfaction is on-line.

We have also studied various continuous and discrete time constraint methods, which can be realized by state integration systems and state transition systems, respectively.

This framework for constraint satisfaction has two advantages. First, the definition of constraint solvers relaxes the condition of solving constraints from finite computation to asymptotic stability. For example, many relaxation methods with the local convergence property are in fact "solvers" under this definition and many

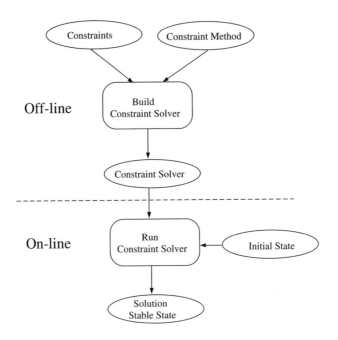

Figure 3.4
Constraint solvers and constraint satisfaction

problems become "semi-computable" in this sense. This concept is very useful in practice and can be used for generalizing Turing computability from discrete domains to continuous domains. Second, dynamic constraints can be solved in this framework as well. The importance of this characteristic is demonstrated here using an application to control synthesis.

3.6   Application to Control Synthesis

One of the significant applications of constraint solvers is the design of robot control systems [15]. A robotic system is a dynamic system consisting of a plant, a controller and an environment (Figure 3.5). The roles of these three subsystems can be characterized as follows:

∗ *Plant*: a plant is a set of entities which must be controlled to achieve certain requirements. For example, a robot arm with multiple joints, a car with throttle and steering, or a nuclear power plant can be considered as the *plant* of a robotic

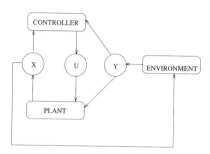

Figure 3.5
A robotic system

system.

* *Controller*: a controller is a set of sensors and actuators, which, together with software/hardware computational systems, senses the states of the plant (X) and the environment (Y), and computes desired inputs (U) to actuate the plant. For example, an analog circuit, a program in a digital computer, various sensors and actuators can be considered as parts of the *controller* of a robotic system.

* *Environment*: an environment is a set of entities beyond the (direct) control of the controller, with which the plant may interact. For example, obstacles to be avoided, objects to be reached, and rough terrain to be traversed can be considered as the *environment* of a robotic system.

In most cases, desired goals, safety requirements and physical restrictions of a robotic system can be specified by a set of constraints on variables $U \cup X \cup Y$ (Figure 3.5). The controller is then synthesized to regulate the system to satisfy the set of constraints.

A controller is *constraint-based* iff the integration of the controller and the plant solves the set of constraints, in response to the state of the environment. Consider the design of a tracking system S which chases a target T. Let x be the position of S and y be the position of T: the constraint to be satisfied is $x = y$. Suppose the plant follows the dynamics $u = \dot{x}$ where u is the control input. One possible design for the controller uses the following feedback control law $u = k(y - x), k > 0$ where the distance between the target and the current position $y - x$ can be sensed. This controller is constraint-based since $\dot{x} = k(y - x)$ solves $x = y$ for any parameter y.

The constraint techniques we have introduced can be applied to control synthesis and behavior verification for robotic systems [22].

Acknowledgments We wish to thank Uri Ascher, Peter Lawrence, Dinesh Pai, Nick Pippenger and Runping Qi for valuable discussions and suggestions. This research was supported by the Natural Sciences and Engineering Research Council, the Canadian Institute for Advanced Research and the Institute for Robotics and Intelligent Systems.

References

[1] S. Agmon. The relaxation method for linear inequalities. *Canadian Journal of Mathematics*, 6:382–392, 1954.

[2] A. Aiba, K. Sakai, Y. Sato, and D. J. Hawley. Constraint logic programming language CAL. In *Proceedings of the International Conference on Fifth Generation Computer Systems*, pages 263 –276, 1988.

[3] Y. Censor and T. Elfving. New method for linear inequalities. *Linear Algebra and Its Applications*, 42:199–211, 1982.

[4] R. Dechter. Constraint networks. In S. C. Shapiro, editor, *Encyclopedia of Artificial Intelligence*, pages 285 – 293. Wiley, N.Y., 1992.

[5] M. Dincbas, P. Van Hentenryck, H. Simonis, A. Aggoun, T. Graf, and F. Berthier. The constraint logic programming language CHIP. In *Proceedings of the International Conference on Fifth Generation Computer Systems*, pages 693 – 702, 1988.

[6] E. C. Freuder. Complexity of k-tree structured constraint satisfaction problems. In *Proceeding of AAAI-90*, 1990.

[7] E. C. Freuder. Completable representations of constraint satisfaction problems. In *KR-91*, pages 186 – 195, 1991.

[8] L. G. Gubin, B. T. Polyak, and E. V. Raik. The method of projections for finding the common point of convex sets. *U.S.S.R. Computational Mathematics and Mathematical Physics*, pages 1–24, 1967.

[9] J. Jaffar and J. L. Lassez. Constraint logic programming. In *ACM Principles of Programming Languages*, pages 111 – 119, 1987.

[10] D. G. Luenberger. *Introduction to Dynamic Systems: Theory, Models and Applications*. John Wiley & Sons, 1979.

[11] A. K. Mackworth. Constraint satisfaction. In S. C. Shapiro, editor, *Encyclopedia of Artificial Intelligence*, pages 276 – 285. Wiley, N.Y., 1992.

[12] A. K. Mackworth. The logic of constraint satisfaction. *Artificial Intelligence*, 58:3–20, 1992.

[13] M. D. Mesarovic and Y. Takahara. *General Systems Theory: Mathematical Foundations*. Academic Press, 1975.

[14] U. Montanari. Networks of constraints: Fundamental properties and applications to picture processing. *Information Science*, 7:95–132, 1974.

[15] D. K. Pai. Least constraint: A framework for the control of complex mechanical systems. In *Proceedings of American Control Conference*, pages 426 – 432, Boston, 1991.

[16] J. Platt. Constraint methods for neural networks and computer graphics. Technical Report Caltech-CS-TR-89-07, Department of Computer Science, California Institute of Technology, 1989.

[17] F. Rossi and U. Montanari. Exact solution in linear time of networks of constraints using perfect relaxation. In *Proceedings First Int. Principles of Knowledge Representation and Reasoning, Toronto, Ontario, Canada*, pages 394–399, May 1989.

[18] D. E. Rumelhart and J. L. McClelland, editors. *Parallel Distributed Processing — Exploration in the Microstructure of Cognition*. MIT Press, 1986.

[19] J. T. Sandfur. *Discrete Dynamical Systems: Theory and Applications*. Clarendon Press, 1990.

[20] V. A. Saraswat, M. Rinard, and P. Panangaden. Semantic foundations of concurrent constraint programming. Technical Report SSL-90-86, Palo Alto Research Center, 1990.

[21] K. Yang and K. G. Murty. New iterative methods for linear inequalities. Unpublished.

[22] Y. Zhang. A foundation for the design and analysis of robotic systems and behaviors, 1994. PhD thesis, forthcoming.

[23] Y. Zhang and A. K. Mackworth. Parallel and distributed constraint satisfaction: Complexity, algorithms and experiments. In Laveen N. Kanal, editor, *Parallel Processing for Artificial Intelligence*. Elsevier/North Holland, 1993.

[24] Y. Zhang and A. K. Mackworth. Constraint Nets: A semantic model for hybrid dynamic systems, 1994. Accepted for TCS Special Issue on Hybrid Systems.

[25] Y. Zhang and A. K. Mackworth. Will the robot do the right thing? In *Proc. Artificial Intelligence 94*, pages 255 – 262, Banff, Alberta, May 1994.

4 Robot Programming and Constraints

Dinesh K. Pai

Abstract

Constraints play a central role in the analysis and planning of robot motion. We suggest that constraints form an appropriate language with which to program robot motion as well and describe the Least Constraint framework.

4.1 Introduction

Robot programming has largely been based on specifying motions in terms of trajectories in a configuration space or a state space. For example, motions of industrial robot manipulators are usually specified in terms of the trajectory of the hand.

Such specifications are simple and intuitive and adequate for some applications. But their deficiencies are increasingly apparent. For example, consider the problem of programming a human-like robot to walk dynamically in three dimensions [17]. The robot has a large number joints which have to be used to achieve a desired motion of the body. One approach to programming such a task is to pick some periodic trajectory for the joints, and attempt to track it. However, it is not clear that this is the natural characterization of the task.

Some important issues:

- How to specify trajectories for high degree of freedom (also called "redundant") robots? Such robots are increasingly common since they improve versatility and fault tolerance.

  Most natural specifications for these robots will only partially constrain the motion. There has been considerable research into "redundancy resolution", i.e., the generation of unique trajectories from partial specifications by the introduction of other criteria such as singularity avoidance (e.g., [9]). But the problem of "redundancy maintenance," i.e., accepting and maintaining partial specifications remains.

- How should a trajectory specification deal with objects in the robot's environment? It was quickly realized that in order to perform interesting tasks, a robot has to interact with its environment — to avoid some objects (obstacles) [12] and to manipulate others [15]. A motion specification should account for the geometric constraints imposed by the objects. This problem has usually been solved by using a separate motion planner which generates a safe trajectory for a low-level trajectory executor. However since the motion constraints are not known at run-time, the executor cannot safely alter the planned trajectory in response to sensed events.

- How to combine motions at run-time? The motion planning task is often divided among different modules whose outputs are combined to produce the actual motion. Since trajectory specifications are entirely procedural most researchers have used mutual exclusion to arbitrate among the modules, leading to run-time behavior that is difficult to anticipate.

Returning to our example of the human-like walking machine, we would instead like to program such a machine incrementally, by specifying assertions about its behavior. We can specify several requirements for walking: for instance, (i) the foot should clear the ground during the swing phase of the leg, (ii) the swing foot should be moved to a location suitable for dynamic balance by foot placement, and so on. The machine is controlled to satisfy these requirements at run-time.

It may turn out that the initial requirements were inadequate — for example, one may find that there is nothing to prevent knee flexion from becoming so large that walking is impossible. In this case one would like to modify the existing program by merely adding new assertions: for example, by adding the assertion that the pelvis should be above a certain height. This is not possible in current robot programming languages.

The Least Constraint (LC) framework was designed to address these problems [16, 18]. It has been successfully used to program dynamic walking in a simulated human-like biped and will be used to program a new class of high degree of freedom robots that are under construction in our lab.

4.2 Constraints in Robotics

4.2.1 Robot Domains: Configuration Space, Task Space

The behavior of robots is usually described in two types of spaces. A *configuration space* of the robot is a space whose points uniquely describe all possible positions and orientations of every part of the robot. It is usually understood that the dimension the configuration space is the minimum required. Otherwise, it can be called a *descriptor space*. The desired behavior, on the other hand, may be more conveniently expressed in other spaces called *task spaces*. For example, the position and orientation of the gripper of a robot is a task space used by most industrial robot programming languages.

The configuration and task spaces are usually differentiable manifolds, but not necessarily covered by a single chart. The space of rigid body rotations, $SO(3)$, is a common example.

Typical spaces include:

- Joint space: the configuration space of a chain of rigid bodies with one degree of freedom joints. Most industrial robots are of this type. A robot with r revolute joints and p prismatic joints has a joint space $\equiv T^r \times \mathbb{R}^p$.

- The space of rigid motions: In three dimensions, this is the manifold of the Special Euclidean group, $SE(3) \equiv \mathbb{R}^3 \times SO(3)$. In two dimensions, this is $SE(2) \equiv \mathbb{R}^2 \times S^1$. The desired configuration of an object manipulated by the robot or of a link of the robot could be expressed in this space.

4.2.2   Geometric Constraints

Interaction between a robot and solid objects in its environment impose a natural set of constraints on its motion and have been extensively studied in motion planning (see e.g., [23, 11]). The solid objects are usually modeled in world coordinates and can be transformed into configuration space (see [13, 7, 11]).

For example, consider the configuration space of a mobile robot modeled as a rectangle free to move in the plane; its configuration space $\mathcal{C}$ is $\mathbb{R}^2 \times S^1$ with coordinates $\mathbf{x}$ for $\mathbb{R}^2$ and θ for S^1. A configuration space obstacle CO_{jk} due to a convex subset $\mathcal{A}_j$ of the robot interacting with a convex subset $\mathcal{B}_k$ of the obstacle can be defined by a family of constraints [13, 8],

$$C_i^{jk} := (\theta \in A_i) \rightarrow (f_i(\mathbf{x}, \theta) \leq 0). \tag{4.2.1}$$

Here $f_i : \mathcal{C} \mapsto \mathbb{R}$ with positive f_i corresponding to free space. A_i is the applicability set, which in this case is of the form

$$(\theta \leq \theta_{max,i}) \bigwedge (\theta_{min,i} \leq \theta). \tag{4.2.2}$$

The configuration space obstacle is given by

$$\bigwedge_{i \in cfamily(\mathcal{A}_j, \mathcal{B}_k)} C_i^{jk}. \tag{4.2.3}$$

In the general case when the robot $\mathcal{A}$ and obstacles $\mathcal{B}$ are non-convex, they can be decomposed into (possibly overlapping) convex polygons $\mathcal{A}^j$ and $\mathcal{B}^k$, so the general form of the free configuration space around the obstacle is

$$\neg \left(\bigvee_{j,k} \bigwedge_{i \in cfamily(\mathcal{A}_j, \mathcal{B}_k)} C_i^{jk} \right).$$ (4.2.4)

4.2.3 Motion Constraints

The physics of the robot and its interaction with the world imposes additional constraints on its motion. The exact constraints depend on our model of the robot and its world. Modeling remains a task involving engineering judgement regarding the significant physics. It is important to note that unlike the geometric constraints above these are *differential-algebraic* constraints.

The following are constraints resulting from some commonly useful models.

Differential Kinematic Constraints Simple examples of such constraints are bounds due to actuator limits or safety considerations of the form

$$\dot{q}_{min} \leq \dot{q} \leq \dot{q}_{max}$$ (4.2.5)

$$\ddot{q}_{min} \leq \ddot{q} \leq \ddot{q}_{max}$$ (4.2.6)

More interesting constraints arise from motion involving rolling without slipping, such as in wheels and fingers. In the above example of the mobile robot with $\mathbf{x} = (x, y)^T$, the constraint that the instantaneous motion of the center of a wheel is restricted to the plane of the wheel leads to a differential kinematic constraint

$$\dot{x} \sin \theta - \dot{y} \cos \theta = 0.$$ (4.2.7)

This constraint can be shown to be *non-holonomic*, i.e., it can not be integrated to produce a geometric constraint involving x, y, and θ only.

Dynamic Constraints The dynamics of the rigid bodies in the robot and the dynamics of the actuators can be significant for high performance robots. These lead to a system of highly non-linear, coupled differential equations which impose additional constraints. The formulation of these constraints for control and simulation has been extensively studied (see e.g. [21]). These can be broadly classified as

- State space constraints: the equations of motion are formulated in terms of a minimal set of Lagrangian coordinates $\mathbf{q}$, leading to a system of ordinary differential equations. For example if a robot is constructed as a chain of rigid bodies, the equations of motion are of the form

$$\dot{\mathbf{q}} = \mathbf{v},$$ (4.2.8)

$$M(\mathbf{q})\dot{\mathbf{v}} = \tau - f(\mathbf{q}, \mathbf{v}),$$ (4.2.9)

where M is a symmetric positive-definite inertia tensor and τ_i is the general-ized force applied along q_i.

- Descriptor space constraints: the equations of motion are formulated in terms of a sufficient, but not necessarily minimal, set of coordinates, $\mathbf{x}$. Additional constraints are imposed between the coordinates, leading to differential-algebraic equations of the form

$$\dot{\mathbf{x}} \;=\; \mathbf{v}, \tag{4.2.10}$$
$$M(\mathbf{x})\dot{\mathbf{v}} \;=\; f(\mathbf{x}, \mathbf{v}) + G^T(\mathbf{x})\lambda \tag{4.2.11}$$
$$0 \;=\; g(\mathbf{x}), \tag{4.2.12}$$

where M is a (different) symmetric positive-definite inertia tensor, $G = Dg$ the constraint Jacobian matrix, and λ are Lagrange multipliers. A common example is to take the position and orientation of each rigid body as descriptors, and introduce constraints for each joint of the robot. It is easier to formulate the dynamics of closed kinematic chains using this approach. However, equations in descriptor form can be difficult to integrate for high index problems [2, 1].

4.3   Least Constraint (LC)

4.3.1   Program Constraints

While the system constraints above have been used in the analysis and planning of robot motion, user specification of desired robot behavior has been in terms of either a trajectory of the robot or a goal state [1]. In the former case the motion is explicitly specified and the main focus has been on the control of the robot to track this trajectory. In the latter case, the motion of the robot is implicitly specified and the focus has been on motion planning, i.e. the construction of a trajectory which reaches the goal.

We believe that specifying robot motions with constraints is appropriate and natural in many situations. A simple example is toleranced motion, in which we want to follow a trajectory but within a generous tolerance of the nominal trajectory. Most robot motions are of this type. Another example is the idea of a "funnel" [14]. Here we only require that the robot lie in a set that contracts over time until

---

[1] A notable exception is the potential field approach to obstacle avoidance [10] which shares many features with LC. LC generalizes obstacles to constraints in arbitrary domains. See [18] for a discussion.

a desired set of configurations is attained.

4.3.2   LC

In the LC framework, motions are expressed by means of time- and state-dependent assertions [18]. These assertions are defined using inequality constraints which describe the set of allowed states as a function of time. The constraints are solved at run time to produce a satisfying motion.

Since complex mechanical systems have large state spaces, it is not convenient or natural to express all of the constraints in a single space. For instance, even the simple walking machine simulated in [17] has a 28-dimensional state space. For convenience of expression, users define derived variables in terms of the basic (e.g., state) variables — an example of this is the definition of task and end-effector coordinates for robot manipulators. LC generalizes such constructions to allow the creation of arbitrary, user definable quantities which are natural to the tasks and the constraints being expressed. One can isolate small groups of variables into domains on which to focus. For example, the foot collision constraints in the above walking example are best expressed in a separate foot position domain.

In LC, users define a *domain system*, $\{\mathcal{D}^i : i \in I\}$, related by *linking functions*

$$l_{ij} : \mathcal{D}^i \to \mathcal{D}^j, \quad (i,j) \in L \subset I \times I, \tag{4.3.13}$$

which satisfy the basic consistency condition that all diagrams of the following form commute.

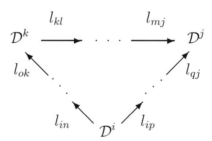

All domains $\mathcal{D}^i$ are connected to a *basic domain* $\mathcal{D}^0$ by compositions of linking functions :

$$\mathcal{D}^0 \xrightarrow{l_{0j}} \cdots \xrightarrow{l_{ki}} \mathcal{D}^i.$$

Briefly, the motivation for using domain systems is that they allow a constraint on a subdomain $\mathcal{D}^i$ to be lifted to an equivalent constraint on the basic domain $\mathcal{D}^0$

using compositions of linking functions. $\mathcal{D}^0$ is usually the configuration space or state space.

A *motion specification* in LC consists of a system of time-varying inequality constraints $C_\alpha, \alpha \in A$, on the domains $\mathcal{D}^i$; here each constraint C_α is expressed by

$$C_\alpha := f_\alpha(\mathbf{x}^i, \dot{\mathbf{x}}^i, t) \leq 0,$$

where $f_\alpha : \mathcal{D}^i \times T\mathcal{D}^i \times \mathbb{R} \to \mathbb{R}$ is a smooth map and $\mathbf{x}^i(t)$ denotes a time-dependent trajectory in $\mathcal{D}^i$. Such C_α and their conjunctions

$$C := \bigwedge_\alpha C_\alpha$$

are executable LC motion programs. The meaning of the constraint is that the robot is controlled to make the specified expressions $C_\alpha := f_\alpha(\mathbf{x}, \dot{\mathbf{x}}, t) \leq 0$ true at all times t.

4.3.3   Constraint Satisfaction

LC programs are executed by satisfying constraints at run-time. This produces a trajectory $\mathbf{x}(t) \in \mathcal{D}^0$ such that the derived constraints

$$\bar{C}_\alpha := f_\alpha((l_{ki} \circ \dots \circ l_{0j})(\mathbf{x}(t)), t) \leq 0$$

obtained by lifting the original constraints using the linking maps are satisfied at all times t. In LC, this is done at discrete time steps $t_{(n)}$: at every time step $t_{(n)}$, a feasible point $x(t_{(n)})$ is produced, and is used to compute the control u.

Criteria for good constraint satisfaction algorithms for LC constraints are quite different than those encountered in other domains such as finite constraint satisfaction and large scale optimization. We first describe features of a suitable constraint satisfaction algorithm and then describe the constraint satisfaction algorithm we currently use.

- On-line constraint satisfaction. This is required since many of the constraints will only be known at run time.

- Any time solution [6]. The constraint satisfaction should be interruptible – if a feasible solution cannot be found in the allotted time an improved estimate should be returned.

- Exploit continuity. The constraints typically vary slowly relative to the rate at which they are satisfied. Since a similar problem was solved at the previous time step, a good starting guess is available.

- Exploit "large" feasible sets due to inequality constraints.

LC separates the specification of constraints and the techniques used for satisfying them. Different constraint satisfaction algorithms can be used. We first discretize the constraint function in time using numerical methods with good stability properties such as linear multistep methods or implicit Runge-Kutta methods [2]. The step size $h > 0$ is taken to be the servo rate. For example, using the simple implicit backward-Euler scheme, the constraint

$$\dot{x} - \cos(\theta)v \leq 0$$

is discretized as

$$x_{(n)} - x_{(n-1)} - h\cos(\theta_{(n)})v_{(n)} \leq 0.$$

The discretization yields a set of algebraic constraints in $x_{(n)}$ at time $t_{(n)}$.

Next, the inequalities are solved to produce a solution at $t_{(n)}$. The solution is usually advanced a few time steps beyond the present time to produce a trajectory segment, combining simulation with trajectory generation. We have had good results with relaxation methods [18], barrier methods [22], and a conjugate direction method with a quadratic penalty function. These methods are local and iterative. The locality is a limitation but makes the methods fast enough to be implementable in real time. The methods exploit knowledge of a good starting point for iteration. Since the feasible sets specified with inequality constraints are usually of non-zero measure and typically large, overrelaxation is used to speed convergence. The gradients are computed cheaply using automatic differentiation [20], which enables us to compute each update within only a small factor of the time to evaluate the constraint functions.

Finally, the satisfying trajectory segment is sent to a low-level tracking controller which drives the actuators.

The method is fast and effective in practice. We should point out that the numerical solution of non-linear systems is a delicate matter. There are several practical considerations such as pre-scaling of constraints, maintaining active constraints and selecting numerical tolerances that are important for implementing such constraint solvers.

4.4   Example: Mobile Robots

Here we demonstrate the LC approach in programming the motion of a mobile robot. This work is part of the Dynamo mobile robotics project at UBC led by

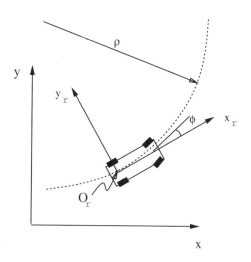

Figure 4.1
Mobile Robot Notation

Mackworth and Pai. The Dynamo facility includes the Dynamite testbed consisting
of radio controlled cars whose absolute position is sensed at video rates using off-
board vision (see e.g. [3]).

While mobile robots are relatively low degree of freedom machines, a collection of
mobile robots may be viewed as a single high degree of freedom robot. The presence
of non-holonomic constraints also adds to the difficulty of specifying the motion of
a wheeled robot. These constraints do not lower the dimension of configuration
space, but on the other hand, the user cannot specify an arbitrary trajectory to
track. By specifying the desired motion weakly in terms of the constraints on the
required motion, the constraints can be solved at run-time to produce a motion
that satisfies the constraint.

The dynamite mobile robots are front-wheel steered with a steering angle ϕ and
can be controlled by setting a throttle value and steering angle. We have implemented a low-level PI controller which servos the robot to track a specified speed
v_d and turning radius ρ_d. To a first approximation, the robot can be modeled as
a kinematic machine, with two inputs v_d and ρ_d. Experiments with programming
these mobile robots with LC are in progress, but we describe a simple example here.

Following the notation in [11] (see Figure 4.4), let the configuration space $\mathcal{C}$ of
the mobile robot be the space of displacements of a coordinate frame (O_r, x_r, y_r)
attached to robot. $\mathcal{C}$ has coordinates x, y, θ. For simplicity, we take $\theta \in \mathbb{R}$ so $\mathcal{C}$ is a

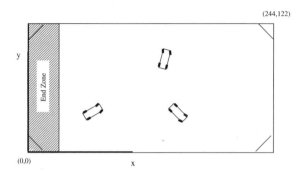

Figure 4.2
Dynamite robot pen

covering space of $SE(2)$. Define the forward speed $v = \dot{x}\cos(\theta) + \dot{y}\sin(\theta)$ and the turning radius $\rho = v/\dot{\theta}$. Note that ρ is a signed quantity, with $\rho > 0$ corresponding to the center of rotation of the robot lying to the "left" of the robot, i.e., having $y_r > 0$. However, since $\rho = \infty$ when the robot is moving along a straight line, we use the less natural but more convenient quantity, the curvature $\varsigma = 1/\rho$.

The robot has the following constraints

Motion constraints

1. Rolling constraint:

$$C_1 := \dot{x}\sin(\theta) - \dot{y}\cos(\theta) = 0 \qquad (4.4.14)$$

2. Speed limit:

$$C_2 := (v_{min} \leq v) \bigwedge (v \leq v_{max}) \qquad (4.4.15)$$

3. Steering limit:

$$C_3 := (\varsigma_{min} \leq \varsigma) \bigwedge (\varsigma \leq \varsigma_{max}) \qquad (4.4.16)$$

Geometric constraints

4. Wall and obstacle constraints: The robot is in a convex, enclosed pen populated by other robots (see figure 4.2). The pen and the robots are well represented by convex polygons. Details of representing the free space of the robot among such obstacles can be found in [13, 8, 5]. Here only type-B contact between an edge of the pen and a vertex of the robot needs to be

considered and each contact mode generates a constraint in the configuration space. Let an edge w be at a distance d_w along the unit normal to the edge $(n_{w,x}, n_{w,y})$ oriented in the direction of free space. Contact between the edge and the vertex u of the robot whose coordinates are $(p_{u,x}, p_{u,y})$ in the (O_r, x_r, y_r) frame generates the configuration space obstacle constraint (see Equation 4.2.1)

$$
\begin{aligned}
C_u^w := (\theta \in A_{u,w}) \quad \rightarrow \quad & ((x + p_{u,x}\cos\theta - p_{u,y}\sin\theta)n_{w,x}) \\
& +((y + p_{u,x}\sin\theta + p_{u,y}\cos\theta)n_{w,y}) \qquad (4.4.17) \\
& -d_w \le 0
\end{aligned}
$$

User constraint

5. Pusher: The task is to reach the "end zone" $0 \le x \le 25$ at the left wall (see figure 4.2). This can be achieved by the constraint

$$ C_p := x - x_{w,max} + st \le 0 \qquad (4.4.18) $$

where s is the speed of the pusher and $x_{w,max}$ is the x-coordinate of the right wall.

With more complicated obstacles, a motion planner can be used to process the constraints into a form suitable for LC. For example, Brooks [4] describes a method for extracting a net of "freeways" which are generalized cylinders covering the free space of the robot. However instead of traveling along the spines of the cylinders as in [4] we can use the freeways as constraints. The robot is pushed through a freeway by pusher constraint. The advantage of this approach is that additional constraints such as those due to unforeseen obstacles can be added run time.

4.5 Future Work

We are developing a new version of LC with a better software architecture, improved performance, and with additional capability to handle differential-algebraic constraints. This is required for new applications such as programming modular legged robots [19]. The new implementation of LC in progress is designed to be efficient enough to run on a network of small embedded controllers.

In the long term, we are interested in the problem of verifying the correctness of LC programs for appropriate notions of correctness (see [24] for recent work in the area). This involves exact or approximate methods for detecting topological changes to the feasible set of system states and for estimating whether a connected component of the feasible set will collapse.

References

[1] U. Ascher and L. R. Petzold. Stability of computational methods for constrained dynamics systems. Technical Report, Computer Science Department, University of British Columbia, May 1991.

[2] K. Brenan, S. Campbell, and L.Petzold. *Numerical Solution of Initial Value Problems in Differential-Algebraic Equations*. North Holland, 1989.

[3] R. Barman, S. Kingdon, J. J. Little, A. K. Mackworth, D. K. Pai, M. Sahota, H. Wilkinson, and Y. Zhang. Dynamo: real-time experiments with multiple mobile robots. In *Proceedings of the IEEE Intelligent Vehicles Conference*, pages 261–266, Tokyo, Japan, July 1993.

[4] R. A. Brooks. Solving the find-path problem by good representation of free space. *IEEE Transactions on Systems, Man, and Cybernetics*, SMC-13(3):190–196, 1983.

[5] John Canny. Collision detection for moving polyhedra. *IEEE Trans. PAMI*, 8(2), March 1986.

[6] T. Dean and M. Boddy. An analysis of time dependent planning. In *AAAI-88*, 1988.

[7] B. R. Donald. A search algorithm for motion planning with six degrees of freedom. *Artificial Intelligence*, 31(3), 1987.

[8] B. R. Donald. A geometric approach to error detection and recovery for robot motion planning with uncertainty. *Artificial Intelligence*, 37((1-3)):223–271, Dec. 1988.

[9] J. M. Hollerbach and K. C. Suh. Redundancy resolution of manipulators through torque optimization. In *IEEE International Conference on Robotics and Automation*, pages 1016 – 1021, 1985.

[10] Oussama Khatib. Real-time obstacle avoidance for manipulators and mobile robots. *International Journal of Robotics Research*, 5(1):90 – 98, 1986.

[11] J. C. Latombe. *Robot Motion Planning*. Kluwer, 1991.

[12] Tomás Lozano-Pérez. Automatic planning of manipulator transfer movements. *IEEE Transactions on Systems, Man, and Cybernetics*, SMC-11(10):681–689, 1981.

[13] Tomás Lozano-Pérez. Spatial planning: A configuration space approach. *IEEE Transactions on Computers*, C-32(2):108–120, February 1983.

[14] Matthew T. Mason. The mechanics of manipulation. In *Proceedings of the IEEE International Conference on Robotics and Automation*, pages 544–548, 1985.

[15] Matthew T. Mason and J. Kenneth Salisbury, Jr. *Robot Hands and the Mechanics of Manipulation*. M.I.T. Press, 1985.

[16] Dinesh K. Pai. Programming parallel distributed control of complex systems. In *Proceedings of the IEEE International Symposium on Intelligent Control*, pages 426–432, September 1989.

[17] Dinesh K. Pai. Programming anthropoid walking: Control and simulation. Cornell Computer Science Tech Report TR 90-1178, 1990.

[18] Dinesh K. Pai. Least constraint: A framework for the control of complex mechanical systems. In *Proceedings of the American Control Conference*, pages 1615 – 1621, 1991.

[19] Dinesh K. Pai, Roderick A. Barman, and Scott K. Ralph. Platonic beasts: a new family of multilimbed robots. In *Proceedings of the IEEE International Conference on Robotics and Automation*, pages 1019 – 1025, San Diego, May 1994.

[20] D. K. Pai and T. H. S. Ser. Simultaneous computation of robot kinematics and differential kinematics with automatic differentiation. In *Proceedings of the IEEE/RSJ International Conference on Intelligent Robots and Systems '93*, pages 775–780, July 1993.

[21] R. E. Roberson and R. Schwertassek. *Dynamics of Multibody Systems*. Springer-Verlag, 1988.

[22] R. Spiteri. Ph.d. thesis, university of british columbia. forthcoming.

[23] C. Yap. Algorithmic motion planning. in *Advances in Robotics: Volume 1*, edited by J. Schwartz and C. Yap, Lawrence Erlbaum Associates, 1987.

[24] Ying Zhang. *A Foundation for the design and analysis of robotic systems*. PhD thesis, University of British Columbia, 1994.

5 Constraint Logic Programming: Hybrid Control, Logic as Linear Programming

Wolf Kohn, Anil Nerode[1], and V.S.Subrahmanian

Abstract

We summarize two independent recent developments in a research program coordinated by A. Nerode, which bear on aspects of the constraint logic programming paradigm. The first development is the Kagan-Nerode-Subrahmanian [26] extension of the Boole-Jeroslow paradigm [11], [46] for implementing propositional logic by integer linear programming to a paradigm for implementing predicate logic (resp. Horn clause logic) by integer linear programming (resp. real linear programming) plus unification, based on a new complete correct proof procedure for predicate logic using integer linear programming plus unification. The second development is the Kohn-Nerode hybrid system theory [39], [40], [41], [42] for extraction of digital control programs for continuous systems. The extraction program has been implemented by Kohn as a constraint logic program with several domains.

5.1 Logic as Unification plus Linear Programming

An important motivating application for constraint logic programming is its ability to represent efficiently those logic programs which, in the course of execution, query for answers to linear programming optimization problems. The answers to these optimization problems are computed in a constraint domain designed for linear programming and the answers are returned to the logic program in the course of execution. The usual unification-resolution algorithm for implementing the logic program and the usual linear programming algorithms for implementing linear optimization, such as Dantzig's simplex algorithm and Gomory's integer linear programming algorithm at first may seem to have little in common. But finding an answer substitution for a finite set of propositional logic statements, that is, solving the satisfaction problem of finding a truth valuation simultaneously making them all true, reduces to finding a zero-one valued solution to a corresponding system of real linear inequalities. This observation goes all the way back to Boole [11]. The proposition "$(a \vee b)$ is true" corresponds to the linear inequality $X_a + X_b \geq 1$, while $\neg a$ is replaced by $1 - X_a$. Boole reduces the corresponding set of inequalities by the Fourier-Motzkin method and checks the reduced system for a zero-one valued solution. This is a prohibitive computation except for simple examples.

---
[1]Research supported by ORA Corp., DARPA-US ARMY AMCCOM (Picatinny Arsenal,NJ) contract DAAA21-92-C-0013, the U. S. Army Research Office contract DAAL03-91-C-0027.

As observed by Dantzig in the 1950s, it is an easy exercise that solving a system of real inequalities is the same as solving a linear optimization problem. So finding a propositional answer substitution for a finite set of propositional logic statements directly reduces to an integer linear programming problem solvable by Gomory's method.

In the early 1980s, Nerode mentioned Boole's work to R. Jeroslow, Professor of Operations Research at Georgia Tech, a specialist in integer programming. Jeroslow (d. 1988) got his Ph.D. under Nerode in proof theory in 1968. Jeroslow reported back the simple but beautiful Jeroslow-Wang theorem of 1985 (see [46]) which asserts that for a propositional Horn clause program, there is an answer substitution if and only if the corresponding system of real inequalities has a real valued solution. This implies that answer substitutions for propositional Horn clause programs can be obtained by first applying the Dantzig simplex method and then checking for a zero-one valued extreme point. Jeroslow raised the question of how to extend this idea to predicate Horn clause logic and to full predicate logic in his book [46] and other papers. He did not resolve this question.

By ignoring the gloss that thirty years of Robinson unification-resolution theorem proving has imposed on Herbrand's method, Kagan, Nerode and Subrahmanian [26] gave a complete, correct proof procedure for full predicate Horn clause logic with function symbols which is based on unification plus real linear programming. This suggests implementing declarative Prolog by replacing SLD resolution-unification by real linear programming-unification using the simplex or similar method. We have undertaken this as an activity of the Cornell-Maryland LOPS (Logical Optimization) effort. The possible advantages are several. The natural implementations of this algorithm are purely declarative, and incremental updates are easy to make as the knowledge base increases. This proof procedure uses partial instantiation, not grounding out. Similar to what happens in the case of unification-resolution, unification-linear programming condenses cases and partially instantiated atomic formulas are treated as atomic when answering propositional satisfaction. But here one uses linear programming rather than resolution to answer propositional satisfaction questions. This method leads easily also to a complete correct proof procedure for full predicate logic based solely on unification and integer linear programming. As Colmerauer has remarked, unification can also be done by linear programming. Thus, if one wishes, one could use integer linear programming for all parts of all predicate logic proofs.

These methods also apply to non-monotonic logics. These logics model the set of all beliefs of an agent as well as objective rules and facts. These logics will not become useful in the intended computer science applications, expert systems and decision aids, until sufficiently large fragments are shown to be computationally feasible and implemented. There are several, basically equivalent, systems. These include stable models of logic programs, extensions of default theories, extensions of truth maintenance systems, belief sets in autoepistemic logics, etc. A general algebraic version of non-monotonic systems which shows transparently why these systems are really the same is the theory of non-monotonic rule systems of Marek-Nerode-Remmel [51], [48], [49], [50], [52], [53], [54].

Bell-Nerode-Ng-Subrahmanian [9], [10] gave a complete correct proof procedure for stable models of Datalog programs (finite Prolog programs without function symbols) based on integer linear programming and implemented a compiler which uses linear programming to answer queries and enumerate stable models. This has led to similar implementations for computing views for databases, default theories, truth maintenance systems, and pointwise circumscription. But all these optimization algorithms proceeded by first "grounding out" and then using linear programming to answer ground instance propositional satisfaction questions. The explosion of ground instances makes this impractical for large databases. But now this can be reworked using the complete correct unification-linear programming procedures without grounding out.

Marek-Nerode-Remmel [55] will give a complete correct proof procedure which, applied to a logic program P, generates by inference rules all statements ϕ which are in all stable models of a logic program P. One of these rules of inference has an infinite recursive set of premises. This can be modified to produce a complete correct proof procedure for generating the set of statements in all stable models of a finite logic program P based solely on unification plus integer linear programming, but again with an inference rule with a recursive infinite set of premises.

Note: The set of statements in all stable models of a finite predicate logic program is generally only a Π_1^1- set. See Marek-Nerode-Remmel [50] for related results.

In the rest of this paper, we will overview the independent work of Kohn and Nerode on hybrid systems, and show how the work on integer linear programming methods for logic computations, due to Nerode, Subrahmanian, and their co-workers, may be applied to the Kohn-Nerode hybrid systems effort.

5.2   Hybrid Systems

Hybrid systems are networks of digital automata and continuous plants under the influence of external disturbances. Hybrid control is the control of continuous

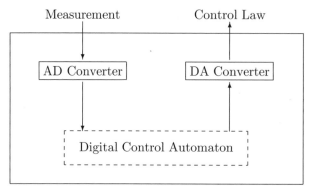

Measurement   Control Law

AD Converter   DA Converter

Digital Control Automaton

Figure 5.1

plants by finite control automata in a hybrid system in which a digital control automaton receives sampled sense data about the state of a continuous plant and, occasionally, issues a change in the control law for a plant controller. The control automaton enforces plant performance specifications by making frequent changes in the control applied to the plant. How and when to make these control law changes is the business of the finite control automaton. For real time systems, digital control programs can be modeled as input-output nondeterministic sequential automata. We call these control automata. The input to such a control automaton is a sensor measurement on the plant, the output is a change in control parameters governing the behavior of the physical plant controller.

The fundamental problem of hybrid systems is to extract from simulation models for the continuous plants and performance specifications for the hybrid system suitable digital control programs, or control automata which are such that if the control automaton is incorporated into the hybrid system, then the hybrid system satisfies its performance specification. The performance is simply a set of acceptable plant histories (plant state trajectories). Here is a short description of the Kohn-Nerode extraction method [43], [28], [29], [30], [31], [33], [33], [34], [35], [36], [37], [38], [39], [40], [41], [42]. A monograph with a complete development is in preparation by Kohn, Nerode, and Remmel.

1. Allow control functions of time that are measure valued, the so called relaxed control functions. The measures are probability measures on the space of control values as introduced by Warga [69], and earlier by Young [68] in their theory of optimal relaxed control. These can be approximated arbi-

trarily closely by piecewise constant control functions, and therefore can be implemented.

2. Form a non-negative cost function on plant trajectories evaluating their relative worth, which is an integral of a non-negative "Lagrangian" defined along trajectories so that the smaller the value of the integral along the trajectory, the better the trajectory. Ordinary differential equations and logical decision rule constraints are incorporated in the cost function.

3. For each plant state, find a relaxed control function minimizing the integral of the cost function over the trajectory produced by that control. We refer to this as an optimal feedback control function. To repeat, an optimal feedback control function assigns to the current plant state a control function yielding a trajectory minimizing the cost function on trajectories.

4. Weaken the optimality condition to an $\epsilon-$ optimality for an ϵ representing an acceptable margin of deviation from the minimal cost.

5. Approximate the optimal feedback control function by a finite control automaton meeting the same $\epsilon-$ optimality condition as the underlying optimal feedback control function.

The Kohn-Nerode theory [41] is distinguished from those offered previously by others by its extraction of continuous topological finite control automata from optimal feedback control functions given by relaxed optimal control to guarantee controllability and observability. The topologies involved are finite subtopologies of spaces of controls, sensor measurements, and trajectories, which we call small topologies. The control automata come equipped with small topologies provided by the extraction process.

The source of approximating finite control automata and digital to analog and analog to digital converters was identified in [Kohn-Nerode [41], appendix II]. The automata arise from relaxing optimality to $\epsilon-$ optimality and finding finite open covers of an optimal feedback control function in the space of all possible optimal feedback control functions. These open covers are also the source of the small topology on measurements and the small topology on control values used to discuss controllability and observability for hybrid systems in [41]. The finite topology on the space of sense measurements describes the analog to digital converter from the sense measurement space to the control automaton and tells roughly how accurate the sensors have to be (how expensive?) to guarantee $\epsilon-$ optimality using the extracted finite control automaton. The finite topology on the space of control values describes the digital to analog converter from control orders issued by the

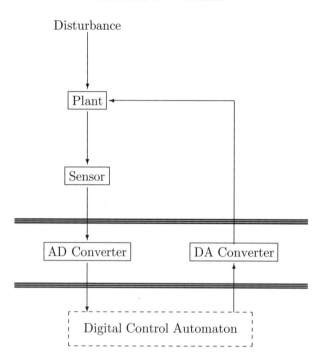

ANALOG WORLD

DIGITAL WORLD

Figure 5.2

digital control automaton to control values imposed on the physical actuator of the plant and tells roughly how accurate the actuators have to be to guarantee ϵ−optimality using the extracted finite control automaton. The smaller the ϵ, the tighter the finite cover needed for the optimal feedback control function and the tighter the resulting requirements on both sensors and actuator. This topological theory gives rise to Figure 2.

Extracting finite automata approximations to feedback control functions has nothing to do with the optimality of feedback control function. It is solely based on covering a feedback control function by an open cover in the space of such feedback control functions. Extracting control automata approximating feedback control functions from covers is a very general new tool, not restricted to optimal or relaxed control strategies, but which can be combined with any control theory that yields feedback control functions as its product.

5.3 Agents

In addition, due to unmodeled dynamics or other errors, the digital control automaton may be observed while operating in the hybrid system to fail to enforce the desired plant performance specification. We introduce the concept of an agent which senses when this happens, and then computes a new control automaton which it simulates or substitutes for the old to restore compliance [42]. That is, the newly available information about failure is incorporated to deduce and simulate a new control automaton.

This is our form of adaptive control. It is a form of non-monotonicity, since previous beliefs about the model, that is equations and constraints, have been replaced by new ones. We implement the agent as a metaprolog program.

In distributed autonomous hybrid control [42] there is a network of plants. Each plant has a continuous plant controller, a finite digital control automaton, and an agent monitoring its digital control program and plant controller. That agent monitors its plant process and its plant process controller and its digital control program, passes and receives messages to and from other agents for other plant processes. In our particular model each agent receives from every other agent a term of the cost function optimized by that agent when extracting a control automaton for that agent's plant. The agent occasionally computes and installs a new finite digital control automaton for its plant process controller, based on deviations it observes from performance specifications. We call this multiple agent hybrid control. It is to be emphasized that the purpose of the agents is to construct new finite control automata to replace old ones on the fly whenever performance and stability criteria are violated, and that the agents have no central supervisor. The tools used are distributed message passing of information about Lagrangians from agent to agent, and the Lagrangian variational-automata method described above for extracting digital control automata. In distributed autonomous hybrid control, each agent has two classes of inputs which provide updates to its knowledge base: messages passed from other agents, and communications of measurements from sensors monitoring plant states, the digital control program, and the environment. Similarly, each agent has two classes of outputs: messages passed to other agents, and simulations of new control automata for its plant controller.

Kohn has implemented this as a constraint logic program in which the program calls, in the course of execution, for the solution of linear optimization problems in infinite dimensional function spaces. This is based on the Kohn-Nerode model for extraction of digital control programs from simulation models and performance specifications described above. In the course of execution, this program queries a relaxed calculus of variations solver for an approximate answer to a problem of minimizing a non-negative lower semicontinuous linear cost functional on an infinite dimensional function space of possible control functions. The formal solution from the calculus of variations using Bellman's equation is loosened to ϵ-optimal form and becomes an implicit set of equations with automata as solutions of the Kleene-Schutzenberger [15], [45] form. That is, finite control automata which will provide control yielding trajectories within ϵ of being optimal are implicitly described by a set of Kleene-Schutzenberger automata equations. The logic program uses its Prolog features to extract the desired control automaton and simulate it.

These algorithms and models are an extension of Kohn's previous declarative control paradigm. The modeling and extraction algorithms have been implemented by Kohn, first at Boeing, then at Intermetrics, as a constraint logic program ERI with metaprolog features which has domains for symbolic calculus, Lie algebras of controls, relaxed variational calculus, optimal control, and the Kleene-Schutzenberger automata equation calculus. We are using these models and that software to investigate real time control for a variety of military and industrial systems including aircraft, traffic control, and industrial plants. Using this method successfully requires substantial sophistication in differential equations and variational calculus modeling. Further, if we wish to achieve stringent performance specifications, we need to have accurate simulation models of the underlying plants. This is a fertile area for establishing real time applications for constraint logic programming.

5.4   Final Remark

There may be a role for direct use of the logic as linear programming paradigm in executing distributed agent logic programs. This is because hybrid system control automaton extraction uses linear optimization in infinite dimensional function spaces, Prolog can be implemented using linear optimization in finite dimensional spaces, and these can be done as a single optimization.

References

[1] V. M. Alekseev, V. M. Tikhomirov, S. V. Fomin, *Optimal Control*, Consultant's Bureau, Plenum Press, 1987.

[2] M. Arbib and R. E. Kalman, *Topics in Mathematical Systems Theory*, McGraw-Hill, N. Y., 1969.

[3] M. Arbib and L. Padulo, *Systems Theory*, Saunders, Philadelphia, 1974.

[4] J. P. Aubin, *Convex Analysis and Optimization*, Pitman, 1982.

[5] J. P. Aubin, *Differential Inclusions, Set Valued Maps, and Viability*, Springer-Verlag, 1984.

[6] J. P. Aubin, *Set Valued Analysis*, Birkhauser, 1990.

[7] J. P. Aubin, *Viability Theory*, Birkhauser, 1991.

[8] J. P. Aubin and I. Ekeland, *Applied Non-Linear Analysis* , Wiley, 1984.

[9] C. Bell, A. Nerode, R. Ng and V.S. Subrahmanian. (1992), Implementing Deductive Databases by Linear Programming, Tech. Report CS-TR-2747, University of Maryland, College Park. Preliminary version in: Proc. 1992 ACM Symp. on Principles of Database Systems.

[10] C. Bell, A. Nerode, R. Ng and V.S. Subrahmanian, Mixed Integer Programming Methods for Computing Nonmonotonic Deductive Databases, accepted for publication in Journal of the ACM.

[11] G. Boole, *An Investigation of the Laws of Thought, on which are founded the Mathematical Theories of Logic and Probability*, MacMillan, London. 1854.

[12] K. L. Clark, Negation as failure, in H. Gallaire and J. Minker, editors, *Logic and Databases*, pages 293–322. Plenum Press, 1978.

[13] J. de Kleer, An Assumption-Based TMS, Artificial Intelligence, 28:127–162, 1986.

[14] J. Doyle, A Truth Maintenance System, Artificial Intelligence, 12:231–272, 1979.

[15] S. Eilenberg, *Automata, Languages, and Machines* (vol. A), Academic Press, New York, 1974.

[16] I. Ekeland, *Infinite Dimensional Optimization and Convexity*, University of Chicago Lecture Notes in Mathematics, University of Chicago Press, 1983.

[17] A. Friedman, *Differential Games*, Wiley-Interscience, 1971.

[18] M. Gelfond and V. Lifschitz, The Stable Semantics for Logic Programs, in R. Kowalski and K. Bowen, editors, *Proceedings of the 5th International Symposium on Logic Programming*, 1070–1080, MIT Press, 1988.

[19] M. Gelfond and V. Lifschitz, Logic Programs with Classical Negation, in D. Warren and P. Szeredi, editors, *Logic Programming: Proceedings of the 7th International Conference*, 579–597, MIT Press, 1990.

[20] J. Goldstine, A Rational Theory of AFL's, LNCS 71, 271-281, 1979.

[21] R. L. Grossman, A. Nerode, H. Rischel, A. Ravn, eds., *Hybrid Systems*, Springer Lecture Notes in Computer Science, October, 1993.

[22] R. L. Grossman and R. G. Larson, Viewing Hybrid Systems as Products of Control Systems and Automata, Proc. IEEE 31st CDC,vol. 3, 2953-2955, Tucson, 1992.

[23] J. Guckenheimer, A. Back, M. Myers, A Dynamical Simulation Facility for Hybrid Systems, MSI Tech. Report 92-6, Cornell University, 1992.

[24] J. Guckenheimer and A. Nerode, Simulation for Hybrid and Nonlinear Control, Proc. IEEE 31st CDC, vol. 3, 2981-2983, 1992.

[25] J. Hilgert, K. H. Hofmann, J. Lawson, Lie Groups, Convex Cones, and Semigroups, Oxford Clarendon Press, 1988.

[26] V. Kagan, A. Nerode, and V.S. Subrahmanian. Computing Definite Logic Programs by Partial Instantiation, Annals of Pure and Applied Logic, 1994.

[27] Y. Kesten and A. Pnueli, Timed and Hybrid Statecharts and their Textual Representation, in *Formal Techniques in Real Time and Fault Tolerant Systems*, LNCS 571, Springer-Verlag, 1992.

[28] W. Kohn, Application of Declarative Hierarchical Methodology for the Flight Telerobotic Servicer, Boeing Document G-6630-061, Final Report of NASA-Ames Research Service Request 2072, Job Order T1988, Jan 15, 1988.

[29] W. Kohn, A Declarative Theory for Rational Controllers, Proc. 27th IEEE CDC, pp. 130-136, 1988.

[30] W. Kohn, The Rational Tree Machine: Technical Description and Mathematical Foundations, IR and D BE-499, Technical Document 905-10107-1, July 7, 1989, Boeing Computer Services.

[31] W. Kohn, Cruise Missile Mission Planning: A Declarative Control Approach, Boeing Computer Services Technical Report, 1989.

[32] W. Kohn, Rational Algebras: A Constructive Approach, IR and D BE-499, Technical Document D-905-10107-2, July 7, 1989.

[33] W. Kohn, Declarative Multiplexed Rational Controllers, Proc. 5th IEEE Int. Symp. Intelligent Cont., pp. 794-803, 1990.

[34] W. Kohn, Declarative Hierarchical Controllers, Proc. DARPA Workshop on Software Tools for Distributed Intelligent Control Systems, Domain Specific Software Initiative, pp. 141-163, Pacifica, Ca., July 17-19, 1990.

[35] W. Kohn, Advanced Architecture and Methods for Knowledge-Based Planning and Declarative Control, Boeing Computer Services Technical Document IRD BCS-021, 1990, in ISMIS 91.

[36] W. Kohn and K. Carlsen, Symbolic Design and Analysis in Control, Proc. 1988 Grainger Lecture Series, U. of Illinois, pp. 40-52, 1989.

[37] W. Kohn and C. Johnson, An Algebraic Approach to Formal Verification of Embedded Systems, IRD Tech. Rpt. D-180-31989-1, Boeing Computer Services, 1990.

[38] W. Kohn and A. Murphy, Multiple Agent Reactive Shop Control, ISMIS91.

[39] W. Kohn and A. Nerode, An Autonomous Control Theory: An Overview, Proc. IEEE CACSD92, Napa Valley, March, 1992.

[40] W. Kohn and A. Nerode, Multiple Agent Autonomous Control Systems, Proc. 31st IEEE CDC Tucson, Ar., 2956-2966, 1993.

[41] W. Kohn and A. Nerode, Models for Hybrid Systems: Automata, Topologies, Controllability, Observability, in [21], 1993.

[42] W. Kohn and A. Nerode, Multiple Agent Autonomous Control, A Hybrid Systems Architecture, in *Logical Methods: A Symposium in honor of Anil Nerode's 60th birthday*, Birkhauser, 1993.

[43] W. Kohn and T. Skillman, Hierarchical Control Systems for Autonomous Space Robots, Proc. AIAA, 382-390, 1988.

[44] N.N. Krasovskii and A.I. Subbotin, *Game-Theoretical Control Problems*, Springer-Verlag, 1988.

[45] W. Kuich and A. Salomaa, *Semirings, Automata, Languages*, Springer-Verlag, 1985.

[46] R. Jeroslow, *Logic-Based Decision Support: Mixed Integer Method Formulation*, Elsevier, 1989.

[47] O. Maler, Z. Manna, and A. Pnueli, From Timed to Hybrid Systems, in *Proc. Rex Workshop, Real Time in Theory and Practice*, J. W. DeBakker, C. Huizing, W. P. de Roever, G. Rozenberg, eds., LNCS 600, Springer Verlag, 1992.

[48] W. Marek, A. Nerode, and J.B. Remmel, Nonmonotonic rule systems i, Annals of Mathematics and Artificial Intelligence, 1:241–273, 1990.

[49] W. Marek, A. Nerode, and J.B. Remmel, How Complicated is the Set of Stable Models of a Recursive Logic Program?, Annals of Pure and Applied Logic, 33:229–263, 1992.

[50] W. Marek, A. Nerode, and J. B. Remmel, The Stable Models of Predicate Logic Programs, in K.R. Apt, editor, Proceedings of International Joint Conference and Symposium on Logic Programming, 446–460, Boston, MA, 1992. MIT Press.

[51] W. Marek, A. Nerode, and J.B. Remmel, Nonmonotonic Rule Systems ii. Annals of Mathematics and Artificial Intelligence, 5:229–263, 1992.

[52] W. Marek, A. Nerode, and J. B. Remmel, Computing Jumps With A Normal Nonmonotonic Rule System, in prep.

[53] W. Marek, A. Nerode, and J. B. Remmel, A Context for Belief Revision: Normal Nonmonotonic Rule Systems, MSI technical report, 1993.

[54] W. Marek, A. Nerode, and J. B. Remmel, Forward Chaining, Well-Ordering, and Non-Monotone Rule Systems, in prep.

[55] W. Marek, A. Nerode, and J. B. Remmel, Π_1^1- Completeness theorems for Non-monotone Predicate Logics, in prep.

[56] A. Nerode, Modeling Intelligent Control, Proc. DARPA Workshop on Software Tools for Distributed Intelligent Control Systems, Domain Specific Software Initiative, Pacifica, Ca., July 17-19, 1990.

[57] A. Nerode and J.B. Remmel, A Model for Hybrid Systems, *Hybrid System Workshop Notes*, MSI, Cornell University, Ithaca, NY, June 10-12, 1991.

[58] A. Nerode, A. Yakhnis, Modeling Hybrid Systems as Games, *Proc. CDC92*, pp.2947-2952, Dec., 1992.

[59] A. Nerode, A. Yakhnis, V. Yakhnis, Concurrent Programs as Strategies in Games, in *Logic from Computer Science*, Y. Moschovakis, ed., Springer-Verlag, 1992.

[60] A. Nerode, A. Yakhnis, V. Yakhnis, Distributed Concurrent Programs as Strategies in Games, to appear in *Logical Methods: A Symposium in honor of Anil Nerode's 60th birthday*, Birkhauser, 1993.

[61] A. Nerode, J.B. Remmel, A. Yakhnis, Hybrid Systems and Continuous Sensing Games, presentation at the 9th IEEE Conference on Intelligent Control, August 25-27, 1993.

[62] A. Nerode, J.B. Remmel and A. Yakhnis, Playing Games on Graphs: Extracting Concurrent and Hybrid Control Programs, in prep.

[63] A. Nerode, R. Ng and V.S. Subrahmanian, Computing Circumscriptive Databases, Part I: Theory and Algorithms, to appear in Information and Computation.

[64] J.J. E. Slotine and Weiping Li, *Applied Nonlinear Control*, Prentice Hall, 1991.

[65] E. D. Sontag, *Mathematical Control Theory*, Springer-Verlag, 1990.

[66] H. J. Sussman and V. Jurdjevic, Controllability of Non-linear Systems, *J. Diff. Equations*, 12 pp.95-116, 1972.

[67] A. Yakhnis, Hybrid Games, Technical Report 92-38, Mathematical Sciences Institute, Cornell University, October, 1992.

[68] L. C. Young, *Lectures on Calculus of Variations and Optimal Control Theory*, Saunders, 1969. (Reprinted by Chelsea, 1980)

[69] J. Warga, *Optimal Control of Differential and Functional Equations*, Academic Press, 1972.

III LANGUAGES AND ENVIRONMENTS

6 2LP: Linear Programming and Logic Programming

Ken McAloon and Carol Tretkoff[1]

Abstract

The 2LP language has been designed to provide a programming environment for combining AI and OR methods for decision support software systems. In the dialogue between AI and OR, there are two basic themes: (1) declarative programming and the notion of logical consequence and, (2) procedural programming and the search algorithm in its many variations. Integrating AI and OR requires an environment that combines a modeling language with a logic based language. 2LP, which stands for "linear programming and logic programming," has the simplex based search mechanism of linear programming and the backtracking mechanism of logic programming built in. It is both an algebraic modeling language and a logical control language. The 2LP language has standard C style syntax and links easily to C and C++ code.

6.1 Introduction

In this paper, we discuss the relationship of 2LP to other programming paradigms and introduce some of the features of the language. We also present some examples of 2LP applications. For a full treatment of 2LP, we refer the reader to [17].

The design decisions that led to 2LP were based on the following considerations:

- The syntax of the language should be based on that of a mainstream programming language such as C.

- The language should support linear constraints on continuous variables.

- The language should support the logical connectives in the manner of logic programming.

- The programmer should have access to standard procedural programming tools.

- The array rather than the linked-list is the natural data structure for mathematical modeling.

- The system should be callable as a library routine from external code and it should be possible to call external routines from source code.

[1]Part of this research supported by NSF Grant # CCR-9102896 and ONR Grant N00014-94-1-0035.

As a result, 2LP programs have declarations such as

```
continuous X[10][20];
extern double a[][20],b[];
```

and code fragments such as

```
    and(int i=0;i<10;i++)
            sigma(int j=0;j<20;j++) a[i][j]*X[i][j] <= b[i];
```

The semantics of this code are discussed below.

6.2 2LP and Other Programming Paradigms

The 2LP language has evolved out a series of smaller languages which were developed step by step to maintain the best balance among the logic module of the language, the linear programming module and the intended applications. The decision to restrict the mathematical solver to linear constraints was based in part on the fact that the atomic operations of a programming language should be efficient. This was also motivated by the fact that the range of applications that can be handled with the combination of logic and linear constraints is remarkably rich. The theoretical basis for this work was developed in [8] which contains an analysis of the CLP scheme [11] in terms of the computational complexity of the "halting problem" of languages which are instances of the scheme. The analysis also calibrates the role of the underlying logic used - propositional, relational, functional. Let D denote the ordered additive group of the real numbers as a Z-module. Then in the terminology of that paper, implementations of minimal-CLP(D) and conservative-CLP(D) were done before the current version of the language was designed and implemented, e.g. [13]. The minimal and conservative languages are based on propositional and relational logic respectively. The logic of full 2LP has a more complex character. All along an important consideration was the challenge of compiling this new kind of programming language building on the work of [23], [12] and others.

Since 2LP is designed to combine AI and OR methods, let us compare and contrast it with AI and OR languages.

For classical AI applications, LISP and Prolog have well known strengths. Both support symbolic data and very flexible handling of types. Each is built on one mighty algorithm, lambda conversion in the case of LISP and unification in the case of Prolog. This brings a uniformity and a declarative quality to programming [14]. Both make programming with recursion very natural and recursion is the control mechanism of choice when working with data structures whose semantics are free in the mathematical sense. This is in contrast to classical imperative languages which are oriented toward numerical processing with its well-understood underlying mathematical semantics. Moreover, the remarkable transparent memory management of LISP and Prolog, made possible by the role of the linked-list as the basic data structure, makes writing code for various search strategies very elegant in these languages: the stacks and queues are managed by the system and garbage is collected in the background. To this Prolog adds its built-in logical control and more declarative programming facilities.

The development of the CLP languages, e.g. Prolog III, CLP(**R**), CHIP and Charme, was motivated to a certain extent by the aim of integrating numerical computation naturally into the declarative framework of logic programming. Although 2LP has its roots in CLP, as a language 2LP is markedly different from CLP languages, perhaps being closest in spirit to Charme. The syntax of 2LP is based on that of C. The data types of 2LP are **int**, **double** and **continuous**, which is a new type for working with constraints. In 2LP techniques such as hill climbing, branch and bound search, constraint propagation, etc. can be coded with an integrated declarative and procedural approach. The trade-off is that the memory management picture is like that of C *sans* recursive data structures.

2LP is different from OR modeling languages such as GAMS [7] and AMPL [10] in several ways. First, it is a logical control language as well as a modeling language and so supports AI methods not available to the MIP modeler. Second, it can directly code disjunctive programs, [5], [6], and bypass recoding logic in terms of 0-1 variables as in a MIP model. In fact 2LP appears to be the first programming language that supports this extension of MIP programming. Third, 2LP supports parameter passing, procedure based modularity and other structured programming constructs while the GAMS and AMPL models basically consist of global variables and loops to generate constraints. Fourth, the data types **int** and **double** in 2LP are the same as in C and so the 2LP model can be passed pointers to data directly from C avoiding a detour through a data file. In fact, 2LP can call external C functions during run time and the fact that 2LP follows the C picture of memory allocation, parameter passing and overall arithmetic syntax makes this integration of C functions very natural. Moreover, this ability to link with external code enables 2LP models to call distributed programming libraries such as PVM or DP, [4], [2]. Thus parallelization of a 2LP program can take place at the level of 2LP source code.

6.3   The 2LP language

The basic data types of 2LP are **int, double** and **continuous**, which is a new
type for working with constraints. The data structures are individual elements and
arrays of elements of a given basic type. Arrays are the natural data structure for
mathematical programming and are indispensable when working with linear constraints. In a 2LP program, variables of type **continuous** function in the declarative manner of the variables of linear algebra or linear programming. As a program
progresses, linear constraints on the continuous variables are generated and define
an evolving polyhedron in n-dimensional space, where n is the number of continuous
variables declared in the program. This polyhedron is called the *feasible region*.

While the fundamental operation on variables of types **int** and **double** is assignment, the continuous variables in a 2LP program are constrained by linear equalities
and inequalities. Thus 2LP overloads the numerical operators and the comparison
operators ==, <= and >= and extends them to this new type. (The = operator
is used for assignment as in C.) By default continuous variables are constrained to
be non-negative unless a negative lower bound is explicitly imposed. A program
consists of declarations of global storage including external storage and external
functions, a main procedure called **2lp_main()** and other procedures. All array
storage locations created in the program are either global variables, external global
variables or are declared in **2lp_main()**; otherwise automatic storage is restricted
to individual identifiers including loop control variables which are created in the
loop header. Procedures take parameters by value or by reference following C and
C++ conventions. Loop control variables can only be passed by value; continuous
variables can only be passed by reference. As in logic programming, procedures may
contain disjunctive control constructs which generate "choice points" in the computation. These are nodes in the logic programming search to which the program
can return later in its run. The system uses depth-first search and chronological
backtracking. Upon "failure" the backtracking mechanism resets the constraints
and the continuous variables to their state at the previous choice point; the loop
control variables are also reset to their values at the choice point. The state of the
other variables is left unchanged by backtracking. In classical logic programming,
the "logical variable" is not assigned values but is monotonically constrained by
unification. Thus the continuous variables and the loop variables capture the role
of the "logical variable."

The 2LP system takes a structured approach to logical modeling. It supports
and loops, **or** loops and other logical constructs. This has the advantage of making
the structure of the logic of a program clear and high-level, since it makes the

alternating structure of a program easier to grasp. In contrast, in classical logic programming languages, logical loops must be expressed by means of recursion using both multiple procedure definitions and cut. In 2LP logical loops and logical alternation can be expressed in a structured way. In fact, in 2LP one can often write an alternating **and/or** loop which directly codes the structure of an NP-Complete problem, since these loops capture the structure of CNF.

As a programming language, 2LP is small; its ambitions are circumscribed and focused. It is designed to be embedded in the larger programming scheme of things. Arrays of types **double** and **int** and C-functions can be provided by the principal system and addressed as extern by the 2LP model. The interpreter for the language is built on an abstract machine model called the S-CLAM which is an analog of the WAM and CLAM in the smaller 2LP context [15]. The 2LP architecture provides for a very modular linkage between the logical control and the mathematical constraint solver. As a result, the 2LP interpreter can use optimization libraries such as Cplex, XA and OSL This means that 2LP can be used for applications that require state-of-the-art optimization software and the system can move with changes in the mathematical programming world.

2LP provides language tools for programming the desired semantics for an optimization application. For a classical linear program the semantics of optimization are straightforward. When a richer mix of programming constructs and logic is introduced, there are many possible interpretations to **max: Z; subject_to ....** For that reason, 2LP supports control mechanisms and some built in optimization constructs for writing code that expresses the semantics intended by the modeler. This is especially helpful when optimization routines occur as subroutines in a larger application. The logic programming negation-as-failure is supported by 2LP. It turns out that in programming with constraints, it is double-negation-as-failure that is a most powerful and useful tool. The reason for this is simple; a call to **not not add_constraints()** is a test for the consistency of the constraints generated by a call to **add_constraints()** with the current feasible region; this test for consistency leaves the object unchanged. It is this type of query that is needed for Land and Doig search, for A* search, for computing heuristics, for hillclimbing search, for lookaheads etc.

During the run of a 2LP program, the representation of the feasible region includes a distinguished vertex, called the *witness point* or the *incumbent solution*. Other structural information and communication routines are also connected with this polyhedron. This collection forms an "object" to use object-oriented programming terminology. In fact, C++ libraries are being developed for constraint programming. An idea shared by the 2LP approach and the C++ approach is that the constraint solving apparatus should be couched in a library to be used as a tool within a larger programming environment. This is also true of MINTO, [21]. For the C++ approach in the context of linear programming, see [19].

6.4   Alternation

The **and/or** loop combination can be used to enumerate the possibilities for a search problem. It is the **and** that moves the search forward to the next level. When a failure occurs, the **or** has kept track of where to start trying next. The loop control variables are handled declaratively in 2LP in that their proper values are restored upon backtracking. By way of example the following 2LP code uses an **or** loop nested in an **and** loop to generate permutations of $0, ..., N-1$ in lexicographical order. It is a variation of the classical algorithm given, for example, in [20]. This method of generating permutations is useful in 2LP because the lexicographic order meshes correctly with backtracking mechanism of the logic programming search. The point is that this kind of procedural apparatus can be used in connection with constraints. The following code fragment addresses the problem of finding a permutation schedule that meets priority constraints and delivery constraints. The code also uses the **find_min** construct to conduct a branch and bound search to find a solution which minimizes the average finishing time.

```
#define N ... // number of tasks to schedule

double prod[N]; //prod[i] is time required for task i
double  dt[N]; // dt[i] is delivery time for task i

int permu[N];  // to keep track of permutation
int p[N][N];

2lp_main()
{

continuous Start_time[N];
        //Start_time[i] is the start time for the ith task

        data();  // initialize prod and dt

        //priority constraints such as
```

```
    //task i depends on task j
    Start_time[i] >= Start_time[j] + prod[j];
    ...


    //delivery constraints such as
    //task i must be finished by time dt[i]
    Start_time[i] + prod[i] <= dt[i];
    ...


    //procedural part of program
    if schedule_all(Start_time);
    then and(int i=0;i<N;i++)
          printf("Schedule task %d at time %f\n",
                     i, Start_time[i]);
    else printf("There is no feasible schedule\n");
}

schedule_all(continuous S[])
{

    and(int i=0;i<N;i++)
          p[0][i] = i; // initialize identity permutation

                 // average finishing time
    find_min: (1.0/N) sigma(int k=0;k<N;k++) (S[k] + prod[k]);
    subject_to
          and(int i=0;i<N;i++)
                or(int j=0;j<N-i;j++) {
                      if j == 0;
                      then and(int k=i+1;k<N;k++)
                          // copy forward symbols for level i+1
                          p[i+1][k] = p[i][k];

                      // schedule task p[i][i+j]
                      S[p[i][i+j]] ==
                          sigma(int k=0;k<i;k++) prod[permu[k]];
                          // fails if inconsistent with setup
                          // constraints and those generated
```

```
                // thus far by this statement
        permu[i] = p[i][i+j]; //record new job
        if j != 0;
        then p[i+1][i+j] = p[i][i+j-1];
        // reset symbols for level i+1
    }
}

data()
{
    // array assignment, same as initialization in C
    prod = { ... };
    dt = { ... };
}
```

The code requires some explanation. The array **permu** keeps track of initial segments of candidate permutations. The consistency of the partial schedule determined by the initial segment of a permutation is accounted for by the constraints set up in the main procedure together with those generated in the **schedule_all** procedure:

```
        S[p[i][i+j]] ==
            sigma(int k=0;k<i;k++) prod[permu[k]];
```

Checking that the initial segments of the permutations are being traversed in lexicographical order is best done with an analytical tool, the *logical loop invariant* which is designed for verifying **and/or** loop combinations, [17]. To check the operational semantics of this code in rough *ad hoc* terms, the **i**th row of the matrix **p** contains the integers that are to be permuted until backtracking returns to level **i-1**. Also, associated with each **i**, there is a **j**, which indicates not only the current backtracking position, but also the number of elements to the right of the diagonal in the permutation currently being generated. Also note that when **i** is freshly incremented, **j** is set to 0 and **p** at row **i+1** is completely reset to reflect the elements that it must keep track of. Thereafter, upon backtracking, when **j** > **0**, row **i+1** is updated.

In the next section, we consider an example where critical procedural information is provided by the witness point on the feasible region.

6.5   Branch and Cut

2LP has been designed with the purpose of bringing into the model itself control
over search mechanisms which normally must be specially built in to mathematical
programming code.

   By way of example, we consider an application which is very much a classic -
the Capacitated Warehouse Location Problem. The goal is to supply the needs
of customers from a group of proposed warehouses and to minimize monthly cost.
Running a warehouse requires a fixed monthly charge and there is the cost of
supplying all or part of a customer's requirements from a given warehouse. The
problem is to determine which warehouses to open so as to minimize cost while
meeting demand. The solution requires logic and can not be done by a linear
program because of the "all-or-nothing" character of the fixed-charge.

   The way we will model this application is by introducing continuous variables $Y[i]$
to represent warehouse i and $X[i][j]$ to represent the fraction of client j's demand
that is provided by warehouse i. So the idea is to use $Y[i]$ as a fuzzy boolean
variable which will be 1.0 if the warehouse is to be opened and 0.0 otherwise. The
program will start with symbolic constants, declarations of continuous variables
and also of arrays of type **double** to hold the data.

```
// This is code for the Capacitated Warehouse Location Problem.

#define M 16          // number of warehouses
#define N 50          // number of clients


continuous X[M][N];
continuous Y[M];
continuous Cost;      // for the objective function

double c[M][N];       // objective function coefficients
double fc[M];         // the fixed cost of opening warehouse i
double kap[M];        // capacity of warehouse i
double d[N];          // demand of client j


int node_cnt;         // for counting nodes
```

The data can be entered by a call to a procedure and array assignment:

```
data()
{
c = { ... }; // analogous to initialization in C
fc = { ... };
kap = { ... };
d = { ... };
}
```

The constraints that link the warehouses and client demand can be loaded by means
of a setup routine such as the following:

```
setup_constraints()
{
        and(int i=0;i<M;i++)
                Y[i] <= 1.0; // bound on fuzzy boolean
        and(int i=0;i<M;i++)
                and(int j=0;j<N;j++)
                        X[i][j] <= 1.0;   // bound on fraction

        and(int i=0;i<M;i++) // capacity can not be exceeded
                sigma(int j=0;j<N;j++) d[j]*X[i][j]
                                        <= kap[i]*Y[i];

        and(int j=0;j<N;j++) // demand must be met
                sigma(int i=0;i<M;i++) X[i][j] == 1;

        Cost ==   // the objective function
                sigma(int i=0;i<M;i++) fc[i]*Y[i]
                +
                sigma(int i=0;i<M;i++)
                        sigma(int j=0;j<N;j++) c[i][j]*X[i][j];
}
```

What is needed is a way to set the **Y**[i] all equal to 0.0 or 1.0. The idea of branch
and cut is to minimize the amount of branching required to achieve this. The
constraints **X**[i][j] <= **Y**[i] are called *valid cuts*, because they must hold at every
solution where **Y**[i] is either 0.0 or 1.0. However, until **Y**[i] is forced either to 0.0

or 1.0, these cuts can be violated. The simplest thing would be to add all these cuts as part of the setup constraints. If the problem size is large, however, adding **M*N** constraints could well slow things down unacceptably. The trick is to add only those cuts $X[i][j] <= Y[i]$ which are violated by the current witness point after the objective function has been optimized. The value of the $X[i][j]$ coordinate of the witness point is returned by the built-in function **wp**. So we can add cuts in a loop which ends when there are no more violated cuts.

```
add_cuts(continuous X[][N],Y[],Cost)
{
int flag,cnt;

        minimize(Cost);
        flag = -1;
        cnt = 0;
        and(;flag != cnt;){
                flag = cnt;
                and(int i=0;i<M;i++)
                        and(int j=0;j<N;j++)
                                if wp(X[i][j]) > wp(Y[i]);
                                then {
                                        X[i][j] <= Y[i];
                                        cnt=cnt+1;
                                        minimize(Cost);
                                }
        }
        printf("The number of cuts generated is %d\n",cnt);
}
```

After adding cuts, the code can proceed to a branch and bound search. So the main routine will be

```
2lp_main()
{
        data();
        setup_constraints();
        add_cuts(X,Y,Cost);
        branch_and_bound(Cost,X,Y);
}
```

It remains to write the branch and bound code. When this code is called the
witness point will be optimal for the objective function. If all the variables **Y**[**i**] are
already integral, then the optimal solution has been found. Otherwise, a variable
Y[**i**] which is not currently integral is chosen to branch on - one branch will fix it
at 1.0, the other at 0.0. A very important part of this and other search programs
is the choice of the branching variable. In the code below, the branching variable
is chosen to be the factory which has the greatest number of customers.

```
branch_and_bound(continuous Cost, X[][N], Y[])
{
int bv;

        node_cnt = 0;

        find_min: Cost; // restores optimal solution upon exiting
        subject_to
             and(;;) {
                    determine(bv,Y,X); // find branching variable
                    if bv == M;
                    then break; // exit the loop
                    fix(Y[bv],X[bv]);
                    minimize(Cost);
             }

        output(Y);
        printf("Number of nodes visited is %d\n",node_cnt);
}

determine(int & bv,continuous Y[],X[][N])
{
int cnt,xijcnt;

     cnt = -1;
     bv = M; // unchanged if all Y[i] integral
     and(int i=0;i<M;i++)
          if not integral(Y[i]);
          then {
                xijcnt = 0;
```

```
            and(int k=0;k<N;k++) // count number of clients
                if wp(X[i][k]) > 0;
                then xijcnt = xijcnt+1;
            if xijcnt > cnt; // select i with largest
            then {              // number of clients
                bv=i;
                cnt=xijcnt;
            }
        }
}

fix(continuous Y, X[])
{
    either {
        node_cnt = node_cnt+1;
        Y == 1.0;   // open the warehouse
    }
    or {
        node_cnt = node_cnt+1;
        Y == 0.0   // close the warehouse
        and(int j=0;j<N;j++)
            X[j] == 0.0; // good programming practice
    }
}


output(continuous Y[])
{
    printf("The optimal cost is %f\n",Cost);

    and(int k=0;k<M;k++)
        if nint(Y[k]) == 1;
        then printf("Build warehouse %d\n",k);
}
```

In the case the data is to be obtained from some external source, a file say, we can link the 2LP model to C code for doing this. The external C code would create the arrays **c**, **fc**, **kap** and **d** and intialize them in a call to a routine, say **data()**. The arrays would be declared in the 2LP model as

```
extern double c[][N];    // objective function coefficients
extern double fc[];      // the fixed cost of opening warehouse i
extern double kap[];     // capacity of warehouse i
extern double d[];       // demand of client j
```

and the **data** function would be declared as

```
extern void data();
```

The external C code will include a function with declaration

```
void * GetExtDataAdd(char *);
```

which the 2LP interpreter will call to find the addresses of the function **data** and the arrays **fc**, **kap**, **c** and **d**.

For further examples of 2LP models, we refer the reader to [4],[2], [16],[17]. This example of branch and cut is relatively simple; for a discussion of branch and cut and more complex examples, we refer the reader to [18].

6.6   Concluding Remarks

The 2LP system currently runs on UNIX workstations and 386/486/Pentium PCs. For code, tech reports etc., ftp as anonymous to acc5.its.brookly.cuny.edu. A parallel implementation which basically is an or-parallelization of the depth-first 2LP stack mechanism was reported on in [4]. More recent work which exploits the ability of 2LP to call external C functions is given in [2]; an important aspect of this work is that the parallel control constructs of a distributed processing library such as DP [1] or PVM [22] can be directly imported into the 2LP model.

References

[1] D. Arnow, DP: - A library for building portable, reliable distributed applications, Brooklyn College CIS Tech Report 94-12, submitted for publication.

[2] D. Arnow, K. McAloon and C. Tretkoff, Disjunctive programming and distributed programming, Sixth IASTED-ISMM International Conference on Parallel and Distributed Computing and Systems, October 1994.

[3] C. Atay, Parallelization of the Constraint Logic Programming Language 2LP, Ph.D. Thesis, City University of New York, June 1992.

[4] C. Atay, K. McAloon and C. Tretkoff, 2LP: a highly parallel constraint logic programming language, Sixth SIAM Conference on Parallel Processing for Scientific Computing, March 1993.

[5] E. Balas, Disjunctive programming and a hierarchy of relaxations for discrete optimization problems, SIAM J. Alg. Disc. Meth., **6** (1985) 466-486.

[6] N. Beaumont, An algorithm for disjunctive programming, European Journal of Operational Research **48** (1990) 362-371.

[7] A. Brooke, D. Hendrick and A. Meeraus, GAMS: A User's Guide, The Scientific Press, 1992.

[8] J. Cox, K. McAloon, C. Tretkoff, Computational complexity and constraint logic programming, Annals of Mathematics and Artificial Intelligence, **5** (1992) 163-190.

[9] M. Dincbas, P. Van Hentenryck, H. Simonis, A. Aggoun, T. Graf, F. Berthier, The Constraint Logic Programming Language CHIP, Proceedings of the International Conference on Fifth Generation Computing Systems, 1988.

[10] R. Fourer, D. Gay and B. Kernighan, AMPL: A Modeling Language for Mathematical Programming, The Scientific Press, 1993.

[11] J. Jaffar and J.-L. Lassez, Constraint logic programming, *Proceedings of POPL 87*, Munich.

[12] J. Jaffar, S. Michaylov, Methodology and Implementation of a CLP System, *Proceedings of the 1987 International Logic Programming Conference*, edited by J.-L. Lassez, MIT Press, 1987.

[13] Geun-Sik Jo and K. McAloon, Constraint solving in CLP languages, *Proceedings of the 2nd Pacific Rim Conference on Artificial Intelligence*, Seoul.

[14] J.-L. Lassez, From LP to LP: Programming with Constraints, Proceedings of Theoretical Aspects of Computer Software, Sendai 91 Springer Verlag. Also in Database Programming Languages, P. Kanellakis and J.W. Schmidt Editors, Morgan Kaufmann 1991.

[15] K. McAloon and C. Tretkoff, Subrecursive constraint logic programming, Proceedings of the NACLP 1990 Workshop on Logic Programming Architectures and Implementation, edited by J. Mills.

[16] K. McAloon and C. Tretkoff, AI/OR Modeling in 2LP, Brooklyn College Computer Science Technical Report 93-4.

[17] K. McAloon and C. Tretkoff, *Optimization and Computational Logic*, J. Wiley and Sons, to appear.

[18] G. Nemhauser and P. Wolsey, *Integer and Combinatorial Optimization*, J. Wiley and Sons, 1989.

[19] S. Nielsen, A C++ class library for mathematical programming. Technical Report, Management Science and Information Systems, University of Texas at Austin, 1993.

[20] E. Reingold, J. Nievergeld, and N. Deo, *Combinatorial Algorithms: Theory and Practice*, Prentice-Hall, Englewood Cliffs NJ, 1977.

[21] M. Savelsbergh, G. Sigismondi and G. Nemhauser, Functional description of MINTO, a MIxed INTeger Optimizer, Georgia Institute of Technology Tech Report 30332, May 1992.

[22] Sunderam, V.S.: PVM- A framework for parallel distributed computing. Concurrency: Practice and Experience 2 (1990).

[23] D.H.D. Warren, An Abstract Prolog Instruction Set, Technical Report 309, SRI International, 1983.

7 A Constraint-Based Scientific Programming Language

Richard Zippel

7.1 Introduction

Due to their size and complexity, the creation of scientific programs tends to be quite difficult and error prone. To address this problem we have been pursuing a program transformation approach to the creation of scientific programs. The transformations we are building include conventional compiler optimizations like loop unrolling, strength reduction and common subexpression elimination, and more mathematical transformations like applying Newton's method to a coupled system of algebraic equations or applying a Runge-Kutta method to a system of ordinary or partial differential equations.

The language to which these transformations are applied, called SPL, contains a combination of conventional programming constructs (loops, arrays, variables, bindings, etc.) and continuous mathematics constructs such as continuous functions, differential equations, integrals and function spaces. The core of SPL is a relatively conventional programming language in which the type system has been extended to include concepts from continuous mathematics. Relationships between continuous objects are specified using various types of constraints. These constraints are indicated in SPL using special control structures. Thus, SPL is a *constraint* programming language, but one built on an imperative base, rather the logic programming base that is so common now.

A somewhat similar approach to constraints was proposed by Steele and Sussman [2] with the goal of using constraints to model the behavior of physical systems. Their approach required that the constraint language be directly executable or interpretable, which limits the types of constraints and combinations of constraints that could be handled. Our constraint programs are not intended to be directly executable, but are *specifications* of the desired computation. By sequences of user-directed source-to-source transformations, these specifications are "compiled" into executable code. These transformations capture the mathematical techniques used to convert the equations of physics (differential equations, etc.) into effective computational schemes.

This paper consists of three parts. In Section 7.2 we describe the basic philosophy behind SPL and the transformation approach and the goals we are trying achieve. SPL itself is described in Section 7.3, along with a few examples of how computations may be specified in SPL. An example of an algebraic transformation for SPL programs and how such a transform is expressed is given in Section 7.4.

A companion paper discusses transformations that convert differential equations to difference equations and other non-algebraic transformations.

7.2 SPL Design Goals

Two different communities are engaged in program transformations, but each uses rather different techniques and ways of expressing their techniques. First, there are those involved in compilers, program transformations, partial evaluation and graph rewriting in the computer science community. These communities are interested in source-to-source transformations of programming languages such as loop unrolling, common subexpression elimination and strength reduction. It is this community that one usually thinks of when the phrase "program transformation" is mentioned.

Second, there is the numerical analysis/scientific computing community, who have developed transformations of mathematical objects like differential equations. Typical of their transformations are the following:

- Approximation

$$\sin x \Longrightarrow x - \frac{x^3}{6} + \frac{x^5}{120}$$

- Horner's rule

$$x - \frac{x^3}{6} + \frac{x^5}{120} \Longrightarrow x \cdot \left(1 - x^2 \cdot \left(\frac{1}{6} - \frac{x^2}{120}\right)\right)$$

- discretization

$$\frac{dx}{dt} = f(x) \Longrightarrow \begin{array}{l} x^{n+1} \\ \overline{\Delta t} \end{array} \begin{array}{l} \leftarrow x^n + \Delta t\, f(x^{n+1}), \\ \leftarrow \dots \end{array}$$

These transformations are usually viewed as operating on mathematical expressions, not programs, and are usually performed by hand before the program is coded. However, some transformations generate control structures in addition to performing formula manipulation. For instance, consider a discretization transformation for an ordinary differential equation. In addition to the discretization given above, we usually also indicate how the step size (Δt) is to be changed. This rather complex step is not reflected in the equations that result from the transformations, but in the final code.

A goal of the design of SPL is to support both types of transformations and to serve as a basis for communication between these two communities. As a consequence, SPL must be able to represent the constructs of conventional programming languages: variables, arrays, structures, loops, recursion, etc., and SPL must support the constructs of the scientific computing community: continuous functions, differential equations, function spaces, etc.

In addition, we feel it important that it be possible to specify scientific computations in SPL in a way that does not bias how the computation is actually performed. Thus we want to be able to say that a certain function is the solution of a differential equation, without specifying the numerical method to be used to compute the function. This means that by specifying the proper program transformations one is able to produce programs that use computational methods that are appropriate for different architectures.

7.3   SPL Language

SPL is a simple imperative language with some extensions for dealing with continuous mathematical objects. The main role of SPL is to serve as both the source and target language for program transformations. Since the program transformations operate on the parse tree, not the surface syntax, more effort has been devoted to the data structures used to represent SPL than the surface syntax. Nonetheless, the surface syntax is used to describe SPL programs in papers like this. For now, a simple parenthesized prefix syntax, much like Common Lisp, will be used. At some point, an infix front end will also be provided.

This section is divided into four parts. The type system used by SPL is described in Section 7.3.1, while Section 7.3.2 describes the imperative core of SPL and gives an example of its use. The mathematical constructs of SPL are described in Section 7.3.3.

7.3.1   Types

As with Weyl [3], the *type* of an object in SPL is split into two components: the *structure type* and the *domain type* of the object. The structure type describes how an object is implemented, while the domain type describes the abstract structure of which the object is an element. To first order, the structure type of an object describes its syntax, while the domain type describes the objects semantics. For clarity we call a full type, one with both a structure and domain type, a *bi-type*.

An element of the rational integers, Z, that is represented as a 32-bit integer would have a bi-type of [(fixnum 32), Z]. The structure type of the number is (fixnum 32), while the domain type is Z. Often it is useful to specify the domain type and structure type of a variable separately. For instance, a variable x may be described as an element of the ring of rational numbers Q, without indicating its structure type. Q is the *domain* of x. We would denote the bi-type of x by [nil, Q], with the nil indicating that the structure type of x is unspecified. At some later point, x might be implemented as a pair of 32-bit integers or as a floating point number.

The primitive structure types of SPL are strings of characters, signed integers and floating point numbers. More complex structure types can be created using the structure-type constructors vector for homogeneous data structures and struct for heterogeneous ones.

The domain types of SPL are precisely the domains of Weyl. Thus, the base domain are Z (the rational integers) and R (the real numbers). More complex domains can be built fom the primitive domains using the constructors ring-of-fractions, quotient-ring, polynomial-ring, vector-space and differentiable-functions.

For instance the algebraic number field $Q[\sqrt{2}]$ can be constructed by first constructing a polynomial in α over the rational numbers Q and then dividing out by the ideal $(\alpha^2 - 2)$:

$$\text{(polynomial-ring } Q\ '(x)) \implies Q[\alpha],$$
$$\text{(quotient-ring } Q[\alpha]\ (\alpha^2 - 2)) \implies Q[\alpha]/(\alpha^2 - 2) \equiv Q[\sqrt{2}].$$

Structure types and domain types are orthogonal in the sense that elements of a particular domain can be implemented with different structure types, and a particular structure type can be used to implement elements of several different domains. In Weyl this occurs frequently. For instance, the elements of a polynomial domain, like $k[X, Y, Z]$, are represented using either a recursive or expanded structure depending on the algorithms that are applied. Elements of this ring can have either structure type. Similarly, some structures are so helpful that they are used to represent elements of very different domains. For instance, the same structure types are used by Weyl to represent elements of abelian monoids and vector spaces.

In general, it is difficult to support the use of different structure types for elements of the same domain using the static run-time control structures used in high-performance scientific programming. A feature of Weyl's (and SPL's) type system that is helpful in these situations is the existence of multiple isomorphic

```
(defprogram factorial (n)
  (bind ((ans 1 Z))
    (sequence
      loop: (if (< n 2) (go end))
            (set! ans (* n ans))
            (set! n (- n 1))
            (go loop)
       end: ans))))
```

Figure 7.1
Simple SPL Program

domains. This feature can be useful in situations where different variables that
represent objects of the same algebraic structure are to be implemented in different
fashions. In this case, the variables are declared to be elements of different domains,
and the elements of the domains are represented differently.

7.3.2   Imperative Core

An SPL program is initially specified using a parenthesized prefix syntax using
ASCII characters. This is the form that is stored in files. Once parsed, the program
is converted into a graph (not a tree) that is decorated with with typing and other
information. Some nodes in this graph may be Weyl expressions, while other nodes
indicate programming constructs. All program transformations operate on the
parse tree. When the parse is printed it is presented using a parenthesized prefix
syntax similar to the ASCII form of the program, but which uses an infix syntax
for Weyl expressions and additional fonts (when available) to make the program
more readable.

SPL uses two types of constructs: function invocations and special forms, both
of which are specified in the ASCII form as lists. For function invocations, the
first element of the list is the function to be invoked; for special forms, the first
element indicates the special form. An effort has been made to reduce the number
of special forms in SPL to as small a set as possible. Currently, SPL has five special
forms: a variable binding statement "bind;" a conditional evaluation form "if"; two
for sequencing "sequence" and "goto;" and a form for assignment "←." Programs
are indicated using the defprogram special form, which is just an abbreviation for
an assignment of lambda expression to the name of the program.

The program in Figure 7.1 illustrates the use of the imperative core of SPL to
compute the factorial of n. The declaration indicates that ans is an element of the

real numbers, but it does not indicate how ans should be implemented. (The most common implementation would use single-word integers, but the intent of allowing the use of arbitrary precision integers is also clear.)

7.3.3   Mathematical Constructs

The ability to specify the domains of variables, without specifying their structure makes it possible in SPL to express computational specifications in terms of mathematical abstractions rather than discretizations and numerical approximations. Consider the problem of computing the evolution of a system of n particles, each of unit mass, that interact via gravitation. Denote the position of particle i by $\vec{r}_i(t)$ and the force induced by particle i on a test particle at location $\vec{r}$ by $\vec{f}_i(\vec{r})$. Thus the equations of motion of the system are

$$\frac{d^2}{dt^2}\vec{r}_i(t) = \sum_{i \neq j} \vec{f}_j(\vec{r}_i).$$

The major computational cost in this problem is the evaluation of the sums on the right hand side. There are $O(n^2)$ terms, and direct evaluation requires $O(n^2)$ time.

   The key idea behind Greengard's fast multipole algorithm is that we can write these sums in a fashion that can be evaluated using only $O(n)$ time. Write $\vec{F} = \vec{f}_1 + \vec{f}_2 + \cdots + \vec{f}_n$, where $\vec{F}$ is the sum of the *functions* $\vec{f}_i$, not the sum of the values of the functions. With $\vec{F}$ defined in this fashion, we can write the equations of motion of the system as

$$\frac{d^2}{dt^2}\vec{r}_i(t) = (\vec{F} - \vec{f}_i)(\vec{r}_i).$$

If functions can be added and subtracted in constant time, then this will yield a $O(n)$ algorithm.[1]

   In SPL we can say that the $\vec{f}_i$ and $\vec{F}$ are elements of the vector space of functions $C^\infty(R^3 \to R^3)$, and can then write the fast multipole expansion (for the far field computation) concisely, as illustrated in Figure 7.2.

   At some later point, a representation for the functions is chosen. In the fast multipole method the functions are represented as truncated series expansions in terms of spherical harmonics. Later, arithmetic with mathematical functions can be replaced by operations on the array of coefficients used to represent each function. For different types of interaction forces, and for different distributions of particles, other representations of the functions can be used without modifying the initial code

---

[1] We have left out a large number of details here relating to the difference between near field and far field interactions, but these considerations do not affect the main point of this example.

$$
\begin{aligned}
&(\text{bind } ((i\ 1\ Z) \\
&\qquad (\vec{F}\ 0\ C^\infty(R^3 \rightarrow R^3))) \\
&\quad (\text{sequence} \\
&\qquad \text{L1: } (\text{set! } \vec{F}\ \vec{F} + \vec{f_i}) \\
&\qquad\quad (\text{set! } i\ (+\ i\ 1)) \\
&\qquad\quad (\text{if } (<\ i\ N + 1)\ (\text{go L1})) \\
&\qquad\quad (\text{set! } i\ 1) \\
&\qquad \text{L2: } (\text{set! } \vec{F_i}\ \vec{F} - \vec{f_i}) \\
&\qquad\quad (\text{set! } i\ (+\ i\ 1)) \\
&\qquad\quad (\text{if } (<\ i\ N + 1)\ (\text{go L2})))))
\end{aligned}
$$

Figure 7.2
Fragment of Far Field Fast Multipole Computation

that describes the basic ideas in the fast multipole algorithm. A simple example of this approach is given by the transform discussed in Section 7.4, which converts programs involving complex numbers to code that use only real numbers. In one case, the complex numbers are represented in terms of the real and imaginary parts, while in the other the final computations are in terms of their absolute value and angle.

Not all mathematical objects, however, are best specified by direct computation as was the case with the force evaluation in the fast multipole scheme. Often, mathematical concepts are specified by *constraints*. The simplest of these are equality constraints. For instance, in a thermodynamic calculation one typically makes use of the ideal gas law $PV = nRT$, where P is the pressure of the gas, V its volume, T its temperature and n a measure of the amount of gas involved. R is the ideal gas constant and is know *a priori*. To indicate that this equality must hold throughout the computation, one writes

$$
\begin{aligned}
&(\text{constrain } (P\ V\ n\ T) \\
&\qquad\qquad (PV = nRT) \\
&\qquad \ldots)
\end{aligned}
$$

This expression indicates that P, V, n and T are constrained, within the scope of the constrain statement, to satisfy the ideal gas law. However, *this statement does not indicate how the quantities are to be determined.*

The constraints on variables can also be differential equations. For instance, an ideal pendulum of length ℓ. The angle the pendulum makes with vertical at time t, $\theta(t)$, is constrained to satisfy the equation

$$\ell\frac{d^2\theta(t)}{dt^2} + g\sin\theta(t) = 0, \tag{7.3.1}$$

where g is the acceleration due to gravitation. This equation constrains the function θ—not the expression $\theta(t)$.

One might express (7.3.1) as the SPL constraint:

$$\text{(constrain } (\theta) \ (\ell\frac{d^2\theta(t)}{dt^2} + g\sin\theta(t) = 0)$$
$$\ldots)$$

However, we object to this form because of the appearance of the free variable t in the constraint. Instead it is more accurate to say that (7.3.1) applies for *each* t in R. Thus, we actually have an infinite set of *algebraic constraints* that relate $\theta(t)$ and $\ddot{\theta}(t)$, indexed by R. In SPL these constraints can be expressed as

$$\text{(constrain } (\theta) \ (\{\forall t \in R \ . \ \ell\frac{d^2\theta(t)}{dt^2} + g\sin\theta(t) = 0\})$$
$$\ldots)$$

Similarly, the electrostatic and magnetic fields of a system can be constrained to satisfy Maxwell's equations; the velocity vectors of a fluid can be constrained to satisfy the Navier-Stokes equations and the geometry of space-time is constrained to satisfy Einstein equations.

For some problems it is more natural to specify the properties of variables, or functions, as minimization or maximization principles. For instance, the behavior of a mechanical system is governed by the paths through its configuration space that minimize the "action" of the system. The motion of (relativistic) particle minimizes the length of the path taken. This types of "constraints" can be specified in SPL by using the minimize and maximize statements.

A simple example of the use of these forms is to determine the rectangle with perimeter P and with the largest area. Denote the width of the rectangle by W and the height by H. The constraints on H and W are easily expressed as

$$\text{(constrain } (W \ H) \ (H + W = \frac{P}{2})$$
$$\text{(minimize } (W \ H) \ (HW)$$
$$\ldots)$$

Similarly, to determine the shortest path between the two points P_0 and P_1 on the unit sphere we might write:

$$\text{(constrain } (x \ y \ z) \ (\langle x(0), y(0), z(0) \rangle = P_0, \ \langle x(1), y(1), z(1) \rangle = P_1,$$
$$\{\forall t \in [0, 1] \ . \ x^2(t) + y^2(t) + z^2(t) = 1\})$$
$$\text{(minimize } (x \ y \ z) \ (\int_0^1 \sqrt{x^2(t) + y^2(t) + z^2(t)} \, dt)$$
$$\ldots \text{)}$$

In this case, we have parameterized the path by t, which ranges from 0 to 1. The second constraint forces the curve to lie on the unit sphere. Notice that the quantity minimized in this case is a functional.

Thus far, all the functions mentioned have been dependent only on time, which can be accurately modeled by R or R^+. Other physical phenomenon involve functions that depend on regions of space. To deal with this properly, we need to add geometric domains to Weyl and thus to SPL. For instance, the flow of a fluid in a domain $D \subseteq R^3$ might be described by

$$\text{(bind } ((u \text{ nil } C^\infty (R \times D \to R^3)))$$
$$\text{(constrain } (u) \ (\{\forall t \in R, \ (x, y, z) \in D \ . \ \frac{\partial u(t, x, y, z)}{\partial t} + (u \cdot \nabla) u = -\nabla p\})$$
$$\ldots \text{)}$$

7.4 Domain Type Realization

One of the simplest types of program transformations is data refinement. In SPL this corresponds to a transform that represents elements of some domain as combinations of elements in a simpler domain. A very useful example occurs with complex numbers. While it is convenient to write programs using complex numbers, there is often a substantial performance penalty for doing so. Complex numbers are usually implemented as pairs of floating point numbers, so a block of storage must be allocated to them. The additional storage allocation and reclamation process can be expensive, as will the cost of the additional memory reference required to obtain the real and imaginary part from a pointer to the pair of floating point numbers.

This section describes the **realify** transformation, which replaces all occurrences of variables whose domain is C by pairs of variables whose domain is R. Realify is a simple application of **walk-form**, the code walking technology we use for most of our transformations. The code walker applies a user provided function to each node of the parse parse tree of the source function. The user function can return a modified parse tree which the code walker splices into the parse tree and with which it continues. In addition the code walker maintains information about the bound variables, type information, etc. which it makes available to the user function.

For modularity and clarity, the realify transform is coded as collection of pieces, each of which applies to a different SPL programming construct. Each of these transforms program structures involving complex quantities into combinations of operations involving real quantities. For instance, an assignment statement

$$(x \leftarrow f(y, z))$$

is transformed into the pair of assignments

$$
\begin{array}{l}
(\text{sequence} \\
\quad (xr \leftarrow \text{RealPart}(f(y, z))) \\
\quad (xi \leftarrow \text{ImagPart}(f(y, z)))))
\end{array}
$$

For this transformation to be valid, x must be declared to be an element of C. Variables xr and xi are created to shadow the real and imaginary parts of x, when the code walker encounters the binding of x. To illustrate these techniques consider the following simple program:

$$
\begin{array}{l}
(\text{defprogram Complex1} \; ((x \; C) \; (y \; C) \; (z \; R)) \\
\quad (x \leftarrow xy + yz))
\end{array}
$$

To avoid changing the input characteristics of the function, the arguments that are complex numbers are re-bound inside the body of Complex1, as illustrated in Complex1b.[2] This will allow later transformations to split the inner copies of x and y into two other variables corresponding to their real and imaginary parts.

$$
\begin{array}{l}
(\text{defprogram Complex1b} \; ((x \; C) \; (y \; C) \; (z \; R)) \\
\quad (\text{bind} \; ((x \; x \; C) \\
\qquad\quad (y \; y \; C)) \\
\quad (x \leftarrow xy + yz))
\end{array}
$$

This transformation is accomplished by the following walk function fragment for a program.

---

[2] Successive steps in the transformation process are indicated by appending an alphabetic letter to the name of the program.

```
(define-realify-walker program :eval (form env)
    (let (bindings var type)
        (loop for arg in (args-of form) do
            (when (listp arg)
                (setq var (first arg) type (second arg))
                (if (complex-num-type? type)
                    (push (make-binding (make-variable (symbol-of var)) var type)
                        bindings))))
        (if bindings
            (values (make-program (name-of form) (args-of form)
                        (make-bind (reverse bindings) (term-of form)))
                    :recurse)
            form)))
```

The walk routine used by realify would be very large if written as a single large routine. Instead, fragments of the walk routine are defined using the macro define-realify-walker, and the main walk routine dispatches to the appropriate fragment. The walk routine fragment above is applied when a program node in the parse tree is encounted in an evaluation context. This fragment is quite simple—it merely looks for arguments of the program that are elements of C and, when found, adds them to a list of new bindings. If any such new bindings are encountered, a bind form is wrapped around the term of the program. Notice that the :recurse continuation indicator in used.

Next, each binding is examined to see if the type of the variable being bound is C. If so, two new variables are created corresponding to the real and imaginary parts of the original variable. In the case of Complex1b this leads to:

```
(defprogram Complex1c ((x C) (y C) (z R))
    (bind ((xr realpart(x) R) (xi imagpart(x) R)
           (yr realpart(y) R) (yi imagpart(y) R))
        (x ← xy + yz))
```

This transformation is performed by the fragment given below.

```
(define-realify-walker binding :binding (form env)
  (let ((type (type-of form))
        real rvalue imag ivalue)
    (cond ((complex-num-type? type)
           (setq real (make-variable (intern (string-append (var-of form) "r"))))
           (setq imag (make-variable (intern (string-append (var-of form) "i"))))
           (if (null (value-of form))
               (setq rvalue nil ivalue nil)
               (multiple-value-setq (rvalue ivalue) (split-real-imag (value-of form) env)))
           (push (list (var-of form) :realify (list real imag)) *new-envs*)
           (list (make-binding real rvalue (get-real-numbers))
                 (make-binding imag ivalue new-type)))
          (t form))))
```

When a binding of a complex variable is encountered, a list of two bindings is returned by the code walker—one for the real part and one for the imaginary part. The names of these variables are the name of the old variable with r and i added to the end. If the original variable had an initial value, then the new variables are initialized to the real and imaginary parts of the old initial value. Also notice the use of *new-envs* to indicate that the real and imaginary parts of the old variable are the new variables.

The final part of the conversion is the transformation of the assignment statement, which will yield the following program.

```
(defprogram Complex1d ((x C) (y C) (z R))
  (bind ((xr realpart(x) R) (xi imagpart(x) R)
         (yr realpart(y) R) (yi imagpart(y) R))
    (sequence
```
$$(xr \leftarrow z \cdot yr + yr \cdot xr - (yi \cdot xi))$$
$$(xi \leftarrow z \cdot yi + yr \cdot xi + yi \cdot xr))))$$

The walker fragment that performs it is quite simple. It merely converts each assignment statement into a pair of assignment statements, one for the real part and one for the imaginary part.

```
(define-realify-walker assignment :eval (form env)
  (multiple-value-bind (rloc iloc) (split-real-imag (location-of form) env)
    (multiple-value-bind (rval ival) (split-real-imag (value-of form) env)
      (values (make-sequence (list (make-assignment rloc rval)
                                   (make-assignment iloc ival)))
              :done))))
```

The essential tool used in these transformations was the Weyl function split-real-imag, which returns the real and imaginary parts of a Weyl expression.

Transforming Constraints

The program to which realify was applied using complex variables in the simplest possible fashion. However, there are many other contexts in which the realify transformation can be of value. For instance, assume we want to find the complex solutions of the equation $x^2 + x + 1 = 0$. The SPL version of this program can be written as

$$(\text{defprogram complex2 ()}$$
$$(\text{bind } ((x \text{ nil } C))$$
$$(\text{constrain } (x) \ (x^2 + x + 1 = 0)$$
$$\cdots \ )))$$

The realify transform can be extended to deal with the constrain statement in the same fashion as has been described in this section. When applied to complex2 we get:

$$(\text{defprogram complex2b ()}$$
$$(\text{bind } ((xi \text{ nil } R) \ (xr \text{ nil } R))$$
$$(\text{constrain } (xr \ xi) \ (1 + xr + xr^2 - xi^2 = 0, \ 2xr \cdot xi + xi = 0)$$
$$\cdots \ )))$$

As before, the the complex variable x is replaced by two real variables, xr and xi. The single algebraic constraint on x is replaced by two coupled algebraic constraints on xr and xi.

Going one step further, this approach of realify constraints can be also be applied to constrains on complex valued functions. For instance, the following SPL program expresses a differential equation constraint on the complex valued function z:

$$(\text{defprogram complex3 ()}$$
$$(\text{bind } ((z \text{ nil } C^\infty([0,\infty) \to C)))$$
$$(\text{constrain } (z) \ (\{\forall t \in [0,\infty) \ . \ \tfrac{dz}{dt}(t) = z(t) + (z(t))^2\})$$
$$\cdots \ )))))$$

When the realify transformation is applied to this program we get

$$(\text{defprogram complex3 ()}$$
$$(\text{bind } ((x \text{ nil } C^\infty([0,\infty) \to R))$$
$$(y \text{ nil } C^\infty([0,\infty) \to R)))$$
$$(\text{constrain } (x \ y) \ (\{\forall t \in [0,\infty) \ . \quad \dot{x}(t) = x^2(t) - y^2(t) + x(t), \ \})$$
$$\dot{y}(t) = 2x(t)y(t) + y(t)$$
$$\cdots \ )))))$$

For clarity, we have used x and y as the real and imaginary part of z and have used $\dot{x}$ to indicate derivatives.

On important issue that is not addressed by the realify transformation is the conversion of continuity and analyticity properties of complex valued function into the appropriate properties for the real valued functions. This will become more important when the discretization transforms for differential equations are guided by these properties of functions of this type. This appears to a particularly appropriate place to take advantage of the theorem proving properties of Nuprl [1].

The basic ideas used in Realify can easily extended to deal with other compound objects that need to be handled especially efficiently. For instance, physical simulations in three dimensions frequently make heavy use of 3-vectors. The efficiency of these programs can often be improved by replacing the each 3-vector valued variable by a triple of variables corresponding to each coordinate. Such a transformation is a simple extension of realify. Perhaps more importantly, this allows the programmer to express the differential equation constraints of the physical system in vector notation. The "de-vectorizing" transform would convert the vector differential equations to constraining differential equations on the components of the vectors.

7.5   Conclusions

We have presented a very high level language for scientific computing, which allows one to specify what one wants to compute without, necessarily, indicating how the computation should be performed. This language allows one to express computations using standard mathematical structures like continuous functions. The relationships between these mathematical structures are expressed using constraints that can take the form of algebraic and differential equations.

Programs in this language are converted into executable form using a library of program transformations, which spans compiler optimizations, parallelizations and mathematical discretizations.

References

[1] R. L. Constable, S. F. Allen, H. M. Bromley, W. R. Cleaveland, J. F. Cremer, R. W. Harper, D. J. Howe, T. B. Knoblock, N. P. Mendler, P. Panangaden, J. T. Sasaki, and S. F. Smith. *Implementing Mathematics with the Nuprl Proof Development System*. Prentice-Hall, Englewood Cliffs, NJ, 1986.

[2] Guy Lewis Steele Jr. and Gerald Jay Sussman. Constraints. AI Memo 502, Massachusetts Institute of Technology, Artificial Intelligence Laboratory, Cambridge, MA, November 1978.

[3] Richard Eliot Zippel. The Weyl computer algebra substrate. Technical Report 90–1077, Department of Computer Science, Cornell University, Ithaca, NY, 1990.

8   Designing Constraint Logic Programming Languages Using Computational Systems

Claude Kirchner, Hélène Kirchner, and Marian Vittek

Abstract

This work presents computational systems, a framework for describing computational logics, and ELAN, an interpreter of computational systems whose expressive power is examplified on several examples of constraint solving and operational semantics design. The rewriting logic, proposed by J. Meseguer, provides a logical framework in which other languages can be represented and a semantic framework for the specification of languages and systems. Here we enrich the notion of rewrite theories in rewriting logic with a notion of strategy to build computational systems. This allows expressing for example equational programming, Horn clause programming and constraint solvers as computational systems. We thus get a framework in which rewriting techniques can be used to reason about termination, confluence, combination and enrichment of computational systems.

The ELAN system implements computational systems using a specific language for expressing strategies. The system is presented and its specificities illustrated on examples.

8.1   Introduction

This work stems from the fact that logic programming in a broad sense, theorem proving and constraint solving can be described in a uniform way by giving the syntax of formulas, a set of axioms, a set of deduction rules, a proof calculus making precise how proofs are built, altogether with one or a class of models. These three computational processes can be formulated as instances of a common schema that consists of applying rewrite rules on formulas with some strategy, until getting specific forms. In logic programming the emphasis is on efficiency in reaching a successful solved form characterizing an answer, in theorem proving on completeness in detecting trivially false or true formulas, and in constraint solving on getting some predefined solved form of a constraint.

The rewriting logic, as shown in [26] starting from the notion of general logic [24], provides a logical framework in which other logics can be represented and a semantic framework for the specification of languages and systems. Here we also want to cover specification of constraint solving systems, in the case where the constraint solving process is described with rewrite rules that compute solved forms of constraints. This includes for now constraint languages built from elementary constraints that may be equations [17, 14], disequations [5], inequations on terms compared with simplification orderings [27], membership constraints [4]. Computational systems allow expressing nicely the proof calculus of a given logic, in order to describe a computational version, if any, of the logic under consideration.

A computational system is given by a signature providing the syntax, a set of conditional rewrite rules describing the deduction mechanism, and a strategy to guide application of rewrite rules. Formally, this is the combination of a rewrite theory in rewriting logic, together with a notion of strategy to efficiently compute with given rewrite rules. The underlying framework is first-order, since the formulas, sets of formulas and proofs are considered as first-order terms. Computation is exactly application of rewrite rules on a term and a strategy describes the intended set of computations, or equivalently in rewriting logic, a subset of proof terms. Computational systems may be generic in the sense that they can be parameterized by a class of signatures and axioms. In this case to each program, i.e. each pair of a signature and a set of axioms, corresponds by instantiation, a computational system.

To validate these ideas, we develop a prototype called ELAN, to describe, experiment and study the combination of different computational systems that provide basis for constraint solving and logic programming paradigms. Computational systems have several advantages: first of all, since the framework is based on first-order tools and the rewriting logic, it is conceptually simple to understand. Second, we benefit from the work on (equational) rewriting and efficient implementation techniques both on sequential models [11] and distributed models [21, 10]. Third, we can define rewriting in the ELAN language itself, and we will see in Section 8.4.5 how easily this can be achieved. Last and even more important, we can reason about computational systems, for instance prove abstract properties of the rewrite rules like termination or confluence with rewrite-based techniques. We can also reason about combination and enrichment of computational systems and build new ones in a modular way, once we know how systems theoretically interact.

So our main contributions are the notion of computational system, the description of the ELAN interpreter of computational systems and several simple but non-trivial and meaningful examples of applications of the introduced concepts. The paper is an elaborated version of ideas first presented in [19]. In the next section, we give the definition of computational systems based on rewriting logic, which is first briefly recalled. We explain what we mean by implementing a specific logic by a computational system. We illustrate the concepts by a simple equational programming language whose operational semantics is narrowing, and by a constraint solver process for unification problems modulo commutativity. The ELAN system is then presented with its specificities, illustrated on the example of a simple Horn clause programming language. Reflexivity of the system is addressed before the conclusion in which we give further perspectives for the development of ELAN.

8.2   General Setting

This section first presents our view of the main concepts of general logic [23] and rewriting logic [24] both due to J. Meseguer. The computational systems are then defined as rewrite theories in rewriting logic together with strategies to restrict the computation space. This provides the semantical foundation of the ELAN system, as an environment in which computational systems can be described and then executed.

8.2.1   Rewriting Logic

The definitions below are given in the one-sorted case. The many-sorted and order-sorted cases can be handled in a similar, although more technical, manner. Our definitions are consistent with [6, 14] to which the reader is referred for more detailed considerations on universal algebra, term rewriting systems and unification.

We consider a set $\mathcal{F}$ of ranked function symbols where $\mathcal{F}_n$ is the subset of functions of arity n, a set $\mathcal{X}$ of variables and the set of first-order terms $\mathcal{T}(\mathcal{F}, \mathcal{X})$ built on $\mathcal{F}$ using variables in $\mathcal{X}$. The set of variables of a term t is denoted $Var(t)$ and this notation is extended in a natural way to any object based on terms. The set of ground terms (i.e. terms without variables) is denoted $\mathcal{T}(\mathcal{F})$. A $\mathcal{T}(\mathcal{F}, \mathcal{X})$-equality is a multiset of terms $\{t, t'\}$ in $\mathcal{T}(\mathcal{F}, \mathcal{X})$, denoted as usual $(t = t')$. For a set of equalities E, $\mathcal{T}(\mathcal{F}, \mathcal{X})/E$ denotes the free algebra of terms modulo E. The equivalence class of a term t modulo E is denoted $\langle t \rangle_E$. To support intuition, the reader can think of E as being the empty set of axioms, or the associativity commutativity axioms for some binary symbol. For details and general results on calculus modulo equational axioms, the reader is invited to consult for example [13]. To simplify notation, we denote a sequence of objects $(a_1, \ldots, a_n)$ by $\bar{a}$.

In rewriting logic, proofs are first-order objects and are represented by proof terms. In order to build proof terms and strategies, rules are labeled with a set $\mathcal{L}$ of ranked label symbols, i.e. of symbols with a fixed arity. In order to compose proofs, we introduce the infix binary operator ";". A *proof term* is by definition a term built on equivalence classes of $\mathcal{T}(\mathcal{F}, \mathcal{X})/E$, function symbols in $\mathcal{F}$, label symbols in $\mathcal{L}$ and the concatenation operator ";". In other words, a proof term is an element of the term algebra $\mathcal{PT} = \mathcal{T}(\mathcal{L} \cup \{;\} \cup \mathcal{F} \cup \mathcal{T}(\mathcal{F}, \mathcal{X})/E)$.

A logic is defined by a syntax, an entailment system, a class of models and a satisfaction relation. These four components respectively denoted by $(Synt, \vdash, Model, \models)$ are more precisely defined below, first for a general logic and second in the case of rewriting logic.

Syntax. The syntax needed for defining a logic is provided by a *signature* which allows building *sentences*. Typically a signature for first-order logic consists of two sets of ranked function symbols and predicate symbols. Since we need to be generic, we consider $Synt$ a class of pairs (Σ, sen) consisting of a signature Σ together with a mapping sen associating to Σ the set of all legal sentences built on this signature.

▶ In rewriting logic, a signature consists of a 3-tuple $\Sigma = (\mathcal{L}, \mathcal{F}, E)$, where $\mathcal{L}$ and $\mathcal{F}$ are sets of ranked function symbols and E is a set of $\mathcal{T}(\mathcal{F}, \mathcal{X})$-equalities. Equalities in E must be understood as structural axioms forming part of the signature. Typically in a signature allowing a conjunction operator $\wedge$, E consists in the associativity and commutativity axioms for $\wedge$. Sentences built on a given signature are defined as sequents of the form $\pi : \langle t \rangle_E \rightarrow \langle t' \rangle_E$ where $t, t' \in \mathcal{T}(\mathcal{F}, \mathcal{X})$ and $\pi \in \mathcal{PT}$. The informal meaning of such sentences is that the proof π allows to derive t' from t.

Entailment systems. For a given class of syntax $Synt$ and (Σ, sen) in $Synt$, a *theory* is a pair $T = (\Sigma, \Phi)$ where $\Phi \subseteq sen(\Sigma)$. We say that T is *presented* by the set of axioms Φ.

Given a signature Σ, an entailment system is an abstract description of the provability relation of a sentence ϕ starting from a given set of sentences (also called axioms) Φ and using logical rules. Formally, given a class of syntax $Synt$, an *entailment system* is a pair $(Synt, \vdash)$ such that $\vdash$ is a function associating to each $(\Sigma, sen) \in Synt$ a binary relation $\vdash_\Sigma \subseteq \mathcal{P}(sen(\Sigma)) \times sen(\Sigma)$ such that:

1. $\forall \phi \in sen(\Sigma), \{\phi\} \vdash_\Sigma \phi,$ (Reflexivity)

2. If $\Phi \vdash_\Sigma \phi$ and $\Phi \subseteq \Phi'$ then $\Phi' \vdash_\Sigma \phi,$ (Monotonicity)

3. If $(\forall i \in I, \Phi \vdash_\Sigma \phi_i)$ and $(\Phi \bigcup_{i \in I} \{\phi_i\} \vdash_\Sigma \phi)$ then $\Phi \vdash_\Sigma \phi,$ (Transitivity)

4. For any signature morphism H:
   if $\Phi \vdash_\Sigma \phi$, then $H(\Phi) \vdash_{H(\Sigma)} H(\phi).$ (Translation)

Reflexivity	
	$\langle t \rangle_E : \langle t \rangle_E \rightarrow \langle t \rangle_E$
	if $t \in \mathcal{T}(\mathcal{F}, \mathcal{X})$
Congruence	$\pi_1 : \langle t_1 \rangle_E \rightarrow \langle t_1' \rangle_E, \ldots, \pi_n : \langle t_n \rangle_E \rightarrow \langle t_n' \rangle_E$
	$\vdash\!\!\rightarrow$
	$f(\pi_1, \ldots, \pi_n) : \langle f(t_1, \ldots, t_n) \rangle_E \rightarrow \langle f(t_1', \ldots, t_n') \rangle_E$
	if $f \in \mathcal{F}_n$
Replacement	$\pi_1 : \langle t_1 \rangle_E \rightarrow \langle t_1' \rangle_E \ldots \pi_n : \langle t_n \rangle_E \rightarrow \langle t_n' \rangle_E$
	$\vdash\!\!\rightarrow$
	$\ell(\pi_1, \ldots, \pi_n) : \langle g(t_1, \ldots, t_n) \rangle_E \rightarrow \langle d(t_1', \ldots, t_n') \rangle_E$
	if $\ell : g(x_1, \ldots, x_n) \rightarrow d(x_1, \ldots, x_n) \in R$
Transitivity	$\pi_1 : \langle t_1 \rangle_E \rightarrow \langle t_2 \rangle_E, \ \pi_2 : \langle t_2 \rangle_E \rightarrow \langle t_3 \rangle_E$
	$\vdash\!\!\rightarrow$
	$\pi_1 ; \pi_2 : \langle t_1 \rangle_E \rightarrow \langle t_3 \rangle_E$

Figure 8.1
REW: The rules of rewrite deduction

▶ In rewriting logic, in order to build the entailment system, the notion of rewrite theory is introduced and an appropriate deduction system allows to inductively define (in fact itself using a rewrite theory) the entailment relation.

A *labeled rewrite theory* is a 5-tuple $\mathcal{R} = (\mathcal{X}, \mathcal{F}, E, \mathcal{L}, R)$ where $\mathcal{X}$ is a given countably infinite set of variables, $\mathcal{L}$ and $\mathcal{F}$ are sets of ranked function symbols, E a set of $\mathcal{T}(\mathcal{F}, \mathcal{X})$-equalities, and R a set of labeled rewrite rules of the form $\ell : g \rightarrow d$ where $\ell \in \mathcal{L}$ and $g, d \in \mathcal{T}(\mathcal{F}, \mathcal{X})$ satisfying $\mathcal{V}ar(d) \subseteq \mathcal{V}ar(g)$ and where the arity of ℓ is exactly the number of distinct variables in g. The labels are of crucial use both in the definition of strategies and in the definition of models for the rewriting logic, in which they allow tracing deductions. Note also that the definitions can be extended to conditional rewriting at the cost of more technically complicated definitions. The reader is referred to [24] for a full treatment of this case.

A given labeled rewrite theory $\mathcal{R}$ entails the sequent $\pi : \langle t \rangle_E \rightarrow \langle t' \rangle_E$, which is denoted $\mathcal{R} \vdash \pi : \langle t \rangle_E \rightarrow \langle t' \rangle_E$, if $\pi : \langle t \rangle_E \rightarrow \langle t' \rangle_E$ is obtained by some finite application of the deduction rules in Figure 8.1. Note that because of the rules **Reflexivity** and **Replacement**, if the rule $r = (\ell : g \rightarrow d) \in R$, then the sequent $seq(r) = (\ell(\langle x_1 \rangle_E, \ldots, \langle x_n \rangle_E) : \langle g \rangle_E \rightarrow \langle d \rangle_E)$ can be derived. The set of all sequents $\{seq(r) | r \in R\}$ is denoted $seq(R)$ and is used to present the theory.

The entailment system is then defined for a signature $\Sigma = (\mathcal{L}, \mathcal{F}, \mathcal{X}, E)$ and a labeled rewrite theory $\mathcal{R}$, by $seq(R) \vdash_\Sigma (\pi : u \rightarrow v)$ if $\mathcal{R} \vdash (\pi : u \rightarrow v)$. The set of

$$\forall \pi_1, \pi_2, \pi_3 \in \mathcal{PT} \quad \pi_1; (\pi_2; \pi_3) = (\pi_1; \pi_2); \pi_3 \qquad\qquad \text{Associativity}$$

$$\forall \pi : \langle t \rangle_E \to \langle t' \rangle_E, \quad \pi; \langle t' \rangle_E = \pi, \text{ and } \langle t \rangle_E; \pi = \pi \qquad \text{Local Identities}$$

For all $f \in \mathcal{F}_n, n \in \mathbf{N}$, $\forall \pi_1, \ldots, \pi_n, \pi'_1, \ldots, \pi'_n$:
$$f(\pi_1; \pi'_1, \ldots, \pi_n; \pi'_n) = f(\pi_1, \ldots, \pi_n); f(\pi'_1, \ldots, \pi'_n) \qquad \text{Independence}$$

For all $f \in \mathcal{F}_n, n \in \mathbf{N}$:
$$f(\langle t_1 \rangle_E, \ldots, \langle t_n \rangle_E) = \langle f(t_1, \ldots, t_n) \rangle_E \qquad \text{Preservation of } E$$

$$\forall \ell : g \to d \in R, \forall \pi_1 : \langle t_1 \rangle_E \to \langle t'_1 \rangle_E, \ldots, \pi_n : \langle t_n \rangle_E \to \langle t'_n \rangle_E$$
$$\ell(\pi_1, \ldots, \pi_n) = \ell(\langle t_1 \rangle_E, \ldots, \langle t_n \rangle_E); d(\pi_1, \ldots, \pi_n) \text{ and}$$
$$\ell(\pi_1, \ldots, \pi_n) = g(\pi_1, \ldots, \pi_n); \ell(\langle t'_1 \rangle_E, \ldots, \langle t'_n \rangle_E) \qquad \text{Parallel Move Lemma}$$

Figure 8.2
$\mathcal{E}_{\mathcal{PT}(R)}$: Equivalence of proof terms

variables in the definition of a rewrite signature is often implicit. It is not difficult to verify that the desired properties of an entailment system are fulfilled.

Models. For a given syntax $\mathcal{S}ynt$, to each signature and associated set of sentences $(\Sigma, sen) \in \mathcal{S}ynt$ is associated a class $Mod(\Sigma)$ of objects called Σ-models and a satisfaction relation denoted $\models_\Sigma \subseteq Mod(\Sigma) \times sen(\Sigma)$ which is compatible with signature morphisms (see [23] for more details).

For a given set of sentences Φ, $Mod(\Sigma, \Phi)$ is the class of all Σ-models M such that $\forall \phi \in \Phi, M \models_\Sigma \phi$, called the models satisfying Φ. $Mod(\Sigma, \Phi) \models_\Sigma \phi$ means that $M \models_\Sigma \phi$ for all $M \in Mod(\Sigma, \Phi)$.

▶ A model of rewriting logic can be chosen as the computation space of the considered rewrite theory $\mathcal{R}$. Such a computation space is determined by the set of proof terms π computed in the sequents $\pi : \langle t \rangle_E \to \langle t' \rangle_E$ modulo the equivalence of computations. This equivalence is given by E and a set $\mathcal{E}_{\mathcal{PT}(R)}$ of equational axioms on the set of proof terms described in Figure 8.2. So the considered model is the quotient set $\{\pi \mid \mathcal{R} \vdash \pi : \langle t \rangle_E \to \langle t' \rangle_E\}/(E \cup \mathcal{E}_{\mathcal{PT}(R)})$.

Logic. We have now defined the ingredients of a logic $\mathcal{L}$, which is given by five components $\mathcal{L} = (\mathcal{S}ynt, sen, \mathcal{M}od, \vdash, \models)$ such that $(\mathcal{S}ynt, sen, \vdash)$ is an entailment system and $(\mathcal{S}ynt, sen, \mathcal{M}od, \models)$ a class of models that satisfy furthermore the *soundness* condition:

$$\forall(\Sigma, sen) \in \mathcal{S}ynt, \Phi \subseteq sen(\Sigma), \phi \in sen(\Sigma), \quad \Phi \vdash_\Sigma \phi \Rightarrow Mod(\Sigma, \Phi) \models_\Sigma \phi.$$

The logic is *complete* when the above implication is also an equivalence.

▶ This specializes trivially to the notion of rewriting logic, using the basic ingredients defined before.

Proof calculus. When a logic is defined this way, it is quite abstract since there is a priori no constructive hint about how the entailment relation is built. Thus this approach only gives a formal description of the relations $\vdash$ and $\models$ and of their relationship. What we need also is to describe how to prove sentences starting from a set of axioms Φ. This description of proofs should allow the flexibility to define subcalculi that are complete for proving theorems in a specific subclass of the set of sentences. For example linear resolution is a (correct and) complete proof method for Horn clause logic and this induces the well-known refutation as computation paradigm. Thus we require that a proof calculus operationally describes the relation $\vdash$; indeed there may exist several proof calculi for a logic, as it is the case for first-order logic.

A proof calculus associates to each theory T an algebraic structure $P(T)$ using axioms of T as hypotheses and using deduction rules as operators to build new proofs. The set $proofs(T)$ consists of all proofs of all theorems of the theory T. To each proof is associated the theorem it is a proof of: τ_T maps each proof $p \in proofs(T)$ to the sentence ϕ such that p is a proof of $\phi = \tau_T(p)$. A *proof subcalculus* formalizes the restriction of an entailment system to a specific syntax and to specific forms of sentences as axioms or conclusions. This allows us to consider only a subset of all proofs and thus to account for efficiency. A proof calculus or subcalculus is formally given by an entailment system and for each theory T, the associated triple $(P(T), proofs(T), \tau_T)$.

▶ In rewriting logic, the set of proofs is defined as the set of proof terms and the proof calculus is thus built by the same set of deduction rules defining the entailment system in Figure 8.1.

8.2.2 Computational Systems

In [26], it is shown how various logics can be represented in rewriting logic, as for example equational logic, Horn logic, linear logic and the natural semantics [16].

We will rather focus now on the specification of operational semantics of languages and systems like constraint solving. So, we need to express not only a rewrite theory but also computations in this theory that mirror computations in various logical systems, e.g. how a deduction in Horn logic is mapped to a proof in rewriting logic.

Computations. The first ingredient of a computational system is a labeled rewrite theory from which we define a notion of computation.

Let us first concentrate on a one-step computation. For a given rewrite theory $\mathcal{R}$, and for the sequent $\pi : \langle t \rangle_E \rightarrow \langle t' \rangle_E$ with the proof term $\pi = t[\ell(\sigma \overline{x})]_\omega$, then

$$\langle t \rangle_E \Rightarrow_{\ell,\sigma,\omega} \langle t' \rangle_E$$

is called a *single rewrite step*. Note that this corresponds exactly to the usual definition of one step of rewriting at occurrence ω using the rule labeled ℓ and the match σ.

Indeed, we are interested in a canonical representation of all computations that are equivalent modulo the axioms $\mathcal{E}_{\mathcal{PT}(R)}$ (see Figure 8.2). This can be done thanks to the following result [24] which shows that up to associativity of the ";" symbol, any sequent can be decomposed into a composition of elementary (sequential) ones: for any sequent $\pi : \langle t \rangle_E \rightarrow \langle t' \rangle_E$, either $\pi = \langle t \rangle_E = \langle t' \rangle_E$, or there exists $n \in \mathbf{N}$ such that:

$$\langle t \rangle_E = \langle t_0 \rangle_E \Rightarrow_{\ell_0} \langle t_1 \rangle_E \Rightarrow_{\ell_1} \langle t_2 \rangle_E \cdots \Rightarrow_{\ell_{n-1}} \langle t_n \rangle_E = \langle t' \rangle_E,$$

and $\pi =_{A(;)} (\pi_0; \pi_1; \pi_2; \ldots; \pi_{n-1})$, where $A(;)$ denotes the associativity of ";". When π is the proof term above, $\langle t_n \rangle_E$ is called the *result of π applied to* $\langle t_0 \rangle_E$ and this is also denoted $\langle t \rangle_E \overset{\pi}{\Longrightarrow} \langle t' \rangle_E$.

Indeed the equivalence relation generated by $(E \cup \mathcal{E}_{\mathcal{PT}(R)})$ on proof terms induces an equivalence on computations: two computations are equivalent (they lead to the same result) if their proof terms are equivalent.

Strategies. In general, we are not interested in all computations, but only in those guided by a strategy, which is in this work a description of the single rewrite steps sequence allowed in the computations. From a formal point of view, a *strategy* is a subset of the set of proof terms which is closed under concatenation.

The result of applying a strategy $\mathcal{S}$ on a term t, denoted functionally $\mathcal{S}(t)$, is the set of all $\langle t' \rangle_E$ for which there exists $\pi \in \mathcal{S}$ such that $\langle t' \rangle_E$ is the result of π applied to $\langle t \rangle_E$:

$$\mathcal{S}(t) = \{\langle t' \rangle_E \mid \exists \pi \in \mathcal{S}, \langle t \rangle_E \overset{\pi}{\Longrightarrow} \langle t' \rangle_E\}.$$

It should be noted from this definition that a strategy applied to a term may have several different terms as results.

A first way to describe a strategy is to extensively enumerate the intended subset of the proof terms. But this is of course not satisfactory in practice and the problem indeed is to define a language to describe subsets of the proof terms. We will see later how is implemented in ELAN an instance of this language which is powerful enough to deal with the examples we are interested in.

Computational systems. We are now in position to define the main concept of this paper: A *computational system* is a labeled rewrite theory $\mathcal{R} = (\mathcal{X}, \mathcal{F}, E, \mathcal{L}, R)$ together with a strategy $\mathcal{S}$.

In order to show the expressivity of this concept, we give below examples of languages and systems design in this formalism. Before entering into these examples, we first present the way strategies can be expressed.

8.2.3   Expressing Strategies

In this section, we present one possibility, adopted in the current version of the language ELAN, to express a subset of proof terms using a first-order language. We intend to make the strategy description conceptually easy and such that the structure of the denoted proof terms can be straightforwardly guessed from it.

In the strategy language, we first want to include the rule names, an iterator operator that describes the iteration of a computation zero and more times, a concatenation operator and a selecting operator that, given n arguments, provides a possible choice of one of them. To raise the expressive power of expressions built on this vocabulary, we need the possibility to express application of a strategy on subterms. Moreover the strategies can be named from a set of strategy names $\mathcal{N}$, and the names of strategies can be used in the definition of other strategies. With these requirements, a simple language for defining strategies can be designed. A strategy expression in this language is a term built up on a set of rule labels $\mathcal{L}$, a set of strategy names $\mathcal{N}$, a set of function symbols $\mathcal{F}$, the binary and associative concatenation symbol ";", a unary function symbol **iterate** and a function symbol **choose** with a variable arity.

- The strategy expression consisting just in one rule name corresponds to all computations obtained by exactly one application of this rule.

- The concatenation $s_1; s_2$ of two strategy expressions s_1 and s_2 in $\mathcal{S}$ denotes all computations made with respect to the strategy s_1 then to the strategy s_2.

- The expression **choose**$(s_1, \ldots, s_n)$ where $s_1, \ldots, s_n$ are in $\mathcal{S}$, describes a possible choice of one of the strategies given as argument.

- The expression **iterate**(s) where s is in $\mathcal{S}$, describes the iteration of a computation zero, one, two, ... times.

- The expression $f(s_1, \ldots, s_n)$ where $s_1, \ldots, s_n$ are in $\mathcal{S}$ and f is a functional symbol from $\mathcal{F}$ with arity n, expresses the fact that the term to be reduced must be of the form $f(t_1, \ldots, t_n)$ and that each subterm t_i will be reduced following the strategy s_i.

- A strategy name in $\mathcal{N}$ is just an abbreviation for a complex expression s. A name n has to be defined by an equality $n = s$ where $s \in \mathcal{S}$. It is enough for our purpose to have non-recursive equalities here, but the case of recursive definitions of strategies is described in [30].

On the set of all strategy expressions $\mathcal{S} = \mathcal{T}(\mathcal{L} \cup \mathcal{N} \cup \mathcal{F} \cup \{;, \mathbf{iterate}, \mathbf{choose}\})$, we define a function $\mathcal{PF} : \mathcal{S} \rightarrow \mathcal{PT}$ giving the set of proof terms corresponding to each expression in $\mathcal{S}$. $\mathcal{PF}$ is recursively defined as follows:

- If ℓ is the name of a rule, with variables $x_1, \ldots, x_n$;
$\mathcal{PF}(\ell) = \{\ell(\langle t_1 \rangle_E, \ldots, \langle t_n \rangle_E) \mid \forall i = 1, \ldots, n, t_i \in \mathcal{T}(\mathcal{F}, \mathcal{X})\}$.

- If s_1 and s_2 are in $\mathcal{S}$;
$\mathcal{PF}(s_1; s_2) = \{\pi_1; \pi_2 \mid \pi_1 \in \mathcal{PF}(s_1), \pi_2 \in \mathcal{PF}(s_2)\}$

- If $s_1, \ldots, s_n$ are in $\mathcal{S}$;
$\mathcal{PF}(\mathbf{choose}(s_1, \ldots, s_n)) = \{\pi_i \mid \pi_i \in \mathcal{PF}(s_i), 1 \leq i \leq n\} = \bigcup_{1 \leq i \leq n} \mathcal{PF}(s_i)$.

- If s is in $\mathcal{S}$;
$\mathcal{PF}(\mathbf{iterate}(s)) = \{\langle t \rangle_E \mid t \in \mathcal{T}(\mathcal{F}, \mathcal{X})\} \cup \{\pi_1; \ldots; \pi_n \mid \pi_i \in \mathcal{PF}(s), 1 \leq i \leq n, n \in \mathbf{N}\}$, where the first part of this union stands for the zero iteration case.

- If $s_1, \ldots, s_n$ are in $\mathcal{S}$ and $f \in \mathcal{F}_n$;
$\mathcal{PF}(f(s_1, \ldots, s_n)) = \{f(\pi_1, \ldots, \pi_n) \mid \pi_i \in \mathcal{PF}(s_i), 1 \leq i \leq n\}$.

- If n is a name from $\mathcal{N}$ defined by $n = s$;
$\mathcal{PF}(n) = \mathcal{PF}(s)$.

8.2.4 Mapping to Rewriting Logic

Our goal is now to use computational systems to express and compute with various logics describing the operational semantics of languages and systems. Formally programs in such languages are theories (Σ, Φ) and each entailment $\Phi \vdash \phi$ in the given logic has a proof built by the proof calculus. We need to map this proof to a computation in a computational system that describes the construction of proofs with labeled rewrite rules and a strategy. To do that, we need to map a theory (Σ, Φ) to a rewrite theory (Σ', Φ') in such a way that any proof from (Σ, Φ) is mirrored by a proof from (Σ', Φ').

Given an entailment system $(\mathcal{S}ynt, \vdash)$ for a logic $\mathcal{L}$, a *mapping to rewriting logic* is defined by a theory mapping

$$\mathcal{M} : T = (\Sigma, \Phi) \mapsto \mathcal{M}(T) = (\mathcal{M}(\Sigma), \mathcal{M}(\Phi))$$

and a proof mapping $\alpha : proofs(T) \mapsto proofs(\mathcal{M}(T))$, such that for any proof p of a theorem ϕ in T, $\alpha(p)$ is a proof of $\mathcal{M}(\phi)$ in $\mathcal{M}(T)$. Mappings of interest are those in which moreover proofs in rewriting logic actually correspond to proofs in the original logic.

Since our goal logic is rewriting logic, $(\mathcal{M}(\Sigma), \mathcal{M}(\Phi))$ is a labeled rewrite theory, $\mathcal{M}(\phi)$ is a sequent of the form $\pi : \langle t \rangle_E \rightarrow \langle t' \rangle_E$. So for a given logic, we have to build a computational system that realises this mapping. Since we want to abstract from the theories, we actually need to define a *generic computational system* that realises this mapping for any theory in the original logic. Indeed this is in general a non-trivial problem to prove that a computational system realises the required mapping and we give examples of such correct constructions in the two next sections.

8.3 Examples of Computational Systems

8.3.1 Mapping Equational Programs to Computational Systems

The first example we consider is equational programming based on narrowing. Such languages have been considered for instance (among many others) in [9, 7, 25].

Using the framework of the previous section, equational programs are theories built on a first order signature where the axioms are finite sets of equalities denoted $Pg = \{l_i \sim r_i | i \in I\}$, which once oriented from left to right form a convergent term rewrite system $PgR = \{l_i \rightarrowtail r_i | i \in I\}$. In order to avoid confusing the reader, we distinguish between the rewrite system underlying rewriting logic and the rewrite system PgR, systems that are a priori different: we call PgR a set of oriented equalities and we denote the arrow symbol with the special symbol $\rightarrowtail$. This difference between the rewrite relation of the computational system and the one defined by the user in a specification of his choice is further discussed in the later section on reflexivity.

The query to solve is assumed to be of the form $g(\overline{x}) = d(\overline{x})$ and the underlying proof calculus is the basic narrowing process [12] that computes a complete set of Pg-unifiers of the query. In order to better understand how basic narrowing is described in rewriting logic, let us briefly explain this process. The reader interested by deeper details and references on narrowing can refer to [14]. The initial query is transformed into an expression of the form $(\exists\emptyset : g = d \parallel \top)$, where $\top$ denotes the empty conjunction of equations, and $\exists\emptyset$ is a trivial quantification over an empty set of variables. The basic narrowing process transforms expressions of the form $(\exists X, g = d \parallel S)$ where $g = d$ is an equation to be solved modulo the equational theory generated by Pg and S a conjunction of equations to be solved in the empty theory. The process tries to unify a subterm of g at position ω with a left-hand side of an oriented equality $l \rightarrowtail r \in PgR$, taking care, by the use of a *Variant* function, that its variables are disjoint from those of g. This gives rise to a unification problem $(g_{|\omega} =^?_\emptyset l)$ and a new goal $(g[r]_\omega = d)$ to be further solved. So a current query $(\exists X, g = d \parallel S)$, where the existentially quantified variables are the "new" variables introduced by the narrowing process, is transformed into the following one:

$$(\exists X \cup Var(l \rightarrowtail r),\ g[r]_\omega = d \parallel S \wedge (g_{|\omega} =^?_\emptyset l))$$

such that the two systems of equations $(\exists X, g =^?_{Pg} d \wedge S)$ and $(\exists X \cup Var(l \rightarrowtail r),\ g[r]_\omega =^?_{Pg} d \wedge S \wedge (g_{|\omega} =^?_\emptyset l))$ have the same set of solutions. Furthermore a query $(\exists X, g = d \parallel S)$ has an obvious solution when g and d are syntactically unifiable and this is exactly the solution of the system $S \wedge (g =^?_\emptyset d)$. Note that a successful computation transforms a problem in the theory Pg (or equivalently PgR) into unification problems in the empty theory. Indeed there is a lot of undeterminism in the choices of the oriented equality $(l \rightarrowtail r)$ and the position ω where the narrowing step is applied. All possible choices have to be explored when completeness of the returned set of solutions is required (see [28]), which is indeed what we want here.

To define a mapping from equational programming to rewriting logic, we consider a rewrite theory whose signature is taken from the program and enriched by the symbols $\rightarrowtail$ for building program rules, $\exists$, $=$ and $\parallel$ for building queries, $=^?_\emptyset$ and $\wedge$ for building equations and equation systems. The rewrite rules of the rewrite theory, that apply to formulas built on this enriched signature, are as follows:

Narrow $(\exists X, g = d \parallel S)$

$\rightarrow$

$(\exists X \cup Var(l, r),\ g[r]_\omega = d \parallel S \wedge (g_{|\omega} =^?_\emptyset l))$
if $l \rightarrowtail r \in Variants(PgR)$ and $(S \wedge (g_{|\omega} =^?_\emptyset l))$ is satisfiable

Block $(\exists X, g = d \parallel S)$

$\rightarrow$

$(\exists X, \top \parallel S \wedge (g =_\emptyset^? d))$

if $(S \wedge (g =_\emptyset^? d))$ is satisfiable

Since the queries are of the form $g(\overline{x}) = d(\overline{x})$, which is the same as $(\exists \emptyset, g = d \parallel \top)$, the formula to prove in rewriting logic is:

$$((\exists \emptyset, g = d \parallel \top) \rightarrow (\exists X, \top \parallel S)),$$

where S is a system of equations solvable in the empty theory. This last condition is ensured using a unification process itself described by a computational system, as this is done in the next section for commutative unification.

The results on correctness and completeness of basic narrowing state that each computation proving such a formula consists of several applications of rule **Narrow** followed by exactly one application of rule **Block**. So, to complete the definition of the computational system, it remains to define a strategy $\mathcal{S}$ that expresses this completeness result. With the notations defined before, we can take for strategy $\mathcal{S} = \mathbf{iterate}(\mathbf{Narrow}); \mathbf{Block}$, which describes the following application of rewrite rules:

$$\{\mathbf{Block},\ \mathbf{Narrow}; \mathbf{Block},\ \mathbf{Narrow}; \mathbf{Narrow}; \mathbf{Block}, \ldots\}.$$

The result of the application of this strategy is the set of all expressions $(\exists X, \top \parallel S)$ such that $(\exists X, \top \parallel S) \in \mathcal{S}(\exists \emptyset, g = d \parallel \top)$.

8.3.2   Constraint Solving as Computational systems

The description of constraint solving using rule-based algorithms as in [5, 14], allows easier correctness and completeness proofs of constraint solvers, partly thanks to the explicit distinction made in this approach between deduction rules and control. At the light of the framework described in this paper, this rule approach to constraint solving can now be seen as the expression of the constraint solving process as a computational system. A constraint solver for symbolic constraints such as equations, inequations or disequations on terms is viewed as a computational system aimed at computing solved forms for a class of considered formulas called constraints.

For instance, unification in commutative theories is a constraint solving process that can be described with a computational system where the signature of underlying rewriting logic consists of first-order terms with an equality symbol denoted $=_C^?$ (C stands for commutative). As rewrite rules, we use rules proposed in [14], which are proved correct and complete for the computation of a complete set of C-unifiers. These rules transform conjunctions of equations of the form $(P \wedge s =^?_C t)$ and are given in Figure 8.3. They use an implicit universal quantification on the variables of conjunction of equations (P), on terms (t_i, s_i) and on the operator symbols (f, g). These later symbols are in fact instantiated when the program, i.e. the rewrite theory, is known. The $+$ symbol is assumed to be the only one which is commutative; when several commutative symbols are needed, general results on combining unification algorithms have to be invoked [3, 29]. The symbol $\mathbf{F}$ denotes a problem without solution (i.e. failure), and for any term t, $|t|$ denotes its size, i.e. the number of its function symbols.

Following [14], solving a given equation $s =^?_C t$ consists in finding the set of its (tree) solved forms. A solved form is either $\mathbf{F}$ if the equation has no solution or a system of equations with the same set of solutions as $s =^?_C t$, and of the form $\bigwedge_{i \in I} x_i =^?_C t_i$ where the variables x_i do not appear elsewhere in the system. Thus, in rewriting logic, we are interested by proofs of the formula: $(s =^?_C t) \rightarrow S$, where S is a solved form. This is expressed using an appropriate strategy: let $\mathcal{S}$ be a strategy that causes application of rules in any order until the normal form is obtained. Then solving the constraint $(s =^?_C t)$ amounts to look for each S such that: $S \in \mathcal{S}(s =^?_C t)$.

Describing constraint solving processes as computational systems has several advantages over constraint solving systems where solvers are encapsulated in black boxes.

1. Although completeness may be in some cases, like syntactic unification, proved for any normalizing strategy, the solved forms are in general reached more efficiently with smart choices of rules. Through the design of rules and strategies, the developer has a direct access to the constraint solver and this point is crucial for discovering and experimenting new solvers.

2. To be able to formalize constraint solving by rewrite rules also makes termination proofs easier and possibly partly automated. This also opens the door to non-trivial applications of termination proof techniques.

3. Constraint handling like simplification, entailment or propagation can be described in a very abstract way.

4. Another interest of this point of view is the conceptually easy combination of constraint solving with other computational systems. Indeed a computational system for a language involving now formulas with constraints $(\varphi \parallel c)$, where φ is a formula (a Horn clause for instance) and c is a constraint, is incrementally built by importing a computational system for the constraint language

Delete	$P \wedge s =^?_C s$
	$\rightarrow$
	P
Decompose	$P \wedge f(s_1, \ldots, s_n) =^?_C f(t_1, \ldots, t_n)$
	$\rightarrow$
	$P \wedge s_1 =^?_C t_1 \wedge \ldots \wedge s_n =^?_C t_n$
ComMutate	$P \wedge s_1 + s_2 =^?_C t_1 + t_2$
	$\rightarrow$
	$P \wedge s_1 =^?_C t_2 \wedge s_2 =^?_C t_1$
Conflict	$P \wedge f(s_1, \ldots, s_n) =^?_C g(t_1, \ldots, t_p)$
	$\rightarrow$
	$\mathbf{F}$
	if $f \neq g$
Coalesce	$P \wedge x =^?_C y$
	$\rightarrow$
	$\{x \mapsto y\}P \wedge x =^?_C y$
	if $x, y \in \mathcal{V}ar(P)$ and $x \neq y$
Merge	$P \wedge x =^?_C s \wedge x =^?_C t$
	$\rightarrow$
	$P \wedge x =^?_C s \wedge s =^?_C t$
	if $0 < |s| \leq |t|$
Check	$P \wedge x =^?_C s$
	$\rightarrow$
	$\mathbf{F}$
	if $x \in \mathcal{V}ar(s)$ and $s \notin \mathcal{X}$
Eliminate	$P \wedge x =^?_C s$
	$\rightarrow$
	$\{x \mapsto s\}P \wedge x =^?_C s$
	if $x \notin \mathcal{V}ar(s), s \notin \mathcal{X}, x \in \mathcal{V}ar(P)$

Figure 8.3
ComUnif: The rules for commutative unification

in which c is expressed. Statements are sets of formulas with constraints, like in $CLP(X)$ [15]. It is yet possible to define rewrite rules on formulas with constraints, as mentioned later in Section 8.5, but such combinations generates delicate problems concerning completeness.

8.4   The ELAN Interpreter

Sketched in a few words, ELAN can be understood as a specification language
that allows first to describe the syntactic part of a logic and the transformation of
its proofs into proofs in the rewriting logic, and second to perform actual proofs
using the computational system. Thus ELAN is a language for designing and
executing computational systems. As such, it provides an implementation of the
concepts presented in Section 8.2, where some slight adaptations and restrictions
with respect to the general case were made and are detailed in this section. A full
description of the language and its implementation is given in [30].

ELAN is a modular language, so a computational system description is usually
divided into modules. Each module represents a particular computational system and is combined with other ones to build the whole system. Modules can be
parametrized. ELAN works with many-sorted rewriting logic, and the definition of
a signature permits mixfix notation of symbols. These facilities are largely used in
examples presented in the rest of this paper.

8.4.1   Expressing Mappings in ELAN

To smartly implement the theory mapping from a given theory to a computational
system in the sense of Section 8.2.4, ELAN provides a special kind of parametrization of computational systems by abstracting from the actual signature and axioms
of specifications.

A non-standard construction of parametrization in ELAN is a **FOR EACH**
construction, which allows the generation of rewrite rules with respect to an actual
theory, as illustrated on examples in the following sections. This parametrization
tool in ELAN is very powerful and also permits internalization of objects as shown
in Section 8.4.5.

8.4.2   Expressing Rewrite Rules in ELAN

In full generality, the underlying term algebra of a rewrite theory is defined as the
quotient term algebra modulo some given set of equations E. All rewrite rules are
then working on these equivalence classes rather than on simple terms. This concept
is implemented in ELAN, in the restricted case of associativity and commutativity
axioms. In practice, this means that symbols can be marked to be associative and
commutative.

A labeled rewrite rule in ELAN is obviously defined as a pair of terms built
on functional symbols and local variables. In addition, rules can be conditional

and a kind of local assignment can be used inside the rules. The purpose of local assignment is mainly to introduce strategy control on subterms. Rules are named by labels that are just identifiers, but variables are also specified. We shall see later in examples that more than one rule can be labeled by the same label. The concrete syntax of a labeled rewrite rule is :

    $<rwrule>$ ::= **rule** $<rule\ name>$ **for** $<sort>$
               declare { $<local\ variable\ declaration>$ }$^+$
               body $<rbody>$
               end of rule

    $<rbody>$ ::= $<term>$ => $<term>$

    $<rbody>$ ::= $<rbody>$ **if** $<boolean\ term>$

    $<rbody>$ ::= $<rbody>$ **where** $<variable>$:= ([$<strategy\ name>$]) $<term>$

   Here and in the rest of the paper, we use a version of BNF-notation to express concrete syntax. In this notation, the expressions written in italics and enclosed into <> parentheses are nonterminal symbols; the reserved words are written in bold, as well as special symbols from the language; an expression enclosed into { }* parentheses is iterated zero and more times; an expression enclosed into { }$^+$ parentheses is iterated one and more times, and finally an expression enclosed into [ ] brackets can be omitted.

   A successful application of a rewrite rule on a given term is processed in the expected way: the left-hand side of the rule has to match a subterm of the given term; this causes instantiation of variables occurring in the left-hand side. Then the local assignments and conditions are evaluated, in reverse order, so that the evaluation starts with the last one and stops with the first one. The conditions have to be evaluated to a constant *true* and the local assignments must instantiate all remaining variables. At the end, the original subterm is replaced by the instantiated right-hand side of the rule. In the **where** assignments, the terms $<term>$ are reduced with respect to strategies named $<strategy\ name>$ and the results are then assigned to the variables on the left-hand sides of the := assignement signs.

   We can consider local assignment as syntactic sugar, because, for example, using a rule of the form:

$$\ell :\ g\ =>\ d[x]_\omega\ \textbf{where}\ x := (s)\ t$$

in a strategy $S[\ell]_v$ is equivalent to using the rule:

$$\ell' :\ g\ =>\ d[t]_\omega$$

with ℓ' a new label, in the strategy $S[(\ell'; d[s]_\omega)]_v$.

8.4.3   Expressing Strategies in ELAN

Strategy definitions in ELAN are based on the expressions defined in Section 8.2.3, with a few more specific points. Based on practical experience, rewrite rules are divided into two groups: the labeled rewrite rules, whose application is controlled by user-defined strategies, and the non labeled rules, whose application is controlled by a default normalization strategy, which consists in applying non-labeled rules at any position of a term until the normal form is reached. The normalization strategy is used with rules defining functions and is applied after each reduction produced by a labeled rewrite rule. This corresponds to the intuition that, after each application of a labeled rewrite rule, functions introduced by the right-hand side of rule must be evaluated.

In the current ELAN implementation, strategies built up from functional symbols application and strategies calling other strategies are not yet implemented. But this is not really a limitation since these constructions can be simulated using the **where** local assignment. On the other hand, mainly for efficiency reasons, we have introduced deterministic strategies in our language.

The syntax for describing strategies in ELAN is the following:

$<strategy\ def>$ ::= **strategy** $<strategy\ name>$
            $<strategy>$
            end of strategy

$<strategy>$ ::= **dont know choose** ({ $<rule\ name>$ }$^+$)
            | **dont know choose** ({ $<strategy>$, }* $<strategy>$)
            | **dont care choose** ({ $<rule\ name>$ }$^+$)
            | **dont care choose** ({ $<strategy>$, }* $<strategy>$)
            | **iterate** $<strategy>$ **enditerate**
            | **repeat** $<strategy>$ **endrepeat**
            | $<strategy>$ $<strategy>$

In this syntax, concatenation is omitted, the constructor **iterate** corresponds to the iterator and the **dont know choose** constructor corresponds to the selecting operator. Note that rule names are always encapsulated in the selecting operator. This is because a rule name represents in general a set of rules, so a selecting operator has always to be specified. The **dont care choose** constructor is what we call a deterministic strategy. It corresponds to the selecting operator, but contrary to **dont know choose**, it selects only one of substrategies giving a non-empty set of results. Another deterministic strategy is the **repeat** strategy, which corresponds to the iterate operator, but only the largest chains of iterations are considered. This means that only proof terms to which no other substrategy can be concatenated, are allowed. These two deterministic strategies are used to significantly restrict the search space and to drop redundant results. For example, in the case of syntactic unification, we know that unification rules can be applied in any order and that all solved forms are equivalent.

8.4.4 Horn Clause Programming Language

To illustrate the ELAN environment, we define in this section a simple programming language based on Horn clause logic and we describe the top level of its implementation.

This allows us to introduce an important point: there are two kinds of users of ELAN. The first ones, let us call them super-users, are those describing in ELAN a computational system in order to design for example a logic programming language. The second ones are those using ELAN *and* a (super-user defined) computational system in order to evaluate a query in the context of a given specification.

In Horn clause logic, formulas are of the form $A \Leftarrow B_1, \cdots, B_n$ with A, B_i being atoms, and a theory is given by a signature and a set of formulas. An example of Horn clause theory to be given as input to ELAN (where a theory is called specification) is:

> **specification** member
>   signature
>   vars   X , Y , Z
>   ops   cons:2, nil:0, a:0, b:0, c:0
>   predicates member:2
>   clauses
>   member(X,cons(X,Y)).
>   member(X,cons(Y,Z)) :- member(X,Z).
> **end of specification**

The syntax of a specification is fully defined by the ELAN super-user; the heading of a specification and the division on named parts (here *signature* and *clauses*) have to be respected by the user, since they are part of the Horn clause programming language syntax.

An implementation of this programming language must be able to solve queries of type: $\exists \overline{x} P(\overline{x})$ where the quantifier can be omitted under the assumption that all variables occurring in P are implicitly existentially quantified. The expected proof calculus must correspond to SLD resolution and give a complete set of substitutions satisfying the query.

Intuitively, our intention is to specify a computational system with a strategy which, applied on the initial term $(P(\overline{x}) \,\|\, true)$, produces a set of final terms of form $(nil \,\|\, \sigma)$, where σ represents a solution. The rewrite rules of the computational system apply to an execution state that is a formula made of a first component which is a list of goals, initially reduced to one element $P(\overline{x})$ and a second component which is a conjunction of equalities in solved forms, initially reduced to an empty conjunction denoted $true$.

The main rule of the computation system is:

$$(P, x \,\|\, \theta) \Rightarrow (B_1, \cdots, B_n, x \,\|\, \theta \circ \theta') \qquad \textbf{where } \theta' = mgu(\theta P, \theta A)$$

for a variant with fresh variables of any clause $A \Leftarrow B_1, \cdots, B_n$ in the specification. This rule is written below in ELAN syntax. The quantification **FOR EACH** $\cdots$ { *<rule>* } means that *<rule>* will be generated for all clauses in the specification with an atom A as head and a list of atoms B as body. The infix operator @ used inside the rule is an append function on lists; the variable sigma is set to a renaming substitution which is applied on the clause $A \Leftarrow B$ to obtain a variant with fresh variables; the variable RRS denotes a set of equations which is checked to be satisfiable by the strategy p_unifys.

FOR EACH C:clause; A:pred_atom; B:pred_atom_list
    SUCH THAT clause(C) & head(C,A) & body(C,B) : {

        rule trans **for** ex_state
        declare RS,RRS : system;
                rest : pred_atom_list;
                h : pred_atom;
                sigma : substitution;
        body
          (h,rest $\|$ RS) => (sigma(B) @ rest $\|$ RRS)
                where RRS := (p_unifys) sigma(A)=h & RS
                where sigma := () rename_subst from vars (A,B) w.r.t. h,rest
        end of rule

}

If after some applications of this rule trans, the empty list of goals is obtained, then a solution is reached. To test emptiness of the list, we add the rule:

rule trans_successfin **for** ex_state
declare sigma1,sigma2 : system;
body
   (nil || sigma1) => (nil || sigma2)
        where sigma2 := (delete_new_vars) sigma1
end of rule

which also deletes non interesting variables (i.e. variables added during execution) from the result.

Of course, this is only the top level description of the computational system, since all details of the implementation of e.g. replacement, substitution, unification, have to be given. This is done using appropriate computational systems, and thus the description of this simple Prolog interpreter (as well as other examples) reduces completely to a conditional term rewriting system.

We finish this example by giving a strategy defining the application of these two rules.

        strategy eval_strat
           iterate
               dont know choose (trans)
           enditerate
               dont know choose (trans_successfin)
           end of strategy

8.4.5 Reflexivity

In order to illustrate two different ways to encode rewriting in the rewriting logic itself, let us assume now that we wish to specify an equational logic language, where formulas are rewrite rules forming a convergent term rewriting system and whose proof calculus is given by normalization of terms. An example of program in this language is:

        specification rwspec
          signature
            Vars: X, Y, Z
            Ops: nil, cons:2, append:2, a, b, c
          rwrules
            append(cons(Y,Z),X) -> cons(Y,append(Z,X)),
            append(nil,X) -> X
        end of specification

This means that the user wants to define variables X, Y, Z and an operators nil, a, b, c of arity zero (by default), and binary operators cons and append that satisfy the usual semantics of lists.

There are two ways for encoding term rewriting in ELAN. The first one consists in describing the steps of matching, substituting and replacement involved in an elementary rewrite step and how to iterate them. In this case, the implementor has to specify completely all details of the implementation of rewriting. But ELAN itself contains the notion of rewriting, so the second possibility is to simply transfer the rewrite rules from the specification level to the execution level.

The first situation is for example expressed by the following **rewrite** rewrite rule who describes how to apply the rule $L \rightarrow R$ at occurrence *occ* on the term *s*, with the substitution *theta*.

FOR EACH L,R:term **SUCH THAT** rwrule(L,R) : {

> **rule** rewrite **for** term
> **declare** ME : system; s : term; theta : substitution; occ : occurrence;
> **body**
>   s => s[theta(R)] at occ
>   **where** theta := () system_to_subst(ME)
>   **where** ME := (matchs) s at occ = L
>   **where** occ := (occ) non-var-occ(s)
> **end of rule**

}

strategy rewriting
> **repeat**
>   **dont care choose** (rewrite)
> **endrepeat**

end of strategy

The strategy expresses the fact that rewrite rules must be applied until the normal form is reached. In this case, the following call of ELAN which uses the computational system described in the file **rewriting** and the specification described in the file **rwspec** returns, when reducing the term $append(cons(a, cons(b, nil)), cons(c, nil))$:

```
--> elan rewriting rwspec
        ******** ELAN-Nancy v0.08 (10/06/93.22:50) ********
...
enter query term:
append(cons(a,cons(b,nil)),cons(c,nil))
[] start with term : append(cons(a,cons(b,nil)),cons(c,nil))

[] result term : cons(a,cons(b,cons(c,nil)))
```

```
number of labeled rules applied: 225
number of labeled rules tried: 3032
number of non labeled rules applied: 364
time: 5.483333 secs
-->
```

On the contrary, we can make an explicit use of rewriting capabilities of ELAN by describing the rewriting in the following reflexive way:

FOR EACH L,R:term **SUCH THAT** rwrule(L,R) : {

    rule for term
    declare FOR EACH X:identifier **SUCH THAT** var(X): { X : term ; }
    body
        L => R
    end of rule

}

which simply consists to internalize any rewrite rule $L \rightarrow R$ of the specification into an ELAN rewrite rule. The line:

    declare FOR EACH X:identifier **SUCH THAT** var(X): { X : term ; }

means that each identifier X, Y, Z declared as variable in the specification rwspec is now declared as a variable of sort term in the rewrite rule $L \Rightarrow R$. Then calling ELAN on the same query solved in this new description gives the same answer in a quite different manner!

```
--> elan intRewriting rwspec
        ******** ELAN-Nancy v0.08 (10/06/93.22:50) ********
...
enter query term:
append(cons(a,cons(b,nil)),cons(c,nil))
[] start with term : append(cons(a,cons(b,nil)),cons(c,nil))

[] result term : cons(a,cons(b,cons(c,nil)))

 number of labeled rules applied: 0
 number of labeled rules tried: 0
 number of non labeled rules applied: 3
 time: 0.000000 secs
-->
```

As quoted also in [26], these two translations of rewriting into a computational system correspond to the identity functor in the second case and an explicit description of the rewrite process in the first case.

8.5   Further Perspectives and Conclusion

Up to now, we have expressed in a uniform framework constraint solving and deduction and achieved a high level of modularity. Our objective of designing and
experimenting with new computational systems leads us to consider different combination problems. Let us mention two kinds of theoretical problems that arise in
this context:

- Putting together a computational system for equality and constraint solving
  like unification leads to interesting but non-trivial problems from the point
  of view of their properties. Performing deduction independently on equality
  formulas and on constraints is not complete in general. This problem is solved
  in a general way in [18] by restructuring formulas and constraints. Such
  restructuration has been shown useless with additional syntactic restrictions
  on formulas [2].

- Putting together two constraint solvers in two different first-order structures
  like for instance booleans and a quotient term algebra cannot be reduced to a
  blind use of both constraint solvers. Typically interactions between theories
  may appear and must be solved [3, 20].

In the challenge of specifying safe software and executing them efficiently, it is
of great importance to present in the same framework, the operational semantics
of a programming language, the prover (as far as possible automated) of desired
properties of programs, and the efficient execution of the proved safe programs. The
constraint paradigm provides a logical foundation to efficient improvements of the
deductive process both in programming languages and theorem provers. We believe
that the similarity mentioned in the introduction between specifying, proving and
computing can rely on the notion of computational systems.

As already emphasized, we expect the ELAN system to provide a uniform framework for describing computational systems, experimenting new combinations and
performing proofs of their properties. Completion-based approaches implemented
in theorem provers like REVE, RRL or OTTER, to prove properties such as confluence or consistency of enrichments, can also be designed in the conceptual setting
of rewrite rules and strategies [1]. However, this view is not to obtain efficient
theorem provers at once, but rather first to allow for experiments and designs of
better proof strategies.

A complementary direction is worth considering to get high efficiency: this is the
parallelisation of deduction obtained for free through parallelisation of rewriting

(see [21, 24]). This argument that needs further investigations is an additional point in favor of the choice of the evaluation mechanism of ELAN.

Indeed some aspects of this work can be compared with other logical frameworks like ELF, proof development systems like NuPRL and interactive theorem provers like Isabelle, Clam or 2OBJ. However we think that, because of its emphasized ability to express, execute and combine computational systems and the crucial role of constraint solving, ELAN provides interesting and original features.

Acknowledgments

This work took great benefit from discussions with José Meseguer and we sincerely thank him for illuminating explanations on rewriting logic and stimulating comments on our own approach. We also thank Patrick Viry for his very pertinent comments on the previous version of this paper.

References

[1] L. Bachmair. *Canonical equational proofs*. Computer Science Logic, Progress in Theoretical Computer Science. Birkhäuser Verlag AG, 1991.

[2] L. Bachmair, H. Ganzinger, C. Lynch, and W. Snyder. Basic paramodulation and superposition. In *Proceedings 11th International Conference on Automated Deduction, Saratoga Springs (N.Y., USA)*, pages 462–476, 1992.

[3] F. Baader and K. Schulz. Unification in the union of disjoint equational theories: Combining decision procedures. In *Proceedings 11th International Conference on Automated Deduction, Saratoga Springs (N.Y., USA)*, pages 50–65, 1992.

[4] H. Comon. Equational formulas in order-sorted algebras. In Paterson, editor, *Proceedings ICALP'90*, volume 443 of *Lecture Notes in Computer Science*, pages 674–688. Springer-Verlag, 1990.

[5] H. Comon. Disunification: a survey. In J.-L. Lassez and G. Plotkin, editors, *Computational Logic. Essays in honor of Alan Robinson*, chapter 9, pages 322–359. MIT Press, Cambridge (MA, USA), 1991.

[6] N. Dershowitz and J.-P. Jouannaud. Rewrite Systems. In J. van Leuven, editor, *Handbook of Theoretical Computer Science*, chapter 6, pages 244–320. Elsevier Science Publishers B. V. (North-Holland), 1990.

[7] N. Dershowitz and D. A. Plaisted. Equational programming. In J. E. Hayes, D. Michie, and J. Richards, editors, *Machine Intelligence 11: The logic and acquisition of knowledge*, chapter 2, pages 21–56. Oxford Press, Oxford, 1988.

[8] J. A. Goguen, C. Kirchner, H. Kirchner, A. Mégrelis, J. Meseguer, and T. Winkler. An introduction to OBJ-3. In J.-P. Jouannaud and S. Kaplan, editors, *Proceedings 1st International Workshop on Conditional Term Rewriting Systems, Orsay (France)*, volume 308 of *Lecture Notes in Computer Science*, pages 258–263. Springer-Verlag, July 1987.

[9] J. A. Goguen and J. Meseguer. EQLOG: Equality, types and generic modules for logic programming. In D. De Groot and G. Lindstrom, editors, *Logic Programming. Functions, relations and equations*, pages 295–364. Prentice-Hall, 1986.

[10] J. A. Goguen. The rewrite rule machine project. In *Proceedings of the second international conference on supercomputing*, Santa Clara, California, May 1987.

[11] G. Huet and J.-J. Lévy. Computations in orthogonal rewriting systems, I. In J.-L. Lassez and G. Plotkin, editors, *Computational Logic*, chapter 11, pages 395–414. The MIT Press, 1991.

[12] J.-M. Hullot. Canonical forms and unification. In W. Bibel and R. Kowalski, editors, *Proceedings 5th International Conference on Automated Deduction, Les Arcs (France)*, volume 87 of *Lecture Notes in Computer Science*, pages 318–334. Springer-Verlag, July 1980.

[13] J.-P. Jouannaud and H. Kirchner. Completion of a set of rules modulo a set of equations. *SIAM Journal of Computing*, 15(4):1155–1194, 1986. Preliminary version in Proceedings 11th ACM Symposium on Principles of Programming Languages, Salt Lake City (USA), 1984.

[14] J.-P. Jouannaud and C. Kirchner. Solving equations in abstract algebras: a rule-based survey of unification. In J.-L. Lassez and G. Plotkin, editors, *Computational Logic. Essays in honor of Alan Robinson*, chapter 8, pages 257–321. MIT Press, Cambridge (MA, USA), 1991.

[15] J. Jaffar and J.-L. Lassez. Constraint logic programming. In *Proceedings of the 14th Annual ACM Symposium pn Principles Of Programming Languages*, pages 111–119, Munich (Germany), 1987.

[16] G. Kahn. Natural semantics. Technical Report 601, INRIA Sophia-Antipolis, February 1987.

[17] C. Kirchner. *Méthodes et outils de conception systématique d'algorithmes d'unification dans les théories équationnelles.* Thèse de Doctorat d'Etat, Université de Nancy I, 1985.

[18] C. Kirchner, H. Kirchner, and M. Rusinowitch. Deduction with symbolic constraints. *Revue d'Intelligence Artificielle*, 4(3):9–52, 1990. Special issue on Automatic Deduction.

[19] C. Kirchner, H. Kirchner, and M. Vittek. Implementing computational systems with constraints. In P. Kanellakis, J.-L. Lassez, and V. Saraswat, editors, *Proceedings of the first Workshop on Principles and Practice of Constraint Programming, Providence (R.I., USA)*, pages 166–175. Brown University, 1993.

[20] H. Kirchner and C. Ringeissen. A constraint solver in finite algebras and its combination with unification algorithms. In K. Apt, editor, *Proc. Joint International Conference and Symposium on Logic Programming*, pages 225–239. MIT Press, 1992.

[21] C. Kirchner and P. Viry. Implementing parallel rewriting. In B. Fronhöfer and G. Wrightson, editors, *Parallelization in Inference Systems*, volume 590 of *Lecture Notes in Artificial Intelligence*, pages 123–138. Springer-Verlag, 1992.

[22] P. Le Chenadec. On the logic of unification. In C. Kirchner, editor, *Unification*, pages 157–216. Academic Press, London, 1990.

[23] J. Meseguer. General logics. In H.-D. E. et al., editor, *Logic Colloquium'87*, pages 275–329. North-Holland, 1989.

[24] J. Meseguer. Conditional rewriting logic as a unified model of concurrency. *Theoretical Computer Science*, 96(1):73–155, 1992.

[25] Moreno-Navarro and Rodriquez-Artalejo. Logic programming with functions and predicates: the language BABEL. *Journal of Logic Programming*, 12(3):191–223, February 1992.

[26] N. Martì-Oliet and J. Meseguer. Rewriting logic as a logical and semantical framework. Technical report, SRI International, May 1993.

[27] R. Nieuwenhuis and A. Rubio. Theorem proving with ordering constrained clauses. In D. Kapur, editor, *Proceedings of CADE-11*, volume 607 of *Lecture Notes in Computer Science*, pages 477–491. Springer-Verlag, 1992.

[28] W. Nutt, P. Réty, and G. Smolka. Basic narrowing revisited. In C. Kirchner, editor, *Unification*, pages 517–540. Academic Press, London, 1990.

[29] C. Ringeissen. *Combinaison de Résolutions de Contraintes.* Thèse de Doctorat d'Université, Université de Nancy 1, December 1993.

[30] M. Vittek. *ELAN: Un cadre logique pour le prototypage de langages de programmation avec contraintes*. Thèse de Doctorat d'Université, Université de Nancy 1, to appear October 1994.

9 Aggregation in Constraint Databases

Gabriel M. Kuper

Abstract

We show how to add aggregation to a constraint database query language. One example of the use of aggregation in such a database is computing the area of a region in a geographic database. We show how aggregation can be added to the algebra and tuple calculus, and discuss the problems that arise from the interaction of aggregate operators and constraints.

9.1 Introduction

The idea of of combining relational databases with constraint formalisms is introduced in [6] (see also [5] [9]). The key idea is the generalization of the notion of a tuple to a conjunction of constraints.

One important aspect of relational databases that is missing in these papers is a discussion of how aggregate operators interact with constraints. In a standard relational database, typical aggregate operators are: **sum**, **average**, **max** and **count**. In a constraint database, besides these operations, we also want to compute functions such **length**, **area** and **volume**. Other possible aggregate operators include **nearest** (finding the object in the database closest to a given point or object), and averaging an attribute (such as rainfall) over a given region.

In this paper, we outline a method to add aggregation to the languages of [6]. Our approach generalizes the paper of Klug [8] to constraint databases. The current paper has three main parts: We first show how Klug's approach can be generalized to the constraint framework, considering only the semantics of the database, not its representation. We show how to generalize the relational algebra and calculus under this assumption. We then examine the consequences of requiring a finite representation for the result (the *closure* property). Our results here are negative: We show that for the **area** aggregate operator, the closure property does not hold for any of the interesting classes of constraints, i.e., dense order, linear, or polynomial constraints. The third part of the paper is devoted to a discussion of ways around this problem. They include restricting the query language, restricting the class of aggregate operators, and using a typed language to restrict the way aggregate operators can be used.

9.2   Constraint Databases

The classes of constraints that we consider in this paper are:

DEFINITION 9.1

1. *Real polynomial inequality constraints* are formulas of the form

$$p(x_1, \ldots, x_j) \; \theta \; 0$$

   where p is a polynomial with real coefficients and variables x_1, ..., x_j, and θ is one of $=$, $<$, $>$. The variables range over the domain D of real numbers.

2. *Dense linear order inequality constraints* are all formulas of the form $x\theta y$ and $x\theta c$, where x, y are variables, c is a constant, and θ is one of $=$, $<$, $>$. The variables range over a countably infinite set D (e.g., the rational numbers) with a binary relation $<$ that is a dense linear order.

3. *Linear inequality constraints* are all formulas of the form

$$f(x_1, \ldots, x_j) \; \theta \; 0$$

   where f is a linear combination, with real coefficients, of the variables x_1, ..., x_j, and θ is one of $=$, $<$, $>$. The variables range over the set D of real numbers.

The basic definitions of constraint databases are (see [6] for more details):

DEFINITION 9.2 Let Φ be a class of constraints.

1. A *generalized k-tuple* (over variables x_1, ..., x_k) is a finite conjunction $\varphi_1 \wedge \cdots \wedge \varphi_N$, where each $\varphi_i, 1 \le i \le N$, is a constraint in Φ. Furthermore, the variables in each φ_i are all free and among x_1, ..., x_k.

2. A *generalized relation of arity k* is a finite set $r = \{\psi_1, \ldots, \psi_M\}$, where each $\psi_i, 1 \le i \le M$ is a generalized k-tuple over the same variables x_1, ..., x_k.

3. The *formula corresponding to a generalized relation r* is the disjunction $\psi_1 \vee \cdots \vee \psi_M$. We use ϕ_r to denote the quantifier-free formula corresponding to relation r.

4. A *generalized database* is a finite set of generalized relations.□

In database theory, a k-ary relation r is a finite set of k-tuples (or points in a k-dimensional space) and a database is a finite set of relations. However, the relational calculus and algebra can be developed without the finiteness assumption for relations. We will use the term *unrestricted relation* for finite or infinite sets of points in a k-dimensional space. In order to be able to do something useful with such unrestricted relations, we need a finite representation that we can manipulate. This is exactly what the generalized tuples provide.

DEFINITION 9.3 Let Φ be a class of constraints interpreted over domain D, r a generalized relation of arity k with constraints in Φ, and let $\phi_r = \phi_r(x_1, \ldots, x_k)$ be the formula corresponding to r with free variables $x_1, \ldots, x_k$. The generalized relation r represents the unrestricted k-ary relation which consists of all $(a_1, \ldots, a_k)$ in D^k such that $\phi_r(a_1, \ldots, a_k)$ is true. A generalized database represents the finite set of unrestricted relations that are represented by its generalized relations. □

In [6] the relational tuple calculus is extended to generalized relations. This language is the same as the language we describe below, if we have no aggregate operators.

In the next two sections, we shall discuss the extension of the relational algebra and calculus with aggregation to unrestricted relations, i.e., we ignore, for now, the issue of representation of the result.

9.3   The Algebra

In [8], for each aggregate function, e.g., **sum**, we have a parameterized family of **sum** functions

$$\mathbf{sum}_1, \mathbf{sum}_2, \ldots, \mathbf{sum}_i, \ldots$$

$\mathbf{sum}_i$ sums the numbers in the ith column of its input, taking duplicates into account.

Aggregate functions such as **sum**, **count**, **average** are still available in our language, but they are defined only when the corresponding instances are finite. We also have aggregate functions such as **area**, **volume**, etc. Note that **area** is a *binary* function, and we therefore need to have a family of functions $\{\mathbf{area}_{i,j}\}$, where $\mathbf{area}_{i,j}$ computes the area of the set of points described by the ith and jth columns of the relation.

Note that this set of points can contain duplicates. The idea behind Klug's approach is to let the user specify whether duplicates should or should not be considered when applying the aggregate functions. We can allow this in our language by assigning a number to each point in the region, representing how many times it occurs. Under appropriate measurability assumptions (that hold for all the classes of constraints defined above), we can define the area as the integral of this function [3].

Some care is needed to ensure that queries are safe. Finite aggregation functions (such as **sum**) can only be applied when the corresponding relation is finite, and infinite functions (such as area) can only be applied when the result is well-defined (in this case, when the region is bounded). This is a topic that needs more research: For now, we shall assume that all queries, and all their subqueries, are well-defined. Our results show that the calculus/algebra equivalence holds for all queries that satisfy this assumption.

We now describe the algebra formally. We have a set

$$\text{Agg} = \{f_\alpha, f_\beta, \ldots\}$$

of aggregate functions. Each function is from the set of all relations to the domain D of the constraints. We need a "uniformness" condition, that basically says that whenever we have an aggregate function, such as **area**$_{1,2}$ in Agg, we also have "similar" functions **area**$_{i,j}$, for all $i \neq j$, that operate on all other possible sets of columns.

DEFINITION 9.4 Agg has the following property. For every $f \in Agg$, and every relation S, if S' is a constant expansion of S, i.e., if there is a projection such that $\Pi_X(S') = S$ and $\Pi_{\neg X}(S')$ contains exactly one tuple, then there is a $f' \in Agg$ such that $f(S) = f'(S')$.

DEFINITION 9.5 The relational algebra is defined in exactly the same way as for languages without aggregation, with the following additional rule.

- If e is a relational expression of arity n, X a sublist of e's attributes, and $f \in \text{Agg}$, then $e \langle X, f \rangle$ is a relational expression of arity $n + 1$.

The semantics of such an expression are defined as follows.

DEFINITION 9.6 Let e be a relational expression of arity n, let X, f be as above and let I be an instance. Then

$$e \langle X, f \rangle (I) = \{t[X] \circ y \mid t \in e(I) \wedge y = f(\{t' \mid t' \in e(I) \wedge t'[X] = t[X]\})\}$$

Note that f is applied to a set of tuples, rather than a multiset, and therefore that all duplicate *tuples* are removed. All treatment of duplicates is "hidden" in the definitions of the aggregate functions, since the set of columns on which the aggregation is actually performed may contain duplicates.

We illustrate the algebra by several examples, based on the rectangle example in [7].

EXAMPLE 9.1 Let $R(z, x, y)$ be a ternary relation that represents a set of rectangles. We interpret a tuple (z, x, y) in R to mean that (x, y) is a point in the rectangle with name z.

There are various ways in which we could apply the **area** function to this relation.

- Suppose we want to compute the area of each rectangle separately. In other words, we want to compute a relation $S(n, a)$, where a is the area of the rectangle with name n. This can be computed by the query

$$R \langle 1, \mathbf{area}_{2,3} \rangle$$

  i.e., for each z we compute the area of the set of points with name z.
- Now suppose that we are interested in the total area covered by the points of the database, counting points that are in several rectangles only once. We can do this by projecting R onto the second and third columns, thus generating a flat representation of the data, without the rectangle names. We then apply the aggregate operator to the result. Formally, the query is:

$$(\Pi_{2,3}(R)) \langle \emptyset, \mathbf{area}_{1,2} \rangle$$

- Finally, suppose that we want to compute the total area, but this time counting points that are in several rectangles multiple times. This is simply

$$R \langle \emptyset, \mathbf{area}_{2,3} \rangle$$

  since the aggregate operator is now applied without eliminating duplicate points. An alternative way to express this query would be to apply the **sum** operator to the result of the first example, i.e.,

$$R \langle 1, \mathbf{area}_{2,3} \rangle \langle \emptyset, \mathbf{sum}_2 \rangle$$

We should mention that even though this example is of a database of rectangles, the queries will also work for a database that consists of any type of geometric objects for which the **area** function is well-defined.

9.4 The Calculus

The definition of the calculus with aggregation is significantly more complicated than that of the relational calculus. Basically, the reason for this is that the relational calculus uses quantification only on the base relations. We, on the other hand, have to be able to quantify over relations that are the result of an aggregate operation, and the only way to do this is to actually compute the result. The calculus, therefore, has to have a way to construct intermediate relations.

For this reason, Klug's tuple calculus is defined via mutual recursion on 3 type of expressions: terms, formulas, and alphas. Closed alphas are the "top level", i.e., the queries themselves.

DEFINITION 9.7 A term is one of

- A constant
- $x.A$, where x is a (tuple) variable and A a column number
- $f(\alpha)$, where α is an alpha

DEFINITION 9.8 A formula is one of

- $\alpha(x)$, where α is a closed alpha, and x is a variable
- $\mu(t, \ldots, t_k)$ where μ is a constraint and $t_1, \ldots, t_k$ are terms
- Disjunctions and negation of formulas
- $(\exists r)\psi$, where ψ is a formula, and r a range formula.

Range formulas are defined as follows.

DEFINITION 9.9 Let x be a variable and let $\alpha_1, \ldots, \alpha_k$ be closed alphas. Then

$$\alpha_1(x) \vee \cdots \vee \alpha_k(x)$$

is a range formula.

Such a formula means that x is is in the union of the relations defined by the α_i's. Finally, we define alphas.

DEFINITION 9.10

- For each relation R symbol of arity i, R is an alpha of degree i.
- If $t_1, \ldots, t_n$ are terms, $r_1, \ldots, r_m$ are range formulas for the free variables in these terms, and ψ is a formula, then

$$(t_1, \ldots, t_n) : r_1, \ldots, r_m : \psi$$

is an alpha of degree n.

Free variables, closed objects, etc. are then defined as usual. The one subtle point is that a variable can be bound by a quantifier, or by being in the range fragment $(r_1, \ldots, r_m)$ of an alpha. In the latter case, variables in $t_1, \ldots, t_n$ also become bound.

We will not describe the semantics here; the corresponding definitions of [8] carry over with no problems.

EXAMPLE 9.2 We show how to express calculus queries equivalent to the algebraic queries in the previous example.

- Compute the area of each rectangle separately.

$$(x.1, (\mathbf{area}_{1,1}(y.2, y.3) : R(y) : y.1 = x.1)) : R(x) : -$$

- Total area, without duplications.

$$(\mathbf{area}_{1,2}((x.2, x.3) : R(x) : -)) : - : -$$

- Total area, with duplications.

$$(\mathbf{area}_{2,3}(R)) : - : -$$

The following example illustrates the advantages of the calculus over the algebra.

EXAMPLE 9.3 Consider a relation R that stores information about rainfall. R is a ternary relation, where (r, x, y) in R means that the total rainfall at point (x, y) was r. Suppose that we want to compute, for each r, the area of the region with total rainfall $\geq r$. This could be done by the following query

$$(x.1, \mathbf{area}_{1,2}((y.2, y.3) : R(y) : y.1 \geq x.1)) : R(x) : -$$

It would be much harder to express this query directly in the algebra.

In the result of this query, the first column only contains values that actually appear in the database. To be able to look up arbitrary values, we use the following query

$$(x, \mathbf{area}_{1,2}((y.2, y.3) : R(y) : y.1 \geq x)) : D(x) : -$$

where $D(x)$ means that x is in the domain D.

We can now show that the algebra and calculus are equivalent. Klug's proof works in our setting—the only things that have to be verified are that the proof does not depend on finiteness of the relations, or on the fact that aggregate functions have only one subscript. Note that we make rather stringent safety requirements, i.e., we show equivalence only between queries that are safe, and all of whose subqueries are safe. Further research is needed to see whether these requirements can be relaxed.

9.5   Closure under Aggregate Operations

So far, we have discussed the relational algebra and calculus on unrestricted relations. In constraint databases, we require that each relation instance be representable as a generalized relation. This means that the result of applying an aggregate operator to a generalized relation, must be a generalized relation. In other words, the result must be representable by the same class of constraints.

In this section, we show that for all the classes of constraints under consideration, this is false.

9.5.1   Linear Constraints

Let $R(x, y, z)$ be a ternary relation over the class of linear constraints, and suppose we want to compute, for each z, the area of the corresponding set of (x, y) points in R. This means that we want to evaluate the calculus query

$$(x.3, \mathbf{area}_{1,2}((y.1, y.2) : R(y) : y.3 = x.3)) : R(x) : -$$

or the (equivalent) algebraic query

$$R\,\langle 3, \mathbf{area}_{1,2}\rangle$$

Consider the following instance I of R

$$I = \{x - y - z \leq 0 \wedge x \geq 0 \wedge y \geq 0\}$$

The result of the query is a binary relation $S(z, t)$, where $S(z, t)$ holds iff $z^2 = 2t$, and this cannot be expressed using linear constraints.

Intuitively, this should not be too surprising. Computing are is basically the same as integrating a function—and of course the integral of a linear function is a quadratic one. It turns out, less intuitively, that the same problem arises for dense linear order and polynomial constraints.

9.5.2   Dense Linear Order

As before, let $R(x, y, z)$ be a ternary relation, with the same query,

$$R\,\langle 3, \mathbf{area}_{1,2}\rangle$$

Let I be the instance

$$I = \{0 < x < y < z < 1\}$$

The result once again is the binary relation $S(z, t)$ where $S(z, t)$ holds iff $z^2 = 2t$, and this cannot be expressed as a generalized relation using order constraints.

9.5.3   Polynomial Constraints

Let R be as before, with the same query $R\langle 3, \mathbf{area}_{1,2}\rangle$. Let I now be the instance

$$I = \left\{ \begin{array}{l} x^2 + y^2 \leq 1 \\ x \leq z \\ x, y, z \geq 0 \end{array} \right\}$$

The result is a relation $S(z,t)$ where $R(z,t)$ holds iff t is the area of the part of the unit circle that is above the x-axis, and between the lines $y = 0$ and $y = 1 - z$. This means that $S(z,t)$ holds iff

$$t = \int_0^{1-z} \sqrt{1 - x^2} dx$$

or

$$t = \frac{1}{2}\left((1-z)\sqrt{z(2-z)} + \sin^{-1}(1-z) \right)$$

This cannot be expressed by polynomial constraints.

9.6   Attempts to Deal with the Closure Problem

So far, we have seen that we can add aggregation to the query language with unrestricted relations, but that if we try to add aggregation to generalized relations we immediately encounter closure problems. This is clearly unsatisfactory. We describe three approaches to dealing with this problem: restricting the query language, restricting the aggregate operators, and restricting the interaction between the aggregation and the rest of the database, via typing.

9.6.1   Restricting the Query Language

It may well be the case, that for many applications, the full power of the relational query language with aggregation is not needed. For example, it might suffice to be able to apply the **area** operator as the final step of a query, without being interested about how the area varies with respect to some other parameter. In such a case the result would be a single number, or set of numbers, and no problems would arise.

We shall not discuss this approach in any more detail here. This approach will probably involve ad. hoc. decisions for specific applications, and at the present time it is not clear what general rules should be used to design such a query language. Some of the discussion in Section 6.3 is relevant to this approach as well.

9.6.2 Restricting the Aggregation Operators

The negative results in the previous section were for a specific aggregate operator **area**. A natural question to ask is whether there are any aggregate operators for which the corresponding query language is closed. In turns out that for the **max** operator, the language is indeed closed.

We outline a proof that the algebra with the **max** operator, over the domain of dense linear order constraints is closed. In fact, we actually show more than this. We show that the **max** operator can be defined directly in the language. This of course, immediately implies that the language with **max** is closed.

For example, suppose that R is a ternary relation. The query

$$R\langle 3, \mathbf{max}_2\rangle$$

is equivalent to the (calculus query,

$$\{(z, n) \mid (\exists x)R(x, n, z) \wedge (\forall x, y)(R(x, y, z) \rightarrow y \leq n))\}$$

and this is a relational calculus query without aggregation. It is not hard to generalize this to arbitrary relational queries with **max**.

An interesting problem is to characterize, for different classes of constraints, which aggregate operators satisfy the closure property. In particular, it is an open problem whether the query language is closed under *any* interesting aggregate operator that strictly increases the expressive power of the language. Some work in this direction is described in [1].

9.6.3 Using a Typed Language

Consider the **area** function. Up to now, we have assumed that **area** is a function from $\mathcal{P}(R \times R)$ to R. If we consider the physical units of the domain and range of **area**, we see that they are in fact different. Since arbitrary constraints between arguments that represent different physical dimensions have no physical meaning, there is no goo reason to allow such constraints in our language.

We propose that, by appropriate typing of the domains, we limit the way in which aggregate operators can be applied. This enables us to express many interesting queries, without the closure problem arising.

We illustrate this by an example. Consider a typed language with three types τ_1, τ_2, and τ_3. The interpretation of these types will be

- τ_1: Length. Constraints on variables of type τ_1 are polynomial constraints

- τ_2: Time. Constraints on variables of type τ_1 are dense linear order constraints

- τ_3: Area. Constraints on variables of type τ_1 are linear constraints

The **area** function is of type $2^{\tau_1 \times \tau_1} \to \tau_3$.

We do not allow arbitrary application of **area**–the set Agg contains functions **area**$_{i,j}$ only when columns i and j are of type τ_1 and the remaining columns are of type τ_2.

One example where such a language could be used is in a land use database. In such a database, the boundaries of the spatial regions change only at discrete points of time, and area is computed only relative to this parameter. On the other hand, in a meterological database, where the data varies continuously, this model would be inappropriate. We can then define an algebraic query language using these restricted aggregate functions, and this language will then be closed.

This has just been a rough sketch. More work is needed to formalize such a notion of typed language, to classify which typed languages and aggregate functions yield closed languages, and to define a tuple calculus equivalent to this typed algebra.

Acknowledgments

I would like to thank Paris Kanellakis for useful discussions, in particular for providing some of the motivation for this paper.

References

[1] J. Chomicki and G. M. Kuper, Measuring Infinite Relations. *in preparation.*

[2] M. Dincbas, et al. The Constraint Logic Programming Language CHIP. *Proc. Fifth Generation Computer Systems*, Tokyo Japan, 1988.

[3] P. Halmos. Measure Theory. *Van Nostrand Reinhold*, 1950.

[4] J. Jaffar, J.L. Lassez. Constraint Logic Programming. *Proc. 14th ACM POPL*, 111–119, 1987.

[5] P. C. Kanellakis and D. Q. Goldin. Constraint programming and database query languages. In *Proc. 2nd Conference on Theoretical Aspects of Computer Software (TACS)*, April 1994. (To appear in LNCS Spring-Verlag volume).

[6] P. Kanellakis, G. Kuper and P. Revesz. Constraint Query Languages. *Proc. 9th ACM PODS*, pp. 299–313, 1990.

[7] P. Kanellakis, G. Kuper and P. Revesz. Constraint Query Languages. JCSS, to appear.

[8] A. Klug. Equivalence of Relational Algebra and Relational Calculus Query Languages Having Aggregate Functions. *J. ACM* 29 (3), pp. 699–717, 1982.

[9] P.Z. Revesz. A Closed Form for Datalog Queries with Integer Order. *Proc. 3rd International Conference on Database Theory*, 1990.

[10] P. Van Hentenryck. *Constraint Satisfaction in Logic Programming*. MIT Press, 1989.

10 Synthesis of Constraint Algorithms

Douglas R. Smith and Stephen J. Westfold[1]

10.1 Introduction

In Constraint Programming, a constraint set partially characterizes objects of interest and their relationships. Constraint propagation is one of the key operations on constraints in Constraint Programming. As committments are made that further characterize some object, we want to infer consequences of those committments and add those consequences as new constraints. Efficiency concerns drive us to look closely at (1) the representation of constraints, (2) inference procedures for solving constraints and deriving consequences, and (3) the capture of inferred consequences as new constraints.

We report here on our current efforts at developing automated methods for deriving problem-specific constraint propagation code. This effort is part of a broader development of automated tools for transforming formal specifications into efficient and correct programs. The KIDS system [10] serves as the testbed for our experiments and provides tools for performing deductive inference, algorithm design, expression simplification, finite differencing, partial evaluation, data type refinement, and other transformations. We have used KIDS to derive over 60 algorithms for a wide variety of application domains, including scheduling, combinatorial design, sorting and searching, computational geometry, pattern matching, and mathematical programming.

A transportation scheduling problems motivated our constraint propagation work [11, 13]. We used KIDS semiautomatically to derive a global search (backtrack) scheduler. The derivation included inferring pruning conditions and generating constraint propagation code. The resulting code is given in [11] and has proved to be dramatically faster than other programs running the same data. The pruning and constraint propagation are so strong that the program does not backtrack on the data we have tried. For example, on a transportation problem involving 15,460 movement requirements obtained from the U.S. Transportation Command, the scheduler produces a complete feasible schedule in about one minute. A straightforward constraint network formulation based on this problem data would have over 31,000 variables and 120,125,000 constraints. Incorporating some of the structure

---

[1] This research was supported in part by the Office of Naval Research under Grant N00014-90-J-1733 and N00014-93-C-0056, in part by the Air Force Office of Scientific Research under Contract F49620-91-C-0073, and in part by DARPA/Rome Laboratories under Contract F30602-91-C-0043.

of the problem, such as the linearity of time, allows reformulating this to a system of about 108,700 constraints. However, this is still a such large formulation that it seems an implicit representation is necessary to find feasible schedules efficiently.

Any constraint programming system depends on an abstract datatype of constraints. What are some of the basic operations on constraints? First, constraints are expressed in the language of some theory (e.g. linear arithmetic with inequalities) and there must be a representation of constraints[2]. Second, in that theory there must be procedures for solving constraints and extracting solutions. Third, there must be a procedure for inferring consequences of constraints and capturing their content in a new constraint (perhaps by weakening or approximation). Fourth, there must be a way to compose two constraints (e.g. to assimilate a new constraint).

Current constraint programming languages, such as PROLOG III [2], CLP(R) [6], and CHIP [5], effectively carry out these operations via representations and operations specialized to the theory of the constraint language. However for the sake of efficiency it may be necessary to go farther and to design representations and operations that exploit not only the general background theory, but the intrinsic structure of the particular problem being solved.

10.2   Global Search Theory

Our studies of constraint propagation take place within a formal model of a class of constraint programs called *global search* algorithms. Global search generalizes the well-known algorithm concepts of binary search, backtrack, and branch-and-bound [9].

The basic idea of global search is to represent and manipulate sets of candidate solutions. The principal operations are to *extract* candidate solutions from a set and to *split* a set into subsets. Derived operations include (1) *filters* which are used to eliminate sets containing no feasible or optimal solutions, and (2) cutting constraints that are used to eliminate nonfeasible elements of a set of candidate solutions. Global search algorithms work as follows: starting from an initial set that contains all solutions to the given problem instance, the algorithm repeatedly extracts solutions, splits sets, eliminates sets via filters and propagates constraints until no sets remain to be split. The process is often described as a tree (or DAG) search in which a node represents a set of candidates and an arc represents the split

---

[2] We will not distinguish constraints and constraint sets, since a constraint set usually denotes the constraint that is a conjunction of the constituent constraints.

relationship between set and subset. The filters and constraint propagators serve to prune off branches of the tree that cannot lead to solutions.

The sets of candidate solutions are often infinite and even when finite they are rarely represented extensionally. Thus global search algorithms are based on an abstract data type of intensional representations called *space descriptors* (denoted by hatted symbols). The space descriptors can be thought of as constraints or representations of constraints.

Global search can be expressed axiomatically via a global search theory [9] which we elide here. In the following we present just those parts needed to discuss the formal derivation of constraint propagation code.

A problem can be specified by presenting an *input domain* D, an *output domain* R, and an *output condition* $O : D \times R \rightarrow boolean$. If $O(x, z)$ then we say z is a *feasible* solution with respect to input x. In other words, the output condition defines the conditions under which a candidate solution is feasible or acceptable. Global search theory extends the components of a problem with a datatype of *space descriptors* (constraint representations) $\hat{R}$ and a predicate *Satisfies* $: R \times \hat{R} \rightarrow boolean$ that gives the denotation of space descriptors; if *Satisfies*$(z, \hat{r})$ then z is in the set of candidate solutions denoted by $\hat{r}$ and we say that z satisfies $\hat{r}$. Also, the predicate *Split* $: D \times \hat{R} \times \hat{R} \rightarrow boolean$ is used to split a space descriptor into alternative subspace descriptors and the predicate *Extract* $: R \times \hat{R} \rightarrow boolean$ is used to extract solutions from a descriptor. $\hat{R}$ contains a distinguished space descriptor $\hat{r}_0$ that contains all feasible solutions. A basic global search program scheme follows:

$$F(x, z) \; :- \; F\_gs(x, \hat{r}_0(x), z)$$

$$F\_gs(x, \hat{r}, z) \; :- \; Extract(z, \hat{r}), \; O(x, z)$$

$$F\_gs(x, \hat{r}, z) \; :- \; Split(x, \hat{r}, \hat{s}), \; F\_gs(x, \hat{s}, z)$$

It can be proved within global search theory that this scheme is correct (see e.g. [9]), so that any instance of it can be used to enumerate all feasible solutions to a given problem. For details of the procedure for constructing global search theories for given problems see [9, 10, 12].

One version of the transportation scheduling problem can be specified as follows. The input is a set of movement requirements and a collection of transportation resources. A movement requirement is a record listing the type of cargo, its quantity, port of embarkation, port of debarkation, due date etc. Schedules are represented as maps from resources to sequences of trips, where each trip includes earliest-start-time, latest-start-time, port of embarkation, port of debarkation, and manifest (set of movement requirements). The type of schedules has the invariant (or subtype characteristic) that for each trip, the earliest-start-time is no later than the latest-start-time. A partial schedule is a schedule over a subset of the given movement records.

A variety of constraints characterize a feasible schedule for this problem, including:

1. *Consistent POE and POD* – The POE and POD of each movement requirement on a given trip of a resource must be the same.

2. *Consistent PAX and Cargo Capacity* – The capacity of each resource cannot be exceeded.

3. *Consistent Release Time* – The start time of a trip must not precede the available to load dates of any of the transported movement requirements.

4. *Consistent Arrival time* – The finish time of a trip must not precede the earliest arrival date of any of the transported movement requirements.

5. *Consistent Due time* – The finish time of a trip must not be later than the latest arrival date of any of the transported movement requirements.

6. *Consistent Trip Separation* – Movements scheduled on the same resource must start either simultaneously or with enough separation to allow for return trips. The inherently disjunctive and relative nature of this constraint makes it more difficult to satisfy than the others.

These constraints are expressed concisely as quantified first-order sentences.

A simple global search theory of transportation scheduling has the following form. A set of schedules is represented by a partial schedule. The split operation extends the partial schedule by adding one movement requirement in all possible ways. The initial set of schedules is described by the empty partial schedule – a map from each available resource to the empty sequence of trips. A partial schedule is extended by first selecting a movement record *mvr* to schedule, then selecting a resource *r*, and then a trip *t* on *r* (either an existing trip or a newly created one). Finally the extended schedule has *mvr* added to the manifest of trip *t* on resource *r*. The alternative ways that a partial schedule can be extended naturally gives rise to the branching structure underlying global search algorithms. The formal version of this global search theory of scheduling can be found in [11].

When a partial schedule is extended it is possible that some problem constraints are violated in such a way that further extension to a complete feasible schedule is impossible. In global search algorithms it is crucial to detect such violations as early as possible. The next two subsections discuss two general mechanisms for early detection of infeasibility and techniques for mechanically deriving them.

10.2.1   Pruning Mechanisms

Pruning tests are derived in the following way. Let x be a problem input and $\hat{r}$ be a space descriptor. The test

$$\exists(z : R)\ (Satisfies(z, \hat{r})\ \wedge\ O(x, z)) \tag{10.2.1}$$

decides whether there exist any feasible solutions satisfying $\hat{r}$. If we could decide 10.2.1 at each node of a global search algorithm then we would have perfect search – no deadend branches would ever be explored. In practice it would be impossible or horribly complex to compute it, so we rely instead on an inexpensive approximation to it. In fact, if we approximate (10.2.1) by weakening it (deriving a necessary condition of it) we obtain a sound pruning test. That is, suppose we can derive a test $\Phi(x, \hat{r})$ such that

$$\exists(z : R)\ (Satisfies(z, \hat{r})\ \wedge\ O(x, z))\ \implies\ \Phi(x, \hat{r}). \tag{10.2.2}$$

By the contrapositive of (10.2.2), if $\neg\Phi(x, \hat{r})$ then there are no feasible solutions satisfying $\hat{r}$, so we can eliminate $\hat{r}$ from further consideration. More generally, necessary conditions on the existence of feasible (or optimal) solutions below a node in a branching structure underlie pruning in backtracking and the bounding and dominance tests of branch-and-bound algorithms [9].

Pruning is incorporated into the basic global search program scheme as follows:

$$F(x, z) \ :-\ \Phi(x, \hat{r}_0(x), z),\ F\_gs(x, \hat{r}_0(x), z)$$

$$F\_gs(x, \hat{r}, z) \ :-\ Extract(z, \hat{r}),\ O(x, z)$$

$$F\_gs(x, \hat{r}, z) \ :-\ Split(x, \hat{r}, \hat{s}),\ \Phi(x, \hat{s}, z),\ F\_gs(x, \hat{s}, z).$$

It appears that the bottleneck analysis advocated in the constraint-directed search projects at CMU [4, 8] leads to a semantic approximation to (10.2.1) that is neither a necessary nor sufficient condition. Such a *heuristic* evaluation of a node is inherently fallible, but if the approximation to (10.2.1) is close enough it can provide good search control with relatively little backtracking.

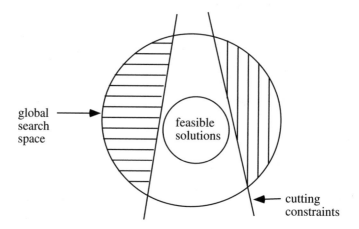

Figure 10.1
Global Search Subspace and Cutting Constraints

In KIDS, a filter Φ is derived using a general-purpose first-order inference system. The inference of Φ takes place within the theory of the specified problem. Potentially, any special problem structure captured by the axioms and theorems of this theory can be exploited to obtain strong problem-specific pruning mechanisms. Analogous comments apply to the constraint propagation mechanisms discussed next. For details of deriving pruning mechanisms for various problems see [9, 10].

10.2.2 Cutting Constraints and Constraint Propagation

Pruning has the effect of removing a node (set of solutions) from further consideration. In contrast, constraint propagation has the effect of changing the space descriptor so that it denotes a smaller set of candidate solutions. Constraint propagation is based on the notion of *cutting constraints* which are necessary conditions $\Psi(x, \hat{r})$ that all candidate solutions z satisfying $\hat{r}$ are feasible:

$$\forall(x : D, \hat{r} : \hat{R}) \ (\forall(z : R)(Satisfies(z, \hat{r}) \ \wedge \ O(x, z)) \ \Longrightarrow \ \Psi(x, \hat{r})) \tag{10.2.3}$$

The cutting constraint Ψ distinguishes subsets of solutions satisfying $\hat{r}$ that are all infeasible. So we can try to incorporate Ψ into $\hat{r}$ to obtain a new descriptor, without losing any feasible solutions. See Figure 10.1.

Constraint propagation can be characterized as the means to make Ψ an invariant of subspace descriptors. Assuming that $\hat{r}$ splits into $\hat{s}$ (so $\Psi(x, \hat{r})$ and $Split(x, \hat{r}, \hat{s})$),

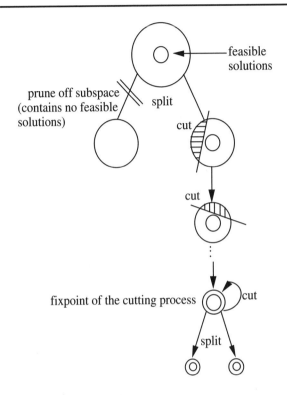

Figure 10.2
Pruning and Constraint Propagation

then $Propagate(x, \hat{s}, \hat{t})$ holds if $\hat{t}$ is a descriptor for a maximal size subset of $\hat{s}$ such that that $\Psi(x, \hat{t})$. *Propagate* is implemented as a fixpoint iteration where the iteration steps can be thought of as a collection of demons derived from Ψ – each is triggered by a violation of Ψ and has the effect of changing a variable component of $\hat{s}$ to restore the violated component (which can itself cause further violations and trigger other demons and so on.). See Figure 10.2.

Propagation is incorporated into the global search program scheme as follows:

$$F(x, z) \ : -$$
$$\quad \Phi(x, \hat{r}_0(x)),$$
$$\quad Propagate(x, \hat{r}_0(x), \hat{r}_0'),$$
$$\quad \hat{r}_0' \neq \perp,$$

$$F\_gs(x, \hat{r}_0', z)$$

$$F\_gs(x, \hat{r}, z) \ :- \ Extract(z, \hat{r}), \ O(x, z)$$

$$F\_gs(x, \hat{r}, z) \ :-$$
$$Split(x, \hat{r}, \hat{s}),$$
$$\Phi(x, \hat{s}),$$
$$Propagate(x, \hat{s}, \hat{t}),$$
$$\hat{t} \neq \bot,$$
$$F\_gs(x, \hat{t}, z).$$

The effect of constraint propagation is to spread information through the subspace descriptor resulting in a tighter descriptor and possibly exposing infeasibility. There are several reasons for constraint propagation. First, it shrinks the space of candidate solutions and may thus reduce the branching required to explore it. Second, the generated descriptors may be inconsistent ($\bot$), allowing early termination.

This model of constraint propagation generalizes the concepts of Gomory cutting planes [7] and the forms of propagation studied in the constraint satisfaction literature (e.g. [5]).

The mechanism for deriving cutting constraints is similar to (in fact a generalization of) that for deriving pruning mechanisms. For transportation scheduling, each iteration of the *Propagate* operation has the following form, where est_i denotes the earliest-start-time for trip i and est_i' denotes the next value of the earliest-start-time for trip i (analogously, lst_i denotes latest-start-time), and $roundtrip_i$ is the roundtrip time for trip i on resource r. For each resource r and the ith trip on r,

$$est_i' = max \begin{cases} est_i \\ est_{i-1} + roundtrip_i \\ max\text{--}release\text{--}time(manifest_i) \end{cases}$$

$$lst_i' = min \begin{cases} lst_i \\ lst_{i+1} - roundtrip_i \\ min\text{--}finish\text{--}time(manifest_i) \end{cases}$$

Here $max\text{--}release\text{--}time(manifest_i)$ computes the max over all of the release times of movement requirements in the manifest of trip i and $min\text{--}finish\text{--}time(manifest_i)$ computes the minimum of the finish times of movement requirements in the same manifest. Boundary cases must be handled appropriately.

After adding a new movement record to some trip, the effect o the *Propagate*
will be to shrink the

$$\langle earliest\text{--}start\text{--}time, latest\text{--}start\text{--}time\rangle$$

window of each trip on the same resource. If the window becomes negative for any
trip, then the partial schedule is necessarily infeasible and it can be pruned.

10.3   Concluding Remarks

The global search design tactic has been implemented in KIDS and extensively
tested [10]. The tactic has been recently extended to derive cutting constraints and
propagation code for various problems, including transportation scheduling.

The message of this work is that there are knowledge-based tools that can be
used to synthesize highly specialized and efficient implementations of constraint
programs. The idea is to exploit not only the structure of the theory within which
the constraints are stated, but the local theory of the particular problem being
solved. The local structure supports the inference of specialized pruning and constraint propagation code. The use of a datatype refinement system [1] also allows
specialized representations of objects, constraints, and efficient implementation of
their operations. The result can be much more efficient code than is possible using
general-purpose representations, solvers, and inference procedures.

Constraint propagation can be viewed as run-time inference. From this view
emerges the issue of how to design specialized inference procedures. Global search
theory provides a natural setting in which to explore constraint propagation algorithms. The resulting code is naturally expressed in constraint logic programming
languages.

References

[1] BLAINE, L., AND GOLDBERG, A. DTRE – a semi-automatic transformation
system. In *Constructing Programs from Specifications*, B. Möller, Ed. North-
Holland, Amsterdam, 1991, pp. 165–204.

[2] COLMERAUER, A. An introduction to PROLOG III. *Communications of the
ACM 33*, 7 (1990), 69–90.

[3] DINCBAS, M., VANHENTENRYCK, P., SIMONIS, H., AND AGGOUIN, A. The
constraint logic programming language CHIP. In *Proceedings of the Second In-*

ternational Conference on Fifth Generation Computer Systems (Tokyo, November 1988), pp. 249–264.

[4] Fox, M. S., Sadeh, N., and Baykan, C. Constrained heuristic search. In *Proceedings of the Eleventh International Joint Conference on Artificial Intelligence* (Detroit, MI, August 20–25, 1989), pp. 309–315.

[5] Hentenryck, P. V. *Constraint Satisfaction in Logic Programming*. Massachusetts Institute of Technology, Cambridge, MA, 1989.

[6] Jaffar, J., Michaylov, S., Stuckey, P., and Yap, R. The CLP(R) language and system. *ACM Transactions on Programming Languages and Systems 14*, 3 (July 1992), 339–395.

[7] Nemhauser, G. L., and Wolsey, L. A. *Integer and Combinatorial Optimization*. John Wiley & Sons, Inc., New York, 1988.

[8] Sadeh, N. Look-ahead techniques for micro-opportunistic job shop scheduling. Tech. Rep. CMU-CS-91-102, Carenegie-Mellon University, March 1991.

[9] Smith, D. R. Structure and design of global search algorithms. Tech. Rep. KES.U.87.12, Kestrel Institute, November 1987.

[10] Smith, D. R. KIDS – a semi-automatic program development system. *IEEE Transactions on Software Engineering Special Issue on Formal Methods in Software Engineering 16*, 9 (September 1990), 1024–1043.

[11] Smith, D. R. Transformational approach to scheduling. Tech. Rep. KES.U.92.2, Kestrel Institute, November 1992.

[12] Smith, D. R. Constructing specification morphisms. *Journal of Symbolic Computation, Special Issue on Automatic Programming 16*, 5-6 (June 1993).

[13] Smith, D. R., and Parra, E. A. Transformational approach to transportation scheduling. In *Proceedings of the Eighth Knowledge-Based Software Engineering Conference* (Chicago, IL, September 1993), pp. 60–68.

11 Exploiting Constraint Dependency Information for Debugging and Explanation

Walid T. Keirouz, Glenn A. Kramer, and Jahir Pabon

Abstract

Constraint programming is another form of programming and, as such, should be supported by appropriate environments that provide debugging, explanation and optimization capabilities. We are building tools needed for such an environment and using them in the context of geometric constraint programming for graphics and mechanical design. In this paper, we present the components of such an environment and their capabilities. We describe the use of constraint dependency graphs for debugging and explanation, and present an algorithm for identifying constraints that cause a model to be over-constrained.

11.1 Introduction

Constraints between entities in a model form a declarative specification used by a constraint solver to satisfy and maintain relations between entities in the model. The solution steps taken by a solver to satisfy these constraints can be collected in a "solution plan" and can be viewed as a procedural program for solving these constraints. Thus, a constraint model forms a declarative specification of a procedural program that is generated automatically to solve the model's constraints. As such, constraint programming is another form of programming and should be supported by appropriate environments for debugging, explanation and optimization. We are building tools needed in such an environment and using them in the context of geometric constraint programming for graphics and mechanical design.

Graphics was one of the first domains to which constraint-based techniques were applied [33, 3]. Since then, commercial constraint-based computer-aided design (CAD) systems have emerged [8]. While they are considered far superior to previous CAD tools, engineers experience difficulty understanding the constraint models that underlie their designs (constraints may be specified by users or inferred by CAD systems). At times, the constraints in a large model become so confusing that a designer might scrap a design and start anew [11]. Furthermore, when a designer returns to the same design several months later, there is no record of how the constraints were solved and what the design dependencies are; the designer must rediscover the original design intent.

People typically develop their own mental models of the plan generated by a constraint solver to satisfy constraints. However, these models often do not reflect the

Constraint name	Explanation
dist:point-point(G_1, G_2, d)	Distance between point G_1 and point G_2 is d.
dist:point-line(G_{pt}, G_ℓ, d)	Distance between point G_{pt} and line G_ℓ is d.
dist:point-plane(G_{pt}, G_{pl}, d)	Distance between point G_{pt} and plane G_{pl} is d.
dist:line-circle(G_ℓ, G_c, d)	Distance between line G_ℓ and circle G_c is d.*
angle:vec-vec(G_1, G_2, α)	Angle between vector G_1 and vector G_2 is α.

* In two dimensions, $d = 0$ represents a tangency constraint.

Table 11.1
Constraints used in GCE

true solution plan. The difficulties users encounter are then compounded because there is no way to view and understand the dependencies in the constraint models they have built.

11.2 Geometric Constraint Engine

We have developed a Geometric Constraint Engine (GCE) that is currently used in a sketching product [2]. GCE is based on research in the use of geometric constraints in kinematics and conceptual design [5, 9] and is described in detail in [6, 7]. We are exploring the use of constraint dependency information in the context of GCE.

GCE finds positions, orientations and dimensions of geometric entities in 3D that satisfy a set of constraints relating different entity features. Geometric entities can be nested hierarchically in a part-whole relationship; *aggregate* entities are composed of combinations of *primitive* ones—points, vectors and dimensions.

With the exception of dimensional constraints, all constraints used in GCE are binary constraints—they relate two geometric entities. These constraints may additionally involve real parameters. Examples of constraints used in GCE are shown in Table 11.1. Dimensional constraints are unary; they relate one geometric entity to a real-valued dimension parameter. Constraints may apply to subparts of a given entity. For example, to constrain two lines to be parallel, one constrains the vectors of those lines to have an angle of zero.

GCE addresses an issue currently outside the major focus of constraint-based systems research: solving highly nonlinear constraint problems over the domain of real numbers.[1] To solve these problems, GCE imposes an operational semantics for

---

[1] In the special volume of *Artificial Intelligence* concerned with constraint-based reasoning, seven of the eleven articles address the finite constraint satisfaction problem [1]. Three of the remaining four address problems using a (linear) interval representation, while [7] addresses non-

constraint satisfaction in the geometry domain. It does so by employing a metaphor of *incremental assembly;* geometric entities are moved to satisfy constraints in an incremental manner. The assembly process is virtual, as geometric entities are treated as *ghost* objects that can pass through each other during assembly. Such an assumption is allowed because the goal of the constraint satisfaction process is to determine globally-consistent locations of the geometric entities rather than the paths required for a physical assembly of that geometry.

GCE assembles geometric entities incrementally to satisfy the constraints acting on them. As the objects are assembled, their degrees of freedom are consumed by the constraints, and geometric invariants are imposed. An operational semantics is imposed: *measurements* and *actions* are used to satisfy each individual constraint. GCE uses information about an entity's degrees of freedom to decide which constraint to solve and to ensure that an action being applied to a geometric entity does not invalidate any geometric invariants imposed by previously-satisfied constraints. This ensures that the solution algorithm is confluent.

The solution algorithm in GCE can handle fully- as well as under- and over-constrained models. The solution of a set of constraints can be captured as a plan that may be replayed to satisfy the constraints when one or more numerical constraint parameters are changed.[2]

11.3 Reasoning Tasks for Constraint Models

The reasoning performed on a constraint model depends on the state of that model. This section enumerates and discusses the various states of constraint models. The following notation will be used: $\mathbf{ls}_i$ denotes line segment i; $\mathbf{l}_i\mathbf{p}_1$ denotes end-point 1 of $\mathbf{ls}_i$; $\mathbf{l}_i\mathbf{p}_2$ denotes end-point 2 of $\mathbf{ls}_i$; $\mathbf{v}_i$ denotes the direction vector of $\mathbf{ls}_i$. In the examples in Figure 11.1, a tick mark in the center of a line segment denotes a fixed dimension constraint for the line segment, an arc with label α_{ij} denotes an angle constraint between the vectors of $\mathbf{ls}_i$ and $\mathbf{ls}_j$, and coincident end-points in the figure indicate a coincidence constraint exists between those end-points.

11.3.1 States of Constraint Models

A constraint model is *fully constrained* when there are no remaining degrees of freedom after all constraints have been satisfied, and where no constraint in the

---

linear real-valued CSPs.

[2]Note that some parameter changes can alter the topology of the constraint problem and hence require finding another plan. For example, in a **dist:point-point** constraint, changing the distance parameter from zero to non-zero alters the degrees of freedom removed by the constraint.

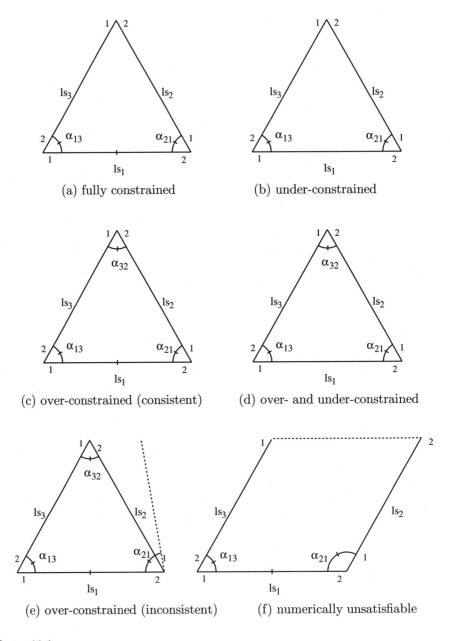

Figure 11.1
Various states of geometric constraint systems

system is redundant. An example is shown in Figure 11.1(a). Here, the length of $\mathbf{ls}_1$ is fixed and two angles are known. This corresponds to using the "angle-side-angle" formula of elementary geometry to find all parts of a triangle.

A constraint model may be *under-constrained*. Figure 11.1(b) is similar to Figure 11.1(a) except that the dimension of $\mathbf{ls}_1$ has been freed. This example describes an infinite family of "similar" triangles, which can be parameterized by fixing the length of any one of the three line segments.

Over-constrained models result from adding more constraints to a fully constrained model (or by adding a constraint restricting m degrees of freedom to a model with n remaining degrees of freedom, where $m > n$). Figure 11.1(c) is similar to Figure 11.1(a), except that constraint α_{32} has been added. In this case, we have chosen α_{32} to be equal to $\pi - (\alpha_{13} + \alpha_{21})$ so the model is numerically consistent. Identifying and correctly solving such cases is important in real-world design (*e.g.*, only one hinge is needed to hold a door on a frame in a constraint-based world; the remaining hinges are mathematically redundant, but are quite useful in the physical world).

Over- and under-constrained situations can coexist in the same constraint model. Figure 11.1(d) shows such an example. The angles are over-constrained but consistent, as in Figure 11.1(c), but the lengths are under-constrained as in Figure 11.1(b).

An over-constrained model can also be *inconsistent*, as shown in Figure 11.1(e). Here, the three angle constraints do not sum to π. If α_{13} and α_{32} are satisfied, the problem is fully constrained. When α_{21} is asserted, $\mathbf{ls}_2$ would need to be rotated to the dashed position to satisfy the new constraint. However, $\mathbf{ls}_2$ is already fully constrained and hence cannot move to the new position.

Fully constrained systems can be *numerically unsatisfiable*, as shown in Figure 11.1(f). Here, α_{13} and α_{21} are chosen so that $\mathbf{ls}_3$ and $\mathbf{ls}_2$, both still of indeterminate length, are parallel. Thus, the desired coincidence constraint between $l_3\mathbf{p}_1$ and $l_2\mathbf{p}_2$, shown as a dashed line, cannot be satisfied. The number of degrees of freedom removed from the system by the constraints is the same as in Figure 11.1(a); only the numerical values have changed.

11.3.2 Reasoning Tasks for Consistent Models

For fully- and under-constrained models, a user may want to replay the solution with different parameter values. Single stepping through the constraint solution can help explain the solution to the user, and allow exploration alternative solutions (by varying the constraint set).

For over-constrained but consistent models, the user may want to compute the sets of over-constraining constraints to determine which constraints should be removed from the model. The user may also want to replay portions of the solution, perhaps in single-step mode, to help explain where the over-constraint lies.

11.3.3 Reasoning Tasks for Inconsistent Models

There are two modes of failure for constraint models. The first one is when the model is over-constrained and inconsistent because of a conflict between some constraints in the model. The model cannot be made consistent unless some constraints are removed from the model.

In this case, the model's *over-constraining set* of constraints must be identified, and one or more constraints from this set must be selected and removed from the model to alleviate the over-constrained situation. The over-constraining set is defined as the set of constraints C such that only retraction of constraints in C can remove the source of over-constraint, and retraction of any constraint not in C has no effect on the over-constraint. This set includes, but is not limited to, the most recently added constraint[3] and the constraints with which it conflicts directly.

The second failure mode is when a model is not over-constrained, but cannot be satisfied due to numerical inconsistencies. In this case, we can identify the unsatisfiable constraints. A plan stepper, which is described below, can then be used to explain where and why the conflict arises.

11.4 Constraint Dependency Graphs

A constraint system's solution algorithm solves the constraints in a "particular" order that respects the dependencies built into the model and captures this order in a solution plan. However, the order of solving constraints, as encoded in the captured plan, is only one of many possible orders in which the constraints may be solved. Ordering relationships can be extracted from the solution plan and collected into a dependency graph for the constraint model. The solution plan then describes one of several possible traversals of the nodes in the graph.

Dependency graphs provide a mechanism for constraint dependency analysis which supports debugging and explanation, consistency analysis, user interaction, parameterization of models, and computational optimization.

Example: an Over-Constrained Model

Figure 11.2 shows an over-constrained model. The two triangles are fully determined by the coincidence constraints for the line segments' end-points, and by the

---

[3]Assuming the constraint system is solved each time a new constraint is added.

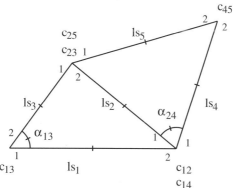

Figure 11.2
An over-constrained model.

lengths of the line segments (all of which are fixed). The notation c_{ij} indicates one end-point of $\mathbf{ls}_i$ is coincident with one end-point of $\mathbf{ls}_j$; the end-points are numbered in the diagram. $\mathbf{l}_1\mathbf{p}_1$ and $\mathbf{v}_1$ are fixed in space, which "grounds" the assembly in space. The two angle constraints are then added; these are redundant and lead to over-constraint. While these angle constraints are the direct cause of the over-constraint, removing other constraints could alleviate the problem just as easily.[4]

Figure 11.3 shows the dependency graph for the model of Figure 11.2. A special node labeled "S" (for "Start"), is the source node. Square nodes indicate constraints, while circular nodes indicate primitive geometric entities whose locations have become known—or fixed—by having been moved to satisfy the constraint immediately preceding it in the graph.

The constraint nodes labeled "g" depict the unary constraints which ground the location of $\mathbf{l}_1\mathbf{p}_1$ and the orientation of $\mathbf{v}_1$, as well as the dimensions of all the line segments. The c_{ij} and α_{ij} nodes correspond to the constraints in Figure 11.2. The square nodes marked "I" denote *inference* nodes: since the representation of line segments is redundant, some information can be inferred after a constraint is satisfied. For example, given $\mathbf{l}_1\mathbf{p}_1$, $\mathbf{v}_1$ and dimension $\mathbf{d}_1$, the location of the other end-point $\mathbf{l}_1\mathbf{p}_2$ may be inferred.

In this graph, the dimensions $\mathbf{d}_2$ and $\mathbf{d}_5$ are found through two different paths (one by grounding, and another by inference from other knowns). These nodes indicate two areas of over-constraint in the model. Each will have its own over-constraining set which will be derived in Section 11.5.1.

---

[4]Removing the constraints grounding the assembly in space does not effect the over-constrained situation and leads to an under- and over-constrained model.

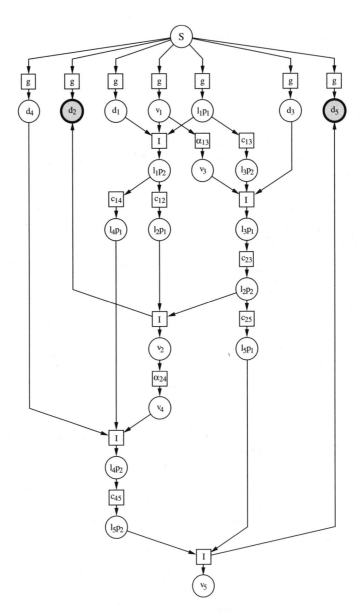

Figure 11.3
Dependency graph of example of Figure 11.2.

11.5   Debugging and Explanation

Debugging and explanation involve analyzing the consistency of a constraint model and identifying the over-constraint sets if needed, analyzing the degrees of freedom in the model, and replaying and modifying the order in which the constraints are solved.

11.5.1   Over-Constrained Models

Although an over-constrained situation is directly caused by the addition of a single constraint to a model, several constraints are involved in such a situation. The over-constraining set consists of the constraint that "caused" the over-constraint and a subset of the model's constraints that conflict with that constraint, directly or indirectly. Selecting one constraint from this set and removing it[5] from the model reduces the over-constrained state to a fully- or under-constrained one. We must now identify the over-constraining set; a potentially different set exists for each over-constrained situation within the same model.

The over-constraint set for an over-constrained situation can be computed by exhaustively searching for the constraints whose removal from the model eliminates the over-constrained situation. However, this approach is computationally very expensive and does not take advantage of the information encoded in the dependency graphs. We have developed an algorithm for identifying over-constraint sets for a restrictive class of constraint models; this algorithm is described below.

Over-Constraint Set Algorithm

Consider the case of the twice-determined dimension d_2. One determination of d_2 comes from the inference node that points to d_2. That inference node states that if l_2p_1 and l_2p_2 are both known, then we can determine d_2 and v_2. If this inference were not possible, then the source of over-constraint would disappear. We indicate this on the graph of Figure 11.4 by "reversing" the direction of the arc (originally from "I" to d_2) to be from d_2 to the "I" node. Continuing the reasoning, the inference would not be possible if *either* l_2p_1 or l_2p_2 were unknown. This is indicated by reversing both arcs. Continuing backward from l_2p_1, this point's location would not be known if l_1p_2 were unknown, so removing the coincident constraint c_{12} would alleviate the over-constraint.

This chain of reasoning continues back through d_1, but not through v_1 or l_1p_1. The reason is due to the reconvergence of the fanout at those nodes where informa-

---

[5]Or altering its numerical parameters such that the constraint removes fewer degrees of freedom.

tion, derived from a given node, v_1, and used in two separate chains of constraint solution, is recombined by an inference node later on. The cycles created when reversing arcs along a solution chain violates the causality that is used in performing the various inferences captured in the dependency graph. The concept is analogous to the notion of reconvergent fanout in the digital test generation literature [4]. The algorithm for finding the over-constraining set is then as follows:

1. Beginning with the node at which the over-constraint is detected (*i.e.*, the node which has two arcs leading to it), flip the arcs backward through the next set of nodes.

2. Continue reversing the arcs backward until a node is reached where there is reconvergent fanout (such a node is guaranteed to exist due to the existence of node "S").

3. All constraints for which both input and output arcs are members of the set of reversed arcs are members of the over-constraining set.

The over-constraining sets for the graph of Figure 11.3 are depicted in Figure 11.4. The set in long dashes corresponds to the constraints that over-determine d_2. The set in short dashes corresponds to the constraints that over-determine d_5. Note that the reconvergent fanout termination criterion for arc reversal is considered separately for each over-constraining set, *i.e.*, two reversed arcs, one from the d_2 set and one from the d_5 set, do not interact and hence are not reconvergent.

Note that the over-constraint of d_5 has no dependence on d_2, although the over-constraining sets have members in common. One might conclude that, since ls_2 is a part of triangle $\langle ls_1, ls_2, ls_3 \rangle$ (call it **T1**) and that triangle $\langle ls_2, ls_4, ls_5 \rangle$(call it **T2**) depends on triangle **T1**, that the over-constraint of **T2** would be dependent on everything in **T1**. However, a closer examination of the particular constraints shows that, even if d_2 were not specified, the location of l_2p_2 would be found. Also, **T2** is not dependent on l_2p_1 at all; rather it is dependent on the location of l_1p_2, to which l_2p_1 is made coincident.

Some of the constraints identified may remove more degrees of freedom than occur in the the over-constrained situation; removing such a constraint would result in an under-constrained model. For example, the over-determination of d_2 indicates over-constraint of one degree of freedom. Thus, removing an angle constraint like α_{13} removes the over-constraint, but removing a coincidence constraint such as c_{12} removes two degrees of freedom, leading to under-constraint. To avoid this, our tools will suggest altering the constraint to require a non-zero distance between l_1p_2 and l_2p_1, which relaxes one degree of freedom. Such suggestions are easy to

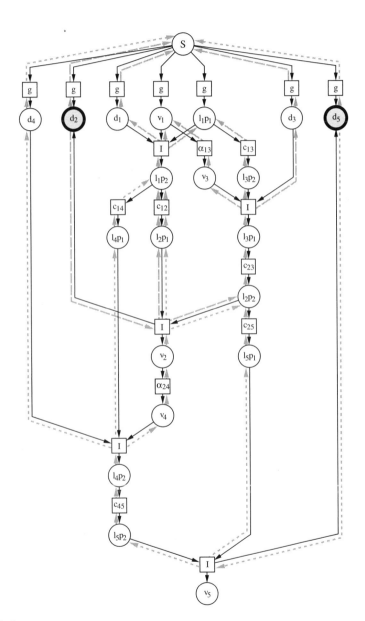

Figure 11.4
Over-constraining sets for the dependency graph of Figure 11.3.

make automatically.

From a theoretical point of view, all the constraints in an over-constraining set are candidates for removal from a model. However, these sets may need to be filtered depending on the context. For example, in geometric constraint models, constraints that reflect topological relationships (*e.g.*, coincident-points constraints) may have precedence over constraints that specify dimensions.

Limitations of Algorithm

At present, we have studied the case where the constraints can be solved by pure propagation; we have not yet explored solutions which require the hierarchical structuring utilized by GCE's strategies of loop and chain analyses. Furthermore, the algorithm described above does not identify the *true* over-constraining set. It omits constraints that contribute to the over-constraint but whose removal would require loop or chain analysis to solve the constraint system. We are currently working to extend the algorithms to handle these cases.

11.5.2   Plan Stepper and Debugger

Since a constraint solution plan is a procedural program that is generated automatically, we are exploring the creation of tools, similar to conventional programming tools, for assisting users in understanding what the program does and how it was generated. One such tool is a *plan debugger* which will provide facilities found in debuggers for procedural programming languages: stepping forward and backward, setting breakpoints, and examining the status of constraints and constrained entities.

A plan debugger uses the already-generated plan to allow a user to replay the plan in single-step mode and review the choices made by the constraint solver when it was generating the plan. The constraint solver may be able to solve more than one constraint at a time, but "arbitrarily" chooses one of the possible constraints at each choice point. These choices reflect the fact that a plan is one possible traversal of the dependency graph. A user may also explore alternative traversals of the dependency graph by modifying the choices made by the constraint solver. Exploring alternative solution orders may give the user insight into the nature of conflicting or unsatisfiable constraints. The debugger calls on the solver to add a new branch to the plan if the user's new choice has not been explored before.

11.5.3   Parameterizing Under-Constrained Models

An under-constrained model may be parameterized by identifying a set of independent model parameters that can be used to determine, completely and irredundantly, the behavior of the model. These parameters represent the degrees of freedom remaining in the model after all of its constraints have been satisfied.

In the graphics and geometric modeling domains, GCE adds "defaulting" constraints to a model whenever it runs out of constraints to solve and there are still some remaining degrees of freedom in the model [7]. Each defaulting constraint consumes one degree of freedom of a geometric entity. Defaulting constraints allow GCE to generate a solution to the now fully-constrained model and tell the user the number of remaining degrees of freedom that may be consumed by additional constraints. These constraints are captured in the solution plan.

11.5.4   Improving Computational Efficiency

The dependency graph of a constraint model specifies a partial order for satisfying the constraints in the model. This partial order can be used to parallelize the solution of the constraint model. Subgraphs in a dependency graph, which correspond to subplans in the solution, can be traversed in parallel and provide coarse grain parallelism.[6] As in dataflow models of parallelism, fine grain parallelism can be identified because the solution of a constraint may proceed as soon as its predecessors in the dependency graph have been satisfied.

The dependency graph may also be used to minimize regeneration of a solution plan when a constraint is added or removed from a model. Graph traversal algorithms can identify portions of the dependency graph that are not affected by the addition or removal of a constraint from a model. The new solution plan reuses the unaffected portion of the previous solution plan (i.e., the unaffected constraints are satisfied) and proceeds to solve the remaining constraints.

11.6   Conclusion

Constraint dependency information can be exploited in a number of areas: debugging and explanation of constraints, consistency analysis, parameterization of models, and computational optimization. As such, the explicit representation of this information in a dependency graph is valuable. The results obtained so far look promising and warrant further study.

---

[6]Subgraphs result from the hierarchical strategies of chain analysis and loop analysis used in GCE. These are not discussed in this paper due to space limitations.

References

[1] *Artificial Intelligence* (Special Volume: Constraint-Based Reasoning), volume 58, December 1992.

[2] Laureen Belleville. Applicon's intelligent approach to modeling. *Computer Graphics World*, page 17, November 1992.

[3] Alan H. Borning. *ThingLab: A Constraint-Oriented Simulation Laboratory.* PhD thesis, Stanford University, July 1979.

[4] Melvin A. Breuer and Arthur D. Friedman. *Diagnosis and Reliable Design of Digital Systems.* Computer Science Press, Rockville, MD, 1976.

[5] Glenn Kramer. Solving geometric constraint systems. In *Proceedings of the 8th National Conference on Artificial Intelligence*, pages 708–714, Boston, MA, August 1990. American Association for Artificial Intelligence, MIT Press.

[6] Glenn Kramer. *Solving Geometric Constraint Systems: A Case Study in Kinematics.* MIT Press, Cambridge, MA, 1992.

[7] Glenn A. Kramer. A geometric constraint engine. *Artificial Intelligence*, 58:327–360, December 1992.

[8] Robert Mills. Terms of endearment. *Computer-Aided Engineering*, pages 48, 50, 54, October 1992.

[9] Jahir Pabon, Robert Young, and Walid Keirouz. Integrating parametric geometry, features, and variational modeling for conceptual design. *Systems Automation: Research and Applications*, 2:17–36, 1992.

[10] Ivan E. Sutherland. *Sketchpad: A Man-Machine Graphical Communication System.* PhD thesis, Massachusetts Institute of Technology, Cambridge, MA, 1963.

[11] Cynthia Tee. Human factors in geometric feature visualization. Master's thesis, Massachusetts Institute of Technology, Cambridge, MA, June 1992.

12 Constraining the Structure and Style of Object-Oriented Programs

Scott Meyers, Carolyn K. Duby, and Steven P. Reiss

Abstract

Object-oriented languages fail to provide software developers with a way to say many of the things about their systems that they need to be able to say. To address this need, we have designed and implemented a language for use with C++ that allows software developers to express a wide variety of constraints on the designs and implementations of the systems they build. Our language is specifically designed for use with C++, but the issues it addresses are applicable to other object-oriented languages, and the fundamental software architecture used to implement our system could be applied without modification to similar constraint languages for other object-oriented programming languages.

12.1 Introduction

C++ is an expressive language, but it does not allow software developers to say many of the things about their systems that they need to be able to say. In particular, C++ offers no way to express many important constraints on a system's design, implementation, and stylistic conventions. Consider the following sample constraints, none of which can be expressed in C++:

- *The member function M in class C must be redefined in all classes derived from C.* This is an example of a **design constraint**, because the constraint is specific to a particular class, C, and a particular function in that class, M. This kind of constraint is common in general-purpose class libraries. For example, the NIH class library [7] contains many functions which must always be redefined if the library is to function correctly.

- *If a class declares a pointer member, it must also declare an assignment operator and a copy constructor.* This is an example of design-independent **implementation constraint**. Failure to adhere to this constraint almost always leads to incorrect program behavior [17].

- *All class names must begin with an upper case letter.* This is an example of one of the most common kinds of **stylistic constraint**. Most software development teams adopt some set of naming conventions that developers are required to follow.

Constraints such as these exist (usually only implicitly) in virtually every system implemented in C++, but different systems require very different sets of constraints. That fact makes it untenable for C++ compilers to search for constraint violations. Our approach to this problem is the development of a new language, CCEL ("Cecil") — the C++ Constraint Expression Language — a language for use with C++ that allows software developers to specify a wide variety of constraints and to automatically detect violations of those constraints.

We took as our original inspiration the lint tool for C programmers, but we quickly discovered that the kinds of errors C programmers need to detect are qualitatively different from the errors that C++ programmers need to detect [18]. lint concentrates on type mismatches and data-flow anomalies, but the stronger typing of C++ obviates the need for lint's type-checking, and data flow analysis is typically unrelated to the high-level perspective encouraged by the modular constructs of C++. Instead, C++ programmers are concerned with concepts such as the structure of a design-specific inheritance hierarchy, but lint offers no provision for design-specific error detection. The most fundamental difference, then, between lint and CCEL is that CCEL was designed from the outset to allow for the addition of *programmer-defined* constraints.

An earlier working paper describing CCEL has already been published [5], but since the time of that publication we have made significant improvements to both the language and the software architecture built around it. Such improvements include a simpler, more uniform syntax; a set of predefined types that is more expressive and is easier to understand and use; and an implementation architecture that is more portable, more robust, and has a more convenient user interface.

12.2   Design Considerations, Syntax, and Semantics

Our primary requirements in designing CCEL were these:

- It must offer sufficient expressive power to allow programmers to specify a wide variety of constraints, including constraints on both concrete syntax (stylistic constraints) and semantics (design and implementation constraints).

- It must be relatively easy to learn and use. In particular, the syntax and semantics of the language should mesh well with the syntax and semantics of C++. We chose as our point of departure C++ itself and the well-known assert macro.

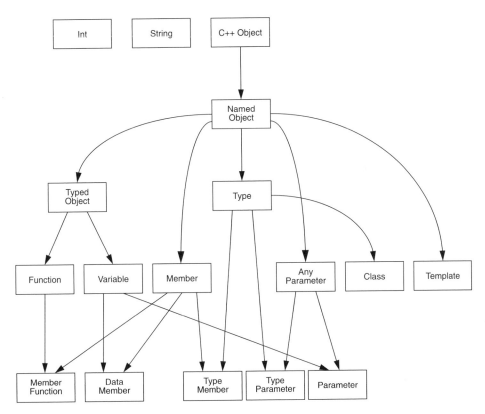

Figure 12.1
CCEL Class Hierarchy

Like the programs C++ is used to build, CCEL has an object-oriented basis. CCEL classes represent the concepts of C++. The CCEL classes are arranged in a multiple inheritance "isa" hierarchy (see Figure 12.1), and each class supports a particular set of member functions (see Tables 12.1 and 12.2).

Syntactically, CCEL constraints resemble expressions in the predicate calculus, allowing programmers to make assertions involving existentially or universally quantified CCEL variables. In general, constraint violations are reported for each combination of CCEL variable bindings that causes an assertion to evaluate to false.

There are five parts to a CCEL constraint:

1. A unique *identifer* that serves as the name of the constraint.

CCEL Class	Member Function
AnyParameter	Int position()
C++Object	String file()
	Int begin_line()
	Int end_line()
Class	
DataMember	
Function	Int num_params()
	Int is_inline()
	Int is_friend(Class)
Int	Int operator == (Int)
	Int operator < (Int)
	Int operator ! ()
	Int operator && (Int)
	Int operator || (Int)
	Int operator != (Int)
	Int operator > (Int)
	Int operator <= (Int)
	Int operator >= (Int)
Member	Int is_private()
	Int is_protected()
	Int is_public()
MemberFunction	Int is_virtual()
	Int is_pure_virtual()
	Int overrides(MemberFunction)
NamedObject	String name()
	Int scope_is_global()
	Int scope_is_file()
Parameter	Int has_default_value()
String	Int operator == (String)
	Int operator < (String)
	Int matches(String)
	String operator + (String)
	Int operator != (String)
	Int operator > (String)
	Int operator <= (String)
	Int operator >= (String)

Table 12.1
CCEL Class Member Functions

CCEL Class	Member Function
Template	Int is_class_template()
	Int is_function_template()
Type	Int has_name(String)
	Type basic_type()
	Int operator == (Type)
	Int is_convertible_to(Type)
	Int is_enum()
	Int is_class()
	Int is_struct()
	Int is_union()
	Int is_friend(Class)
	Int is_child(Class)
	Int is_descendant(Class)
	Int is_virtual_descendant(Class)
	Int is_public_descendant(Class)
	Int operator != (Type)
TypedObject	Type type()
	Int num_indirections()
	Int is_reference()
	Int is_static()
	Int is_volatile()
	Int is_const()
	Int is_array()
	Int is_long()
	Int is_short()
	Int is_signed()
	Int is_unsigned()
	Int is_pointer()
TypeMember	
TypeParameter	
Variable	Int scope_is_local()

Table 12.2
CCEL Class Member Functions (continued)

2. A set of *declarations* for universally quantified CCEL variables. Such variables take as their values components of C++ programs. Each CCEL variable has a type; this type is one of the CCEL classes shown in Figure 12.1.

3. An *assertion* that comprises the essence of the constraint. Assertions may use universally quantified CCEL variables and may declare and use existentially quantified CCEL variables.

4. A *scope specification* that determines the region of applicability of the constraint in relation to the C++ source being checked. By default, constraints are globally applicable, but they may be restricted on the bases of file, function, or class names.

5. A *message specification* describing how violations of the constraint should be reported.

Of these five parts, only the constraint identifier and the assertion are required. If omitted, the set of CCEL variables is empty, the scope of applicability is global, and constraint violations are indicated by a message in a default format.

As an example of a CCEL constraint, consider Meyers' admonition [17] that every base class in C++ should declare a virtual destructor:

```
BaseClassDtor (
    Class B;
    Class D | D.is_descendant(B);
    Assert(MemberFunction B::m; |
        m.name() == "~" + B.name() &&
        m.is_virtual());
);
```

This constraint is called "BaseClassDtor":
For all classes B,
for all classes D such that D is a descendant of B,
there must exist a member function m in B such
that m's name is a tilde followed by B's name and
m is a virtual function.

Within this constraint, the variables B and D are universally quantified,[1] and m is existentially quantified. The scope of the constraint has been omitted, so it applies to all classes. The violation message has also been omitted.

The assertion inside a constraint is evaluated only if it is possible to find a binding for each of the universally quantified variables declared in the constraint. It can therefore be useful to write constraints containing assertions that always fail, the goal being to detect the ability to bind to a universally quantified variable. For example, class templates in C++ may take either type or non-type parameters, but function templates may take only type parameters, and this inconsistency (as well

---

[1] B and D are both of type Class, which technically corresponds to C++ classes, structs, and unions, i.e., any language construct that may contain member functions. Hence B and D may be bound to any of these language constructs. This use of the term "class" is consistent with that employed by the C++ language reference manual [6]. Member functions in the CCEL class Class allow programmers to distinguish between C++ classes, structs, and unions.

as other considerations) may make it advisable to avoid non-type parameters in templates of any kind. This rule can be formalized in CCEL as follows:

```
// Templates should take only type parameters:
TypeParametersOnly (
    Template t;                          For all templates t and
    Parameter t<p>;                      all non-type parameters p of t,
    Assert(FALSE);                       issue a violation message.
);
```

Individual constraints are useful, but it is often convenient to group constraints together. This is especially the case with stylistic constraints, because a consistent style can typically be achieved only through adherence to a number of individual constraints. CCEL provides for this grouping capability through support for *constraint classes*, which comprise a set of individual constraints. For example, suppose there are several constraints on naming conventions. They could be grouped together into a constraint class called NamingConventions:

```
NamingConventions {
    // Every class name must begin with an upper case letter:
    CapitalizeClassNames (
        Class C;
        Assert(C.name().matches("^[A-Z]"));
    );

    // Every function name must begin with a lower case letter:
    SmallFunctionNames (
        Function F;
        Assert(F.name().matches("^[a-z]"));
    );
};
```

Syntactically, the extent of constraint classes is demarcated by brackets {...}, while individual constraints use parentheses as their delimiters.

Sometimes what is a single conceptual constraint is best expressed using a set of simpler constraints bundled into a constraint class. The following example consists of a pair of constraints that detects undeclared assignment operators for classes that contain a pointer member or are derived from classes containing a pointer member. This is an important constraint in real-world C++ programs [17] and is one that cannot be specified in C++ itself:

```
PointersAndAssignment {
    // If a class contains a pointer member, it must declare an assignment operator:
    AssignmentMustBeDeclaredCond1 (
        Class C;
        DataMember C::cmv | cmv.is_pointer();
        Assert(MemberFunction C::cmf; | cmf.name() == "operator=");
    );

    // If a class inherits from a class containing a pointer member, the
    // derived class must declare an assignment operator:
    AssignmentMustBeDeclaredCond2 (
        Class B;
        Class D | D.is_descendant(B);
        DataMember B::bmv | bmv.is_pointer();
        Assert(MemberFunction D::dmf; | dmf.name() == "operator=");
    );
};
```

By default, a constraint applies to all code in the system. This is not always desirable. For example, a programmer might have one set of naming conventions for a class library and a different set of naming conventions for application-specific classes. CCEL explicitly provides for the need to restrict the applicability of constraints to subsets of the system being checked. In particular, the scope of a constraint may be restricted on the bases of file, function, and/or class names. For file names, scopes are specified in terms of UNIX shell wildcard expressions. For function and class names, scopes are specified in terms of UNIX regular expressions. For example, if we wanted to limit the applicability of CapitalizeClassNames to the file file.h, we could declare a scope for the constraint. Such scope specifications precede the name of the constraint:

```
    // The name of every class declared in "file.h" must begin with a capital letter:
    File "file.h" : CapitalizeClassNames (
        Class C;
        Assert(C.name().matches("^[A-Z]"));
);
```

Sometimes it is more convenient to specify where an otherwise global constraint does *not* apply. This can be accomplished by creating a new constraint with a restricted scope of application. The new constraint does nothing but *disable* the constraint that should not apply to the specified scope. Such disabling occurs through the Disable keyword. For example, to set things up so that CapitalizeClassNames applies to every C++ class *except* class X, we could disable CapitalizeClassNames for that class as follows (note the use of a regular expression to specify only the class name "X"):

```
// Do not report violations of CapitalizeClassNames in class X:
Class "^X$" : DontCapitalizeInX (
  Disable CapitalizeClassNames;
);
```

Like individual constraints, constraint classes may be disabled. This is most frequently combined with a scoping specification:

```
// Ignore naming conventions for the file "importedFromC.h":
File "importedFromC.h" : NamingConventionsOff (
  Disable NamingConventions;
);
```

Individual members of a constraint class may be disabled by referring to them using the C++ scoping operator("::"):

```
// Turn off the constraint NamingConventions::CapitalizeClassNames for file.h only:
File "file.h" : SomeNamingConventionsOff (
  Disable NamingConventions::CapitalizeClassNames;
);
```

When a constraint violation is detected, a message to that effect is issued identifying the location of the CCEL constraint, the name of the C++ object bound to each universally quantified variable, and the location of each object so bound. Locations consist of a file name and a line number corresponding to the beginning of the source code for the object being identified. For example, consider this declaration for an array template:

```
template<class T, int size> class BoundedArray { ... };
```

This template violates the TypeParametersOnly constraint discussed earlier, so a violation message in the following format would be issued:

"constraints.ccel", line 100: TypeParametersOnly violated:
   t = BoundedArray ("BArray.h", line 15)
   p = size ("BArray.h", line 15)

CCEL allows this default message format to be overridden by a programmer-defined format on a per-constraint basis. Details are available in the CCEL language specification [10].

12.3   A Software Architecture

The architecture for our prototype constraint-checking environment is shown in Figure 12.2. CCEL constraints may be specified in one or more files and/or within a C++ program in the form of specially formatted comments. All features of CCEL may be used inside C++ source, but we expect programmers will use this capability primarily to specify constraints specific to a class or file, i.e. to associate a constraint with the C++ source to which it applies. For example, a constraint stating that all subclasses of a class must redefine a particular member function might be best put in the C++ source file for the class so that programmers know that they will need to define that member function. A more generic constraint, such as that every class name must begin with an upper case letter, might go in a file containing nothing but stylistic constraints.

The constraints specified in CCEL constraint files and the constraints specified in special comments in C++ source code together comprise the set of applicable constraints for the software system to be checked. This set of constraints is brought together by a program called gather that creates from the possibly many CCEL and C++ source files a single database of CCEL constraints. gather invokes the C++ preprocessor on its input files prior to constructing the constraint database, so the power of the preprocessor is available for use in conjunction with CCEL itself.

The constraint database generated by gather is one of two inputs to ccheck, which is the program that actually determines whether any constraints have been violated. ccheck's second input is the name of an "oracle" about the C++ system being checked. The oracle is in essence a virtual database system containing information about C++ programs. There are many actual database systems containing such information (e.g., Reprise[21], CIA++[8], and XREFDB[13]), and our virtual database interface allows us to decouple ccheck from any particular database. In

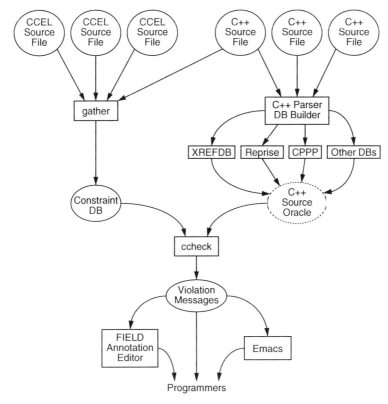

Figure 12.2
CCEL System Architecture

fact, our eventual virtual database interface will be OQL [20], a virtual interface to many database systems. For the time being, however, we are using XREFDB as our repository of information about C++ programs.

The output of ccheck is a series of violation messages. These may be viewed in their raw textual form, or they may be parsed by higher-level tools, such as Emacs [23] or the annotation editor inside FIELD [19]. Use of such tools allows programmers to see not only CCEL constraint violation diagnostics, but also the CCEL and C++ sources giving rise to the violations. This makes it much easier to locate and eliminate errors.

Our earlier working paper [5] described a prototype implementation of CCEL that was less elaborate than that shown in Figure 12.2. We are currently implementing a second-generation prototype that corresponds to the current (much expanded) language specification [10] and that, as noted above, is based on XREFDB.

12.4 Examples

The CCEL constraints that follow serve to demonstrate not only the expressiveness of CCEL itself, but also the kinds of constraints that C++ programmers might well want to express.

The following two constraints are taken from Meyers' book [17]:

```
// Subclasses must never redefine an inherited non-virtual
// member function:
NoNonVirtualRedefines (
    Class B;
    Class D | D.is_descendant(B);
    MemberFunction B::bmf;
    MemberFunction D::dmf | dmf.overrides(bmf);
    Assert(bmf.is_virtual());
);

// The return type of operator= must be a reference to the class:
ReturnTypeOfAssignmentOp (
    Class C;
    MemberFunction C::mf | mf.name() == "operator=";
    Assert(mf.is_reference() && mf.type().basic_type() == C);
);
```

The constraint that structs in C++ should be the same as structs in C (useful for maintaining data structure compatibility between the two) consists of three separate constraints: (1) no struct may contain a non-public member, (2) no struct may contain a function member, and (3) no struct may have a base class. These constraints may be combined into a single constraint class StructsAreSimple as follows:

```
// Structs in C++ should be just like structs in C:
StructsAreSimple {

    Class s | s.is_struct();

    AllMembersPublic (
```

```
        DataMember s::mv;
        Assert(mv.is_public());
    );

    NoMemberFunctions (
        MemberFunction s::mf;
        Assert(FALSE);
    );

    NoBaseClasses (
        Class base | s.is_descendant(base);
        Assert(FALSE);
    );
};
```

Here is another constraint from Meyers' book, this one also employing a constraint class:

```
// All classes declaring or inheriting a pointer member must
// declare a copy constructor:
NecessaryCopyConstructors {

  // All classes declaring a pointer member must declare
  // a copy ctor:
  PtrDeclImpliesCopyCtor (
      Class C;
      DataMember C::mv | mv.is_pointer();
      Assert(MemberFunction C::mf; Parameter mf(p); |
              mf.name() == C.name() && mf.num_params() == 1  &&
              p.type().basic_type() == C && p.is_reference() &&
              p.is_const());
  );

  // All classes inheriting a pointer member must declare
  // a copy ctor:
  InherPtrImpliesCopyCtor (
      Class B;
      Class D | D.is_descendant(B);
      DataMember B::mv | mv.is_pointer();
```

```
    Assert(MemberFunction D::mf; Parameter mf(p); |
            mf.name() == D.name() && mf.num_params() == 1  &&
            p.type().basic_type() == D && p.is_reference() &&
            p.is_const());
  );
};
```

The following constraint enforces a common rule of style:

```
// Members must be declared in this order:
//      public, protected, private:
MemberDeclOrdering {

    Class  C;
    Member C::pub  | pub.is_public();
    Member C::prot | prot.is_protected();
    Member C::priv | priv.is_private();

    PublicBeforeProtected (
        Assert(pub.begin_line() < prot.begin_line());
    );

    PublicBeforePrivate (
        Assert(pub.begin_line() < priv.begin_line());
    );

    ProtectedBeforePrivate (
        Assert(prot.begin_line() < priv.begin_line());
    );
};
```

12.5   Application to Other Languages

The classes supported by CCEL and the member functions of those classes are
clearly specific to C++. The more fundamental design principles behind CCEL,
however, apply equally well to other object-oriented languages. The kinds of constraints described earlier exist for languages like Smalltalk and CLOS as much as
they do for C++ [11]. The desireability of choosing a syntax, semantics, and conceptual model that is familiar to programmers is as important for an Eiffel constraint

language as it is for CCEL. The software engineering considerations that allow
CCEL constraints to be bundled into constraint classes, to be explicitly disabled,
and to have user-specified scopes and violation messages are as important for Object Pascal programmers as they are for C++ software developers. Furthermore, the
software architecture depicted in Figure 12.2 contains nothing that tailors it to the
idiosyncrasies of C++. In short, the primary design considerations — both in terms
of the language itself and the implementation of that language — are divorced from
the specifics of C++ and can be directly applied to constraint languages for other
object-oriented languages.

12.6   Related Work

In their analysis of the CLOS Metaobject Protocol [11], Kiczales and Lamping
identified a number of issues germane to the design of extensible class libraries,
and they proposed a set of informal techniques by which to specify requirements
and restrictions on classes inheriting from the library. CCEL is an important step
towards formalizing such requirements and restrictions and toward making them
amenable to automatic verification.

Support for formal design constraints in the form of assertions or annotations
was designed into Eiffel [15], has been grafted onto Ada in the language Anna [14],
and has been proposed for C++ in the form of A++ [3, 2]. This work, however,
has grown out of the theory of abstract data types, and has tended to limit itself
to formally specifying the semantics of individual functions and/or collections of
functions (e.g., how the member functions within a class relate to one another).
In general, violations of these kinds of constraints can only be detected at run-
time. Our work on CCEL has a different focus. We are interested in constraints
whose violations can be detected at compile time, and we are further interested in
addressing the need to constrain relationships between classes, which Eiffel, A++,
and Anna are unable to do. CCEL can also express constraints on the concrete
syntax of C++ source code (e.g., CCEL class-specific naming conventions); this is
also outside the purview of semantics-based constraint systems.

The commercial product CodeCheck [4] allows for the specification of user-defined
constraints in a similar spirit as CCEL, but the model behind CodeCheck is procedural, not object-oriented. This is a reflection of the fact that CodeCheck was
originally designed to express constraints on C programs.

Formal specification languages such as Z [22], VDM [24], and Larch [9] are designed to allow developers to specify the behavior of software systems independent

of the language(s) used to implement the systems. Such specification languages can express a wide variety of powerful constraints, but their semantic model and syntactic appearance is unfamiliar to most practicing programmers, and as a result they have not seen wide adoption. CCEL, though less expressive than general-purpose specification languages, is at once simpler and more intuitive for C++ programmers, and we believe this will lead to its being more readily embraced by the development community.

Acknowledgments

Several people not listed as authors on this paper have made important contributions to the CCEL project. Yueh hong Lin made important design decisions affecting the current state of the CCEL language, and he wrote the formal language specification. Anir Chowdhury implemented gather, and he compiled a list of many of the programming guidelines we have used to make sure that CCEL has practical applicability. Joshua Spiewak implemented much of ccheck, and Supriya Wickrematillake is currently in the process of implementing the CCEL-to-emacs interface. Support for this research was provided by the NSF under grants CCR 9111507 and CCR 9113226, by ARPA order 8225, and by ONR grant N00014-91-J-4052.

References

[1] David R. Barstow, Howard E. Shrobe, and Erik Sandewall, editors. *Interactive Programming Environments*. McGraw-Hill, 1984.

[2] Marshall P. Cline and Doug Lea. The Behavior of C++ Classes. In *Proceedings of the Symposium on Object-Oriented Programming Emphasizing Practical Applications (SOOPPA)*, pages 81–91, September 1990.

[3] Marshall P. Cline and Doug Lea. Using Annotated C++. In *Proceedings of C++ at Work - '90*, pages 65–71, September 1990.

[4] Loren Cobb. *C Code Analysis Using Codecheck*. Abraxas Software, 1992.

[5] Carolyn K. Duby, Scott Meyers, and Steven P. Reiss. CCEL: A Metalanguage for C++. In *USENIX C++ Conference Proceedings*, August 1992. Also available as Brown University Computer Science Department Technical Report CS-92-51, October 1992.

[6] Margaret A. Ellis and Bjarne Stroustrup. *The Annotated C++ Reference Manual*. Addison Wesley, 1990.

[7] Keith E. Gorlen, Sanford M. Orlow, and Perry S. Plexico. *Data Abstraction and Object-Oriented Programming in C++*. John Wiley & Sons, 1990.

[8] Judith E. Grass and Yih-Farn Chen. The C++ Information Abstractor.

[9] John V. Guttag, James J. Horning, and Jeannette M. Wing. The Larch Family of Specification Languages. *IEEE Software*, September 1985.

[10] Yueh hong Lin and Scott Meyers. CCEL: The C++ Constraint Expression Language. Technical Report CS-93-23, Brown University Department of Computer Science, May 1993.

[11] Gregor Kiczales and John Lamping. Issues in the Design and Specification of Class Libraries. In Andreas Paepcke, editor, *Proceedings of the 1992 Conference on Object-Oriented Programming Systems, Languages and Applications (OOPSLA '92)*, pages 435–451, October 1992.

[12] Moises Lejter, Scott Meyers, and Steven P. Reiss. Adding Semantic Information To C++ Development Environments. In *Proceedings of C++ at Work - '90*, pages 103–108, September 1990.

[13] Moises Lejter, Scott Meyers, and Steven P. Reiss. Support for Maintaining Object-Oriented Programs. *IEEE Transactions on Software Engineering*, 18(12), December 1992. Also available as Brown University Computer Science Department Technical Report CS-91-52, August 1991. An earlier version of this paper appeared in the *Proceedings of the 1991 Conference on Software Maintenance* (CSM '91), October 1991. The paper is largely drawn from two other papers [16, 12].

[14] D. Luckham, F. von Henke, B. Krieg-Bruckner, and O. Owe. *Anna, A Language for Annotating Ada Programs: Reference Manual*, volume 260 of *Lecture Notes in Computer Science*. Springer-Verlag, 1987.

[15] Bertrand Meyer. *Object-Oriented Software Construction*. Prentice Hall International Series in Computer Science. Prentice Hall, 1988.

[16] Scott Meyers. Working with Object-Oriented Programs: The View from the Trenches is Not Always Pretty. In *Proceedings of the Symposium on Object-Oriented Programming Emphasizing Practical Applications (SOOPPA)*, pages 51–65, September 1990.

[17] Scott Meyers. *Effective C++: 50 Specific Ways to Improve Your Programs and Designs*. Addison-Wesley, 1992.

[18] Scott Meyers and Moises Lejter. Automatic Detection of C++ Programming Errors: Initial Thoughts on a lint++. In *USENIX C++ Conference Proceedings*, pages 29–40, April 1991. Also available as Brown University Computer Science Department Technical Report CS-91-51, August 1991.

[19] Steven P. Reiss. Connecting Tools using Message Passing in the FIELD Program Development Environment. *IEEE Software*, pages 57–67, July 1990. Also available as Brown University Computer Science Department Technical Report CS-88-18, "Integration Mechanisms in the FIELD Environment," October 1988.

[20] Steven P. Reiss and Manojit Sarkar. Generating Program Abstractions. Working paper, September 1992.

[21] David S. Rosenblum and Alexander L. Wolf. Representing Semantically Analyzed C++ Code with Reprise. In *USENIX C++ Conference Proceedings*, pages 119–134, April 1991.

[22] J. M. Spivey. *Understanding Z : A Specification Language and its Formal Semantics*. Cambridge University Press, 1988.

[23] Richard M. Stallman. EMACS: The Extensible, Customizable, Self-Documenting Display Editor. In *Proceedings of the ACM SIGPLAN/SIGOA Symposium on text Manipulation*, pages 147–156, June 1981. Reprinted in [1, pp. 300–325].

[24] *VDM '90: VDM and Z: Formal Methods in Software Development: Third International Symposium of VDM Europe*, 1990. Held in Kiel, Germany, April 17-21.

IV CONSTRAINT-SOLVING ALGORITHMS

13 An Approach for Solving Systems of Parametric Polynomial Equations

Deepak Kapur[1]

13.1 Abstract

An approach for solving nonlinear polynomial equations involving parameters is proposed. A distinction is made between parameters and variables. The objective is to generate from a system of parametric equations, solved forms from which solutions for specific values of parameters can be obtained without much additional computations. It should be possible to analyze the parametrized solved forms so that it can be determined for different parameter values whether there are infinitely many solutions, finitely many solutions, or no solutions at all. The approach is illustrated for two different symbolic methods for solving parametric equations – Gröbner basis computations and characteristic set computations. These methods are illustrated on a number of examples.

13.2 Introduction

Many complex phenomena can be modeled using nonlinear polynomial equations. Examples include imaging transformations in computer vision, computing geometric invariants, geometric and solid modeling, constraint-based modeling, reasoning about geometry problems, properties of chemical equilibrium, kinematics, robotics; an interested reader may consult [13, 14, 7, 5] for many examples. Variables in these equations can be classified into two subsets: *independent* variables and *dependent* variables. Independent variables often correspond to input to a phenomenon or the features of a physical subsystem in a phenomenon. Henceforth, independent variables will also be called *parameters*; dependent variables will be called just *variables* . For different parameter values, dependent variables have different behavior. A designer is usually interested in studying the phenomenon on a wide range of parameter values.

Given as input is a system of polynomial equations in variables and parameters, henceforth called a *system of parametric equations.* In certain cases, a set of constraints on parameters specifying parameter values of interest may be given sep-

[1]Supported in part by a grant from United States Air Force Office of Scientific Research AFOSR-91-0361. This approach was first discussed in September 1990 in a proposal entitled *Integrated Symbolical and Numerical Methods for Advanced Computer Vision* to the United Air Force Office of Scientific Research. A preliminary version of this paper was presented at the Chinese Academy of Science, Chengdu, China, in July 1992.

arately as part of the input. An equation can be viewed as a nonlinear polynomial equation in variables, with the coefficient of a term in a polynomial being an expression (henceforth called a *parametric constraint expression* or simply a *constraint* purely in terms of parameters).[2] Instead of having to repeatedly solve polynomial equations for many different specific parameter values, the objective is to solve the equations once for all, and compute solved parametric forms. Solutions for specific parameter values can be obtained from a solved parametric form without much additional computations.

A simple approach for solving systems of parametric equations is proposed. The approach is used first to develop an algorithm for computing a *parametric Gröbner basis* from a system of parametric polynomials. The construction is illustrated using many examples. Then the approach is used to develop an algorithm for computing a *parametric characteristic set*. For this construction, the discussion is brief because of space limitations. The construction is illustrated using an example. More details can be found in an expanded version of this paper [9]. From a parametric Gröbner basis and characteristic set, solutions of parametric polynomial equations can be extracted.

The discussion in this paper is limited to parametric constraints expressed as polynomials over the parameters. When parameters are specialized to specific concrete values from some ground field, then a constraint expression evaluates to a value in the ground field also; the ground field used in this paper is that of the field of complex numbers. The proposed approach should be applicable for more general parametric constraints also (in particular, constraint expressions could be transcendental, trigonometric or radical expressions, or even differential polynomials) insofar as they constrain the coefficients of the polynomials, and constraints can be manipulated to determine whether they are consistent or not.

13.2.1   Properties of Solved Parametric Forms

Below are listed desirable features of a solver for a system of parametric equations and the output generated by the solver.

1. The output should be in a solved form with constraints on parameters. The output should be in sufficient detail so that for particular parameter values, minimal (preferably no) additional computation has to be performed to obtain a solved form from which solutions can be extracted. For example, a

---

[2]We apologize for the abuse of the terminology since often by a constraint, we would mean a formula and not a constraint expression. We are hoping that the context would be able to disambiguate the use of the phrase constraint without causing any confusion.

parametric Gröbner basis should remain a Gröbner basis under a *specialization*, i.e. when specific values for parameters are substituted. A parametric characteristic set should remain a characteristic set under a specialization.

2. The output should generate results for all possible values of parameters (that satisfy the constraints on parameters in case such constraints are specified as a part of the input).

3. Parametric constraints under which the system of equations does not have a solution should be clearly identified, and should not be mixed with parametric constraints for which the system has a solution.

4. Parametric constraints under which the system of equations has finitely many solutions should also be separately identified, and not mixed with parametric constraints for which the system has infinitely many solutions. It will be preferred that a solver does not mix parametric constraints leading to solution spaces of different dimensions.

13.2.2   Overview of the Approach

The approach discussed here is straightforward and easy to understand. Polynomial computations are performed by making assumptions about the parametric constraint expressions arising in the leading coefficient of the polynomials. For Gröbner basis constructions, polynomials are manipulated in their distributed representation, whereas for characteristic set constructions, polynomials are manipulated in their recursive representation. Assumptions about parametric constraint expressions are collected as constraint sets. The concept of a constrained polynomial is introduced as a pair consisting of a finite set of constraints and a polynomial such that the coefficients of its terms are interpreted with respect to the constraint set.

The leading coefficient of a constrained polynomial may or may not be nonzero with respect to its associated constraint set. If the leading coefficient cannot be determined to be nonzero with respect to its constraint set, the constrained polynomial is considered ambiguous; otherwise, it is considered unambiguous. Additional constrained polynomials may be generated from an ambiguous constrained polynomial by extending its constraint set to make its leading coefficient nonzero. Apart from that, the basic structure of computations generated by algorithms remains the same.

For Gröbner basis construction, the concepts of reduction (simplification) of a constrained polynomial by another constrained polynomial and S-polynomial of constrained polynomials are defined. For characteristic set construction, the concept of a chain of constrained polynomials and pseudodivision of a constrained polynomial using the chain are defined. In the exposition here, algorithmic aspects have been emphasized rather than theoretical aspects because algorithmic constructions are viewed as the main contributions of the paper. Theoretical results are essentially obtained in a straightforward way by modifying proofs for Gröbner basis and characteristic set constructions on polynomial systems so that they work for parameterized systems. The reader is assumed to be familiar with Gröbner basis and characteristic set constructions; otherwise, the reader can consult an introductory paper by Kapur and Lakshman [10].

13.2.3   Organization

In the next section, assumptions about constraints on parameters are stated. Minimal requirements on a constraint solver are discussed. The notion of constrained polynomials is introduced. The definitions of degree, head term, head coefficient, and head monomial are extended to constrained polynomials in distributed representation. Unambiguous and ambiguous constrained polynomials are defined.

Section 13.3 extends Gröbner basis constructions to constrained polynomials. Key concepts such as S-polynomials and reduction are extended. A parametric Gröbner basis is defined for a set of parametric polynomials. Parametric Gröbner bases can be used for analyzing solutions of parametric polynomials, computing dimension, and other properties of solution sets. These constructions are illustrated on a number of examples.

Section 13.4 extends characteristic sets to constrained polynomials. Degree, head term, initial, class, etc. are defined for constrained polynomials in recursive representation. Definitions of pseudodivision and chains are extended to work on constrained polynomials. Parametric characteristic sets in Wu's sense are defined. They can be used to analyze solutions of parametric polynomial equations. An example illustrating the construction is briefly discussed.

During the development of this approach, we came to know about related approaches for linear equations by Sit [16, 17], and for nonlinear polynomial equations based on Wu's characteristic set method by Chou and Gao [4], and also for nonlinear polynomial equations based on the Gröbner basis method by Weispfenning [18]. Apart from the fact that the proposed approach is simpler and easier to understand, there appear to be considerable differences between the methods outlined here and in the above cited papers. Some of these differences are illustrated later using examples.

13.3   Constraints and Constrained Polynomials

13.3.1   Constraints

A constraint is, in general, viewed as a formula over parameters, which is true or false based on values substituted for free parameters appearing in the constraint. Let P, called a *parameter space*, stand for the set of values that a free parameter appearing in a constraint can take.[3] Given a substitution σ of parameters from P (also called a *specialization* or *instantiation*), written as $\{u_1 \leftarrow v_1, \cdots, u_m \leftarrow v_m\}$, where $u_1, \cdots, u_m$ are parameters, and $v_1, \cdots, v_m \in P$, a constraint c and a constraint expression cp specializes or evaluates under σ. If all free variables in c (cp respectively) are specialized, then $\sigma(c)$ ($\sigma(cp)$, respectively) specializes to a truth value (a value, respectively).

A constraint c is satisfiable (or consistent) if there is a specialization σ such that $\sigma(c)$ is true; otherwise c is unsatisfiable (or inconsistent). Similarly, a set C of constraints, called a *constraint set*, is consistent if and only if there is a specialization such that the constraints in C are satisfiable using that specialization; a constraint set C is thus a conjunction of constraints. C is *inconsistent* if the constraints in C cannot be simultaneously satisfied no matter what specialization is used. Let $spcl(C)$ be the set of all specializations satisfying constraints in C.

Given a constraint c, let $neg(c)$ stand for the negation of c to mean that for a given σ substituting for all free parameters in c, $\sigma(c)$ is true if and only if $\sigma(neg(c))$ is false, as well as that the set $\{c, neg(c)\}$ is inconsistent. Given a consistent constraint c and a consistent constraint set C, $C \cup \{c\}$ or $C \cup \{neg(c)\}$ is consistent; c is consistent with C iff $C \cup \{c\}$ is consistent. A constraint c is *dependent* with respect to a consistent C if and only if exactly one of $C \cup \{c\}$ and $C \cup \{neg(c)\}$ is consistent. A constraint c is *independent* of a constraint set C if both $C \cup \{c\}$ as well as $C \cup \{neg(c)\}$ are consistent. Further, $C \models c$ iff for every specialization σ, if $\sigma(C)$ is true, $\sigma(c)$ is true, i.e. $C \cup \{neg(c)\}$ is inconsistent.

Requirements on Constraint Solver

The main requirement on a constraint solver is that it should be a decision procedure for determining consistency of a constraint set C. For efficiency, it should be preferably incremental in the sense that the consistency check of $C \cup \{c\}$ as well as $C \cup \{neg(c)\}$ should be able to use intermediate results from the consistency check of C.

---

[3] In general, parameters may be typed, i.e. different parameters may range over different sets of values. The proposed approach generalizes to typed parameters.

Polynomial Equations and Inequations as Constraints

In the above discussion, a logical view of constraints has been adopted without fixing a language for expressing constraints. In the rest of the paper, however, constraints are assumed to be of the following forms: $cp = 0$ or $cp \neq 0$, where cp is a polynomial over the parameters. If c is an equation $cp = 0$, then $neg(c)$ is the inequation $cp \neq 0$ and similarly, if c is an inequation $cp \neq 0$, then $neg(c)$ is $cp = 0$. The parameter space P is assumed to be an algebraically closed field, for example, the field of complex numbers. The constraint $cp = 0$ (respectively, $cp \neq 0$) is *satisfiable* (or *consistent*) iff there exists a specialization σ such that $\sigma(cp)$ evaluates to 0 (respectively, does not evaluate to 0), and $cp = 0$ (respectively, $cp \neq 0$) is not satisfiable if for every possible specialization σ, $\sigma(cp)$ evaluates to a value different from 0 (respectively, evaluates to 0).

When constraints are polynomial equations and inequations, a Gröbner basis algorithm or a characteristic set algorithm can be used for consistency check. However, in the discussion below, it is assumed that some constraint solver is available for querying whether $C \cup \{(cp = 0)\}$ and $C \cup \{(cp \neq 0)\}$ are consistent assuming that C is consistent.

13.3.2   Constrained Polynomials

A parameterized polynomial is interpreted in the context of a set of constraints on parameters. For different values of free parameters satisfying the set of constraints, a parameterized polynomial has different structure (i.e. different terms) since the coefficients of terms may become 0. A *constrained polynomial* is defined as a pair $< C, p >$, where p is a polynomial over parameters and variables, C is a finite set of constraints over parameters. To contrast, a polynomial (without any constraints) is *an unconstrained* polynomial p and is written as $< \emptyset, p >$. Similarly, a constrained polynomial $< C, p >$ such that for every specialization σ, $\sigma(C)$ is true, is the same as the unconstrained polynomial p. As a formula, $< C, p >$ can be viewed as $C \Rightarrow p = 0$. A constrained polynomial $< C, p >$ in which C is inconsistent (unsatisfiable), is said to be *undefined*. Such constrained polynomials will never be generated in a computation. Below, by a constrained polynomial $< C, p >$, we mean the one in which C is consistent, unless stated otherwise. Further $< \sigma(C), p >$ can also be written as $< C \cup E_\sigma, p >$, where E_σ are the equations $\{u_1 = v_1, \cdots, u_m = v_m\}$ corresponding to $\sigma = \{u_1 \leftarrow v_1, \cdots, u_m \leftarrow v_m\}$. A specialization σ can be applied on a set of constrained polynomials CP as well; $\sigma(CP) = \{< \sigma(C), \sigma(p) > \mid < C, p > \in CP\}$. If a specialization σ instantiates all parameters in $< C, p >$, then either $\sigma(C)$ is inconsistent or $\sigma(C)$ is consistent and equivalent to $\emptyset$ and in that case, $\sigma(< C, p >)$ is equivalent to $\sigma(P)$, an unconstrained polynomial without any parameters.

Two constrained polynomials $< C, p >$ and $< D, q >$ are equivalent iff for every specialization σ, either both $\sigma(C)$ and $\sigma(D)$ are unsatisfiable, or both $\sigma(C)$ and $\sigma(D)$ are true and $\sigma(p) = \sigma(q)$. A constrained polynomial $< C, p >$ is *nonzero* (written as $< C, p > \neq 0$) if there exists a satisfying specialization σ of C such that $\sigma(p) \neq 0$. By slightly abusing the notation, a constrained polynomial $< C, p >$ subsumes another constrained polynomial $< D, q >$ if for every specialization σ satisfying D, $\sigma(C)$ is true and $\sigma(p) = \sigma(q)$; this implies that $\{< C, p >, < D, q > \} = \{< C, p >\}$. Obviously, $< C, p >$ is equivalent to $< D, q >$ if $< C, p >$ subsumes $< D, q >$ and $< D, q >$ subsumes $< C, p >$. Given $< C, p >$, its *simplified form* is $< D, q >$, where D is a simplified form of C and q only includes those terms of p whose coefficients cannot be deduced to be 0 from C.

A set of constrained polynomials CP can be simplified by removing any constrained polynomial from CP that is subsumed by another constrained polynomial in CP. Two sets of constrained polynomials CP and DP are equivalent if and only if for every specialization σ, $\sigma(CP) = \sigma(DP)$.

13.3.3 Degree, Head Term

The degree, head term, and head coefficient of a constrained polynomial are determined by its constraint set. As in the case of polynomials, a constrained polynomial can be viewed as a constrained univariate polynomial in one of its variables (recursive representation), or a constrained multivariate polynomials (distributed representation). Recursive representation is useful for univariate resultant computation and for computing characteristic sets, whereas distributed representation is useful for multivariate resultant computation and for Gröbner basis computations. In this subection and the section on Gröbner basis computations, distributed representation of polynomials is discussed. In the section on characteristic set computations, recursive representation of polynomials will be used.

In distributed representation, the coefficient of a term in a polynomial is a constraint expression. This coefficient may or may not be zero depending upon a constraint set associated with the polynomial. Let $>$ be a total admissible ordering on terms [2]. The *potential degree* of a constrained polynomial $< C, p >$ is defined as the degree of the highest term t in p such that (i) it is not the case that $C \models (c = 0)$, where c is the coefficient of t in p, and and (ii) for all terms $t' > t$, c', the coefficient of t' in p, is such that $C \models (c' = 0)$. Term t is then called the *potential head term* of $< C, p >$; c and ct are, respectively, called the *potential head coefficient* and *potential head monomial* of $< C, p >$. Let phm, pht, phc stand, respectively, for functions for computing the potential head monomial, potential head term and potential head coefficient of a constrained polynomial.

The *degree* of a constrained polynomial $< C, p >$ is defined as the degree of the highest term, say t, in p whose coefficient, say c, is such that $C \cup \{c = 0\}$ is inconsistent, i.e. c cannot be 0 with respect to C. Head term, head coefficient and head monomial of a constrained polynomial are defined in a similar manner. Let hm, ht, hc stand, respectively, for functions for computing the head monomial, head term and head coefficient of a constrained polynomial.

The distinction between the potential degree and degree of a constrained polynomial $< C, p >$ is that its potential degree is greater than or equal to its degree because p may have terms whose coefficients may or may not be 0 with respect to C.

13.3.4   Unambiguous and Ambiguous Constrained Polynomials

A constrained polynomial $< C, p >$ is *unambiguous* if the potential head monomial of $< C, p >$ is also the head monomial of $< C, p >$, i.e. (i) $phm(< C, p >) = a_i t_i$ (ii) $C \cup \{a_i = 0\}$ is inconsistent, and (iii) $C \cup \{a_i \neq 0\}$ is consistent. Otherwise, $< C, p >$ is called *ambiguous*. Further, as more constraints are added to C without destroying its consistency, the head term of an unambiguous $< C, p >$ does not change, i.e. for an unambiguous $< C, p >$, for each consistent constraint set D such that $spcl(D) \subseteq spcl(C)$, $pht(< C, p >) = pht(< D, p >)$. But for an ambiguous constrained polynomial, its potential head term and head coefficient may change as more constraints are added to C.

For example, consider $p = ux^2y + v^3x^2y + vy + ux = (u + v^3)x^2y + vy + ux$, where u, v are parameters and x, y are variables. In the distributed representation, in which p is viewed as a multivariate polynomial, under the total degree ordering induced by the variable ordering $y > x$, the degree of p relative to the empty constraint set is 0; the potential degree of $< \emptyset, p >$ is 3, and the potential head term is x^2y with $u + v^3$ being the potential head coefficient. The degree of p relative to $\{u + v^3 \neq 0\}$ is 3 and the head term is x^2y. The degree of p relative to $\{u + v^3 = 0\}$ is still 0 since it cannot be said whether $v = 0, u = 0$ or not. The degree of p relative to $\{u + v^3 = 0, v \neq 0\}$ is, 1, and the head term is y. The simplified form of $< \{u + v^3 = 0\}, p >$ is $< \{u + v^3 = 0\}, vy + ux >$.

Unambiguous Polynomials From an Ambiguous Polynomial

From an ambiguous constrained polynomial $< C, p >$ with the potential head coefficient a_i, an equivalent finite set of unambiguous constrained polynomials can be generated based on the following property: $\{< C, p >\} = \{< C \cup \{a_i \neq 0\}, p >$ $, < C \cup \{a_i = 0\}, p >\}$. The first element is an unambiguous constrained polynomial, whereas the second element could be ambiguous for which the construction is repeated till all the constrained polynomials generated are unambiguous.

LEMMA 13.1 Given a finite set of ambiguous constrained polynomials, there exists an equivalent finite set of unambiguous constrained polynomials, and this set can be obtained using the above algorithm.

Compactification

It is also possible to define a transformation from unambiguous constrained polynomials to possibly ambiguous constrained polynomials, especially if a set includes constrained polynomials with the same polynomial component but possibly with different constraint sets. Using the property that $\{< C \cup \{a_i \neq 0\}, p >, < C \cup \{a_i = 0\}, p >\} = \{< C, p >\}$ if $phc(< C, p >) = a_i$, and neither $C \models (a_i = 0)$ nor $C \models (a_i \neq 0)$. In general, given two constrained polynomials $< C, p >$ and $< D, p >$, $\{< C, p >, < D, p >\} = \{< E, p >\}$ if it is possible to generate a constraint set E that corresponds to the disjunction of constraint sets C and D since $spcl(E) = spcl(C) \cup spcl(D)$. Often this may be possible because of the way constraints get associated with a constrained polynomial.

13.4 Gröbner Basis Computation

In this section, Gröbner basis computations are extended to constrained polynomials. The reader is assumed to be familiar with concepts and definitions related to Gröbner basis computations, in particular the notions of reduction of a polynomial by another polynomial, S-polynomials and completion algorithm. For an introduction to Gröbner basis, the reader may consult [1, 2, 7, 10]. In a constrained polynomial $< C, p >$, the constraint set C is assumed to be consistent. Further a specialization σ is assumed to substitute values for all parameters in a set of constrained polynomials.

DEFINITION 13.1 A finite set GCB of constrained polynomials is a parametric Gröbner basis if and only if for every specialization σ of parameters in GCB, $\sigma(GCB)$ is equivalent to a finite set GB of polynomials that is a Gröbner basis.

The above definition captures the fact that for any specialization, a Gröbner basis can be obtained from a parametric Gröbner basis by substituting for the parameters and simplifying the constrained polynomials, thus satisfying one of the requirements for solved forms stated in the introduction.

DEFINITION 13.2 A finite set GCB of constrained polynomials is a parametric Gröbner basis of a set CB of constrained polynomials if and only (i) GCB is a parametric Gröbner basis, and (ii) if for every specialization σ of parameters in CB, $\sigma(GCB)$ is equivalent to a finite set GB of polynomials, which is a Gröbner basis, generating the same ideal as the ideal generated by the set B of polynomials equivalent to $\sigma(CB)$.

13.4.1 S-polynomial Computations

An important operation in a Gröbner basis computation is that of computing an *S-polynomial* of a pair of distinct polynomials (also called *critical pair* in the term rewriting literature). The simplification of a polynomial by another polynomial can be viewed as a special case of S-polynomial computation. Below we extend the concept of an S-polynomial to constrained polynomials.

For two nonequivalent constrained polynomials $< C, p >$ and $< D, q >$ such that $C \cup D$ is consistent, their *constrained S-polynomial* is defined as: Let $phm(< C \cup D, p >) = a_i t_i$ and $phm(< C \cup D, q >) = a_j t_j$ such that there exist smallest f_i, f_j, $f_i t_i = f_j t_j$, $f_i \neq t_j$, and $f_j \neq t_i$,

$$s - poly(< C, p >, < D, q >) = < C \cup D, a_j f_i p - a_i f_j q > .$$

For example, given

$$cp_1 = < \{v \neq 0\}, vxy + ux^2 + x >, \quad cp_2 = < \{u \neq 0\}, uy^2 + x^2 >,$$

since the combined constraint set $\{u \neq 0, v \neq 0\}$ is consistent, and assuming a lexicographic order on terms defined by the variable order $y > x$, $phm(< \{u \neq 0, v \neq 0\}, vxy + ux^2 + x >) = vxy$ and $phm(< \{u \neq 0, v \neq 0\}, uy^2 + x^2 >) = uy^2$; $a_1 = v, a_2 = u, t_1 = xy, f_1 = y, t_2 = y^2, f_2 = x$. The S-polynomial of cp_1 and cp_2 is

$$cp_3 = < \{u \neq 0, v \neq 0\}, u^2 x^2 y + uxy - vx^3 > .$$

The S-polynomial of two unambiguous constrained polynomials need not be unambiguous.

LEMMA 13.2 For any specialization σ satisfying $C \cup D$ and the constrained S-polynomial $< C \cup D, a_j f_i p - a_i f_j q >$ of $< C, p >$ and $< D, q >$, let p', q', r' be the polynomials equivalent to $\sigma(< C, p >), \sigma(< D, q >),$

$\sigma(< C \cup D, a_j f_i p - a_i f_j q >)$, respectively. Then, r' is the S-polynomial of p' and q'.

The above lemma establishes the soundness of S-polynomial computation. It is not necessary to assume that any of $< C, p >$ and $< D, q >$ be unambiguous, because even if a_i or a_j is 0 for a particular specialization, the result is still in the required ideal. It is perhaps better to define S-polynomials for pairs of unambiguous polynomials only; however, we do not have much experimental experience with these two different heuristics to say which one is better. All the calculations below are illustrated using unambiguous polynomials.

13.4.2 Reduction

For reduction (rewriting), it is more useful to have both the constrained polynomials to be unambiguous as otherwise polynomials may not be reducing!! If the constrained polynomial being reduced is ambiguous and its head coefficient can be 0, the result may not be smaller than the original constrained polynomial. If the constrained polynomial used to reduce another polynomial is ambiguous and its head coefficient can be 0, then again no reduction is taking place.

Reduction as a Special Case of S-polynomial Computation

Given two unambiguous constrained polynomial $< C, p >$ and $< D, q >$, $< C, p >$ can be reduced (rewritten) by $< D, q >$ if $C \cup D$ is consistent, $hm(< C \cup D, p >)$ $= hm(< C, p >) = a_i t_i$, $hm(< C \cup D, q >) =$ $hm(< D, q >) = a_j t_j$ and $t_i = f_j t_j$ for some f_j. In that case, $< C \cup D, a_j p >$ is said to reduce to (or, rewrite to) $< C \cup D, a_j p - a_i f_j q >$ in a single step.[4] It is easy to see that the result is smaller than the $< C \cup D, a_j p >$ in a well-founded order on the polynomial part of the constrained polynomials. This ensures that the reduction process always terminates. The reader would have noticed that this computation is a special case of S-polynomial computation discussed above.

Unlike in the case of the classical Gröbner basis construction, $< C \cup D, a_j p - a_i f_j q >$ cannot replace $< C, p >$ unless $C \models D$ as otherwise for a specialization σ satisfying C but not D, the ideal would not be the same. If $C \models D$, then $< C, p >$ can be replaced by $< C, a_j p - a_i f_j q >$ or deleted if $< C, a_j p - a_i f_j q >$ is equivalent to $< C, 0 >$.

---

[4]Since p is in an ideal implies $a_j p$ is also in the ideal, it is okay to reduce $a_j p$ instead of p.

Reduction as Replacement

It is possible to define reduction so that the constrained polynomial being reduced can always be replaced by a finite set of constrained polynomials. If
it is not the case that $C \models D$, then $< C, p >$ can be replaced by $< C \cup
D, a_j p - a_i f_j q >$ and the set $T = \{< C \cup \{neg(d)\}, p > \ | \ d \in D, C \cup
\{neg(d)\}$ is consistent and p does not simplify to 0 with respect to $C \cup \{neg(d)\}\}$.
The family of constraint sets $\{C \cup \{neg(d)\} \ | \ d \in D\}$ represents all specializations
which satisfy C but do not satisfy D.[5] A constrained polynomial $< C, p >$ is said
to reduce in a single-step to $\{< C \cup D, a_j p - a_i f_j q >\} \cup T$ in which at least one
polynomial is smaller than p and all other constrained polynomials have constraint
sets which are strictly implied by C.

A single-step reduction on a finite set S of constrained polynomials is defined as
follows: S reduces to S' in one step by $< D, q >$ if there is a constrained polynomial
$< C, p >\in S$ that reduces by $< D, q >$ in a single-step to a finite set T of constrained
polynomials and $S' = S -
\{< C, p >\} \cup T$. The multi-step reduction is then the transitive closure of the single-
step reduction. Multi-step reduction terminates because at least one polynomial
in the polynomial components of constrained polynomials is getting smaller in the
well-founded order.

An unambiguous constrained polynomial $< C, p >$ is *reduced* (or, in a *normal
form*) with respect to a set of unambiguous constrained polynomials CP if it cannot
be reduced by any element in CP. Similarly, a set S of unambiguous constrained
polynomials is reduced with respect to CP if every polynomial in S is reduced with
respect to CP.

A constrained polynomial $< C, p >$ reduces to 0 with respect to a set of unambiguous constrained polynomials CP if $< C, p >$ reduces in finitely many steps to
a finite set of constrained polynomials equivalent to 0.

LEMMA 13.3 Given two nonequivalent unambiguous $< C, p >$ and $< D, q >$ such
that $C \cup D$ is consistent, and $hm(< C \cup D, p >) = hm(< C, p >) = a_i t_i$, $hm(<
C \cup D, q >) = hm(< D, q >) = a_j t_j$, $t_i = f_j t_j$ for some f_j, and $< C, a_j p >$ reduces
by $< D, q >$ to $S = \{< C \cup D, a_j p - a_i f_j q >\} \cup \{< C \cup \{neg(d)\}, p > \ | \ d \in
D, C \cup \{neg(d)\}$ is consistent, $< C \cup \{neg(d)\}, p >\neq 0, \}$. For every specialization
σ satisfying C, if σ also satisfies D, then p' reduces by q' to r', where p', q', r' are

---

[5]If we use complex constraints that are propositional formulas built from basic constraints of
the form $ce = 0$, then an alternate and more compact representation would be $C \cup \{neg(d_1) \vee
\cdots \vee neg(d_k) \ | \ d_1, \cdots, d_k \in D\}$. A disjunction of constraints that are equations can be replaced
by the product of the polynomials in the equations, i.e. $ce_1 = 0 \vee ce_2 = 0$ can be replaced by
$ce_1 * ce_2 = 0$.

equivalent to $\sigma(< C, p >)$, $\sigma(< D, q >)$, $\sigma(< C \cup D, a_j p - a_i f_j q >)$, respectively, and r' is in the ideal of p' and q'. Further, if σ does not satisfy D, then S includes a constrained polynomial $< D', p >$, where D' is satisfied by σ.

13.4.3   Test for a Parametric Gröbner Basis

A test for a set of unambiguous constrained polynomials to be a parametric Gröbner basis can be given using S-polynomial computation. (If the set includes ambiguous constrained polynomials, they can be replaced by an equivalent set of unambiguous constrained polynomials; the test applies to a set including ambiguous polynomials also.)

THEOREM 13.1 A set CP of constrained polynomials is a parametric Gröbner basis if and only if for every pair of nonequivalent unambiguous constrained polynomials $< C, p >$ and $< D, q >$ from CP such that $C \cup D$ is consistent, their S-polynomial (i.e. the set of unambiguous constrained polynomials equivalent to it) reduces to 0 by CP.

The proof of the theorem follows the pattern of a proof in the case of the classical Gröbner basis test for polynomials.

13.4.4   Parametric Gröbner Basis Algorithm

The above test can be used to design an algorithm for computing a parametric Gröbner basis from a set of constrained polynomials as in the case of a classical Gröbner basis algorithm on polynomials. A simple version of such an algorithm takes a finite set of polynomials as input, makes constrained polynomials out of them by associating the empty constraint set with each polynomial and repeatedly performs the following steps:

1. replace every ambiguous constrained polynomial by an equivalent set of un-ambiguous constrained polynomials,

2. for every pair of nonequivalent unambiguous constrained polynomials,

   (a) generate an S-polynomial, if any,

   (b) find an equivalent set of unambiguous constrained polynomials to it,

   (c) reduce each of these unambiguous constrained polynomials to a normal form, which itself is a finite set of constrained polynomials, and

   (d) if a nonzero normal form is generated, add all nonzero constrained poly-nomials in a normal form to the basis, and compute new S-polynomials with other polynomials in the basis.

This process is continued until all S-polynomials among pairs of constrained polynomials have been considered or reduce to 0. Suitable data structures and book keeping mechanisms can be developed to avoid unnecessary computations. Optimizations suggested in the literature for identifying unnecessary S-polynomials extend to parametric Gröbner basis computations also.

The termination of the above algorithm is based on Hilbert's basis condition and the following additional argument. Every term in a constrained polynomial could possibly become a head term. At any given iteration, there are only finitely many possibilities for generating different possible Gröbner bases assuming that all parameters are specialized. If the above algorithm does not terminate, there is an infinite path by König's lemma since the branching factor is finite in the tree of possible Gröbner bases. And, the existence of an infinite path is impossible since that contradicts Hilbert's basis condition.

The method presented here has been tried on many examples including those in [18] and [4]. Our outputs are different from the ones reported in [18]. Example 1 in [18], for instance, is a discussion of a set of two generic univariate quadratic polynomials; a Gröbner basis given in [18] includes two parametric cubic polynomials. In our computation, higher degree polynomials will not be computed.

From a parametric Gröbner basis consisting of unambiguous constrained polynomials, a subset which constitutes a parametric Gröbner basis with respect to a constraint set C can be extracted, and this subset serves as a parametric Gröbner basis with respect to C. For every constrained polynomial $< D, p >$ in a parametric Gröbner basis such that $C \cup D$ is consistent, a new constrained polynomial $< D \cup C, p >$ is included. For a specialization σ, the subset of constrained polynomials whose constraints are satisfied by σ, is equivalent to a set of polynomials that constitute a Gröbner basis in the usual sense. A Gröbner basis thus obtained may have redundant elements; any polynomial in a Gröbner basis whose head monomial can be simplified using other polynomials is redundant.

Using Parametric Gröbner Basis for Analyzing Solutions

Just like Gröbner basis for polynomials, a parametric Gröbner basis can be used to study and analyze the solution space of a system of parametric polynomial equations with respect to a constraint set on parameters. It is possible to compute the dimension of different components of the variety, as well as compute other properties of the associated ideal and variety for different constraints on parameters. This is done in a way similar to computing dimension of a polynomial ideal from its Gröbner basis. For parametric polynomials in which for every parameter, the ideal generated is zero-dimensional, it is possible to use the basis conversion algorithm of [6] to obtain a parametric Gröbner basis with respect to a lexicographic ordering from a Gröbner basis constructed using another term ordering such as degree ordering or reverse lexicographic ordering. Computations of solutions from parametric Gröbner bases are briefly illustrated later.

EXAMPLE 13.1 We illustrate the Gröbner basis construction on a simple example that models a chemical system and explains chemical equilibrium. The example is discussed in [18] and [4] so it also contrasts the proposed approach with methods discussed in [18] and [4] as well as illustrates differences in computational steps and outputs. The set of input polynomials is:

$$\{p_1 = x_4 - (a_4 - a_2), \ p_2 = x_1 + x_2 + x_3 + x_4 - (a_1 + a_3 + a_4),$$

$$p_3 = x_1 x_3 x_4 - a_1 a_3 a_4,$$

$$p_4 = x_1 x_3 + x_1 x_4 + x_2 x_3 + x_3 x_4 - (a_1 a_4 + a_1 a_3 + a_3 a_4)\},$$

where a_1, a_2, a_3, a_4 are parameters, and x_1, x_2, x_3, x_4 are variables. The lexicographic ordering on terms defined by $x_1 > x_2 > x_3 > x_4$ is used.

The corresponding unambiguous constrained polynomials are:

$$1 : \ < \emptyset, p_1 >, \quad 2 : \ < \emptyset, p_2 >, \quad 3 : \ < \emptyset, p_3 >, \quad 4 : \ < \emptyset, p_4 > .$$

Polynomials 3 and 4 can be simplified using 1 and 2 in the classical way since the associated constraint sets are empty. Polynomial 3 gets simplified to 3' and replaces 3. $3' : \ < \emptyset, q_3 >$, where $q_3 = (a_4 - a_2) x_2 x_3 + (a_4 - a_2) x_3^2 - (a_1 + a_2 + a_3)(a_4 - a_2) x_3 + a_1 a_3 a_4$. Similarly, 4 can be replaced by: $4' : \ < \emptyset, q_4 >$, where $q_4 = (a_4 - a_2) x_2 + x_3^2 - (a_1 + a_2 + a_3) x_3 + (a_1 a_2 + a_2^2 + a_2 a_3 + a_1 a_3 - a_2 a_4)$. Neither 3' nor 4' is unambiguous; from 4' we get: $5 : \ < \{a_4 - a_2 \neq 0\}, q_4 >$ and $6 : \ < \{a_4 - a_2 = 0\}, q_4 >$, both of which are unambiguous. Similarly, from 3', we get: $7 : \ < \{a_4 - a_2 \neq 0\}, q_3 >$ and $8 : \ < \{a_4 - a_2 = 0\}, q_3 > $. Polynomial 8 is ambiguous and exhibits an interesting case since after simplification, it is equivalent to $< \{a_4 - a_2 = 0\}, a_1 a_3 a_4 > $. Unambiguous polynomials equivalent to it are: $9 : \ < \{a_4 - a_2 = 0, a_1 a_3 a_4 \neq 0\}, a_1 a_3 a_4 >$, and $10 : \ < \{a_4 - a_2 = 0, a_1 a_3 a_4 = 0\}, 0 > $.

This reveals that the original system is inconsistent for the constraint set $\{a_4 - a_2 = 0, a_1 a_3 a_4 \neq 0\}$. This also follows from the original system of parametric polynomials above; for parameter values satisfying these constraints, there is indeed inconsistency since if $a_4 = a_2$, then $x_4 = 0$ simplifying p_3 to a constant $a_1 a_3 a_4$.

Polynomial 5 can be used to simplify polynomial 7 and the result, $7' : \ < \{a_4 - a_2 \neq 0\}, q_7 >$, where $q_7 = x_3^3 - (a_1 + a_4 + a_3) x_3^2 + (a_1 a_4 + a_3 a_4 + a_1 a_3) x_3 - a_1 a_3 a_4$, replaces 7.

The set $\{1, 2, 5, 6, 7', 9\}$ constitutes a parametric Gröbner basis.

It can be easily checked that every specialization of the above parametric Gröbner basis that satisfies one of these constraint set $\{a_4 - a_2 \neq 0\}$, $\{a_4 - a_2 = 0, a_1 a_3 a_4 = 0\}$ as well as $\{a_4 - a_2 = 0, a_1 a_3 a_4 \neq 0\}$ is a Gröbner basis. Further, the above constraint sets constitute a complete cover in the sense every specialization satisfies exactly one of the constraint sets. For each constraint set, its Gröbner basis can be used to analyze solutions of the original parametric system. For the constraint set $\{a_4 - a_2 = 0, a_1 a_3 a_4 \neq 0\}$, the parametric equations are inconsistent; the dimension of the associated solution set is -1 because for such specializations, there are no solutions. If a specialization satisfies $\{a_4 = a_2, a_1 a_3 a_4 = 0\}$, then $x_4 = 0$, and x_3 can be obtained by solving q_4, and x_1 and x_2 are related by p_2, resulting in a solution set of dimension 1. For specializations in which $a_4 \neq a_2$, the solution set is zero-dimensional since for every variable, there is a polynomial in the Gröbner basis whose leading term is a powerproduct in that variable alone: $x_4 = a_4 - a_2$, values of x_3 are given by q_7, from which the corresponding values of x_2 and x_1 can be obtained using q_4 and p_2.

This result is different from the comprehensive Gröbner basis given in [18] or ascending sets given in [4].[6] In [18], many extra and complicated polynomials appear in the comprehensive basis given as the result. In [4], there are too many cases given which can be easily combined; in contrast the above result is compact, very much in Sit's sense [16].

EXAMPLE 13.2 Let us consider another example from [4] to contrast the proposed approach with Chou and Gao's approach. Consider the following set of polynomials:

$$\{y^2 - zxy + x^2 + z - 1, xy + z^2 - 1, y^2 + x^2 + z^2 - r^2\},$$

in which r is a parameter. The computations are performed using the lexicographic term ordering defined by $y > x > z$.

Unambiguous constrained polynomials generated from the input are:

$1 : <\emptyset, y^2 - zxy + x^2 + z - 1>$, $\quad 2 : <\emptyset, xy + z^2 - 1>$,

$3 : <\emptyset, y^2 + x^2 + z^2 - r^2>$.

Polynomial 1 can be simplified using 3 and 2 in the classical way (because of empty constraint sets) to give: $1' : <\emptyset, z^3 - z^2 + r^2 - 1>$, which replaces 1. The S-polynomial of 2 and 3 is also computed in the classical way to produce:

---

[6] Because of space limitations, definitions of comprehensive and reduced Gröbner bases as given in [18] and ascending sets in [4] cannot be reproduced. The reader may consult the original papers for definitions and other details.

$4 : < \emptyset, z^2y - y - x^3 - z^2x + r^2x >$. The S-polynomial of 1' and 4 gives a new polynomial:

$5 : < \emptyset, zy - 2y + r^2y + zx^3 - x^3 + z^3x - zr^2x - z^2x + r^2x >$.

The S-polynomial of 2 and 4 gives a new polynomial:

$6 : < \emptyset, x^4 + z^2x^2 - r^2x^2 - z^2 - r^2z + z + 2 - r^2 >$.

The S-polynomial of 3 and 4 reduces to 0. The S-polynomial of 2 and 6 also reduces to 0. Polynomial 5 simplifies 4 to: $4' : < \emptyset, q_4 >$, where $q_4 = (r^4 - 4r^2 + 3)y - (z^2 - (r^2 - 1)z + r^2 - 1)x^3 + ((r^2 - 1)z^2 - (r^4 - 2r^2 + 1)z - 2 + 2r^2)x$; 4' replaces 4. Since 4' is ambiguous, equivalent unambiguous polynomials are: $7 : < \{r^4 - 4r^2 + 3 \neq 0\}, q_4 >$, and $8 : < \{r^4 - 4r^2 + 3 = 0\}, q_4 >$. Using polynomial 7, polynomials 2, 3, and 5 reduce to 0 under the constraint set $\{r^4 - 4r^2 + 3 \neq 0\}$.

The set $\{1', 2, 3, 5, 6, 7, 8\}$ constitutes a parametric Gröbner basis. A compactified Gröbner basis consists of $\{1', 2, 3, 4', 5, 6\}$.

For any specialization satisfying any of the constraint systems $\{r^4 - 4r^2 + 3 \neq 0\}$ and $\{r^4 - 4r^2 + 3 = 0\}$, the equivalent set of polynomials obtained from the above parametric Gröbner basis is a Gröbner basis. These constraint sets obviously constitute a complete cover.

Solution sets can be generated from the above parametric Gröbner basis. The dimension of the solution set is 0 irrespective of the value of r. Since $r^4 - 4r^2 + 3 = (r^2 - 1)(r^2 - 3)$, each factor can be considered to lead to a distinct case. For $r^2 - 1 = 0$, i.e. $r = 1, -1$, the Gröbner basis is: $\{ 1' : z^3 - z^2, \ 2 : xy + z^2 - 1, \ 3 : y^2 + x^2 + z^2 - 1, \ 4' : z^2x^3, \ 5 : zy - y + zx^3 - x^3 + z^3x - zx - z^2x + x, \ 6 : x^4 + z^2x^2 - x^2 - z^2 + 1\}$. By factoring 1', we get $\{z = 0, x^4 - x^2 + 1 = 0, y^2 + x^2 - 1 = 0\}$ giving one set of solutions, and $\{z = 1, x = 0, y = 0\}$ as another solution. Similarly, for $r^2 - 3 = 0$, the following solutions are obtained from its Gröbner basis: $\{z = -1, x = 0, y^2 = 2\}$, $\{z = -1, x^2 = 2, y = 0\}$; there are additional solutions for which the z component satisfies the $\{z^2 - 2z + 2 = 0\}$. Similarly, for $(r^2 - 1)(r^2 - 3) \neq 0$, solutions can also be computed.

The ascending sets given for this example in [4] are different from the above parametric Gröbner basis, in particular they are far too many; many of these ascending sets can be combined and described using a single ascending set. The above description is much more compact and comprehensive much in the spirit of [16, 17].

EXAMPLE 13.3 Here is a slighly complicated example picked from [18]. Consider the set of two parametric polynomials: $\{f = vxy + ux^2 + x, \ g = uy^2 + x^2\}$, in which u, v are parameters and x, y are variables. From f, the unambiguous constrained polynomials are: 1: $< \{v \neq 0\}, f >$, 2: $< \{v = 0, u \neq 0\}, f >$; 3: $< \{v = 0, u = 0\}, f >$. From g, the unambiguous constrained polynomials are: 4: $< \{u \neq 0\}, g >$, 5: $< \{u = 0\}, g >$.

The S-polynomial of 1 and 4 is: $< \{u \neq 0, v \neq 0\}, -vx^3 + u^2x^2y + ux >$; its normal form is $< \{u \neq 0, v \neq 0\}, h >$ where $h = (u^3 + v^2)x^3 + 2u^2x^2 + ux$. This constrained polynomial is ambiguous; the unconstrained polynomials equivalent to it are: 6 : $< \{v \neq 0, u \neq 0, u^3 + v^2 \neq 0\}, h >$, 7 : $< \{v \neq 0, u \neq 0, u^3 + v^2 = 0\}, h >$. The S-polynomial of 1 and 5 is: $< \{v \neq 0, u = 0\}, ux^3 + x^2 >$, which reduces to 0 using 5. Polynomial 5 reduces by polynomial 3 to $\{< \{v = 0, u = 0\}, 0 >, < \{v \neq 0, u = 0\}, x^2 >\}$. So we can replace 5 by 5' : $< \{v \neq 0, u = 0\}, x^2 >$. The S-polynomial of 1 and 6 is: $< \{u \neq 0, v \neq 0, u^3 + v^2 \neq 0\}, (u^3 + v^2)ux^4 + (u^3 + v^2)x^3 - 2u^2vx^2y - uvxy >$, which simplifies to 0 by using constrained polynomials 1 and 6. Similarly, the S-polynomial of 1 and 7 also simplifies to 0.

It can be easily verified that the set of unambiguous constrained polynomials $\{1, 2, 3, 4, 5', 6, 7\}$ constitute a parameterized Gröbner basis because every S-polynomial reduces to 0. For the case when $\{u \neq 0, v \neq 0, u^3 + v^2 \neq 0\}$, $\{1, 4, 6\}$ is a Gröbner basis. Its solution set is zero-dimensional since the Gröbner basis includes polynomials whose head terms are powers of x and y. For $\{u \neq 0, v \neq 0, u^3 + v^2 = 0\}$, $\{1, 4, 7\}$ is a Gröbner basis, and its solution set is also zero-dimensional. In the case when $\{u \neq 0, v = 0\}$, $\{2, 4\}$ is a Gröbner basis and its solution set is also zero-dimensional. The set $\{1, 5'\}$ is a Gröbner basis for the case $\{u = 0, v \neq 0\}$, and for when $\{u = 0, v = 0\}$, $\{3\}$ is a Gröbner basis. In both cases, the solution set is of dimension 1 since the Gröbner bases do not include polynomials in y.

Constrained polynomials in the above parametric Gröbner basis can be compactified easily. For example, constrained polynomials 6 and 7 can be compactified to $< \{u \neq 0, v \neq 0\}, h >$; constrained polynomials 1, 2, 3 can be compactified to unconstrained polynomial f; similarly, 4 and 5' can be compactified to g. Compactification would result in $\{f, g, < \{u \neq 0, v \neq 0\}, h >\}$ as a Gröbner basis. The reader can check that for different constraints on parameters, the resulting Gröbner basis from the compactified parametric Gröbner basis, after deleting redundant elements, is the same as above.

The above parametric Gröbner basis of $\{f, g\}$ is different from a Gröbner system, a reduced Gröbner system, as well as a comprehensive Gröbner basis given in [18]. This suggests that even though there may be many similarities in the two approaches, they are different as they produce different answers. In particular, Weispfenning's algorithm produced the polynomial $2v(u^3 + v^2)x^3y + 2(u^3 + v^2)x^3 - ux$

in a Gröbner system as well as a comprehensive Gröbner basis which is not in the above answer. Further there are many additional polynomials in the result reported in [18].

13.5 Characteristic Set Construction

The concept of a characteristic set of a set of polynomials was introduced by Ritt in [15], and has been popularized by Wu because of its success in geometry theorem proving as well as solving systems of polynomial equations [19, 20]. In [8], we developed a characterization of characteristic sets as defined by Ritt, which is different from Wu's definition of a characteristic set. The characteristic set algorithm given by Wu transforms a system of polynomial equations into a triangular form whose zero set is "roughly equivalent" to the zero set of the original system. Below, we discuss characteristic sets in Wu's sense as the readers are likely to have better familiarity with them. But the approach discussed below extends to Ritt's characteristic sets discussed in [8].[7] We extend characteristic set construction to constrained polynomials. We assume the reader is familiar with the characteristic set method; for details, the reader may consult [15, 19, 10].

13.5.1 Definitions for Recursive Representation of Polynomials

In characteristic set computations, recursive representation of polynomials is used. A total ordering on variables is assumed to be given. A polynomial is viewed as a univariate polynomial in the highest variable appearing in it. Degree, head term, head monomial and initial of a constrained polynomial are defined using recursive representation similar to the definitions for distributed representation.

Let $>$ be a total ordering on variables $x_1 < x_2 < \cdots < x_n$. A constrained polynomial $< C, p >$ is defined to be of *potential class* i if and only if (i) for every variable $x_j > x_i$, the coefficient a_j of a term $x_j^{d_j}$ in p is 0 with respect to C, where $d_j > 0$, i.e. $< C, a_j >=< C, 0 >$, and (ii) there is a term $x_i^{d_i}$, where $d_i > 0$, whose coefficient a_i in p is such that $< C, a_i >$ is not equivalent to $< C, 0 >$. The coefficient a_i is a polynomial in parameters as well as variables. The highest such term $x_i^{d_i}$ is called the *potential* head term of $< C, p >$, and d_i its potential degree;

---

[7]Ritt's definition of a characteristic set of a set Σ of polynomials is that in addition to being a chain, every polynomial in the ideal generated by Σ pseudodivides to 0 using the characteristic set. That is not necessarily the case for a characteristic set as defined by Wu's algorithm.

The major difference in the algorithm discussed in [8] for constructing Ritt's characteristic set is that when a chain is used for pseudodivision, it is ensured that the initial of a polynomial in the chain is invertible with respect to the polynomials lower in the chain. This may result in splitting of the system of polynomials into many subsystems.

the coefficient a_i is called the *potential* initial of $< C, p >$.

For example, consider $p = ux^2y + v^3x^2y + vy + ux$ discussed earlier assuming $y > x$. In recursive representation, p is viewed as a univariate polynomial in y and is written as: $((u + v^3)x^2 + v)y + ux$; the degree of p relative to $\{u + v^3 \neq 0\}$ is 1, and the head term is y. The head coefficient of p, also called its *initial*, is $((u + v^3)x^2 + v)$. The degree of p relative to $\{v \neq 0\}$ is also 1, and the head term is y; the head coefficient of p remains to be $((u + v^3)x^2 + v)$ since $((u + v^3)x^2 + v) \neq 0$. The potential class of $< \emptyset, p >$ is 2; its potential degree is 1, and the potential initial is $((u + v^3)x^2 + v)$.

Given a constrained polynomial $< C, p >$ in recursive form, an equivalent simplified form $< C, q >$ can be defined in a way similar to the one for distributed representation: $< C, q >$ is obtained from $< C, p >$ by deleting terms whose coefficients are 0 with respect to C. For example, the simplified form of $< \{u + v^3 = 0, v \neq 0\}, p >$ is $<< \{u + v^3 = 0, v \neq 0\}, vy + ux >$, and the simplified form of $< \{u + v^3 = 0, v = 0\}, p >$ is $< \{u = v^3 = 0, v = 0\}, 0 >$.

13.5.2   Ambiguous and Unambiguous Constrained Polynomials

If there is a consistent superset D of C such that $< D, a_i >$ is equivalent to $< D, 0 >$, then p is ambiguous. Otherwise, $< C, a_i >$ cannot be made equivalent to 0, and p is unambiguous in which case, i, $x_i^{d_i}$ d_i and a_i are, respectively, the class, head term, degree, and initial of p also. From an ambiguous constrained polynomial $< C, p >$ (implying that its initial a_i is such that $< C, a_i >$ is ambiguous), unambiguous constrained polynomials equivalent to it can be generated. Unlike in the distributed representation case, we cannot require that $a_i \neq 0$ since a_i is itself a polynomial in parameters and variables. In fact, it is necessary to keep checking for the head coefficient until a constraint expression is arrived at; then the constraint set C is appropriately extended as in the case of distributed representation. In general, the constraint set C is extended based on the structure of a_i to make a_i unambiguous with respect to an extended constraint set that includes C. This process can be repeated till all constrained polynomials thus obtained are unambiguous. Corresponding to an ambiguous constrained polynomial, there is a finite set of unambiguous constrained polynomials equivalent to it.

For example, assuming $y > x$, consider $p = ((u+v^3)x^2+v)y+ux$. The constrained polynomial $< \emptyset, p >$ is ambiguous because its initial, the polynomial $(u+v^3)x^2 + v$, is ambiguous with respect to the empty set of constraints. However, $(u + v^3)x^2 + v$ is nonzero with respect to $\{u + v^3 \neq 0\}$; so $< \{u + v^3 \neq 0\}, p >$ is unambiguous, its degree is 1, and its initial is $(u + v^3)x^2 + v$. Similarly, the initial remains nonzero with respect to the constraint set $\{u + v^3 = 0, v \neq 0\}$; the degree of

$< \{u+v^3 = 0, v \neq 0\}, p >$ is also 1, and the initial remains $(u+v^3)x^2+v$. The initial $(u + v^3)x^2 + v$ becomes zero with respect to the constraint set $\{u + v^3 = 0, v = 0\}$, so the degree of $< \{u + v^3 = 0, v = 0\}, p >$ drops to 0, and the potential initial is ux, which is zero with respect to $\{u + v^3 = 0, v = 0\}$. So $< \{u+v^3 = 0, v = 0\}, p >$ is equivalent to 0.

Compactification of unambiguous constrained polynomials into ambiguous constrained polynomials can be defined for recursive representation also.

13.5.3   Pseudodivision

There are three important concepts in characteristic set computations: (i) a polynomial being reduced with respect to another polynomial, (ii) the reduction of a polynomial by another polynomial by pseudodivision [12], and (iii) the initial of a polynomial being invertible [8]. The first two must be extended for Wu's algorithm.

A constrained polynomial $< C, p >$ is *reduced* with respect to an unambiguous $< D, q >$ if and only if (i) the constraint set $C \cup D$ is consistent, and (ii) the class of $< D, q >$ is i and the potential degree of x_i in $< C \cup D, p >$ is $<$ the degree of x_i in $< D, q >$.

An unambiguous $< C, p >$ *reduces* (*pseudodivides*) by another unambiguous $< D, q >$ to $< C \cup D, r >$ if (i) $C \cup D$ is consistent, (ii) $< C, p >$ is not reduced with respect to $< D, q >$, and (iii) there exist a number k (preferably the smallest such number, but is $\leq (d - d_i) + 1$, where i is the class of $< D, q >$, d_i is the degree of $< D, q >$, and d is the degree of x_i in $< C, p >$), a polynomial b (preferably not involving parameters) and another polynomial r such that

$$< C \cup D, I_q{}^k p >=< C \cup D, bq > + < C \cup D, r >,$$

where I_q is the initial of $< C \cup D, q >$, and the potential degree of x_i in r is $< d_i$; this calculation can be done in the classical way by first simplifying p and q with respect to $C \cup D$. Note that $< C \cup D, r >$ need not be unambiguous.

It is easy to see that for every specialization σ satisfying $C \cup D$, the common zeros of $\sigma(p)$ and $\sigma(q)$ are also the zeros of the remainder $\sigma(r)$; further, if $r = 0$, then the common zeros of $\sigma(p)$ and $\sigma(q)$ are the same as the zeros of $\sigma(q)$ insofar as they are not the zeros of $\sigma(I_q)$. And, $\sigma(r)$ is in the ideal generated by $\sigma(p)$ and $\sigma(q)$. Unlike in the case of Gröbner basis computations, $< C \cup D, r >$ does not replace any of $< C, p >$ and $< D, q >$; instead, it gets added to the basis.

In order for the definitions to extend naturally, we define that an unambiguous constrained polynomial $< C, p >$ reduces by another unambiguous $< D, q >$ to 0 if $C \cup D$ is inconsistent. Thus an unambiguous constrained polynomial $< C, p >$ is *not reduced* with respect to another unambiguous $< D, q >$ if their constraint sets clash.

DEFINITION 13.3 A set $\{< C_1, p_1 >, \cdots, < C_l, p_l >\}$ of unambiguous constrained polynomials is called a chain if (i) $l = 1$ and $< C_1, p_1 >$ is not equivalent to 0, or (ii) $0 < i_1 < i_2 < \cdots < i_l$, where i_j is the the class of $< C_j, p_j >$, and $D = C_1 \cup \cdots \cup C_l$ is consistent, and $< C_j, p_j >$ is reduced with respect to each $< C_i, p_i >$, $i < j \le l$.

A chain is also called a *triangular* form; each element in the chain is said to introduce a new variable, i.e. $< C_j, p_j >$ introduces x_{i_j}. Also notice that the chain is relevant for only those parameter values that satisfy the constraint set D. The above definition can be weakened to define a chain in the loose sense or a chain in the weak sense as defined by Wu for polynomials, in which only the initial of $< C_j, p_j >$ is reduced with respect to $< C_i, p_i >$'s [19].

Pseudodivision of a constrained polynomial can be defined with respect to a chain in the obvious way. The constrained polynomial is pseudodivided by the polynomial of the largest class in the chain, then the result is pseudodivided by the next polynomial lower in the chain and so on, until the result that is reduced with respect to every polynomial in the chain is generated.

13.5.4 Computing Parametric Characteristic Set

A parametric characteristic set should cover all values of parameters satisfying parametric constraints if given as a part of the input. A parametric characteristic set may thus include many chains, but they are disjoint in covering different parameter values. A parametric characteristic set is defined based on the definition of a characteristic set.

DEFINITION 13.4 A finite set CCP of unambiguous constrained polynomials is a parametric characteristic set if (i) for any two nonequivalent $< C, p >$ and $< D, q >$ of class i in CCP, $C \cup D$ is inconsistent, and (ii) for every specialization σ of parameters, $\sigma(CCP)$ is equivalent to a set CP of polynomials that constitutes a characteristic set.

DEFINITION 13.5 A finite set CCP of unambiguous constrained polynomials is a parametric characteristic set of a finite set BCP of parametric polynomials if and only if (i) CCP is a parametric characteristic set, and (ii) for every specialization σ, $\sigma(CCP)$ is equivalent to a set CP of polynomials that constitutes a characteristic set of the set of polynomials equivalent to $\sigma(BCP)$.

A parametric characteristic set can be computed using a method similar to a method used to compute a characteristic set of polynomials as discussed in [19, 20, 3, 11]. A simple algorithm for computing a parametric characteristic set works as follows. Firstly, for every ambiguous polynomial, generate an equivalent set of unambiguous polynomials. Secondly, identify a minimal chain of constrained polynomials in the basis: From a given set BCP of constrained polynomials, let $S = BCP$, $B = \emptyset$, $CB = \emptyset$.

1. Pick a minimal element, say $< C, p >$, in S, i.e. a constrained polynomial of the smallest class, say i, and of the smallest degree, say d_i, in its largest variable x_i, and include it in B. Let $CB = CB \cup C$.

2. Remove from S any constrained polynomial $< D, q >$ such that the degree of x_i in $< D, q >$ is $\geq d_i$ or either $CB \cup D$ is inconsistent.

3. Repeat the above two steps until S is empty.

It can be easily shown that $B \subseteq BCP$ is a chain. Polynomials in BCP are pseudodivided by B. Let T be the nonzero remainders obtained. If T is $\emptyset$, then we have identified a chain belonging to a parametric characteristic set. Otherwise BCP is augmented to include T, and the above procedure of identifying a chain in BCP is repeated. This process terminates since T includes polynomials of lower degrees than those in B.

If a chain B in BCP is identified such that every constrained polynomial in BCP has a clashing constraint set with B or pseudodivides to 0 using B, we extract that chain out of BCP and compute the remaining chains. B is a chain in a parametric characteristic set of BCP; the constraint set CB associated with B represents parameter values for which B is a characteristic set. For every specialization σ satisfying CB, every polynomial in the set Σ of polynomials equivalent to $\sigma(BCP)$ pseudodivides to 0 using B', the set of polynomials equivalent to $\sigma(B)$.

One simple (but naive) way to extract out B from BCP is to define

$$BCP' = \{< D, p > \mid < C, p > \in BCP, D = C \cup \{neg(cb)\} \text{ is consistent,}$$
$$cb \in CB, < D, p > \neq < D, 0 >\}$$

It is easy to see that for every specialization σ satisfying CB, $\sigma(BCP')$ is the empty set, and further, for every specialization σ not satisfying CB, $\sigma(BCP') = \sigma(BCP)$.[8]

---

[8] As in the case of Gröbner basis construction, a compact representation of BCP' can be constructed using constraints which are propositional formulas over basic constraints.

If BCP' is not the empty set, assign BCP' to S and repeat the above steps of identifying and extracting out additional chains of a parametric characteristic set. The set of all chains collected in this way is a parametric characteristic set.

Many variations of the above simple algorithm are possible and many heuristics can be incorporated. Many examples, including those in [18, 4], have been successfully worked out using the above algorithm.

13.5.5 Example

Let us consider Example 13.1 of the previous section used for illustrating Gröbner basis computations, and apply the characteristic set construction. The input is $\{f = vxy + ux^2 + x, \ g = uy^2 + x^2\}$ with $y > x$. Unambiguous constrained polynomials equivalent to f are: $1 : < \{v \neq 0\}, f >$, $2 : < \{v = 0, u \neq 0\}, f >$, $3 : < \{v = 0, u = 0\}, f >$. Unambiguous constrained polynomial equivalent to g are:

$4 : < \{u \neq 0\}, g >$, $5 : < \{u = 0\}, g >$.

Applying the above algorithm, we get $\{3\}$ as a chain of a parametric characteristic set for the case when $\{u = 0, v = 0\}$. This chain is extracted giving a replacement of 5 by $5' : < \{u = 0, v \neq 0\}, g >$. From $\{1, 2, 4, 5'\}$, another chain $\{5', 1\}$ for the case when $\{u = 0, v \neq 0\}$ is generated. After extracting this chain, we have: $\{1', 2, 4\}$, where $1' : < \{u \neq 0, v \neq 0\}, f >$. There is another chain $\{2, 4\}$ for $\{u \neq 0, v = 0\}$. After extracting this chain, we get: $\{1', 4'\}$, where $4' : < \{u \neq 0, v \neq 0\}, g >$.

Polynomial 1' is used to pseudodivide 4' and the result is: $< \{v \neq 0, u \neq 0\}, r >$, where $r = (u^3 + v^2)x^4 + 2u^2x^3 + ux^2$. Since the result is ambiguous, we get additional unambiguous polynomials equivalent to it: $6 : < \{v \neq 0, u \neq 0, u^3 + v^2 \neq 0\}, r >$, and $7 : < \{v \neq 0, u \neq 0, u^3 + v^2 = 0\}, r >$. There are two more chains: $\{1', 6\}$ for the constraint set $\{v \neq 0, u \neq 0, u^3 + v^2 \neq 0\}$, and $\{1', 7\}$ for the constraint set $\{v \neq 0, u \neq 0, u^3 + v^2 = 0\}$.

A parametric characteristic set consists of:

$3 : < \{v = 0, u = 0\}, f >$, $\quad 5' : < \{u = 0, v \neq 0\}, g >$,

$2 : < \{v = 0, u \neq 0\}, f >$, $\quad 4'' : < \{u \neq 0, v = 0\}, g >$,

$1'' : < \{u = 0, v \neq 0\}, f >$, $\quad 1''' : < \{u \neq 0, v \neq 0, u^3 + v^2 \neq 0\}, f >$,

$1'''' : < \{u \neq 0, v \neq 0, u^3 + v^2 = 0\}, f >$,

$6 : < \{v \neq 0, u \neq 0, u^3 + v^2 \neq 0\}, r >$,

$7 : < \{v \neq 0, u \neq 0, u^3 + v^2 = 0\}, r >$.

In [20], Wu gave a structure theorem and showed how it could be used for computing zeros of polynomial equations from their characteristic sets. This construction can be extended to constrained polynomials. Below we illustrate how solutions can be obtained from some of the chains in the above parametric characteristic set.

The chain $\{1''', 6\}$ can be used to generate the zeros as follows: For $1'''$, the initial vx should be nonzero which requires that $x \neq 0$; this condition can be used to simplify $\{1''', 6\}$, to give a new set $\{1''', 6'\}$, where $6' : < \{v \neq 0, u \neq 0, u^3 + v^2 \neq 0\}, (u^3 + v^2)x^2 + 2u^2x + u >$. From constrained polynomials $1'''$ and $6'$, zeros can be computed by solving $6'$ and then substituting the values of x to get the corresponding values of y.

It is also necessary to consider the case when the initial $x = 0$. It is not enough to add the polynomial $x = 0$ to the chain $\{1''', 6\}$; instead this condition of an initial not being zero needs to be added to the whole basis from which the chain was generated. Alternately, $x = 0$ can be added to the original set and a parametric characteristic set can be computed for $\{u \neq 0, v \neq 0, u^3 + v^2 \neq 0\}$.

When $x = 0$ is added to the original basis, f becomes 0, and g becomes uy^2. We thus get a parametric characteristic set consisting $< \{u \neq 0\}, uy^2 >, < \emptyset, x >$, which gives the zero $x = 0, y = 0$ for the case when $u \neq 0$. For the case when $u = 0$, we get a 1-dimensional zero set, which is $x = 0$.

From the chain $\{1''', 7\}$, we get $7'$ under the condition that $x \neq 0$: $< \{u \neq 0, v \neq 0, u^3 + v^2 = 0\}, 2u^2x + u >$, which gives a zero-dimensional zero set whose x component is $-\frac{1}{2u}$. Zero sets can be computed from other chains in a similar manner. Chain $\{5\}$ for the case $u = 0, v = 0$, also gives a 1-dimensional zero set, which is $x = 0$.

For computing zero sets, optimizations such that factoring and splitting can be performed to speedup the computations of chains insofar as the zero sets are preserved.

13.6   Concluding Remarks and Future Research

A simple but powerful approach for solving systems of parametric polynomial equations has been discussed. The approach was applied to define and illustrate parametric Gröbner basis construction from a system of parametric polynomial equations. As was evident from examples discussed above, different values for parameters may result in different systems and associated solution sets, including cases when for some parameter values, system may be inconsistent and thus have no solution, as well as for other parameter values, the same system may have infinitely many solutions. The approach was also briefly illustrated for characteristic set constructions and generating solutions using characteristic sets. The same approach should extend to other symbolic elimination techniques including univariate resultants and multivariate resultants.

From the discussion, the reader must have noticed that sometimes unnecessary and excessive branching may be done because it is guided by considering the coefficient of the leading term in a parametric polynomial. Further research is necessary to study how branching can be avoided. In [16, 17], some ideas are discussed in the context of solving linear systems of parametric equations, which may be useful for nonlinear polynomial equations also.

Given that symbolic computation algorithms do not often finish on many large examples (often because of lack of space since large intermediate computations may be generated), numerical algorithms such as those based on homotopy and continuation techniques must be employed. It would be interesting to study how this approach can be used for solving systems of parametric polynomial equations using numerical methods.

Acknowledgments: Comments by Lakshman Y.N. and a referee on an earlier draft helped in improving the presentation of the paper.

References

[1] B. Buchberger (1965), *Ein algorithmus zum auffinden der basiselemente des restklassenringes nach einem nulldimensionalen polynomideal*, Ph.D. Thesis (in German), Universitat Innsbruck.

[2] B. Buchberger (1985), "Gröbner bases: An Algorithmic method in Polynomial Ideal theory", in *Multidimensional Systems Theory*, N.K. Bose, ed., D. Reidel Publishing Co., 184-232.

[3] S.-C. Chou and X.-S. Gao (1990), "Ritt-Wu's decomposition algorithm and geometry theorem proving," Proc. *10th Intl. Conf. on Automated Deduction (CADE-10)*, Kaiserslautern, Germany, LNCS Springer Verlag, 207-220.

[4] S.-C. Chou and X.-S. Gao (1992), "Solving parametric algebraic systems," Proc. *ISSAC 1992*, Berkeley, CA. Also in Mathematics-Mechanization Research Reprints, No. 7, March 1992.

[5] B. Donald, D. Kapur, and J.L. Mundy (eds.) (1992), *Symbolic and Numerical Computation for Artificial Intelligence*, Academic Press.

[6] J.C. Faugère, P. Gianni, D. Lazard, and T. Mora (1989), *Efficient computation*

of zero-dimensional Gröbner bases by change of ordering, Technical Report 89–52, LITP, Université de Paris.

[7] C.M. Hoffman (1989), *Geometric and solid modeling: An introduction,* Morgan Kaufmann.

[8] D. Kapur (1992), A theory of characteristic sets, Unpublished Manuscript, Department of Computer Science, State University of New York, Albany, NY.

[9] D. Kapur (1992), Solving systems of parametric polynomial equations, Unpublished Manuscript, Department of Computer Science, State University of New York, Albany, NY.

[10] D. Kapur and Lakshman Y.N. (1992), "Elimination Methods: An Introduction," in *Symbolic and Numerical Computation for Artificial Intelligence,* Donald, Kapur and Mundy (eds.), Academic Press, 1992.

[11] D. Kapur and H. Wan (1990), "Refutational Proofs of Geometry Theorems via Characteristic Set Computation," Proc. of *the SIGSAM 1990 Intl. Symp. on Symbolic and Algebraic Computation - ISSAC '90,* Japan, August 1990.

[12] D.E. Knuth (1980), *Seminumerical algorithms: The art of computer programming,* 2, Second Edition, Addison Wesley, 407-408.

[13] A.P. Morgan (1987), *Solving Polynomial Systems using Continuation for Scientific and Engineering Problems,* Prentice Hall, Englewood Cliffs, NJ.

[14] V.-D. Nguyen, J.L. Mundy, and D. Kapur (1991), "Modeling Generic Polyhedral Objects by Constraints," Proc. of *Computer Vision and Pattern Recognition,* Hawaii, June 1991,

[15] J.F. Ritt (1950), *Differential Algebra,* AMS Colloquium Publications.

[16] W.Y. Sit (1991), "A theory for parametric linear systems," Proc. *ISSAC 1991,* Bonn, Germany, 112-121.

[17] W.Y. Sit (1992), *An algorithm for solving parametric linear systems.* Unpublished Manuscript. To appear in *J. Symbolic Computation.*

[18] V. Weispfenning (1990), *Comprehensive Gröbner bases,* MIP-9003, Fakultät für Mathematik und Informatik, Universität Passau, Germany.

[19] W. Wu (1986), "Basic principles of mechanical theorem proving in geometries", *J. of System Sciences and Mathematical Sciences,* 4(3), (1984), 207-235. Also appeared in *J. of Automated Reasoning,* **2,** (1986), 221-252.

[20] W. Wu (1986), "On zeros of algebraic equations - an application of Ritt's principle", *Kexue Tongbao,* **31**(1), 1-5.

14 Fourier's Elimination: Which to Choose?

Jean-Louis Imbert

Abstract

This paper is concerned with variable elimination methods in linear inequation systems, related to Fourier's elimination [8]. Our aim is to make visible the links between the different contributions of S.N. Cernikov [3], D.A. Kolher [17], R.J. Duffin [6], JL.J. Imbert [10], and J. Jaffar, M.J. Maher, P.J. Stuckey and R.H.C. Yap [14]. We show that the three methods proposed by Cernikov, Kolher and Imbert produce exactly the same output (without more or less redundant inequations), up to multiplying by a non-zero positive scalar. We present and discuss the improvements of Cernikov, Duffin, Imbert and Jaffar et al., and propose a new improvement. We give a short analysis of the complexity of the main improvements and discuss the choice of the method in relation to the problem at hand. We propose a pattern algorithm. Finally, we conclude with a comparative assessment through a brief example and a few remarks.

14.1 Introduction

Variable elimination is of major interest for Constraint Logic Programming Languages [12], and Constraint Query Languages [15], where we would like to eliminate auxiliary variables introduced during the execution of a program. This elimination is always suitable for final results. It can also increase the efficiency of the intermediary processes. We focus on linear inequalities of the form $ax \leq b$, where a denotes a n-real vector, x an n-vector of variables, b a real number, and the juxtaposition ax denotes the inner product. This type of constraint occurs in CLP languages such as CHIP [7, 22], CLP($\Re$) [13], and Prolog III [4, 5]. A constraint system is a conjunction of constraints. Using matrix notation, an inequation system $\{a_i x \leq b_i \mid i = 1, \ldots, m\}$ can be written $Ax \leq b$, where A denotes an $(m \times n)$-matrix, and b an m-real vector. The main problem we face during the variable elimination process in linear inequation systems, is the size of the output. It is doubly exponential. Variable elimination in inequation systems has been extensively investigated. Among these investigations one can cite the C. and JL. Lassez method [18], which globally eliminates in one single operation the set of unwanted variables. It is based on semantic properties of projection and of convex hull. It makes it possible to obtain approximations. Nevertheless, so far, mainly methods derived from Fourier's elimination [8] are used in CLP languages. For example, the programming language CLP($\Re$) outputs its results after eliminating undesirable variables using a method related to Fourier [14]. This kind of method carries out an incremental elimination of variables, one after another. The major problem comes from the size of intermediary systems.

In this paper, our interest will be exclusively focused on methods derived from Fourier's elimination. Among the improvements in these eliminations are the contributions of S.N. Cernikov [3], D.A. Kolher [17], R.J. Duffin [6], JL.J. Imbert [10], and J.Jaffar, M.J. Maher, P.J. Stuckey and R.H.C. Yap [14]. There are basically three approaches represented in these methods: the general algebraic approach of Cernikov, the matricial algebraic approach of Kohler, and the graph, or more specifically, the tree approach of [10]. These trees reflect the way in which the new inequations are constructed as the elimination proceeds. This last approach shows clearly that the methods proposed by Cernikov, Kohler and Imbert are equivalent. This is far from being obvious as Kohler remarks (see Section 14.4).

The aim of this paper is to make visible the links between these different abovementioned contributions. This study, which has not been done before, is of great interest. We show that the three methods proposed by Cernikov, Kolher and Imbert produce exactly the same output (without more or less redundant inequations), up to multiplying by a non-zero positive scalar. We present and discuss improvements by Cernikov, Duffin, Imbert and Jaffar et al., and propose a new improvement. We give a short analysis of the complexity of the main improvements and discuss the choice of the method depending on the problem at hand. We propose a pattern algorithm. Finally, we conclude with a comparative assessment using a brief example and a few remarks.

The rest of this paper is organized in the following way: Section 14.2 presents basic concepts necessary for understanding the other Sections. In Section 14.3, we introduce the parts of the initial system (called minimal parts) which can produce a relevant final inequation, and present the Cernikov-Fourier algorithm [3]. In Section 14.4, we introduce the characterization of minimal parts and give the Kohler-Fourier algorithm [17]. Moreover, in this Section, we show that the algorithms of Cernikov-Fourier and Kohler-Fourier produce exactly the same final system (without more or less redundant inequations), up to multiplying each inequation by a non-zero positive scalar. Section 14.5 successively presents improvements by Cernikov, Duffin, Imbert and Jaffar et al., and introduces some new precisions about redundancy. Furthermore, we show (subsection 14.5.4) a new improvement of the Cernikov minimal part method, dividing in half the average number of comparisons. In Section 14.6, we discuss the complexity of the various improvement contributions and the choice between the minimal part method (Cernikov) and the matricial method (Kohler). Then we give a pattern variable elimination algorithm for inequation systems. Section 14.7 compares, through a brief example, the contributions of Cernikov, Kohler and Imbert [10]. Finally, in Section 14.8, we conclude with a few remarks.

14.2 Preliminaries

Let x denote the vector $(x_1, \ldots, x_n)$. Let x' be the vector of variables to be retained, and let x'' be the vector of variables to be eliminated. We will abuse the language by writing $x = (x', x'')$. In the same way, $a = (a_1, \ldots, a_n)$ denotes a real or rational vector, and a will be written (a', a''), respective of the subscripts of x' and x''. The inequation system $Ax \leq b$ can then be written $A'x' + A''x'' \leq b$. To eliminate the variables of x'', the problem at hand is to find a system $Cx' \leq d$ as concise as possible for which, if (a', a'') is in the solution set of $A'x' + A''x'' \leq b$, then a' is in the solution set of $Cx' \leq d$, and reciprocally, if a' is a solution of system $Cx' \leq d$, then there is a'' such that (a', a'') is a solution of system $A'x' + A''x'' \leq b$. We will say that $Cx' \leq d$ and $A'x' + A''x'' \leq b$ are *equivalent* on x'. It can be shown that each inequation of the final system $Cx' \leq d$ is a linear combinatory with positive coefficients of inequations of initial system (this is a consequence of Fourier's elimination).

14.2.1 Fourier's Algorithm

Let $a_1 x \leq b_1$ and $a_2 x \leq b_2$ be two inequations, and let $a_{1,1}$ and $a_{2,1}$ be the coefficients of the variable x_1 respectively in the first and second inequations. Let us assume that $a_{1,1} > 0$ and $a_{2,1} < 0$. Then

$$-a_{2,1}(a_1 x) + a_{1,1}(a_2 x) \leq -a_{2,1} b_1 + a_{1,1} b_2 \tag{14.2.1}$$

is a consequence of the two initial inequations, and x_1 does not occur in it. Let $Ax \leq b$ be an inequation system, and V the variables which occur in it. Let $\tilde{A}x \leq \tilde{b}$ be the system obtained from $Ax \leq b$, by removing all inequations which x_1 occurs in, and replacing them with all the inequations of type (14.2.1) above, we can construct from any pair of removed inequations. It can be proven that $\tilde{A}x \leq \tilde{b}$ and $Ax \leq b$ are equivalent on $V - \{x_1\}$. This operation must be successively repeated for each variable to be eliminated.

14.2.2 Redundancy and Size of the Intermediary Systems

A drawback of Fourier's elimination is the production of redundancies which overwhelms the system. It is here that the improvements of S.N. Cernikov [3], D.A. Kolher [17], R.J. Duffin [6], JL.J. Imbert [10], and J.Jaffar, M.J. Maher, P.J. Stuckey and R.H.C. Yap [14], come. One way to mitigate this drawback is to associate each inequation with information to memorize the way in which it has been produced. This information deals with: the inequations of the initial system used to produce this inequation, the variables which are effectively eliminated during pair gathering, and, finally, the other variables eliminated during the previous variable eliminations. Some relations between the quantities of elements occurring in these three kinds of variables, make it possible to detect whether a new inequation is redundant or not.

Another drawback of Fourier's method is the large increase in the number of constraints in the intermediary systems. One of the main reasons is that the historic method quickly detects most of the redundancies, but it does not detect all of them (only those due to the construction, i.e. due to $A''x''$, but not those due to $A'x'$). Besides, redundancies have a tendency to spread because they multiply very quickly. The other reason concerns the nature of Fourier's method: independently of the redundancies, the number of inequations has a tendency to increase, before decreasing when few variables remain to be eliminated. A remedy for the first cause is to use a general method of redundancy removing [20, 16, 19, 11]. As for the second cause, which is structural, it cannot be suppressed. Other methods are necessary for remedying this inconvenience. Numerous methods have been proposed, including one already cited and set out in [18] which is particularly interesting as it creates a minimal representation of the final system and does not use intermediary systems.

14.2.3 Some Results

Let S be the linear inequation system $\{a_1x \leq b_1, \ldots, a_nx \leq b_n\}$. It is known (Farkas [21, p87-90]), that the inequation $cx \leq d$ is a consequence of S if and only if there exist positive coefficients (≥ 0) $\alpha_0, \alpha_1, \ldots, \alpha_n$, such that $c = \alpha_1a_1 + \ldots + \alpha_na_n$ and $d = \alpha_0 + \alpha_1b_1 + \ldots + \alpha_nb_n$. The inequation $cx \leq d$ is said to be an *affine combinatory with positive coefficients* of inequations of S. A *linear combinatory* is an affine combinatory such that $\alpha_0 = 0$. Hence, an inequation of S is redundant in S if and only if it is an affine combinatory with positive coefficients of the other inequations of S. It is *weakly redundant* if $\alpha_0 = 0$ in each affine combinatory, *strongly redundant* in other cases.

Lastly, let us notice that, from Fourier's elimination, each inequation obtained after variable elimination in an inequation system S, is a linear combinatory with positive coefficients of the inequations of S.

14.3 Minimal Subset

As a result of Fourier's elimination (the last remark of Section 14.2.3), each inequation of the final system $Cx' \leq d$ is a linear combinatory with non-negative coefficients of inequations of the initial system $A'x' + A''x'' \leq b$. Hence, we look at the real-vectors $w = (w_1, \ldots, w_m)$ such that $wA'' = 0''$. ($0''$ denotes the vector a'' with all its components equal to zero. The vector a'' has been introduced in Section 14.2. We will abuse the language by writing 0 instead of $0''$ if there is no ambiguity. In the same way, we will write 0 instead of $0'$). A vector w_1 is less than or equal to a vector w_2 (written $w_1 \leq w_2$), if each component of w_1 is less than or equal to its corresponding component of w_2. Let F be the cone[1] of non-negative solutions $0 \leq w$ of $wA'' = 0$. From the last remark of Section 14.2.3, it is evident that:

LEMMA 14.1 The system $\{wA'x' \leq wb \mid w \in F\}$ is equivalent to the final system $Cx' \leq d$.

However, this system is unnecessarily large. Indeed, on the one hand, if w_1 and w_2 are two elements of F identical up to multiplying by a non-zero scalar, then the inequations $w_1 A'x' \leq w_1 b$ and $w_2 A'x' \leq w_2 b$ are equivalent. On the other hand, from [1, Section 3 p 297-298] it suffices that the number of non-zero components of w is less than or equal to the number of non-zero components of x'' plus 1. As a matter of fact, according to [3], it is sufficient to take a base of F. A *base* of F is an irreducible subset of elements of F which generates F. Here, irreducible is for inclusion. Since F is a cone, a vector is *generated* by other vectors if it is a linear combinatory with non-negative coefficients of these other vectors.

Two elements of F are *essentially different* if they do not differ from one another by a positive scalar multiple. A *minimal vector* is a non-zero vector of F such that the only essentially different vector of F less than itself, is the zero-vector. Let G be a base of essentially different minimal vectors of F. Then, using lemma 14.1, it is evident that:

THEOREM 14.1 The systems $Cx' \leq d$ and $\{wA'x' \leq wb \mid w \in G\}$ are equivalent.

Moreover,

COROLLARY 14.1 If w_1 and w_2 are two elements of G, the zero-components of which coincide with each other, then $w_1 = w_2$.

---

[1] a cone is a point set containing all the linear combinatories with positive coefficients of any finite number of its elements.

PROOF: If $w_1 \neq w_2$, there is a linear combinatory of these two vectors which produces a non-zero element of F less than each of them. Indeed, it can be found $k > 0$, such that $kw_1 \leq w_2$. Then, continuously increase k with $kw_1 \leq w_2$, until at least one non-zero component of kw_1 is equal to the corresponding component of w_2. Then, $w_2 - kw_1$ is non-zero positive and is in F. So, w_1 and w_2 are not minimal and are not in G. $\square$

Each minimal vector of F or G, is associated with an inequation subset of $A'x' + A''x'' \leq b$ (the lines of the initial subset corresponding to the non-zero components of the minimal vector). This subset is said to be *minimal for x''*, or simply *minimal* if there is no ambiguity.

From [1, section 3 p 297-298] and [3], theorem 14.1 can be used at each step in Fourier's elimination, yielding a correct algorithm. Then, for each inequation i, we memorize the subset H_i of initial inequations (i.e., of initial system $Ax \leq b$) which produced i. H_i is called a *historical subset* (a *label* in [14]). Clearly, for each initial inequation i, $H_i = \{i\}$. In Fourier's algorithm, only inequations with minimal historical subsets are retained. An algorithm using these properties is given in Figure 14.1.

Notice that the historical subset of the new inequation, and the comparison can be processed before producing the inequation. Hence, the inequation is not created if at least one existing historical subset is included in its historical subset.

EXAMPLE 14.1 Let us consider the following system:

$$
\begin{array}{ll}
(1) & x_1 - x_4 - x_5 \leq 2 \\
(2) & x_2 - 2x_4 + x_5 \leq 0 \\
(3) & -x_1 + x_2 + x_4 - x_5 \leq 0 \\
(4) & -x_3 + x_4 + 2x_5 \leq 0
\end{array}
$$

Assume that $x' = (x_1, x_2, x_3)$ and $x'' = (x_4, x_5)$. This system can be written in matricial form:

$$
\begin{pmatrix} 1 & 0 & 0 \\ 0 & 1 & 0 \\ -1 & 1 & 0 \\ 0 & 0 & -1 \end{pmatrix} \begin{pmatrix} x_1 \\ x_2 \\ x_3 \end{pmatrix} + \begin{pmatrix} -1 & -1 \\ -2 & 1 \\ 1 & -1 \\ 1 & 2 \end{pmatrix} \begin{pmatrix} x_4 \\ x_5 \end{pmatrix} \leq \begin{pmatrix} 2 \\ 0 \\ 0 \\ 0 \end{pmatrix}
$$

The vectors $w_1 = (3, 0, 1, 2)$, $w_2 = (5, 2, 5, 4)$, $w_3 = (1, 1, 2, 1)$ and $w_4 = (0, 3, 5, 1)$ are in F. The vector w_1 is minimal in F because each non-zero vector w of F in which the second component is 0, is of the form $(3k, 0, k, 2k)$ where k is a real.

Input: $Ax \leq b$, a system of inequations.
   Assume that $x = (x', x'')$, where $x'' = (x_1, \ldots, x_k)$ is the vector of variables to be eliminated.
Output: A system $Cx' \leq d$ equivalent to $Ax \leq b$ on x'

begin

1. At the start, the inequation system S is equal to $Ax \leq b$.
2. **For** x_j being successively the variables $x_1, \ldots, x_k$,
   2.1. Remove from S, each inequation with a non-zero coefficient of x_j.
   2.2. For each pair of removed inequations $a_1 x \leq b_1$ and $a_2 x \leq b_2$, with components $a_{j,1}$ and $a_{j,2}$ of x_j respectively positive and negative, insert the inequation $a_{j,1} a_2 x - a_{j,2} a_1 x \leq a_{j,1} b_2 - a_{j,2} b_1$ in S. If the historical subsets of the inequations of the pair are H_1 and H_2 respectively, then, the historical subset of the new inequation is $H_1 \bigcup H_2$.
   2.3. Remove from S each inequation with a historical subset including at least one historical subset of the remaining inequations.
3. Return the system S which is then of the form $Cx' \leq d$.

end

Figure 14.1
Cernikov-Fourier's Algorithm

The corresponding minimal part is formed of the three inequations (1), (3) and (4). The vectors w_2 and w_3 are not minimal since the vector $1/3\ w_1$ is less than and essentially different from each of them. And for any non-negative real k, the vector $k\ w_1$ is in F.

   Moreover, $G = \{w_1, w_4\}$ is a base of F, since $w_2 = 5/3\ w_1 + 2/3\ w_4$ and $w_3 = 1/3\ w_1 + 1/3\ w_4$.

14.4 Characterization of Minimal Subsets

The main problem we face in the previous method is that the historical subset of each inequation of $Cx' \leq d$ must be compared to the historical subset of every other inequation of $Cx' \leq d$. The following theorem makes it possible to overcome this drawback. In the following, the notion of rank of vector space, affine space, vector system and matrix is assumed known.

THEOREM 14.2 Let $A'x' + A''x'' \leq b$ be an inequation system. Let F be the cone defined in Section 14.3. An element w of F is minimal iff the sub-matrix A''_w formed from lines of A'' related to non-zero components of w has as its rank, the number of lines of A''_w minus 1.

PROOF: Since $wA'' = 0$, this rank is at most the number of lines of A''_w minus 1. If it is smaller, there exists a vector v of F with at least one non-zero positive component, such that for each non-zero component of v, the corresponding component of w is non-zero, and such that $vA'' = 0$. Without loss of generality, v can be assumed less than or equal to w, with equality for at least one non-zero component (if necessary, multiply by an appropriate scalar). As a result, $w - v$ is a non-zero vector of F, then w is not minimal. $\square$

EXAMPLE 14.2 Let us take up again the previous example. Then w_1 is minimal since the matrix

$$A''_{w_1} = \begin{pmatrix} -1 & -1 \\ 1 & -1 \\ 1 & 2 \end{pmatrix},$$

evidently has rank 2 with three rows.

But, w_2 is not a minimal vector, since the matrix

$$A''_{w_2} = \begin{pmatrix} -1 & -1 \\ -2 & 1 \\ 1 & -1 \\ 1 & 2 \end{pmatrix},$$

has rank 2 and four rows.

In fact, Cernikov defines a minimal vector (which he calls *fundamental element*) as a vector w for which the rank of the matrix A''_w is the number of its lines minus 1 [3, p 1520]. He then says that the maximal systems of essentially different minimal elements of F are identical with its bases. Kohler used this result in Fourier's elimination algorithm. In the algorithm of Figure 14.2, if H is the historical subset associated with an inequation, A''_H will denote the matrix formed from lines and columns of A'' which respectively correspond to elements of H and to columns of $x_1, \ldots, x_j$.

Input: $Ax \leq b$, an inequation system.
  Assume that $x = (x', x'')$, where $x'' = (x_1, \ldots, x_k)$ is the vector of variables to be eliminated.
Output: A system $Cx' \leq d$ equivalent to $Ax \leq b$ on x'

begin

1. we begin with the system of inequations S equal to $Ax \leq b$.

2. **For** x_j being successively the variables $x_1, \ldots, x_k$,

    2.1. Remove from S, each inequation with a non-zero coefficient of x_j.

    2.2. **For each** pair of removed inequations $a_1 x \leq b_1$ and $a_2 x \leq b_2$, with components $a_{j,1}$ and $a_{j,2}$ of x_j respectively positive and negative,

      2.2.1 If the historical subsets of the inequations of the pair are H_1 and H_2 respectively, then, the historical subset of the new inequation is $H_1 \bigcup H_2$.

      2.2.2 If the rank of A''_H is its number of lines minus 1, insert in S the new inequation
      $$a_{j,1} a_2 x - a_{j,2} a_1 x \leq a_{j,1} b_2 - a_{j,2} b_1.$$

3. Return the system S which is then of the form $Cx' \leq d$.

end

Figure 14.2
Kohler-Fourier's Algorithm

Note that, contrary to the Cernikov-Fourier Algorithm, the detection of minimal subsets is performed at the time of the creation of the new inequations. That is to say, whether a subset is minimal or not is detected at the time of its creation. This is the opposite of the Cernikov-Fourier Algorithm, in which some inequations are temporarily kept until a new inequation with a smaller historical subset is created. As a result, time used for creating non-retained inequations, and an non-negligible place used for intermediary storage can be saved.

However, it can be asked whether this method detects when the same inequation can be obtained from the same minimal subset in more than one way. Kohler [17, p 23]: *"I have been unable to prove that we can discount the possibility of the Fourier-Motzkin Method generating more than one extreme vector from the same half-line. Should this occur we need only keep one of them"*. The tree approach of [10] makes it possible to give a simple answer to this question using its unicity theorem (p 121). This theorem can be translated as follows:

THEOREM 14.3 (UNICITY THEOREM) For each minimal subset, Fourier's algorithm, modified by Cernikov or Kohler, can produce only one inequation and only in one way.

COROLLARY 14.2 The Cernikov-Fourier and Kohler-Fourier algorithms rigorously produce the same final system without more or less redundant inequation.

PROOF: It is an immediate consequence of the previous theorem, since, as a result of Theorem 14.2, the Kohler-Fourier algorithm produces all the inequations produced by the Cernikov-Fourier algorithm, and eventually, some double inequations.
□

Remark : Theorem 14.3 is valid only if, at each Fourier step, each inequation associated with a non-minimal historical subset is discarded. Otherwise uniqueness is not guaranteed and the Cernikov method is preferred. In addition, it can be remarked that this theorem involves the result of corollary 14.1.

Another very interesting result shown in [10] is the independence of the order in which the variables are eliminated:

THEOREM 14.4 Whatever the order in which the variables are eliminated, the Cernikov-Fourier algorithm or the Kohler-Fourier algorithm rigorously produce the same final system (up to multiplied by a positive scalar), without more or less redundant inequation.

14.5   Quick Detection of Minimal or Non-Minimal Subsets

The main problem we face in the previous two methods is that the minimal subset detection operation is very costly. In this section, we present various known solutions to this problem and we give some new answers. Most of these improvements can be applied independently to both methods.

14.5.1   Upper Limit of the Rank

The first improvement was provided by the precursor of the previous two methods. Though Cernikov presents the following improvement in [3], we can find its foundation in [1, p 296 corollary 2].

THEOREM 14.5 After k variable eliminations, if the historical subset associated with an inequation has more than $k + 1$ elements, then this historical subset is not minimal.

PROOF: It can be immediately deduced from theorem 14.2, and from the fact that the matrix A''_w has k columns, and then its rank is less than or equal to k. $\square$

In this case, the detection cost is very low. Cernikov and Kohler included this detection in their algorithms.

14.5.2   Passive Variables

Duffin, in [6, p 90], introduces the active or passive variable concept. A variable is *active* during its elimination if there is at least one pair of inequations in the sense of Fourier's elimination. Otherwise the variable is said to be *passive*. Let x_j be a passive variable. Its elimination can suppress some inequations from the system, but does not add any. This comes from the fact that the coefficients of x_j in the inequations are either all positive $(0 \leq)$ or all negative (≤ 0). Then if we delay the elimination of such a variable, since Fourier's elimination uses only linear combinatories with positive coefficients, the coefficients of x_j will all have the same sign in all generated inequations. In particular, the inequations with non-zero coefficients of x_j, generate inequations with non-zero coefficients of x_j. These inequations will all be rejected in a subsequent elimination of this variable. Thus,

THEOREM 14.6 After the elimination of k variables, p of which are passive, if in a historical subset more than $k + 1 - p$ elements occur, then this historical subset is not minimal.

14.5.3   Upper and Lower Limits of the Rank

So far, we have looked at the improvements at a global level. However, the minimal subset is a local concept in that a minimal part depends only on what is included within it. Hence, it is sufficient to look at the eliminated variables occurring in at least one inequation of the historical subset [10].

Assume that the variables eliminated from the initial system are $x_1, \ldots, x_k$. We will say that they are *officially eliminated*, and will write O_k the set of these variables. For each inequation i produced, the set O_k can be divided into three disjointed subsets: the subset of *effectively eliminated* variables denoted E_i, the subset of *implicitly eliminated* variables denoted I_i, and the other variables. A variable is said to be effectively eliminated for i, if its official elimination produces at least one of its ancestors (initial or intermediate inequations used to produce i). A variable is said to be implicitly eliminated for i, if the following three conditions are satisfied: it occurs in at least one inequation of H_i, it does not occur in i, it is not effectively eliminated for i. In practice, in I_i we also find some implicitly eliminated variables which are not in O_k.

EXAMPLE 14.3 Let us consider the following system from which we want to eliminate the variables x_1, x_2, x_3 and x_4:

$$
\begin{array}{ll}
(1) & x_1 - 2x_3 - x_4 + x_6 + x_7 \leq 2 \\
(2) & -x_1 + 2x_3 - x_5 - x_6 \leq 1 \\
(3) & x_1 + x_3 + x_4 + 2x_7 \leq 0 \\
(4) & -x_1 - x_3 \leq -1
\end{array}
$$

Among the inequations produced by the elimination of x_1 are the two following $((5) = (1) + (2)$ and $(6) = (3) + (4))$.

$$
\begin{array}{ll}
(5) & -x_4 - x_5 + x_7 \leq 3 \\
(6) & +x_4 + 2x_7 \leq -1
\end{array}
$$

The variables x_2 and x_3 do not occur in the inequations (5) and (6). The elimination of these two variables retains these two inequations. To eliminate x_4, we only have to add (5) and (6).

$$
(7) \quad -x_5 + 3x_7 \leq 2
$$

The officially eliminated variables are x_1, x_2, x_3 and x_4. The variables effectively eliminated for the inequation (7) are x_1 and x_4. The variable x_3 has been implicitly eliminated for the inequation (7), as has been the variable x_6 which is not officially eliminated. The variable x_2 is eliminated neither effectively nor implicitly for (7), since it does not occur in any of the four original inequations used to produce (7).

In [10] the following two theorems are shown, where $Card(S)$ denotes the number of elements of S:

THEOREM 14.7 (FIRST ACCELERATION THEOREM) If H_i is a minimal subset, then the following relation is satisfied:

$$
1 + Card(E_i) \quad \leq \quad Card(H_i) \quad \leq \quad 1 + Card(E_i \bigcup (I_i \bigcap O_k))
$$

In this same paper it is shown that whatever H_i, minimal part or not, the left inequality is satisfied. The right inequality gives an upper limit less than or equal to the one of Theorem 14.5 above. In fact, from Theorem 14.2, Theorem 14.5 says that the rank of the A''_w matrix can be more than the number of columns. Theorem 14.7 suppresses from this number the zero columns. Moreover, the Duffin improvement is always global and still applicable: we only have to suppress passive variables from O_k. When the first acceleration theorem quickly detects non-minimal parts, the second acceleration theorem quickly detects minimal parts:

THEOREM 14.8 (SECOND ACCELERATION THEOREM) Let i be an inequation such that $1 + Card(E_i) = Card(H_i)$, then H_i is minimal.

This theorem avoids a heavy verification burden. The cost of these two theorems is very low. It linearly depends on the number of eliminated variables. The costly research operation of minimal subsets, either by comparison of minimal parts, or by computing a matrix rank, needs to be done only when

$$1 + Card(E_i) \quad < \quad Card(H_i) \quad \le \quad 1 + Card(E_i \bigcup (I_i \bigcap O_k)).$$

Thus, if there is no implicitly eliminated variable, these two theorems are sufficient. Usually, this happens when the constraints are randomly generated. In return, the algorithm performances decrease when the number of implicitly eliminated variables increases.

An example using these two theorems is given in section 14.7.

14.5.4 Comparison Number

The following improvement deals only with the Cernikov-Fourier method. The set G is a base of F, and there is a one-to-one map between G and the set of minimal subsets. Then, for each element j of a non-minimal subset P, there is a minimal part included in P, in which j occurs. As a result, if we take an ordering on the initial inequations, the comparison between subsets with the same first element is sufficient. So, the average number of comparisons is divided in half. However, more storage space is needed for intermediary results.

EXAMPLE 14.4 Let us take up again Example 14.1. The vector w_2 produces the inequation $7x_2 - 4x_3 \le 10$ associated with the historical set $\{(1), (2), (3), (4)\}$. This historical set is not minimal. Then it includes a minimal historial set in which occurs the inequation (1). Indeed, the vector w_1 produces the inequation $2x_1 + x_2 - 2x_3 \le 6$ associated with the historical set $\{(1), (3), (4)\}$. In fact, if the original system is without redundancy, it can be shown that $H_{w_2} = H_{w_1} \bigcup H_{w_4}$, since $w_2 = 5/3 \, w_1 + 2/3 \, w_4$ and since the vector w_4 produces the inequation $-5x_1 + 8x_2 - x_3 \leq 0$ associated with the historical set $\{(2), (3), (4)\}$.

14.5.5 Redundancies

Let us consider the initial inequation system $A'x' + A''x'' \leq b$. So far, the only redundancies suppressed during the elimination process of x'', are the ones due to A''. However, if we take into account $A'x'$, other redundancies may appear. I do not know a method which suppresses all redundancies, compatible with one of Fourier elimination methods presented above. However, in some cases, coexistence is possible. In [14], it is shown that strong redundancies[2] produced by Fourier's algorithm with the previous improvements, can be suppressed without subsequent damage.

THEOREM 14.9 Every inequation, at least one ancestor of which is strongly redundant, is strongly redundant.

PROOF: Let $ux \leq v$ be a strongly redundant inequation. Let us assume that this inequation is equal to the linear combinatory $(\mathbf{sum}_{i=1}^{i=p} \, \alpha_i a_i)x \leq (\mathbf{sum}_{i=1}^{i=p} \, \alpha_i b_i) + \alpha_0$. The proof is then trivial since $uv \leq v - \alpha_0$ is a logical consequence of the inequation system and since each produced inequation is a linear combinatory with positive coefficients of the inequations of the system. □

The systematic detection of strong redundancies is very costly. However, there are some cases in which the detection cost is lower. The quasi-redundancy is a special case of strong redundancy. An inequation $ux \leq v$ is quasi-redundant in $Ax \leq b$ if there is another inequation of that system written $ux \leq v - r$ up to multiplied by a positive scalar, where r is a non-zero positive constant [19]. The quasi-redundancy detection is not excessively expensive because it is roughly a one-to-one comparison of constraints with each other.

Remark : Assume that all or part of the strong redundancies are suppressed from an intermediary system $\mathcal{C}_i$, and that $\mathcal{C}_i$ is obtained by a derived Fourier's elimination method $\mathcal{M}$. Let $\mathcal{K}_i$ be the subsystem of $\mathcal{C}_i$ so obtained. To take advantage of this, we have to be sure that in the next steps all the redundancies detected by $\mathcal{M}$ applied on $\mathcal{C}_i$, will not occur in $\mathcal{K}_{i+1}$ when this same method is applied on $\mathcal{K}_i$. If this is the case, we will say that the method $\mathcal{M}$ is *fully compatible* with the

---

[2]the supporting hyperplane of which is far from the solution set of the inequation system.

partial or full deletion of strong redundancies. Otherwise we have to find a means to detect all strong redundancies at each step, and this detection is too costly, and thus impracticable.

The methods of Cernikov-Fourier and Kohler-Fourier, are opposed in that the first detects the minimal subset by comparison with each of the others, whereas the second only needs to know the inequations of its historical subset. As a result, if some minimal subsets are missing due to strong redundancy deletions, the comparison method can be put on the wrong track. On the contrary, this is not the case for the matricial method. In conclusion we have the following result

PROPOSITION 14.1 *Any partial deletion of strong redundancies is fully compatible with the Kohler-Fourier elimination method but is not fully compatible with the Cernikov-Fourier elimination method.*

Thus, the partial deletion of strong redundancies is not suitable for the Cernikov-Fourier elimination method.

14.6   Comparison or Matricial Computation?

14.6.1   Complexity

The incorporation of improvements from theorems 14.5, 14.6, 14.7 and 14.8, results in a great reduction in the cost of the elimination algorithm. If m_0 is the number of inequations of the initial system, and if k is the number of variables to be eliminated, the cost of theorems 14.5, 14.7 and 14.8 is at most $O(m_0 + k)$ for each produced inequation. Note that the detection of the minimality of historical subsets can always be done before the creation of the new inequations. Thus, time can be saved in cases of rejection.

The cost of minimal subset detection using comparison is, at most, $O(m_0 m)$ for each produced inequation where m is the maximal number of inequations occurring in the intermediary system during the process of elimination. It must be noted that in the case of the Cernikov-Fourier method, the comparison must be done in both directions of the inclusion. If we use the improvements of theorems 14.7 and 14.8, the comparison must be done only for inequations satisfying theorem 14.7: in both directions of the inclusion between historical subsets of two new inequations which do not satisfy theorem 14.8, only in one direction when one of the new inequations satisfies theorem 14.8, no comparison is needed when the two inequations satisfy this same theorem.

The cost of minimal subset detection using matricial computation is, for each produced inequation, at most $O(k^5)$ in infinite precision, $O(k^3)$ otherwise. Thus, when k is low, it is better to use matricial computation and to change methods during the elimination process when k and m move. Theorem 14.3 and its corollary allow for this change at every moment.

Furthermore, in the choice of method, we have to take into account the fact that the matricial method allows for an independent process of produced inequations. Conversely, if during the elimination of a variable, the comparison is used, there will be comparisons to do until the end of the elimination of that variable. Moreover, the comparison method does not always immediately detect redundancies, as a result, this leads to an additional cost because of the intermediary storage. Consequently, the matricial method allows for a degree of parallelism higher than the comparison method. And then, the matricial method is better suited to an additional redundancy deletion such as quasi-redundancy than the comparison method is. In all cases, these two methods need to be used only when both theorems 14.7 and 14.8 fail.

14.6.2   Modified Fourier's Algorithm

In order to take into account the results of theorems 14.7 and 14.8, each inequation i is associated with three sets: the set H_i of initial inequations from which i is produced, the set E_i of its effectively eliminated variables, and the set I_i of its implicitly eliminated variables. When i is an initial inequation, $H_i = \{i\}$, and E_i and I_i are empty. The pattern algorithm is described in Figure 14.3.

In practice, it does not matter that some variables not implicitly eliminated occur in I_i, if each of these variables occur in at least one inequation of H_i. This comes from the fact that I_i is used only in theorem 14.7. So, these variables which are officially eliminated, are effectively eliminated, and then occur in E_i.

Note that steps 2.3.4 and 2.3.5 can be interchanged. Particularly, if the inequations are ordered, one can quickly see when an inequation is quasi-redundant and avoid the minimality detection for its historical subset [14].

If the strong redundancies are suppressed, (step 2.3.5), it is advisable to use the matricial computation at step 2.3.4.

14.7   An Example

In the following example, each inequation is associated with a triplet $(H; E; I)$. H is the historical subset of the inequation, E the set of its implicitly eliminated

Input: S an inequation system $Ax \leq b$.
Let us assume that $x = (x', x'')$, where $x'' = (x_1, \ldots, x_k)$ is
the vector of variables to be eliminated.
Output: A system $Cx' \leq d$ equivalent to $Ax \leq b$ on x'

begin

1. The set O of officially eliminated variables, is empty.
2. **For** x_j being successively the variables $x_1, \ldots, x_k$,
   2.1. Suppress from S all the inequations in which the coefficient of x_j is non-zero.
   2.2. If there is at least one pair of suppressed inequations with opposite sign coefficients of x_j, put x_j into O (*Duffin improvement*), and continue to 2.3, otherwise continue to 2.
   2.3. **For each** pair of suppressed inequations $a_1 x \leq b_1$ and $a_2 x \leq b_2$, of which the coefficients $a_{j,1}$ and $a_{j,2}$ of x_j are respectively positive and negative,
      2.3.1 Assume that the sets associated with these inequations are respectively H_1, E_1, I_1 and H_2, E_2, I_2. Compute $H = H_1 \bigcup H_2$, $E = E_1 \bigcup E_2$ and $I = I_1 \bigcup I_2$.
      2.3.2 If $Card(E \bigcup (I \bigcap O)) < Card(H)$ then continue to 2.3. (*Theorem 14.7*).
      2.3.3 If $Card(E) = Card(H)$ then go to 2.3.5. (*Theorem 14.8*).
      2.3.4 Analyze using comparison [3] or matricial computation the set H. If it is a minimal part then go to 2.3.5, else continue to 2.3.
      2.3.5 Suppress some strongly redundant inequations (*Theorem 14.9*). If the new inequation is strongly redundant then continue to 2.3, else continue to 2.3.6.
      2.3.6 Put in S the inequation
      $$a_{j,1} a_2 x - a_{j,2} a_1 x \leq a_{j,1} b_2 - a_{j,2} b_1.$$
3. Return the system S which is then of the form $Cx' \leq d$.

end

---

[3] When the comparison method is chosen, also suppress from the system the inequations of which the historical subsets include that of the new inequation.

Figure 14.3
Pattern Modified Fourier's Algorithm

variables and I the set of its implicitly eliminated variables. In the following notation, a hyphen will denote the empty-set, and a non-empty set will be denoted by the juxtaposition of its elements separated by dots. Let x_i, $i = 1, \dots, 5$ be the variables to be eliminated in the following system:

$$
\begin{aligned}
&(1) && 0 \le -1x_3 - 1x_4 - 1x_5 + 1 && (1;\ -;\ -) \\
&(2) && 0 \le +1x_1 + 2x_4 - 1y_2 + 2 && (2;\ -;\ -) \\
&(3) && 0 \le +1x_2 + 2x_5 - 1y_3 + 2 && (3;\ -;\ -) \\
&(4) && 0 \le -2x_2 - 3x_5 + 1y_3 - 1 && (4;\ -;\ -) \\
&(5) && 0 \le +1x_2 && (5;\ -;\ -) \\
&(6) && 0 \le +1x_3 && (6;\ -;\ -) \\
&(7) && 0 \le -1x_1 - 1x_2 + 2x_3 - 1y_1 + 3 && (7;\ -;\ -) \\
&(8) && 0 \le -1x_1 - 1x_2 - 2x_3 - 2x_4 - 2x_5 + 1y_1 + 1y_2 + 1y_3 - 5 && \\
& && && (8;\ -;\ -) \\
&(9) && 0 \le -1x_2 - 1x_5 + 2y_2 && (9;\ -;\ -)
\end{aligned}
$$

The elimination of x_1 gives $O_1 = \{x_1\}$, suppresses the inequations (2), (7) and (8), and proposes two pairs to create new inequations. These two new inequations are all accepted as a result of theorem 14.8. The cost is then minimal. The new system is:

$$
\begin{aligned}
&0 \le -1x_3 - 1x_4 - 1x_5 + 1 && (1;\ -;\ -) \\
&0 \le +1x_2 + 2x_5 - 1y_3 + 2 && (3;\ -;\ -) \\
&0 \le -2x_2 - 3x_5 + 1y_3 - 1 && (4;\ -;\ -) \\
&0 \le +1x_2 && (5;\ -;\ -) \\
&0 \le +1x_3 && (6;\ -;\ -) \\
&0 \le -1x_2 - 1x_5 + 2y_2 && (9;\ -;\ -) \\
&0 \le -1x_2 + 2x_3 + 2x_4 - 1y_1 - 1y_2 + 5 && (2.7;\ x_1;\ -) \\
&0 \le -1x_2 - 2x_3 - 2x_5 + 1y_1 + 1y_3 - 3 && (2.8;\ x_1;\ x_4)
\end{aligned}
$$

The elimination of x_2 gives $O_2 = \{x_1, x_2\}$, suppresses six inequations, and proposes eight pairs to create new inequations. These eight new inequations are all accepted as a result of theorem 14.8. The new system is:

$$0 \le -1x_3 - 1x_4 - 1x_5 + 1 \qquad (1; \ -; \ -)$$
$$0 \le +1x_3 \qquad (6; \ -; \ -)$$
$$0 \le +1x_5 - 1y_3 + 3 \qquad (3.4; \ x_2; \ -)$$
$$0 \le +1x_5 + 2y_2 - 1y_3 + 2 \qquad (3.9; \ x_2; \ -)$$
$$0 \le +2x_3 + 2x_4 + 2x_5 - 1y_1 - 1y_2 - 1y_3 + 7 \quad (2.3.7; \ x_1.x_2; \ -)$$
$$0 \le -2x_3 + 1y_1 - 1 \qquad (2.3.8; \ x_1.x_2; \ x_4.x_5)$$
$$0 \le -3x_5 + 1y_3 - 1 \qquad (4.5; \ x_2; \ -)$$
$$0 \le -1x_5 + 2y_2 \qquad (5.9; \ x_2; \ -)$$
$$0 \le +2x_3 + 2x_4 - 1y_1 - 1y_2 + 5 \qquad (2.5.7; \ x_1.x_2; \ -)$$
$$0 \le -2x_3 - 2x_5 + 1y_1 + 1y_3 - 3 \qquad (2.5.8; \ x_1.x_2; \ x_4)$$

So far, each pair produces a retained inequation. The elimination of x_3 gives $O_3 = \{x_1, x_2, x_3\}$ and proposes nine pairs for the creation of inequations. Among these nine pairs, two are rejected according to theorem 14.7. The other seven pairs are accepted as a result of theorem 14.8. The new system is then:

$$0 \le +1x_5 - 1y_3 + 3 \qquad (3.4; \ x_2; \ -)$$
$$0 \le +1x_5 + 2y_2 - 1y_3 + 2 \qquad (3.9; \ x_2; \ -)$$
$$0 \le -3x_5 + 1y_3 - 1 \qquad (4.5; \ x_2; \ -)$$
$$0 \le -1x_5 + 2y_2 \qquad (5.9; \ x_2; \ -)$$
$$0 \le -1x_4 - 1x_5 + 1 \qquad (1.6; \ x_3; \ -)$$
$$0 \le +1y_1 - 1 \qquad (2.3.6.8; \ x_1.x_2.x_3; \ x_4.x_5)$$
$$0 \le -2x_5 + 1y_1 + 1y_3 - 3 \qquad (2.5.6.8; \ x_1.x_2.x_3; \ x_4)$$
$$0 \le -1y_1 - 1y_2 - 1y_3 + 9 \qquad (1.2.3.7; \ x_1.x_2.x_3; \ x_4.x_5)$$
$$0 \le +2x_4 + 2x_5 - 1y_2 - 1y_3 + 6 \quad (2.3.7.8; \ x_1.x_2.x_3; \ x_4.x_5)$$
$$0 \le -2x_5 - 1y_1 - 1y_2 + 7 \qquad (1.2.5.7; \ x_1.x_2.x_3; \ x_4)$$
$$0 \le +2x_4 - 2x_5 - 1y_2 + 1y_3 + 2 \quad (2.5.7.8; \ x_1.x_2.x_3; \ x_4)$$

The elimination of x_4 gives $O_4 = \{x_1, x_2, x_3, x_4\}$ and proposes two pairs for the creation of inequations. According to theorem 14.7 no new inequation is created. The new system is then:

$$0 \le +1x_5 - 1y_3 + 3 \qquad (3.4; \ x_2; \ -)$$
$$0 \le +1x_5 + 2y_2 - 1y_3 + 2 \qquad (3.9; \ x_2; \ -)$$
$$0 \le -3x_5 + 1y_3 - 1 \qquad (4.5; \ x_2; \ -)$$
$$0 \le -1x_5 + 2y_2 \qquad (5.9; \ x_2; \ -)$$
$$0 \le +1y_1 - 1 \qquad (2.3.6.8; \ x_1.x_2.x_3; \ x_4.x_5)$$
$$0 \le -2x_5 + 1y_1 + 1y_3 - 3 \qquad (2.5.6.8; \ x_1.x_2.x_3; \ x_4)$$
$$0 \le -1y_1 - 1y_2 - 1y_3 + 9 \qquad (1.2.3.7; \ x_1.x_2.x_3; \ x_4.x_5)$$
$$0 \le -2x_5 - 1y_1 - 1y_2 + 7 \qquad (1.2.5.7; \ x_1.x_2.x_3; \ x_4)$$

The elimination of x_5 gives $O_5 = \{x_1, x_2, x_3, x_4, x_5\}$ and proposes eight pairs for the creation of inequations. Two are accepted according to theorem 14.8. Two are rejected according to theorem 14.7. And four are rejected using comparison or matricial computation methods. The final system is:

$$
\begin{array}{ll}
0 \leq +1y_1 - 1 & (2.3.6.8;\ x_1.x_2.x_3;\ x_4.x_5) \\
0 \leq -1y_1 - 1y_2 - 1y_3 + 9 & (1.2.3.7;\ x_1.x_2.x_3;\ x_4.x_5) \\
0 \leq -1y_3 + 4 & (3.4.5;\ x_2.x_5;\ -) \\
0 \leq +4y_2 - 1y_3 + 2 & (3.5.9.;\ x_2.x_5;\ -)
\end{array}
$$

Let us compare, on this small example, the cost of the Cernikov-Fourier and Kohler-Fourier Algorithms using Theorem 14.5 (column entitled "Cernikov/Kohler" in the table below), and the cost of these algorithms by replacing Theorem 14.5 by Theorem 14.7 and Theorem 14.8 (column entitled "+ Theorems 14.7 and 14.8"). The detailed account of realized operations is given in the table below. In the Cernikov or Kohler methods column, the first number represents the usage number of Theorem 14.5, the right number is the usage number of comparison or matricial method. In the right column, the first number represents the usage number of Theorem 14.7, the second number represents the usage number of Theorem 14.8, and the third number represents the usage number of the comparison or matricial method.

step	Cernikov/Kohler	+ Theorems 14.7 and 14.8
1	0 / 2	0 / 2 / 0
2	0 / 8	0 / 8 / 0
3	2 / 7	2 / 7 / 0
4	2 / 0	2 / 0 / 0
5	0 / 8	2 / 2 / 4
total	4 / 25	6 / 19 / 4

It can be seen, in this example, that the proportions of heavy detection methods used, are completely exchanged depending on the use of theorem 14.7 and 14.8: (4/29), or theorem 14.5: (25/29). The advantage supplied by the two acceleration theorems is greater insomuch as the number of implicitly eliminated variables is lower. The extreme case is the one where this number is zero. In this extreme case, only these two theorems are needed for all decisions. This is generally the case when the coefficients of the constraints are randomly generated.

14.8 Conclusion

After presenting the approaches of Cernikov and Kohler for improving the Fourier elimination algorithm, we have shown that these two approaches produce exactly the same final inequation system. The use of theorems 14.7 and 14.8 introduced in [10] considerably decreases the use of costly minimal subset detection methods. We have seen that the matricial minimal subset detection method is better suited to an additional redundancy deletion than the comparison detection method.

In addition, we have tested the heuristic which eliminates, at each Fourier step, the variable with the least production of inequations. The results obtained are clearly not as good as with any other choice, even at random. In some cases, the computation time increases from half a minute to more than an hour, with an overwhelming production. The lower initial production can quickly become disastrous.

Finally, the generalization of the passive variable concept to variables which only produce non-retained constraints, is incorrect, as is shown in the following example. Let the initial system be:

$$
\begin{array}{lll}
(1) & 0 \leq +x + y + z + t & (1; -; -) \\
(2) & 0 \leq -x - y + z & (2; -; -) \\
(3) & 0 \leq +x - y - z & (3; -; -) \\
(4) & 0 \leq -x + y - z & (4; -; -)
\end{array}
$$

The elimination of x gives

$$
\begin{array}{ll}
0 \leq +2z + t & (1.2;\ x;\ y) \\
0 \leq -2z & (3.4;\ x;\ y) \\
0 \leq +2y + t & (1.4;\ x;\ z) \\
0 \leq -2y & (2.3;\ x;\ z)
\end{array}
$$

The elimination of y gives the system

$$
\begin{array}{ll}
0 \leq +2z + t & (1.2;\ x;\ y) \\
0 \leq -2z & (3.4;\ x;\ y)
\end{array}
$$

and the elimination of z gives the final system

$$
0 \leq t \quad (1.2.3.4;\ x.z;\ y).
$$

If we had not taken the variable y into account, the inequation $0 \leq t$ would be rejected. Then the final system would be incorrect. This also shows the importance of the implicitly eliminated variables.

For new improvements of the Fourier algorithm, it would be interesting to see under which conditions the weakly redundant inequations (the ones for which the supporting hyperplanes are adjacent to the solution set of the inequation system) can be deleted without putting the previous improvements of the Fourier elimination on the wrong track. Whatever the future improvements however, we cannot prevent the Fourier elimination from producing a great deal of constraints, with a significant increase in the intermediary steps, before this number decreases when few variables remain in the system.

Acknowledgments

This research was supported by the ACCLAIM Esprit Research Project (PE7195). We are grateful to David Wonnacott who have read and commented on earlier version of this paper. I would also like to thank Pamela Morton for her help in the English correctness of this paper.

References

[1] S.N. Cernikov. Contraction of Systems of Linear Inequalities. In *Soviet mathematics* DOKLADY 1, 1960.

[2] S.N. Cernikov. The Solution of Linear Programming Problem by Elimination of Unknowns. In *Soviet mathematics* DOKLADY 2, 1961.

[3] S.N. Cernikov. Contraction of Finite Systems of Linear Inequalities. In *Soviet mathematics* DOKLADY 4, 1963.

[4] A. Colmerauer. Opening the Prolog III Universe. In *BYTE*, p177–182, August 1987.

[5] A. Colmerauer. An Introduction to Prolog III. In *Communications of the ACM*, 33, vol 7, July 1990.

[6] R.J. Duffin. On Fourier's Analyse of Linear Inequality Systems. In *Mathematical Programming Study* 1 71–95. North-Holland Publishing Company. (1974)

[7] M. Dincbas, P. Van Hentenryck, H. Simonis, A. Aggoun, T. Graf and F. Berthier. The Constraint Logic Programming Language CHIP. In *Proceedings of the International Conference on Fifth Generation Computer Systems*, Tokyo, Japan, December 1988.

[8] J.B.J Fourier. reported in : Analyse des travaux de l'Académie Royale des Sciences, pendant l'année 1824, Partie mathématique. *Histoire de l'Académie*

Royale des Sciences de l'institut de France 7 1827, xlvii-lv. (Partial English translation in: D.A. Kohler, Translation of a Report by Fourier on his work on Linear Inequalities, *Opsearch 10* pages 38–42, 1973).

[9] JL. Imbert. Simplification des Systèmes de Contraintes Numériques Linéaires. *Thèse de Doctorat de l'Université d'Aix-Marseille II*, faculté des Sciences de Luminy, Mai 1989.

[10] JL. Imbert. About Redundant Inequalities Generated by Fourier's Algorithm. In P. Jorrand, editor, *Proceedings of the Fourth International Conference on Artificial Intelligence*, AIMSA'90, p 117-127.Varna, Bulgaria. North-Holland. 1990.

[11] JL. Imbert and P. Van Hentenryck. A Note on Redundant Linear Constraints. *Technical Report CS-92-11*, CS Department, Brown University, 1992. 13 pages.

[12] J. Jaffar and JL. Lassez. Constraint Logic Programming. *Technical Report 86/73*. Dept. of computer science. Manash University (June 1986). An abstract appears in *Proceedings of the 14th Principles of Programming Languages*. Munich. p 111–119, 1987.

[13] J.Jaffar, S. Michaylov. Methodology and Implementation of a CLP System. In *Proceedings of the Logic Programming Conference*. Melbourne, M.I.T. Press, 1987.

[14] J.Jaffar, M.J. Maher, P.J. Stuckey and R.H.C. Yap. Output in CLP($\Re$). In *Proceedings of the International Conference on Fifth Generation Computer Systems*, pages 987–995, Tokyo, Japan. June 1992,

[15] P.C. Kanellakis, G.M. Kuper and P.Z. Revesz. Constraint Query Languages. in *Proceedings of the ACM Conference on Principles of Database Systems*. Nashville 1990.

[16] M.H Karwan, V. Lofti, J. Telgen and S. Zionts. Redundancy in Mathematical Programming: a State-fo-the-Art survey. In *Lecture Notes in Computer in Economics and Mathematical Systems*, Vol 206, springer Verlag 1983.

[17] D.A. Kohler. Projection of Convex Polyhedral Sets. *PhD Thesis*, University of California, Berkeley, 1967.

[18] C. Lassez and JL. Lassez. Quantifier Elimination for Conjunctions of Linear Constraints via a Convex Hull Algorithm. To Appear 1991.

[19] JL. Lassez, T. Huynh and K. McAloon. Simplification and Elimination of Redundant Arihtmetic Constraints. In *Constraint Logic Programming: Selected Research.*, edited by F. Benhamou and A. Colmerauer. MIT Press, 73–87 Sept 1993.

[20] J. Telgen. Redundancy and Linear Programming. *Mathematical Center Tracts 137*, Mathematisch Centrum, Amsterdam, 1981.

[21] A. Schrijver. Theory of Linear and Integer Programming. *Interscience Series in Discrete Mathematics and Optimization.* John Wiley & Sons, 1987.

[22] P. Van Hentenryck. Constraint Satisfaction in Logic Programming. *M.I.T. Press*, 1989.

15 Verifying Logic Circuits by Benders Decomposition

J. N. Hooker and H. Yan[1]

Abstract

We describe a new tautology checking algorithm that can determine whether a logic circuit correctly implements a given boolean function. Although nonnumeric, the algorithm is equivalent to a numeric algorithm obtained by applying Benders decomposition to an integer programming formulation of the circuit verification problem. Computational testing suggests that the algorithm may be superior to methods based on binary decision diagrams on certain types of circuits.

15.1 Introduction

One of the fundamental problems of VLSI design is checking whether a logic circuit implements a desired boolean function. This can be done by checking whether the circuit is equivalent to another circuit known to implement the desired function. The two circuits are typically compared by constructing binary decision diagrams (BDD's) for them or, when BDD's require too much computer memory, simply by simulating the circuits and comparing their outputs for every possible input (if it is practical to do so) [6, 1, 16, 4].

We propose here a new algorithm for verifying circuits that, to our knowledge, is unlike any existing methods. It compares the outputs of the two circuits in question, but (if all goes well) for only a small fraction of the possible inputs. The algorithm is actually a general tautology checking algorithm; i.e., it determines whether a circuit has the same output for all possible inputs. The circuit verification problem is readily put into this form.

The algorithm works roughly as follows. If the circuits disagree for a given input, they are obviously nonequivalent, and the algorithm terminates. But if they agree, the algorithm identifies analytically a large number of other inputs it need not try. It generates a logical constraint violated by precisely these superfluous inputs, and the next input tried must satisfy the constraints generated so far. If at some point no input satisfies the constraints, the circuits are equivalent.

The distinguishing feature of this algorithm is that each input enumerated gives rise to a class of inputs that need not be enumerated. Precisely the same strategy is

---

[1]Partially supported by AFOSR grant 87-0292 and NSF grant 1-55093 through the Engineering Design Research Center, Carnegie Mellon University. The authors thank Karl Brace, Edmund Clarke, Allan Fisher and Bruno Repetto, all of Carnegie Mellon University, for generously offering their advice as well as assistance in implementing software and obtaining test problems.

used by Benders decomposition, a well known technique for solving mathematical programming problems [2, 18]. In fact we discovered our algorithm by formulating the circuit verification problem as an integer programming problem and solving it with Benders decomposition. We found that the resulting algorithm is formally equivalent to the nonnumeric algorithm we describe here. For this reason we refer to our algorithm as a "Benders approach" to circuit verification (or, more generally, to tautology checking), even though we do not solve the problem numerically, as is normally done in a Benders approach. By forging this link between circuit theory and mathematical programming, we believe we have made available to the former a new solution strategy.

We emphasize that our algorithm, like the BDD algorithm, is exact and not a heuristic. It, the BDD algorithm and simulation all have exponential complexity in the worst case, which is not surprising in view of the fact that the tautology checking problem is NP-complete.

A key step of the algorithm is finding an input that satisfies the current set of constraints. This is a satisfiability problem in propositional logic. Satisfiability problems can be hard, but the problems we solve are small (only as many variables as inputs). We also benefit from the enormous improvement in satisfiability algorithms over the past few years [3, 7, 8, 10, 11, 13, 15, 16] [17, 19, 20]. In particular, we rely on a fast incremental satisfiability algorithm that repeatedly rechecks satisfiability after adding a new logical constraint [12]. We find that, on the average, solving the satisfiability problems requires less time than generating the constraints.

Computational testing indicates that our preliminary implementation of the Benders approach is superior to BDD's on certain problems but inferior on many common circuits. If the comparison is based solely on problems for which BDD benchmarks have been published [16, 4], Benders is usually slower than BDD's. For some of these circuits, including adders and multipliers, our algorithm actually tries all or nearly all possible inputs, so that one could do better by simulation. But there is reason to believe that a Benders approach can be very effective on circuits that do not contain many "irreducible" gates (or subcircuits that are equivalent to irreducible gates). These are gates with the property that for any input to the gate, reversing any one of the input signals causes the output of the gate to reverse. An exclusive OR, for instance, is irreducible, whereas AND and OR gates or not. We randomly generated a set of problems with only AND, OR and NOT gates and found that our algorithm used an extremely small fraction of possible inputs and was an order of magnitude faster than the most recent available BDD code. A Benders approach may therefore be somewhat complementary to BDD's, in that it is effective on some circuits on which they are not.

When considered apart from its mathematical programming roots, our algorithm can be readily understood by persons with no acquaintance with Benders decomposition. Several sections of this paper therefore explain the algorithm without mention of Benders decomposition. Section 15.2 illustrates our algorithm on a small example problem, and Section 15.3 provides a precise statement of the algorithm. Section 15.6 addresses implementation issues, and Section 15.7 reports computational results.

We also think it important to reveal the connection between integer programming and logic circuits that led us to discover the algorithm. The connection is not only interesting in its own right, but similar connections between logic and mathematics have led to new algorithms in other areas [5, 9]. We therefore prove in Sections 15.4 and 15.5 that our algorithm is equivalent to a Benders algorithm applied to the integer programming formulation of the problem. The correctness of the algorithm therefore follows from the theory of Benders decomposition.

15.2 An Illustration of the Algorithm

A circuit represents a tautology if its output is 1 for all possible inputs. The circuit verification problem can be formulated as a tautology checking problem as illustrated in Fig. 15.1. A and B are circuits whose equivalence is to be tested. They have the same output signals for every input if and only if the combined circuit has output 1 for every input.

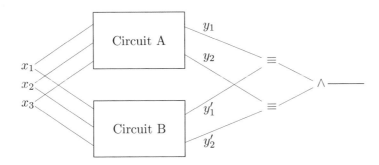

Figure 15.1
Verifying circuit A by comparing with circuit B

We next illustrate our algorithm on a small tautology checking problem. Consider the simple logic circuit of Fig. 15.2, which has three input signals x_1, x_2 and x_3.

The output y_i of each remaining node i of the network is a boolean function of the values on the incoming arcs. Node 6, for instance, is an AND node whose output is $y_6 = x_1 \wedge \neg x_2 \wedge x_3$. The cross hatch on the arc from x_2 to node 6 indicates that the input x_2 is negated, so that 0 becomes 1 and 1 becomes 0.

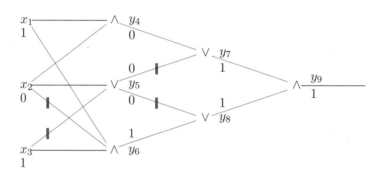

Figure 15.2
A small example

We begin with an arbitrary input, such as $(x_1, x_2, x_3) = (1, 0, 1)$. The resulting output of each gate is indicated in Fig. 15.2. If the output of the network were 0, the algorithm could terminate with a negative answer. But since the output is 1, we continue.

Note that if we fix only the two inputs $(x_2, x_3) = (0, 1)$, the output is still 1, no matter what the value of x_1. This means that if y_9 is to be 0, the input must satisfy,

$$x_2 \vee \neg x_3 \tag{15.2.1}$$

We call (15.2.1) a *circuit cut* with respect to the input $(x_1, x_2, x_3) = (1, 0, 1)$. The complete set of input signals $(x_1, x_2, x_3) = (1, 0, 1)$ also corresponds to a trivial circuit cut,

$$\neg x_1 \vee x_2 \vee \neg x_3 \tag{15.2.2}$$

We now continue our search for an input that makes y_9 equal to 0. We can restrict ourselves to inputs that satisfy the circuit cuts (15.2.1) and (15.2.2). (Actually we could drop (15.2.2), because (15.2.1) implies it.) To do this we solve a *satisfiability* problem. That is, we try to find an assignment of truth values to x_1, x_2, x_3 that satisfies both (15.2.1) and (15.2.2). If there is no satisfying assignment, then the output of the circuit is necessarily 1. In the present case, however, there are several satisfying assignments, such as $(x_1, x_2, x_3) = (1, 0, 0)$. This makes y_9 false, and we conclude that the circuit's output need not be 1. If it had made y_9 true, we would have continued to accumulate cuts until the satisfiability problem is insoluble or we find an input that makes y_9 false.

It remains to illustrate how we generate circuit cuts with respect to a given input. Note that the input $(x_1, x_2, x_3) = (1, 0, 1)$ makes the two input signals to node 9, y_7 and y_8, equal to 1. Since node 9 is an AND node, y_9 is not 1 unless both of these signals are 1. Thus any input to the circuit that makes y_9 true makes y_7 and y_8 true.

We now treat nodes 7 and 8 similarly. $y_5 = 0$ is enough to make y_7 true (whereas $y_4 = 0$ is not). As for node 8, either $y_5 = 0$ or $y_6 = 1$ is enough to make y_8 true. For the moment we will enforce $y_5 = 0$. Now any circuit input that makes y_5 false will make y_9 true. Since $(x_2, x_3) = (0, 1)$ makes y_5 false, $x_2 \vee \neg x_3$ is a circuit cut.

To obtain the other circuit cut (15.2.2), we can make y_8 true by forcing $y_6 = 1$ rather than $y_5 = 0$. This means that any circuit input that makes y_5 false and y_6 true makes y_9 true. But again $(x_2, x_3) = (0, 1)$ makes y_5 false, and $(x_1, x_2, x_3) = (1, 0, 1)$ makes y_6 true. Combining these, we have the second circuit cut $\neg x_1 \vee x_2 \vee \neg x_3$.

15.3   Formal Statement of the Algorithm

We begin with some terminology. A logical *clause* is a disjunction of literals, which are atomic propositions or their negations. A formula is in *conjunctive normal form (CNF)* if it is a conjunction of clauses. Any formula of propositional logic is equivalent to a formula in CNF. A clause C *absorbs* a clause D if and only if all the literals of C occur in D. C logically implies D if and only if C absorbs D.

Given a vector $x = (x_1, \cdots, x_m)$, a *subvector* x_J of x is a vector consisting of the components indexed by the elements of $J \subseteq \{1, \cdots, m\}$ in increasing order. For instance, $x_{\{1,3\}} = (x_1, x_3)$.

A logic circuit implements a boolean function $F(x)$, where $x = (x_1, \cdots, x_m)$ is the vector of input variables and $F(x)$ is the output. The output of every node i is represented by a variable y_i. (It will be convenient to reserve variables $y_1, \ldots, y_m$ to represent the input signals $x_1, \ldots, x_m$.) The nodes are indexed so that $i < j$ whenever node i is a predecessor of j. Each node i is associated with a boolean function f_i, where we set $y_i = f_i(y_{J_i})$. The argument y_{J_i} of f_i is the vector of variables y_j associated with the input signals to i. The output node of the circuit has the largest index t, and $F(x) = f_t(y_{J_t})$.

Given input $x^* = (x_1^*, \cdots, x_m^*)$ for which $F(x^*) = 1$, we wish to find, if possible, subvectors $x_{\overline{J}}$ of input signals for which $F(x) = 1$ whenever $x_{\overline{J}} = x_{\overline{J}}^*$. Each subvector $x_{\overline{J}}$ gives rise to a circuit cut $C(\overline{J}, x^*)$, where

$$C(\overline{J}, x^*) = \left(\bigvee_{\substack{j \in \overline{J} \\ x_j^* = 1}} \neg x_j \right) \vee \left(\bigvee_{\substack{j \in \overline{J} \\ x_j^* = 0}} x_j \right)$$

Circuit cuts are generated as follows. We will indicate by a starred variable $(y_i^*, y_{J_i}^*, etc.)$ the value of that variable when the input is $x = x^*$. We first find a subvector $y_{\overline{J}_t}$ of y_{J_t} such that $f(y_{J_t}) = 1$ whenever $y_{\overline{J}_t} = y_{\overline{J}_t}^*$. Then for each variable y_i in $y_{\overline{J}_t}$, other than inputs x_j, we find a subvector $y_{\overline{J}_i}$ of y_{J_i} such that $f_i(y_{J_i}) = y_i^*$ whenever $y_{\overline{J}_i} = y_{\overline{J}_i}^*$. We continue the process in a recursive manner as far as possible. The desired set $\overline{J}$ consists of all indices j of input variables that occur in $\overline{J}_i$ for some i. We can often get several circuit cuts, since there may be more than one subvector $y_{\overline{J}_i}$ to choose from at a node, and a different choice may result in a different cut.

We have already illustrated how to find $y_{\overline{J}_i}$ when f_i is an AND or an OR function. $y_{\overline{J}_i}$ can be found in general by writing f_i (if $y_{i*} = 1$) or $\neg f_i$ (if $y_i^* = 0$) in disjunctive normal form (DNF). The details are given in Algorithm 1, which is a formal statement of the cut generation algorithm. The subroutine CUTS generates circuit cuts for a given input x^*.

Algorithm 1.
Let $S = \emptyset$.
While S is a satisfiable set of clauses do:
      Let x^* be any satisfying solution for S.
      If $F(x^*) = 0$, stop; $F(x)$ is not 1 for all inputs.
      Call $CUTS(\{t\}, \emptyset, \emptyset)$ to generate a set $\hat{S}$ of cuts.
      If desired, remove from S any cuts dominated by the cuts in $\hat{S}$.
      Let $S = S \cup \hat{S}$.
Stop; $F(x) = 1$ for all inputs.

Procedure $CUTS(P, \overline{J}_F, \overline{J}_T)$.
If $P = \emptyset$ then generate the cut $C(\overline{J}_F \cup \overline{J}_T, x^*) = \bigvee_{j \in \overline{J}_F} x_j \vee \bigvee_{j \in \overline{J}_T} \neg x_j$.
Else
      Pick any $i \in P$.
      If $y_i^* = 1$ then
          Put f_i in DNF $D_1 \vee \cdots \vee D_K$, where each $D_k = \bigvee_{j \in I_k} w_{kj}$.

Else put $\neg f_i$ in DNF similarly.
For each $k \in \{1, \cdots, K\}$ do:
    If $D_k^* = 1$ then
        Let $\hat{J}_F = \overline{J}_F$, $\hat{J}_T = \overline{J}_T$, and $\hat{P} = P$.
        For each $j \in I_k$ do:
            If $w_{kj} = y_j$ then
                If $j \leq m$ (i.e., y_j is an input) then put j into $\hat{J}_T$.
                Else put j into $\hat{P}$.
            Else
                If $j \leq m$ then put j into $\hat{J}_F$.
                Else put j into $\hat{P}$.
        If $I_k \neq \emptyset$ then call $CUTS(\hat{P} \setminus \{i\}, \hat{J}_F, \hat{J}_T)$.
End CUTS.

When the algorithm sets $\hat{J}_F = \overline{J}_F$ (or $\hat{J}_F = \overline{J}_T$), it could just as well let $\hat{J}_F$ be any subset of $\hat{J}_F \cup I_k$ (or $\hat{J}_T \cup I_k$). But this could result in a longer circuit cut.

15.4   Some Definitions

Before showing the connection with Benders decomposition, we must introduce some more terminology. Note that the clause $x_1 \vee \neg x_2 \vee \neg x_3$ is true if and only if the linear inequality $x_1 + (1 - x_2) + (1 - x_3) \geq 1$ is satisfied, provided $x \in \{0, 1\}$, and we interpret x_j to be true when $x_j = 1$ and false when $x_j = 0$. Thus any clause can be written as a *clausal* inequality, in this case $x_1 - x_2 - x_3 \geq -1$.

We can check whether a set S of clauses logically implies a clause C by solving an integer programming problem. Let $c^T x \geq \gamma$ be a clausal inequality representing C, and let $Ax \geq a$ be a system of clausal inequalities representing the clauses in S. Then S implies C if and only if the minimum value of $c^T x$ in the following integer programming problem is at least γ.

$$\text{min} \quad c^T x$$
$$\text{s.t.} \quad Ax \geq a$$
$$x_j \in \{0, 1\}, \quad \forall j. \tag{15.4.3}$$

Given two clauses C and D, if there is exactly one variable x_j that is posited in one clause and negated in the other, the *resolvent* (on x_j) of the two clauses (called the *parents*) consists of the clause containing all the literals occurring in C and D except x_j and $\neg x_j$. For instance, the resolvent of $x_1 \vee \neg x_2$ and $\neg x_1 \vee x_3$ is $\neg x_2 \vee x_3$. *Resolution* is the process of generating a resolvent. *Unit resolution* occurs when at least one parent of the resolvent is a *unit clause*, i.e., a clause consisting of exactly one literal. A *resolution proof* of a clause C from a set S of clauses is a finite sequence of clauses, beginning with the clauses in S and ending with C, such that every clause in the sequence is in S or is the resolvent of two clauses that occur previously in the sequence. A *unit resolution proof* is a proof in which every resolution is unit resolution. A *unit support proof* [11] of C from S is a resolution proof that becomes a unit resolution proof of $\emptyset$ when all variables in C are removed from every clause of the proof.

We will need the following easy lemma, in which two inequalities are equivalent if they have the same 0-1 solutions.

LEMMA 15.1 ([3]) Let clause E be the resolvent of clause C and unit clause D, and let e be a vector of ones. Then if $c^T x \geq \gamma$ and $d^T x \geq \delta$ are clausal inequalities equivalent to C and D, then $(c + d)^T x \geq (\gamma + \delta)$ is a clausal inequality equivalent to E, and

$$\{x \mid c^T x \geq \gamma, d^T x \geq \delta, 0 \leq x \leq e\} = \{x \mid (c + d)^T x \geq (\gamma + \delta), 0 \leq x \leq e\}.$$

15.5   Interpretation as Benders Decomposition

To apply Benders decomposition [2, 18] to the circuit verification problem we must write it as an integer programming problem. We first write each equation $y_i = f_i(y_{J_i})$ as a conjunction of clauses. To do this we use the fact that a logical equivalence $A \equiv B$ can be written $(\neg A \vee B) \wedge (A \vee \neg B)$. Recall that $f_i(y_{J_i})$ is written in DNF as $D_1 \vee \ldots \vee D_k$, where each $D_k = \bigwedge_{j \in I_k} w_{kj}$, and each w_{kj} is y_j or $\neg y_j$. We therefore have the equivalence

$$y_j \equiv (D_1 \vee \ldots \vee D_k),$$

which can be written as the conjunction of the two formulas,

$$D_1 \vee \ldots D_k \vee \neg y_i \tag{15.5.4}$$

$$\neg(D_1 \vee \ldots D_k) \vee y_i. \tag{15.5.5}$$

But (15.5.4) is a conjunction of the clauses

$$\bigvee_{k=1}^{K} w_{ks(k)} \vee \neg y_i, \quad \text{for all } s, \tag{15.5.6}$$

where s is any function satisfying $s(k) \in I_k$ for $k = 1, \ldots, K$. Applying De Morgan's law to (15.5.5), we obtain the conjunction of the following clauses.

$$\bigvee_{j \in I_k} \neg w_{kj} \vee y_i, \quad k = 1, \ldots, K. \tag{15.5.7}$$

Therefore, $y_i = f_i(y_{J_i})$ can be represented by the conjunction of the clauses (15.5.6) and (15.5.7).

This means that the problem of verifying that $F(x) = 1$ for all inputs x is equivalent to the integer programming problem,

$$\min \quad y_t \tag{15.5.8}$$
$$\text{s.t.} \quad \mathbf{sum}_{k=1}^{K} \hat{w}_{ks(k)} + (1 - y_i) \geq 1, \quad \forall s, \ \forall i. \tag{15.5.9}$$
$$\mathbf{sum}_{k=1}(1 - \hat{w}_{ks(k)}) + y_i \geq 1, \quad \forall s, \ \forall i. \tag{15.5.10}$$
$$y \in \{0, 1\} \ \forall i \in \{1, \ldots, m\}, \ 0 \leq y \leq 1 \ \forall i, \tag{15.5.11}$$

where $\hat{w}_{kj}$ is y_j if $w_{kj} = y_j$ and is $1 - y_j$ if $w_{kj} = \neg y_j$. Then $F(x) = 1$ for all x if and only if the minimum value of y_t is 1. The variables y_i for $i > m$ are not explicitly required to be integral, but we will see shortly that they are necessarily integral in any feasible solution.

The integer programming problem for the example of Section 15.2 (Fig. 15.2)) appears in Table 15.1. (Note that the x_j's have been moved to the right-hand side of the inequalities. The numbers in italic on the right are explained below.)

The first three constraints encode $y_4 \equiv (x_1 \wedge x_2)$, which defines the output of node 4. The other constraints are similar.

It is convenient to write the integer programming problem (15.5.8)-(15.5.11) in the following form.

$$\min \quad y_t \tag{15.5.12}$$
$$\text{s.t.} \quad Ax + B\bar{y} \geq \alpha$$
$$x_i \in \{0, 1\}, \ i \in \{1, \ldots, m\}, \ 0 \leq y_j \leq 1, \ \forall j,$$

where $\bar{y}$ is the vector of all y_j's except the inputs $y_1, \ldots, y_m \ (= x_1, \ldots, x_m)$. To apply Benders' decomposition we formulate a "master problem" that contains only the x_j's and y_t,

$$\min \quad y_t \tag{15.5.13}$$
$$\text{s.t.} \quad y_t \geq (u^r)^T (\alpha - Ax) - (v^r)^T e, \quad r = 1, \ldots, R,$$
$$x_j \in \{0, 1\}, \ j = 1, \ldots, m.$$

			RHS	Dual		
Min		y_9				
s.t.	$-y_4$	$\geq$	$0-x_1$	-1		
	$-y_4$	$\geq$	$0\quad -x_2$	0		
	$+y_4$	$\geq$	$-1+x_1+x_2$	0		
	$-y_5$	$\geq$	$-1\quad -x_2+x_3$	0	2	1
	$+y_5$	$\geq$	$0\quad x_2$	0		
	$+y_5$	$\geq$	$1\quad -x_3$	0		
	$-y_6$	$\geq$	$0-x_1$	-1		
	$-y_6$	$\geq$	$-1\quad +x_2$	-1		1
	$-y_6$	$\geq$	$0\quad -x_3$	-1		
	$+y_6$	$\geq$	$-1+x_1-x_2+x_3$	1		
	$+y_4-y_5\quad -y_7$	$\geq$	-1	-1		
	$-y_4\qquad +y_7$	$\geq$	0	0		
	$+y_5\quad +y_7$	$\geq$	1	1	1	1
	$-y_5+y_6\quad -y_8$	$\geq$	-1	-1		
	$+y_5\qquad +y_8$	$\geq$	1	1	1	
	$-y_6\quad +y_8$	$\geq$	0	0		1
	$+y_7\quad -y_9$	$\geq$	0	0		
	$+y_8-y_9$	$\geq$	0	0		
	$-y_7-y_8+y_9$	$\geq$	-1	-1	1	1

$x_j \in \{0,1\}, \ 0 \leq y_j \leq 1.$

Table 15.1
An example of Benders decomposition.

Here each (u^r, v^r) is a solution of the dual of the subproblem, which we display below, and e is a vector of ones. Each constraint of (15.5.13) is known as a *Benders cut*. The subproblem is,

$$\min \quad y_t \tag{15.5.14}$$
$$\text{s.t.} \quad B\bar{y} \geq \alpha - Ax$$
$$0 \leq y_j \leq 1, \ j = 1, \ldots, m.$$

where x is regarded as fixed. The dual of the subproblem is,

$$\max \quad u^T(\alpha - Ax) - v^T e \tag{15.5.15}$$
$$\text{s.t.} \quad u^T B - v^T \leq e_t,$$

$$u, v \geq 0,$$

where e_t is a vector consisting of all zeros except a 1 in the t-th place.

The Benders solution procedure begins by solving the dual (15.5.15) of the subproblem (15.5.14) that results when x is set to some arbitrary value x^*. If the solution value of the dual is zero, then the same is true of the primal (15.5.14), which indicates that $F(x^*) = 0$, and we can stop. Otherwise each solution of the dual gives rise to a Benders cut, which we add to the master problem (15.5.13). We then solve the master problem for a new value x^* of x. If the solution value is 1, then $F(x) = 1$ for all inputs x, and we can stop. Otherwise we continue as before. So long as we generate at least one Benders cut whenever one exists, the theory of Benders decomposition guarantees that the algorithm terminates with the correct solution after finitely many iterations.

Since $F(x^*) = 1$ whenever the dual gives rise to a Benders cut, we know that there is a circuit cut whenever there is a Benders cut. If nothing else, $C(\{1, ..., m\}, x^*)$ is a circuit cut, since $F(x^*) = 1$. But we will show below that any circuit cut is equivalent to a Benders cut when $y_t = 0$. Thus the master problem has solution value 0 precisely when the circuit cuts generated so far are satisfiable. Since circuit cuts exist whenever Benders cuts exist, the correctness and finiteness of the Benders algorithm imply the same for the algorithm of Section 15.4. It remains therefore to prove the following theorem.

THEOREM 15.1 Any circuit cut is equivalent to a Benders cut for (15.5.12) when $y_t = 0$.

EXAMPLE 15.1 Before proving the theorem we will illustrate it using the example discussed earlier. Recall that the input $(x_1, x_2, x_3) = (1, 0, 1)$ gives rise to the two circuit cuts (15.2.1) and (15.2.2). When we substitute this input for x_1, x_2, x_3 in (15.5.12) we obtain the subproblem (15.5.14). The resulting right-hand sides are shown in italics in (15.5.12). Two solutions of the dual problem are indicated in the last two columns of italics in (15.5.12). The value of each positive u_i is indicated to the right of the corresponding constraint (the remaining u_i's are zero). The first dual solution generates the Benders cut $y_9 + 2x_2 - 2x_3 \geq -1$. When $y_9 = 0$ this is equivalent to the circuit cut $x_2 \vee \neg x_3$. The second dual solution generates the Benders cut $y_9 - x_1 + 2x_2 - 2x_3 \geq -2$, which is equivalent to the second circuit cut $\neg x_1 \vee x_2 \vee \neg x_3$ when $y_9 = 0$.

The following lemma is fundamental to the proof of Theorem 15.1.

LEMMA 15.2 If algorithm CUTS yields $x_{\overline{J}}$ for some input $x = x^*$, then there is a unit resolution proof of y_t from the set of clauses consisting of (15.5.6), (15.5.7), unit clauses x_j for all $j \in J$ with $x^* = 1$, and unit clauses $\neg x_j$ for all $j \in J$ with $x^* = 0$.

PROOF: The proof is by induction on node indices. In fact, we show by induction that if the algorithm yields a vector $y_{\overline{J}_i}$ for any node i, then there is a unit resolution proof of y_i (if $y^* = 1$) or $\neg y_i$ (if $y^* = 0$) from the clauses indicated above. This is clearly true for the inputs $y_1, \cdots, y_m (= x_1, \cdots, x_m)$, since if $x^* = 1$ and $j \in \overline{J}$, x_j is already a premise, and similarly if $x^* = 0$. Suppose, then, that the claim is true for all nodes with indices less than i, and consider a node i, for which algorithm CUTS yields $y_{\overline{J}_i}$. Write f_i in DNF as above. There are two cases. i) $y^* = 1$, so that D_k is true for some k, say $\overline{k}$. This means $w_{\overline{k}j}$ is true for each $j \in I_k$. Thus by resolving the unit clause $w_{\overline{k}j}$ (for each $j \in I_k$) with the constraint in (15.5.10) that corresponds to i and $\overline{k}$, we obtain y_k. But by the induction hypothesis, there is a unit resolution proof of each $w_{\overline{k}j}$, since if $w_{\overline{k}j} = y_j$, there is such a proof of y_j because $y^* = 1$, and similarly if $w_{\overline{k}j} = \neg y_j$. Thus there is a unit resolution proof of y_i. ii) On the other hand, suppose that $y^* = 0$, so that all D_k are false. Then for each k, w_{kj} is false for at least one j, which we may denote $s(k)$. Then we can resolve the unit clause $\neg w_{kj}$ for each such w_{kj} with the constraint in (15.5.9) corresponding to i and s to obtain $\neg y_i$. Again by the induction hypothesis, there is a unit resolution proof of each $\neg w_{kj}$, and we have such a proof of $\neg y_i$. □

COROLLARY 15.1 Any feasible solution of (15.5.8)-(15.5.11) is integral.

PROOF: Given any input $x = x^*$, it is consistent with algorithm CUTS to set $y_{\overline{J}(i)} = y_{J_i}$ at each node i, so that $x_{\overline{J}} = x$. Then by Lemma 15.2 there is a unit resolution proof of y_i if $y^* = 1$ and $\neg y_i$ if $y^* = 0$. By Lemma ??, the linear constraint set of (15.5.8) forces $y_i = 1$ in the former case and $y_i = 0$ in the latter. □

COROLLARY 15.2 If algorithm CUTS yields $x_{\overline{J}}$ for some input $x = x^*$, then there is a unit support proof of $y_t \vee C(\hat{J}, x^*)$ from the set of clauses consisting of (15.5.6) and (15.5.7).

PROOF: We can assume without loss of generality that each $x^* = 0$ for $j \in \overline{J}$, since if $x^* = 1$ we can redefine x_j to be its complement and set $x^* = 0$. From Lemma 15.2, there is a unit resolution proof of y_t from (15.5.6), (15.5.7) and the unit clause premises x_j for $j = \bar{J}$. Note that whenever a premise from (15.5.6) or (15.5.7) is used in the proof, it is resolved with a series of unit clauses so as to yield a variable y_i. So, the variable x_j can occur in a premise only if $j \in \bar{J}$, and it must occur positively except in a unit clause premise. Furthermore, any x_j with $j \in \bar{J}$ appears in the proof. So, if we remove the unit clause premises from the proof, we obtain a unit support proof of $y_t \vee \bigvee_{j \in \bar{J}} x_j$, which is $y_t \vee C(\bar{J}, x^*)$. $\square$

We also need the following result.

THEOREM 15.2 ([11]) For a given clause C, let $Q = \{0 \le x_j \le 1 | C \text{ contains } x_j\}$. Then if C is the result of a unit support proof from a set S of clausal inequalities, then there is a positive linear combination of inequalities in $S \cup Q$ that yields a clausal inequality representing C when the right-hand side is rounded up.

In particular we need the following corollary.

COROLLARY 15.3 There is a linear combination like that in Theorem 15.2 with the additional property that when the bounds in Q are removed from the linear combination, the resulting inequality is equivalent to C.

PROOF: Since the unit support proof never resolves on variables in C, these variables always occur in S with the same sign. We can assume without loss of generality that they are all positive, since otherwise we can replace x_j with $1 - x_j$. Since the positive linear combination guaranteed by Theorem 15.2 results in an inequality in which the variables in C have coefficient 1, the weights in this combination given the inequalities in Q must therefore sum to less than 1. This means that if the inequalities of Q are removed from the combination, the resulting inequality is the same as before, except that the coefficients of the variables in C are reduced from 1 to a positive number no greater than 1. It is easy to verify that this inequality is satisfied by the same 0-1 points as the original. $\square$

We can now prove the main theorem.
PROOF: [Theorem 15.1] Let C be a circuit cut for some input $x = x^*$. We can again suppose without loss of generality that every literal in C is positive. Let $x_{\bar{J}}$ be the corresponding subvector of x. By Corollary 15.2, there is a unit support proof of $y_t \vee \bigvee_{j \in \bar{J}} x_j$ from (15.5.6) and (15.5.7). By Theorem 15.2, there is a positive linear combination of inequalities in (15.5.6) and (15.5.7), along with bounds in $Q = \{y_t \ge 0, x_j \ge 0 | j \in \bar{J}\}$, that yields an inequality $y_t + \mathbf{sum}_{j \in \bar{J}} x_j \ge \gamma$ that becomes $y_t + \mathbf{sum}_{j \in \bar{J}} x_j \ge 1$ when γ is rounded up. For each constraint i of

(15.5.12), let $\bar{u}_i$ be the weight of the corresponding clause in this linear combination (with $\bar{u}_i = 0$ if the clause does not occur in the linear combination), and let $\bar{v}_j$ be the weight attached to $x_j \geq 0$. Then if $\bar{u}$ and $\bar{v}$ are vectors of the $\bar{u}_i$'s and $\bar{v}_j$'s respectively, we have $u^T B\bar{y} = c_t y_t$ for $0 \leq c_t \leq 1$, $\bar{u}^T Ax + \bar{v}^T = \mathbf{sum}_{j \in \bar{J}} x_j$, and $\bar{u}^T \alpha = \gamma$. We will show that $y_t + (1/c_t)\bar{u}^T Ax \geq (1/c_t)\gamma$ is a Benders cut that is equivalent to the circuit cut $\mathbf{sum}_{j \in \bar{J}} x_j \geq 1$ when $y_t = 0$.

We first note that $y_t + (1/c_t)\bar{u}^T Ax \geq (1/c_t)\gamma$ is equivalent to $c_t y_t + \bar{u}^T Ax \geq \gamma$ (since one is a positive multiple of the other), which in turn is equivalent to $y_t + \mathbf{sum}_{j \in \bar{J}} x_j \geq 1$ by Corollary 15.3 . This last is equivalent to the circuit cut $\mathbf{sum}_{j \in \bar{J}} x_j \geq 1$ when $y_t = 0$. To show that $y_t + (1/c_t)\bar{u}^T Ax \geq (1/c_t)\gamma$ is a Benders cut, we need only show that $u = (1/c_t)\bar{u}$ and $v = 0$ solve the dual of (15.5.14). Since $(1/c_t)\bar{u}^T B\bar{y} = y_t$, the dual constraints are all satisfied as equalities. Thus any feasible solution of (15.5.14) satisfies complementary slackness with respect to the dual solution $(u, v) = (\bar{u}, 0)$. Since (15.5.14) clearly has a feasible solution when $x = x^*$ (namely, $y = y^*$), $(u, v) = (\bar{u}, 0)$ is optimal in the dual. $\square$

COROLLARY 15.4 The algorithm of Section 15.3 terminates with the correct solution after finitely many iterations.

15.6   Implementation Issues

We found in preliminary testing that algorithm CUTS tends to generate a large number of circuit cuts in each iteration, many of which are identical. We therefore modified the algorithm to generate only one cut per iteration. We also employed a heuristic that tends to result in strong cuts. (The algorithm as a whole is not a heuristic and remains exact; the heuristic used here is only a subprocedure that chooses which cut to generate.)

Since we generate only one logic cut, we can accumulate a cut while propagating values in a forward pass through the network. We associate with every node i an active set A_i of input signals that may become part of the cut. The active set associated with an input to the circuit consists of the input itself. Now suppose, for instance, that we compute $y_i = f_i(y_{J(i)})$ for an OR node i. If $y_i = 0$, then we need all of i's predecessors to make y_i false, so that $\bar{J}(i) = J(i)$. Thus the active set A_i is the union $\bigcup_{y \in J(i)} A_j$ of the active sets associated with all the predecessors. But if $y_i = 1$, we need only one true predecessor to make y_i true. Since our goal is to generate a strong cut, we let A_i be the smallest active set associated with a true predecessor. The active set A_t associated with the circuit's output determines the circuit cut $C(A_t, x^*)$.

The algorithm is displayed as Algorithm 2. Our implementation indexes each active set A_i it generates and associates an index with each node to indicate its active set. Thus when a node has the same active set as an immediate predecessor, only the index need be copied.

Algorithm 2.
Let $S = \emptyset$.
While S is satisfiable do:
      Let x^* be a satisfying solution for S.
      For $i = m + 1, \cdots, t$ do:
            Let $y_i^* = f_i(y_{J(i)}^*)$.
            If $y_i^* = 1$ then
                  Put f_i in DNF $D_1 \vee \cdots \vee D_k$, where each $D_k = \bigwedge_{j \in J_k} w_j$.
            Else put $\neg f_i$ in DNF similarly.
            Let $A_i = \bigcup_{j \in J_k^*} A_j$, where $|J_k^*| = \min_{k \in K_1} |J_k|$ and $K_1 = \{k | D_k^* = 1\}$.
      Enddo.
      If $y_t^* = 0$ then stop; $F(x)$ is not 1 for all inputs.
      Add cut $C(A_t, x^*)$ to S.
Enddo.
Stop; $F(x) = 1$ for all inputs.

The satisfiability algorithm [12] uses a variation of the Davis-Putnam-Loveland procedure, which is a tree search for a satisfying solution. At each node, two child nodes are created by fixing a chosen variable to true and then to false. The resulting subproblems are simplified and the procedure repeated for each. Key to the success of the method is the heuristic used to choose which variable to fix at each node. When the satisfiability problem is re-solved after the addition of a new circuit cut, the algorithm exploits the information obtained in the solution of the previous problem. This tends to make re-solution at least an order of magnitude faster than solving the incremented problem from scratch.

We wrote the algorithm in FORTRAN, compiled it with a Sun FORTRAN compiler, and tested it on a Sun Spar Station 330 in a Unix environment (Suns 4.1).

15.7 Computational Results

Tables 15.2 and 15.3 display computational results for 51 circuit verification problems for which benchmarks have been published [16, 4]. Here "n" is the number of inputs and "o" the number of outputs of the circuit in question. "op" is the total number of nodes in the two circuits compared. The total number of nodes (op) is lower than the total number of operators appearing in two circuits as reported in [16] because we use a different convention for counting gates. The tables show the total number of circuit cuts and break the running time down into that required by the Benders subproblem (cut generation) and the master problem (solving the satisfiability problem).

For comparison we solved the same problems on the same computer using a state-of-the-art BDD code, since BDD methods are the principal competitor other than simulation. We used the code KBDD written very recently at Carnegie Mellon University by Karl Brace. The tables also show the BDD running times. The single decimal place reflects the limited accuracy we could obtain by using the procedure Brace recommended for separating the loading time from the actual solution time.

The Benders code ran as fast as or faster than the BDD code on ten of the benchmark problems. (Lack of precision in time measurement makes it impossible to resolve several ties.) It ran much slower on a number of problems. For the adders (add1-add4) it appears to generate all 2^n cuts, and it generates nearly 2^n cuts for the multipliers (mul03-mul08), which result in exponential solution time for BDD's as well.

The BDD code benefits from several years of refinements in BDD-based methods, whereas our implementation of the Benders approach is preliminary. But even if this is taken into account, the Benders approach is clearly ineffective on many circuits, namely those for which it generates more than a small fraction of the 2^n possible circuit cuts.

One factor that results in a large number of cuts is the presence of what we might call "irreducible" gates. An irreducible gate is characterized by the property that all of its inputs must belong to its active set, regardless of its output. For instance, and exclusive OR (as well as its negation) is irreducible, because all of its inputs belong to its active set, whether the output is true or false. That is, one can always change the output of an XOR by reversing any one of the inputs. Most of the benchmark problems contain a number of XOR's in addition to AND's and OR's. This suggests that a Benders approach could be more effective on circuits without XOR's.

To test this hypothesis we generated a number of random circuits containing only AND, OR and NOT gates. We fixed the number n of inputs to the circuit and the number d of inputs to each node (the "in-degree"). We provided each circuit with one output. We randomly assigned each interior and output node inputs from d nodes with smaller indices. We designated the node AND or OR

Problem	Size			Benders		BDD
lem	n	o	op	cuts	sec	sec
cath						
add1	9	5	166	512	1.89	0.1
add4	29	12	609	*		2.8
add2	13	7	257	2068	14.81	0.4
addsub	29	14	523	*		0.9
add3	21	11	408	*		1.0
alu	11	4	137	1283	5.88	0.5
plasco						
in1	15	17	428	1383	78.17	10.7
mul	7	7	52	27	0.07	0.1
counter	6	12	90	63	0.19	0.2
pitch	16	48	644	5413	280.30	5.9
d3	7	9	303	0	0.02	2.1
rom2	13	7	141	108	0.79	0.8
hostint1	5	7	85	25	0.07	0.1
werner	6	7	37	0	0.00	0.0
mp2d	14	14	229	609	8.85	0.9
table	17	5	339	1642	19.68	0.9
mul						
ex2	4	1	13	7	0.00	0.0
rip02	4	3	33	16	0.02	0.1
mul03	6	6	85	55	0.15	0.1
rip04	8	5	75	256	0.55	0.1
mul04	8	8	161	233	1.10	0.3
rip06	12	6	115	3569	24.73	0.2
mul05	10	10	261	971	7.81	1.0
rip08	16	9	159	*		0.2
mul06	12	12	386	3976	50.75	4.0
transp	4	2	18	9	0.02	0.0
mul07	14	14	507	16137	337.51	12.2
ztwaalf1	12	1	57	258	0.63	0.1
mul08	16	16	675	*		41.6
ztwaalf2	12	1	56	231	0.57	0.1

*The problem is not solved within 30,000 cuts.

Table 15.2
Benchmark circuits.

Problem	Size			Benders		BDD
lem	n	o	op	cuts	sec	sec
hachtel						
mlp4	8	8	300	256	2.16	0.9
rd73	7	3	128	128	0.44	0.3
alupla20	19	1	57	470	2.74	0.9
risc	8	31	134	43	0.18	0.2
alupla21	22	1	72	50	13.66	4.0
root	8	5	137	130	0.58	0.3
alupla22	25	1	97	2351	81.25	15.6
vg2	25	8	122	18034	2108.7	0.3
alupla23	25	1	96	2791	193.73	9.6
sqn	7	3	97	109	0.31	0.2
alupla24	20	1	84	1199	12.82	3.2
x1dn	27	6	122	7938	342.51	0.2
dc2	8	7	136	253	1.01	0.2
x6dn	39	5	219	4882	334.30	1.0
dk17	10	11	148	531	2.21	0.2
z4	7	4	57	128	0.19	0.1
dk27	9	9	73	104	0.27	0.1
5xpl	7	10	165	128	0.51	0.2
f51m	8	8	164	256	1.12	0.2
z9sym	9	1	203	172	1.07	0.7
misg	56	23	145	*		0.2

*The problem is not solved within 30,000 cuts.

Table 15.3
Benchmark circuits (continued).

Problem	Size			Benders		BDD
lem	n	o	op	cuts	sec	sec
circ31	32	1	347	36	0.35	0.8
circ41	32	1	424	21	0.17	1.2
circ32	32	1	370	9	0.06	2.4
circ42	32	1	420	58	0.49	1.5
circ33	32	1	354	55	0.42	1.2
circ43	32	1	445	19	0.17	1.0
circ34	32	1	367	29	0.32	1.6
circ44	32	1	429	4	0.05	1.7
circ35	32	1	348	25	0.17	1.8
circ45	32	1	421	40	0.35	1.3
circ51	64	1	537	*		2.2
fcir11	64	1	575	*		3.9
circ52	64	1	546	22	0.25	2.0
fcir12	64	1	583	2	0.09	3.8
circ53	64	1	542	21	0.19	2.7
fcir13	64	1	585	11	0.14	2.3
circ54	64	1	528	15	0.16	1.8
fcir14	64	1	580	7	0.06	2.6
circ55	64	1	547	3	0.01	3.0
fcir15	64	1	579	10	0.11	5.7
circ61	64	1	486	10	0.09	0.8
fcir21	64	1	614	5	0.05	2.7
circ62	64	1	506	9	0.09	0.8
fcir22	64	1	618	11	0.13	2.4
circ63	64	1	522	*		1.0
fcir23	64	1	609	13	0.16	5.1
circ64	64	1	501	7	0.08	0.7
fcir24	64	1	613	*		3.0
circ65	64	1	482	4	0.05	0.8
fcir25	64	1	606	10	0.12	2.9

*The problem is not solved within 30,000 cuts.

Table 15.4
Random circuits.

Problem	Size			Benders		BDD
lem	n	o	op	cuts	sec	sec
circ11	8	1	148	2	0.01	0.2
circ21	16	1	286	5	0.02	0.7
circ12	8	1	142	8	0.03	0.2
circ22	16	1	292	4	0.03	0.4
circ13	8	1	150	4	0.02	0.2
circ23	16	1	287	4	0.03	0.6
circ14	8	1	147	3	0.01	0.2
circ24	16	1	289	6	0.04	0.6
circ15	8	1	142	7	0.02	0.2
circ25	16	1	289	25	0.17	0.7
circ81	25	1	376	8	0.04	1.1
circ91	25	1	385	4	0.03	0.8
circ82	25	1	371	17	0.12	0.8
circ92	25	1	385	6	0.05	1.1
circ83	25	1	379	3	0.04	1.4
circ93	25	1	376	20	0.15	1.3
circ84	25	1	366	90	0.74	0.9
circ94	25	1	385	4	0.02	0.9
circ85	25	1	371	5	0.03	1.1
circ95	25	1	378	9	0.06	0.9
circ71	96	1	713	4	0.06	4.8
circ74	96	1	734	3	0.02	2.1
circ72	96	1	730	8	0.11	3.1
circ73	96	1	711	3	0.05	2.5
circ75	96	1	702	3	0.05	3.5

*The problem is not solved within 30,000 cuts.

Table 15.5
Random circuits (continued).

with equal probability, and negated each input with probability $1/2$. We generated an equivalent circuit by a process that essentially uses De Morgan's law to move all NOTs inward so that they attach only to input variables. For every node i in the original circuit C (including inputs), we generate two nodes i, $\bar{i}$ in the equivalent circuit C'. (We do not regard NOTs as nodes.) For every unnegated arc (i, j) in C we generate arcs (i, j) and $(\bar{i}, \bar{j})$ in C', and for every negated arc we generate $(i, \bar{j})$ and $(\bar{i}, j)$ in C'. Then for each input i in C, we remove $\bar{i}$ and all incident arcs from C'. We add to C' a negated arc (i, j) for each arc $(\bar{i}, j)$ that was in C' and a negated arc $(i, \bar{j})$ for each arc $(\bar{i}, \bar{j})$ that was in C'.

The results appear in Tables 15.4 and 15.5. In almost every case, the Benders algorithm runs at least an order of magnitude faster than the BDD code. It also generates a remarkably small number of cuts (only a handful) out of the theoretical maximum of 2^n. This suggests that a Benders approach can be very effective on circuits that do not contain irreducible gates.

We also noted that Benders is faster than BDD on the few benchmark problems in which the comparison circuits are nonequivalent.

References

[1] Akers, B. S., Binary decision diagrams. *IEEE Trans. on Computers* **27** (1978) 509-516.

[2] Benders, J. E. Partitioning procedures for solving mixed-variables programming problems. *Numerical Mathematics* **4** (1962) 238-252.

[3] Blair, C. E., R. G. Jeroslow and J. K. Lowe. Some results and experiments in programming techniques for propositional logic. *Computers and Operations Research* **13** (1988) 633-645.

[4] Bryant, R. E. Graph-based algorithm for boolean function manipulation. *IEEE Trans. on Computers* **35** (1986) 677-691.

[5] Chandru, V., and J.N. Hooker. *Optimization Methods for Logical Inference.* Wiley, New York, to appear.

[6] Fujiwara, H. *Logic Testing and Design for Testability.* MIT Press, Cambridge, 1985.

[7] Gallo, G., and G. Urbani. Algorithms for testing the satisfiability of propositional formulae. *Journal of Logic Programming* **7** (1989) 45-61.

[8] Harche, F., J. N. Hooker and G. Thompson. A computational study of satisfiability algorithms for propositional logic. To appear in *ORSA Journal on Computing*.

[9] Hooker, J. N. A quantitative approach to logical inference. *Decision Support Systems* **4** (1988) 45-69.

[10] Hooker, J. N. Resolution vs. cutting plane solution of inference problems: some computational experience. *Operations Research Letters* **7** (1988) 1-7.

[11] Hooker, J. N. Input proofs and rank one cutting planes. *ORSA Journal on Computing* **1** (1989) 137-145.

[12] Hooker, J. N. Solving the incremental satisfiability problem. *Journal of Logic Programming* **15** (1933) 177-186.

[13] Hooker, J. N., and C. Fedjki. Branch and cut solution of inference problems in propositional logic. *Annals of Mathematics and AI* **1** (1990) 123-139.

[14] Jeroslow, R. G., and J. Wang. Solving propositional satisfiability problems. *Annals of Mathematics and Artificial Intelligence* **1** (1990) 167-187.

[15] Kamath, A. P., N. K. Karmakar, K. G. Ramakrishnan and M. G. C. Resende. Computational experience with an interior point algorithm on the satisfiability problem. *Integer Programming and Combinatorial Optimization*, ed. by R. Kannan and W.R. Pulleyblank, University of Waterloo Press (1990) 333-349.

[16] Minato, S., N. Ishiura and S. Yajima. Fast tautology checking using shared binary decision diagram. *IMEC IFIP International Workshop on Applied Formal Methods for Correct VLSI Design*, Belgium (1989).

[17] Mitterreiter, I., and F. J. Radermacher. Experiments on the running time behavior of some algorithms solving propositional logic problems. To appear in *Annals of Operations Research*.

[18] Nemhauser, G. L. and L. A. Wolsey. *Integer and Combinatorial Optimization*. Wiley, New York, 1988.

[19] Spera, C. Computational results for solving large general satisfiability problems. Technical report, Centro di Calcolo Elettronico, Universitá degli studi di Siena, Italy, 1990.

[20] Truemper, K., and F. J. Radermacher. Analyse der Leistungsfähigkeit eines neuen Systems zur Auswertung aussagenlogisher Probleme. Technical report FAW-TR-90003, Forschungsinstitut für anwendungsorientierte Wissensverarbeitung, Ulm, Germany, 1990.

16 An Incremental Hierarchical Constraint Solver

Francisco Menezes and Pedro Barahona

Abstract

This article presents an incremental method to solve hierarchies of constraints over finite domains, which borrows techniques developed in intelligent backtracking, and finds best solutions according to some criteria as *globally-predicate-better*. A prototype implementation of this method, IHCS, was written in C and can be integrated with different programming environments. In particular, with Prolog producing an instance of an HCLP language. Possible applications of IHCS are briefly illustrated with a time-tabling and a set covering problem. Because of its portability and incremental nature, IHCS is well suited for reactive systems, allowing the interactive introduction and removal of preferred constraints.

16.1 Introduction

Since real problems are usually over constrained, the best answer a constraint solver should give is a partial solution satisfying all but the least important constraints. Preferences among constraints may be declared explicitly by associating a strength denoting the degree of requirement to preferred or non-required constraints, in contrast with required constraints that are mandatory. In particular, a general scheme has been proposed for Hierarchical Constraint Logic Programming languages, parameterized by $\mathcal{D}$ and denoted by $\mathrm{HCLP}(\mathcal{D}, \mathcal{C})$, the domain of the constraints and by $\mathcal{C}$, a comparator that allows different possible solutions to be matched and the best ones selected [1].

A *constraint hierarchy* $\mathcal{H}$ is a set of *labelled constraints* c@*level* relating a set of variables ranging over finite domains, where c is a constraint on some variables and *level* the strength of c in the hierarchy. Level 0 corresponds to the required constraints and the other levels to the non-required (or preferred) constraints. The higher the level, the weaker a constraint is.

A *valuation* to a constraint hierarchy $\mathcal{H}$, is a mapping of the free variables in $\mathcal{H}$ to elements in their respective domains, that satisfies all the required constraints (level 0). Given two valuations θ and σ, the comparator $\mathcal{C}$ supplies the criteria to decide which valuation is better. Without loss of generality and due to space limitations, we will restrict this paper to the use of the *globally-predicate-better* comparator: θ is *globally-predicate-better* than σ if a) θ and σ both satisfy exactly the same number of constraints in each level until some level k, and b) in level $k{+}1$ θ

satisfies more constraints than σ. $\mathcal{GPB}$ (the *globally-predicate-better* comparator) is an adaptation of the *globally-better* comparator defined in [1], using weight 1 for each constraint and the trivial error function that returns 0 if the constraint is satisfied and 1 if it is not.

The Incremental Hierarchical Constraint Solver (IHCS) that we have developed may be the kernel of a HCLP($\mathcal{FD}, \mathcal{C}$) instance of this scheme, where $\mathcal{FD}$ stand for finite domains and $\mathcal{C}$ stand for a general comparator. Operationally, our approach diverges from the one presented in [1] because it is incremental. Instead of delaying the non-required constraints until the complete reduction of a goal, IHCS tries, in its forward phase, to satisfy constraints as soon as they appear. In case of inconsistency, a special backward algorithm is evoked.

This can be seen as an "optimistic" treatment of preferred constraints (i.e. we bet they will participate in the search for a solution), as opposed to the "pessimistic" view of [1] where non-required constraints (source of possible inconsistency) are delayed as much as possible. The advantage is to actively use these constraints for pruning the search space. This approach nevertheless requires a specialized backward phase where dependencies between constraints, caused by their handling of common variables, are exploited to identify pertinent causes of failure. This is done much in the same way as in intelligent backtracking [3, 9], although IHCS identifies pertinent non-required constraints to be relaxed, instead of pertinent choice points.

Because of its portability and incremental nature, IHCS is well suited for reactive systems requiring constraint facilities, allowing the interactive introduction and removal of preferred constraints to further refine any solution found. Possible applications of IHCS are briefly illustrated with a time-tabling and a set covering problem.

This article is organized as follows. Some preliminary definitions about hierarchies are specified in Section 16.2. The formal description of IHCS is presented in Section 16.3. A dependency graph is presented in Section 16.4. Extensions to cope with disjunctions of constraints are described in Section 16.5. The set-covering and time-tabling applications are presented in Section 16.6 and final remarks in Section 16.7.

16.2   Preliminary Definitions

A constraint hierarchy $\mathcal{H}$ is a tuple $\langle \mathcal{V}ars, \mathcal{C}ons, \mathcal{D}, \text{level}, D \rangle$, where $\mathcal{V}ars = \{v_1, v_2, \ldots, v_n\}$ is the set of variables, $\mathcal{C}ons = \{c_1, c_2, \ldots, c_m\}$ the set of constraints, $\mathcal{D}$ is a finite domain, level : $\mathcal{C}ons \longrightarrow \mathcal{N}$ is a mapping from constraints to their hierarchical levels, and function : $Vars \longrightarrow \wp(\mathcal{D})$ is a mapping from variables to their domains.

In our notation, c or c_i designates any constraint from $Cons$, and v or v_j any variable from $Vars$. A constraint store is any set of constraints $S \subseteq Cons$. Given any constraint store S, $S_{[i]}$, $S_{[<i]}$ and $S_{[>i]}$ designate the subsets of S containing all constraints of levels equal, lower and higher then i, respectively. Since $Cons$ itself is a constraint store, $Cons_{[0]}$ is the set of all required constraints and $Cons_{[>0]}$ the set of all non-required constraints. For convenience, elements in a constraint store may be labeled with their hierarchical level, like in $S = \{c_1@1, c_2@0, c_3@2\}$, to simplify the definition of function level (for example, with this instance, level(c_1) = 0). Finally, we will express that a store S is consistent by $S \nvdash_X \bot$, where X designates some consistency axiomatization (e.g. $X = $ AC for Arc-Consistency [6]).

The axiomatization X is not required to ensure a strong consistency condition. Although with weaker conditions, such as arc-consistency for finite domains, global consistency is not guaranteed, inconsistency is eventually detected when enough variables become instantiated. This is a trade off, since arc-consistency may be implemented in polynomial time for the general case [7] and in linear time for a number of important classes of constraints [10], while methods to verify strong K-consistency are exponential for $K > 2$ [5].

16.2.1 Configurations of a Hierarchy

DEFINITION 16.1 Configuration A *configuration* Φ of hierarchy $\mathcal{H}$ is a triple of constraint stores $\langle AS \bullet RS \bullet US \rangle$, where AS is the *Active Store*, RS the *Relaxed Store* and US the *Unexplored Store*, with the following properties:

1. $(AS \cup US) \subseteq Cons$ and $RS \subseteq Cons_{[>0]}$;
2. $AS \cap RS = \emptyset$ and $AS \cap US = \emptyset$ and $RS \cap US = \emptyset$.

DEFINITION 16.2 Total/Partial Configuration Φ is a *total configuration* if $AS \cup RS \cup US = Cons$, otherwise it is a *partial configuration*.

A total/partial configuration may be seen as a state/sub-state of the evaluation of a hierarchy where the active store contains all active constraints (i.e. those that upon activation might have reduced some domains of its variables), the relaxed store is composed by the relaxed constraints and the unexplored store is the set of candidates "queuing" for activation. In our notation, any index or prime character used in a configuration symbol, is also used in the correspondent constraint stores. For example, Φ_i or Φ' correspond respectively to the configurations $\langle AS_i \bullet RS_i \bullet US_i \rangle$

and $\langle AS' \bullet RS' \bullet US' \rangle$. Operations on configurations are defined in Figure 16.1, together with the inclusion relation.

Union	:	$\Phi_i \cup \Phi_j = \langle AS_i \cup AS_j \bullet RS_i \cup RS_j \bullet US_i \cup US_j \rangle$
Intersection	:	$\Phi_i \cap \Phi_j = \langle AS_i \cap AS_j \bullet RS_i \cap RS_j \bullet US_i \cap US_j \rangle$
Subtraction	:	$\Phi_i \setminus \Phi_j = \langle AS_i \setminus AS_j \bullet RS_i \setminus RS_j \bullet US_i \setminus US_j \rangle$
Inclusion	:	$\Phi_i \subseteq \Phi_j \equiv AS_i \subseteq AS_j,\ RS_i \subseteq RS_j,\ US_i \subseteq US_j$

Figure 16.1
Operations on configurations

DEFINITION 16.3 Simplified Configuration For each configuration Φ, there is a corresponding *simplified configuration* $|\Phi| = \langle NS \bullet RS \rangle$, where $NS = AS \cup US$ is the *Non-relaxed Store*.

Simplified configurations will be used whenever no distinction is to be made between active and unexplored constraints, since they are both constraints intended to be active. Operations on simplified configurations are defined in a similar way as for normal configurations. The word "simplified" will be dropped whenever the context makes it unnecessary.

DEFINITION 16.4 W(S) Given $S \subseteq Cons$, let W(S) be the space of all possible simplified configurations $\langle NS \bullet RS \rangle$ of $\mathcal{H}$ such that $NS \cup RS = S$, i.e,

$$W(S) = \{\langle NS \bullet RS \rangle \mid NS \subseteq S,\ RS \subseteq S_{[>0]},\ NS \cup RS = S,\ NS \cap RS = \emptyset\}$$

EXAMPLE 16.1 Given $S = \{c_1@0, c_2@1, c_3@1, c_4@2\}$, then

$$\begin{aligned}
W(S) = \{ & |\Phi_1| = \langle\{c_1, c_2, c_3, c_4\} \bullet \emptyset\rangle,\ |\Phi_2| = \langle\{c_1, c_2, c_3\} \bullet \{c_4\}\rangle, \\
& |\Phi_3| = \langle\{c_1, c_2, c_4\} \bullet \{c_3\}\rangle,\ |\Phi_4| = \langle\{c_1, c_3, c_4\} \bullet \{c_2\}\rangle, \\
& |\Phi_5| = \langle\{c_1, c_2\} \bullet \{c_3, c_4\}\rangle,\ |\Phi_6| = \langle\{c_1, c_3\} \bullet \{c_2, c_4\}\rangle, \\
& |\Phi_7| = \langle\{c_1, c_4\} \bullet \{c_2, c_3\}\rangle,\ |\Phi_8| = \langle\{c_1\} \bullet \{c_2, c_3, c_4\}\rangle\ \}
\end{aligned}$$

16.2.2   Criteria to Select Best Configurations

DEFINITION 16.5 $\preceq$ Given a constraint store S and $|\Phi|, |\Phi'| \in W(S)$, $|\Phi|$ is *globally-predicate-better* than $|\Phi'|$, denoted $|\Phi| \preceq |\Phi'|$, iff:

1. $|\Phi| = |\Phi'|$;
   or

2. $(\exists k > 0, \forall i < k), \#RS_{[i]} = \#RS'_{[i]}$ and $\#RS_{[k]} < \#RS'_{[k]}$.

EXAMPLE 16.2 Given the configuration space $W(S)$ of Example 16.1,

$$\langle W(S), \preceq \rangle = \Phi_1 - \Phi_2 \Big\langle \begin{array}{c} \Phi_3 \\ \Phi_4 \end{array} \displaystyle\bigtimes \begin{array}{c} \Phi_5 \\ \Phi_6 \end{array} \Big\rangle \Phi_7 - \Phi_8$$

It is trivial to see that given any constraint store S, $\preceq$ is reflexive, anti-symmetric and transitive in $W(S)$, and it has top element $\langle S_{[0]} \bullet S_{[>0]} \rangle$ and bottom element $\langle S \bullet \emptyset \rangle$. Consequently, $\langle W(S), \preceq \rangle$ is a complete partial order. As will be seen later, to ensure a sound and complete behavior of the constraint solver, a total order is also necessary in order to systematically enumerate configurations of a hierarchy. Definition 16.6 introduces a total order relation, related to the partial order defined by $\preceq$. This total order simply extends the $\preceq$-order by sorting the not $\preceq$-comparable configurations, using any suitable criteria such as the order in which constraints where introduced in the hierarchy (for example, if two configurations are not $\preceq$-comparable, then the configuration with older active constraints is $\preceq_t$-better then the other).

DEFINITION 16.6 $\preceq_t$ Given any constraint store S, let $\preceq_t$ be a relation associated to $\preceq$ such that the following properties hold:

1. $(\forall |\Phi_i|, |\Phi_j| \in W(S))$, $|\Phi_i| \preceq_t |\Phi_j|$ or $|\Phi_j| \preceq_t |\Phi_i|$;
2. $(\forall |\Phi_i|, |\Phi_j| \in W(S))$, $|\Phi_i| \preceq |\Phi_j| \Rightarrow |\Phi_i| \preceq_t |\Phi_j|$.

The first property of Definition 16.6 ensures that all elements are $\preceq_t$-comparable (total order), and the second property preserves the partial ordering of $\preceq$. Given a constraint store S and $\Phi \in W(S)$, $succ(\Phi, \preceq_t)$ denotes the successor of Φ in $\langle W(S), \preceq_t \rangle$.

EXAMPLE 16.3 Given the configuration space $W(S)$ of Example 16.1, a possible chain
$\langle W(S), \preceq_t \rangle$ is $\Phi_1 - \Phi2 - \Phi_3 - \Phi_4 - \Phi_5 - \Phi_6 - \Phi_7 - \Phi_8$.

PROPOSITION 16.1 Given S_1, S_2 and S_3 such that $S_1 \cap S_3 = \emptyset$ and $S_2 \cap S_3 = \emptyset$, then $\forall \Phi_1 \in W(S_1), \forall \Phi_2 \in W(S_2), \forall \Phi_3 \in W(S_3)$,

$$|\Phi_1| \preceq_t |\Phi_2| \Rightarrow |\Phi_1| \cup |\Phi_3| \preceq_t |\Phi_2| \cup |\Phi_3|.$$

The demonstration of Proposition 16.1 is obvious, since adding new constraints (Φ_3) to both Φ_1 and Φ_2, will keep their relative positions.

A relation $\propto$, related to $\preceq$, is now defined, which is used to state that a configuration is "as good as" another configuration, regarding the $\preceq$-order. This relation is convenient to prove Proposition 16.2, discussed next.

DEFINITION 16.7 $\propto$ The "as good as" relation $\propto$ is defined as follow:

$$|\Phi| \propto |\Phi'| \quad \equiv \quad (|\Phi| = |\Phi'|) \text{ or } (|\Phi| \npreceq |\Phi'| \text{ and } |\Phi'| \npreceq |\Phi|)$$

As a consequence of its definition, $\propto$ is always reflexive and symmetric and it is trivial to prove that $\propto$ also is transitive, and hence it is an equivalence relation. In the configuration space $W(S)$ of Example 16.1, $\propto$ defines the following equivalence classes: $C_1 = \{\Phi_1\}$, $C_2 = \{\Phi_2\}$, $C_3 = \{\Phi_3, \Phi_4\}$, $C_4 = \{\Phi_5, \Phi_6\}$, $C_5 = \{\Phi_7\}$ and $C_6 = \{\Phi_8\}$. Each configuration of a given class is "as good as" any other configuration of the same class, in the sense that they can not be $\preceq$-compared. Any configuration from class C_i is always better then any configuration from class C_j if $i < j$.

PROPOSITION 16.2 Given any constraint store S the following condition holds:

$$(\forall \Phi_1, \Phi_2, \Phi_3 \in W(S)) \quad (|\Phi_1| \preceq |\Phi_2|, |\Phi_2| \preceq_t |\Phi_3|) \Rightarrow |\Phi_1| \preceq |\Phi_3|$$

Informally, this proposition state that if $|\Phi_2|$ is $\preceq$-worse then $|\Phi_1|$, then any successor of $|\Phi_2|$ in any chain $\langle W(S), \preceq_t \rangle$ is also $\preceq$-worse then $|\Phi_1|$.

PROOF: Since $|\Phi_2| \preceq_t |\Phi_3|$, either i) $|\Phi_2| \preceq |\Phi_3|$ and by transitivity of $\preceq$, $|\Phi_1| \preceq |\Phi_3|$ or ii) $|\Phi_2| \propto |\Phi_3|$ (they both belong to the same equivalence class), and consequently $|\Phi_3|$ is also $\preceq$-worse then $|\Phi_1|$. $\square$

DEFINITION 16.8 Final Configuration A total configuration Φ is a *final configuration*, denoted FC(Φ), if 1) $AS \nvdash_X \bot$ and 2) $US = \emptyset$.

Notice the similarity between a final configuration, which only presents two stores (the unexplored store is always empty), and a simplified configuration. Actually, given any configuration Φ, its simplified form $|\Phi| = \langle NS \bullet RS \rangle$ corresponds to a possible final configuration $\langle NS \bullet RS \bullet \emptyset \rangle$. W($Cons$) may thus be seen as the domain of possible final configurations and $\langle W(Cons), \preceq_t \rangle$ defines the order in which final configurations are searched, as will be discussed later.

DEFINITION 16.9 Best Configuration A final configuration Φ is a *best configuration*, denoted $BC(\Phi)$, if there is no other final configuration Φ' such that $|\Phi'| \preceq |\Phi|$.

DEFINITION 16.10 Promising Configuration A   total   configuration Φ is a *promising configuration*, denoted $PC(\Phi)$, if i) $AS \nvdash_X \bot$ and ii) there is no final configuration $\Phi' \neq \langle NS \bullet RS \bullet \emptyset \rangle$ such that $|\Phi'| \preceq |\Phi|$.

PROPOSITION 16.3 If Φ is a promising configuration and $NS \nvdash_X \bot$, then $\Phi' = \langle NS \bullet RS \bullet \emptyset \rangle$ is a best configuration.

PROOF: By Definition 16.10 there is no final configuration $\Phi'' \neq \Phi$ such that $|\Phi''| \preceq |\Phi|$. Since $|\Phi'| = |\Phi|$ and $NS \nvdash_X \bot$, Φ' is a best configuration. $\square$

16.3   The Basic IHCS

IHCS aims at computing best configurations incrementally: given a hierarchy $\mathcal{H}$ with a known best configuration $\langle AS \bullet RS \bullet \emptyset \rangle$, if a new constraint c is inserted into $\mathcal{H}$, then starting from the promising configuration $\langle AS \bullet RS \bullet \{c\} \rangle$ several transitions will be performed until a best configuration is reached undoing and redoing as little work as possible. The basic rules which define the valid transitions for configurations are displayed in Figure 16.2.

Forward rule: $\dfrac{PC(\Phi) \qquad\qquad\qquad \exists c \in US}{\Phi \longrightarrow \langle AS \cup \{c\} \bullet RS \bullet US \setminus \{c\} \rangle}$ bellow = eol
  (fw)

Backward rule: $\dfrac{AS \vdash_X \bot \qquad \exists \Phi_{conf} \subseteq \Phi \qquad \exists \mathcal{Reset} \subseteq AS}{\Phi \longrightarrow \Phi'}$ bellow = eol
  (bw)

where $\begin{cases} \langle \mathcal{Activate} \bullet \mathcal{Relax} \rangle & \leftarrow \quad succ(|\Phi_{conf}|, \preceq_t) \setminus |\Phi_{conf}| \\ AS' & \leftarrow \quad AS \setminus (\mathcal{Relax} \cup \mathcal{Reset}) \\ RS' & \leftarrow \quad (RS \setminus \mathcal{Activate}) \cup \mathcal{Relax} \\ US' & \leftarrow \quad (US \setminus \mathcal{Relax}) \cup \mathcal{Reset} \cup \mathcal{Activate} \end{cases}$

Figure 16.2
Basic Rules

The forward rule is used to activate a new unexplored constraint if the current configuration is a promising one, while the backward rule searches for an alternative promising configuration for the hierarchy when a conflict is raised (i.e. the active store becomes inconsistent), relaxing some constraints and possibly reactivating other constraints previously relaxed.

The backward rule, assumes the existence of Φ_{conf} and $\mathcal{R}eset$. Φ_{conf}, the *conflict configuration*, is composed of only those constraints *pertinent* to the conflict. A constraint is pertinent if, directly or indirectly, has caused the removal of values from the domains of the variables involved in some constraint that became unsatisfiable, or if it was involved in some previous conflict related to the present one. Φ_{conf} represents the sole part of the whole configuration which is worth changing to solve the conflict, by relaxing some constraints (the $\mathcal{R}elax$ set) and re-activating constraints previously relaxed (the $\mathcal{A}ctivate$ set), so that $|\Phi_{conf}|$ is transformed into $\text{succ}(|\Phi_{conf}|, \preceq_t)$.

The $\mathcal{R}eset$ set is composed of active constraints that must be temporarily deactivated (moved to the unexplored store), in a backtracking like strategy, where all constraints introduced after any of the constraints being relaxed must be reevaluated. Values returned to current variables domains due to the relaxation of constraints, are then checked again for consistency. Not all constraints introduced after those relaxed must be included in the $\mathcal{R}eset$ set, since some of them may be fully independent of the relaxing ones. The $\mathcal{R}eset$ set should therefore be restricted, according to some notion of constraint dependency, as discussed in Section 16.4 where a dependency graph is introduced - this is equivalent to adopt am intelligent backtracking strategy. Notice that resetting constraints in a configuration does not change the corresponding simplified configuration, since it simply moves constraints from the active to the unexplored store. For the time being let us assume that Φ_{conf} and $\mathcal{R}eset$, with the properties described above, exist and can be computed (the actual computation is dealt with in Section 16.4.1).

LEMMA 16.1 (Uniqueness) Given a configuration Φ, there is at most one transition $\Phi \longrightarrow \Phi'$.

PROOF: The forward rule is only applicable to promising configurations, which implies $AS \nvdash_X \bot$ (Definition 16.10), while the backward rule is only applicable when $AS \vdash_X \bot$. Since these conditions are mutually exclusive, at most one rule can be applied to Φ and therefore there is at most one possible transition from Φ. $\square$

PROPOSITION 16.4 If $\Phi \longrightarrow \Phi'$, then $|\Phi| \preceq_t |\Phi'|$.

PROOF: This Proposition is trivially true with a forward transition since $|\Phi| = |\Phi'|$. In the backward case, $\Phi \xrightarrow{\text{bw}} \Phi'$, we have $|\Phi| = |\Phi_{conf}| \cup |\Phi_{rest}|$ and

$|\Phi'| = \text{succ}(|\Phi_{\text{conf}}|, \preceq_t) \cup |\Phi_{\text{rest}}|$, i.e., $|\Phi_{\text{conf}}|$ is changed to its successor while $|\Phi_{\text{rest}}|$ is kept unchanged. Since $|\Phi_{\text{conf}}| \preceq_t \text{succ}(|\Phi_{\text{conf}}|, \preceq_t)$ then, by Proposition 16.1, $(|\Phi_{\text{conf}}| \cup |\Phi_{\text{rest}}|) \preceq_t (\text{succ}(|\Phi_{\text{conf}}|, \preceq_t) \cup |\Phi_{\text{rest}}|)$. $\square$

One consequence of Proposition 16.4 is that in a transition $\Phi \longrightarrow \Phi'$, $|\Phi'| \not\preceq |\Phi|$, i.e., the configuration obtained is never globally-predicate-better then the original one. The search for a solution is always performed in increasing $\preceq_t$-order of configurations.

THEOREM 16.1 If $\Phi \longrightarrow \Phi'$, then there is no final configuration Φ_k such that $\Phi_k \neq \Phi$ and $\Phi_k \neq \Phi'$ and $\Phi \preceq_t \Phi_k \preceq_t \Phi'$.

PROOF: We want to prove that no final configuration is missed in any transition $\Phi \longrightarrow \Phi'$. In a forward transition, we have $|\Phi| = |\Phi'|$ and consequently there is no final configuration in between.

In the case of a backward transition, $|\Phi| \preceq_t |\Phi'|$, but $|\Phi'|$ is possibly not the immediate successor of $|\Phi|$, i.e. $|\Phi'| \neq \text{succ}(|\Phi|, \preceq_t)$. All the intermediate configurations are the result of also relaxing or activating constraints in $\Phi \setminus \Phi_{\text{conf}}$ which are irrelevant to the conflict raised: either the current conflict would not be solved or previously solved conflicts would be re-produced. Therefore these intermediate configurations do not lead to any final configuration, and $|\Phi'|$ is thus the first successor of $|\Phi|$ which is worth considering. $\square$

DEFINITION 16.11 Dead-end Φ is a *dead-end* if no transition rule is applicable to Φ, i.e.:

1. $AS \not\vdash_X \bot \quad \Rightarrow \quad \exists \Phi' \preceq \Phi, \text{FC}(\Phi')$
   (the forward rule is not applicable);

2. $AS \vdash_X \bot \quad \Rightarrow \quad NS_{\text{conf}[>0]} = \emptyset$
   (the backward rule is not applicable, because
   there is no $\text{succ}(|\Phi_{\text{conf}}|, \preceq_t)$).

LEMMA 16.2 If Φ is a promising configuration of $\mathcal{H}$, then there is a finite sequence of transitions $\Phi \longrightarrow \Phi_1 \longrightarrow \cdots \longrightarrow \Phi_n$, with n bounded by $\#US$, such that Φ_n is either a final configuration, a dead-end or a new promising configuration such that $|\Phi_n| \neq |\Phi|$.

PROOF: Starting with the promising configuration Φ, at most $\#US$ transitions performed by the forward rule will be made until either a final configuration is reached or a conflict is raised.

Suppose that after transition $\Phi_{j-1} \xrightarrow{\text{fw}} \Phi_j$ ($j \le \#US$), $AS_j \vdash_X \bot$, i.e., a conflict is raised. If $NS_{\text{conf}[>0]} = \emptyset$ ($\Phi_{\text{conf}} \subseteq \Phi_j$), then Φ_j is a dead-end and the derivation stops ($n = j$). Otherwise, the backward rule is applied to produce an alternative configuration Φ_n ($n = j + 1$).

Since all the affected constraints are reset, $AS_n \not\vdash_X \bot$. Additionally, and since no final configuration exists between $|\Phi|$ and $|\Phi_n|$ (c.f. Theorem 16.1), we can conclude that either Φ_n is also a promising configuration, or there is some final configuration Φ' such that $|\Phi'| \preceq_t |\Phi|$ and $|\Phi'| \not\preceq |\Phi|$ and $|\Phi'| \preceq |\Phi_n|$ in which case Φ_n is a dead-end and the derivation stops. This exception may arise when looking for alternative best configurations as will be seen in Section 16.3.1. $\square$

DEFINITION 16.12 Unsuccessful Derivation An *unsuccessful derivation* is a sequence of transitions $\Phi \xrightarrow{*} \Phi'$, such that Φ' is a dead-end.

DEFINITION 16.13 Successful Derivation A *successful derivation* is a sequence of transitions $\Phi \xrightarrow{*} \Phi'$, such that Φ' is a final configuration.

THEOREM 16.2 (Decidability) If Φ is a promising configuration of $\mathcal{H}$, then there is one and only one derivation $\Phi \xrightarrow{*} \Phi'$, either successful or unsuccessful, and this derivation is finite.

PROOF: Starting from a promising configuration Φ, after a finite number of transitions either a final configuration or a dead-end or another promising configuration Φ_j will be reached (Lemma 16.2). In the two first cases the finiteness is proved. In the latter case, since Φ_j is exactly in the same conditions as Φ (i.e. it is also a promising configuration), this reasoning can be re-iterated. There will be one such re-iteration for each conflict raised, but since the number of possible conflicts[1] is bounded by $\#W(\mathcal{C}ons)$, and transitions are always made in increasing order of $\preceq_t$ comparisons (Proposition 16.4), the derivation will end after a finite sequence of transitions. The uniqueness of the derivation is an obvious consequence of Lemma 16.1. $\square$

THEOREM 16.3 (Soundness) If Φ is a promising configuration of $\mathcal{H}$ and $\Phi \xrightarrow{*} \Phi_n$ is a successful derivation, then Φ_n is a best configuration.

---

[1]in the worst case there will be a conflict for each possible simplified configuration

PROOF: As shown in Proof 16.3, a successful derivation always ends in a sequence of zero or more transitions using only the forward rule and starting from some promising configuration Φ_j, i.e. $\Phi \xrightarrow{*} \Phi_j \xrightarrow{fw} \Phi_{j+1} \xrightarrow{fw} \cdots \xrightarrow{fw} \Phi_n$. Since $\Phi_n = \langle NS_j \bullet RS_j \bullet \emptyset \rangle$ and $NS_j \nvdash \perp$, by Proposition 16.3, Φ_n is a best configuration. □

EXAMPLE 16.4 Given variables X and Y with initial domains $D(X) = D(Y) = 1..10$, consider the following constraints: $c_1 \equiv X+Y = 15@1$; $c_2 \equiv 3\cdot X-Y < 5@1$; $c_3 \equiv X > Y+1@2$; $c_4 \equiv X < 7@2$. The incremental insertion of each constraint is given by the following transitions:

Action	Configuration			$D(X)$	$D(Y)$	Relaxeds @1 @2	Next Rule
add c_1	$\langle\{$	$\}\bullet\{$	$\}\bullet\{c_1\}\rangle$	1..10	1..10	0 0	fw
	$\langle\{c_1$	$\}\bullet\{$	$\}\bullet\{\ \}\rangle$	5..10	5..10	0 0	
add c_2	$\langle\{c_1$	$\}\bullet\{$	$\}\bullet\{c_2\}\rangle$	5..10	5..10	0 0	fw
	$\langle\{c_1,c_2$	$\}\bullet\{$	$\}\bullet\{\ \}\rangle$	$\emptyset$	$\emptyset$	0 0	bw
	$\langle\{c_1$	$\}\bullet\{c_2$	$\}\bullet\{\ \}\rangle$	5..10	5..10	1 0	
add c_3	$\langle\{c_1$	$\}\bullet\{c_2$	$\}\bullet\{c_3\}\rangle$	5..10	5..10	1 0	fw
	$\langle\{c_1,c_3$	$\}\bullet\{c_2$	$\}\bullet\{\ \}\rangle$	7..10	5..8	1 0	
add c_4	$\langle\{c_1,c_3$	$\}\bullet\{c_2$	$\}\bullet\{c_4\}\rangle$	7..10	5..8	1 0	fw
	$\langle\{c_1,c_3,c_4\}\bullet\{c_2$	$\}\bullet\{\ \}\rangle$		$\emptyset$	$\emptyset$	1 0	bw
	$\langle\{c_1,c_3$	$\}\bullet\{c_2,c_4\}\bullet\{\ \}\rangle$		7..10	5..8	1 1	

16.3.1 Obtaining Alternative Best Configurations

There may be several best configurations to a hierarchy $\mathcal{H}$, since the $\preceq$ ordering is not a total ordering, i.e., more than a final configuration of $\mathcal{H}$ may exist with exactly the same number of relaxed constraints in each level. Of course the system using the rules described so far is not exhaustive in the sense that it cannot find all these best configurations. Such exhaustiveness is achieved by IHCS using a new rule, the *alternative* rule (Figure 16.3). Given the current best configuration, this rule allows IHCS to find the next promising configuration.

The main difference between this and the backward rule is that here an alternative to a best configuration is being computed, rather then an alternative to a conflicting one. The successor of $|\Phi|$ is computed, instead of only the successor of some subconfiguration $|\Phi_{\text{conf}}|$.

If the configuration Φ' determined by the alternative rule is $\preceq$-worse then Φ, then it is not a promising configuration, since Φ is a final configuration (c.f. Definition

Alternative rule: $\dfrac{\mathrm{BC}(\Phi) \qquad \exists \mathcal{R}eset \subseteq AS}{\Phi \longrightarrow \Phi'}$ bellow = eol
(alt)

$$\text{where} \begin{cases} \langle \mathcal{A}ctivate \bullet \mathcal{R}elax \rangle & \leftarrow & \mathrm{succ}(|\Phi|, \preceq_t) \setminus |\Phi| \\ AS' & \leftarrow & AS \setminus (\mathcal{R}elax \cup \mathcal{R}eset) \\ RS' & \leftarrow & (RS \setminus \mathcal{A}ctivate) \cup \mathcal{R}elax \\ US' & \leftarrow & \mathcal{R}eset \cup \mathcal{A}ctivate \end{cases}$$

Figure 16.3
Extra rule to search for an alternative

16.10), and the search for an alternative best configuration fails. Otherwise, Φ' is subsequently handled by the basic rules. If any future transition $\Phi_j \xrightarrow{\text{bw}} \Phi_{j+1}$ is such that $|\Phi_j| \preceq |\Phi_{j+1}|$, then the search fails since Φ_{j+1} is no longer a promising configuration (Φ_{j+1} is a dead-end).

THEOREM 16.4 (completeness) Given a hierarchy $\mathcal{H}$, there is always a successful derivation leading to any best configurations of $\mathcal{H}$, starting from the promising configuration $\langle \emptyset \bullet \emptyset \bullet \mathcal{C}ons \rangle$.

PROOF: Given $\Phi = \langle \emptyset \bullet \emptyset \bullet \mathcal{C}ons \rangle$, $|\Phi|$ is the bottom element of $\mathrm{W}(\mathcal{C}ons)$. Since transitions are performed in increasing $\preceq_t$-order of configurations (c.f. Proposition 16.4) and no final configuration is missed (c.f. Theorem 16.1), the first final configuration reached by a sequence of transitions made by the forward and backward rules alone is the first best configuration. Applying the alternative rule to each best configuration Φ_j found will either produce a dead-end or a new promising configuration Φ_k. In the later case, since $|\Phi_k| = \mathrm{succ}(|\Phi_j|, \preceq_t)$, there is no other final configuration between Φ_j and Φ_k. Further forward and backward transitions will lead Φ_k to the next best configuration, if any, otherwise a dead-end will be reached (c.f. Theorem 16.2). Whenever a dead-end is reached, by Proposition 16.2 all the successor in the chain $\langle \mathrm{W}(\mathcal{C}ons), \preceq_t \rangle$ are $\preceq$-worst and consequently the search may fail immediately. $\square$

EXAMPLE 16.5 All alternatives to the solution found in Example 16.4 are computed by the following transitions:

Action	Configuration	$D(X)$	$D(Y)$	Relaxeds @1 @2		Next Rule
more	$\langle\{c_1,c_3\} \bullet \{c_2,c_4\}\ \}\bullet\{\ \}\rangle$	7..10	5..8	1	1	alt
	$\langle\{c_1\ \} \bullet \{c_2,c_3\}\ \}\bullet\{c_4\}\rangle$	5..10	5..10	1	1	fw
	$\langle\{c_1,c_4\} \bullet \{c_2,c_3\}\ \}\bullet\{\ \}\rangle$	5..6	9..10	1	1	
more	$\langle\{c_1,c_4\} \bullet \{c_2,c_3\}\ \}\bullet\{\ \}\rangle$	5..6	9..10	1	1	alt
	$\langle\{\ \} \bullet \{c_1,c_3\}\ \}\bullet\{c_2,c_4\}\rangle$	1..10	1..10	1	1	fw
	$\langle\{c_2\ \} \bullet \{c_1,c_3\}\ \}\bullet\{c_4\}\rangle$	1..4	1..10	1	1	fw
	$\langle\{c_2,c_4\} \bullet \{c_1,c_3\}\ \}\bullet\{\ \}\rangle$	1..4	1..10	1	1	
more	$\langle\{c_2,c_4\} \bullet \{c_1,c_3\}\ \}\bullet\{\ \}\rangle$	1..4	1..10	1	1	alt
	$\langle\{c_2\ \} \bullet \{c_1,c_4\}\ \}\bullet\{c_3\}\rangle$	1..4	1..10	1	1	fw
	$\langle\{c_2,c_3\} \bullet \{c_1,c_4\}\ \}\bullet\{\ \}\rangle$	$\emptyset$	$\emptyset$	1	1	bw
	$\langle\{\ \} \bullet \{c_2,c_3,c_4\} \bullet \{c_1\}\rangle$	1..10	1..10	1	2	—

The final search for an alternative in Example 16.5 fails, because the last transition performed by the backward rule produced a configuration worse then the previous one (with an extra constraint relaxed in level 2).

16.3.2 Incremental Removal of a Constraint

Given a best configuration of hierarchy $\mathcal{H}$, the removal of a constraint c from $\mathcal{H}$ is straightforward if c is a relaxed constraint, and a final configuration is immediately obtained by the relaxed removal rule (Figure 16.4).

Relaxed removal rule:
(rr)
$$\dfrac{BC(\Phi) \qquad c \in RS}{\Phi \longrightarrow \langle AS \bullet RS \setminus \{c\} \bullet \emptyset\rangle}\ bellow = eol$$

Active removal rule:
(ar)
$$\dfrac{BC(\Phi) \qquad c \in AS \qquad \exists Reset \subseteq AS}{\Phi \longrightarrow \Phi'}\ bellow = eol$$

$$where\ \begin{cases} AS' & \leftarrow & AS \setminus (\{c\} \cup Reset) \\ RS' & \leftarrow & RS \setminus Activate \\ US' & \leftarrow & Reset \cup Activate \end{cases}$$

Figure 16.4
Removal of a constraint

THEOREM 16.5 If $\Phi_i \xrightarrow{\text{rr}} \Phi_j$, then Φ_j is a best configuration.

PROOF: Let $\mathcal{H}$ and $\mathcal{H}'$ be respectively the hierarchy before and after the removal of relaxed constraint c. Let us also assume, by absurd, that there is a final configuration Φ_k of $\mathcal{H}'$ such that $|\Phi_k| \preceq |\Phi_j|$ and let $\Phi_l = \Phi_k \cup \langle \emptyset \bullet \{c\} \bullet \emptyset \rangle$. Then,

$$|\Phi_k| \preceq |\Phi_j| \Rightarrow |\Phi_k \cup \langle \emptyset \bullet \{c\} \bullet \emptyset \rangle| \preceq |\Phi_j \cup \langle \emptyset \bullet \{c\} \bullet \emptyset \rangle| \Leftrightarrow |\Phi_l| \preceq |\Phi_i|.$$

If there were such Φ_k, then there would also exist a final configuration Φ_l of $\mathcal{H}$ such that $|\Phi_l| \preceq |\Phi_i|$, and therefore Φ_i would not be a best configuration of $\mathcal{H}$, contrary to the initial premises in the relaxed removal rule. Therefore, we can conclude that there is no such Φ_k and Φ_j is indeed a best configuration of $\mathcal{H}'$. $\square$

To remove an active constraint, the *active removal* rule is used instead (Figure 16.4). The $\mathcal{Reset}$ set is composed of constraints affected by c, that must be reset. The $\mathcal{Activate}$ set contains all relaxed constraints that were previously in some conflict with c. Those constraints are candidates for activation since the removal of c will hopefully resolve those previous conflicts.

PROPOSITION 16.5 If $\Phi \xrightarrow{\text{ar}} \Phi'$, then Φ' is a promising configuration.

PROOF: Let c be the constraint to be removed and $\mathcal{H}$ and $\mathcal{H}'$ be respectively the hierarchy before and after the removal of c. We have to prove that conditions i) and ii) of Definition 16.10 hold for Φ':

i) Given that Φ is a best configuration, $AS \not\vdash_X \bot$. It is trivial to see that in transition $\Phi \xrightarrow{\text{ar}} \Phi'$, $AS' \subset AS$ (c.f. the active removal rule). Consequently, $AS' \not\vdash_X \bot$;

ii) Let us assume, by absurd, that there is a final configuration Φ_j of $\mathcal{H}'$ such that $|\Phi_j| \preceq |\Phi'|$ and let $\Phi_k = \langle (AS_j \setminus \mathcal{Activate}) \cup \{c\} \bullet RS_j \cup \mathcal{Activate} \bullet \emptyset \rangle$. Then,

$$\begin{aligned}
|\Phi_j| &\preceq |\Phi'| \Rightarrow \\
&\Rightarrow |\Phi_k| \preceq \langle (NS' \setminus \mathcal{Activate}) \cup \{c\} \bullet RS' \cup \mathcal{Activate} \rangle \Leftrightarrow \\
&\Leftrightarrow |\Phi_k| \preceq |\Phi|
\end{aligned}$$

We can conclude that there is no such Φ_j, otherwise there would be a final configuration Φ_k of $\mathcal{H}$, contrary to the premise that Φ is a best configuration of $\mathcal{H}$. $\square$

If $\Phi \xrightarrow{ar} \Phi'$ then there is always a successful derivation $\Phi' \xrightarrow{*} \Phi_n$, since there is at least a final configuration $\Phi_m = \langle AS \setminus \{c\} \bullet RS \bullet \emptyset \rangle$ after Φ', and $|\Phi_n| \preceq_t |\Phi_m|$.

EXAMPLE 16.6 Removing the active constraint c_3 from the solution obtained in Example 16.4 produces the following transitions:

Action	Configuration	$D(X)$	$D(Y)$	Relaxeds @1 @2		Next Rule
remove c_3	$\langle \{c_1, c_3\} \bullet \{c_2, c_4\} \bullet \{\ \ \} \rangle$	7..10	5..8	1	1	ar
	$\langle \{c_1\ \ \} \bullet \{c_2\ \ \ \ \} \bullet \{c_4\} \rangle$	5..10	5..10	1	0	fw
	$\langle \{c_1, c_4\} \bullet \{c_2\ \ \ \ \} \bullet \{\ \ \} \rangle$	5..6	9..10	1	0	

EXAMPLE 16.7 Removing the active constraint c_4 from the second alternative obtained in Example 16.5 produces the following transitions:

Action	Configuration	$D(X)$	$D(Y)$	Relaxeds @1 @2		Next Rule
rem. c_4	$\langle \{c_2, c_4\} \bullet \{c_1, c_3\} \bullet \{\ \ \ \ \} \rangle$	1..4	1..10	1	1	ar
	$\langle \{c_2\ \ \} \bullet \{\ \ \ \ \ \} \bullet \{c_1, c_3\} \rangle$	5..10	5..10	1	0	fw
	$\langle \{c_1, c_2\} \bullet \{\ \ \ \ \ \} \bullet \{c_3\ \ \} \rangle$	$\emptyset$	$\emptyset$	1	0	bw
	$\langle \{c_1\ \ \} \bullet \{c_2\ \ \} \bullet \{c_3\ \ \} \rangle$	5..10	5..10	1	0	fw
	$\langle \{c_1, c_3\} \bullet \{c_2\ \ \} \bullet \{\ \ \ \ \} \rangle$	7..10	5..8	1	0	

16.4   The Dependency Graph

To cope with hierarchical constraints, a *dependency graph* ($\mathcal{DG}$) with information about the dependency between active constraints, must be kept and updated. When a conflict is raised, $\mathcal{DG}$ is analysed to find out the pertinent causes of the failure (the *conflict configuration* Φ_{conf}) and what will be affected by the relaxation of some constraints (the *Reset* set).

Given a constraint c, let the set of its variables be denoted by $\mathcal{V}_c$ and given a variable v let the set of the constraints on v be denoted by $\mathcal{C}_v$.

DEFINITION 16.14 Constrainer c ($c \in AS$) is a *constrainer* of v ($v \in \mathcal{V}_c$) if it actually caused the reduction of D_v, i.e., values where removed from the domain of v during some revision of c. We also designate c as a constrainer (without mentioning of which variable) if it is a constrainer of some variable.

Notice that a constraint may be redundant for some of its variables, i.e. it never becomes a constrainer of these variables.

DEFINITION 16.15 Immediate Dependency\Support c_k is *immediately dependent* of c_j (or c_j is an *immediate supporter* of c_k), written $c_j \hookrightarrow c_k$, iff $\exists v \in \mathcal{V}_{c_k}$ such that c_j is a constrainer of v.

PROPOSITION 16.6 $c \hookrightarrow c$ iff c is a constrainer.

This proposition is a trivial consequence of Definition 16.15.

DEFINITION 16.16 $\mathcal{DG}$ $\mathcal{DG}$ is a direct graph whose nodes are the constraints in AS and there is an arc from c_j to c_k $(\forall c_j, c_k \in AS)$ iff $c_j \hookrightarrow c_k$.

DEFINITION 16.17 Dependent\Supporter c_k is *dependent* of c_j (conversely c_j is a *supporter* of c_k) iff $c_j \overset{*}{\hookrightarrow} c_k$, i.e, there is a path from c_j to c_k in $\mathcal{DG}$.

DEFINITION 16.18 Immediately Connected c_j is *immediately connected* to c_k , written $c_j \rightleftharpoons c_k$, iff $c_j \hookrightarrow c_k$ or $c_k \hookrightarrow c_j$.

DEFINITION 16.19 Connected c_j is *connected* to c_k iff $c_j \overset{*}{\rightleftharpoons} c_k$, i.e. there is a path between c_j and c_k in the underlying undirected graph of $\mathcal{DG}$.

The dependency relation is based on *local propagation* of constraints in the following way: whenever a constraint c_j $(c_j \in AS)$ makes a restriction on some v $(v \in \mathcal{V}_{c_j})$, any other constraint c_k $(c_k \in AS)$ such that $v \in \mathcal{V}_{c_k}$ will be reactivated and probably cause the reactivation of further constraints, even if they do not share any variable with c_j. The restrictions performed by c_j may consequently affect all those constraints and for this reason they all become dependent of c_j.

A simple way to implicitly maintain $\mathcal{DG}$ is to record for each variable v the set of its constrainers, $\bar{\mathcal{C}}_v$ $(\bar{\mathcal{C}}_v \subseteq \mathcal{C}_v)$, and for each constraint c the set of its constrained variables, $\bar{\mathcal{V}}_c$ $(\bar{\mathcal{V}}_c \subseteq \mathcal{V}_c)$. Observe that, following intelligent backtracking techniques, we record dependencies at the level of the constraint network, as opposed to [4] where a truth-maintenance system is coupled with a finite domains constraint solver. All necessary operations on $\mathcal{DG}$ will be made through the functions of Figure 16.5.

PROPOSITION 16.7 Given $S \subseteq AS$, IS(S) returns the set of all immediate supporters of any constraint in S, i.e.

$$\mathrm{IS}(S) = \{c_k \in AS \mid (\exists c_j \in S),\ c_k \hookrightarrow c_j\}$$

vars	:	$\wp(Cons) \longrightarrow \wp(Vars)$,	$\mathrm{vars}(S)$	$= \bigcup_{c \in S} \mathcal{V}_c$
cvars	:	$\wp(Cons) \longrightarrow \wp(Vars)$,	$\mathrm{cvars}(S)$	$= \bigcup_{c \in S} \bar{\mathcal{V}}_c$
IS	:	$\wp(Cons) \longrightarrow \wp(Cons)$,	$\mathrm{IS}(S)$	$= \bigcup_{v \in \mathrm{vars}(S)} \bar{\mathcal{C}}_v$
SUP	:	$\wp(Cons) \longrightarrow \wp(Cons)$,	$\mathrm{SUP}(S)$	$= \mathrm{IS}(S){\uparrow}\omega$
ID	:	$\wp(Cons) \longrightarrow \wp(Cons)$,	$\mathrm{ID}(S)$	$= \bigcup_{v \in \mathrm{cvars}(S)} \mathcal{C}_v$
IR	:	$\wp(Cons) \longrightarrow \wp(Cons)$,	$\mathrm{IR}(S)$	$= \mathrm{IS}(S) \cup \mathrm{ID}(S)$
REL	:	$\wp(Cons) \longrightarrow \wp(Cons)$,	$\mathrm{REL}(S)$	$= \mathrm{IR}(S){\uparrow}\omega$

Figure 16.5
Manipulation of $\mathcal{DG}$

PROOF: By Definition 16.15, an immediate supporter of a constraint c is any con-strainer of any variable belonging to $\mathcal{V}_c$. $\mathrm{IS}(S)$ is the union of all the constrainers of each variable appearing in some constraint in S, consequently it contains all the possible immediate supporters of any constraint in S and nothing else. $\square$

Considering the set union operation as a unit operation (with a bitmap representation of sets one can roughly obtain set union as a constant time operation), functions $\mathrm{vars}(S)$ and $\mathrm{IS}(S)$ are respectively computable in time $O(nc)$ and $O(nc+nv)$, being nc the number of constraints in S (the length of S) and nv the number of variables in S.

PROPOSITION 16.8 Given $S \subseteq AS$, $\mathrm{ID}(S)$ returns the set of all constraints which are immediately dependent of any constraint in S, i.e.

$$\mathrm{ID}(S) = \{c_k \in AS \mid (\exists c_j \in S),\ c_j \hookrightarrow c_k\}$$

PROOF: By Definition 16.15, if $c_j \hookrightarrow c_k$ then c_k is any constraint over any vari-able produced by c_j. $\mathrm{ID}(S)$ is the union of all the constraints over each variable produced by some constraint in S, consequently it must contain all constraints im-mediately dependent of any constraint in S. $\square$

Functions $\mathrm{cvars}(S)$ is computable in time $O(nc)$ and $\mathrm{ID}(S)$ in time $O(nc+nv)$, being nc and nv respectively the number of constraints and the number of constrained variables in S.

PROPOSITION 16.9 Given $S \subseteq AS$, IR(S) returns the set of all constraints which are immediately connected to any constraint in S, i.e.

$$\text{IR}(S) = \{c_k \in AS \mid (\exists c_j \in S),\ c_j \rightleftharpoons c_k\}$$

This proposition is a trivial consequence of Propositions 16.7 and 16.8 and Definition 16.18. IR(S) is also computable in time $O(nc+nv)$. Additionally, it is trivial to see that $\wp(Cons)$ (the powerset of C) is a complete partial order under the inclusion relation, and that functions IS, ID and IR are all monotonic and continuous. Therefore they all contain some fix points in their domains.

DEFINITION 16.20 Straight Path A path of $\mathcal{DG}$ from c_j to c_k is a *straight path* if it does not contains repeated nodes and there is no other path of $\mathcal{DG}$ from c_j to c_k with smaller length.

PROPOSITION 16.10 Given $S \subseteq AS$, SUP(S) is a fix point of IS which represents the set of all supporters of any constraint in S, i.e.

$$\text{SUP}(S) = \{c_k \in AS \mid (\exists c_j \in S),\ c_k \overset{*}{\hookrightarrow} c_j\}$$

PROOF: Let $S_1 = \text{IS}(S), S_2 = \text{IS}(S_1) = \text{IS}(S)\!\uparrow\!2, \ldots, S_n = \text{IS}(S_{n-1}) = \text{IS}(S)\!\uparrow\!n$. Suppose that S_n is the fix point reached by this iterations. Since S_i ($1 \leq i \leq n$) only contains constrainers, by Proposition 16.6 $S_i \subseteq \text{IS}(S_i)$, i.e, each iteration preserves the elements collected so far. S_1 is composed of the immediate supporters, that is, the supporters distanced by a single link in a straight path of $\mathcal{DG}$, from constraints in S. Applying IS to S_1, and thus obtaining S_2, will add all the supporters distanced by two links. This iterative process keeps adding new supporters with longer straight paths of $\mathcal{DG}$ leading to constraints in S. If n is the maximal length of a straight path of $\mathcal{DG}$ leading to some constraint in S, then $\text{IS}(S_n) = S_n$ since there are no more new supporters to add. Consequently, $\text{IS}(S)\!\uparrow\!\omega = \text{SUP}(S)$ is the set of all possible supporters of any constraint in S. $\square$

Notice that in each iteration of the computation of SUP(S), one has only to consider the new variables introduced by the new constraints in the previous iteration in order to collect new supporters. Function SUP(S) is thus computable in time $O(nc + nv)$, being nc and nv respectively the total number of constrains and variables of the hierarchy.

PROPOSITION 16.11 Given $S \subseteq AS$, $\text{REL}(S)$ is a fix point of IR which represents the set of all constraints connected to any constraint in S, i.e.

$$\text{REL}(S) = \{c_k \in AS \mid (\exists c_j \in S), \ c_j \overset{*}{\rightleftharpoons} c_k\}$$

The proof for this proposition is analogous to the one used for Proposition 16.10 and similarly $\text{REL}(S)$ is computable in time $O(nc + nv)$, which concludes that all required operations on the dependency graph are computable with linear time complexities on the size of the hierarchy (given in terms of the number of constraints and variables).

16.4.1 Conflict Configurations and Reset Sets

The Dependency Graph is mainly used to find out the pertinent causes of failures and which active constraints are affected by the relaxation of some constraints, as explained before. In this section two conventions are made to the use of indexes in both configurations and constraints. The index in a configuration is used to indicate the order in which that configuration was produced, i.e., starting from some initial configuration Φ_0, transitions are represented by $\Phi_0 \longrightarrow \Phi_1 \longrightarrow \Phi_2 \longrightarrow \cdots$. The index in a constraint represents the order in which this constraint was introduced in the hierarchy, i.e. the first constraint is c_1, the second is c_2 and so on.

Conflict Sets. Let c_i be the unexplored constraint activated in a transition $\Phi_{j-1} \overset{fw}{\longrightarrow} \Phi_j$. If a conflict is raised (i.e. $AS_j \vdash_X \bot$), then let $CS_j \subseteq AS_j$, the *conflict store*, be the set of relaxable supporters of c_i, i.e. the relaxable active constraints pertinent to the conflict raised by the activation of c_i. These supporters are responsible for the elimination of some values from the domains of variables, required to satisfy c_i:

$$CS_j = \text{SUP}(\{c_i\})_{[>0]}.$$

Conflict Configurations. As seen in Section 16.3, when solving a conflict in some Φ_j with the backward rule, constraints from the conflict configuration $\Phi_{\text{conf}} \subseteq \Phi_j$ may be relaxed or reactivated. Consequently, on addition to include the conflict store CS_j (the direct responsible for the current conflict), Φ_{conf} must also include previous conflict stores related to the current one. This is necessary to ensure a "best configuration" policy, since the resolution of the current conflict may work as an alternative for the resolution of previously related conflicts, thus allowing the reactivation of some constraints relaxed before. Two conflicts are related if they involve common constraints. The conflict configuration is thus given by:

$$\Phi_{\text{conf}} = |\Phi_j| \cap \{CS_i, i \leq j \mid CS_i \cap CS_j \neq \emptyset\}.$$

Reset Sets. Whenever constraints are relaxed or removed from the hierarchy, active constraints related to these constraints must be reset , in a backtracking strategy, to ensure that values returning to the domains of variables due to the relaxation (or removal) of constraints are checked again for consistency. Given $\mathcal{Relax}$, a set of constraints to be relaxed (or removed), the $\mathcal{Reset}$ set is given by:

$$\mathcal{Reset} = \bigcup_{c_j \in \mathcal{Relax}} \{c_i \in \text{REL}(\{c_j\}) \mid i \geq j\}.$$

16.5   Disjunctive Constraints and Inter-Hierarchies

In logic programming the alternatives to solve a goal are usually specified as different rules for the same literal. This fact raises some problems, since different choices of rules in the logic program may produce solutions from different constraint hierarchies, sometimes producing non-intuitive solutions. In [11] the HCLP scheme is extended with some non-monotonic properties of comparators to cope with inter-hierarchy comparisons.

This problem was dealt with in IHCS by extending it with disjunctive constraints of the form $c = c^1 \vee c^2 \vee \cdots \vee c^n$, where c^i is a normal constraint representing the i-th alternative of c. A disjunctive constraint c can only be relaxed if $\text{level}(c) > 0$ and all alternatives have already failed.

This extension enables the specification of more complex constraint hierarchies and we take advantage of the dependency graph to backtrack intelligently to alternative choices.

Disjunctions however complicates the overall IHCS algorithm, as non exhausted disjunctions must be integrated in conflict sets. Since we want to minimize the number of constraints to be relaxed, it is preferable whenever possible to try an alternative choice rather than relaxing extra constraints. As in intelligent backtracking methods, we have to associate an *alternative set* for each disjunction – cf. the $\mathcal{Alt}$ sets of [3] – and to restart from the first alternative disjunctions to be re-inserted – cf. the selective reset of [2].

The use of disjunctive constraints is very useful for the final generation of solutions, specially in incomplete inference systems such as the ones that use arc-consistency for finite domains. After the pruning due to all constraints being treated, some variables may still have several possible values in their do-mains. If the domain of a variable v is $\{w_1, \ldots, w_n\}$ then adding a constraint $v = w_1 \bigvee \cdots \bigvee v = w_n$ will ensure that a single value will be assigned to v within a best solution. We used such constraint as the basic definition for the built-in value generator - predicate $indomain(v)$.

16.5.1   The Disjunctive Rule

With the introduction of disjunctions, conflicts may be solved not only by relaxing non-required constraints, but also by trying different choice points. An extra tran-sition rule, the *disjunctive rule* (Figure 16.6) and some changes in the backward, active removal and alternative rules are required, to cope with this extension. One of the revisions on the backward and alternative rules it is to exclude their appli-cability when there is some alternative choice to try, in order to keep the mutual exclusivity of the rules. Consequently, priority is given to trying alternative choices rather than relaxing extra constraints to solve a conflict or search for alternatives. This conforms with the goal of minimizing the number of constraints to be relaxed. In what follows, c or c^i designate any constraint (disjunctive or not), where i is the current choice. If c^i is a non disjunctive constraint, then i is always 1, since there is only one choice.

Disjunctive rule: $\dfrac{AS \vdash_X \bot \quad \exists c_{\text{disj}} \in AS \quad \exists Reset \subseteq AS}{\Phi \xrightarrow{\text{dj}} \Phi'}$ bellow $=$ eol
   (dj)

$$\text{where} \begin{cases} c_{\text{disj}} & = & c^i_j \\ Reset' & = & \{c^1 \mid c^i \in Reset\} \\ AS' & = & AS \setminus (\{c^i_j\} \cup Reset) \\ RS' & = & RS \\ US' & = & US \cup \{c^{i+1}_j\} \cup Reset' \end{cases}$$

Figure 16.6
New rule to cope with disjunction

A constraint is *exhausted* if there are no more alternative choices to try (a non disjunctive constraints is always exhausted). The disjunctive rule is applied when-ever a conflict is raised and there are some non-exhausted constraints pertinent to the conflict. $c_{\text{disj}} = c^i_j$ is the most recent of such constraints, i.e., the last one intro-duced in the hierarchy. c^i_j is removed and its next choice c^{i+1}_j is inserted instead. The $Reset$ set is composed of active constraints affected by the removal of c^i_j and

that must be reset. Notice however, that constraints to be reset are introduced in
the unexplored store at their first choices (*Reset'* set). This will ensure a correct
tree search, since backtracking to some early node always implies restarting the
search in all subtrees. This is also done in the backward rule with constraints to
be reset and re-activated (*Activate'* set), for the same reason.

The alternative and active removal rules are similarly revised in order to insert
disjunctive constraints in the unexplored store at their first choice. Additionally,
when searching for alternative solutions, the alternative rule is only applicable if all
active constraints are exhausted. Otherwise, the disjunctive rule is applied instead,
with the difference that c_{disj} is simply the most recent of the non-exhausted active
constraints, since there is no conflict to solve.

16.6   Applications

We integrated IHCS with Prolog to create a HCLP($\mathcal{FD}, \mathcal{GPB}$) language, using pre-
processing methods. At present we are employing YAP Prolog running on a NeXT
Station 68040.

In this section we describe the use of our HCLP language in two problems, namely
a set-covering problem and a time-tabling problem, to illustrate the applicability
and declarativity of hierarchical constraints and the efficiency of our incremental
approach to solve them.

In the set-covering problem, the goal is to minimize the number of services required to cover a set of needs (the problem variables designated by $X_1, \ldots, X_m$).
Each variable ranges over the set of services that cover that need. The approach
that we took to solve this problem is depicted in the HCLP program of Figure 16.7.

For m needs, predicate *cover/1* states $m-1$ disjunctive constraints of level 1. This
set of constraints will try to ensure that the service assigned to variable X_i will also
be assigned to at least some X_j, $j > i$. Predicate *labeling/1* simply uses the built-in
predicate *indomain* to generate values for each variables. A best solution (one that
relaxes the minimum number of constraints) will correspond to the minimization
of services. Table 16.1 presents results obtained using several real life instances,
taken from a Portuguese Bus company. The time presented concerns the first (best)
solution found and column *Min* reports the minimum number of services required
to cover the needs.

The time-tabling problem is taken from the experience in the Computer Science
Department of our University, but it is simplified so that no spatial constraints are
considered (it is assumed that there are enough rooms) and each subject is already

$$\text{cover}([X_1, \ldots, X_m]) :-$$
$$X_1 = X_m \bigvee \cdots \bigvee X_1 = X_4 \bigvee X_1 = X_3 \bigvee X_1 = X_2 @ 1,$$
$$X_2 = X_m \bigvee \cdots \bigvee X_2 = X_4 \bigvee X_2 = X_3 @ 1,$$
$$X_3 = X_m \bigvee \cdots \bigvee X_3 = X_4 @ 1,$$
$$\vdots$$
$$X_{m-1} = X_m @ 1,$$
$$\text{labeling}([X_1, \ldots, X_m]).$$

Figure 16.7
Set-covering problem

Table 16.1
Results for the set-covering problem

Needs	Services	Time	Min
13	43	0.33s	6
24	293	3.98s	7
38	67	3.57s	11

assigned to a teacher (c.f. [8] for a full description). For this problem we used a multi-level hierarchy to model preferences of different strength regarding the layout of blocks of subjects in a time-table. There are many preferred constraints that may be added in order to customize a time-table, for example, taking into account teachers priorities. In this example we only use the preferences bellow, regarding the distribution of blocks, since they are sufficiently illustrative of our approach:

level 1 two consecutive blocks of a subject should not take place at consecutive days;

level 2 two consecutive blocks of a subject should not be apart by more then two days;

level 3 no block from a subject with only two blocks per week should take place on mondays;

level 4 blocks of the same subject should take place at the same hour.

Constraints of level 1 try to ensure a uniform distribution of blocks throughout

the week. A three block subject will have to be placed on monday, wednesday and
friday to satisfy these constraints. Level 2 constraints will prevent two blocks of the
same subject from being too far apart. Along with level 1 and 2, level 3 constraints
will help centering two block subjects, which will preferably be placed on Tuesday
and Thursday (or Wednesday and Friday). This hierarchy of preferred constraints,
reflects the priority given to each criterion. For example, in case of conflict it is
preferable to place two blocks at different hours rather than in consecutive days.

Table 16.2 presents results obtained from the generation of time-tables for three
semesters. The first line reports the results obtained by specifying only required
constraints (teachers availability, blocks for the same subject at different days, non
overlapping of classes for the same semester or given by the same teacher). Each
of the other lines shows the effect of adding an extra hierarchical level.

Table 16.2
Results for the time-tabling problem

Max. level	Number of constraints	Time	Relaxed Constraints			
			@1	@2	@3	@4
0	356	1.80s	(16)	(1)	(7)	(15)
1	+21 = 377	1.86s	2	(4)	(7)	(11)
2	+21 = 398	1.98s	2	1	(5)	(10)
3	+11 = 409	1.98s	2	1	1	(10)
4	+21 = 430	2.33s	2	1	1	0

The *Relaxed Constraints* columns report the number of preferred constraints
relaxed in each level (in fact, values inside round brackets do not represent relaxed
constraints, since that level was not being used, but rather the number of those
that are not satisfied by the solution).

The introduction of the preferred constraints of each level, significantly increases
the quality of the solution. The last solution satisfies 95% of the preferences against
only 47% satisfied by the first one with a mere slowdown penalty of 32%.

16.7   Conclusion

This article presents the formalization and implementation of IHCS, and some of
its properties are proven, namely a) soundness (only best solutions with respect
to the criterion are obtained), b) completeness (all such solutions are computed),

and c) non redundancy (no repeated solutions). The experimental results obtained are quite promising with respect to its performance, and the algorithm complexity (both in time and memory requirements) are being currently accessed. Although this paper only considers a Global-Predicate-Better comparator, a more general constraint solver allowing a diversity of comparators to be used and their performances compared in real cases has been developed.

Acknowledgments

This work was started at INRIA/Rocquencourt and at the AI Centre of UNI-NOVA and was funded by Délégation aux Affaires Internationales (DAI) and Junta Nacional de Investigação Científica e Tecnológica (JNICT), as part of a Réseaux-Formation-Recherche Franco-Portugais between the Institute Nationale the Recherche en Informatique et Automatique (INRIA) and the Universidade Nova de Lisboa (UNL). We thank Philippe Codognet for all the helpful suggestions and discussions.

References

[1] A. Borning, M. Maher, A. Martindale, and M. Wilson. Constraints hierarchies and logic programming. In Levi and Martelli, editors, *Logic Programming: Proceedings of the 6th International Conference*, pages 149–164, Lisbon, Portugal, June 1989. The MIT Press.

[2] C. Codognet and P. Codognet. Non-deterministic Stream AND-Parallelism based on Intelligent Backtracking. In *Proceedings of 6th ICLP*, Lisbon, 1989. The MIT press.

[3] C. Codognet, P. Codognet, and G. Filé. Yet Another Intelligent Backtracking Method. In *Proceedings of 5th ICLP/SLP*, Seattle, 1988.

[4] William S. Havens. Intelligent Backtracking in the Echidna Constraint Logic Programming System. Research Report CSS-IS TR 92-12, Simon Fraser University, Canada, 1992.

[5] Vipin Kumar. Algorithms for Constraint-Satisfaction-Problems: A Survey. *AI Magazine*, pages 32–44, Spring 1992.

[6] Alan K. Mackworth. Consistency in Networks of Relations. *Artificial Intelligence*, 8:99–118, 1977.

[7] Alan K. Mackworth and Eugene C. Freuder. The Complexity of Some Plynomial Network Consistency Algorithms for Constraint Satisfaction Problems.

Artificial Intelligence, 25:65–74, 1985.

[8] F. Menezes, P. Barahona, and P. Codognet. An Incremental Hierarchical Constraint Solver Applied to a Time-tabling Problem. In *Proceedings of Avignon 93*, 1993.

[9] Luis Moniz Pereira and M. Bruynooghe. Deduction Revision by Intelligent Backtracking. In *Implementations of Prolog*, pages 194–215. J.A. Campbell, 1984.

[10] P. Van Hentenryck, Y. Deville, and C.-M. Teng. A Generic Arc Consistency Algorithm and its Specializations. Technical Report RR 91-22, K.U. Leuven, F.S.A., December 1991.

[11] M. Wilson and A. Borning. Extending Hierarchical Constraint Logic Programming: Nonmonotonocity and Inter-Hierarchy Comparison. In *Proceedings of the North American Conference 1989*, 1989.

V ARTIFICIAL INTELLIGENCE

17 A Disjunctive Decomposition Control Schema for Constraint Satisfaction

Eugene C. Freuder and Paul D. Hubbe

Abstract

The paper[1] presents a control schema for constraint satisfaction. Several algorithms, old and new, are formulated as instances of this schema by specifying different methods of problem decomposition. This formulation facilitates description and comparison of the algorithms and suggests directions for further research. A new decomposition method is described that is virtually guaranteed to reduce problem size, while always retaining at least one of the solutions to the original problem.

17.1 Introduction

A *solution* to a *constraint satisfaction problem (CSP)* is an assignment of a value to each problem variable that satisfies all the *constraints*, or restrictions, on which combinations of variables are permitted. We will focus here on binary CSPs where the constraints involve two variables. Two values for two variables are *consistent* if they are permitted by the constraint (if any) between the variables. The potential values for a variable constitute its *domain*. We will assume finite domains.

We propose a disjunctive divide and conquer control schema for constraint satisfaction. The schema encompasses a wide variety of specific algorithms. It facilitates description, implementation and comparative analysis of older algorithms and suggests new algorithmic possibilities. In particular, the problem decomposition offers new opportunities for ordered search in a space of alternative problems, and for parallel and distributed processing.

A *possibility* is a choice of one value for each variable, i.e. a candidate for a solution. We present a specific decomposition technique that is virtually guaranteed to reduce the number of possibilities, while always retaining at least one of the actual solutions to the original problem.

Our basic CSP algorithm schema can be stated very simply:

Disjunctive Decomposition Algorithm Schema:
Place the initial problem on the Agenda
Until Agenda empty:

---

[1] This material is based upon work supported by the National Science Foundation under Grant No. IRI-9207633.

Remove a problem P from Agenda
If P has only instantiated variables
      then Exit with their values
        else
                Decompose P into a set of subproblems $\{P_i\}$
                Place each non-empty P_i onto the Agenda
Exit with no solution

Initially all variables are *uninstantiated*; the decomposition methods mark variables as *instantiated*. Intuitively, the instantiated variables are the variables for which values have been chosen. Note that while normally the domains of instantiated variables will be single values, occasionally we will extend the usual connotation of the term "instantiated" to allow an instantiated variable to have several values. Upon exit the Cartesian product of the instantiated variable domains is the set of reported solutions. (This is not necessarily all the solutions, but some of our algorithms will naturally find sets of solutions even while searching for a first solution.)

A *subproblem* P_i of P is formed by reducing some (in the extremes none or all) of the domains of the variables (and simply updating the constraints so that they do not refer to eliminated values). *Problem size* can be measured as the number of possibilities, i.e. the product of the domain sizes for each variable. A problem is *empty* if any of its domains is empty, i.e. it has no possibilities.

A *disjunctive decomposition* produces from a problem P a set of subproblems $\{P_i\}$. We will refer to the set of subproblems as a decomposition. We require that it has the following properties:

1. *Consistency*: Any pair of values from a pair of instantiated variables is consistent.
2. *Simplification*: Each of the $\{P_i\}$ has fewer possibilities or more instantiated variables than P.
3. *Semi-completeness*: If there is a solution to P, then there will be a solution to at least one of the $\{P_i\}$.

PROPOSITION 17.1 A disjunctive decomposition guarantees that the disjunctive decomposition algorithm schema will produce a solution to solvable problems and terminate without a solution when none exists.

The simplification property, together with the finite nature of the variable domains, ensures that eventually all subproblems will either be empty or will have all their variables instantiated. Consider any branch of the "decomposition tree" produced by the schema: the original problem is the root and each decomposition performed by the schema is reflected in the tree by establishing the decomposed problem as the parent of its subproblems. This tree cannot be infinite. No branch can be infinite. Each succeeding subproblem as we move down a branch either has more instantiated variables or fewer possibilities. Eventually we must either reach an empty problem or a fully instantiated one. Obviously the tree cannot have an infinite number of branches either: for any problem, there are only a finite number of distinct possible subproblems. Semi-completeness ensures that, if the original problem has a solution, at least one branch of the decomposition tree will contain a solution in every problem on that branch. Obviously this branch cannot terminate in an empty leaf. Therefore it terminates with all variables instantiated. The consistency property ensures that solutions are returned. □

Disjunctive decompositions break a problem into subproblems such that a solution for any one of them will be a solution to the original problem. *Conjunctive decompositions* break a problem into subproblems such that all the subproblems must be solved, and the solutions must fit together properly, for the original problem to be solved. Of course, disjunctive problem decomposition is a very basic problem solving paradigm; however, it has not received a great deal of attention in the CSP literature. *Domain splitting*, dividing a variable domain into two disjoint sets of values, is a basic disjunctive technique, which, as we emphasize here, is implicit even in the fundamental backtrack search technique. The domain splitting in the NC algorithm [6], discussed further below, best anticipates our approach. We have found that viewing CSP algorithms in terms of subproblem decomposition, as opposed to searching a tree of values, has facilitated our recent work on new CSP algorithms.

There are other optional properties that we might seek in a decomposition, among them:

1. *Completeness*: Any solution to P will be a solution to at least one of the $\{P_i\}$.
2. *Non-redundancy*: Any possibility for P appears in at most one of the $\{P_i\}$.
3. *Reducibility*: The sum of the sizes of the P_i may be less than the size of P, i.e. there are problems P for which at least one possibility does not appear in any of the $\{P_i\}$.

Notice that if we are only looking for one solution, we do *not* need to require that every solution to P will be a solution to some Pi. However, if the decomposition is complete, the schema can easily be modified to find all solutions. Non-redundancy is obviously related to efficiency. This schema immediately suggests two avenues of exploration:

1. How is the decomposition performed?
2. How is the agenda organized?

Different answers to these questions produce a family of divergent algorithms.

Notice that if the agenda is maintained as a stack we have a form of depth-first search, which does not need to present a serious space problem. Stack size requirements are $O(nD)$, for n variables and a maximum of D problems in any decomposition $\{P_i\}$. (In fact if we represent all but the first component as a continuation, generating the individual subproblems as needed, stack size can be reduced to $O(n)$.) On the other hand, if we are more flexible in the agenda ordering, it permits opportunities for heuristic ordering that may save processing time. (If ordering is limited to ordering a set $\{P_i\}$ before placing it on the agenda, stack size requirements can still be $O(nD)$.) All of our examples will assume a stack organization for the agenda. However, that still leaves open questions about which problems to place next on the stack, and in what order. We will discuss five different decompositions that when used with the schema produce versions of the following five algorithms:

1. backtrack [3]
2. forward checking [4]
3. network consistency [6]
4. backtrack with Cartesian product representation [5]
5. inferred disjunctive constraints [1]

The decomposition schema facilitates synthesizing an appropriate algorithm for a given application, by plugging in an appropriate decomposition. It also facilitates utilizing several decompositions alternately as deemed heuristically appropriate, or in response to problem feedback.

We will specify each decomposition abstractly and then illustrate it with a simple example. Each of these decompositions is consistent, simplifying and semi-complete. Most are complete, non-redundant and reducing as well. We will specify which properties the decompositions have, and prove the properties where they are not obvious.

The abstract decomposition descriptions will refer to a *decomposed problem*, P, with n variables. Each of the subproblems in the decomposition will be specified by describing the domains of the variables (domains that remain unchanged from

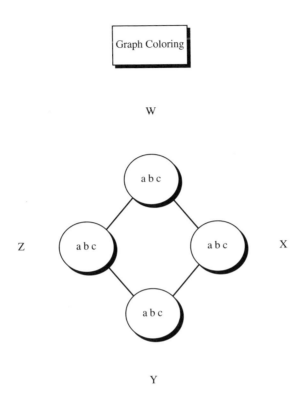

Figure 17.1
Sample Problem.

P will not be listed), and by specifying which variables are marked instantiated. (More procedural descriptions of the decompositions are provided in the references.) The domain of variable V will be indicated by the notation $d(V)$. As an example of the notation we will use,

$$d(U_1) = d(U_1) - \{u_1\}$$

is to be interpreted as: the domain of variable U_1 in the subproblem is the domain of variable U_1 in P with value u_1 removed.

The subproblems are placed on the decomposition schema's stack so that they reside on the stack in the same order as they are specified. (In other words the first subproblem specified will be the first to be removed from the stack.) We will often refer to the "first" uninstantiated variable, U_1, or the "first" value in its domain, u_1, assuming the variables and values are stored in some order. We specify "first" rather than "any" in order to present a more specific algorithm, rather than another schema, parameterized around the method of variable and value choice. However, we could also impose a heuristic variable or value search ordering scheme to choose the variables or values (or provide their initial ordering), and such schemes are of considerable interest. More generally we will use the notation U_i to refer to the ith uninstantiated variable.

We will use as an example a simple graph coloring problem. The variables are vertices, the values are colors, the constraints specify that vertices that share an edge cannot have the same color. We will have four vertices (variables): W, X, Y and Z. Each vertex has three possible colors (values): a(qua), b(lue), and c(oral). The vertices are arranged in a "ring": W and X are joined by an edge, as are X and Y, Y and Z, Z and W (Figure 17.1).

Coloring problems and subproblems will be represented by listing the domains for W, X, Y and Z in order. Thus the original problem can be represented:

a b c

a b c

a b c

a b c

The domains of instantiated variables will be underlined. We will carry out the decomposition depth-first until a solution is found. We will show all the sibling subproblems for each decomposition, even though in practice we need not generate all siblings at once. Empty domains will be represented by the symbol "O".

This example is purposely trivial for pedagogical purposes. It is not intended to illustrate the relative merits of the different algorithms. However, it may provide some insight into their potential, as well as their operation.

17.2   Backtrack (BT)

Decomposition:
P1: if $u1$ is consistent with all the values in the domains of previously instantiated variables, then $d(U_1) = \{u_1\}$, else $d(U_1) = O$
    instantiate U_1
P2: $d(U_1) = d(U_1) - \{u_1\}$

Example:
Figure 17.2. The first two children in the tree represent the decomposition of the original problem. The disjunctive decomposition algorithm schema, using the backtrack decomposition, takes the first child off the stack and uses the backtrack decompositon on it to produce the two subproblems shown at the third level of the

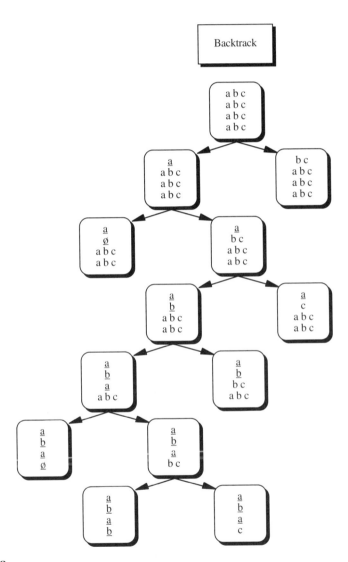

Figure 17.2
Backtrack.

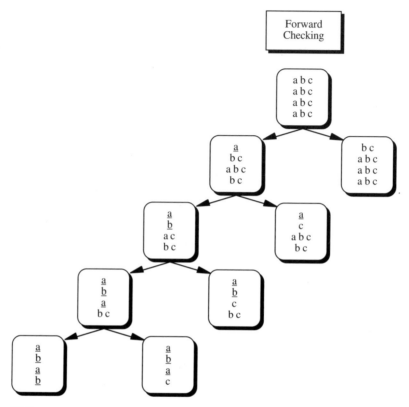

Figure 17.3
Forward checking.

subproblem tree. The leaf node with all variables instantiated represents a solution: aqua for W, blue for X, aqua for Y and blue for Z.

Properties:

consistency: yes; simplification: yes; semi-completeness: yes

completeness: yes; non-redundancy: yes; reducibility: no

Analysis:

We use this basic decomposition to introduce the schema. The properties are all pretty obvious here.

17.3   Forward Checking (FC)

Decomposition:
P1: $d(U_1) = \{u_1\}$
   for all other uninstantiated variables, $U : d(U) = \{u \ \varepsilon \ d(U) \mid u$ is consistent with $u_1\}$
   instantiate U_1
P2: $d(U_1) = d(U_1) - \{u_1\}$

Example: Figure 17.3.
Properties:
consistency: yes; simplification: yes; semi-completeness: yes
completeness: yes; non-redundancy: yes; reducibility: yes
Analysis:
   Again the properties are pretty obvious. Note that when we instantiate a variable it is already known to be consistent with previous instantiations; any inconsistent values were already removed. Thus the consistency property is established. While in theory forward checking can do more work than backtracking, in practice it often proves more efficient.
   The effective minimal domain size variable ordering [4] can be naturally incorporated as a decomposition decision. We can choose as the "first" uninstantiated variable, one with a minimal domain size.

17.4   Network Consistency (NC)

Decomposition:
   Let S_1 and S_2 be a partition of $d(U_1)$ into two disjoint halves. Let $AC(Q)$ be the result of processing a problem Q to make it arc consistent. Q_1 and Q_2 are specified as follows, for $i = 1, 2$:
   $Q_i : d(U_1) = S_i$
   Now the decomposition is specified, for $i = 1, 2$:
   $P_i : AC(Q_i)$
      instantiate each variable that has only one element in its domain
      if all but one variable is instantiated, instantiate that variable also

Example: Figure 17.4.
Properties:
consistency: yes; simplification: yes; semi-completeness: yes

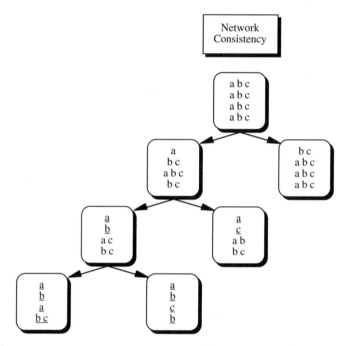

Figure 17.4
Network consistency.

completeness: yes; non-redundancy: yes; reducibility: yes
Analysis:
   The original NC algorithm explicitly operated in a recursive divide and conquer form, alternating local consistency processing with variable domain splitting. The schema formulation helps suggest a variety of NC variations to explore, and clarifies the relationship between NC and FC.

   The divide and conquer approach is clearly non-redundant and simplifying. Enforcing arc consistency cannot remove any solutions, so completeness is maintained; it can remove inconsistent values, making the decomposition reducible. When a non-empty problem, with at most one variable with a domain containing more than one value, is arc consistent, the Cartesian product of the domains represents a set of solutions. Thus the consistency property is guaranteed.

   The decomposition schema encourages us to view forward checking and network consistency as widely separated points in a space of possible algorithms, parameterized by how we partition U_1 and the amount of arc consistency processing we do after the partition. In forward checking we partition into maximally unequal pieces; in network consistency into maximally equal pieces. In forward checking we only seek partial arc consistency, removing values arc inconsistent with u_1 from the uninstantiated variable domains of the first subproblem. In network consistency we make the entire subproblems arc consistent after partitioning U_1. Intermediate degrees of arc consistency processing are possible [4].

Different points along this spectrum might work better for different classes of problems or different computational resources. As an obvious example, partioning into more than two pieces might be desirable in a distributed computing environment.

Note that in employing this decomposition in the disjunctive decomposition schema the arc consistency processing does not actually have to be done until we take the subproblem off the agenda.

17.5   Backtrack With Cartesian Product Representation (BT-CPR)

Decomposition:
Let $\{S_i\}$ be the partition of $d(U_1)$ into disjoint subsets S_i such that two values are in the same subset iff they are consistent with exactly the same values in the domains of each of the instantiated variables. For each S_i there will be a subproblem P_i:

   P_i: for all instantiated variables, V: $d(V) = \{v\ \varepsilon\ d(V) \mid v$ is consistent with the elements of $S_i\}$
      $d(U_1) = S_i$
      instantiate U_1

Example: Figure 17.5.
Properties:
consistency: yes; simplification: yes; semi-completeness: yes
completeness: yes; non-redundancy: yes; reducibility: yes
Analysis:
The schema formulation, similar to that used in the original presentation of the algorithm, facilitates viewing backtracking as a degenerate case of backtracking with CPR. This in turn facilitates the demonstration [5] that adding CPR can not increase the number of *constraint checks* (a standard measure of CSP algorithm performance) when searching for all solutions, or finding that none exist (and may reduce the number of checks significantly). ("Cartesian product" was termed "cross product" in [5].) A similar formulation is possible for forward checking with CPR.

Instantiation is done in a manner to ensure consistency. This is easily seen with a recursive argument. If we assume that the Cartesian product of instantiated domains contains mutually consistent values, when a new instantiated domain is added any values inconsistent with the values in this domain are eliminated, so mutual consistency is maintained. (Consistency obtains trivially when we begin.) Simplification is obvious. Only inconsistencies are removed, ensuring completeness. The partitioning into disjoint sets ensures non-redundancy. Reducibility is obvious.

The Cartesian product of instantiated domains represents a set of tuples each of which satisfies all the constraints on the instantiated variables. This representation can save both space and time. Imagine a problem with 10 values for variable X, each consistent with each of 10 values for variable Y. The Cartesian product of the two sets of 10 values represents 100 pairs of mutually consistent values. If X and Y are the first two variables instantiated, these 100 pairs can be represented in a single subproblem using the Cartesian product decomposition, while they would be distributed among 100 different subproblems in the basic backtracking decomposition schema (or among 100 branches in the standard backtrack search tree). When testing a value, v, for the next variable against these 100 possibilities, the most we need to do is check the consistency of v against each of the 20 values once. When testing v against these 100 possibilities with the basic backtracking algorithm, we might need to check the consistency of v against each of these 20 values 10 times.

17.6   Inferred Disjunctive Constraint (IDC)

Decomposition:
$P_1 : d(U_1) = \{u_1\}$
    for all other uninstantiated variables, U: $d(U) = \{u \; \varepsilon \; d(U) \mid u \text{ is consistent with } u_1\}$
        instantiate U_1
        if there is only one uninstantiated variable remaining, instantiate it

$P_j, j = 2...m$, where m is the number of uninstantiated variables:
    $d(U_1) = d(U_1) - \{u_1\}$
    $1 < i < j : d(U_i) = \{u \; \varepsilon \; d(U_i) \mid u \text{ is consistent with } u_1\}$
    $i = j : d(U_i) = \{u \; \varepsilon \; d(U_i) \mid u \text{ is inconsistent with } u_1\}$

Example: Figure 17.6.
Properties:
consistency: yes; simplification: yes; semi-completeness: yes

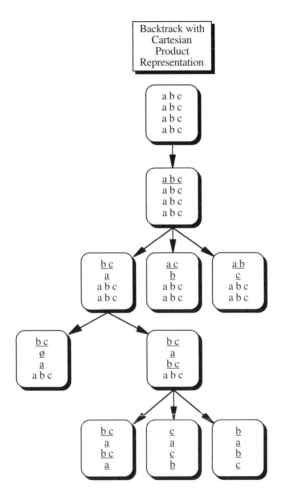

Figure 17.5
Backtrack with Cartesian product representation.

completeness: no; non-redundancy: yes; reducibility: yes

Analysis:

The intuition behind the IDC decomposition is that given a value v, there are two cases:

1) there is a solution involving v, in which case the other values in the solution are obviously consistent with v

2) there is no solution involving v, in which case any solution must involve some value inconsistent with v (otherwise we could substitute v and still have a solution).

In the IDC decomposition the first subproblem accounts for the first case, the remaining subproblems account for the second case. Note any uninstantiated variable, U_k, for which there is no constraint between U_k and U_1, will automatically lead to an empty subproblem, P_k. In P_k, $d(U_k)$ will be empty, since nothing will be inconsistent with u_1. Thus the number of subproblems is equal to one more than the number of variables, V, for which there is a constraint between V and U_1.

IDC is the first of our decompositions to take advantage of semi-consistency. It takes advantage of the fact that some solutions may be thrown away in the search for a single solution. IDC is not complete; it can throw away solutions. This can be seen in our example. However, it will not throw away all solutions. We will prove semi-completeness.

First we establish the following proposition:

PROPOSITION 17.2 The possibilities in P that are left out of the IDC decomposition are the possibilities discarded by the pruning of inconsistent values in the first subproblem, plus the possibilities in the subproblem:

$C : d(U_1) = U_1 - \{u_1\}$

for all other uninstantiated variables, $U : d(U) = \{u \ \varepsilon \ d(U) \mid u$ is consistent with $u_1\}$

We will refer to C as the *consistent subproblem* discarded by the decomposition, and to the possibilities left out of the first subproblem as the precluded possibilities.

First we establish that if a possibility p, is in one of the subproblems in the decomposition, then p is not in C and not a precluded possibility. If p is in P_1, then it contains u_1 and so it is not in C. If p is in one of the other P_j, then the value for U_j is inconsistent with u_1 , and thus p cannot be in C. Obviously if p is in P_1 it is not a precluded possibility. If p is in any other subproblem it does not contain u_1 and so is not a precluded possibility.

Next we establish that if p is not in C and not a precluded possibility, then it is in one of the subproblems in the decomposition. If p contains u_1, then it must be in P_1, since it is not a precluded poccibility. If p does not contain u_1, it must contain one or more values inconsistent with u_1. Let U_k be the first uninstantiated variable for which p has one of these inconsistent values. P_k will contain p. □

PROPOSITION 17.3 The IDC decomposition is semi-complete.

The possibilities discarded by removing inconsistent values in the first subproblem of a decomposition are not solutions. The only other possibilities discarded by a decomposition are those in the consistent subproblem. Suppose there is a solution, s, in the consistent subproblem. Substitute u_1 for the U_1 value in s. The result will be another solution. It will be a solution because the other values of s are all consistent with u_1. It is not a possibility in the consistent subproblem or one discarded from the first subproblem so it will be in the IDC decomposition. □

PROPOSITION 17.4 The IDC decomposition is non-redundant.

We will show that for each subproblem none of its possibilities are in any of the succeeding subproblems. For P_1 this is obvious as all the possibilities in P_1 contain u_1 and none of the succeeding subproblems contains u_1. For $Pi, i > 1$, all the possibilities contain a value for U_i inconsistent with u_1, while each succeeding subproblem only has possibilities with values for U_i consistent with u_1. □

The IDC decomposition subsumes the forward checking decomposition in a sense. The first subproblem of each decomposition is the same as that produced by forward checking. (Except for a refinement, which could be added also to forward checking, that observes that the last remaining uninstantiated variable can be immediately instantiated.) Thus an IDC decomposition does the pruning that an FC decomposition does, plus often additional pruning. The pruning in FC and the additional pruning in IDC complement one another so that in IDC some possibilities will almost always be removed. If there are lots of values inconsistent with u_1, they will be removed by the FC pruning; if there are lots of values consistent with u_1, they will be removed by the IDC pruning. Only in the degenerate case where there are no inconsistent values and u_1 is the only value in U_1 will there be no pruning. Thus the IDC decomposition virtually always reduces problem size, i.e. the sum of the sizes of the subproblems will virtually always be less than the size of the decomposed problem.

The additional possibilities removed by IDC beyond FC alone can be precisely measured, as the size of the consistent subproblem. This facilitates comparison of

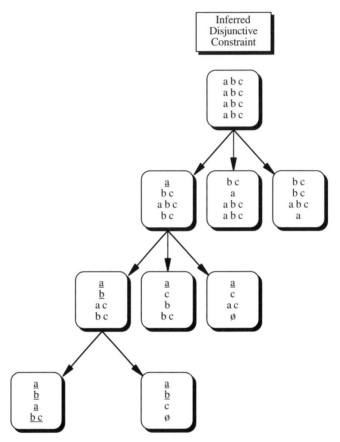

Figure 17.6
Inferred disjunctive constraint

the two decompositions. In particular, the IDC algorithm implemented in [1] uses this information to choose between IDC and FC decomposition dynamically during search. (The additional pruning in IDC is not guaranteed to be cost effective; in particular, IDC could conceivably prune a solution that would be found quickly by FC.) This algorithm was explicitly developed as a disjunctive decomposition algorithm. Consistency holds for the same reason that it holds for the forward checking decomposition. (When there is only one variable remaining, all its values will already be consistent with all previous chouces.) Simplification is obvious. Reducibility is obvious, and the size of the consistent subproblem tells us exactly how many possibilities are pruned.

17.7 Conclusion

Decomposition can provide a tool for algorithm analysis and synthesis. Viewing CSP algorithms as instances of the decomposition schema helps us to compare them, and suggests new variations and combinations. Ordering heuristics for subproblem consideration provide a new avenue to explore. We can view ourselves as searching in a metalevel "subproblem space". This subproblem space obviously lends itself to distributed and parallel processing, especially given the disjunctive nature of our decompositions. Sophisticated algorithm synthesizers may someday mix and match decomposition techniques as most appropriate for the problem at hand.

Most intriguing of all is the possibility that useful new forms of decomposition are waiting to be discovered. Indeed we have already made some progress in that direction by defining a disjunctive decomposition schema that generalizes the sub-problem extraction demonstrated by IDC, and applying it to an algorithm FOF (Factor Out Failure) that dynamically extracts previously failed subproblems during search [2].

References

[1] E. Freuder and P. Hubbe. Using inferred disjunctive constraints to decompose constraint satisfaction problems. *Proceedings of the Thirteenth IJCAI.* 254-260.

[2] E. Freuder and P. Hubbe. Extracting constraint satisfaction subproblems. University of New Hampshire TR 94-1.

[3] S. Golumb and L. Baumert. Backtrack programming. *JACM 12.* 516-524.

[4] R. Haralick and G. Elliott. Increasing tree search efficiency for constraint satisfaction problems. *Artificial Intelligence 14.* 263-313.

[5] P. Hubbe and E. Freuder. An efficient cross product representation of the constraint satisfaction problem search space. *Proceedings of the Tenth National Conference on Artificial Intelligence 421-427.*

[6] A. Mackworth. On reading sketch maps. *Proceedings of the Fifth IJCAI.* 598-606.

18 Local Consistency in Parallel Constraint-Satisfaction Networks

Simon Kasif and Arthur L. Delcher[1]

Abstract

In this paper we present several basic techniques for achieving parallel execution of constraint networks. The major result supported by our investigations is that the parallel complexity of constraint networks is critically dependent on subtle properties of the network that do not influence its sequential complexity.

18.1 Introduction

One of the key problems facing Artificial Intelligence (AI) is performing efficient inferences over large knowledge bases. Viewed in the context of parallel computation this problem brings forth fundamental research issues such as knowledge representation in parallel environments, problem-decomposition methods, parallelization of classes of AI problems, the role of incremental methods, parallel matching, and parallel search strategies that eliminate redundancy.

Our research is aimed at deriving a precise characterization of the utility of parallelism in constraint networks. In this paper, we relate parallel constraint networks to standard models of computation (Parallel Random Access Machines or PRAM's). We present several basic techniques for achieving parallel execution of constraint networks. We are interested primarily in developing a classification of constraint networks according to whether they admit massively parallel execution. We analyze parallel execution for dense constraint networks, chain networks, tree networks, two-label networks, directed-support networks and path consistency in general networks. For example, we show that contrary to common intuition, chain networks do admit parallel solutions (as in fact do all acyclic graphs). While the obvious parallel algorithm for local consistency in constraint networks should work well in practice, we would like to obtain lower and upper bounds on the complexity of the problem on ideal parallel machines (such as the PRAM).

This study may have significant practical implications since it should indicate which parallel primitives are fundamental in the solutions of large constraint systems. Once such primitives are implemented in hardware, they execute in essentially constant time for all practical purposes, e.g., parallel prefix on the Connection Machine. The original design of the Connection Machine was motivated by these

---

[1]Originally published in *Artificial Intelligence* **69**:307–327, 1994.

considerations. The ultimate goal of our research is to produce a set of primitives that are critical to the solution of constraint problems. In a view of parallelism advocated by many AI researchers, we associate a small simple processor with each data element (thus loading data does not require time). In this perspective logarithmic-time parallel algorithms have important implications since they show how to represent the data and perform parallel search in almost constant time for any reasonable size network.

It is generally believed that humans perform many tasks efficiently (*i.e.*, in almost constant time) by exploiting the massive parallelism in the brain (*e.g.*, Feldman's 100-instruction-step metaphor). One of the main underlying assumptions of the Connectionist school of thought is that their approach is naturally amenable to a parallel (distributed) implementation. Moreover, the claim is often made that the symbolic approach does not have this advantage. Our analysis suggests that parallel implementations are possible for symbolic constraint systems. In fact, we conjecture that both connectionist and symbolic constraint systems share the same limitations which are caused by the structure of the particular problem or algorithm. The major result supported by our investigations reported in this paper is that the parallel complexity of constraint networks is critically dependent on subtle properties of the network that do not influence its sequential complexity.

18.2   Constraint Satisfaction, Local Consistency and Discrete Relaxation

Constraint satisfaction networks are used extensively in many AI applications such as planning, scheduling, natural language analysis, truth-maintenance systems, and logic programming [3, 10, 18, 23, 29, 26]. These networks use the principle of local constraint propagation to achieve global consistency (*e.g.*, consistent labelling in vision).

A constraint satisfaction network can be defined as follows. Let $V = \{X_1, \ldots, X_n\}$ be a set of variables. With each variable X_i we associate a set of labels L_i. Now let $\{R_{ij}\}$ be a set of binary predicates that define the compatibility of assigning labels to pairs of variables. Specifically, $R_{ij}(a, b) = 1$ iff the assignment of label a to X_i is compatible with the assignment of label b to X_j.

The Constraint Satisfaction Problem (CSP) is defined as the problem of finding an assignment of labels to the variables that does not violate the constraints given by $\{R_{ij}\}$. More formally, a solution to CSP is a vector $(a_1, \ldots, a_n)$ such that a_i is in L_i and for each i and j, $R_{ij}(a_i, a_j) = 1$.

A standard approach to model CSP problems is by means of a constraint graph, (e.g., v. [18, 22]). The nodes of the constraint graph correspond to variables of the constraint network, and the edges correspond to the binary constraints. In this context, each edge in the constraint graph is labelled with a matrix that shows which assignments of labels to the objects connected by that edge are permitted. In this interpretation CSP can be viewed as generalized graph coloring.

In this paper we also will use an *explicit* constraint graph representation, which expresses constraint information in a more detailed fashion. Specifically, for any constraint network $G = (V, E)$, we define its explicit representation $G_{\text{expl}} = (V', E')$ to be the graph in which $V' = \cup_{i=1}^n L_i$ and $E' = \{(a_{ij}, b_{k\ell}) \mid a_{ij} \in L_j, \; b_{k\ell} \in L_\ell$ and $R_{j\ell}(a_{ij}, b_{k\ell}) = 1\}$.

We illustrate this construction by an example. Assume the set of labels is $\{0, 1\}$ for each variable. For each variable X we create 2 nodes $\langle X, 0 \rangle$ and $\langle X, 1 \rangle$. For each edge connecting variables X and Y we connect $\langle X, a \rangle$ with an arc to $\langle Y, b \rangle$ iff assigning a to X is consistent with assigning b to Y. An example is shown below for the relation R_{XY}.

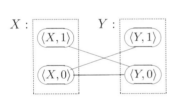

X	Y	R_{XY}
$\langle X, 0 \rangle$	$\langle Y, 0 \rangle$	1
$\langle X, 0 \rangle$	$\langle Y, 1 \rangle$	1
$\langle X, 1 \rangle$	$\langle Y, 0 \rangle$	1
$\langle X, 1 \rangle$	$\langle Y, 1 \rangle$	0

Since CSP is known to be $\mathcal{NP}$-complete, several local-consistency algorithms have been used extensively to filter out impossible assignments.

Arc consistency allows an assignment of a label a to an object X iff for every other object X' in the domain there exists a valid assignment of a label a' which does not violate the constraints [18, 22]. More formally, we define arc consistency as follows.

Given a constraint network, a solution to the *local version of CSP* or *arc consistency* (AC) is a vector of sets $(M_1, \ldots, M_n)$ such that M_i is a subset of L_i and label a is in M_i iff for every M_j, $i \neq j$ there is a label b in M_j, such that $R_{ij}(a, b) = 1$. Intuitively, a label a is assigned to a variable iff for every other variable there is at least one valid assignment of a label to that other variable that supports the assignment of label a to the first variable.

We call a solution $(M_1, \ldots, M_n)$ a *maximal* solution for AC iff there does not exist any other solution $(S_1, \ldots, S_n)$ such that $M_i \subseteq S_i$ for all $1 \leq i \leq n$. We are

interested only in maximal solutions for an AC problem. By insisting on maximality
we guarantee that we are not losing any possible solutions for the original CSP.
Therefore, in the remainder of this paper a solution for an AC problem is identified
with a maximal solution. The sequential time complexity of AC is discussed in
[19, 21, 14]. Discrete relaxation is the most commonly used method to achieve
local consistency. Starting with all possible label assignments for each variable,
discrete relaxation repeatedly discards labels from variables if the AC condition
specified above does not hold.

18.3   Parallel Processing of Constraint Networks

The standard approach for achieving arc consistency is the following discrete-
relaxation procedure:

Procedure Parallel-AC

Step 1 Start by setting $M_i = L_i$, for $1 \leq i \leq n$.

Step 2 Repeat the following:

> For each constraint between X_i and X_j test whether for
> each label $a \in M_i$ there exists a label $b \in M_j$ that permits
> it. If there is no such b then remove a from M_i.

until no label is removed from any M_i.

It is easy to see that this algorithm will terminate in $O(EK^2nK)$ time, where
E is the number of edges in the constraint-network graph and K is the number of
labels for each variable, (recall that EK^2 is the size of the input). In fact, much
better sequential algorithms for the problem are discussed in [19, 21, 13, 14].

Clearly, procedure Parallel-AC can be parallelized in a straightforward way. If
we assume a CRCW PRAM as our model of parallel computation,[2] we have the
following simple result:

PROPOSITION 18.1 The parallel complexity of procedure Parallel-AC is $O(nK)$ on
a CRCW PRAM with EK^2 processors.

PROOF: Simply assign K processors to each arc and label, and perform the test
for arc consistency in Step 2 in parallel. Arc consistency is essentially a logical OR

---

[2]CRCW PRAM is a standard shared-memory parallel computation model that permits concurrent reads and writes into the same location. Concurrent writes are permitted if they agree on
the data being written.

Figure 18.1
A Chain Symmetric-Constraint Graph

on set membership of a set of labels, and can be performed in constant time on a CRCW PRAM. At each parallel step, if the algorithm does not halt, then at least one label must be dropped and there are a total of nK labels. □

On a more realistic model of computation, such as an EREW PRAM (exclusive read/exclusive write), we can perform the above procedure in $O(nK \log K)$ parallel time, the extra $\log K$ factor being required to compute the logical OR.

The usual way to see parallel computation of constraint networks in the AI community is not via shared-memory models such as the CRCW PRAM. We usually assume that we have processors associated with nodes/arcs of the network. The processors communicate to their neighbors. This perspective requires the full power of a CRCW PRAM model for the following reasons:

1. We assume constant overhead for communication between processors, which in the worst case implies complete graph connectivity.

2. We assume that in constant time all the neighbors of a node can communicate with the node (*i.e.*, propagate constraints, remove labels, etc.), which is equivalent to concurrent read/write capabilities.

It is easy to see that the procedure above has a lower bound of nK steps, *i.e.*, in the worst case it does not fully parallelize in the sense of achieving polylogarithmic parallel time (this a well known observation). As a simple example, consider a chain constraint graph as shown in Figure 18.1 with label sets $L_i = \{0, 1\}$, $2 \leq i \leq n$ and $L_1 = \{1\}$, and assume the only supporting assignment for label 0 is 0. Then procedure Parallel-AC will drop only one 0-label in each parallel iteration of Step 2. In Section 18.6 we show that, in fact, it is possible to achieve full parallelization of chain networks using a different technique.

In [14] we proved the following much stronger result, namely, that AC is inherently sequential in the worst case for general constraint networks.

THEOREM 18.1 (Kasif 90) The propositional Horn clause satisfiability problem is log-space reducible to the AC problem. That is, AC is $\mathcal{P}$-complete.

Local consistency belongs to the class of inherently sequential problems called log-space complete for $\mathcal{P}$ (or $\mathcal{P}$-complete). Intuitively, a problem is $\mathcal{P}$-complete iff a polylogarithmic-time parallel solution (with a polynomial number of processors) for the problem will produce a polylogarithmic-time parallel solution for every deterministic polynomial-time sequential algorithm. This implies that unless $\mathcal{P} = \mathcal{NC}$ ($\mathcal{NC}$ is the class of problems solvable in polylogarithmic parallel time with polynomially many processors) we cannot solve the problem in polylogarithmic time using a polynomial number of processors. The above theorem implies that to achieve polylogarithmic parallel time one (probably) would need a superpolynomial number of processors. We emphasize that this is a worst-case result and indeed several groups have reported successful experiments with massively parallel constraint processing [7, 24, 27, 9, 2, 30].

One common but incorrect interpretation of Theorem 18.1 is that inherent sequentiality is caused by long constraint chains such as the one in Figure 18.1. In Section 18.6 we give a simple technique for parallel processing of constraint chains, and in Section 18.7 we extend these results to trees. Most importantly we show that while the degree of parallelism is dependent on the diameter of the constraint graph, a high diameter is not a sufficient condition for inherent sequentiality of constraint networks.

We first make an observation which is critical to the understanding of the procedural semantics, and consequently the complexity, of achieving arc consistency. In [12, 13, 14] we provided a two-way reduction between arc consistency and Propositional Horn Satisfiability (PHS). Specifically, given a constraint satisfaction problem S one can construct a propositional Horn formula (AND/OR graph) G such that arc consistency of S can be achieved by (essentially) running a satisfiability algorithm for G. For a formal construction see [14]. We sketch the intuition here. For each label a and a variable X we construct a propositional atom $P_{X,a}$ which means a drops from X. We also use a propositional atom $Q_{X,a,Y}$ to mean that variable Y has no label that supports label a in X. Consider, for example, a variable X connected in the constraint graph to variables Y and Z. Assume that Y has labels a_1, a_2 and Z has labels a_3, a_4 that support a at X. Thus, we construct the formulae:

$$
\begin{aligned}
P_{X,a} &\leftarrow Q_{X,a,Y} \\
P_{X,a} &\leftarrow Q_{X,a,Z} \\
Q_{X,a,Y} &\leftarrow P_{Y,a_1} \wedge P_{Y,a_2} \\
Q_{X,a,Z} &\leftarrow P_{Z,a_3} \wedge P_{Z,a_4}
\end{aligned}
$$

We can apply one iteration of procedure Parallel-AC to determine which labels will be dropped initially and add the corresponding assertions.

Note that if the constraint graph has E edges and K labels per variable, the size of the formulae is potentially EK^2. More importantly, the sequential complexity of solving satisfiability of this graph is $O(EK^2)$ (see [14] for details). This is a slight improvement over the result in [19] and it matches the algorithm in [21]. The advantage is that we can use this reduction to derive optimal algorithms for AC when the resulting Horn-clause formula is of small size. Thus, for example, when the size of the formula is $O(EK)$ we get an $O(EK)$ algorithm. We also can devise efficient parallel algorithms when the resulting Horn-clause formula has some special graph structure. Note that this reduction is from AC to PHS, as opposed to the reduction from PHS to AC used to prove Theorem 18.1.

18.4   AC in Dense Graphs

It has been noted by several researchers that for many P-complete problems such as depth-first search, circuit evaluation and unification, optimal speed-up is possible if the underlying graph is very dense, *i.e.*, the number of edges in the graph is quadratic [28]. We illustrate this simple principle with an example. Assume we are given a boolean circuit that consists of NAND gates only. The circuit contains N gates and E edges. We also are given an input to the circuit. Clearly, any sequential algorithm must take $O(E)$ time to evaluate the output of this circuit. The standard technique for evaluating circuits uses a counter for each gate. The initial value of the counter is set to the number of inputs the gate has. We maintain a queue of gates whose value has been computed (initially, just the input gates). We pick any gate on the queue and traverse all its outgoing edges. For each such edge we decrement the counter associated with the gate incident to the edge and drop the edge. If the counter becomes zero we simply add the gate to the queue. For the special case of NAND gates one can obviously reset the counter of a gate to zero when one of the inputs is zero. Note that this simple algorithm is in fact the same algorithm that yields optimal sequential time for both PHS (propositional Horn satisfiability) and AC [21, 14]. PHS and AC problems may generate circuits with cycles but this does not fundamentally change the algorithm, as was pointed out in [14].

But now consider a brute-force parallel algorithm, where we essentially perform the sequential algorithm above, with one exception. When we choose a gate g from the queue we use N processors to update the counters of all the gates that are connected to g. This can be done trivially in constant time on a PRAM (parallel shared-memory machine). When any counter becomes zero, we add the gate to the queue as in the sequential version (on some models of parallel computation the above two steps may take logarithmic time). Since we are visiting at most N nodes the procedure terminates in $O(N)$ steps using N processors. Thus we achieve linear speed-up when the number of edges in the circuit is $O(N^2)$. This observation holds for Propositional Horn Satisfiability. It also holds for Arc Consistency and Path Consistency by using the reduction to Propositional Horn Satisfiability (or circuit evaluation). For AC, this observation yields $O(nK)$ performance with nK processors (details are left as an exercise to the reader).

THEOREM 18.2 AC can be solved in $O(nK)$ time with nK processors.

The algorithm above will work well on any machine that can support broadcasts (to implement traversing edges) and some kind of fast selection operation (to pick the next node from the queue). Parallel prefix on the connection machine can support both primitives efficiently in logarithmic time. Note, that the parallel algorithm described above can be improved in practice by retrieving (in parallel) all nodes (gates) from the queue. Thus, for a tree-structured graph we obviously will achieve performance proportional to the depth rather than the size of the tree. Since in this paper we are primarily concerned with asymptotic performance, we do not discuss obvious improvements that may work in specific problem instances.

18.5   Path Consistency

While arc consistency is useful in many applications, it does not always succeed in pruning the search space. Therefore, arc consistency has been generalized to i-consistency as follows [8]. A network of constraints is said to be i-consistent (or path consistent) iff for every consistent assignment of labels to a subnetwork of $i-1$ variables, there is a label consistent with the subnetwork for any choice of an ith variable. Several i-consistency-enforcing algorithms have been proposed [8, 21]. In this section we extend the simple observation from the previous section and derive optimal i-consistency algorithms. We believe that the methodology we use here is important since several published path consistency algorithm had errors and our derivation is very simple and easy to prove correct.

Earlier we mentioned the two-way reduction between AC and PHS. Here, we observe that a similar two-way reduction can be provided between path consistency and PHS. We illustrate the reduction from 3-consistency to PHS. The key to solving 3-consistency is deriving all assignments of pairs of labels to two variables that violate the 3-consistency condition. Without loss of generality, assume all labels are unique (otherwise, we can rename the labels). For each pair of labels a and b

we create a proposition $P_{a,b}$ that is true iff the pair $\langle a, b \rangle$ violates the 3-consistency condition, and therefore is dropped from consideration. However, $P_{a,b}$ is true iff there is at least one other variable to which it cannot be extended. We denote this condition by a predicate $Q_{a,b,i}$ which is true iff this assignment cannot be extended to variable X_i. Thus,

$$
\begin{aligned}
P_{a,b} &\leftarrow Q_{a,b,1} \\
P_{a,b} &\leftarrow Q_{a,b,2} \\
P_{a,b} &\leftarrow Q_{a,b,3} \\
&\vdots
\end{aligned}
$$

Now, $Q_{a,b,i}$ is true iff $P_{b,c}$ or $P_{a,c}$ is true for all labels c that potentially support the assignment $\langle a, b \rangle$ at variable X_i. Thus,

$$
\begin{aligned}
Q_{a,b,1} &\leftarrow Q'_{a,b,c_1} \wedge Q'_{a,b,c_2} \wedge \cdots \\
Q'_{a,b,c_1} &\leftarrow P_{a,c_1} \\
Q'_{a,b,c_1} &\leftarrow P_{b,c_1} \\
&\vdots
\end{aligned}
$$

We have $O(EK^2)$ predicates of the form $P_{a,b}$. Therefore, the size of the PHS formula is dominated by the clauses of the form

$$
Q_{a,b,1} \leftarrow Q'_{a,b,c_1} \wedge Q'_{a,b,c_2} \wedge \cdots .
$$

The total size is therefore $O(EK^2nK) = O(nEK^3)$, or alternatively $O(n^3K^3)$. The assertions of the program are obtained by applying a 3-consistency check once, and asserting all the dropped pairs $\langle a, b \rangle$ as facts $P_{a,b}$.

The important corollary of this construction is that now we can utilize the standard linear time PHS algorithm for local consistency. This immediately yields an algorithm that matches (in asymptotic complexity) the best known algorithm for path consistency. This algorithm is optimal if the number of labels is assumed constant. The same algorithm also would work for k-consistency with similar optimal performance. The bottom-up PHS algorithm has very good performance in practice. The conversion to PHS also can be done efficiently in parallel.

Similar observations were made independently by McAllester, Bibel, Mackworth and Saraswat. Here we have presented a careful analysis of the transformation that leads to optimal complexity results as stated above. The reduction illustrated in this section can be combined with the observation in the previous section to yield an

efficient parallel algorithm for path consistency in dense constraint graphs. Parallel
path consistency is also studied in [21, 17].

18.6   AC in Chains

It is easy to see that a simple separator-based technique can be used to solve constraint satisfaction problems in chain graphs. The technique is based on removing
a variable that separates a constraint chain with n variables into two chains with
$n/2$ variables. Then we create $2K$ recursive subproblems, where K is the number
of labels in each variable. We repeat the process $\log n$ times, so that the complexity
is $O((2K)^{\log n}) = O(n^{\log 2K})$. For details see [13]. Thus, when the number of labels
is large (*i.e.*, is a function of the number of variables n), the complexity is no longer
polynomial.

Here we propose a simple procedure to achieve AC in a constraint chain. We first
construct an explicit constraint graph G_{expl}. The number of nodes in this graph is
nK, one node for each label in each variable. Recall that in G_{expl} two nodes $\langle X, a \rangle$
and $\langle Y, b \rangle$ are connected iff the assignment of a to X is compatible with assigning
b to Y. Without loss of generality, assume the variables are numbered X_1 to X_n
in order on the chain. We now orient all the edges in G_{expl} in the direction from
X_i to X_{i+1}. We mark all nodes reachable from the source nodes contained in X_1,
and discard all other nodes. Next, we reverse the orientation of edges to point from
X_{i+1} to X_i. We then mark all nodes reachable from the remaining nodes in X_n,
and discard the rest. An easy induction argument shows that the nodes that remain
after this last step correspond to the labels in the solution to the AC problem.

THEOREM 18.3 AC in a chain constraint network can be solved either with
$nK^3/\log n$ processors in $O(\log n)$ time, or with $nM(K)/\log n$ processors in
$O(\log K \log n)$ time, on a CRCW PRAM, where $M(K)$ is the number of processors
need to multiply two $K \times K$ boolean matrices in $O(\log K)$ time.

PROOF: By the argument of the preceding paragraph the AC problem is reducible
to reachability in an n-level directed acyclic graph. Let $Reach_{i,j}$ denote the predicate on $L_i \times L_j$ that indicates for each $a \in L_i$ and $b \in L_j$ whether there is a path
from a to b in the directed version of G_{expl}. $Reach_{i,i+1}$ is the constraint relation
given initially, and we must compute $Reach_{1,n}$.

We can successively compute $Reach_{i,i+2^s}$, in parallel for $1 \le i \le n$, in stages
$s = 1, \ldots, \log n$. At stage $s = 1$ we compute $Reach_{i,i+2}$ for $i \equiv 1 \pmod 2$ by
composing the predicates $Reach_{i,i+1}$ and $Reach_{i+1,i+2}$. Then at stage $s = 2$ we

compute $Reach_{i,i+2^2}$ for $i \equiv 1 \pmod{2^2}$ by composing the predicates $Reach_{i,i+2}$ and $Reach_{i+2,i+2^2}$. In general, at stage s we compute $Reach_{i,i+2^s}$ for $i \equiv 1 \pmod{2^s}$ by composing the predicates $Reach_{i,i+2^{s-1}}$ and $Reach_{i+2^{s-1},i+2^s}$. Note that the number of compositions at stage s is $n/2^s$ so that the total number of compositions is n. By performing $n/\log n$ compositions in parallel, we can finish all n compositions in $O(\log n)$ steps.

Each of the $Reach_{i,j}$ predicates is a $K \times K$ boolean matrix and the composition can be performed by matrix multiplication. Specifically, when we compose $Reach_{i,j}$ with $Reach_{j,k}$ to get $Reach_{i,k}$, we have

$$Reach_{i,k}(a, c) = \bigvee_{b \in L_j} Reach_{i,j}(a, b) \wedge Reach_{j,k}(b, c)$$

In the CRCW model, with K^3 processors we can accomplish this composition in $O(1)$ time, or alternatively in $O(\log K)$ time with $M(K)$ processors [11]. □

Note that Dechter and Pearl used a similar technique, *i.e.*, orienting the constraint edges in one direction and then in the opposite direction. They coined the term directed arc-consistency for this approach. However, since they were not studying the parallel complexity of chain networks, they did not note that this approach reduces the problem in chains to two computations of directed components in a graph.

18.7   Trees

In this section we consider the special case of CSP in which the constraint graph contains no cycles, *i.e.*, it is a forest. Since it clearly suffices to consider each connected component of the graph separately, in the remainder of this section we restrict our attention to trees.

18.7.1   Separator-Based Methods

We first show how we can take advantage of the separability properties of the constraint graph in order to achieve a recursive parallel decomposition of the problem. A more powerful (but higher overhead) method was presented for planar constraint networks in [15] (see also [25, 4]).

LEMMA 18.1 Given any constraint tree T, with $|T| = N$, we can construct a corresponding binary constraint tree T', with $|T'| < 2N$, such that T and T' have the same solutions.

Non-Binary Node   Binary Equivalent

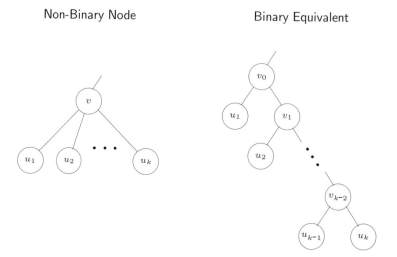

Figure 18.2
Converting a Non-Binary Tree to a Binary Equivalent

PROOF:

Let v be a node in T with k children, $u_1, \ldots, u_k$; let $L_v, L_{u_1}, \ldots, L_{u_k}$ be their respective label sets; and let $R_{u_i,v}$ be the constraint relation between L_{u_i} and L_v. If $k \leq 2$, we make v and its child edges the same in T' as in T. If $k > 2$, then we create a chain of nodes $v_0, \ldots, v_{k-2}$ as shown in Figure 18.2.

To each v_j we assign the same label set L_v, and the constraint relation between u_i and its parent v_j is just $R_{u_i,v}$. Between v_j and v_{j-1}, $1 \leq j \leq k-2$, we assign the identity constraint. It is now an easy exercise to verify that the solutions to T and T' are identical. Since we create at most one new node v_j for each child node u_i, it follows that $|T'| < 2|T|$. $\square$

Notice we are not transforming n-ary constraint networks into binary constraint networks; we are merely modifying the topology of the original constraint tree with a constant increase in size. Thus, without loss of generality we need consider only binary trees.

LEMMA 18.2 Let T be a binary tree, with $|T| = N$. There is a node v in T such that if T_v denotes the subtree of T rooted at v, then $N/3 \leq |T_v| \leq 2N/3$.

PROOF: Starting from the root of T, traverse a path P toward the leaves always moving to the child which roots the larger subtree. Then choose v to be the first node on P with $N/3 \leq |T_v| \leq 2N/3$. Clearly such a node exists, since if u_1 and u_2

are successive nodes on P, $|T_{u_2}| \geq (|T_{u_1}| - 1)/2$. $\square$

PROPOSITION 18.2 If constraint graph G is a tree, with K labels per node, we can solve CSP for G in $O(\log N)$ time with $O(N^{\log_{1.5} K})$ processors.

PROOF: As in Lemma 18.2, let v be a node in G such that $N/3 \leq |T_v| \leq 2N/3$. Disconnect T at v to create two trees, each of size less than $2N/3$. Then in parallel for each possible label of v, recursively solve CSP for these two trees. Finally determine whether there is a solution for each tree with the same label for v. The recurrences for time and processors are, respectively:

$$
\begin{aligned}
T(N) &\leq T(2N/3) + c \quad\quad c \text{ a constant} \\
&= O(\log N)
\end{aligned}
$$

$$
\begin{aligned}
P(N) &\leq K \cdot P(2N/3) \\
&= O(N^{\log_{1.5} K})
\end{aligned}
$$

Thus, we can solve CSP in logarithmic time with a polynomial number of processors, where the degree of the polynomial depends on K, the number of labels per variable. $\square$

A similar method can be used to solve the AC problem. Details are omitted.

18.7.2 Expression Evaluation Methods

In the previous subsection we suggested a separator-based algorithm to solve CSP and AC when the underlying graph is a tree. Similar to chains, the complexity of that algorithm is $O(\log N)$ with $O(K^{\log_{1.5} N})$ processors. Here we propose a different algorithm to solve AC in trees. This algorithm operates in $O(\log N \log K)$ time and uses a polynomial number of processors, where the degree of the polynomial does not depend on K. More importantly, it reduces the consistency problem to reachability and expression evaluation on trees.

For non-constant values of K, the algorithm in this subsection is asymptotically better than the previous algorithm. However, the algorithm is probably impractical, and is presented to demonstrate the substantial difficulty in getting asymptotically optimal parallel algorithms, even for tree-like constraint networks.

Let T be the constraint tree, which without loss of generality we assume is binary and rooted at some arbitrary node. We first construct the explicit constraint graph G_{expl}. Let $\ell_{i,v}$ denote the ith label in node v, and let $R_{u,v}$ denote the compatibility (support) predicate between nodes u and v. Note that $R_{u,v}$ is also the adjacency matrix for the subgraph of G_{expl} restricted to labels in nodes u and v.

The algorithm now proceeds as follows:

Step 1 Mark the following set of labels, defined bottom up in the tree:

- $\ell_{i,v}$ is marked if v is a leaf.
- $\ell_{i,v}$ is marked if for each child w of v in T there exists j such that $\ell_{j,w}$ is marked and $\ell_{i,v}$ and $\ell_{j,w}$ are adjacent in G_{expl}.

The entire system is consistent iff the set of labels marked at the root is non-empty.

Step 2 Discard all unmarked labels, and consider the original problem restricted only to marked labels. Clear all marks, and do the following second marking procedure:

- Mark all labels at the root.
- Mark $\ell_{i,v}$ iff there exists a marked $\ell_{j,w}$ where w is the parent of v and $\ell_{i,v}$ and $\ell_{j,w}$ are adjacent in G_{expl}.

The solution is the set of labels marked at the end of Step 2.

The sequential version of the algorithm outlined above is a version of directed arc-consistency that was originally developed by Dechter and Pearl [4]. The reader should note that while sequentially directed arc-consistency can be implemented optimally for both chains and trees, in the parallel environment the two problems are very different. The parallel implementation of directed arc-consistency that achieves sublinear time is non-trivial and is discussed below.

For completeness, we first discuss the correctness of the algorithm outlined above. By induction on the height of nodes in the tree, it is clear that labels marked in Step 1 are precisely those that potentially have support from nodes below them in the tree. In particular, it follows that labels marked at the root of T will be contained in the solution. We now can argue by induction on the depth of each node in T that nodes marked in Step 2 are precisely those that have support from their parent in the tree. Since we are only considering nodes that already have support from their child edges, it follows that the labels marked in Step 2 are the solutions to the AC problem.

It is easy to see that the sequential version executes in linear time. We now describe how this simple algorithm can be implemented in parallel. Our implementation is non-trivial, but we are unaware of a simpler way to achieve sublinear time for trees in which the depth may be proportional to the size of the tree.

Step 1 can be viewed either as an expression-evaluation calculation, or as a reachability computation.

- As an expression we are computing a bit vector at each node, one bit marker for each label at that node. If $\vec{b}_x$ denotes the bit vector computed at node x, then if nodes v and w are children of node u in T, we have

$$\vec{b}_u = (\vec{b}_v \times R_{v,u}) \odot (\vec{b}_w \times R_{w,u})$$

where $\times$ represents boolean matrix multiplication and $\odot$ is a bitwise AND operation. We can evaluate this expression by parallel expression-evaluation algorithms such as the raking procedure described in [1, 16].

In brief, the raking procedure works by evaluating and removing (in parallel) leaves and their parents from the expression tree. At each stage approximately half of the leaves are removed, so that after $O(\log N)$ stages the entire expression has been evaluated. The partial evaluation results are stored on the edges of the tree. In our case, when a leaf is raked, we are applying an intersection of a known (i.e., constant) bit vector between two matrix multiplications. This is simply a restriction of the matrix product to the rows and columns of the intersection vector. Thus the result of the rake operation can be represented as a single matrix, and can be computed in $O(\log K)$ time using the number of processors required to multiply two $K \times K$-bit matrices, $M(K)$. The entire evaluation can then be done in $O(\log N \log K)$ time with $N \cdot M(K)/\log N$ processors.

- As a reachability computation, we can identify all labels reachable from a leaf label (assuming G_{expl} is now directed with all arcs oriented toward the root of T). We then mark all labels that are reachable from all leaves under them. Finally, restricting ourselves only to these marked nodes, we redo the reachability-from-leaves calculation. Computing reachability as transitive closure by matrix multiplication, we can accomplish Step 1 in this manner also with $N \cdot M(K)/\log N$ processors in $O(\log N \log K)$ time.

Step 2 is a simple calculation of reachability from labels at the root of T, and so can be done within the same processor-time bounds. Thus we have shown:

THEOREM 18.4 If constraint graph G is a tree, with K labels per node, we can solve AC for G in $O(\log N \log K)$ time with $N \cdot M(K)/\log N$ processors.

18.8 2-Label CSP

In this section we reduce 2-label CSP to 2-SAT (satisfiability of formulae in conjunctive normal form with at most two atoms per clause). 2-SAT is equivalent to a reachability problem in directed graphs. Therefore, if the number of possible labels per variable is two or less we can process the constraint graph in polylogarithmic parallel time. Another implication of this result is that 2-label CSP can be solved in linear time.

LEMMA 18.3 Given a CSP P, where $|L_i| \leq 2$, $1 \leq i \leq n$ (i.e., the number of labels for each variable is at most 2), then P can be converted to a 2-SAT problem S such that I is a solution for S iff I is a solution for P.

PROOF: We merely regard the labels in each variable as representing truth values. We then translate each constraint relation R_{ij} into an equivalent 2-CNF form, and take the conjunction over all such relations in P. For instance, the constraint

X	Y	R_{XY}
0	0	0
0	1	1
1	0	1
1	1	0

is converted to the set of clauses $(X \vee Y) \wedge (\neg X \vee \neg Y)$. $\square$

Given a set S of clauses in 2-SAT form, we can create a new, directed constraint graph that captures the constraints of the initial constraint graph more explicitly. For each variable X occurring in S we create two nodes, X and $\neg X$. Then for each clause in S of the form $\alpha \vee \beta$, we create two directed arcs: $\neg \alpha \rightarrow \beta$ and $\neg \beta \rightarrow \alpha$. As an example, for the constraint $(X \vee Y) \wedge (\neg Y \vee Z)$ we generate the following graph:

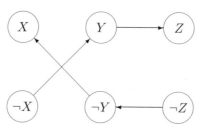

It is known that using the above construction of an explicit directed graph we can find solutions to the original problem by tracing the strongly connected components of the constraint graph. The precise claim is captured in the next intuitive proposition which we state without proof.

PROPOSITION 18.3 Let S be a 2-SAT formula and C its explicit constraint graph constructed as above. Then S is satisfiable iff no strongly connected component of C contains both X and $\neg X$ for any variable X in S. Moreover, if S is satisfiable, the strongly connected components of C can be used to derive satisfying assignments for the variables of S.

In other words, the formula is unsatisfiable iff some node $\neg X$ is reachable from node X and vice versa. However, reachability problems are well-understood and can be done by transitive closure methods in parallel in $O(\log^2 N)$ time with $M(N)$ processors on a CRCW PRAM [11]. Thus, we have the following:

PROPOSITION 18.4 Given a CSP P where $|L_i| \leq 2$, i.e., the number of possible labels (solutions) per variable is at most 2, P can be solved in $O(\log^2 N)$ time with $M(N)$ processors on a CRCW PRAM.

Thus, in the special case when the number of labels per object is at most 2, we can compute the solution in sublinear time with a relatively large number of processors ($N^{1.5}$ processors where N is the size of the entire input). We note that we are actually solving the constraint problem directly without attempting to achieve arc consistency first. Since computing directed components can be done sequentially by depth-first search, we obtain an immediate corollary.

COROLLARY 18.1 Let P be a CSP with $|L_i| \leq 2$. Then P can be solved in linear time by a single processor.

This last result apparently has been known for some time [20], however it first appeared in print in [13, 6]. In fact, a more general version of the above construction seems to be folklore, namely that arc consistency for networks with K labels is easily transformable in linear time to K-SAT. Thus, our translation of 2-CSP to 2-SAT is a special case of this result. We leave the proof to the reader.

18.9   Consistency in Directed Support Networks (DC)

Traditionally, AC was considered as a filtering step used to solve constraint satisfaction problems. However, there is an interesting modal-logic-like interpretation

of AC in the context of support networks. We start with a collection of agents
(variables) each holding a set of beliefs (labels). For each pair of variables X and
Y we define a directional support relation that for each belief states which beliefs
at one agent get supported by beliefs at the other agent.

An agent keeps a belief a iff it is supported by at least one belief at each of the
other agents associated with it. Note that we are not seeking a global interpretation
of the variables, but rather would like to filter unsupported beliefs. This is analogous
to the standard AC problem. In this case, however, the support relations are
directed. Dechter and Pearl have defined the notion of directed arc-consistency,
which is used to compute arc-consistency in trees. The standard directed arc-
consistency allows one to orient the edges from one variable to another in a certain
direction. Our formalization allows one to direct edges from any label to any label
in any prespecified direction (see also [5] for a related idea). The intuition is, that
a certain belief an agent may have could be supported by some beliefs from other
agents, but another belief is independent of other agents. Consistency in directed
support networks (DC) is naturally described by an explicit constraint graph. Edges
in the graph describe directed support (see the example below). The only label that
drops is e from Y.

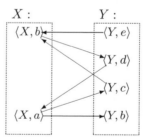

The following surprising result indicates that the parallel complexity of solving
DC is considerably more complicated than standard AC problem. Essentially, this
result indicates that the parallel complexity is dependent on the structure of the
explicit constraint graph, rather than the structure of the constraint graph. This
follows from the fact that we can encode general logical dependency in such a graph.

THEOREM 18.5 Consistency in directed support networks (DC) is P-complete, even
if the underlying graph is a 3-node chain.

PROOF: Our reduction is from Propositional Horn-Clause Satisfiability. Without
loss of generality, we assume the Horn clause program contains a single assertion
T, and that every other variable A_i appears as the head of either exactly one rule

of the form $A_i \leftarrow A_j \wedge A_k$, or else two or more rules of the form $A_i \leftarrow A_j$. Let A_n be the goal of the program.

We construct an instance of DC containing three nodes: L(eft), M(iddle) and R(ight). Let each of these three nodes contain a label for T and for each A_i. Now construct arcs for the explicit support graph as follows:

1. From each label in M to the corresponding label in both L and R.

2. From T_L to T_M and from T_R to T_M.

3. For every clause of the form $A_i \leftarrow A_j, A_k$, construct an arc from $A_{j,L}$ to $A_{i,M}$ and from $A_{k,R}$ to $A_{i,M}$.

4. For every clause of the form $A_i \leftarrow A_j$, construct an arc from $A_{j,L}$ to $A_{i,M}$ and from T_R to $A_{i,M}$.

It is now easy to show that the labels that remain in M correspond exactly to the variables that are true in the Horn-clause program. In particular $A_{n,M}$ remains iff the goal A_n of the program is true. $\square$

18.10   Summary of Parallel AC Results

In this section we summarize our knowledge of the parallel complexity of computing local consistency in constraint satisfaction problems. The results appear in Tables 18.1 and 18.2. We have classified the parallel complexity of problems into two classes: $\mathcal{P}$-complete problems and $\mathcal{NC}$ problems. $\mathcal{P}$-complete problems are perceived to be difficult to parallelize (in the same sense that $\mathcal{NP}$-complete problems are considered intractable), and $\mathcal{NC}$ problems can be solved in polylogarithmic time with a polynomial number of processors. $\mathcal{NC}$ problems are often amenable for optimal speed-up on parallel machines. In both tables R denotes the binary compatibility predicate.

The main practical conclusions that we can draw from our study are as follows:

1. Local consistency in constraint networks is generally $\mathcal{P}$-complete. Practical experience suggests that it is difficult to obtain optimal parallel algorithms for such problems. By optimal parallel algorithms we mean algorithms that obtain P-fold speed-up of the best sequential algorithm with P processors. However, it is often easy to obtain optimal speed-ups for these (and other) problems when the number of processors is small.

Table 18.1
Complexity of Arc Consistency for Arbitrary-Size Label Sets

Arbitrary K (K is the size of the label set L)		
G	CSP	AC
Chain	$\mathcal{NC}$; reachability	Undirected R's: $\mathcal{NC}$; reachability Directed R's: P-complete; reduction from Propositional Horn-Clause Solvability
Tree	$\mathcal{NC}$	Undirected R's: $\mathcal{NC}$; like expression eval where operation at each node is intersection of sets of support for each label (see this paper) Directed R's: P-complete; from above
Simple Cycle	$\mathcal{NC}$; reachability	Undirected R's: $\mathcal{NC}$; cycle detection Directed R's: P-complete; from above
Arbitrary Graph	$\mathcal{NP}$-complete; reduction from graph colouring	Undirected R's: P-complete; reduction from Propositional Horn-Clause Solvability Directed R's: P-complete; from above

2. Substantial speed-ups for parallel local consistency algorithms are possible if the constraint graph is dense. This can be accomplished using a simple obvious algorithm which is likely to be efficient in practice. Specifically, given a constraint network with n nodes and K labels per node, it is easy to obtain an $O(nK)$ algorithm for arc-consistency with nK processors on a shared-memory parallel model of computation.

3. The application of the obvious parallel version of the arc-consistency algo-

Table 18.2
Complexity of Arc Consistency for Fixed-Size Label Sets

Fixed K (K is the size of the label set L)		
G	CSP	AC
Chain	$\mathcal{NC}$	Undirected R's: $\mathcal{NC}$ Directed R's: $\mathcal{NC}$
Tree	$\mathcal{NC}$	Undirected R's: $\mathcal{NC}$ Directed R's: $\mathcal{NC}$; from above
Simple Cycle	$\mathcal{NC}$	Undirected R's: $\mathcal{NC}$ Directed R's: $\mathcal{NC}$; from above
Arbitrary Graph	$K = 2$: Linear sequential algorithm by reduction to 2-SAT which is $\mathcal{NC}$ $K \geq 3$: $\mathcal{NP}$-complete; reduction from 3-colouring graphs	Undirected R's: For $K = 2$, $\mathcal{NC}$ by reachability along "singleton paths"; For $K \geq 3$, P-complete from Propositional Horn-Clause Solvability Directed R's: P-complete for $K \geq 2$

rithm to such networks does not yield a sublinear algorithm. The parallel complexity of local consistency in chain networks has been shown equivalent to reachability problems in directed graphs. While this class of networks can theoretically be solved very fast, in practice our results imply that the "transitive closure" bottleneck may apply to chain networks. It currently is not known how to get optimal speed-ups for transitive closure problems in graphs unless the number of processors is smaller than the number of nodes,

4. For tree networks we suggested several algorithms that achieve sublinear time with many parallel processors. We have been unable to find an obvious practical algorithm to achieve optimal speed-up in tree networks.

5. We provided a reduction from i-consistency to propositional Horn satisfiability which allows us to derive optimal sequential algorithms for problems such as path consistency in a simple manner.

Acknowledgments

This research has been supported partially by the Air Force Office of Scientific Research under grant AFOSR-89-1151, the National Science Foundation under grant IRI-88-09324 and NSF/DARPA Grant CCR-890892. Thanks are due to David McAllester, Judea Pearl and Rina Dechter for their constructive comments.

References

[1] K. Abrahamson, N. Dadoun, D. A. Kirkpatrick, and T. Przytycka. A simple parallel tree contraction algorithm. *Journal of Algorithms*, 10(2):287–302, 1989.

[2] P.R. Cooper and M.J. Swain. Arc consistency: Parallelism and domain dependence. *Artificial Intelligence*, 58:207–235, 1992.

[3] J. de Kleer. An assumption-based TMS. *Artificial Intelligence*, 28:127–162, 1986.

[4] R. Dechter and J. Pearl. Network-based heuristics for constraint satisfaction problems. *Artificial Intelligence*, 34:1–38, 1987.

[5] R. Dechter and J. Pearl. Directed constraint networks: A relational framework ofr causal modelling. In *Proceedings of the 1991 International Joint Conference on Artificial Intelligence*, pages 1164–1170, August 1991.

[6] J. deKleer. A comparison of atms and csp techniques. In *Proceedings of the 1989 International Joint Conference on Artificial Intelligence*, pages 290–296, August 1989.

[7] M. Dixon and J. de Kleer. Massively parallel assumption-based truth maintenance. In *Proceedings of AAAI-88*, pages 199–204, 1988.

[8] E. Freuder. A sufficient condition for backtrack-free search. *JACM*, 29:24–32, 1982.

[9] J. Gu, W. Wang, and T.C. Henderson. A parallel architecture for discrete relaxation algorithms. *IEEE Transactions on Pattern Analysis and Machine Intelligence*, 9:816–831, 1987.

[10] R. M. Haralick and L. G. Shapiro. The consistent labeling problem: Part I. *IEEE Trans. Patt. Anal. Mach. Intel.*, PAMI-1:173–184, 1979.

[11] J. Já Já. *An Introduction to Parallel Algorithms*. Addison-Wesley, 1992.

[12] S. Kasif. On the parallel complexity of some constraint satisfaction problems. In *Proceedings of the 1986 National Conference on Artificial Intelligence*, pages 349–353, August 1986.

[13] S. Kasif. Parallel solutions to constraint satisfaction problems. In *Principles of Knowledge Representation and Reasoning*, pages 180–187, May 1989.

[14] S. Kasif. On the parallel complexity of discrete relaxation in constraint networks. *Artificial Intelligence*, pages 229–241, 1990.

[15] S. Kasif, J. Reif, and D. Sherlekar. Formula dissection: A parallel algorithm for constraint satisfaction. In *Proceedings of the 1987 IEEE Workshop on Computer Architecture for Pattern Analysis and Machine Intelligence*, pages 51–57, October 1987.

[16] S. R. Kosaraju and A. L. Delcher. Optimal parallel evaluation of tree-structured computations by raking. In J. Reif, editor, *VLSI Algorithms and Architectures: Proceedings of 1988 Aegean Workshop on Computing*, pages 101–110. Springer Verlag, 1988. LNCS 319.

[17] P. Ladkin and Maddux R. Parallel path consistency algorithms for constraint satisfaction. In *Proceedings of the 1990 Workshop on Constraint Systems*, August 1990.

[18] A. K. Mackworth. Consistency in networks of relations. *Artificial Intelligence*, 8:99–118, 1977.

[19] A. K. Mackworth and E. Freuder. The complexity of some polynomial network consistency algorithms for constraint satisfaction. *Artificial Intelligence*, 25:65–74, 1985.

[20] David McAllester. Personal communication.

[21] R. Mohr and T.C. Henderson. Arc and path consistency revisited. *Artificial Intelligence*, 28:225–233, 1986.

[22] U. Montanari. Networks of constraints: Fundamental properties. *Inform. Sci.*, 7:727–732, 1974.

[23] A. Rosenfeld, R. Hummel, and S. Zucker. Scene labeling by relaxation operations. *IEEE Trans. Syst. Man Cybern.*, SMC-6:420–433, 1976.

[24] A. Samal and T.C. Henderson. Parallel consistent labelling algorithms. *International Journal of Parallel Programming*, 16:341–364, 1987.

[25] R. Seidel. A new method for solving constraint satisfaction problems. In *Proceedings of the International Joint Conference on AI*, pages 338–342, 1981.

[26] P. Van Hentenryck. *Constraint Satisfaction in Logic Programming*. MIT Press, 1989.

[27] P. Van Hentenryck. Parallel constraint satisfaction in logic programming. In *Proceedings of the International Conference on Logic Programming*, pages 165–180, 1989.

[28] J. S. Vitter and R. A. Simons. New classes for parallel complexity: A study of unification and other complete problems in P. *IEEE Transactions on Computers*, C-35(5):403–418, 1986.

[29] P. H. Winston. *Artificial Intelligence*. Addison-Wesley, 1984.

[30] Y. Zhang and A.K. Mackworth. Parallel and distributed algorithms for finite constraint satisfaction problems. In *Proceedings of the Third IEEE Symposium on Parallel and Distributed Processing*, pages 394–397, December 1991.

19 Terminological Reasoning with Constraint Handling Rules

Thom Frühwirth[1] and Philipp Hanschke[2]

Abstract

Terminological knowledge representation formalisms in the tradition of KL-ONE enable one to define the relevant concepts of a problem domain and their interaction in a structured and well-formed way. In recent years, a wealth of literature has appeared on this topic, e.g. [5]. Sound and complete inference algorithms for terminological logics have been developed using constraint calculi. These terminological reasoning services can be reduced to a single algorithm checking consistency.

We propose constraint handling rules (CHRs) as an implementation language for terminological reasoning. We will give an introduction into the language. CHRs are a flexible means to implement 'user-defined' constraints on top of existing host languages like Prolog and Lisp. In particular, inference rules, which are often used to define constraint calculi, can usually be written as CHRs with little modification. The result of using CHRs for terminological reasoning is an incremental and concurrent consistency checking algorithm.

The implementation provides a natural combination of three layers: (*i*) a constraint layer that reasons in well-understood domains such as rationals or finite domains, (*ii*) a terminological layer providing a tailored, validated vocabulary on which (*iii*) the application layer can rely. As an application example, a configuration problem is modeled. The flexibility of the approach will be illustrated by extending the formalism, its implementation and the example with attributes, a new quantifier and concrete domains.

19.1 Introduction

A reader interested in constraint-based programming may consider this chapter as a case study on user-defined constraints using the CHRs approach. A reader with background in terminological reasoning may learn about a flexible way to implement terminological languages. We tried to tackle the difficulties of serving both audiences. The final judgement is to you, the reader.

---

[1] Partially supported by ESPRIT Project 5291 CHIC

[2] Partially supported by BMFT Projects ARC-TEC (Grant ITW 8902 C4) and IMCOD/VEGA (Grant 413 5839 ITW 9304/3). Work was done while at DFKI, Postfach 2080, D-67608 Kaiserslautern, Germany

Terminological formalisms based on KL-ONE [7] are used to represent the terminological knowledge of a particular problem domain on an abstract logical level. To describe this kind of knowledge, one starts with atomic concepts and roles, and then defines new concepts and their relationship in terms of existing concepts and roles. For example,

> grand_father isa male and some child is parent.

Concepts can be considered as unary relations which intensionally define sets of objects (similar to types). Roles correspond to binary relations over objects (not necessarily of the same kind - properties like color can be roles as well). Then, assertions are added, describing actual objects of the application, e.g.

> john:male.   (john,jack):child.   jack:parent.

Terminological formalisms have a straightforward embedding in first-order logic, so it seems natural to implement them as logic programs. Moreover, the limited expressiveness of terminological formalisms allows for decision procedures for a number of interesting reasoning problems. These problems include consistency of assertions and classification of concepts. The key idea of [17, 23, 8]) for constructing such inference algorithms is to reduce all reasoning services to consistency checking. This essential algorithm can be considered as constraint solving, where concepts and roles are the constraints.

We therefore aim at implementing reasoning with terminologies as constraint logic programs (CLP). In this way, an instance of the CLP scheme results, and we can carry over the declarative and operational semantics from CLP. *Constraint logic programming* [20, 28, 18, 29, 9, 21] combines the advantages of logic programming and constraint solving. In logic programming, problems are stated in a declarative way using rules to define relations (predicates). Problems are solved by the built-in logic programming engine (LPE) using chronological backtrack search. In constraint solving, efficient special-purpose algorithms are employed to solve problems involving distinguished relations referred to as constraints.

A practical problem remains: Constraint solving is usually 'hard-wired' in a built-in constraint solver (CS) written in a low-level language. While efficient, this approach makes it hard to build a CS over a new domain like terminologies, let alone verify its correctness. We proposed *constraint handling rules* (CHRs) [11] to overcome this problem. CHRs are a language *extension* providing a declarative means to introduce *user-defined* constraints into a given high-level host language. In this chapter the host language is Prolog, a CLP language with equality over

Herbrand terms as the only built-in constraint. CHRs define *simplification* of and *propagation* over user-defined constraints. Simplification replaces constraints by simpler constraints while preserving logical equivalence, e.g.

    X>Y,Y>X <=> false.

Propagation adds new constraints which are logically redundant but may cause further simplification, e.g.

    X>Y,Y>Z ==> X>Z.

When repeatedly applied by a constraint handling engine (CHE) the constraints are incrementally solved as in a CS, e.g.

    A>B,B>C,C>A results in `false`.

CHIP was the first CLP language to introduce constructs (demons, forward rules, conditionals) [28] for user-defined *constraint handling* (like constraint solving, simplification, propagation). These various constructs have been generalized into CHRs. CHRs are based on guarded rules, as can be found in concurrent logic programming languages [24], in the Swedish branch of the Andorra family [13], Saraswats cc-framework of concurrent constraint programming [22], and in the 'Guarded Rules' of [25]. However all these languages (except CHIP) lack features essential to define non-trivial constraint handling, namely for handling conjunctions of constraints and defining constraint propagation. CHRs provide these two features using multi-headed rules and propagation rules.

This chapter first introduces CHRs, then terminological reasoning. Next it is shown that CHRs indeed can serve as a flexible implementation layer for an incremental and concurrent version of the consistency test for terminologies. Moreover, the implementation effort turns out to be minimal, as the CHRs directly reflect the inference rules of the tuned tableaux calculus that is used for the consistency test.

Last but not least we illustrate that extensions to the basic terminological formalism proposed in the literature carry over to the implementation with CHRs in a painless manner. One such extension allows to parameterize terminologies with *concrete domains*, e.g. linear constraints over rational numbers [6, 14]. Concrete domains can be either implemented by CHRs or provided as built-in constraints of the host language. In this way we obtain a fairly natural combination of three knowledge representation layers - the constraint, terminological and application layer - on a common implementational basis.

19.2   CLP with Constraint Handling Rules

Here we assume that constraint handling rules extend a a given constraint logic
programming language. The syntax and semantics given reflect this choice. It
should be stressed, however, that the host language for CHRs need not be a CLP
language. Indeed, the work presented here has been done at DFKI in the context
of LISP [16].

19.2.1   Syntax

A CLP+CH program is a finite set of clauses from the CLP language and from
the language of CHRs. Clauses are built from atoms of the form $p(t_1, ...t_n)$ where
p is a predicate symbol of arity n ($n \geq 0$) and $t_1, ...t_n$ is a n-tuple of terms. A
term is a variable, e.g. X, or of the form $f(t_1, ...t_n)$ where f is a function symbol
of arity n ($n \geq 0$) applied to a n-tuple of terms. Function symbols of arity 0 are
also called constants. In this chapter, predicate and function symbols start with
lowercase letters while variables start with uppercase letters. Infix notation may
be used for specific predicate symbols (e.g. $X = Y$) and functions symbols (e.g.
$-X + Y$). There are two classes of distinguished atoms, built-in constraints and
user-defined constraints. In most CLP languages there is a built-in constraint for
syntactic equality over Herbrand terms, =, performing unification. The built-in
constraint `true`, which is always satisfied, can be seen as an abbreviation for `1=1`.
`false` (`1=2`) is the built-in constraint representing inconsistency.

A *CLP clause* is of the form

$$H \text{:- } B_1, \ldots B_n. \ \ (n \geq 0)$$

where the head H is an atom but not a built-in constraint, the body $B_1, \ldots B_n$ is a
conjunction of literals called *goals*. The empty body ($n = 0$) of a CLP clause may
be denoted by the built-in constraint `true`. A *query* is a CLP clause without head.
There are two kinds of CHRs[3]. A *simplification* CHR is of the form

$$H_1, \ldots H_i \text{ <=> } G_1, \ldots G_j \mid B_1, \ldots B_k.$$

A *propagation* CHR is of the form

$$H_1, \ldots H_i \text{ ==> } G_1, \ldots G_j \mid B_1, \ldots B_k. \ \ (i > 0, j \geq 0, k \geq 0)$$

where the multi-head $H_1, \ldots H_i$ is a conjunction of user-defined constraints and
the guard $G_1, \ldots G_j$ is a conjunction of literals which neither are, nor depend on,

---
[3] A third, hybrid kind is described in [4].

user-defined constraints.

19.2.2 Semantics

Declaratively, CLP programs are interpreted as formulas in first order logic. Extending a CLP language with CHRs preserves its declarative semantics. A CLP+CH program P is a conjunction of universally quantified clauses.

A CLP clause is an implication[4]

$$H \leftarrow B_1 \wedge \ldots B_n.$$

A simplification CHR is a logical equivalence provided the guard is true in the current context

$$(G_1 \wedge \ldots G_j) \rightarrow (H_1 \wedge \ldots H_i \leftrightarrow B_1 \wedge \ldots B_k).$$

A propagation CHR is an implication provided the guard is true

$$(G_1 \wedge \ldots G_j) \rightarrow (H_1 \wedge \ldots H_i \rightarrow B_1 \wedge \ldots B_k).$$

Procedurally, a CHR can fire if its guard allows it. A firing simplification CHR *replaces* the head constraint by the body, a firing propagation CHR *adds* the body to the head constraints. No theorem proving in the general sense is required to reason with the formulas expressed by CHRs.

The *operational semantics* of CLP+CH can be described by a transition system. A *computation state* is a tuple

$$< Gs, C_U, C_B >,$$

where Gs is a set of goals, C_U and C_B are constraint stores for user-defined and built-in constraints respectively. A *constraint store* is a set of constraints. A set of atoms represents a conjunction of atoms.

The *initial state* consists of a query Gs and empty constraint stores,

$$< Gs, \{\}, \{\} >.$$

A *final state* is either *failed* (due to an inconsistent built-in constraint store represented by the unsatisfiable constraint `false`),

$$< Gs, C_U, \{\texttt{false}\} >,$$

or *successful* (no goals left to solve),

---

[4]For simplicity of presentation, we do not use Clark's completion.

$$< \{\}, C_U, C_B >.$$

The union of the constraint stores in a successful final state is called *conditional answer* for the query Gs, written $answer(Gs)$.

The built-in constraint solver (CS) works on built-in constraints in C_B and Gs, the user-defined CS on user-defined constraints in C_U and Gs using CHRs, and the logic programming engine (LPE) on goals in Gs and C_U using CLP clauses. The following *computation steps* are possible to get from one computation state to the next.

Solve

$$< \{C\} \cup Gs, C_U, C_B > \longmapsto < Gs, C_U, C'_B >$$
if $(C \wedge C_B) \leftrightarrow C'_B$

The built-in CS updates the constraint store C_B if a new constraint C was found in Gs. To *update* the constraint store means to produce a new constraint store C'_B that is logically equivalent to the conjunction of the new constraint and the old constraint store.

We will write $H =_{set} H'$ to denote equality between the sets H and H', i.e. $H = \{A_1, \dots, A_n\}$ and there is a permutation of H', $perm(H') = \{B_1, \dots, B_n\}$, such that $A_i = B_i$ for all $1 \leq i \leq n$.

Introduce

$$< \{H\} \cup Gs, C_U, C_B > \longmapsto < Gs, \{H\} \cup C_U, C_B >$$
if H is a user-defined constraint

Simplify

$$< Gs, H' \cup C_U, C_B > \longmapsto < Gs \cup B, C_U, C_B >$$
if $(H \texttt{ <=> } G \mid B) \in P$ and $C_B \rightarrow (H =_{set} H') \wedge answer(G)$

Propagate

$$< Gs, H' \cup C_U, C_B > \longmapsto < Gs \cup B, H' \cup C_U, C_B >$$
if $(H \texttt{ ==> } G \mid B) \in P$ and $C_B \rightarrow (H =_{set} H') \wedge answer(G)$

The constraint handling engine (CHE) applies CHRs to user-defined constraints in Gs and C_U whenever all user-defined constraints needed in the multi-head are present and the guard is satisfied. A guard G is *satisfied* if its local execution does not involve user-defined constraints and the result $answer(G)$ is entailed (implied) by the built-in constraint store C_B. Equality is entailed between two terms if they match. To *introduce* a user-defined constraint means to take it from the goal literals Gs and put it into the user-defined constraint store C_U. To *simplify* user-defined constraints H' means to replace them by B if H' matches the head H of a simplification CHR H <=> G | B and the guard G is satisfied. To *propagate from* user-defined constraints H' means to add B to Gs if H' matches the head H of a propagation CHR H ==> G | B and G is satisfied.

Unfold
$$< \{H'\} \cup Gs, C_U, C_B > \longmapsto < Gs \cup B, C_U, \{H = H'\} \cup C_B >$$
if $(H$:- $B) \in P$.

The logic programming engine (LPE) unfolds goals in Gs. To *unfold* an atomic goal H' means to look for a clause H: $- B$ and to replace the H' by $(H = H')$ and B. As there are usually several clauses for a goal, unfolding is nondeterministic and thus a goal can be solved in different ways using different clauses. There can be CLP clauses for user-defined constraints. Thus they can be unfolded as well. This unfolding is called *(built-in) labeling*. The transition below is somewhat simplified, the details can be found in [11, 4].

Label
$$< Gs, \{H'\} \cup C_U, C_B > \longmapsto < Gs \cup B, C_U, \{H = H'\} \cup C_B >$$
if $(H$:- $B) \in P$.

Note that any constraint solver written with CHRs will be *incremental* and *concurrent*. By "incremental" we mean that constraints can be added to the constraint store one at a time using the "introduce"-transition. Then CHRs may fire and simplify the user-defined constraint store. The rules can be applied concurrently, even using chaotic iteration (i.e. the same constraint can be simplified by different rules at the same time), because correct CHRs can only replace constraints by equivalent ones or add redundant constraints.

19.2.3 Implementation

The operational semantics are still far from the actual workings of an efficient implementation. At the moment, there exist two implementations, one prototype in LISP [16], and one fully developed compiler in a Prolog extension.

The compiler for CHRs is available as a library of ECLiPSe [4], ECRC's advanced constraint logic programming platform, utilizing its delay-mechanism and built-in meta-predicates to create, inspect and manipulate delayed goals. All ECLiPSe documentation is available by anonymous ftp from ftp.ecrc.de, directory /pub/eclipse/doc. In such a sequential implementation, the transitions are tried in the textual order given above. To reflect the complexity of a program in the number of CHRs, at most two head constraints are allowed in a rule[5]. This restriction also makes complexity for search of the head constraints of a CHR linear in the number of constraints on average (quadratic in the worst case) by using partitioning and indexing methods. Termination of a propagation CHR is achieved by never firing it a second time with the same pair of head constraints.

The CHRs library includes a debugger and a visual tracer as well as a full color demo using geometric constraints in a real-life application for wireless telecommunication. 18 constraint solvers currently come with the release, for booleans, finite domains (similar to CHIP [28]), also over arbitrary ground terms, reals and pairs, incremental path consistency, temporal reasoning (quantitative and qualitative constraints over time points and intervals [12]), solving linear polynomials over the reals (similar to CLP(R) [19]) and rationals, for lists, sets, trees, terms and the solver described in this chapter. The average number of rules in a constraint solver is as low as 24. Typically it took only a few days to produce a reasonable prototype solver, since the usual formalisms to describe a constraint theory, i.e. inference rules, rewrite rules, sequents, first-order axioms, can be expressed as CHRs programs in a straightforward way. Thus one can directly express how constraints simplify and propagate without worrying about implementation details. Starting from this executable specification, the rules then can be refined and adapted to the specifics of the application.

On a wide range of solvers and examples, the run-time penalty for our declarative and high-level approach turned out to be a constant factor in comparison to dedicated built-in solvers (if available). Moreover, the slow-down is often within an order of magnitude. On some examples (e.g. those involving finite domains with the element-constraint), our approach is faster, since we can exactly define the amount of constraint simplification and propagation that is needed. This means that the solver are intentionally made as incomplete as the application requires it. Some solvers (e.g. disjunctive geometric constraints in the phone demo) would be very hard to recast in existing CLP languages.

19.3   Terminological Reasoning

In this section we will recall the concept language $\mathcal{ALC}$ [23] as our basic terminological logic (TL) and show its implementation in CHRs.

---

[5]Two is the minimal number such that a rule with more head constraints can be rewritten into several number-restricted rules.

Section 19.4 will then proceed with some useful extensions of this formalism demonstrating the flexibility of the CHRs approach.

19.3.1 Terminology

A terminology (T-box) consists of a finite, cycle free set of *concept definitions*

C isa s,

where C is the newly introduced concept name and s is a concept term constructed from concept names and roles. Inductively, *concept terms* are defined as follows:

1. Every concept name C is a concept term.

2. If s and t are concept terms and R is a role name then the following expressions are concept terms:

   s and t (conjunction),

   s or t (disjunction),

   nota s (complement),

   every R is s (value restriction),

   some R is s (exists-in restriction).

Although there is an established notation for terminologies, we use a more verbose syntax so that readers not familiar with the topic can read the expressions easily as sentences in (almost) natural language.

An *interpretation* $\mathcal{I}$ with a set $\mathrm{dom}_\mathcal{I}$ as domain interprets a concept name C as a set $C^\mathcal{I} \subseteq \mathrm{dom}_\mathcal{I}$ and a role name R as a set $R^\mathcal{I} \subseteq \mathrm{dom}_\mathcal{I} \times \mathrm{dom}_\mathcal{I}$. In other words, roles are interpreted as an arbitrary binary relation over $\mathrm{dom}_\mathcal{I}$. It can be lifted to concept terms in a straight-forward manner: Conjunction, disjunction, and complement are interpreted as set intersection, set union, and set complement wrt $\mathrm{dom}_\mathcal{I}$, respectively, and

$a \in (\text{every } R \text{ is } s)^\mathcal{I}$ iff, for all $b \in \mathrm{dom}_\mathcal{I}$, $(a, b) \in R^\mathcal{I}$ implies $b \in s^\mathcal{I}$,

and

$a \in (\text{some } R \text{ is } s)^\mathcal{I}$ iff, there is some $b \in \mathrm{dom}_\mathcal{I}$ such that $(a, b) \in R^\mathcal{I}$, $b \in s^\mathcal{I}$.

An interpretation is a *model* of a terminology T if $C^\mathcal{I} = s^\mathcal{I}$ for all $(C \text{ isa } s) \in T$.

Example: The domain of a configuration application comprises at least devices, interfaces, and configurations. The following concept definitions express that these are disjoint concepts.

```
primitive device.⁶
interface isa nota device.
configuration isa nota (interface or device).
```

Let us assume that a simple device has at least one interface. We introduce a role connector which relates devices to interfaces and employ the exists-in restriction.

```
role connector.
simple_device isa device and
some connector is interface.
```
□

19.3.2 Assertions and Reasoning Services

Objects are (Herbrand) constants or variables. Let a, b be objects, R a role, and C a concept term. Then $b : C$ is a *membership assertion* and $(a, b) : R$ is a *role-filler assertion*. An *A-box* is a collection of membership and role-filler assertions.

Example (contd): We introduce instances of devices and interfaces.

```
pc:device.   rs231:interface.   (pc,rs231):connector.
```
□

An *interpretation of an A-box* $\mathcal{A}$ is a model of the underlying terminology that, in addition, maps Herbrand constants to elements of $\mathrm{dom}_\mathcal{I}$. For these constants we adopt the unique name assumption. An A-box $\mathcal{A}$ is *consistent* if there is an interpretation $\mathcal{I}$ and a variable assignment $\sigma : objects \rightarrow \mathrm{dom}_\mathcal{I}$ such that all assertions of $\mathcal{A}$ are satisfied, i.e., $(a\sigma^\mathcal{I}, b\sigma^\mathcal{I}) \in R^\mathcal{I}$ and $b\sigma^\mathcal{I} \in C^\mathcal{I}$, for all $(a, b) : R$ and $b : C$ in $\mathcal{A}$. An object a is a *member of* a concept C iff for all models $\mathcal{I}$ of the terminology all assignments $\sigma : objects \rightarrow \mathrm{dom}_\mathcal{I}$ that satisfy $\mathcal{A}$ also satisfy $a : C$. A concept C_1 *subsumes* a concept C_2 iff for all models $\mathcal{I}$ of the terminology $C_1^\mathcal{I} \supseteq C_2^\mathcal{I}$. Figure 19.1 shows the subsumption graph of the terminology developed in sections 19.3 and 19.4.

The *consistency test* is the central reasoning service for terminological knowledge representation systems with complete inference algorithms. Various other services can be reduced to this test [17]. In particular, the subsumption (and similarly membership) services can be implemented on the basis of the consistency test of A-boxes:

1. A concept C_1 subsumes a concept C_2 iff an A-box consisting just of the membership assertion $a : C_2$ and nota C_1 is inconsistent.

---

⁶This declaration introduces a concept name that is not defined any further.

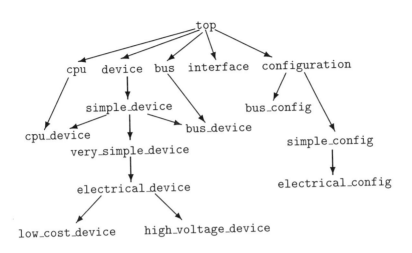

Figure 19.1
Subsumption Graph of the Example Terminology

2. An object a is a member of C wrt the A-box $\mathcal{A}$ iff $\{a : \text{nota } C\} \cup \mathcal{A}$ is inconsistent.

19.3.3 CLP+CH(TL)

Roughly, the consistency test of A-boxes works as follows.

1. Simplify and propagate the assertions in the A-box to make the knowledge more explicit.

2. Look for obvious contradictions ("clashes") such as "X:C, X:nota C".

The consistency test can be implemented with CHRs by regarding assertions as user-defined constraints. CHRs similar to the ones that follow can be found as the unfolding and completion rules in [23] and the propagation rules in [8]. However, the former work does not provide an incremental algorithm and the latter does not simplify constraints.

First we treat the complement operator:

```
I:nota nota S    <=>   I:S.
I:nota (S or T)   <=>   I:(nota S and nota T).
I:nota (S and T)  <=>   I:(nota S or nota T).
I:nota every R is S  <=>   I:some R is nota S.
```

```
I:nota some R is S  <=>  I:every R is nota S.
```

These simplification CHRs show how the complement operator `nota` can be pushed towards the leaves of a concept term.

The conjunction rule generates two new, smaller assertions:

```
I:S and T  <=>  I:S,I:T.
```

An exists-in restriction generates a new object (i.e. variable) that serves as a "witness" for the restriction:

```
I:some R is S  <=>  (I,J):R, J:S.
```

The time-complexity of executing the above CHRs is linear in the size of the concept term.

A value restriction has to be propagated to all role fillers:

```
I:every R is S, (I,J):R  ==>  J:S.
```

In the implementation this propagation rule will be applied only once per matching pair of membership and role-filler assertions. The time-complexity is quadratic in the number of assertions.

Disjunction is treated lazily by two CLP clauses (introducing a disjunction for built-in labeling):

```
I:S or T :- I:S.
I:S or T :- I:T.
```

These are the two rules where the exponential complexity of consistency tests for terminologies surfaces.

The unfolding rules expand concept names to their definitions:

```
I:C  <=>  (C isa S) | I:S.
I:nota C  <=>  (C isa S) | I:nota S.
```

Since concept definitions do not contain cycles, the above two CHRs clearly terminate.

For $\mathcal{ALC}$ we need only the following single clash rule, one may need more for extensions of the formalism.

```
I:nota S, I:S  <=> false.
```

The above solver simplifies terminological constraints until a normal form is reached. In the normal form, the only constraints are `I:C`, `I:nota C`, `I:S or`

T, I:every R is S, (I,J):R, where C is a primitive concept name. The solver is *complete*, i.e. it detects all inconsistencies through the clash rule independent of the order in which constraints are added and CHRs are applied. All CHRs except the clash rule have pairwise disjoint heads (C can only stand for concept names). Therefore for completeness we have to show that the clash rule can still be applied even after an inconsistent pair of membership assertions is reduced by other rules. For example, the inconsistent constraints

> I:nota every R is S, I:every R is S

can be simplified by pushing nota down in the first constraint

> I:some R is nota S, ·I:every R is S $\longmapsto$ (some-rule)
> (I,J):R, J:nota S, I:every R is S $\longmapsto$ (every-rule)
> (I,J):R, J:nota S, I:every R is S, J:S

and the clash rule applies to J:nota S, J:S leading to false. $\square$

19.4 Extensions

In a number of papers (e.g., [17, 23, 8]) the above idea of a tableaux based consistency test as the central reasoning service has been successfully applied to terminological logics with various other language constructs. This flexibility carries over to extensions of our implementation.

19.4.1 Functional Roles

Attributes (also called features) are functional roles, i.e., their interpretation is the graph of a partial function $dom_\mathcal{I} \to dom_\mathcal{I}$. Assuming declarations of attributes of the form attribute F, F an attribute name, we just have to extend our implementation by

> (I,J1):F, (I,J2):F ==> attribute F | J1=J2.

Example (contd): Now we are ready to define a simple configuration which consists of two distinguished simple devices:

> attribute component_1.
> attribute component_2.
> simple_config isa configuration and
>   some component_1 is simple_device and
>   some component_2 is simple_device.

Asking the query

```
:- config1:simple_config, (config1,dev1):component_1,
   (config1,dev2):component_2,
```

the membership service can derive that dev1 and dev2 are simple devices. The reason is that the attribute-rule constrains the witness for some component_1 is simple_device and the second argument of the role (config1,dev1):component_1 to be equal (analogously for dev2).

☐

A more local way to specify functionality of roles is provided through concept terms of the form "at_most_one R", R a role name.[7] An $a \in \mathrm{dom}_{\mathcal{I}}$ is an element of (at_most_one $R)^{\mathcal{I}}$ if there is at most one R-role filler for a. This is implemented through

```
I:at_most_one R, (I,J1):R, (I,J2):R  ==> J1=J2.
```

An object does not belong to at_most_one R if, and only if, there are at least two different role fillers:

```
I:nota at_most_one R  <=>
   (I,J1):R, (I,J2):R, different(J1,J2).
```

The constraint different is unsatisfiable if its arguments are identical.

```
different(X,X)  <=> false.
```

Example (contd):

```
very_simple_device isa simple_device and
   at_most_one connector.
```

☐

19.4.2 Concrete Domains

In [14] restricted forms of quantification over predicates of a *concrete domain* $\mathcal{D}$ have been suggested as concept forming operators. Examples of concrete domains are Allen's temporal interval relations, rational (natural) numbers with comparison operators and linear polynomials over the reals (all of which have been implemented by CHRs). An *admissible* concrete domain has to be closed under complement (since we have to propagate the complement operator nota) and has to provide a satisfiability test for conjunctions of predicates. Unlike in [10], we present an untyped and simpler version of the concrete domains extension for space reasons.

---

[7] The at_most_one construct is a restricted form of the *number restriction* [7].

The syntax for the new operators in the extension $\mathrm{TL}(\mathcal{D})$ of the concept language is as follows:

> every w_0 and ...and w_n is p
> some w_0 and ...and w_n is p,

where w_i is of the form "R_{i1} of ...of R_{ik_i}", R_{ij} are role names, $n > 0$, $k_i \geq 0$, $i = 1, \cdots, n$, and p is an n-ary concrete predicate (constraint) of $\mathcal{D}$. These constructs are inspired by the value restriction and the exists-in restriction. The semantics of the new operators is as follows:

> $a \in$ (every w_0 and ...and w_n is p$)^{\mathcal{I}}$
> iff, for all $b_1, \cdots, b_n \in \mathrm{dom}_{\mathcal{I}}$: $(a, b_i) \in w_i^{\mathcal{I}}$, for $i = 1, \cdots, n$, implies $(b_1, \cdots, b_n) \in p^{\mathcal{I}}$

> $a \in$ (some w_0 and ...and w_n is p$)^{\mathcal{I}}$
> iff, there are $b_1, \cdots, b_n \in \mathrm{dom}_{\mathcal{I}}$ such that $(a, b_i) \in w_i^{\mathcal{I}}$, for $i = 1, \cdots, n$, and $(b_1, \cdots, b_n) \in p^{\mathcal{I}}$

The denotation of $w_i^{\mathcal{I}}$ is defined inductively similar to relational product: $(a, c) \in [R \text{ of } S]^{\mathcal{I}}$ iff there exists a b such that $(a, b) \in S^{\mathcal{I}}$ and $(b, c) \in R^{\mathcal{I}}$.

Note that with R matching the expression "w_0 and ...and w_n" the complement-rules are also applicable to the new constructs for concrete domains. We just have to introduce a CHR to complement predicates over the concrete domain:

> $(X_1, \cdots, X_n)$:nota P   <=>
>   concrete_complement(P,Q) | $(X_1, \cdots, X_n)$:Q,

where concrete_complement is a two place predicate belonging to $\mathcal{I}$ that associates each predicate of the concrete domain with its complement wrt to $\mathrm{dom}_{\mathcal{I}}^n$.

Analogous to the value restriction (resp., the exists-in restriction) CHR we have to collect (resp., generate) objects satisfying the concrete domain predicate. This can be implemented through a fixed, finite set of CHRs that collect (resp., generate) objects according to the roles and attributes occurring in the operators "from left to right" and then restrict the collected (resp., generated) objects with the concrete predicate. To simplify the presentation we give two schemata of propagation (resp., simplification) rules. For each term of the form every w_0 and ...and w_n is P that occurs in the knowledge base or in a query we introduce a rule

$$\texttt{X:every } w_0 \texttt{ and } \dots \texttt{and } w_n \texttt{ is P,}$$
$$(\texttt{X}, \texttt{X}_{11}) : R_{11}, \cdots, (\texttt{X}_{1k_1-1}, \texttt{X}_{1k_1}) : R_{1k_1},$$
$$\dots$$
$$(\texttt{X}, \texttt{X}_{n1}) : R_{n1}, \cdots, (\texttt{X}_{nk_n-1}, \texttt{X}_{nk_n}) : R_{nk_n} \texttt{ ==> } (\texttt{X}_{1k_1}, \cdots, \texttt{X}_{nk_n}) : \texttt{P.}$$

Analogously, for a term **some** w_0 **and** ...**and** w_n **is P** we introduce a rule

$$\texttt{X:some } w_0 \texttt{ and } \dots \texttt{ and } w_n \texttt{ is P } \texttt{<=>}$$
$$(\texttt{X}_{1k_1}, \cdots, \texttt{X}_{nk_n}) : \texttt{P,}$$
$$(\texttt{X}, \texttt{X}_{11}) : R_{11}, \cdots, (\texttt{X}_{1k_1-1}, \texttt{X}_{1k_1}) : R_{1k_1},$$
$$\dots$$
$$(\texttt{X}, \texttt{X}_{n1}) : R_{n1}, \cdots, (\texttt{X}_{nk_n-1}, \texttt{X}_{n,k_n}) : R_{nk_n}.$$

For example, an expression **every f of r1 and r2 is p** leads to a rule

$$\texttt{X:every f of r1 and r2 is P,} \qquad (\texttt{X},\texttt{X}_{11}):\texttt{r1,} \qquad (\texttt{X}_{11},\texttt{X}_{12}):\texttt{f,}$$
$$(\texttt{X},\texttt{X}_{21}):\texttt{r2 ==> } (\texttt{X}_{12},\texttt{X}_{21}):\texttt{P.}$$

As a simple example of a concrete domain we take inequalities over rational numbers. The reasoning in the concrete domain itself is implemented through the following rules which find all contradictions (but do not perform all possible simplifications).

```
X > Y <=>  Y < X.
X >= Y <=>  Y =< X.
X =< X <=>    true.
X < X <=>    false.
X =< Y <=>  number_>(X,Y) |  false.
X < Y <=>  number_>=(X,Y) |  false.
X < Y, Y < Z ==>   X < Z.
X =< Y, Y < Z ==>   X < Z.
X < Y, Y =< Z ==>   X < Z.
X =< Y, Y =< Z ==>   X =< Z.
```

The guard `number_>(X,Y)` (resp., `number_>=(X,Y)`) is true if X and Y are bound to numbers x and y and $x > y$ (resp., $x \geq y$). The predicate `concrete_complement` associating concrete predicates with their complements is defined by the following clauses:

```
concrete_complement(<,>=).
concrete_complement(>=,<).
```

```
concrete_complement(=<,>).
concrete_complement(>,=<).
```

The CHRs for the new operator generates atoms of the form (x, y) : $\langle comparison\ operator\rangle$ and x : $(\langle comparison\ operator\rangle\langle number\rangle)^8$. These atoms have to be translated to the infix syntax of the concrete domain:

```
X:(< N) <=>    X < N.          (X,Y):< <=>    X < Y.
X:(> N) <=>    X > N.          (X,Y):> <=>    X > Y.
X:(>= N) <=>   X >= N.         (X,Y):=< <=>   X =< Y.
X:(=< N) <=>   X =< N.         (X,Y):>= <=>   X >= Y.
```

Example (contd): Now we can associate price and voltage with a device and require that in an electrical configuration the voltages have to be compatible.

```
attribute price.
attribute voltage.
electrical_device isa very_simple_device and
    some voltage is > 0 and some price is > 1 .
low_cost_device isa electrical_device and
    every price is < 200.
high_voltage_device isa electrical_device and
    every voltage is > 15.
electrical_config isa simple_configuration and
    every component_1 is electrical_device and
    every component_2 is electrical_device and
    every voltage of component_1 and
        voltage of component_2 is >=.           □
```

The new operator can also be used to specify upper bounds. This is illustrated by a configuration where several CPUs are plugged onto a bus with the side condition that the maximal frequency of the CPUs must be less than the frequency of the bus.

```
attribute frequency.
primitive bus.
bus_device isa simple_device and bus and
    some frequency is > 0 .
primitive cpu.
```

---

[8] The latter enables the use of numbers in concept terms.

```
cpu_device isa simple_device and cpu and
  some frequency is > 0 .
role main_device.
role sub_device.
bus_config isa configuration and
    some main_device is bus_device and
    every component is cpu_device and
    every frequency of main_device and
    frequency of sub_device is > .    □
```

19.4.3   CLP+CH(TL($\mathcal{D}$))

If we apply the CLP scheme of Höhfeld und Smolka [18] in a straight-forward
manner to A-boxes of TL($\mathcal{D}$), we obtain a CLP language with three representation
and reasoning layers [3].

Example (contd): The following CLP clauses specify the catalog of devices and
describe possible configurations that are based on this catalog.

```
catalog(dev1) :- dev1:electrical_device,
  (dev1,10):voltage, (dev1,100):price.
catalog(dev2) :- dev2:electrical_device,
  (dev2,20):voltage, (dev2,1000):price.
possible_config(C) :-
    catalog(D1), (C,D1):component_1,
    catalog(D2), (C,D2):component_2.
```

The following queries enumerate possible configurations satisfying the requirements.

```
:- possible_config(C).
:- possible_config(C), C:electrical_config.
:- possible_config(C), C:electrical_config,
   (C,D1):component_1, D1:low_cost_device,
   (C,D2):component_2, D2:high_voltage_device.
```

The first query enumerates all possible electrical configurations comprising two
devices based on the catalog, i.e., configurations consisting of two devices dev1, two
dev2, or dev1 and dev2. The second query allows for all configurations involving
dev1 and dev2, except the one where dev1 is component one and dev2 is component
two. Finally, the third query has no solution, because the catalog lists only one
low-cost device and there is no high-voltage device with a compatible voltage.   □

19.5 Conclusions

Constraint handling rules (CHRs) are a language extension for implementing user-defined constraints. Rapid prototyping of novel applications for constraint techniques is encouraged by the high level of abstraction and declarative nature of CHRs.

In this chapter we investigated terminological reasoning as constraint solving with CHRs. The terminological constraint system is related to other term domains like [27, 26, 2], which we currently implement in a similar way. The overall language has some similarities with LOGIN [1]. Flexibility was illustrated by extending the formalism and its implementation with attributes, a special quantifier and concrete domains. Applicability was illustrated by sketching a generic, hybrid knowledge base for solving configuration problems.

References

[1] H. Ait-Kaci and R. Nasr, Login: A Logic Programming Language with Built-In Inheritance, Journal of Logic Programming, 3:185-215, 1986.

[2] H. Ait-Kaci, A. Podelski and S. C. Goldstein, Order-Sorted Feature Theory Unification, DEC PRL Research Report 32, May 1993, DEC Paris Research Laboratory, France.

[3] A. Abecker and P. Hanschke. TaxLog: A flexible architecture for logic programming with structured types and constraints. In Notes of the Workshop on Constraint Processing held in conjunction with CSAM'93, Petersburg, 1993.

[4] ECLiPSe 3.4 Extensions User Manual, ECRC Munich, Germany, July 1994.

[5] R. Bajcsy (ed.), Terminological Logic I-IV, Sessions in Proceedings of the 13th International Joint Conference on Artificial Intelligence, Chambery, France, Morgan Kaufmann, 1993, pp. 662-717.

[6] F. Baader and P. Hanschke. A scheme for integrating concrete domains into concept languages. In Proceedings of the 12th International Joint Conference on Artificial Intelligence, 1991.

[7] R. J. Brachman and J. G. Schmolze. An overview of the KL-ONE knowledge representation system. Cognitive Science, 9(2):171–216, 1985.

[8] M. Buchheit, F. M. Donini and A. Schaerf. Decidable Reasoning in Terminological Knowledge Representation Systems. Journal of Artificial Intelligence Research, 1(1993):109-138.

[9] T. Frühwirth et al, Constraint Logic Programming - An Informal Introduction, Logic Programming Summer School, Zurich, Switzerland, September 1992, Springer LNCS 636, 1992 (also Technical Report ECRC-93-05, ECRC Munich, Germany, February 1993).

[10] Terminological Reasoning with Constraint Handling Rules, Workshop on Principles and Practice of Constraint Programming, Newport, Rhode Island, USA, April 1993 (revised version as Technical Report ECRC-94-06, ECRC Munich, Germany, February 1994, available by anonymous ftp from ftp.ecrc.de, directory pub/ECRC_tech_reports/reports, file ECRC-94-06.ps.Z).

[11] T. Frühwirth, Constraint Simplification Rules (former name for CHRs), Technical Report ECRC-92-18, ECRC Munich, Germany, July 1992 (revised version of Internal Report ECRC-LP-63, October 1991), available by anonymous ftp from ftp.ecrc.de, directory pub/ECRC_tech_reports/reports, file ECRC-92-18.ps.Z.

[12] T. Frühwirth, Temporal Reasoning with Constraint Handling Rules, Technical Report ECRC-94-05, ECRC Munich, Germany, February 1994. (first published as CORE-93-08, January 1993), available by anonymous ftp from ftp.ecrc.de, directory pub/ECRC_tech_reports/reports, file ECRC-94-05.ps.Z.

[13] S. Haridi and S. Janson, Kernel Andorra Prolog and its Computation Model, Seventh International Conference on Logic Programming, MIT Press, 1990, pp. 31-46.

[14] P. Hanschke. Specifying role interaction in concept languages. In Third International Conference on Principles of Knowledge Representation and Reasoning (KR '92), October 1992.

[15] P. Hanschke. A declarative integration of terminological, constraint-based, data-driven, and goal-directed reasoning. PhD Thesis at University of Kaiserslautern, Germany, July 1993.

[16] Eine homogene Implementierungsebene fuer einen hybriden Wissensrepraesentationsformalismus, Master Thesis, in German, University of Kaiserslautern, Germany, April 1993.

[17] B. Hollunder. Hybrid inferences in KL-ONE-based knowledge representation systems. In 14th German Workshop on Artificial Intelligence (GWAI-90), volume 251, pages 38–47. Springer, 1990.

[18] M. Höhfeld and G. Smolka, Definite Relations over Constraint Languages. LILOG Report 53, IBM Deutschland, West Germany, October 1988.

[19] J. Jaffar et al., The CLP(R) Language and System, ACM Transactions on programming Languages and Systems, Vol.14:3, July 1992, pp. 339-395.

[20] J. Jaffar and J.-L. Lassez, Constraint Logic Programming, ACM 14th POPL 87, Munich, Germany, January 1987, pp. 111-119.

[21] J. Jaffar and M. Maher, Constraint Logic Programming: A Survey, Journal of Logic Programming, to appear.

[22] V. A. Saraswat, Concurrent Constraint Programming, MIT Press, Cambridge, 1993.

[23] M. Schmidt-Schauß and G. Smolka. Attributive concept descriptions with complements. In Journal of Artificial Intelligence, 47, 1991.

[24] E. Shapiro, The Family of Concurrent Logic Programming Languages, ACM Computing Surveys, 21(3):413-510, September 1989.

[25] G. Smolka, Residuation and Guarded Rules for Constraint Logic Programming, Digital Equipment Paris Research Laboratory Research Report, France, June 1991.

[26] G. Smolka, Feature Constraint Logics for Unification Grammars, Journal Of Logic Programming, 12:51-87 (1992).

[27] J. Sowa (ed.), Principles of Semantic Networks, Morgan Kaufmann, 1991.

[28] P. Van Hentenryck, Constraint satisfaction in Logic Programming, MIT Press, Cambridge, 1989.

[29] P. Van Hentenryck, Constraint Logic Programming, The Knowledge Engineering Review, Vol 6:3, 1991, pp 151-194.

VI COMPUTER GRAPHICS

20 The SkyBlue Constraint Solver and Its Applications

Michael Sannella

Abstract

The SkyBlue constraint solver uses multi-way local propagation to efficiently maintain constraints organized in a constraint hierarchy. As individual constraints are added and removed, SkyBlue executes *method* procedures associated with each constraint to incrementally resatisfy the constraints. SkyBlue is a successor to the DeltaBlue algorithm, which has two significant limitations: cycles of constraints are prohibited, and constraint methods can only have a single output variable. SkyBlue relaxes these restrictions, satisfying cycles of constraints by calling external solvers and supporting multi-output methods.

This paper compares SkyBlue to other constraint solvers, describes the SkyBlue algorithm and discusses several applications that have been built using Sky-Blue. The SkyBlue algorithm description introduces several new concepts including *method vines* (used to select which methods to execute) and *walkbounds* (a generalization of DeltaBlue's *walkabout strengths*).

20.1 Introduction

User interface toolkits can use constraint solvers to maintain consistency between application data and a graphical display of that data, to maintain consistency among multiple views of data, and to maintain layout relationships among graphical objects. By giving the system responsibility for maintaining the various relationships in a user interface, the programmer is freed from the tedious and error-prone task of maintaining these relationships by hand, making it easier to develop and maintain complex graphical user interfaces. Many user interface development systems have provided integrated constraint solvers, including Garnet [14], Rendezvous [11], and ThingLab II [13]. References [2, 6] contain additional references to constraint-based systems.

One important type of constraint solver accepts a set of linear or non-linear relations over real-valued variables, and sets the variables to values that satisfy the relations. These solvers have been used in the user interfaces for surface modeling tools and graphic editors [8, 10]. However, these constraint solvers are limited to problems where the constraints can be expressed as numeric relations.

More general constraints can be handled by *local propagation* solvers that maintain networks of constraints by calling *method* procedures associated with each constraint. When a constrained variable is changed, a series of methods is executed to propagate the change to other variables and resatisfy the constraints. Often, local propagation is more efficient than numeric solution techniques for solving a given set of constraints. There are two main types of local propagation solvers: one-way and multi-way. One-way solvers allow each constraint to have a single method, that satisfies the constraint in one direction [12, 20]. For example, a one-way solver might represent the constraint $A + B = C$ by the single method $C := A + B$, and execute this method to reset C if A or B is changed. Multi-way solvers allow a constraint to have multiple methods, which the solver can use to satisfy the constraint in different directions [18, 19].

Multi-way solvers are more powerful than one-way solvers, but it may be difficult for the user to understand and control the solutions produced without understanding the implementation of the solver. One way to deal with this problem is to organize the constraints into a constraint hierarchy, where each constraint is labeled with a strength that indicates how important it is to satisfy the constraint [2]. Constraint hierarchies can be used to specify declaratively which solution should be produced without regard for the solver implementation. This paper describes the SkyBlue constraint solver, a multi-way local propagation solver that maintains constraint hierarchies. The following sections compare SkyBlue to the related DeltaBlue algorithm, explain the concepts of method graphs and constraint hierarchies, present a high-level description of the SkyBlue algorithm and examine techniques used to improve its performance. Finally, several applications that currently use SkyBlue are described. More information on SkyBlue, including complete pseudocode, is available in other papers [15, 16]. Contact the author for information on implementations of SkyBlue.

20.2   DeltaBlue and SkyBlue

SkyBlue is a successor to the DeltaBlue algorithm [6, 18], which was used as the basis for the ThingLab II user interface development environment [13]. DeltaBlue has two significant limitations: cycles in the graph of constraints and variables are prohibited (if a cycle is found, an error is signaled and the cycle is broken by removing a constraint) and constraint methods can only have one output variable.[1]

Local propagation techniques do not work well with cycles of constraints. It is

---

[1]Reference [7] presents an algorithm that solves constraint hierarchies with single-output methods, but also allows constructing cycles. This algorithm is less efficient than DeltaBlue in many cases because DeltaBlue uses walkabout strengths (Section 20.6.4) when selecting methods to execute.

generally not possible to satisfy the constraints in a cycle by executing a series of constraint methods. Unlike DeltaBlue, SkyBlue allows cycles of constraints to be constructed without signaling an error. If SkyBlue finds a cycle, it càn call more powerful, specialized constraint solvers (*cycle solvers*) to satisfy the constraints in the cycle. For example, if all of the constraints in a cycle are linear equations, our SkyBlue implementation calls a cycle solver that uses Gaussian elimination to satisfy the constraints in the cycle, and uses local propagation to satisfy the rest of the constraints.

DeltaBlue only supports constraint methods with a single output variable. For example, a constraint $A + B = C$ may be satisfied using a method that sets C (i.e., $C := A + B$), but DeltaBlue would not allow a method to set *both* A and B. SkyBlue supports methods with multiple output variables, which are useful in many situations. For example, suppose the variables X and Y represent the Cartesian coordinates of a point, and the variables ρ and θ represent the polar coordinates of this same point. To keep these two representations consistent, one can define a constraint with one method calculating X and Y from ρ and θ, and another method calculating ρ and θ from X and Y. Multi-output methods are also useful for accessing the elements of compound data structures. For example, one could unpack a compound Cartesian point object into two variables using a constraint with methods $(X, Y) := (Point.X, Point.Y)$ and $Point := CreatePoint(X, Y)$.

The SkyBlue algorithm is substantially different from DeltaBlue. To support multi-output methods and cycles, SkyBlue uses a backtracking search to construct *method vines* when selecting methods to execute (Section 20.5.2) and generalizes the concept of *walkabout strengths* used in DeltaBlue (Section 20.6.4).

Support for cycles and multi-output methods introduces a performance issue. For sets of constraints that DeltaBlue can handle (no cycles, single-output methods), the worst-case time complexity of SkyBlue for adding or removing a constraint is linear in the number of constraints in the set.[2] However, it has been proven that supporting cycles and multi-output methods is NP-complete [13]. Special examples have been constructed where the time for SkyBlue to add or remove a particular constraint is exponential in the number of constraints in the set. These test cases are highly unusual, and it is unlikely that similar sets of constraints would be constructed in a real application. In actual use, SkyBlue typically examines only a small subset of the constraints when a constraint is added or removed, and the performance is sub-linear in the number of constraints in the set.

---

[2] This complexity result assumes that the number of constraint strengths, the maximum number of variables per constraint, and the maximum number of methods per constraint are all bounded by small constants. This has been true in existing SkyBlue applications.

20.3   Method Graphs

A SkyBlue constraint is represented by one or more *methods*. Each method is a procedure that reads the values of a subset of the constraint's variables (the method's *input variables*) and calculates values for the remaining variables (the method's *output variables*) that satisfy the constraint. SkyBlue can satisfy a set of such constraints by selecting one method for each constraint, and executing the selected methods. For example, given the constraint $A + B = C$ (represented by three methods $C := A + B$, $A := C - B$, and $B := C - A$) and the constraint $C + D = E$ (represented by three analogous methods), the two constraints could be satisfied by executing the methods $C := A + B$ and $E := C + D$ in order.

The meaning of a SkyBlue constraint is defined by the set of methods for that constraint. It is acceptable to define a constraint such that some of the constrained variables are input by all of a constraint's methods (read-only variables) or output by all of the methods (write-only variables). In particular, it is possible to define a one-way constraint by only defining one method for a constraint. When SkyBlue satisfies a set of constraints, the resulting variable values are determined by the methods that it executes. One exception occurs when cycle solvers satisfy the constraints around a cycle, using additional information about the constraints in addition to the constraint methods.

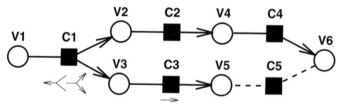

Figure 20.1
A method graph.

To satisfy a set of constraints, SkyBlue chooses one method to execute from each constraint, the *selected method* of the constraint. The set of constraints and variables, together with the selected methods, form a directed *method graph* (or *mgraph*). In this paper, mgraphs are drawn with circles representing variables and squares representing constraints (Figure 20.1). Lines are drawn between each constraint and its variables. If a constraint has a selected method, arrows indicate the outputs of the selected method. If a constraint has no selected method, it is linked to its variables with dashed lines.

If a constraint doesn't have methods in all possible directions ($C3$) or has multi-output methods ($C1$), small diagrams beneath the constraint indicate the possible methods.

The following terminology will be used in this paper. If a constraint has a selected method in an mgraph, then the constraint is *enforced* in that mgraph, otherwise it is *unenforced*. Assigning a method (no method) as the selected method of a constraint is known as *enforcing* (*unenforcing*) the constraint. A variable that is an output of a constraint's selected method is *determined* by that constraint, otherwise it is *undetermined*. Following the arrows leads to *downstream* variables and constraints. Following the arrows in the reverse direction leads to *upstream* variables and constraints.

If two or more selected methods output to the same variable, this is a *method conflict*. Method conflicts are undesirable: Suppose that constraints X and Y both have selected methods that output to V. If we satisfy X by executing its selected method (setting V), and then satisfy Y by executing its selected method (again setting V), then X might no longer be satisfied. To avoid this situation, SkyBlue chooses selected methods so there are no method conflicts in the mgraph.

If an mgraph has no method conflicts and no directed cycles, then it can be used to satisfy the enforced constraints by executing the selected methods so any determined variable is set before it is read (i.e., executing the methods in topological order). For example, all of the enforced constraints in Figure 20.1 can be satisfied by executing the selected methods for $C1$–$C4$ in order.

If there are directed cycles in the mgraph, it is not possible to topologically sort the selected methods. In this case, SkyBlue collapses the selected methods in each directed cycle into a single large method. Each cycle may be either a simple cycle, or a set of constraints containing multiple simple cycles (i.e., a strongly connected component in the directed graph). SkyBlue processes the list of methods and collapsed cycles in topological order, executing method procedures and calling cycle solvers to satisfy the constraints in collapsed cycles.

20.4 Constraint Hierarchies

An important property of any constraint solver is how it behaves when the set of constraints is overconstrained (there is no solution that satisfies all of the constraints) or underconstrained (there are multiple solutions). If the solver is maintaining constraints within a user interface application, it is not acceptable to handle these situations by signaling an error or halting. The theory of *constraint hierarchies*

[2] provides a way to specify declaratively how a solver should behave in these situations. A constraint hierarchy is a set of constraints, each labeled with a *strength*, indicating how important it is to satisfy each constraint.[3] Given an overconstrained constraint hierarchy, a constraint solver may leave weaker constraints unsatisfied in order to satisfy stronger constraints. If a hierarchy is underconstrained, the solver can choose any of the possible solutions. The user can control which solution is chosen by adding weak *stay* constraints to specify variables whose value should not be changed.

The SkyBlue solver uses the constraint strengths to construct *method-graph-better* (or *MGB*) mgraphs. An mgraph is MGB if none of the unenforced constraints could be enforced without introducing a method conflict by choosing different selected methods for the enforced constraints with the same or stronger strength and unenforcing weaker constraints. By constructing MGB mgraphs, SkyBlue ensures that weaker constraints are left unenforced if necessary to enforce stronger constraints. However, weaker constraints can influence which selected methods are used to enforce stronger constraints. As an example, consider the mgraph in Figure 20.2a. This mgraph is not MGB because the *strong* constraint $C2$ could be enforced by choosing the method that outputs to $V2$ and unenforcing the *medium* constraint $C3$, producing Figure 20.2b. Actually, this mgraph is not MGB either since $C3$ could be enforced by unenforcing $C4$, producing Figure 20.2c. This mgraph is MGB since the only unenforced constraint ($C4$) cannot be enforced without introducing a method conflict or unenforcing equal-strength or stronger constraints.

There may be multiple MGB mgraphs for a given set of constraints. Figure 20.2d shows another MGB mgraph for the same constraints. Given these constraints, SkyBlue could construct either one of these mgraphs. The constraint strengths could be modified to favor one alternative over the other. For example, if the strength of $C1$ was changed to *strong*, the only MGB mgraph would be the one in Figure 20.2e. One way for the programmer to control the mgraphs constructed is to add *stay* constraints that have a single null method with no inputs and a single output. A stay constraint specifies that its output variable should not be changed.

The theory of constraint hierarchies describes several different ways to define which variable values "best" satisfy a constraint hierarchy [2]. For many sets of constraints, MGB mgraphs compute *locally-predicate-better* solutions to the constraint hierarchy according to this theory [13, 15].

---

[3]SkyBlue can handle any number of different constraint strengths. Examples in this paper use the strengths *max*, *strong*, *medium*, *weak*, and *min*, in order from strongest to weakest.

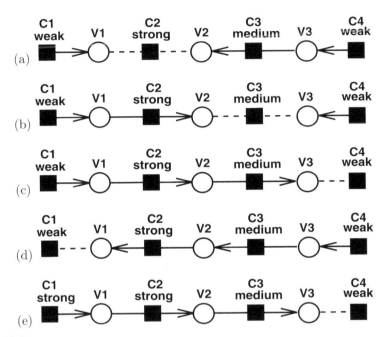

Figure 20.2
MGB and non-MGB Method Graphs.

20.5   The SkyBlue Algorithm

The SkyBlue constraint solver maintains a set of constraints by constructing an MGB mgraph and executing the selected methods to satisfy the enforced constraints. Initially, the MGB mgraph is empty. SkyBlue is invoked by calling two procedures that add a constraint and remove a constraint from the mgraph. Whenever a constraint is added or removed, SkyBlue incrementally updates the mgraph to be MGB and executes the selected methods to resatisfy the enforced constraints.

The MGB mgraph determines how to calculate some variable values from others, but does not specify the values of the undetermined variables. The process of setting variables is a little complicated, since setting a variable that is determined by a method may cause the corresponding constraint to be unsatisfied. To set a variable, one must add and remove a constraint with a single method that sets the variable to the specified value. If the constraint is strong enough, it will be enforced and SkyBlue will propagate the new value to other variables.

20.5.1   Adding and Removing Constraints

SkyBlue performs the same sequence of three steps when adding or removing a constraint. First, SkyBlue adds or removes the specified constraint from the mgraph. If a constraint is being added, it is added as an unenforced constraint. Second, SkyBlue repeatedly tries to enforce each unenforced constraint by constructing an mvine (Section 20.5.2). It has been proven that if no unenforced constraints are *mvine-enforcible* (can be enforced by constructing an mvine), then the mgraph is MGB [15]. Third, SkyBlue executes the selected methods in the mgraph to satisfy the enforced constraints, topologically sorting the selected methods and collapsed cycles as described in Section 20.3.

Each time an unenforced constraint is successfully enforced by constructing a mvine, one or more weaker constraints may become unenforced. These newly-unenforced constraints must be examined to determine whether they are mvine-enforcible. It may be possible to enforce these constraints by constructing a mvine, adding still weaker constraints to the set of unenforced constraints, but this process cannot go on indefinitely. Eventually the second step will stop with a set of unenforced constraints that are not mvine-enforcible.

As an example, suppose that SkyBlue has just added $C2$ (unenforced) to the mgraph shown in Figure 20.2a. One way that an mvine could be constructed is by enforcing $C2$ with the method that outputs to $V2$ and unenforcing $C3$ (20.2b). Given this mgraph, the second step would try constructing an mvine to enforce $C3$, possibly by unenforcing $C4$ (20.2c). It is not possible to construct an mvine to enforce $C4$ so the second step terminates. This mgraph is MGB. Alternatively, if the first mvine had been constructed by unenforcing $C1$ then the MGB mgraph of Figure 20.2d would have been produced immediately and the second step would not have been able to enforce $C1$.

20.5.2   Constructing Method Vines

The SkyBlue algorithm is based on enforcing an unenforced constraint by changing the selected methods of constraints with the same or stronger strength and/or unenforcing constraints with weaker strengths. SkyBlue uses a backtracking depth-first search to enforce unenforced constraints by constructing a *method vine* (or *mvine*).

To construct an mvine, SkyBlue selects a method for the constraint it is trying to enforce (the mvine root constraint). If this method has a method conflict with the selected methods of other enforced constraints, SkyBlue unenforces these conflicting constraints. If a conflicting constraint is equal-strength or stronger than the root constraint, SkyBlue enforces it with another selected method. If the new selected methods for the conflicting constraints conflict with yet other enforced constraints, these new conflicting constraints are handled in the same way, and so on. This process extends through the mgraph, building a "vine" of newly-chosen selected methods growing from the root constraint.

At any point during this process, SkyBlue maintains a set of constraints that are "in the mvine." Initially, this set just includes the root constraint. When constraints are found that conflict with constraints in the mvine, they are unenforced, and added to the mvine. Any unenforced constraints in the mvine that are weaker than the root constraint are just left unenforced. However, any unenforced constraints in the mvine that are equal-strength or stronger than the root constraint (including the root constraint itself) must be enforced. This is done by enforcing such a constraint with one of its methods, collecting other conflicting constraints, and so on. When all of the constraints in the mvine that are equal-strength or stronger than the root constraint are enforced, and there are no method conflicts with other constraints, then the mvine is complete.

When SkyBlue enforces an unenforced constraint in the mvine, it does not select any method that conflicts with the selected methods of the enforced constraints in the mvine. This prevents an infinite loop from occurring where SkyBlue would enforce the constraint X and unenforce the conflicting constraint Y, then enforce Y while unenforcing X, etc. If all of the possible methods conflict with other constraints in the mvine, then SkyBlue backtracks: previously-enforced constraints are unenforced, conflicting constraints are removed from the mvine and enforced with their original methods, and the mvine is extended using other selected methods for the mvine constraints. This backtracking process may unwind the search all the way to the beginning, choosing another selected method for the root constraint. If no method can be chosen for the root constraint that allows a conflict-free mvine to be constructed, then the mgraph is not changed.

Figure 20.3 shows an example of constructing an mvine to enforce $C1$. The newly-selected methods are drawn with thicker lines. Suppose SkyBlue starts with the mgraph of Figure 20.3a. First, $C1$ is enforced with its only method so it determines $V1$, and $C2$ is unenforced and added to the mvine (20.3b). Since $C2$ is stronger than the root constraint $C1$, it will have to be enforced in the mvine. The method that outputs to $V1$ conflicts with $C1$, so $C2$ is enforced with its other method, and $C4$ is unenforced and added to the mvine (20.3c). Since $C4$ is stronger than the root, it will have to be enforced. Suppose SkyBlue enforces $C4$ with the method that sets $V4$, unenforcing $C3$ (20.3d). Since $C3$ is stronger than the root, it will have to be enforced. Both of its methods conflict with other constraints in the mvine

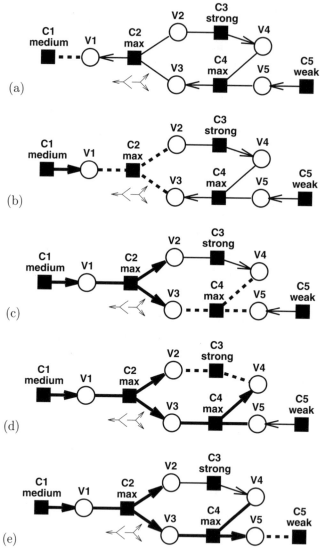

Figure 20.3
Constructing an mvine.

($C2$ and $C4$), so SkyBlue backtracks, removing $C3$ from the mvine, enforcing it with its original method, and unenforcing $C4$. It is still necessary to enforce $C4$, so SkyBlue enforces $C4$ with another method, unenforcing $C5$ and adding it to the mvine (20.3e). Now, $C5$ is the only unenforced constraint in the mvine, and it is weaker than the root constraint, so SkyBlue has successfully constructed an mvine.

20.6   Performance Techniques

The SkyBlue algorithm described in Section 20.5 works correctly, but its performance suffers as the mgraph becomes very large. This happens because larger constraint method may contain greater numbers of unenforced constraints that SkyBlue has to try enforcing, and each attempt to construct an mvine may involve searching through more enforced constraints. This section describes techniques used in SkyBlue to improve its performance with larger mgraphs.

20.6.1   Collecting Downstream Unenforced Constraints

If the mgraph is MGB and a constraint is added or removed, any unenforced constraints in a subgraph unconnected to the added or removed constraint clearly cannot be enforced. It is possible to be more selective: Whenever SkyBlue adds a constraint cn and an mvine is successfully constructed to enforce it, it is sufficient to examine the "redetermined" variables whose determining constraint has changed while constructing the mvine, and any variables downstream from the redetermined variables, and collect any unenforced constraints that constrain these variables. Whenever SkyBlue removes an enforced constraint cn, it is sufficient to examine the variables previously determined by cn, and any downstream variables, and collect any unenforced constraints that constrain these variables.

Whenever SkyBlue successfully constructs an mvine, additional unenforced constraints can be added to the set of collected unenforced constraints by scanning downstream from the newly-redetermined variables. As each of these constraints is processed (it is enforced, or it is determined that it cannot be enforced) it can be removed from the set. When the set is empty there are no more unenforced constraints that can be enforced.

A similar technique can be used to reduce the number of methods executed. Rather than executing the selected methods for all enforced constraints in the mgraph, it is only necessary to collect and execute the selected methods and downstream methods of newly-enforced constraints, and downstream methods of redetermined variables.

20.6.2   Collecting Weak Unenforced Constraints

It has been proven that, whenever an mvine is successfully constructed, the only unenforced constraints that could have become mvine-enforcible are those constraints
that are strictly weaker than the root constraint of the mvine [15]. SkyBlue uses
this fact to extend the technique of Section 20.6.1: After an mvine is constructed,
when SkyBlue traces downstream from redetermined variables to collect unenforced
constraints, it only collects unenforced constraints weaker than the mvine root.

20.6.3   Sorting Unenforced Constraints

Whenever SkyBlue takes an unenforced constraint from the set of collected unenforced constraints, and tries to construct an mvine to enforce it, it always selects
the strongest constraint from the set. As a result, no unenforced constraint will
be processed more than once while updating the mgraph to be MGB. Consider:
each time SkyBlue successfully constructs an mvine, it only collects unenforced
constraints strictly weaker than the root of the mvine (Section 20.6.2). If the set of
collected unenforced constraints is processed in decreasing order of strength, once a
constraint with a given strength is processed, no constraints with the same strength
or stronger will ever be added to the set, including that constraint itself. Therefore,
each constraint will only be processed once.

20.6.4   Walkabout Strengths and Walkbounds

When SkyBlue constructs an mvine as described in Section 20.5.2, it repeatedly
enforces an unenforced constraint in the mvine, unenforces conflicting constraints,
and adds them to the mvine. Figure 20.4a shows the situation where the mvine
constraint $C1$ is being enforced with a selected method that determines $V1$, which
is currently determined by the selected method of $C2$. In order to construct a
complete conflict-free mvine, it is necessary to change the mgraph so that $C2$ no
longer determines $V1$. SkyBlue does this by unenforcing $C2$ (20.4b), adding it to
the mvine, and trying to enforce it with another method (if it is not weaker than
the root constraint).

Figure 20.4
Selecting a method for $C1$ and unenforcing $C2$.

In this situation, SkyBlue assumes that it will be possible to change the mgraph
so that $C2$ no longer determines $V1$, without unenforcing any constraints that are

equal-strength or stronger than the mvine root. This assumption may be wrong for various reasons. $C2$ may be such a stronger constraint, and may have no other methods. Stronger constraints with no alternate methods may appear when the mvine is extended after adding $C2$. The constraints in the extended mvine may conflict with each other. In these cases, SkyBlue will eventually backtrack to this point, and choose another selected method for $C1$.

If SkyBlue could predict that it would not be able to change the mgraph so that $C2$ no longer determines $V1$, unless it unenforces constraints that are equal-strength or stronger than the mvine root, then it could immediately reject $C1$'s new selected method without trying to extend the mvine.

The DeltaBlue algorithm predicts whether a constraint can be enforced by using *walkabout strengths* (or *walkstrengths*) [6]. A variable's walkstrength is the strength of the weakest constraint that would have to be unenforced so that the variable is no longer determined by its current determining constraint. This could be the strength of the constraint that currently determines the variable, or the strength of a weaker constraint elsewhere in the mgraph that could be unenforced after switching the selected methods of other constraints. If the variable is not currently determined by any constraint then the walkstrength is defined as *min*, a special strength weaker than any constraint. A variable will also have a walkstrength of *min* if it can be left undetermined by switching selected methods without unenforcing any constraints.[4]

DeltaBlue associates a walkstrength with each variable, and updates this information whenever the mgraph is changed. The walkstrength of a variable determined by a constraint can be calculated from the constraint's strength, its methods, and the walkstrengths of the rest of the constraint's variables, calling `set_walkstrength` in Figure 20.7. This calculates the walkstrength by finding the weakest strength among the constraint's strength and the walkstrengths of the outputs of the unselected methods.

DeltaBlue updates all of the variable walkstrengths by setting the walkstrengths of undetermined variables to *min* and processing each enforced constraint in topological order to set the walkstrength of the variable it determines. For example, Figure 20.5 shows an mgraph with each variable labeled with its walkstrength. These walkstrengths could be computed by setting $V1$'s walkstrength to *min* (since it is undetermined) and calling `set_walkstrength` on $C1$–$C7$ in order. Note that $V5$'s walkstrength is *max* rather than *min* because $C4$ only has one method: if it

---

[4]Another interpretation of the *min* strength is that each variable has an implicit stay constraint with a strength of *min*, which specifies that the variable value doesn't change unless a stronger constraint determines it.

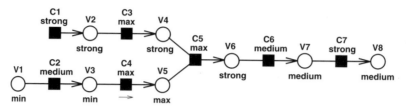

Figure 20.5
A method graph with variable walkstrengths.

had another method that output to $V3$, the walkstrength of $V5$ (and $V6$, $V7$, $V8$) would be *min*.

There is a problem with using walkstrengths in SkyBlue because methods may have multiple outputs, and mgraphs can contain directed cycles of methods. Consider the mgraph of Figure 20.6. DeltaBlue would correctly calculate the walkstrengths of $V1$–$V5$ to be *min*. But what about $V6$? The walkstrengths of $V4$ and $V5$ imply that $V6$ should have a walkstrength of *min*, since the other (multi-output) method for $C5$ can be chosen that outputs to $V4$ and $V5$, which both have *min* walkstrengths. However, it is not possible for a method to set *both* $V4$ and $V5$ simultaneously, without unenforcing one of the *max*-strength constraints. Simply switching methods for $C1$, $C2$, $C3$, and $C4$ would lead to a method conflict with both $C1$ and $C2$ determining $V1$. To calculate the walkstrength of $V6$, more information is needed than just the walkstrengths of $V4$ and $V5$.

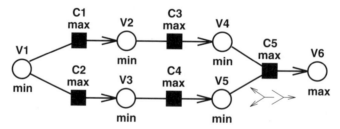

Figure 20.6
DeltaBlue cannot calculate $V6$'s walkstrength correctly.

Unlike DeltaBlue, SkyBlue does not calculate the exact walkstrength for every variable. Instead, SkyBlue associates with every variable a *walkbound*, defined as any strength that is equal to or weaker than the walkstrength of the variable. Note that the walkbound of a variable is not uniquely defined. In particular, *min* is a correct walkbound for any variable in any conflict-free mgraph.

Walkbounds can be calculated using local information to each constraint, even if

```
set_walkstrength(cn)
    out_var := cn.selected_method.output
    min_strength := cn.strength
    For mt in cn.methods do
        If mt.output ≠ out_var then
            max_strength := mt.output.walk_strength
            If weaker(max_strength, min_strength) then
                min_strength := max_strength
    out_var.walk_strength := min_strength

set_walkbounds(cn)
    current_outputs := cn.selected_method.outputs
    For out_var in current_outputs do
        min_strength := cn.strength
        For mt in cn.methods do
            If out_var ∉ mt.outputs then
                max_strength := max_out(mt, current_outputs)
                If weaker(max_strength, min_strength) then
                    min_strength := max_strength
        out_var.walkbound := min_strength

max_out(mt, current_outputs): Strength
    max_strength := min
    For var in mt.outputs do
        If var ∉ current_outputs then
            If weaker(max_strength, var.walkbound) then
                max_strength := var.walkbound
    Return max_strength
```

Figure 20.7
Pseudocode for computing walkabout strengths and walkbounds.

there are multi-output methods and cycles in the mgraph. The procedure
1zset_walkbounds in Figure 20.7 sets the walkbounds of the outputs of an enforced
constraint's selected method. For each of these output variables, set_walkbounds
examines the alternate methods of the constraint that don't output to it (and thus
could be used to enforce the constraint while leaving this variable undetermined).

For each of these methods the strongest walkbound among the method's outputs is found (by calling `max_out`). Note that `set_walkbounds` may ignore some of the alternate method outputs. If an output is currently being determined by the constraint then no additional constraints would need to be unenforced for the constraint to determine this variable.

SkyBlue updates the variable walkbounds whenever the mgraph is changed by using a scheme similar to the one for executing selected methods (Section 20.3). First, the walkbounds of all undetermined variables are set to *min*. Then, all directed cycles in the mgraph are collapsed, and SkyBlue processes the list of methods and collapsed cycles in topological order. Methods are processed by examining the strength and other methods of the method's constraint, much like DeltaBlue.[5] Collapsed cycles are processed by setting the walkbounds for all of the variables determined by the cycle constraints to *min* (guaranteed to be a correct walkbound), and processing each of the constraints in the cycle. SkyBlue applies a version of the technique from Section 20.6.1, processing only the enforced constraints downstream of the redetermined variables.

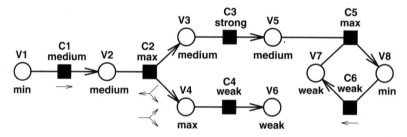

Figure 20.8
A method graph with variable walkbounds.

Figure 20.8 demonstrates how SkyBlue calculates walkbounds. The variables are labeled with walkbounds calculated by setting $V1$'s walkbound to *min*, calling `set_walkbounds` to process $C1$–$C4$, and handling the cycle by setting the walkbounds of $V7$ and $V8$ to *min* and calling `set_walkbounds` to process $C5$ and $C6$. Note that the walkbound of $V4$ is *max* because the unselected method for $C2$ also outputs to this variable. Also note that the walkbound of $V8$ would be set to *weak* rather than *min* if $C6$ had been processed before $C5$, but in either case these are correct walkbounds.

---

[5] If all of the methods of a constraint have single outputs, `set_walkbounds` calculates the same values as `set_walkstrength`. Therefore, for constraint sets without cycles or multi-output methods, the walkbounds will be equal to the walkstrengths.

SkyBlue uses variable walkbounds to reject methods when constructing an mvine: If any of the outputs of a method have walkbounds equal to or stronger than the root constraint, then it is not possible to complete the mvine using this method. The use of walkbounds cannot eliminate all of the backtracking during mvine construction but it can reduce it considerably.

20.7   SkyBlue Applications

The SkyBlue constraint solver has been implemented in several languages, and a number of applications have been developed using it, including an implementation of the Kaleidoscope language [5], the CoolDraw drawing program [4], the TBAG 3D animation system [3], and the VB2 virtual reality system [9]. The following subsections describe two applications in detail, emphasizing how the applications take advantage of the unique features of SkyBlue.

20.7.1   Multi-Garnet

Garnet is a widely-used user interface toolkit that supports one-way required constraints (no hierarchies) [14]. The Multi-Garnet package uses the SkyBlue solver to add support for multi-way constraints and constraint hierarchies to Garnet [15, 17].

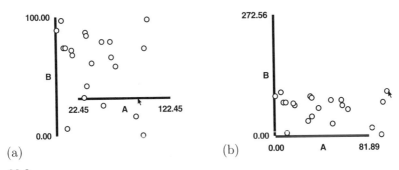

Figure 20.9
Two views of a scatterplot built in Multi-Garnet.

Figure 20.9 shows two pictures of a graphic user interface constructed in Multi-Garnet: a scatterplot displaying a set of points. SkyBlue constraints are used to specify the relationship between the screen position of each point, the corresponding data value, and the positions and range numbers of the axes. As the points and axes are moved with the mouse, SkyBlue maintains the constraints so that the plot continues to display the same data. When an object is moved there may be many possible ways to satisfy the constraints. The scatterplot user interface specifies the behavior of different interactions by adding additional stay constraints to determine which variables are changed to maintain the constraints. During a Move-Axis interaction (Figure 20.9a), dragging one of the axis bars with the mouse will move it without changing the scatterplot points or the other axis. The axis range numbers change to be consistent with the position of the axis relative to the point cloud. This allows the axis to be used to examine the value of a data point. During a Scale-Points interaction (Figure 20.9b), dragging a point with the mouse will stretch the point cloud. The axes will not move but their range numbers will change to be consistent with the position and size of the point cloud.

The scatterplot application exploits many of the features of SkyBlue. SkyBlue resatisfies the constraints quickly enough to allow continuous interaction. The constraints are satisfied with different methods during different interactions. Finally, the scatterplot uses constraints with multi-output methods. This application could have been written entirely in Garnet, using one-way constraints to connect the different elements, but each interaction mode would have had to enable exactly the right set of one-way constraints to propagate the values correctly. In contrast, the Multi-Garnet scatterplot program declares the relationships between the scatterplot elements once and uses the SkyBlue constraint solver to choose which methods to execute to maintain the constraints. New interaction modes are specified by adding stay constraints to control constraint propagation.

20.7.2   The Pika Simulation System

SkyBlue is being used as an equation manipulation tool in a version of the Pika simulation system [1]. Pika constructs simulations in domains such as electronics or thermodynamics by collecting algebraic and differential equations representing relationships between object attributes. For example, in a simulation of an electronic circuit, one equation would relate the voltage across and the current through a particular resister. Pika processes these equations and passes them to a numerical integrator that calculates how the object attributes change over time.

Pika uses SkyBlue to manipulate the collected equations. Each equation is expressed as a SkyBlue constraint with one method for each possible output variable. SkyBlue constructs an MGB mgraph, and topologically orders the selected methods. Pika uses the ordered list of selected methods to set up the numerical integrator. Note that Pika does not use SkyBlue to maintain the constraints (equations) directly, but rather uses it to process the equations for the numerical integrator, which will maintain the equations during the simulation.

During equation processing, Pika takes advantage of SkyBlue's support for constraint hierarchies to influence the methods selected. There may be many possible ways to directionalize a given set of equations, leaving different sets of variables constant. Within the simulation, it may be preferable to keep some variables constant over others. This is represented by adding weak stay constraints to variables that should remain constant. SkyBlue will choose an equation ordering that leaves these variables constant, if possible.

Pika uses SkyBlue's facilities for incrementally adding and removing constraints to update the sorted list of equation methods as equations are added and removed. This may occur while the simulation is executing. For example, when the temperature of a container of water increases and it starts to boil, a different set of equations describing its behavior is activated.

Often there are cycles in the sets of selected methods produced by SkyBlue. Currently, Pika handles these cycles by extracting the equations in the cycle, and passing them to an symbolic mathematics system which tries to transform them to a non-cyclic set of equations. Pika replaces the cycle of equations by the reduced equations, SkyBlue (incrementally) updates the mgraph, and Pika processes the new ordered list of selected methods.

Acknowledgments

Thanks to Alan Borning, Ralph Hill, and Brad Vander Zanden for useful discussions and comments on earlier versions of this paper. This research has been supported in part by the U.S. National Science Foundation under grants IRI-9102938, CCR-9107395, IRI-9302249, and CCR-9402551.

References

[1] Franz G. Amador. *Self-Explanatory Simulation for an Electronic Encyclopedia*. PhD thesis, Department of Computer Science and Engineering, University of Washington, June 1994.

[2] Alan Borning, Bjorn Freeman-Benson, and Molly Wilson. Constraint Hierarchies. *Lisp and Symbolic Computation*, 5(3):223–270, September 1992.

[3] Conal Elliott, Greg Schechter, Ricky Yeung, and Salim Abi-Ezzi. TBAG: A High Level Framework for Interactive, Animated 3D Graphics Applications. In *SIGGRAPH '94 Conference Proceedings*, Orlando, Florida, July 1994. ACM.

[4] Bjorn Freeman-Benson. Converting an Existing User Interface to Use Constraints. In *Proceedings of the ACM Symposium on User Interface Software and Technology*, pages 207–215, Atlanta, Georgia, November 1993.

[5] Bjorn Freeman-Benson and Alan Borning. The Design and Implementation of Kaleidoscope'90, A Constraint Imperative Programming Language. In *Proceedings of the IEEE Computer Society International Conference on Computer Languages*, pages 174–180, April 1992.

[6] Bjorn Freeman-Benson, John Maloney, and Alan Borning. An Incremental Constraint Solver. *Communications of the ACM*, 33(1):54–63, January 1990.

[7] Michel Gangnet and Burton Rosenberg. Constraint Programming and Graph Algorithms. In *Second International Symposium on Artificial Intelligence and Mathematics*, January 1992.

[8] Michael Gleicher. Integrating Constraints and Direct Manipulation. In *Proceedings of the 1992 Symposium on Interactive 3D Graphics*, pages 171–174, March 1992.

[9] Enrico Gobbetti and Jean-Francis Balaguer. VB2: An Architecture for Interaction in Synthetic Worlds. In *Proceedings of the ACM Symposium on User Interface Software and Technology*, pages 167–178, Atlanta, Georgia, November 1993.

[10] Richard Helm, Tien Huynh, Kim Marriott, and John Vlissides. An Object-Oriented Architecture for Constraint-Based Graphical Editing. In *Proceedings of the Third Eurographics Workshop on Object-oriented Graphics*, Champery, Switzerland, October 1992. Also in *Advances in Object-Oriented Graphics II*, Springer-Verlag, 1993.

[11] Ralph D. Hill. Languages for the Construction of Multi-User Multi-Media Synchronous (MUMMS) Applications. In Brad Myers, editor, *Languages for Developing User Interfaces*, pages 125–143. Jones and Bartlett, Boston, 1992.

[12] Scott E. Hudson. Incremental Attribute Evaluation: A Flexible Algorithm for Lazy Update. *ACM Transactions on Programming Languages and Systems*, 13(3):315–341, July 1991.

[13] John Maloney. *Using Constraints for User Interface Construction*. PhD thesis, Department of Computer Science and Engineering, University of Washington, August 1991. Published as Department of Computer Science and Engineering Technical Report 91-08-12.

[14] Brad A. Myers, Dario A. Giuse, Roger B. Dannenberg, Brad Vander Zanden, David S. Kosbie, Ed Pervin, Andrew Mickish, and Philippe Marchal. Garnet: Comprehensive Support for Graphical, Highly-Interactive User Interfaces. *IEEE Computer*, 23(11):71–85, November 1990.

[15] Michael Sannella. *Constraint Satisfaction and Debugging for Interactive User Interfaces.* PhD thesis, Department of Computer Science and Engineering, University of Washington, August 1994.

[16] Michael Sannella. SkyBlue: A Multi-Way Local Propagation Constraint Solver for User Interface Construction. In *Proceedings of the ACM Symposium on User Interface Software and Technology*, Marina Del Rey, California, November 1994.

[17] Michael Sannella and Alan Borning. Multi-Garnet: Integrating Multi-Way Constraints with Garnet. Technical Report 92-07-01, Department of Computer Science and Engineering, University of Washington, September 1992.

[18] Michael Sannella, John Maloney, Bjorn Freeman-Benson, and Alan Borning. Multi-way versus One-way Constraints in User Interfaces: Experience with the DeltaBlue Algorithm. *Software—Practice and Experience*, 23(5):529–566, May 1993.

[19] Brad Vander Zanden. A Domain-Independent Algorithm for Incrementally Satisfying Multi-Way Constraints. Technical Report CS-92-160, Computer Science Department, University of Tennessee, July 1992.

[20] Brad Vander Zanden, Brad Myers, Dario Giuse, and Pedro Szekely. The Importance of Pointer Variables in Constraint Models. In *Proceedings of the ACM Symposium on User Interface Software and Technology*, pages 155–164, Hilton Head, South Carolina, November 1991.

21 Practical Issues in Graphical Constraints

Michael Gleicher

Abstract

Use of constraint-based techniques in interactive graphics applications poses a variety of unique challenges to system implementors. This paper begins by describing how interface concerns create demands on interactive, constraint-based, graphical applications. We will discuss why such applications must be able to handle systems of non-linear constraints, and survey some of the techniques available to solve them. Employing these numerical algorithms in the contexts of interactive systems poses challenges, including dynamically setting up the equations to be solved and achieving acceptable performance and scalability. This paper will explore these issues and describe the methods we have used in our efforts to address them.

21.1 Introduction

The ability to represent and maintain relationships among objects can be an extremely useful tool in a graphical application. Ever since Sketchpad [33], one of the earliest interactive graphical applications, the use of such constraint techniques has been demonstrated in applications including drawing, 3D modeling, user interface construction, animation, and design.

In employing constraint-based techniques in such graphical applications, system designers must face a variety of new challenges. This paper describes some of these challenges and discusses techniques to address them. We begin by looking at how usability concerns for such applications create requirements for systems. We will discuss why these applications will often demand the power and generality of non-linear numerical techniques. Issues in employing such algorithms within interactive systems will be surveyed.

Constraints have been used in graphical applications in many ways. Some systems provide constraint-based interfaces, that is, constraints are given to the users to help them with their tasks. Constraint techniques have also been used to aid the programmer of graphical applications, by providing a tool to use in the construction of systems. The two uses of constraints are orthogonal: it is common to write an application with a constraint-based interface using conventional tools, and to use constraint-based tools to write applications with conventional interfaces. These two uses of constraints provide different sets of challenges. This paper focuses on the former, although some of the issues and solutions presented apply to both.

The central idea of a constraint-based graphical interface is that the user is able to make persistent constraints: declarations that the system maintains after they are specified. The canonical example of a constraint-based graphical interface is drawing. In a constraint-based drawing program, the user specifies relationships among parts of the drawing as persistent constraints that the system maintains during subsequent editing. For example, a user can attach an arrow to an object, and the position of the arrow is altered as the object is moved.

For this paper, we are concerned with constraint-based interfaces to applications where user create and edit models made up of a number of graphical objects. An example is an object-oriented drawing program, where the model (or drawing in this case) is made up of lines and circles, as opposed to a painting program in which the model is a bitmap or image.

21.2   The Challenges of Constraint-Based Graphical Applications

An interactive graphical application with constraints must address the same issues as those without constraints. However, there are other challenges that are inherent when constraints among objects are provided. In addition to the graphical objects, constrained models also contain constraints that must be stored, displayed, edited, saved, etc. More significantly, constraints change the nature of interaction in a graphical application. Without them, actions only affect the objects to which they refer. For example, dragging an object in a traditional drawing program moves only the object. With constraints, this locality is lost: altering one object may cause other objects to be affected. This global nature of constraint operations is at the core of many of the difficult issues in employing constraints. It introduces issues in implementation, in performance, and in usability. The latter is potentially most concerning, not only for its difficulty, but also because usability concerns create further challenges for implementation and performance.

Without user specified constraints, graphical objects have fixed behaviors. For instance, an ellipse in a drawing program behaves like an ellipse. The system designer can create a good, usable behavior that the user can learn and apply to all ellipses. When user specified constraints among objects are introduced, the situation changes. To begin with, the behaviors can become more complicated because of interactions among objects. Each combination of objects and constraints will have its own behavior. These behaviors are specified by the user in terms of the constraints; the user is effectively programming.

As in more traditional programming, complexity in the constrained behavior of a graphical model becomes a problem when it has bugs, e.g. when the behavior isn't what is desired or expected. The most obvious form of bug is when the constraints force the model into a configuration that is not what the user desires, or the constraints prevent the user from achieving a desired configuration. Another class of constraint bug stems from bad constraints for which solutions cannot be found, either because of conflicting specifications or solver failures.

Because constraint errors occur, interactive graphical applications that provide constraints to users must deal gracefully with bad situations, such as conflicting or redundant constraints. Underdetermined models also must be handled, as it is impractical to expect the user to specify all possible degrees of freedom. Because of the potential for errors, it is crucial to aid the user in understanding the complex behaviors of constrained models. Providing continuous motion animation seems to be important for helping users understand complicated behaviors as it allows them to use their perceptual skills to connect states. This places demands on systems to solve constraints quickly enough to provide the illusion of continuous motion. Another important weapon in avoiding constraint bugs is the development of specification techniques that help avoid them; this is evidenced by the large effort in automatically inferring constraints, such as [1, 13, 19].

The interactive nature of constraint-based graphical application also necessitates that systems of constraints be dynamic. Typically, as the user edits the model, constraints are added, removed, and altered. While there are some applications, such as [31], where it is possible to separate manipulation and modeling, applications must typically interleave altering the constraints with solving them.

Because constraints are a tool to aid in the process of creating graphical models, the constraint solver should not get in the way of the creative process. This leads to increases the demands for reliability and robustness in solvers. Users should not be forced to deal with equations. Artifacts of the solving process must be hidden from the user. Similarly, we cannot expect the user to tweak algorithms on a per problem basis, as is often the case in numerical analysis.

21.2.1 An Example Application

A constraint-based drawing program demonstrates how the issues in building interactive constraint-based graphical applications manifest themselves. Despite the nearly universal agreement on their utility, constraints have never really caught on in graphical applications. What have been successful are direct manipulation programs. We have built a drawing program called *Briar* [7, 13], depicted in Figure 21.1, that aims to keep the the features of the successful direct manipulation sys-

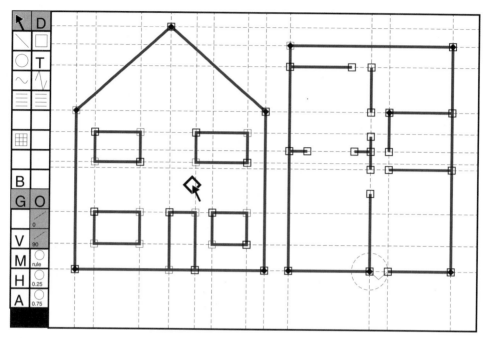

Figure 21.1
The *Briar* graphical editor editing a constrained drawing.

tems, but to augment them with constraints [8]. Briar is based on snap-dragging [2], an existing, highly evolved direct manipulation drawing interface. Snap-dragging automatically positions the cursor to help the user precisely position points, for example to align objects or create objects of a particular size. Unlike previous systems, Briar provides the facility of making these positioning operations into persistent constraints. This can be done without the user explicitly specifying the constraints. Briar's visual language for displaying the constraints closely parallels the specifications. Briar also provides simple methods for deleting constraints.

Despite its constraint features, Briar maintains the fundamental direct manipulation feel of dragging. Like more traditional programs, objects are dragged and move with continuous motion, except that in Briar, constraints among the objects can be maintained. For example, the user can draw a mechanical contraption, and have it stay together when the crank is turned. This requires Briar to resolve constraints many times per second.

Briar only represents two types of constraints: point–on–object and point–on–point. More complicated relationships, such as distance, orientation, or co-linearity, are created by combining these simple elements with special alignment objects. These more complex relationships lead to non-linear equations which Briar's solver must handle. Grouping operations with rotation and curved objects also lead to non-linearities. Briar uses a visual representation for constraints so the user is never confronted with equations.

Another important aspect of the constraints in Briar is that they are dynamic: the user is continually creating and destroying constraints. These changes occur during drawing operations, so it would be unacceptable if adding or deleting a constraint were not instantaneous.

21.3   The Need for General Purpose Solving

A constraint in an interactive graphical application is a relationship, typically geometric, among objects. A constraint is represented by a set of equations that must hold for the constraint to be satisfied. This equation is over the variables that determine the configuration of the model, called the *state vector*. The standard form of these equations is as some function of the state vector set equal to a constant, often zero with no loss of generality. Inequalities are similarly handled by an equation that states that the function is greater than or equal to zero. Such a function is called a *constraint function*. The job of a constraint solver is to find configurations of the state vector for which the constraints hold. If continuous motion is to be achieved, the solver must be called for each frame.

The geometric constraints are expressed as non-linear equations. Such equations are notoriously difficult and expensive to solve. In order to keep up with interactive rates, it is tempting to restrict the types of constraints that the solver can handle. However, the things which it is most tempting to restrict are exactly those which things from which a constraint-based approach derives much of its value. Namely, it is tempting to limit the class of equations that the solver can handle, and to limit the ways that constraints can be combined simultaneously.

One of the most obvious simplifications to a constraint system is to restrict the class of constraints it can handle, as simpler types of constraints have simpler, faster solving algorithms. However, restrictions on the generality of the equation solver, for example limiting it to linear equations, diminish the value of the constraints. Even in the most basic 2D applications, non-linear equations arise; simple geometric relationships, such as distance and orientation, give rise to non-linear equations. Many graphical objects are most easily represented in ways that give rise to non-linear functions.

Figure 21.2
A lamp is manipulated by dragging the point at the center of its illumination area on the floor. The constraint solver can adjust joint angles based on the manipulation of the light's target, as well as positions of the light.

Similarly in 3D, many of the interesting relationships among objects require non-linear equations.

A general purpose non-linear solver frees interface developers to experiment with novel and unusual constraints since they need not worry about how to solve new types of constraints. For example, in our work we have experimented with constraints on a variety of values, cataloged in [10], such as the outcome of viewing transformations [11], on the positions of reflections and shadows, and on the results of lighting calculations, permitting constraints on the colors that objects appear. Such constraints are interesting because they permit users to control models directly in terms of aspects they are interested in, as demonstrated by the example of Figure 21.2, and because they can be used in combination with one another to create other interesting interaction techniques.

The ability to solve constraints simultaneously is one of the biggest advantages for the user of a constraint-based system. Simultaneity helps avoid redundant work, as constraints can keep previously established relationships maintained during subsequent editing operations. The ability to arbitrarily combine constraints permits users to specify parts of models in an unordered fashion, mixing and matching specification tactics to meet their needs. It also aids in explorations of design spaces, by allowing the user to constrain aspects of the design and altering the free parameters to explore which configurations are consistent with these constraints. The ability to combine constraints also can also aid interface designers as it provides an interesting way to define interaction techniques [9].

Although the ability to solve constraints simultaneously is crucial to interactive graphical applications, some common classes of solvers severely restrict how constraints can be combined in an effort to achieve better performance. For example, the popular propagation solvers can only solve combinations of constraints that can be solved one at a time by some ordering. While some solvers, such as DeltaBlue [5], employ sophisticated algorithms to find these orderings, they still place substantial restrictions on which constraints can be combined. Also, the distinction between what the solvers can and cannot do is based on aspects of the data structures, for example that the constraint graph is acyclic, which is probably not what the user of a graphical editor is thinking about.

21.3.1   Properties of Constraint Problems

Not only must the constraint solver in a constraint-based graphical application handle non-linear equations, but it must also manage equations with some other difficult properties. Under-constrained, over-constrained, and redundant constraints may arise.

It is impractical to require the user to specify all aspects of a geometric model. For example, there may be some uncertainty in the design. In general, it is difficult to tell if a model is fully-specified. It is therefore important that the constraint solver can handle these underdetermined cases. This requires the solver to choose from all of the possible solutions in the under-constrained case. The best choice would be for the solver to select the solution that the user wants, something that is impossible without some mind reading. Therefore a heuristic is needed. Even if the goal of choosing an under-constrained solution is relaxed to simply pick the one which will surprise the user the least, e.g. the "Principle of Least Astonishment" [4], some form of operational metric is needed.

A common heuristic for selecting an under-constrained solution is to minimize the amount that the model changes in order to meet the constraints. A justification for this heuristic is that if the user did not ask for something to change, the system should minimize the amount that it is changed. There are many ways to measure the amount the model changes, ranging from minimizing the amount of work done by the solver [15] to optimization metrics such as least-squares norms or even user-defined optimization criteria, as provided by Ascend[26]. A discussion of some of the options for these optimization criteria are given in [4]. In our work, we have chosen least-squares as it provides a global metric that distributes change in a predictable and uniform way, and it can be implemented easily in the context of non-linear constraint techniques.

Although they are often easier to prevent than under-constrained cases, overde-termined constraints still arise in interactive graphical applications. Often, such situations are caused by users attempting to more fully specify their model when heuristics used to choose under-constrained solutions fail. Over-constrained cases are a problem both in the case of redundancy, where many constraints lead to a consistent solution, and conflicts, where there will be no solution that satisfies all the constraints. Redundant constraints are difficult for solvers, as numerical inaccuracy can make them appear to be conflicts. Conflicting constraints are difficult for non-linear solvers as it is not always possible to determine that there is no solution, or that the solver merely has not found it yet.

There are several possible behaviors which may be desirable when constraints conflict. One useful way to resolve conflicts is to attempt to minimize the error residual, for example in a weighted least-squares sense. Weights cause some constraints to be valued more than others in computing the error. Minimizing the magnitude of the error is unacceptable if the constraints are meant to represent rules which cannot be violated. Another option is to provide a preference ordering, or hierarchy, for the constraints [4]. In such a scheme, more important constraints must be satisfied before less important ones. Providing a general hierarchy mechanism for non-linear constraints appears to be a difficult problem. However, the techniques that we have used provide a two-level hierarchy of "hard" and "soft" controls [10, 11].

21.4 Solving Constraints

Solving systems of non-linear equations is difficult. In fact, a guaranteed general method for solving systems of non-linear equations does not exist, and there are arguments that such a method cannot exist [28]. Without knowledge about the equations, it is difficult to predict where solutions will occur. Very little knowledge about arbitrary non-linear equations can be made available to solvers. Most solvers use limited, local information about the equations, such as the derivatives, and iteratively search for a solution. Despite the lack of guarantees, such methods are useful in practice when good initial guesses for the solution are available.

Some methods only operate on one constraint at a time. One example is relaxation which successively solves each constraint. Relaxation was used in several early constraint-based graphical systems including ThingLab [3] and Sketchpad [33]. With relaxation, solving a constraint may break previously solved ones. The process iterates over all the constraints until a solution is found, or the solver gives up. Other methods that treat constraints individually include gradient (steepest) descent and penalty methods, surveyed by Platt [27]. These simple methods do not work reliably for constraint problems and offer slow convergence even on problems that they do solve.

Better solving methods consider all constraints simultaneously to choose each step of the iteration. These iterative methods take a sequence of steps (hopefully) converging on a solution. At each iteration, a linear system is solved to determine what step should be taken. Numerical analysis texts, such as [28], introduce the basic varieties of these methods. The best known are Newton-Raphson methods, which have been used in a number of constraint-based graphics systems including Juno [24] and Converge [30].

We have been using a variant of these iterative approaches in our work, which we call the *differential approach*. Rather than specifying what the desired values for constraint functions are, we instead specify how they are to change, i.e. their time derivatives. For example, we might specify that something is not to change, or is to move towards a target. Such an approach is useful for interaction because we want our objects to move continuously, rather than jump to their goal positions. The derivatives of variables can be computed from the derivatives of the constraint functions by solving a system of linear equations, even if the constraint functions themselves are non-linear. Differential methods are detailed in [10] and [11].

Differential methods and Newton-like methods are very similar. Both repeatedly solve linear systems to iteratively move towards satisfying non-linear equations. One way to describe the difference might be that a Newton-style method attempts to race towards the goal as fast as possible, regardless of the route taken, while the differential methods try to take a controlled continuous route, even if it takes longer. The former method runs more of the risk of speeding off in a wrong direction, but may arrive at its goal sooner.

The method actually used to solve constraints is an implementation detail, that should hidden from the user of a constraint-based application. What is important to making such a system successful, however, is that constraints are solved in a manner that is fast, robust, and reliable.

21.4.1   Solving Linear Systems

Many methods will repeatedly solve systems of linear equations based on the derivatives of the non-linear equations. Linear system solving dominates the computational complexity of constraint-based graphical applications (see section 21.5), and is a key place where stability and reliability concerns must be met.

The linear system solver at the core of the constraint solver must be able to handle ill-conditioned and singular cases. Such cases arise not only when the constraints are over-specified, but also from certain types of geometric configurations. Some linear system methods, such as QR factorization or singular value decomposition [14] can handle such matrices, but are typically expensive to use. We have used a standard method to cope with these problems known as regularization or damping. It alters the linear system by limiting how much any particular equation can contribute to the solution. The method is the basis for the Levenberg-Marquardt method for solving non-linear equations [6]. It has also been applied to the animation of articulated figures by Maciejewski [20], and to the related problem of robotic control by Wampler [34]. Damping methods are equivalent to the robust pseudo-inverse techniques of Nakamura [23].

To solve linear systems in our constraint applications, we have used a conjugate-gradient algorithm. Conjugate-gradient algorithms are detailed in [25] and [29]. Briefly, such algorithms repeatedly refine an estimate of the solution to the linear system until converging on an answer. As discussed in [10], conjugate-gradient algorithms are particularly attractive for interactive constraint-based applications because:

- they permit exploitation of sparsity in the linear systems to enhance performance and memory usage. They can exploit sparsity without any pre-analysis of the matrices;

- they are readily available in standard texts such as [28];

- they permit the specification of stopping criteria, permitting a tradeoff between accuracy and performance to be controlled.

21.5   Scalability and Performance

Performance is important to interactive graphical applications since they must provide the appearance of continuous motion by recreating the image rapidly. In a conventional drawing program this can be achieved easily as only one object is moving at a time. If it is a complicated or compound object, it can be drawn in a simpler form (such as a bounding rectangle) because it cannot change internally. Because of this constant $O(1)$ complexity in the interactive loop, direct manipulation drawing is practical on small computers.

In a constraint-based system, the constant time portions of drawing systems no longer exist. Many objects can potentially change at once. Where this complexity hurts the most is in constraint solving, but the fact that many objects move simultaneously also makes other things, such as redraw, more complicated. Simultaneous movement of multiple objects moving also raises the cognitive complexity of drawing, as the behaviors can become quite complicated.

21.5.1 Computational Complexity

The performance of an interactive graphical application degrades as the size of the problem the user is working on increases. We are interested in understanding how the constraint methods scale as the number of constraints (n) and variables (m) increase. The number of variables is roughly proportional to the number of graphical objects.

We only consider the complexity of one iteration of solving the constraints, although other parts of the system might scale badly: for example, an input technique might need to examine all pairs of objects for intersection (requiring $O(m^2)$ time), or a rendering computation might require solving for interactions among all objects. The time for an iteration is the important quantity for non-linear solving since the number of iterations required is not known in advance, and the intermediate results are sometimes displayed after a fixed number of iterations, as in a differential approach.

With arbitrary constraints, the computation costs are almost unbounded. For example, we might have a constraint on the average center of each combination of 4 objects, requiring a combinatorial explosion just to enumerate the terms in the expression. However, for analysis we make some assumptions that are rarely violated in practice:

1. Objects are independent.

2. Constraints are independent, therefore, the addition of another control neither changes the number of variables a constraint depends on, nor adversely changes the amount of time to compute a constraint's value. Some optimizations, most notably common subexpression sharing, may speed evaluations.

3. Constraints depend on a fixed number of variables, independently of the total number of variables or controls in the system. This restriction eliminates

controls on the aggregate of all objects, for example the center of mass of all objects in the world.

From these three assumptions, it follows that n and m are independent. It also follows that the time to compute the values for the constraints is $O(n)$, because computing each of n controls cannot depend on either n or m. By a similar argument, computing the derivatives of the constraints with respect to the variables the can also be computed in $O(n)$ time. This matrix of derivatives is known as the Jacobian, is denoted ($\mathbf{J}$), and is used in many solving methods.

The fact that the Jacobian of the constraints ($\mathbf{J}$) can be computed in $O(n)$ time is significant, and non-obvious. $\mathbf{J}$ is an $n \times m$ matrix, so it would take $O(nm)$ time just to fill the matrix with 0s. The key observation is that we do not have to store all the values in the matrix because many of them will be zero, that is, the matrix is *sparse*. Each row only depends on the variables that its constraint depends on, which is independent of n or m. Therefore, the entire matrix will only contain $O(n)$ entries. By exploiting sparsity, this can be stored and accessed in $O(n)$ time.

The computational complexity of constraint-based graphical applications using iterative numerical algorithms is dominated by the linear systems which must be solved in order to solve the non-linear equations. Solving a system of linear equations is, in the most general case, an $O(n^3)$ problem. However, because the matrices which arise in graphical constraint problems are sparse, the complexity can be lower. For certain classes of sparse matrices, linear systems can be solved in much less than $O(n^3)$ time. For example, if the matrix has constant bandwidth, solving time is $O(n)$. For certain configurations of constraints, the matrices will have this structure. Surles [31] describes why important problems in molecular biology and other domains have this structure, and describes techniques for solving such constraint systems in [32].

When the user is free to place constraints between objects, there is no guarantee that the matrices to be solved will have any specific structure. However, by using conjugate-gradient solving techniques and placing reasonable restrictions on the required accuracy, the linear systems can be solved in $O(n^2)$ time because the solver requires at most $O(n)$ iterations, and each iteration only accesses the matrix to multiply it by a vector, which can be done in $O(n)$ time.

Another type of sparsity that can often be exploited in solving constraint systems is partitioning. Partitioned systems can be broken into smaller, independent pieces. Solving each piece separately is more efficient when the computational complexity is worse than linear.

21.5.2   Reducing Problem Size

To maintain interactive performance, it is critical to reduce the complexity of the solving algorithm by exploiting the sparsity of the systems that are solved. However, without placing restrictions on the problems, it is unlikely that we can achieve better than $O(n^2)$ complexity for general constraint problems. We must find ways to keep n small, without restricting the size of the problems that the user actually works on. That is, to find methods that give the user the illusion that the system is working on a larger problem, while in fact, the problem's size has been reduced.

If we know how some variables are going to change by some other means, the expense of constraint solving is not required. For example, if we know that an object is frozen in place, we know that it will not change. We can implement the constraints by removing the object's variables from the set of variables solved for, rather than by adding more equations.

For complexity purposes, m and n are really the number of *active* variables and constraints, that is the number that might actually have an effect on the solution. We can discount objects if there are no constraints affecting them or if there is something that requires them not to change. We can ignore a constraint if it does not effect any changeable objects. We call the set of variables and constraints that are actually participating the *working set*.

In general, adding a new control or constraint adds to n and therefore makes constraint solving more expensive to compute. However, constraints realized by removing variables from the working set instead reduce m rather than increasing n, speeding computations. Such constraints are represented implicitly in the structure of the problem, rather than explicitly by an equation.

Freezing an object is a simple example of a constraint that can be implemented implicitly. Specifying that an object is to be frozen, e.g. that it must not change, could be represented by explicitly placing a control on each variable. However, the effects of these controls are known: they will cause the variables not to change. Since the variables will not change, they can be removed from the working set. Without variables in the working set, the object is constrained not to move, however, this constraint is represented implicitly in the structure of the problem.

Implicit constraints generalize to individual variables. For example, a line segment has 4 degrees of freedom. Freezing its length can be implemented by explicitly placing a constraint on its length. However, if the line segment's representation included a separate independent variable for length, this variable could be removed from the working set to implicitly represent the length constraint.

Implicit constraints are representation dependent. In the example above, if the programmer had chosen a different representation for the line segment, for example to represent it by the positions of its endpoints, the length constraint could not be implemented as an implicit constraint.

It is often worthwhile to choose representations that maximize the number of implicit constraints. For example, in a planar mechanisms simulator most line segments represent rigid linkage rods. Therefore, a representation is used that has length as a variable. This way the commonly needed constraint that the line is a rigid length can be realized as a implicit constraint.

Finding new representations of objects is a difficult problem, especially when we cannot anticipate the types of constraints and combinations that will be desired. However, it is possible to create multiple representations for important cases of constraints on objects. It is conceivable to build a system that changes the representation of objects to maximize the number of implicit constraints. This requires solving a combinatorial optimization problem.

Another form of implicit constraint is merging, that is having multiple parameters access the same variable, as seen in Thinglab [3]. Merging is an implicit constraint for equating parameters. Because merged parameters share a single variable, they have exactly the same value. A more general variant of merging allows a variable to be connected to some output. This effectively mixes local propagation into the numerical methods.

Implicit constraints are exact. If an object is frozen, it exactly does not move. Two merged quantities are exactly equal. While this exact equality can be an asset, it can also be a problem as it means the constraint behaves differently than its explicit counterpart. This can be particularly troublesome in cases where the solver might break the equality constraint slightly, for example to achieve a least squares solution to an over-constrained problem.

21.5.3 Trading Accuracy for Performance

For many applications, users are not concerned with extreme accuracy — we are often willing to let our objects be an imperceptible tenth of a pixel apart if it allows our solver to be faster. When we employ iterative numerical solvers, there are several ways in which accuracy can be traded for performance. The simplest is to raise the solver's tolerance, causing it to stop iterating sooner. When an iterative linear system solver is used within the non-linear method, the tolerance for this solver can also raised.

The damping techniques mentioned in section 21.4.1 are another example of trading accuracy for performance. The perturbed, or damped, linear system does not exactly model the problem being solved. However, the new linear system does have properties that permit it to be solved faster.

21.6   Forming Equations

The methods for solving systems of non-linear equations discussed in section 21.4 require evaluating the values and derivatives of the constraint functions. These evaluations must be able to take advantage of sparsity in the resulting derivative matrices to achieve needed performance in evaluations. Since these functions are defined in response to dynamic creation and destruction of constraints, the creation of the functions themselves must be dynamic.

Functions are built by composing other functions together. At a low level, one might consider building functions out of basic mathematical primitives such as addition; however, this composition occurs at higher levels of abstraction in constraint systems too. For example, many constraints are typically defined in terms of points on objects. It is then the job of the objects to compute these point positions in terms of their state variables. This provides an important layer of modularity: the constraints can be defined independently of the objects.

A function can be represented as a directed acyclic graph[1] with composed functions at the nodes, and arcs representing composition. Our approach to providing function composition in the dynamic setting of interactive applications is to provide a tools for managing these function graph structures. In *Snap-Together Mathematics* [12, 10], function elements are "wired" together to make more complicated functions.

Evaluating the values and derivatives of an expression involves traversing the graph. To compute a value, a node requests the values from its predecessors and then performs its local function on these results. The chain rule for derivatives provides a similar method for computing derivatives. To compute the derivative of a node with respect to the global inputs, a node asks its predecessors for their derivatives, and multiplies these intermediate results by the derivative of its internal derivative matrix. This process is called *automatic differentiation*, and is superior to building the global derivative matrix symbolically in most situations [16, 18].

At the leaves of the function graph are the variables over which the function is computed, the state vector of the model. The state vector contains the parameters of the graphical objects which make up the model. The state of the system is distributed among objects, however, numerical algorithms require state to be gathered

---

[1]It is not a tree, as common subexpressions might be shared.

into a single global vector. The positions of variables in this vector are significant as they determine which columns of the derivative matrices correspond to which variables. It would be possible to keep variables in a large vector and have the objects simply look in this larger structure for values. Such an approach, however, violates encapsulation of objects and makes it more difficult to switch variables on and off. In our implementation, variables from object state vectors are gathered into a larger vector when needed. By selecting which variables are gathered, it is simple and fast to switch among sets of variables.

We have implemented function composition and automatic differentiation in an object-oriented Snap-Together Mathematics library. Rather than requiring special graph node objects, the library allows application objects to mix in the ability to "speak mathematics." This permits application objects to participate directly in calculations. They must only respond to a simple protocol. This simplifies applications by reducing the need for special math objects that must be allocated and maintained. Snap-Together Mathematics uses a specially designed sparse matrix representation and does extensive caching to achieve better performance.

21.7   Putting it Together

A wide variety of graphical applications might employ constraints. Any of these applications will face the same issues previously described. Fortunately, the solutions proposed are general enough to apply across many applications, and can be encapsulated into a toolkit to support a variety of applications.

At a low level, any application that employs numerical constraints will gain leverage from a library of mathematical structures and algorithms. Our mathematical toolkit provides support for such elements as vectors, matrices, and differential equations in an object oriented manner. It includes several varieties of sparse matrices, and a variety of linear system, non-linear system, and ordinary differential equation solvers.

Snap-Together Mathematics, described in section 21.6, is built on top of the mathematical library. In addition to the support for dynamically composing and rapidly evaluating functions, it also includes interface to differential and Newton-style solvers. Many applications, including Briar, have been built with these tools.

The Bramble graphics toolkit [9, 10], built on top of Snap-Together Mathematics, aims to provide a framework for building graphical applications with constraints. Previous toolkits, such as Garnet [22], ThingLab II [21], and Rendezvous [17], employ constraints to aid programmers in application development. Bramble, in contrast, primarily aims to provide constraints as for user level services. However, it does appear that the differential constraint techniques provided in Bramble simplify the task of building graphical applications by helping separate manipulation from representation and facilitating general purpose interaction techniques.

There are many drawbacks to the use of iterative numerical algorithms in interactive graphical applications. Such computations can be expensive and have worse computational complexity than their non-numerical counterparts. The techniques only apply to real numbers, which means other techniques must be used for discrete data within applications. Care must be taken to avoid numerical instability. Also, the set of equations for which non-linear constraint solvers will perform satisfactorily is not a well defined set – often such determinations must be done empirically.

Despite these drawbacks, it is still advantageous to employ numerical non-linear constraint methods in graphical applications. The generality in the class of equations allows the constraints typically required by graphical editors, and allows experimentation with new types of constraints. Such constraints can be handled simultaneously. Most non-linear methods require very little information about the constraint functions. That information which they do need can be computed automatically. The iterative non-linear methods can be made to gracefully handle under and overdetermined constraints, using least-squares techniques.

The addition of constraints to an interactive graphical application creates a variety of issues that system builders must be concerned with. Many of these issues stem from interface concerns and the need to handle non-linear relationships. Achieving the needed performance and dynamicness from the non-linear solvers requires careful attention. However, support for these can be provided in a general purpose manner.

References

[1] Sherman R. Alpert. Graceful interaction with graphical constraints. *IEEE Computer Graphics and Applications*, pages 82–91, March 1993.

[2] Eric Bier and Maureen Stone. Snap-dragging. *Computer Graphics*, 20(4):233–240, 1986. Proceedings SIGGRAPH '86.

[3] Alan Borning. The programming language aspects of ThingLab, a constraint-oriented simulation laboratory. *ACM Transactions on Programming Languages and Systems*, 3(4):353–387, 1981.

[4] Alan Borning, Bjorn Freeman-Benson, and Molly Wilson. Constraint hierarchies. *Lisp and Functional Programming*, 5:223–270, 1992.

[5] Bjorn Freeman-Benson, John Maloney, and Alan Borning. An incremental constraint hierarchy solver. *Communications of the ACM*, 33(1):54–63, January 1990.

[6] Phillip Gill, Walter Murray, and Margret Wright. *Practical Optimization*. Academic Press, New York, NY, 1981.

[7] Michael Gleicher. Briar - a constraint-based drawing program. In *SIGGRAPH Video Review*, volume 77, 1992. CHI '92 Formal Video Program.

[8] Michael Gleicher. Integrating constraints and direct manipulation. In *Proceedings of the 1992 Symposium on Interactive 3D Graphics*, pages 171–174, March 1992.

[9] Michael Gleicher. A graphics toolkit based on differential constraints. In Randy Pausch, editor, *Proceedings UIST '93*, pages 109–120, November 1993.

[10] Michael Gleicher. *A Differential Approach to Graphical Interaction*. PhD thesis, School of Computer Science, Carnegie Mellon University, 1994.

[11] Michael Gleicher and Andrew Witkin. Through-the-lens camera control. *Computer Graphics*, 26(2):331–340, July 1992. Proceedings Siggraph '92.

[12] Michael Gleicher and Andrew Witkin. Supporting numerical computations in interactive contexts. In Tom Calvert, editor, *Graphics Interface*, pages 138–145, May 1993.

[13] Michael Gleicher and Andrew Witkin. Drawing with constraints. *The Visual Computer*, To Appear.

[14] Gene H. Gollub and Charles F. Van Loan. *Matrix Computations*. Johns Hopkins Press, 1989.

[15] James Gosling. *Algebraic Constraints*. PhD thesis, Carnegie Mellon University, May 1983.

[16] Andreas Griewank. On automatic differentiation. In M. Iri and K. Tanabe, editors, *Mathematical Programming: Recent Developments and Applications*, pages 83–108. Kluwer Academic, 1989.

[17] Ralph Hill, Tom Brinck, John Patterson, Steven Rohall, and Wayne Wilner. The rendezvous language and architecture. *Communications of the ACM*, 36(1):62–67, January 1993.

[18] Masao Iri. History of automatic differentiation and rounding error estimation. In Andreas Griewank and George Corliss, editors, *Automatic Differentiation of Algorithms: Theory, Implementation and Application*, pages 3–16. SIAM, January 1991.

[19] David Kurlander and Steven Feiner. Inferring constraints from multiple snapshots. *ACM Transactions on Computer Graphics*, 12(4), October 1993.

[20] Anthony Maciejewski. Dealing with the ill-conditioned equations of motion for articulated figures. *IEEE Computer Graphics and Applications*, May 1990.

[21] John Harold Maloney. *Using Constraints for User Interface Construction*. PhD thesis, University of Washington, 1991. Appears as Computer Science Technical Report 91-08-12.

[22] Brad A. Myers, Dario Guise, Roger B. Dannenberg, Brad Vander Zanden, David Kosbie, Ed Pervin, Andrew Mickish, and Phillipe Marchal. Comprehensive support for graphical, highly-interactive user interfaces: The garnet user interface development environment. *IEEE Computer*, November 1990.

[23] Yoshiko Nakamura. *Advanced Robotics: Redundancy and Optimization*. Addison-Wesley, 1991.

[24] Greg Nelson. Juno, a constraint based graphics system. *Computer Graphics*, 19(3):235–243, 1985. Proceedings SIGGRAPH '85.

[25] Christopher Paige and Michael Saunders. LSQR: an algorithm for sparse linear equations and sparse least squares. *ACM Transactions on Mathematical Software*, 8(1):43–71, March 1982.

[26] P. Piela, T. Epperly, K. Westerberg, and A. Westerberg. Ascend: An object-oriented computer environment for modeling and analysis. part 1 - the modeling language. Technical Report EDRC 06–88–90, Engineering Design Research Center, Carnegie Mellon University, 1990.

[27] John Platt. A generalization of dynamic constraints. *CGVIP: Graphical Models and Image Processing*, 54(6):516–525, November 1992.

[28] William Press, Brian Flannery, Saul Teukolsky, and William Vetterling. *Numerical Recipes in C*. Cambridge University Press, Cambridge, England, 1986.

[29] Jonathan Shewchuck. An introduction to the conjugate gradient mathod without the agonizing pain. Technical Report CMU-CS-94-125, School of Computer Science, Carnegie Mellon University, 1994.

[30] Steven Sistare. Interaction techniques in constraint-based geometric modeling. In *Proceedings Graphics Interface '91*, pages 85–92, June 1991.

[31] Mark Surles. Interactive modeling enhanced with constraints and physics – with applications in molecular modeling. In *Proceedings of the 1992 Symposium on Interactive Computer Graphics*, pages 175–182, March 1992.

[32] Mark C. Surles. An algorithm for linear complexity for interactive, physically-based modelling of large proteins. *Computer Graphics*, 26(2):221–230, 1992. Proceedings SIGGRAPH '92.

[33] Ivan Sutherland. *Sketchpad: A Man Machine Graphical Communication System*. PhD thesis, Massachusetts Institute of Technology, January 1963.

[34] Charles W. Wampler. Manipulator inverse kinematic solutions based on vector formulations and damped least-squares method. *IEEE Transactions on Systems, Man, and Cybernetics*, 16(1):93–101, January 1986.

22 Constraint Management in a Declarative Design Method for 3D Scene Sketch Modeling

Stéphane Donikian and Gérard Hégron

Abstract

In this paper, we present a dynamic model associated with an intelligent CAD system aiming at the modeling of an architectural scene sketch. Our design methodology has been developed to simulate the process of a user who tries to give a description of a scene from a set of mental images. The scene creation is based on a script which describes the environment from the point of view of an observer who moves across the scene. The system is based on a declarative method viewed as a stepwise refinement process. For the scene representation, a qualitative model is used to describe the objects in terms of attributes, functions, methods and components. The links between objects and their components are expressed by a hierarchical structure, and a description of spatial configurations is given by using locative relations. The set of solutions consistent with the description is usually infinite. So, either one scene consistent with this description is calculated and visualized, or reasons of inconsistency are notified to the user. The resolution process consists of two steps: firstly a logical inference checks the consistency of the topological description, and secondly an optimization algorithm deals with the global description and provides a solution. Two examples illustrate our design methodology and the calculation of a scene model.

22.1 Introduction

In the current literature, several approaches have been attempted to design CAD systems. A first approach consists of an extension of classical CAD systems with the help of parametric objects or variational geometry [1], but models required by those systems are still very close to the traditional geometrical models and imply a bottom up design methodology by using imperative methods. Furthermore, this approach is not suitable when the design scene is complex or when the designer thinks about his project in a more semantical way. A second approach consists in building expert systems; these systems tend to focus on a particular domain and are only useful for routine design in a well known application domain completely formalized by a set of rules and constraints [2, 3]. Both approaches are far from an architect's considerations during the first stage of design which is more a top-down approach and a stepwise refinement process. A third approach met a constantly increasing interest in all CAD domains [4, 5, 6, 7, 8, 9]. This approach is more declarative and offers to the designer a more progressive and dynamic scene specification, leaving to the system the care of suggesting solutions, detecting inconsistencies and manipulating incomplete knowledge. An important difference between declarative and imperative methods (figure 22.1) is that a declarative method does not provide a unique solution like an imperative method does, but provides a model corresponding to a large number of scenes for which the system proposes one or more solutions.

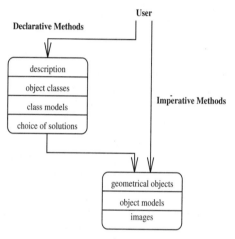

Figure 22.1
Declarative and imperative methods.

Our system is based on the third approach and offers to the designer the ability to describe the topology and geometry of the scene in a declarative way by means of properties and constraints on objects and their spatial configuration. This system deals with under-constrained and over-constrained scene descriptions and proposes to the designer one of the numerous scenes whenever the description is consistent, or explicits the reasons for the inconsistency. The goal of this paper is to put an emphasis on the different sorts of properties and constraints our system can manage, how they are performed and how a particular solution is calcuted from the global description. Other parts are not detailed but are referred to previous papers. The next section gives an overview of our system structure. Section three deals with the two steps involved in the resolution process and section four gives some details about the different kinds of inconsistencies which may occur during the design process. Finally some implementation details and illustrations of our method are given.

22.2   System Overview

We intend to apply the declarative methodology to architectural design. Our goal is not to get the final and precise geometric model of each component of the scene but to assist the designer in creating sketches meeting the main properties and constraints of mental images. The architectural project design we will try to simulate is based on a script which describes the scene from the point of view of a user who moves across the scene [10]. From each viewpoint, the user increases the scene description by adding new objects and new properties and constraints about objects and their spatial configurations, and a current model of the scene is then proposed by the system. For architectural design, the complexity comes from the spatial configuration of objects and from the large amount of data. This observation explains why we are not interested in defining complex geometrical objects but in providing a high level description of object characteristics and spatial configurations.

Our model is composed of a 3-tuple $<O, S, L>$, where O is the set of scene objects, S the scene hierarchical structure and L the set of locative relations and constraints between objects. A dynamic and interactive user interface is used to offer a high level interaction to the designer, and the dialogue is carried out with the help of an object oriented language (figure 22.2). The verification of the scene description consistency and the proposition of a scene (solution of the description) are made during the resolution process.

Each class of objects is a member of an architectural abstraction level (urban, building, architectural space, architectural element, architectural components and architectural constructors). The hierarchical structure of the scene is represented by a directed acyclic graph whose nodes are objects and whose arcs link an object to another one as a *part of* or as a *copy of*. In the example of figure 22.3, *opening2* and *room2* objects inherit *opening1* and *room1* object's characteristics except for their positions.

Each object refers to a particular class, and a class is composed of attributes, functions, methods and of a prototype. Attributes denote characteristics of the object which can be represented by a variable of atomical or numerical type. A function defines the object characteristics represented by an analytical inequation which is composed by:

- usual arithmetic operators +, -, *, /,
- parenthesis (,),
- real constants,
- basic geometrical constraints like volume, surface area, segment length, . . .

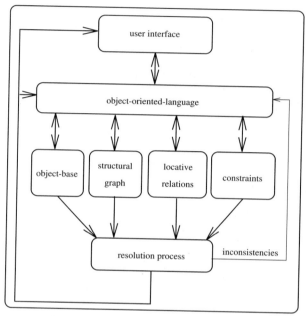

Figure 22.2
The system architecture.

- numerical attributes of the object and its components,
- functions of the object and of its components.

A geometrical constraint will be represented by a function of the object from which all parameters belong to a part of itself. Methods correspond to qualifying adjectives, allow to refine the description of an object, and are described by a sequence of predicates. Some attributes are predefined for every class of objects and represent characteristics useful for locative relation management as well as for the scene visualization. Each object is defined in its own reference system of axes and is included in its bounding box with edges parallel to the axes. Dimensions of the bounding box are either fixed or included in a possible value domain or unknown, and its position depends on locative relations and geometrical constraints.

A locative expression involves a locative prepositional phrase together with whatever the phrase modifies [11]. Each locative expression is given in accordance with the current locator's viewpoint. In our system, a locative expression is composed of a locative syntagma, a verb (to be) and two noun phrases: N_{target} **is**

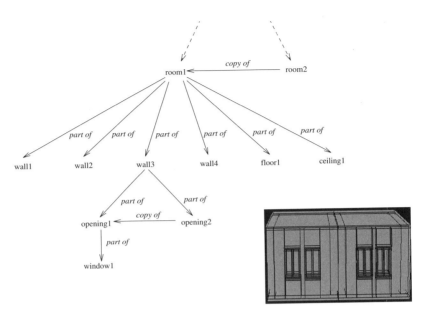

Figure 22.3
A structural graph example and a corresponding scene.

locative syntagma N_{site}. The subject (N_{target}) refers to the located entity and the object (N_{site}) to the reference entity. Each locative syntagma possesses its own semantic defined in the relation reference system. The orientation of this reference system depends on the site orientation and for each locative expression, the site can have three kinds of orientation [12] (intrinsic, deictic and contextual orientations). The description is given for a succession of the locator's viewpoints, and for each of them the locator participates to the scene description. For example, the scene shown in figure 22.3 is one possible scene corresponding to the structural graph, where:

- *room1* and *room2* are in front of the *locator*.

- *room2* is located to the right of *room1* and they have the same front, back, top and bottom sides.

- *opening2* is on the right of *opening1* and they have the same front, back, top and bottom sides.

Some locative relations are given on object bounding boxes, and the locative syntagma semantic [13] is expressed by three constraints (one along each axis of the relation reference system). Constraints are expressed on edges corresponding to the projections of object bounding boxes (figure 22.4). Each constraint $C(X, Y)$ corresponds to a disjunction of some Allen's elementary relations [14], which allows to describe the relative positionning of the two segments X and Y along an axis:

$C(X, Y) = (\vee_{i=1}^{13}\alpha_i.r_i(X, Y))$
with $\alpha_i \in \{0, 1\}$ *and* r_i *one of the thirteen Allen's relations (figure 22.4)*

Other locative relations are given on the sides of the objects. Each side is represented along the axis parallel to its normal by a projection point of the side on the axis. The relative positionning of two parallel sides is expressed by a constraint on corresponding points (figure 22.5). A constraint $c(x, y)$ between two points x and y along an axis is expressed by:

$c(x, y) = (\vee_{i=1}^{3}\alpha_i.r_i(x, y))$
with $\alpha_i \in \{0, 1\}$ *and* $r_i \in \{precede, identical\_to, follow\}$

To have a unique representation for these two kinds of constraints, each segment X is represented by its two extremities X_b and X_e which correspond to the beginning and end points of the segment. Each Allen's relation $r_i(X, Y)$ between the two segments X and Y is then expressed in the following form:

$r_i(X, Y) \equiv precede(X_b, X_e) \wedge precede(Y_b, Y_e) \wedge r_{i_1}(X_b, Y_b) \wedge$
$r_{i_2}(X_b, Y_e) \wedge r_{i_3}(X_e, Y_b) \wedge r_{i_4}(X_e, Y_e)$
with $r_{i_j} \in \{precede, identical\_to, follow\}$.

A description being a conjonction of constraints, each Allen's constraint must be expressed in the following disjunctive normal form to make the union of all constraints on the same segments or extremities:

$C(X, Y) = [(\wedge_{j=1}^{4}(\vee_{k=1}^{3}\alpha_{k_j}.r_k(X_{u_j}, Y_{v_j}))) \wedge precede(X_b, X_e) \wedge precede(Y_b, Y_e)]$,
where $\alpha_{k_i} \in \{0, 1\}$, $(u_j, v_j) \in \{(b, b), (b, e), (e, b), (e, e)\}$, $r_k \in \{precede, follow, identical\_to\}$

Among all Allen's constraints there are only 187 wich are expressible in this form [15]. Constraints expressible in a disjunctive normal form correspond to constraints which present a continuity in their geometrical configuration area. For example the locative relation *The chair is on the left side or on the right side of*

Relation	Symbol	Symbol for inverse	Illustration
x before y	$<$	$>$	
x equal y	$=$	$=$	
x meets y	m	mi	
x overlaps y	o	oi	
x during y	d	di	
x starts y	s	si	
x finishes y	f	fi	

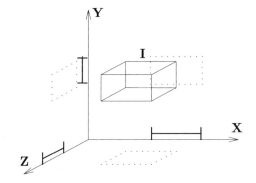

Figure 22.4
The thirteen relations between two intervals and the bounding box projection along the three axes.

the table is not expressible in a disjunctive normal form on the lateral axis. On the other hand, the locative relation *The box X is on the table Y* corresponds to:

- $C_{vertical}(X, Y) = \{m_i\}$,
- $C_{frontal}(X, Y) = \{o \vee o_i \vee d \vee d_i \vee s \vee s_i \vee f \vee f_i \vee =\}$,
- $C_{lateral}(X, Y) = \{o \vee o_i \vee d \vee d_i \vee s \vee s_i \vee f \vee f_i \vee =\}$.

Relation	Symbol	Illustration
x precede y	*precede*	x ● y ●
x identical to y	*identical_to*	x ● y ●
x follow y	*follow*	y ● x ●

Figure 22.5
The three possible relations between two points.

and is expressible in the following normal form:

- $C_{vertical}(X, Y) = [(X_b \, precede \, X_e) \wedge (Y_b \, precede \, Y_e) \wedge (X_b \, identical \, to \, Y_e) \wedge (Y_b \, precede \, X_e) \wedge (X_b \, follow \, Y_b) \wedge (X_e \, follow \, Y_e)]$

- $C_{frontal}(X, Y) = C_{lateral}(X, Y) = [(X_b \, precede \, X_e) \wedge (Y_b \, precede \, Y_e) \wedge (X_b \, precede \, Y_e) \wedge (Y_b \, precede \, X_e) \wedge (X_b \, \{precede \vee follow \vee identical \, to\} \, Y_b) \wedge (X_e \, \{precede \vee follow \vee identical \, to\} \, Y_e)]$

22.3 The Calculation of a Scene Description Solution

At any stage of the design process, a solution *s*, among the infinite set of valid solutions S, can be calculated and visualized. The solution calculation is achieved in two steps: the first step allows to check the consistency of the locative description and to obtain a minimal system of linear inequations; the second step adds to the previous system the set of geometrical constraints (object functions) and proposes one solution of the global description by minimizing an objective function subject to the global system of linear and nonlinear inequalities.

From the set of locative relations, a directed valuated graph is constructed for each axis[16], whose nodes are edge extremities of the bounding box. Graph arcs represent the relative positionning of points by using only {*precede*} and {*precede* ∨ *identical_to*} relations.

There is no creation of an arc connecting two nodes when the disjunctive relation is {*precede* ∨ *identical_to* ∨ *follow*} or {*precede* ∨ *follow*}, because the relative positionning of these two nodes is considered as being free. This description is logi-

$r_i(X_k, Y_l)$	corresponding arc
$\{precede\}$	$X_k \xrightarrow{\text{les}} Y_l$
$\{identical\_to\}$	$X_k \xrightarrow{\text{eq}} Y_l$
	$Y_l \xrightarrow{\text{eq}} X_k$
$\{follow\}$	$Y_l \xrightarrow{\text{les}} X_k$
$\{precede \vee identical\_to\}$	$X_k \xrightarrow{\text{leq}} Y_l$
$\{follow \vee identical\_to\}$	$Y_l \xrightarrow{\text{leq}} X_k$
$\{precede \vee follow\}$	no arc creation
$\{precede \vee follow \vee identical\_to\}$	no arc creation

Figure 22.6
Correspondance between constraints and graph arcs.

cally consistent if there is at least one solution to order extremities of segments. For example, the set of constraints $(Y \ \mathbf{d} \ X)$, $(X \ \mathbf{m} \ Z)$, $(Y \ \mathbf{o} \ Z)$ is logically inconsistent, because points X_e, Y_e and Z_b cannot be ordered $(X_e \xleftrightarrow{\text{eq}} Z_b \xrightarrow{\text{les}} Y_e \xrightarrow{\text{les}} X_e)$. The consistency of the description is checked (in a unique graph traversal) by searching for a circuit.

Each arc is also valuated by the information of its length, which is given by bounding box dimensions or by distance constraints between the sides of the object. Each distance between two nodes is either fixed or included in a possible value domain or unknown :

- $\xrightarrow{d}$: for a fixed distance $\mathbf{d}$,
- $\xrightarrow{[a,b]}$: for a distance in a possible value domain $[\mathbf{a},\mathbf{b}]$,
- $\xrightarrow{nil}$: for an unknown distance.

For each arc from X_k to Y_l whose length is unknown, if there is a path between its two nodes of length higher than one, then the arc is removed by applying antitransitivity rule. After this reduction process, some of the arc lengths are still unknown, and it would be interesting to reduce their possible value domain by propagation of known values, but the global propagation algorithms have a Non-deterministic Polynomial complexity. On the other hand, we can apply local propagation algorithms, according to the local graph structure, and for a low cost.

If no inconsistency has been detected at the preceding step, then a minimal system of linear inequations is obtained from the three graphs. Each arc from X_k to Y_l with *les* or *leq* valuation corresponds to one of the three following expressions:

1. $(X_k \xrightarrow{d} Y_l) \Rightarrow (V(Y_l) - V(X_k)) = d$

2. $(X_k \xrightarrow{[a,b]} Y_l) \Rightarrow a \leq (V(Y_l) - V(X_k)) \leq b$

3. $(X_k \xrightarrow{nil} Y_l) \Rightarrow 0 \leq (V(Y_l) - V(X_k)) \leq L$ (L is the domain length
   along the corresponding axis)

Each graph node X_k is performed by an expression (by using the function V) corresponding to the sum of a variable and a constant as follows:
$\forall X_k$,

- $\forall Y_l \in pred(X_k),\ (Y_l \xrightarrow{[a,b] \vee nil} X_k) \Rightarrow V(X_k) = new\,variable\,(x_i)$
- $\exists Y_l \in pred(X_k),\ (Y_l \xrightarrow{d} X_k) \Rightarrow V(X_k) = V(Y_l) + d$

The function $pred(X)$ defines the set of the direct predecessors of the node X. This allows to reduce the number of variables and inequalities, and also to detect some numerical inconsistencies as for the following system:

$$\left.\begin{array}{l} 30 \leq V(j) - V(k) \leq 50 \\ V(j) = V(i) + 40 \\ V(k) = V(i) + 20 \end{array}\right\} \Longrightarrow 30 \leq 20 \leq 50$$

Our goal is not to detect all inconsistencies of the linear system but only those which can be easily identified during the system construction. Some geometrical constraints are linear, like relations between segment lengths, and are added to the previous linear system; the others form a vector of nonlinear inequations. This system can be well-constrained, but it is generally under or over-constrained; thus it is not possible to enumerate all solutions of the description. The translation of the problem into a system of linear and nonlinear inequalities allows us to solve geometrical and locative constraints simultaneously and to propose one solution among the infinity of possible solutions (when the description is consistent). This system is described by the following equations :

1. $\forall i \in \{1, \ldots, n\},\ l_i \leq x_i \leq u_i,$

2. $\forall j \in \{n+1, \ldots, p\},\ l_j \leq \mathbf{sum}_{i=1}^{n}\, \alpha_i^j . x_i \leq u_j,$

3. $\forall r \in \{p+1, \ldots, q\},\ l_r \leq C_r(x_1, \ldots, x_n) \leq u_r.$

The system is solved by using a resolution algorithm which minimizes a quadratic objective function F as follows:

$$minimize\, F(x)\, (x \in R^n)\, subject\, to\, :\, l \leq \left\{ \begin{array}{c} x \\ A_L x \\ C(x) \end{array} \right\} \leq u$$

where $x = (x_1, \ldots, x_n)$, A_L is an $(p - n)$ by n constant matrix, and $C(x)$ is an $(q - p)$ element vector of nonlinear constraint functions. A numerical solution of the problem is computed by using a NAG[1] library routine, essentially similar to the subroutine SOL/NPSOL described in Gill et al [17]. The objective function F to be minimized is given by the following equation:

$$F(x_1, \ldots, x_n) = \mathbf{sum}_{i=n+1}^{p} \beta_i . (\frac{(u_i + l_i)}{2} - (x_k - x_l))^2, k, l \in \{1, \ldots, n\},$$

where $\beta_i = 1$ if the (i-n) linear equation is in the form $l_i \leq x_k - x_l \leq u_i$, and if $(l_i \neq u_i)$ else $\beta_i = 0$. This particular objective function allows to keep the equilibrium of the object's space distribution.

22.4   Consistency of the Description

At every moment of the design process, an inconsistency can be generated by the description. Firstly we have topological inconsistencies due to an incompatibility between some locative relations. Secondly we may have some geometric inconsistencies: for instance when different values are given for the depth and width of an objet while this object is said to be cubic. A part of this second kind of inconsistency can be detected during the construction of the global system and will also be easily expressed to the user. Other inconsistencies are detected during the numeric resolution process.

22.5   System Implementation and Results

A first version of this system has been carried out[10]. The object-oriented-language and knowledge representation model have been written in Quintus-Prolog and C++. The user interface is composed of a graphic zone written in Phigs included in a Motif window manager environment. The routine of the NAG library, which

---

[1]NAG is a registered trademark of: the Numerical Algorithms Group Limited and The Numerical Algoritms Group Incorporated.

performs the numerical resolution, is directly called by prolog. We use a global illumination rendering algorithm [18] to obtain realistic images of the scene. The following examples illustrate our method.

A first pedagogic example shows the management of objects having some unknown dimensions, and on which the user gives some constraints. The scene is composed of a carpet, a table, two chairs and the following description:

- *The carpet is two centimeters high, five meters wide and three meters deep.*
- *The table is seventy centimeters high and its width and depth are unfixed.*
- *Both chairs are one meter high and their width and depth are unfixed.*
- *The carpet is in front of the locator.*
- *The table and the two chairs are on the carpet.*
- *Both chairs are respectively on the left and on the right of the table.*

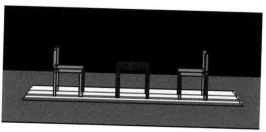

Figure 22.7
Initial solution of the first example.

The scene solution calculated by our system is shown on the figure 22.7. Adding a constraint defining that *the table depth is twice as important as the width of both chairs* modifies the scene only on the locator's frontal axis (figure 22.8) because chairs are intrinsically oriented objects.

Figure 22.9 is obtained after adding a constraint defining that *a quarter of the carpet area is occupied by the two chairs and the table.*

The scene illustrated by figure 22.10 has been produced after the definition of the table width (two meters and eighty centimeters). In this scene, the area occupied by the chairs has decreased proportionnaly to the increase of the table area, maintaining the length relation on the locator's frontal axis. This example shows that locative relations and geometrical constraints are jointly taken into account in our system, which allows us to constantly offer the designer one solution of the global description as long as the scene description is consistent.

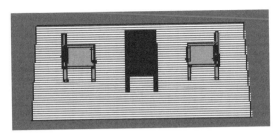

Figure 22.8
The table depth is twice as important as the width of both chairs.

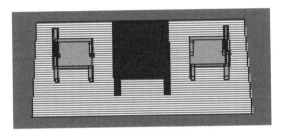

Figure 22.9
A quarter of the carpet area is occupied by the two chairs and the table.

Through an easy description of a building, the second example illustrates that our system is useful even for more complex scenes. This building (figure 22.12) is composed of a ground floor, four identical storeys and a roof. On the front side of the building, each storey is composed of five identical rooms with the same structure as on figure 22.3: there are two identical apertures in the front wall of the rooms in which a window is embedded. The ground floor is composed of four identical pillars, a winding stair and two rooms. The dimensions of the objects are given in

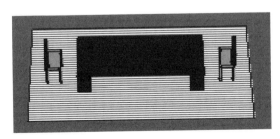

Figure 22.10
The table width is equal to two meters and eighty centimeters.

figure 22.11.

Object	Height	Width	Depth
scene	50.0	50.0	50.0
building	nil	nil	nil
storey	[2.0,4.0]	[8.0,30.0]	[8.0,30.0]
room1	[2.6,3.0]	[2.0,7.0]	[2.0,7.0]
ceiling	[0.1,0.4]	nil	nil
ground	[0.1,0.4]	nil	nil
wall	[1.0,4.0]	nil	[0.1,0.4]
window	[0.8,1.2]	[0.6,0.8]	[0.04,0.12]
roof	[2.0,4.0]	nil	nil
ground floor	nil	nil	nil
pillar	nil	[0.5,1.5]	[0.5,1.5]
winding stairs	nil	[3.0,4.0]	[3.0,4.0]
room2	nil	[3.0,4.0]	[5.0,6.0]
room3	nil	nil	nil
door	[2.4,2.6]	[0.8,1.0]	[0.04,0.12]

Figure 22.11
The dimensions of the objects (in meters).

Here are some locative relations in which the objects of the ground floor occur:

- *The winding stairs is set on the left side of room3 and in front of room2.*
- *The top side of the winding stairs is at the same place as the bottom side of the door.*
- *The right side of the door is located to the left of the right side of room2 at a distance which is included in a possible value domain [0.2,0.3].*
- *The locator is in front of the door.*

Because of the *copy of* links, some geometrical constraints (length equality) are implicit for rooms, storeys, windows and pillars. There are also two other geometrical constraints:

- Height(pillar1) - 3*Height(locator) = 0
- $24 \text{ m}^2 \leq \text{Area(room1)} \leq 30 \text{ m}^2$

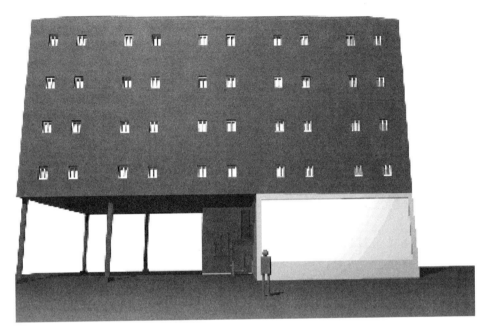

Figure 22.12
A building example.

Conclusion

This paper has presented in detail the management of constraints and properties in our declarative design methodology which provides the ability to manipulate uncertainty for both numerical and locative constraints. The description of objects at a level higher than the geometrical one and the use of prototypes permit to reduce the decomposition/recomposition step. The examples illustrate the capability of our system to jointly deal with a topological and geometrical knowledge. One of its main characteristics is the cooperation between two inference techniques which are most of the time competing: on the one hand a logical inference stemming from Allen's temporal logic and instant logic, on the other hand a numerical inference based on an optimization under constraints algorithm. We are currently extending this model to more complex geometrical objects, and are investigating other design domains involving new kinds of constraints.

References

[1] R. Light and D. Gossard. Modification of geometric models through variational geometry. *Computer Aided Design*, 14(4):209–214, July 1982.

[2] U. Flemming, R. F. Coyne, T. Glavin, H. Hsi, and M. Rychener. *A Generative Expert System for the Design of Building Layouts(Final Report)*. Technical Report EDRC 48-15-89, Carnegy Mellon University, 1989.

[3] P. Quintrand, J. Zoller, R. de Filippo, and S. Faure. A model for the representation of urban knowledge. *planning and design*, 18(1):71–83, 1991.

[4] P.J.W. ten Hagen and T. Tomiyama (Eds.). *Intelligent CAD Systems I. Theoretical and methodological aspects*. Springer-Verlag, 1987.

[5] M. Lucas. Equivalence classes in object space modelling. In T. L. Kunii, editor, *Proc. of Working Conference on Modeling in Computer Graphics*, pages 17–34, IFIP TC 5/WG 5.10, Springer Verlag, Tokyo, Japan, April 1991.

[6] J. S. Gero, editor. *Artificial Intelligence in Design*. Springer-Verlag, 1989.

[7] E. Lang, K. U. Carstensen, and G. Simmons. *Modelling Spatial Knowledge on a linguistic Basis. Lecture Note in Artificial Intelligence*, Springer-Verlag, 1991.

[8] F. Giunchiglia and E. Trucco. *Object Configuration by Incremental Ill-described Spatial Constraints*. Technical Report DAI Research Paper NO. 400, Department of Artificial Intelligence, University of Edinburgh, 1988.

[9] P. Veerkamp and P. J. W. ten Hagen. Qualitative reasoning about design objects. In *5th International Conference on the Manufacturing Science and Technology of the Future*, Enschede, Pays-Bas, June 1991.

[10] S. Donikian. *Une approche déclarative pour la création de scènes tridimensionnelles : application à la conception architecturale*. PhD thesis, University of Rennes I, IRISA, Campus de Beaulieu, 35042 Rennes Cedex, December 1992.

[11] A. Herskovits. *Language and spatial cognition*. Cambridge University Press, 1986.

[12] M. Aurnague. *Contribution à l'étude de la sémantique formelle de l'espace et du raisonnement spatial : la localisation interne en français, sémantique et structures inférentielles*. PhD thesis, Université Paul Sabatier, IRIT, 118, route de Narbonne, 31062 Toulouse Cedex, February 1991.

[13] S. Donikian and G. Hégron. A declarative design method for 3d scene sketch modeling. In *EUROGRAPHICS'93 Conference Proceedings*, Barcelona, Spain, September 1993.

[14] J.F. Allen. An interval based representation of temporal knowledge. In *Proceedings of the seventh International Joint Conference on Artificial Intelligence*, pages 221–226, August 1981.

[15] T. Granier. *Contribution à l'étude du temps objectif dans le raisonnement.* Technical Report 716-I-73, IMAG, Février 1988.

[16] S. Donikian and G. Hégron. The kernel of a declarative method for 3d scene sketch modeling. In *Graphicon'92*, Programming and Computer Science, Moscow, Russia, September 1992.

[17] P.E. Gill, S.J. Hammarling, W. Murray, M.A. Saunders, and M.H. Wright. *User's Guide for LSSOL (version 1.0)*. Technical Report SOL 86-1, Department of Operations Research, Stanford University, 1986.

[18] K. Bouatouch and P. Tellier. A two-pass physics-based global illumination model. In *Proceedings of Graphics Interface 92*, Vancouver, Canada, May 1992.

23 Expressing Constraints for Data Display Specification: A Visual Approach

Isabel F. Cruz

Abstract

In this paper we introduce a constraint-based language that has a visual syntax, and allows for the declarative specification of the display of data. Other features of the proposed language include: (1) simplicity and genericity of the basic constructs; (2) ability to specify a variety of displays (graphs, bar charts, pie charts, etc.); (3) compatibility with the object-oriented framework of the database language DOO-DLE. We provide the syntax and the semantics of the language, and examples of applications that demonstrate the expressiveness of our language.

23.1 Introduction

Mappings between the data domain and the visual domain are commonly used for extracting information from the data by reasoning in the visual domain [3, 12]. For example, Venn diagrams are visual representations of abstract sets and of their inclusion relationships. Other diagrams are close to the concrete entities that they represent, such as transportation and communication networks. Bar charts, pie charts, and plot charts can facilitate the comprehension of large amounts of quantitative data [20].

In this paper we present a visual constraint-based language, called *U-term language*, to specify the geometric layout of pictures (e.g., as displayed on a computer screen), i.e., sets of graphical objects. Syntactically, a picture is a well-formed sentence in a visual language. Pictures in the U-term language are called *U-terms*, and are used to specify pictures on the computer screen. We have designed the U-term language to provide:

- A declarative and visual specification of pictures with simple and generic constructs.

- The ability to specify a variety of pictures such as graphs, bar charts, and pie charts, using Cartesian or polar coordinates.

- Easy integration in an object-oriented framework.

This paper does not address constraint satisfaction issues, which are covered elsewhere [8], and summarized in a later section.

Previous work on data display specification includes constraint-based languages that have a textual syntax, such as TRIP [13], which uses Prolog terms and functors to specify pictures, and IDEAL [21], where textual programs instantiate abstract data types. Visual approaches include GVL [11] for the display of data structures (e.g., lists) that are created during the execution of a program, and ThingLab [1], an object-oriented system, where the constraints are integrated with the visual classes that specify the pictures and visual classes are described visually by means of prototypical symbols. Related research has focused on grammars for visual languages, with either a textual syntax (e.g., [10]) or a visual syntax (e.g.,[17]).

This paper is organized as follows. In Section 23.2, we present an overview of the database language DOODLE that is based on the U-term language. In Section 23.3 we introduce the graphical principles and the objects and constraints that are the basis for the U-term language. In Section 23.4 we present the abstract and concrete syntax of the U-term language, followed by the semantics of the language in Section 23.5. In Section 23.6 we give a short summary of our research on the satisfaction of constraints. Finally, in Section 23.7 we draw some conclusions and discuss topics for future research.

23.2   Background

The U-term language is used within DOODLE (*Draw an Object-Oriented Database LanguagE*) [5]. DOODLE is a meta-language with which the user can define visual query languages [7]. In this section we give an overview of DOODLE. A DOODLE visual program is a set of visual rules. Visual rules are vertically divided by a double bar. We call the entities to the left and to the right of this bar *D-terms* (for DOODLE terms). The DOODLE program of Figure 23.1(i) specifies the visualization of a software engineering database as a graph. The database classes are *block*, *module*, *procedure* (*module* and *procedure* are subclasses of *block*), *calls*, *contains*, and *aggregate* (abbreviated by *agg*). In Figure 23.1(i) there are two kinds of D-terms:

F-terms. These are terms from *F-logic* [15]. F-terms are depicted as strings of characters.

U-terms. These are *user-defined* terms. A U-term is a picture, which is a sentence of the U-term language.

In this program all the terms to the right of the double bar are F-terms, hence the box f-language . For the database facts that make the F-terms true, pictures of the visual language softGraph (for software graph), as indicated by softGraph are specified by the U-terms.

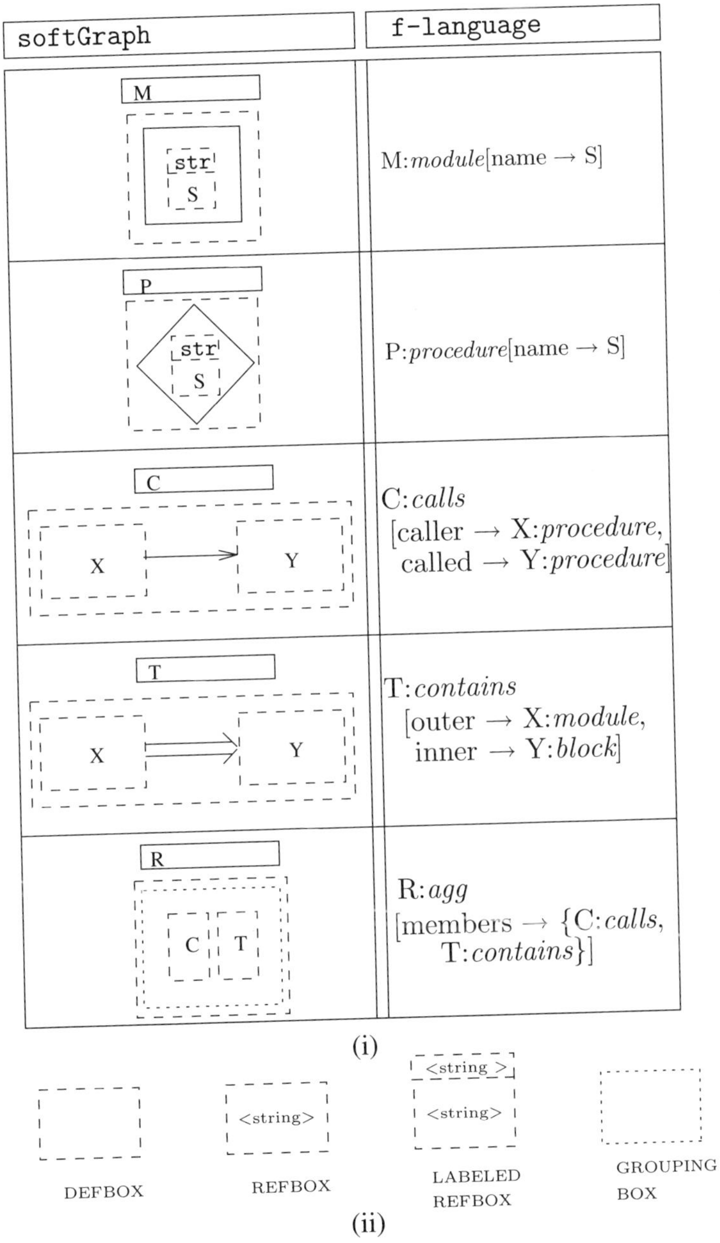

Visual Constraints for Data Display Specification

softGraph	f-language
M ┌str S┐	M:*module*[name → S]
P ◇str S◇	P:*procedure*[name → S]
C X ⟼ Y	C:*calls* [caller → X:*procedure*, called → Y:*procedure*]
T X ⟹ Y	T:*contains* [outer → X:*module*, inner → Y:*block*]
R C T	R:*agg* [members → {C:*calls*, T:*contains*}]

(i)

DEFBOX   REFBOX   <string>   GROUPING
                <string>   LABELED   BOX
                                REFBOX

(ii)

Figure 23.1
(i) Visual program that defines softGraph. (ii) Some key symbols in DOODLE.

In this example the U-terms are formed of three kinds of symbols: (1) *proto-typical symbols*, which specify "by example" the visual attributes (e.g., shape) of the graphical objects to be displayed on the screen; (2) *constraint symbols*, which specify the spatial relationships between these objects (none of which is explicitly represented in this example); (3) *key symbols* (see Figure 23.1(ii)) of the DOODLE language, such as *defbox*, *refbox*, and *grouping box*. For a class of objects a *def-box* defines a set of symbols (those that are physically contained in the defbox); a *refbox* with name X refers to the objects that were defined as belonging to the defbox of the U-term associated with database object X. A *grouping box* defines the visualization of a set of database objects.

In addition, there are *macro symbols* and *generic symbols* that will be described later.

The first rule of the DOODLE program in Figure 23.1(i) states that any object M in class *module* is to be displayed by a box. The second rule states that any object P in class *procedure* is to be displayed by a diamond. In a similar way, objects C of class *calls* are to be displayed by (simple) arrows, while objects T of class *contains* are to be displayed by double arrows. The last rule states that the visual representation of a set of objects R is the set of the visual representations of the members of the set (in this case C and T). We use a grouping box to denote the set of visual representations.

We explain now the rules in greater detail. The U-term in the third rule specifies the following display: *"Draw a solid arrow that starts on the graphical object that displays database object X (represented by the refbox with name X) and ends on the graphical object that displays database object Y (represented by the refbox with name Y."* Therefore, refboxes allow for U-terms to refer to U-terms that were defined elsewhere. For example, in the objects of class *calls*, the refboxes make reference to the graphical symbols inside the defbox of the U-term that specifies the display of objects of class *procedure*, in this case the prototypical symbol diamond and a labeled refbox. The roles of defbox and refbox are analogous to the concepts of procedure definition and of procedure call. The defbox specifies the display, and the refbox "calls" it. Labeled refboxes are a generalization of refboxes. While (simple) refboxes make a call to a defbox in the current visual language (softGraph in the example), the labeled refboxes make a call to the visual language that labels the refbox (e.g., str)) which has been defined elsewhere.

In the third and fourth visual rules, the refboxes that contain X (or Y) can either refer to the defbox in the rule that specifies the display of *procedure* or to the defbox that specifies the display of *module*, depending on the subclass of *block* to which the object belongs.

The semantics of a DOODLE program is given by the semantics of the F-logic program that is obtained by mapping each visual rule to one F-logic rule and a U-term to a set of F-logic objects. The program of Figure 23.1(i) defines a mapping from database objects to graphical objects. We call such mapping a *visualization*. A set of F-logic objects defines a picture in the visual language softGraph if and only if it is a minimal model of the equivalent F-logic program. For example, if we assume that the rules of the DOODLE program of Figure 23.1(i) are the only ones that define the visual language softGraph, then (for any database) a graph where some of the nodes are circles is not a picture in softGraph. Given a database, in general a DOODLE program defines a set of pictures. Each two pictures in the set differ in one or more of the graphical attributes that were not completely specified by the U-terms. For a single picture to be defined, the exact placement of the graphical objects, dimensions of the objects, distances between objects, etc., have to be uniquely specified by the U-terms.

23.3 Objects and Constraints

23.3.1 Visual Objects

Visual objects are instances of the visual classes, and correspond to the graphical objects that can be drawn on the screen. Visual classes include *box*, *diamond*, *text*, *circle*, *sector*, *straightLine*, and *arrow*.

There are attributes that are common to all visual objects, and therefore belong to *visualObject* (the superclass of all visual classes), such as color and texture.

23.3.2 Landmarks and Anchor Points

Landmarks are used to give dimensions to the objects, and to place graphical objects relatively to other objects. Landmarks can belong to the following classes: *landmark*, *cartesianLandmark*, *polarLandmark*, and *lineLandmark*. *Anchor point* objects are user-defined landmarks. From now on, we use *point* to denote a landmark or an anchor point.

Points can be described in two formats: *cartesian* or *polar*. For the cartesian format, there are two values that can be specified: the horizontal coordinate (x) and the vertical coordinate (y). For the polar format, there are two values that can be specified: the length (r) and the angular coordinate (θ). Any point can be positioned on the plane (or referred to) according to any of the formats. This makes it possible to specify the positions of polar objects in the cartesian plane (e.g., a set of pie charts, where the X-coordinate represents the year to which the pie chart refers), or to specify the position of cartesian objects in a polar picture (e.g., text that labels a sector in a pie chart).

The following discusses the different classes of landmarks and the visual objects where they can be used.

Landmarks. All visual objects have the following landmarks : c, for center, and any, which refers to any position on the boundary of the object. For objects of class *text*, c refers to the the center of the bounding box, which is the minimal invisible box that contains the object.

Cartesian landmarks. Polygons and circles have the following cartesian landmarks: mw (for midwest), mn (for midnorth), me (for mideast), ms (for midsouth). We show their position, as located on a box and on a circle in Figure 23.2(i-ii).

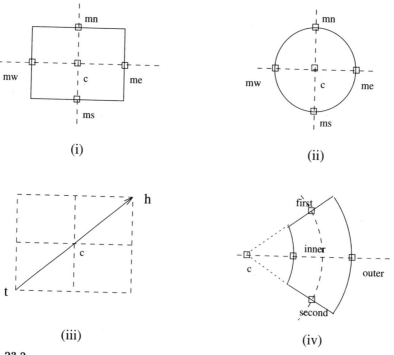

Figure 23.2
Cartesian landmarks: (i) on a box; (ii) on a circle; (iii) on a line. Polar landmarks: (iv) on a sector.

Polar landmarks. Sectors (and therefore circles) have the following polar landmarks: first (for first angle), second (for second angle), inner (the middle point of the inner arc), and outer (the middle point of the outer arc), as shown in Figure 23.2(iii).

Line landmarks. Lines (e.g., arrows, double-headed arrows) have the following line landmarks: h (for head), t (for tail), denoting the endpoints of a line.

23.3.3 Visual Constraint Objects

Visual constraint objects express spatial relationships between one or more visual objects, and are instances of *visual constraint classes*. The constraints are expressed in terms of the objects' points. A visual constraint between two points of the same object can be used to specify one of the dimensions of the object. If the points belong to two different objects, the visual constraint expresses a spatial relationship between those objects. We define two classes: *lengthConstraint* and *overlapConstraint*. We describe the classes using F-logic signatures [15].

Length constraint. The description of the *lengthConstraint* class using an F-logic signature is as follows:

$$lengthConstraint[\text{firstObj} \Rightarrow visualObject;$$
$$\text{secondObj} \Rightarrow visualObject;$$
$$\text{firstLand} \Rightarrow \{landmark,\ anchorpoint\};$$
$$\text{secondLand} \Rightarrow \{landmark,\ anchorpoint\};$$
$$\text{distance} \Rightarrow realNumberExp;$$
$$\text{kind} \Rightarrow kindType]$$

To the left of the the double arrows are the attribute names (e.g., firstObj), and to the right of the arrow are the classes to which the attribute values belong (e.g., visualObject). Braces indicate class union. Objects of class *realNumberExp* are either constants, variables, or different kinds of expressions (e.g., *max(X, Y)*, $Height_1 + Height_2$, ≥ 0) of type *real*. Values of attribute *kind* are vertical, horizontal, absolute (Euclidean distance), and angular.

The class *lengthConstraint* is: (1) general, since it considers a variety of distances and kinds of distances, and (2) generic, because constraints apply to any objects as long as the landmarks are defined for those objects.

Overlap constraint. Given two visual objects, an overlap constraint specifies which object is to be drawn on top of the other object. The class *overlapConstraint* has the following signature:

$overlapConstraint$[firstObj $\Rightarrow$ $visualObject$;

secondObj $\Rightarrow$ $visualObject$;

top $\Rightarrow$ $visualObject$]

Top indicates which of the two objects is to be displayed on top. The default value for the attribute top takes the second object to be the one on top.

23.3.4 Examples

Position between two boxes. Figure 23.3 shows eight distances that can be defined between some of the landmarks of two boxes. These distances are a subset of all the possible distances that could be specified between these landmarks. Not

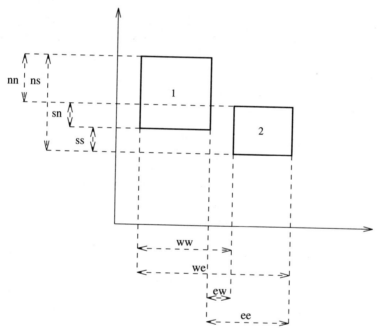

Figure 23.3
Constraining the position of two objects.

all the above distances are needed to specify completely the spatial constraints between two objects. The examples of Figure 23.4 illustrate this point. In these examples we consider the first graphical object to be the one with smallest identity, and we do not specify the absolute dimensions of each object.

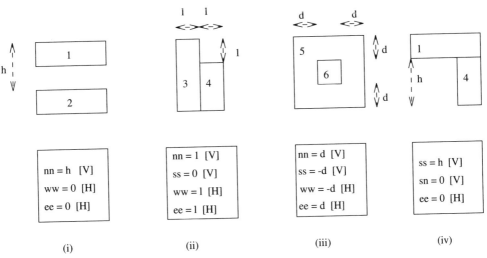

Figure 23.4
Spatial relationships between pairs of objects ("V" denotes vertical and "H" denotes horizontal).

Position between two sectors. Figure 23.5 shows four angular distances and four radial distances that constrain the position of two sectors.

Position of anchor points. The following example shows how the horizontal position of the anchor point labeled "headpoint" is specified using an object lc_1 of class *lengthConstraint*.

lc_1 : *lengthConstraint*[firstObj → 1;
                 secondObj → 1;
                 firstLand → me;
                 secondLand → "headpoint";
                 distance → 0;
                 kind → horizontal]

The vertical position of the anchor point can be specified relatively to the landmark mn. The head of the arrow can be positioned in the following way (see Figure 23.6(i)):

lc_2 : *lengthConstraint*[firstObj → 1;
                 secondObj → 2;
                 firstLand → "headpoint";

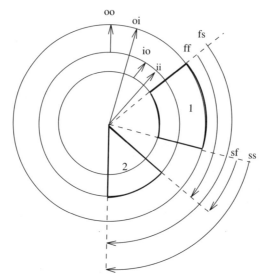

Figure 23.5
Spatial relationship between pairs of sectors.

secondLand → h;
distance → 0;
kind → absolute]

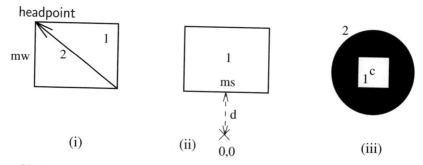

Figure 23.6
(i) Position of anchor point; (ii) Position on the screen; (iii) Overlapping of objects.

Positions on the screen. Absolute, vertical, and horizontal positions on the screen can be defined by considering the origin to be a visual object (see Figure 23.6(ii)).

$lc_3 : lengthConstraint[$firstObj $\rightarrow$ origin;

secondObj $\rightarrow$ 1;

firstLand $\rightarrow$ c;

secondLand $\rightarrow$ ms;

distance $\rightarrow$ d;

kind $\rightarrow$ vertical]

Overlapping of Objects. Object o_1 describes how two objects with identities 1 and 2 overlap, as in Figure 23.6(iii).

$o_1 : lengthConstraint[$firstObj $\rightarrow$ 1;

secondObj $\rightarrow$ 2;

top $\rightarrow$ 1]

The relative position of the two objects is defined by a length constraint, as follows.

$lc_4 : lengthConstraint[$firstObj $\rightarrow$ 1;

secondObj $\rightarrow$ 2;

firstLand $\rightarrow$ c;

secondLand $\rightarrow$ c;

distance $\rightarrow$ 0;

kind $\rightarrow$ absolute]

23.4 Syntax of the U-term Language

23.4.1 Abstract Syntax

In the U-term language there are five kinds of symbols: prototypical symbols, constraint symbols, key symbols, macro symbols, and generic symbols.

Prototypical symbols. A prototypical symbol consists of:

symbol name. The symbol name uniquely identifies the symbol.

symbol class. Symbol classes include shapes (like box), lines (like straight line), and text.

attributes. The attributes depend on the particular symbol class. The value of the attributes specify further the graphical objects. For example the boundary of a box can be solid or dashed. **boundary** is therefore an attribute name and its attribute values include solid and dashed.

set of landmarks. Each symbol has a set of landmarks. Each landmark is defined by a name and by a format. The format of a landmark can be cartesian or polar.

set of anchor points. This set may be empty. The names of the anchor points are strings chosen by the user. The format of the anchor points can be cartesian or polar.

In Figure 23.7 we give some examples of prototypical symbols using the syntax of F-logic.

> b : box[boundary → solid, density → opaque, color → black, texture → plain,
>   landmarks ↠ {[name → mw, format → cartesian], ...},
>   anchorpoints ↠ {[name → "headpoint", format → cartesian]}]
> s : sector[boundary → dashed, density → transparent, color → black, texture → plain,
>   landmarks ↠ {[name → outradius, format → polar], ...},
>   anchorpoints ↠ {}]
> t : text[value → "Draw", font → roman, size → 12pt]

Figure 23.7
Examples of abstract U-terms for prototypical symbols.

Key symbols and constraint symbols. Table 23.1 summarizes the syntax of the key symbols — defbox, refbox, labeled refbox, grouping box — and of constraint symbols in the U-term language. In addition to the attributes that are listed for defbox, refbox, labeled refbox, and grouping box there are two set-valued attributes: landmarks and anchorpoints, similar to the attributes with the same name of the prototypical symbols. In the table, <*any symbol but defbox*> stands for any prototypical, macro or generic symbol (macro and generic symbols are described below).

Figure 23.8 gives examples of abstract U-terms for key and constraint symbols. The following observations complement the summarized information in Table 23.1.

Symbol Class	Attributes Names	Attribute Value Types
defbox	contains	$\{< any\ symbol\ but\ defbox >\}$
refbox	name	$< string >$
labeled refbox	name	$< string >$
	label name	$< string>$
grouping box	contains	$\{< any\ symbol\ but\ defbox\ or\ grouping\ box >\}$
length constraint	first object	$< prototypical\ symbol > \mid < refbox >$
	second object	$< prototypical\ symbol > \mid < refbox >$
	first landmark	$< landmark > \mid < anchorpoint >$
	second landmark	$< landmark > \mid < anchorpoint >$
	distance	$+ (\ < expression >) \mid - (\ < expression >) \mid$ abs $(\ < expression >)$
	kind	horizontal | vertical | absolute | radial | angular
overlap constraint	first object	$< prototypical\ symbol > \mid < refbox >$
	second object	$< prototypical\ symbol > \mid < refbox >$
	top	$< prototypical\ symbol > \mid < refbox >$

Table 23.1
Key symbols and constraint symbols.

d : defbox[contains $\rightarrow$ b]
l : labeledRefbox[name $\rightarrow$ "X", labelname $\rightarrow$ "barChart"]
t : lengthconstraint[firstobject $\rightarrow$ l, secondobject $\rightarrow$ l,
                firstlandmark $\rightarrow$ ms, secondlandmark $\rightarrow$ mn,
                distance $\rightarrow \alpha$ Y, kind $\rightarrow$ vertical]

Figure 23.8
Examples of abstract U-terms for key symbols and constraint symbols.

- The objects that are values for the attribute contains have to be physically contained in the boxes that form a defbox or a grouping box. This means that if the object overlaps but is not within the boundaries then it is not part of any of those constructs. A defbox cannot be contained in another defbox or in a grouping box.

- distance can be either positive, negative or the absolute value of an expression (the distance is restricted to be absolute when the kind of the length constraint is absolute).

- An expression can be either a simple expression or a proportionality expression. Examples of simple expressions were given in Section 3.3. The proportionality expression α, is used, for example, to specify that a visual attribute (e.g., the height of a bar in a bar chart) is proportional to the value of a database attribute (e.g., salary). The syntax of the proportionality expression is as follows:

$$< proportionalityExpression >:: \alpha <simpleExpression > [\text{min} :< num >]$$
$$[\text{max} :< num >][\text{sum} :< num >]$$

The value for max (min) is the greatest (smallest) value in the active domain of the specified attribute. The value of sum is the sum of all the values of an attribute. For example, sum can be used to display pie charts, where it is necessary to know the sum of all the values being represented, so that the sum of the angular widths of each sector (the angular width of a sector being proportional to its value) can be made equal to 2π.

Macro symbols.   There are spatial relationships between objects that result from combining two or more length constraint objects. They are not therefore indispensable, but their existence can simplify the user's task of assembling a picture. Next, we present in some detail two macro symbols: nest and grid alignment. Other macro symbols include: Cartesian position (to specify the placement of a graphical object on the plane), zero distance (to specify that the absolute distance between two points is zero), and macroarrow (to specify that an arrow goes from a point in an object to another point in another object).

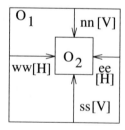

Figure 23.9
nest relationship.

Figure 23.10 shows the four length constraint objects that an instance of nest is equivalent to.

C : nest[firstobject $\rightarrow O_1$, secondObject $\rightarrow O_2$,
nn $\rightarrow \geq 0$, ss $\rightarrow \leq 0$, ee $\rightarrow \geq 0$, ww $\rightarrow \leq 0$]

$\equiv$

$\{Z_1$: lengthConstraint[firstObject $\rightarrow O_1$, secondObject $\rightarrow O_2$,
firstLandmark $\rightarrow$ mn, secondlandmark $\rightarrow$ mn,
distance $\rightarrow \geq 0$, kind $\rightarrow$ vertical],
Z_2 : lengthConstraint[firstObject $\rightarrow O_2$, secondObject $\rightarrow O_1$,
firstLandmark $\rightarrow$ ms, secondLandmark $\rightarrow$ ms,
distance $\rightarrow \geq 0$, kind $\rightarrow$ vertical],
Z_3 : lengthConstraint[firstObject $\rightarrow O_1$, secondObject $\rightarrow O_2$,
firstLandmark $\rightarrow$ me, secondLandmark $\rightarrow$ me,
distance $\rightarrow \geq 0$, kind $\rightarrow$ horizontal],
Z_4 : lengthConstraint[firstObject $\rightarrow O_2$, secondobject $\rightarrow O_1$,
firstLandmark $\rightarrow$ mw, secondlandmark $\rightarrow$ mw,
distance $\rightarrow \geq 0$, kind $\rightarrow$ horizontal]$\}$

Figure 23.10
nest abstract U-term and set of equivalent length constraint abstract U-terms.

Nest   The nest relationship is a macro for four length constraint objects, as outlined in Figure 23.9.

Grid alignment   The principle behind grid alignment is the following: all landmarks and anchor points that are on the same horizontal (vertical) line specify points that have the same horizontal (vertical) coordinates in the picture. Figure 23.11 shows a specification of a bar chart and of two nodes of a linked list, where the grid alignment is enforced. The syntax of this macro symbol is GRID ON (otherwise it is GRID OFF). In Figure 23.11 we have emphasized some of the landmarks for which the vertical or horizontal positions will be enforced.

Generic symbols.   Generic symbols are predefined symbols to the layout program. For example, a set of orthogonal axes (as in Figure 23.12(i)). The parameters for these axes, are the names of two domains, the maximum and minimum values in each of the domains, the space along each axis between each consecutive pair of "labeled ticks" The grid generic symbol is similar to axes, but there the "ticks" are replaced by sets of horizontal and vertical lines (see Figure 23.12(ii)).

23.4.2   Concrete Syntax

Figure 23.13 exemplifies part of the concrete syntax of the U-term language. The

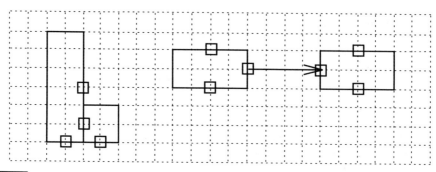

GRID ON

Figure 23.11
The grid alignment option.

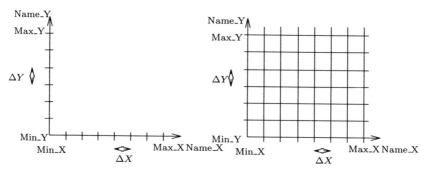

Figure 23.12
(i) X-Y axes; (ii) X-Y grid.

U-term in the figure specifies entity-relationship (E-R) diagrams, such as the one represented in Figure 23.14. In the example, the diamond is specified to be centered at the point with coordinates (20,20). Attached to the diamond there is a box, and a set of (zero or more) circles. There is a defbox that contains the diamond, the set of circles, the box and two straight lines. The defbox has the following anchor points: next and previous. There is a larger box that is also connected to the diamond. This box contains a labeled refbox (with two anchor points), a smaller box, and a line that connects the labeled refbox and the smaller box.

The syntactic description of the picture is given in Figure 23.16. It takes into account the exact position of the objects in the U-term of Figure 23.13. The objects

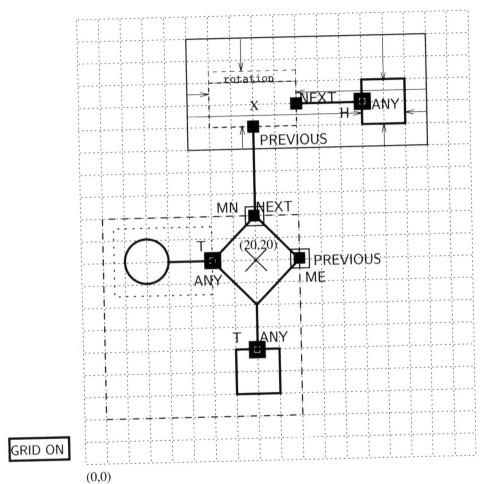

Figure 23.13
U-term that specifies an E-R diagram.

are described by their shape and by their extent. The extent of objects such as boxes and lines is the minimum box that contains the object, and is described by the coordinates of two points in that box (as in [10]). The extent of circles is defined by the coordinates of the center, and the radius. Examples of the extents of two objects are given in Figure 23.15. The abstract syntax for the U-term of

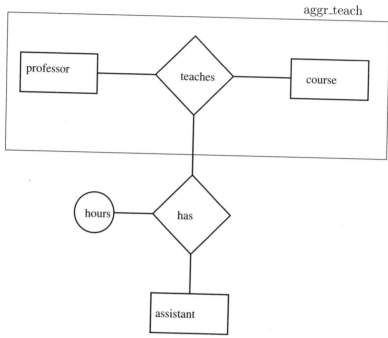

Figure 23.14
E-R diagram with aggregation [16].

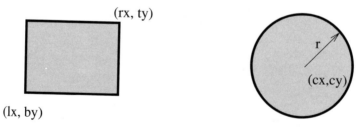

Figure 23.15
The extent of two graphical objects.

Figure 23.13, is given in Figure 23.17. Figures 23.13 and 23.17 demonstrate that it is easier to draw a visual specification using the U-term language than to write all the constraints in textual form.

There may be more than one well-formed U-term that is mapped to the same

box[lx → 7, by → 3, rx → 9, ty → 5, boundary → solid, width → 3]
box[lx → 13, by → 15, rx → 15, ty → 17, boundary → solid, width → 3]
box[lx → 5, by → 14, rx → 16, ty → 19, boundary → solid, width → 2]
groupingbox[lx → 1.5, by → 7.5, rx → 6, ty → 10.5]
labeledrefbox[lx → 5, by → 15, rx → 10, ty → 17.5, name → "X",
                 labelname → "rotation"]
circle[cx → 3, cy → 9, r → 1, boundary → solid]
defbox[lx → 1, by → 2, rx → 10, ty → 11]
diamond[lx → 6, by → 7, rx → 10, ty → 11, boundary → solid, width → 2]
cartesianposition[cx → 8, cy → 9, label → "20,20"]
anchorpoint[cx → 8, cy → 11, name → "next"]
anchorpoint[cx → 10, cy → 9, name → "previous"]
anchorpoint[cx → 10, cy → 16, name → "next"]
anchorpoint[cx → 8, cy → 15, name → "previous"]
straightline[lx → 8, by → 5, rx → 8, ty → 7, boundary → solid, width → 3]
straightline[lx → 4, by → 9, rx → 6, ty → 9, boundary → solid, width → 3]
straightline[lx → 10, by → 16, rx → 13, ty → 16, boundary → solid, width → 3]
nestarrows → {arrow[lx → 7.5, by → 19, rx → 7.5, ty → 17.5],
            arrow[lx → 5, by → 16.5, rx → 6, ty → 16.5],
            arrow[lx → 7.5, by → 14, rx → 7.5, ty → 14],
            arrow[lx → 16, by → 16.5, rx → 10, ty → 16.5]}
nestarrows → {arrow[lx → 14, by → 19, rx → 14, ty → 17]
            arrow[lx → 5, by → 15.5, rx → 13, ty → 15.5],
            arrow[lx → 14, by → 14, rx → 14, ty → 15],
            arrow[lx → 16, by → 15.5, rx → 15, ty → 15.5]}
gridon

Figure 23.16
Description of the U-term of Figure 23.13.

abstract U-term. We can therefore partition the U-terms into equivalence classes. We say that two U-terms are *specification equivalent* if they are described by the same (up to macro symbol equivalence) abstract syntax. On the other hand, U-terms may specify the same display without this condition being true.

23.5   Semantics

The semantics of a U-term is the set of pictures that the U-term specifies. Each U-term is associated with a visual language, V, and with a database class, C. The U-term specifies how each object O in class C (written O:C) is to be displayed. For prototypical objects other than the ones contained in a grouping box, there

a : box[boundary → solid, width → 3]
b : box[boundary → solid, width → 3]
c : box[boundary → solid, width → 2]
d : labeledrefbox[name → "X"; labelname → "rotation";
                anchorpoints ↠ {[name → "next", format → cartesian],
                            name → "previous", format → cartesian]}]
e : circle[boundary → solid]
f : defbox[contains → {a, e, g},
        anchorpoints ↠ {[name → "next", format → cartesian],
                   name → "previous", format → cartesian]}]
g : diamond[boundary → solid]
h : groupingbox[contains → {e, i}]
i : straightline[boundary → solid]
j : straightline[boundary → solid]
k : straightline[boundary → solid]
l : straightline[boundary → solid]
m : cartesianposition[object → g, landmark → c, x_position → 20, y_position → 20]
n : lengthconstraint[firstObject → e, secondObject → i, firstLandmark → any,
                secondLandmark → t, distance → 0, kind → absolute]
o : lengthconstraint[firstObject → i, secondObject → g, firstLandmark → h,
                secondLandmark → mw, distance → 0, kind → absolute]
p : lengthconstraint[firstObject → a, secondObject → j, firstLandmark → any,
                secondLandmark → t, distance → 0, kind → absolute]
q : lengthconstraint[firstObject → j, secondObject → g, firstLandmark → h,
                secondLandmark → ms, distance → 0, kind → absolute]
r : lengthconstraint[firstObject → g, secondObject → f, firstLandmark → mn,
                secondLandmark → "next", distance → 0, kind → absolute]
s : lengthconstraint[firstObject → g, secondObject → f, firstLandmark → me,
                secondLandmark → "previous", distance → 0, kind → absolute]
t : lengthconstraint[firstObject → f, secondObject → l, firstLandmark → "next",
                secondLandmark → t, distance → 0, kind → absolute]
u : lengthconstraint[firstObject → l, secondObject → d, firstLandmark → h,
                secondLandmark → "previous", distance → 0, kind → absolute]
v : lengthconstraint[firstObject → d, secondObject → k, firstLandmark → "next",
                secondLandmark → t, distance → 0, kind → horizontal]
w : lengthconstraint[firstObject → k, secondObject → b, firstLandmark → h,
                secondLandmark → "previous", distance → 0, kind → vertical]
u : contains[firstObject → c, secondObject → d,
        nn →≥ 0, ss →≤ 0, ww →≥ 0, ee →≤ 0]
v : contains[firstObject → c, secondObject → b,
        nn →≥ 0, ss →≤ 0, ww →≥ 0, ee →≤ 0]

Figure 23.17
Abstract U-term for Figure 23.13.

will be one graphical object displayed for each of them. The graphical objects are displayed in such a way that they satisfy the constraints, as specified by the constraint symbols and by the macro symbols. In the case of prototypical symbols inside a grouping box, the corresponding graphical symbols will be displayed zero or more times. Associated with each refbox there is one name, e.g., X, and if it is a labeled refbox there is also a label name (for example `rotation` in Figure 23.13). The name X is the identity of an object, which is a subobject of the object $O{:}C$, and $X{:}D$. The refbox is in place of a set of symbols that are contained in the defbox of the U-term that has been defined for objects of class D and the same visual language V. The labeled refbox is in place of a set of symbols contained in the defbox of the U-term that has been defined for objects of class D and the visual language denoted by the label name (e.g., `rotation`).

Consider for example the signature of objects of class *relationship*:

$$relationship[entity\_1 \Rightarrow entityClass[name \Rightarrow string];$$
$$entity\_2 \Rightarrow aggrClass[relation \Rightarrow relationship;$$
$$entity \Rightarrow entityClass[name \Rightarrow string]];$$
$$relationshipName \Rightarrow string;$$
$$attributes \Rightarrow\!\!\!\Rightarrow attributeClass[name \Rightarrow string]]$$

and that we are specifying the visualization of an object O:*relationship* with a subobject X:*relationship*.

$$O : relationship[entity\_1 \rightarrow entityClass[name \rightarrow "assistant"];$$
$$entity\_2 \rightarrow aggrClass$$
$$[relation \rightarrow X : relationship;$$
$$entity \rightarrow entityClass[name \rightarrow "hours"]];$$
$$relationshipName \rightarrow "has";$$
$$attributes \rightarrow\!\!\!\rightarrow \{attributeClass[name \rightarrow "hours"]\}$$

Given the U-term of Figure 23.13 (modified to specify the placement of the names), the picture of Figure 23.14 is part of the visual language associated with this U-term, for a conveniently defined visualization of X (e.g., the display of objects of class *relationship* is specified by the symbols that are inside the defbox of the U-term of Figure 23.13, rotated by 90°, clockwise).

23.6 Constraint Satisfaction

In a visualization system that uses the U-term language, once the constraints are expressed, there are two additional stages. First, the visualization system will satisfy the constraints by solving the system of constraints associated with the U-term. This is called the *constraint satisfaction stage*. Second, there is the drawing of pictures on the screen that may involve choosing precise coordinate values when they have not been uniquely specified by the previous stage. We call this second stage, the *rendering stage*. In both stages, the algorithms that are used should be efficient and satisfy both the visually-specified constraints and some global aesthetic criteria (e.g., minimize the overlap of graphical objects, minimize the area of the picture).

As is customary in constraint satisfaction [2], we have not looked at this problem as a whole but concentrated on a specific domain. We chose the graph drawing domain [9], and considered the important classes of trees and planar acyclic digraphs. For the kinds of constraints that are needed to specify certain layouts for these classes, we provide algorithms that run in linear time [8].

23.7 Conclusions

We have presented a new constraint-based visual language, the U-term language, to specify the display of data. This language is declarative and visual. The U-term language is geared to the display of database objects, and to fit in an object-oriented framework. The fact that the language has a visual syntax distinguishes it from other approaches such as IDEAL [21]. In ways, our work is closer to (and also drew from) ThingLab [1], in that the user can define visual classes by example, and the language is constraint-based and object-oriented. However, ThingLab is a visual programming language while the U-term language is a language to specify pictures that represent data. Computational power can be given to the U-term language by embedding it in DOODLE [5, 6]. Constraint satisfaction is an important part of ThingLab. We plan to pursue our research on efficient algorithms for constraint satisfaction. Other topics of future research include:

Language design. We are extending the U-term language to specify the display of 3D objects [18, 19]. Incorporating constraint hierarchies [2] in the language in a suitable manner would allow for complex layout specifications, e.g., for VLSI design [4].

Temporal constraints. Another intriguing subject is the use of the U-term language to express temporal constraints. These could use 3D display, where the third dimension is used for time. Simple temporal reasonings can already be expressed by DOODLE, using a 2D display of temporal charts [5].

Constraint query languages. Constraint query languages such as [14] have a textual syntax. The U-term language could provide a visual syntax for such languages.

Design of the user interface. The detail of the U-terms suggests a sophisticated interface to assist the user in the visual specification of constraints. Different levels of detail as in Figures 23.1(i) and 23.13 should also be supported.

Expressive power of DOODLE as a picture generator. The example of Figure 23.1(i) is relatively simple: for instance we have no recursion in the rules. An interesting topic for future research includes the precise comparison of the expressive power of DOODLE with the expressive power of grammars, such as the multiset grammars [10].

Acknowledgments

Thanks to Roberto Tamassia, Theo Norvell, and Ashim Garg for useful discussions. The author is also indebted to an anonymous referee for helpful suggestions. This work was partially carried out at Brown University, Department of Computer Science, and supported in part by the Office of Naval Research and the Advanced Research Projects Agency under contract N00014-91-J-4052, ARPA order 8225.

References

[1] Alan Borning. The Programming Language Aspects of ThingLab, a Constraint-Oriented Simulation Laboratory. *ACM Transactions on Programming Languages and Systems*, 3(4):353–387, October 1981.

[2] Alan Borning, Bjorn Freeman-Benson, and Molly Wilson. Constraint Hierarchies. *Lisp and Symbolic Computation*, 5:223–270, 1992.

[3] B. Chandrasekaran, N. Hari Narayanan, and Yumi Iwasaki. Reasoning with Diagrammatic Representations: A Report on the Spring Symposium. *AI Magazine*, 14(2), Summer 1993.

[4] Umakanta Choudhury and Alberto Sangiovanni-Vincentelli. Automatic Generation of Parasitic Constraints for Performance-Constrained Physical Design of Analog Circuits. *IEEE Transactions on Computer-Aided Design of Integrated Circuits and Systems*, 12(2):208–224, 1993.

[5] Isabel F. Cruz. DOODLE: A Visual Language for Object-Oriented Databases. In *ACM-SIGMOD Intl. Conf. on Management of Data*, pages 71–80, 1992.

[6] Isabel F. Cruz. *Querying Object-Oriented Databases with User-Defined Visualizations*. PhD thesis, Department of Computer Science, University of Toronto, 1993.

[7] Isabel F. Cruz. User-defined Visual Query Languages. In *IEEE Symposium on Visual Languages (VL '94)*, 1994.

[8] Isabel F. Cruz and Ashim Garg. Drawing Graphs by Example Efficiently: Trees and Planar Acyclic Digraphs. Brown University, Department of Computer Science. Manuscript submitted for publication, July 1994.

[9] G. Di Battista, P. Eades, R. Tamassia, and I.G. Tollis. Algorithms for Drawing Graphs: an Annotated Bibliography. Technical report, Department of Computer Science, Brown University, March 1993. To appear in *Computational Geometry: Theory and Applications*.

[10] Eric J. Golin and Steven P. Reiss. The Specification of Visual Language Syntax. *Journal of Visual Languages and Computing*, (1):141–157, 1990.

[11] T. C. Nicholas Graham and J. R. Cordy. GVL: A Graphical, Functional Language for the Specification of Output in Programming Languages. In *Proc. IEEE Intl. Conference on Computer Languages*, pages 11–22, 1990.

[12] James G. Greeno. Conceptual Entities. In Derdre Gentner and Albert L. Stevens, editors, *Mental Models*, pages 227–252. Lawrence Erlbaum Associates, Publishers, Hillsdale, N.J., 1983.

[13] Tomihisa Kamada. *Visualizing Abstract Objects and Relations – A Constraint-Based Approach*. World Scientific, Singapore, 1989.

[14] Paris C. Kanellakis, Gabriel M. Kuper, and Peter Z. Revesz. Constraint Query Languages. In *ACM Symposium on Principles of Database Systems*, pages 299–313, 1990.

[15] Michael Kifer, Georg Lausen, and James Wu. Logic Foundations of Object-Oriented and Frame-Based Languages. Technical Report 90/14 (2-nd revision), Department of Computer Science, SUNY Stony Brook, 1990. To appear in *JACM*.

[16] Henry F. Korth and Abraham Silberschatz. *Database System Concepts*. McGraw-Hill Book Company, New York, NY, 1986.

[17] Fred Lakin. Visual Grammars for Visual Languages. In *Proc. AAAI*, 1987.

[18] Steven P. Reiss. A Framework for Abstract 3D Visualizations. In *IEEE Symposium on Visual Languages (VL '93)*, pages 108–115, 1993.

[19] Steven P. Reiss and Isabel F. Cruz. Practical Software Visualization. In *SIGCHI '94 Workshop on Software Visualization*, 1994.

[20] Edward R. Tufte. *The Visual Display of Quantitative Information*. Graphics Press., Cheshire, Conn., 1983.

[21] Christopher J. Van Wyk. A High-Level Language for Specifying Pictures. *ACM Transactions on Graphics*, 1(2):163–182, April 1982.

Contributors

Pedro Barahona
Departamento de Informática
Universidade Nova de Lisboa
2825 Monte da Caparica,
Portugal
<pb@fct.unl.pt>

Arthur L. Delcher
Computer Science Department
Loyola College in Maryland
Baltimore, MD 21210
USA
<delcher@loyola.edu>

Stéphane Donikian
IRISA / CNRS
Campus de Beaulieu,
35042 Rennes Cedex,
France
<donikian@irisa.fr>

Isabel F. Cruz
Tufts University
Department of Electrical Engineering
and Computer Science
Medford, MA 02155, USA
<isabel@cs.tufts.edu>

Carolyn K. Duby
Cadre Technologies, Inc.
222 Richmond Street
Providence, RI 02903
USA
<ckd@cadre.com>

Eugene C. Freuder
Department of Computer Science
University of New Hampshire
Durham, NH 03824
USA
<ecf@cs.unh.edu>

Thom Frühwirth
ECRC
Arabellastrasse 17
D-81925 Munich
Germany
<thom@ecrc.de>

Michael Gleicher
Apple Computer
1 Infinite Loop M/S 301-3J
Cupertino, CA 95014
USA
<gleicher@apple.com>

Philipp Hanschke
sd&m
Schimmersfeld 7a
D-40880 Ratingen
Germany
<hanschke@uni-duesseldorf.de>

Gérard Hégron
Ecole des Mines de Nantes
3, rue Marcel Sembat,
44049 Nantes Cedex 04
France
<hegron@info.emn.fr>

Martin Henz
Programming Systems Lab
DFKI
Stuhlsatzenhausweg 3
D-66123 Saarbrücken, Germany
<henz@dfki.uni-sb.de>

J.N. Hooker
Carnegie Mellon University
Graduate School of
Industrial Administration
Pittsburgh, PA 15213, USA
<jh38@andrew.cmu.edu>

Paul D. Hubbe
Department of Computer Science
University of New Hampshire
Durham, NH 03824
USA
<pdh@cs.unh.edu>

Jean-Louis Imbert
Laboratoire d'Informatique
de Clermont-Ferrand
Complexe Universitaire des Cezeaux
F–63177 Aubiere Cedex (France)
<imbert@glm.univ-bpclermont.fr>

Deepak Kapur
State University of New York
Department of Computer Science
LI 67A, 1400 Washington Avenue
Albany, NY 12222
<kapur@cs.albany.edu>

Simon Kasif
Department of Computer Science
The Johns Hopkins University
Baltimore, MD 21218
USA
<kasif@cs.jhu.edu>

Claude Kirchner
CRIN-CNRS & INRIA-Lorraine
Batiment LORIA
Campus scientifique, BP 239
54506 Vandœuvre-lès-Nancy, France
<Claude.Kirchner@loria.fr>

Hélène Kirchner
CRIN-CNRS & INRIA-Lorraine
Batiment LORIA
Campus scientifique, BP 239
54506 Vandœuvre-lès-Nancy, France
<Helene.Kirchner@loria.fr>

Wolf Kohn
Itermetrics
1750 112Av. N.E.,Suite D151,
Bellevue, WA
USA
<wfk@minnie.bell.inmet.com>

Walid T. Keirouz
Schlumberger Austin Research
8311 North RR 620 Road,
Austin, Texas 78726
USA
<walid@slb.com>

Glenn A. Kramer
Enterprise Integration Technologies
800 El Camino Real
Menlo Park, CA 94025
USA
<gak@eit.com>

Gabriel M. Kuper
ECRC
Arabellastr. 17
D-81925 München
Germany
<Gabriel.Kuper@ecrc.de>

Alan Mackworth
Department of Computer Science
University of British Columbia
Vancouver, B.C.
Canada V6T 1Z2
<mack@cs.ubc.ca>

Ken McAloon
Logic Based Systems Lab
Brooklyn College CUNY
2900 Bedford Avenue
Brooklyn, NY 11210
<mcaloon@sci.brooklyn.cuny.edu>

Francisco Menezes
Departamento de Informática
Universidade Nova de Lisboa
2825 Monte da Caparica
Portugal
<fm@fct.unl.pt>

Scott Meyers
Software Development Consultant
1855 NW 173rd Avenue
Suite 2004
Beaverton, OR 97006
<smeyers@netcom.com>

Ugo Montanari
University of Pisa
Computer Science Department
Corso Italia 40,
56125 Pisa, Italy
<ugo@di.unipi.it>

Anil Nerode
Mathematical Sciences Institute
Cornell University,
Ithaca, New York 14850
USA
<anil@math.cornell.edu>

Dinesh Pai
Department of Computer Science
University of British Columbia
Vancouver, B.C.
Canada V6T 1Z2
<pai@cs.ubc.ca>

Jahir Pabon
Schlumberger Austin Research
8311 North RR 620 Road,
Austin, Texas 78726
USA
<jahir@slb.com>

Steven P. Reiss
Brown University
Department of Computer Science
Box 1910
Providence, RI 02912, USA
<spr@cs.brown.edu>

Francesca Rossi
University of Pisa
Computer Science Department
Corso Italia 40,
56125 Pisa, Italy
<rossi@di.unipi.it>

Michael Sannella
Department of Computer Science
and Engineering, FR-35
University of Washington
Seattle, Washington 98195 USA
<sannella@cs.washington.edu>

Douglas Smith
Kestrel Institute
3260 Hillview Avenue
Palo Alto, CA 94304
USA
<smith@kestrel.edu>

Gert Smolka
Programming Systems Lab
DFKI
Stuhlsatzenhausweg 3
D-66123 Saarbrücken, Germany
<smolka@dfki.uni-sb.de>

V. S. Subrahmanian
Department of Computer Science
University of Maryland
College Park, Maryland 20742
USA
<vs@cs.umd.edu>

Carol Tretkoff
Logic Based Systems Lab
Brooklyn College CUNY
2900 Bedford Avenue
Brooklyn, NY 11210
<tretkoff@sci.brooklyn.cuny.edu>

Marian Vittek
CRIN-CNRS & INRIA-Lorraine
Batiment LORIA
Campus scientifique, BP 239
54506 Vandœuvre-lès-Nancy, France
<Marian.Vittek@loria.fr>

Stephen J. Westfold
Kestrel Institute
3260 Hillview Avenue
Palo Alto, CA 94304
USA

Jörg Würtz
Programming Systems Lab
DFKI
Stuhlsatzenhausweg 3
D-66123 Saarbrücken, Germany
<wuertz@dfki.uni-sb.de>

H. Yan
Carnegie Mellon University
Graduate School of
Industrial Administration
Pittsburgh, PA 15213
USA

Ying Zhang
Department of Computer Science
University of British Columbia
Vancouver, B.C.
Canada V6T 1Z2
<zhang@cs.ubc.ca>

Richard Zippel
Cornell University
Ithaca, NY 14853
<rz@cs.cornell.edu>